Battleship Missouri

An Illustrated History

NAVAL INSTITUTE PRESS
Annapolis, Maryland

Frontispiece: The *Missouri* lies moored to a buoy in the Hudson River against the backdrop of buildings on the west side of Manhattan. President Harry S Truman visited the ship the following day, Navy Day, October 27, 1945. (*Courtesy Ted Stone*)

Text © 1996 by Paul Stillwell

Drawings © 1996 by Alan B. Chesley

Library of Congress Cataloging-in-Publication Data

Stillwell, Paul, 1944–
    Battleship Missouri : an illustrated history /
Paul Stillwell.
        p.   cm.
    Includes bibliographical references (p.   )
and index.
    ISBN 1-55750-780-5 (alk. paper)
    1. Missouri (Battleship : BB 63)   I. Title.
VA65.M59S75   1995
359.3′252′0973—dc20   95-22241

Printed in the United States of America on
acid-free paper ⊗

02 01 00 99 98 97 96 95   9 8 7 6 5 4 3 2

First printing

PAUL STILLWELL

Battleship Missouri

Contents

Preface

In my mind's eye I can still see President Harry S Truman going down Boonville Avenue in Springfield, Missouri. He and his buddies from the Army's 35th Division, which fought in World War I, were celebrating a reunion in early June 1952 and were marching in this parade more than thirty years after they had been together in France. In my mental picture of the parade are automobiles with white sidewall tires—the ones with three-inch-wide bands of white, rather than the puny ones we see today. I had just completed the second grade at the time and felt a sense of home-state pride that the nation's president had come to our city to be with his comrades-in-arms.

Gradually, as I grew older and more aware of things, I learned that the battleship named for our state had been the site of the surrender ceremony marking the end of World War II in the Pacific. She was still in active service in the fifties, and—probably like almost every boy in America at the time—I put together a plastic model of the *Missouri*. The Revell company must have sold millions of them over the years. My father and I worked together on the project, and I particularly remember applying the glue to the haze-gray 5-inch gun mounts and then using a thumb and forefinger to put each one into its slot along the side of the superstructure. Later, we used sewing thread to run rigging from the foremast to bow and stern and then folded over little paper signal flags and attached them to the thread.

Some fifteen years after that, in the summer of 1969, I first encountered the real battleship *Missouri*. I took a busman's holiday from my

Clad in shirtsleeves and straw hat, sixty-eight-year-old President Harry Truman leads a parade of World War I veterans in Springfield, Missouri, on June 6, 1952. The 35th Division was holding a reunion of soldiers who had served together in France thirty-four years earlier. Springfield was the site of the gathering because it was the home of the president's cousin, General Ralph Truman, who had once commanded the division. A few months later, in September 1952, General Truman was on board the battleship *Missouri* for the first leg of her long journey to the Korean War zone. (Courtesy Mike O'Brien)

After decades out of service, the ship's highly polished bell was installed on the forecastle prior to the *Missouri*'s recommissioning in 1986. (Photo by Michael D. P. Flynn in DoD Still Media Records Center: DN-ST-86-07286)

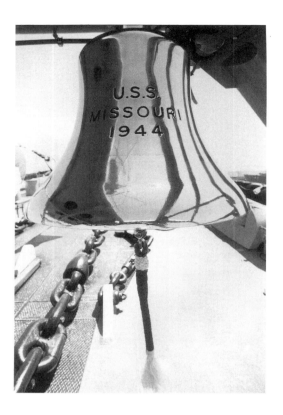

own ship while on liberty in the state of Washington. I caught a ferryboat across the tree-lined Puget Sound and went aboard the mothballed *Missouri* at Bremerton. She was twenty-five years old by that time but still possessed of the graceful lines that have been admired by so many for so long. Instead of the two-foot-long model I once held in my hands, here now was a mammoth structure nearly as long as three football fields.

A few months later, I had the opportunity to walk through the interior and see the compartments in which men had lived and worked and shared each other's company in good times and bad. The crew that had animated the *Missouri* in years past was long gone; left behind were many tangible signs of their experiences as shipmates.

After leaving the Navy, I enrolled in the University of Missouri, which is at Columbia, near the center of the state. It was a short drive one day to go to the state capitol at Jefferson City for a ceremony in which the Navy loaned the ship's bell to Missouri for display. Representing the service was Vice Admiral Edwin B. Hooper, the director of naval history. He was

no stranger to battleships himself. In November 1942, he had been in the USS *Washington* with Rear Admiral Willis A. Lee during a gunnery duel against the Japanese near Guadalcanal.

The idea formed somewhere along the way to write a book about the *Missouri,* and so I interviewed some of the former skippers about their experiences in command. Included were Vice Admiral Roscoe Hillenkoetter, Vice Admiral Taylor Keith, and Admiral Page Smith. In 1991, the project became definite when the Naval Institute Press gave its blessing.

So it was that in December 1991, I had the opportunity to go to sea in this battleship that had first invaded my awareness four decades earlier. The *Missouri* was going to Hawaii to join in the observance of the fiftieth anniversary of the attack on Pearl Harbor. In the process, she was making her final voyage, the last by any battleship. The Desert Storm crewmen were still on board, available for interviews about what they had experienced earlier that year. Two words came up over and over in their conversations: "adrenaline" and "pride." These men had carried the ship through a demanding combat experience; she, in turn, had carried them through it.

On the morning of Thursday, December 5, I joined others in going topside in the predawn twilight. Crew members had already swabbed the decks and donned their white uniforms for the entrance into Pearl Harbor. As the ship steamed along in the semidarkness, the bright lights of the south coast of Oahu moved past the starboard side in a steady procession. Along the shore were thousands of people, standing and waving enthusiastically; they signaled their picture taking with a series of flashes. As the *Missouri* made a turn to starboard and pushed her long, narrow bow into the entrance channel, the dawn was breaking. The sun popped up in the distance, making a silhouette of the crouching Diamond Head promontory.

In steamed the last battleship. To port, up against Ford Island, were white painted mooring quays that marked the December 7, 1941, positions of the old Battleship Row. The *Missouri* swept past quays bearing the name *California.* Farther on were the spots for the *Maryland*

and *Oklahoma*. Ironically, their quays had recently been removed so a dock could be constructed to accommodate the *Missouri*. But she wouldn't be based at Pearl Harbor as planned. Instead, she would be going to mothballs in faraway Bremerton.

On she steamed, shepherded by a gaggle of tugboats. More names showed up on the mooring quays: *Tennessee* and *West Virginia*. I thought of all the still and movie pictures I'd seen of the burning ships. Then came a low white memorial, gleaming in the morning sun. It marked the final resting place of the *Arizona*. Beyond was the spot from which the *Nevada* had embarked on a gallant sortie down the channel fifty years earlier. It was an emotionally moving experience as I thought of the thousands of men who had been in those old ships—and some who still were.

The symbolism was powerful. Over there was the physical place where World War II had started for the United States. A hundred or so feet away from me, down on the *Missouri*'s 01 deck, was the physical place where it had ended. The Japanese had surrendered in this ship because the president at the time was the man from Missouri. The ceremony on that deck had forever sealed the ship's place in history. And yet there was much, much more to her story than that. Those Desert Storm interviews were the precursor to dozens of others, dealing with all periods in the *Missouri*'s existence. The narrative that follows of necessity hits the highlights of dates and places, but even more it attempts to capture the flavor of life and work for the thousands of men who served in the ship over the years. For however long each man spent on board, this great battleship was his home.

Implicit in the stories that follow is the ship's mobility. In the spring of 1945, she was dealing with kamikazes off Okinawa. Six months after that she was the centerpiece for a victorious Navy Day celebration in New York. Six months after that she made a ground-breaking deployment to the Mediterranean to help shore up the U.S. position in the emerging Cold War. The following year she was off to South America to support hemispheric solidarity and to provide a pleasant homeward cruise for the

Truman family. In subsequent years she trained midshipmen. Indicative of that mobility was her presence in August 1950 in New York while training midshipmen; a month later she was bombarding Korea. After a long hiatus in mothballs she returned to the fleet in 1986 and engaged in the ultimate demonstration of mobility—an around-the-world goodwill cruise. In her final years she traveled twice to the faraway Persian Gulf on behalf of U.S. interests.

Longevity is another striking factor. In 1991, when she was bombarding Iraqi positions in Kuwait, the *Missouri* was nearly forty-seven years past her first commissioning. To put that in perspective, conjure up an image of the first U.S. battleships, commissioned in 1895, participating in the 1942 battles around Guadalcanal. Simply unthinkable! Many of the men who served in the *Missouri* in 1991 could easily have been grandsons of the men of the original crew in 1944.

The USS *Missouri* was the last battleship commissioned by the U.S. Navy. She was the last active battleship in any Navy. This is the story of that long career. Above all, it is the story of the men who gave her life over those many, many years.

A constant throughout the battleship's many years of service was the thunderous firepower of her 16-inch guns. She is shown firing here shortly after her deployment to the North Arabian Sea in late 1987. (Courtesy Terry Cosgrove)

Acknowledgments

An invaluable assist to my research for this book was the opportunity to ride the *Missouri* in 1991 when she was still in active service. That enabled me both to interview crew members and to make mental notes on various things I saw. Lieutenant Commander Steve Chesser, then the public affairs officer for Naval Surface Group Long Beach, played an instrumental role in getting me aboard. I am also grateful to Rear Admiral Brent Baker, then the Navy's chief of information, for his assistance.

Once I reached the ship, Lieutenant Commander Terry "T" McCreary and Master Chief John Caffey of the public affairs office made available a variety of material. When the *Missouri* was decommissioned a few months later, McCreary sent me boxes of documents on the ship's history. Included were copies of the interviews from the ship's own oral history program, which was the brainchild of Captain John Chernesky and former crewman Tom O'Malley. Lieutenant Mark Walker, McCreary's predecessor as public affairs officer, conducted dozens and dozens of interviews, which were then transcribed by Ms. Teri Yamaguchi and others. Those transcripts were a most useful adjunct to my own interviews, contributing recollections that would not otherwise have been available. Captain Lee Kaiss, skipper during my visit, was most generous with his knowledge of the *Missouri* and in allowing me free access to both ship and crew.

Mrs. Victoria Washington does a formidable job in her role as lead tech in the central research room of the Washington National Records Center, Suitland, Maryland. She was invariably helpful in arranging for me to have access to the *Missouri* deck logs for the years 1946–55. Barry Zerby of the National Archives facility in downtown Washington, D. C., dug out the 1944–45 logs. Doreen German handles recent deck logs for the ships' histories branch, Naval Historical Center, Washington Navy Yard. She supplied the 1986–92 logs and also guided me to the *Missouri* public affairs files in the branch.

The *Missouri*'s annual command histories for the years 1984 to 1991, stored in the ships' histories branch, provide chronologies and useful summaries of each year's events. Unfortunately, the dates in the chronologies are not as reliable as those in the deck logs. On the other hand, the deck logs in the ship's second term in commission are not as informative on other points as are those for the 1944–55 period. In keeping with more recent directives, current logs too often emphasize trivia over substance.

The operational archives branch of the Naval Historical Center is an indispensable stop for anyone doing research on the wartime activities of U.S. Navy ships. As she has been in the past, Kathy Lloyd was invariably cheerful when digging out folders filled with the *Missouri*'s after-action reports. She also put forth extra effort in supplying other files, particularly the oral history of Lieutenant John Bremyer, who took Commodore Matthew Perry's 1853 flag to Sagami Wan in August 1945 and then did an engaging interview about his experiences once he returned to Washington.

Samuel Loring Morison, grandson of the noted naval historian, possesses a storehouse of valuable material on warships. He provided the negatives for some excellent photos of the *Missouri*'s underwater hull, made in February 1950, when the ship was drydocked at Norfolk after her notorious grounding at Thimble Shoal. He supplied far more pictures than would comfortably fit in the chapter on the grounding. Norman Polmar, editor of *The Naval Institute Guide to the Ships and Aircraft of the U.S. Fleet* (15th edition, 1992), likewise lent pictures from his extensive collection.

The National Archives still photo collection has moved into a sparkling new facility at College Park, Maryland. As usual, Dale Conley proved helpful in locating material. Theresa Roy also displayed considerable patience in digging out a variety of photos. Ed Finney and Chuck Haberlein made available dozens of *Missouri* pictures in the still photo branch of the Naval Historical Center. Chuck Porter of the Department of Defense Still Media Records Center in Anacostia, D. C., provided prompt and helpful service in making available hundreds of images from the *Missouri*'s second tour in commission. Gail Munro of the Navy Art Collection supplied the John Roach painting of the *Missouri* that appears on the dust jacket and in the Desert Storm chapter. The inspiration for the painting came from Roach's discussions with Captain Peter Bulkeley soon after HMS *Gloucester* shot down a Silkworm missile headed for the battleship.

The USS *Missouri* Association has been helpful in a variety of ways, including making me welcome for interviews with former crew members at two annual reunions and putting me in touch with others who were not able to attend the reunions. Herb Fahr, editor of the association's newsletter, does a great deal to keep members informed. I met ever cheerful Tony Alessandro, former president of the organization, when I rode the *Missouri* to Hawaii in late 1991. Ralph Barry, one of Tony's predecessors as president, supplied a number of pictures, relayed through the ship's public affairs office. The fellowship of the former *Missouri* shipmates who get together at the reunions is impressive; they have a strong bond to their ship and to each other. For those interested in joining, the individual to contact is Mr. Richard Reisig, Membership Chairman, USS *Missouri* Association, 54 James Lane, Levittown, New York 11756, telephone 516-731-4398.

Although its main focus is understandably on another ship, the Battleship *New Jersey* Historical Museum Society was nevertheless an extremely valuable ally. Member Robert Kaplan has been indefatigable in providing newspaper clippings, suggestions on people to interview, photos to track down, and other information. For instance, he prompted another member, Dick Landgraff, formerly of the Long Beach Naval Shipyard, to write me. Landgraff has an immense technical knowledge of *Iowa*-class battleships and has been most generous in sharing both photos and his knowledge. Vince Falso, a former *New Jersey* sailor, one day brought me a big box of *Missouri* material that Landgraff had previously shared with him. Leon Morrison, editor of the society's monthly newsletter, has frequently given me good leads. Since the newsletter covers the activities of all four *Iowa*-class battleships, the file of back issues provided considerable source material on the *Missouri*. For those interested in joining, the address for the society is Battleship *New Jersey* Historical Museum Society, Post Office Box BB-62, Middletown, New Jersey 07748.

When I visited the Harry S. Truman Library in Independence, Missouri, I found a wonderful collection of photos, documents, and media articles related to the *Missouri*. The friendly staff could not have been more helpful in responding to my requests, going out of their way to dig useful material out of the files. In particular, I am grateful to Dennis Bilger, Elizabeth Safly, and Pauline Testerman.

Ron Waudé, a major figure in the Seattle chapter of the Navy League, had an instrumental role in helping me obtain material on the *Missouri*'s mothball years in Bremerton, Washington, across Puget Sound from Seattle. He and his wife, Jan, were gracious hosts when I visited the Pacific Northwest. Commander Bob Anderson, an active-duty public affairs officer in the area, was also helpful.

I am grateful to John Gordon and Diane Manning of the Puget Sound Naval Shipyard public affairs office—also in Bremerton—for supplying material. I also had a fruitful visit to the photo lab, meeting with Rick Ellis and with one of my *New Jersey* shipmates, Chief Ralph Wasmer. At the Naval Inactive Ship Maintenance Facility, also in Bremerton, I received warm hospitality on a cold day from Gunnar Watson, Bob Callaham, Harry Ehlert, and Ken Ahl. Ehlert and Ahl gave me a guided tour through the inactive *Missouri* so I could complete the final chapter. Helen Devine, the director of the Bremerton Naval Museum, made available a report on the "un-grounding" of the *Missouri* in 1950, as well as her file of copies of the *Broadside* magazines published by the ship from 1988 to 1991. She has a warm spot in her heart for anyone who has served in the Navy.

On the photographic front, I salute two men who are truly artists with a camera: Rich Pedroncelli and Terry Cosgrove. Rich has been a multi-winner in the Naval Institute's annual photo contests. He took hundreds of on-board pictures during a visit to the *Missouri* in 1987 and generously made them available for inclusion in the book. I wish there were room for even more. Terry, who is now personal photographer for the secretary of the Navy, invited me to his Pentagon office to go through thousands of images shot during his time on board. The *Missouri* cruisebooks from the eighties and nineties contain some spectacular shots, thanks to Terry and his fellow shipboard photographers.

Captain Joe Lee Frank, former executive officer, dug down into his files to supply some excellent images from Desert Storm. Captain Peter Bulkeley, a Naval Academy classmate of Frank's, also supplied memories and a picture from his Desert Storm service in the ship. Robert Sumrall, a friend and fellow battleship author, lent me some *Missouri* photos from his collection. Dick Klug, one of the sailors on the 1947 Truman cruise, gave me a stack of souvenir pictures from that experience. Kermit "Kit" Bonner, a historian and author connected with the naval museum in San Francisco, provided leads on a number of photos from the morgue files of the old *San Francisco Call-Bulletin* newspaper. Ernest Arroyo of Pearl Harbor History Associates made available a number of fine images from his collection of thousands of Navy photos.

James H. Thach III and Robert Brodie III, sons of two *Missouri* commanding officers, provided photos from their fathers' periods in command. Allan E. Smith, Jr., lent photos from his father's book *The Mighty Mo;* his dad was instrumental in the ship's salvage in 1950. Mrs. Emma West provided a photo of her father, Captain Tom B. Hill, who commanded the ship shortly after World War II. Vice Admiral Douglas Plate sent me a box of treasures from his 1944–45 service in the *Missouri*. Included were photos, ship's newspapers, plans of the day (including September 2, 1945), family grams, New York newspapers, cartoons, and magazines. He also shared his memories during two extended interviews. The book is unquestionably better than it would have been without Admiral Plate's kindness. Also in that category is Captain Al Carney, *Missouri* skipper from 1986 to 1988. He lent me a scrapbook on the ship's 1946 and 1986 visits to Turkey and also gave me valuable insights during our recorded conversations.

Two women who were especially generous in sharing illustrations were Mrs. Eleanor Keith and Mrs. Sybil-Carmen North, widows of the last two commanding officers of the *Missouri* prior to the decommissioning in 1955. Mrs. Keith made available her husband's *Missouri* scrapbook, large enough to hold full newspaper pages. Mrs. North lent me dozens of pictures. Harry Levins, military writer for the *St. Louis Post-Dispatch*, was an enjoyable companion during my time on board ship in 1991 and has since kept in touch by supplying material for the book. Another Missouri man I met then was John Lewis, a 1986 plank owner and fellow supporter of the St. Louis Cardinals baseball team. Ted Stone, a friend for many years, has been taking pictures of Navy ships for decades. He supplied several prints from his vast collection of negatives. Included is the October 1945 image on the title pages of this book.

The interviews that really constitute the meat of the book originated in a variety of ways. In particular, I want to thank George Elsey, whom I came to know when I was editing a book on D-Day. A veteran of White House service under both President Roosevelt and President Truman, Elsey paved the way for my interview with Margaret Truman Daniel, the

Missouri's sponsor. John Hird volunteered an interview about his experiences with the Trumans on Navy Day 1945 and also supplied an excellent photo.

Don Giles lent me a book of photos covering the *Missouri*'s 1950–51 cruise to Korea and shared his memories. During the course of the discussion, he told of standing watches with an ensign named Lee Royal, who had met Winston Churchill in 1949. I contacted Royal, who supplied both wonderful stories and photos. The chapter on the first deployment to Korea draws in large part on the recollections of Giles and Royal. Bob Eichenlaub, Dan Williams, Jim Roswell, and Bob Schwenk were other crew members who provided both interviews and illustrations. Schwenk sent a videotape that contained a number of clips from the 1992 decommissioning. Jack Barron contributed photos, ship's papers, and an interview about the 1945 landing party in Japan. Indeed, I am grateful to all who were kind enough to be interviewed. They are listed individually in the section on sources.

Father Lawrence Schmieder, long-ago *Missouri* chaplain, generously gave me a cruisebook from World War II, and Marty Thumudo, a *Missouri* veteran of the Korean War, lent me his cruisebook for the 1952–53 deployment. Both books were invaluable for reference. Jack Zeldes, the editor of the Korean cruisebook, was generous with both recollections and illustrations. Bob Rogers, a Naval Academy graduate, provided a copy of his detailed memoir of the ship's 1953 midshipman cruise to Rio de Janeiro. Walt Urban, a former Army officer who saw the light and joined the naval reserve, has supplied a number of *Missouri* pictures now that he wears the blue suit. Herb O'Quin, a veteran of service in the USS *Maryland*, now lives in the Pacific Northwest. He generously supplied newspaper articles to keep me updated on the *Missouri*'s activities in 1995.

Robert Fisher of San Diego generously donated a copy of his master's thesis, from which I drew a good deal of insight in describing the background for the *Missouri*'s visit to the Mediterranean in the spring of 1946. I am grateful to Tom Grassey, editor of the *Naval War College Review*, for putting me in touch with Fisher. Alan B. Chesley did the superb drawings at the back of the book, as he did for my previous volumes on the *New Jersey* and *Arizona*. His knowledge of the subject and his skill with a pen have produced works of top-notch quality.

Soon after I began my research on the *Missouri* I became friends with the late Captain Fred Edwards and his wife, Lydia. They lived in Annapolis during the final years of their long and productive lives. Captain Edwards, who graduated from the Naval Academy in 1923, lived to be ninety-one. In the course of providing his oral history to the Naval Institute, he told of serving in seven battleships: *Michigan, South Carolina, Florida, West Virginia, Nevada, New Mexico,* and *North Carolina.* When the *North Carolina* went into commission in 1941, two of the department heads were Fred Edwards and Tom Hill. Edwards's assistant, William Maxwell, later became first chief engineer of the *Missouri;* Hill became the *Missouri*'s fourth skipper. Edwards did a prodigious amount of research on the history of battleships, and both he and his wife were quite supportive of my efforts. In a way this book represents a continuation of his work on the subject.

At the Naval Institute, former press director Tom Epley got the book going by approving the concept in 1991. Dottie Sappington and Mary Beth Straight of the photo archives were helpful in providing many of the *Missouri* images that appear in the volume. Their knowledge of both ships and photos is impressive. Linda O'Doughda, a coworker for a number of years now, did the expert editing of the manuscript, was meticulous in overseeing details, and provided considerable moral support as the manuscript was coming together. Karen White did her usual magnificent job of designing the book's physical appearance.

At home, my wife, Karen, and sons Robert and James have endured my situation as part-time husband and father for the months I have been off on research trips or glued to the computer screen. Son Joseph is a college student in the state for which the ship is named and has been supportive from afar. I am grateful to all of them for their love and patience.

Battleship Missouri

1 ❖ The Birth of a Battleship

January 1941–February 1945

The banging of hundreds of trip hammers filled the air of Brooklyn on the morning of January 6, 1941, as a few naval officers and civilian shipbuilders gathered to lay the keel for the future battleship *Missouri*. The noise came from the adjacent shipbuilding ways as shipfitters and riveters went about their work assembling the *Iowa,* lead ship of a new class of forty-five-thousand-ton dreadnoughts. Now, the first keel plates of the *Missouri* were about to come together on shipways number one, vacated the previous spring by the launching of the *North Carolina.* The presiding official was husky Rear Admiral Clark Woodward, commandant of the Third Naval District and the New York Navy Yard. He drove in the first rivet, joining two sixty-foot slabs of steel that were the beginning of the keel.[1]

The ceremony on that brisk winter morning in Brooklyn was low-key and private. The public was specifically excluded, in part to prevent interruption of work on other ships at a time when war appeared likely. Even more compelling was the concern about possible sabotage.[2] (Later that year, director Alfred Hitchcock conceived the film *Saboteur,* produced in early 1942, in which an enemy agent just missed blowing up a battleship being launched at this same New York Navy Yard.)

In the preceding year the German conquest of most of Europe had given dramatic emphasis to the peril faced by Western democracies. The U.S. Congress responded by directing the creation of a two-ocean Navy. Back in 1938, it had officially authorized construction of the *Missouri.* As the threat of war grew ever closer, Congress appropriated the money and shipyards were translating the legislation into reality. The keel of the *Missouri,* which would carry the hull number BB-63, was being laid three months earlier than originally scheduled.[3]

The event was a completely ceremonial one to mark the official beginning of construction. For several months prior, workmen had been fabricating steel sub-assemblies that would be put into place when the schedule directed. In the months that followed the keel-laying, the navy yard had the job of lengthening the *Missouri*'s shipbuilding ways by about three hundred feet to accommodate her length.[4] She and the *Iowa* would eventually be close to nine hundred feet long, and they needed room to grow. By the time the *Missouri* was completed three and a half years later, the navy yard had expended more than three million man-days on the construction.[5]

Nearly three weeks after the *Missouri* ceremony, officials at the Philadelphia Navy Yard laid the keel for the future *Wisconsin.* All told—over fifty-some years, beginning in the early 1890s—the nation laid keels for sixty-six battleships.[6] Construction of nine of those ships was halted while they were in various stages of completion, some in the 1920s because of an international disarmament treaty, some in the 1940s because wartime operating requirements called for resources to go into building other types of warships. The Navy completed fifty-seven frontline battleships. Even though the *Wisconsin* started later and had a higher hull number—BB–64—the *Missouri* was the last battleship built to completion for the U.S. Navy.

Once the *Missouri*'s construction was under way, the inner bottoms started growing as the hull gradually began to take shape. As part of the shipyard's quality-control efforts, Ensign Dick Miller, the assistant hull superintendent, had to spot-check each compartment and each

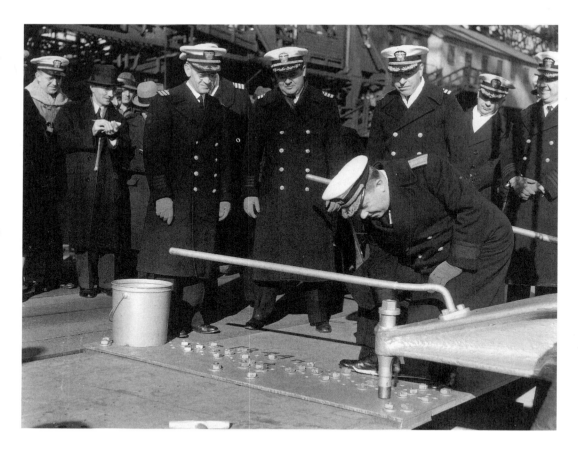

tank to ensure that the welds were complete and neat in appearance, no gaps. He spent many hot hours in July and August 1941 crawling around in those double bottoms.[7]

One day Ensign Miller met with Lieutenant Commander Wilbur Landers, who was in charge of design changes for both the *Iowa* and *Missouri*. Landers showed him the arrangement plans for the second deck spaces outboard of the extension of the holding bulkhead above the torpedo protection system. Contemplating possible improvements, he said, "Look at all these unassigned spaces, Dick. We don't have any need for them."[8] It was good, though, that the original designers had left some extra space because the demands of the war were heavy in the months to come. The ships needed much more in several categories—light antiaircraft guns, personnel, ammunition, fire control systems, and electronics—than originally planned. Space then became a premium item. At some point, for instance, a powder magazine on the starboard side of the fourth deck

was converted to serve as the combat information center for the ship's radar systems.[9]

One of the thousands of individuals involved in bringing together the materials that became part of the structure of the *Missouri* was Ensign Herbert Johnson, who was assigned to the new-construction section of the navy yard's supply department. A number of ships were being built at a time when the nation was involved in a full-fledged military construction program. In addition to building the fast battleships, the New York Navy Yard was also assembling the aircraft carriers *Bennington, Bon Homme Richard, Kearsarge,* and *Franklin D. Roosevelt,* and smaller ships and craft—along with repairing damage to ships such as the battle-ravaged *South Dakota* that was back from the South Pacific.[10]

For a time Johnson's particular specialty was electrical systems and equipment. Large items such as turbo-generators and emergency diesel generators arrived from the manufacturers shortly before they were to be installed, but

many other items needed to be stored until they were ready for installation in the gigantic jigsaw puzzle that was gradually taking the shape of a battleship. Thus, Johnson controlled the contents of five warehouses in Brooklyn. The Navy contracted for space in these commercial warehouses because the demands of the construction program were so heavy that not all the parts could be accommodated in the Navy's own spaces.[11]

In the electrical area, for instance, the ship required miles and miles of cabling to connect the users of the power with the generators. There were outlets, light switches, motors, communication equipment, appliances, and connectors for all sorts of gunnery and fire control devices, and so forth. The demands in the electrical area were, of course, multiplied by the thousands of items needed in a growing steel structure nearly as long as three football fields.[12] By the time she was finished, the *Missouri* would include—among many other components—90 miles of piping, 15,000 valves, 900 electric motors, 844 doors, 852 manholes, and 161 hatches.[13]

The shipyard's planning department worked with the blueprints and specifications for the *Missouri* and other ships to determine just what would be needed—when—and how much. The yard then sent the requisitions to the headquarters of the Third Naval District at 90 Church Street in Manhattan. From there, working in conjunction with the Bureau of Ships, the naval district sent out orders to the various suppliers, including both Navy facilities and those in private industry. The purpose was to ensure that manufacturing and delivery schedules matched up with the schedule for the items going into place on board ship.[14]

The shipyard organization was like a giant octopus, with its tentacles reaching throughout American industry. For critical material, individuals known as expediters made numerous telephone calls to impart a sense of urgency to those who needed to produce needed items. If things didn't arrive when they were supposed to, the builders had to use their ingenuity and work around the shortages until they were finally alleviated. Fortunately, the shipyard included a cadre of men who had worked there

for decades. Their experience enabled them to anticipate the requirements and keep on schedule. The *Missouri*'s construction, remembered Johnson, was never slowed by a shortage of component parts; she was given the highest priority.[15]

So it was that such diverse items as guns, turrets, armor, boilers, piping, coffee vats, radars, propellers, steel plates, gyrocompasses, furniture, lathes, ladders, hatches, and so forth were gathered for the step-by-step assembly process. Sometimes the supply people sent material to shops where sub-assemblies were manufactured, sometimes directly to the shipbuilding ways for installation. During his time at the shipyard in 1943–44, it was a source of considerable satisfaction for Ensign Johnson to go aboard the *Missouri* at her construction site, to see her growing on practically a daily basis.[16]

It was a busy time for everybody in the yard, with workers covering three shifts a day to see that the ship was completed as quickly as possible. Construction of a battleship was necessarily a lengthy process, but it was shortened to the extent that it could be. Another ingredient in the process, observed Johnson, was the enthusiastic spirit of the civilian work force. Their sense of patriotism and selflessness has seldom been seen since then. Now a retired captain, Johnson laments the national loss of that spirit of cooperation.[17]

Gradually, the sides of the *Missouri* climbed high enough for the installation of the side armor belt. It was put in at an angle from the vertical so that a torpedo approaching horizontally would have slightly more depth to penetrate than the actual thickness of the steel. When the fifty-ton armor plates arrived, they were put together in three-piece sub-assemblies linked by interlocking joints known as key ways. The bond was further strengthened by welding butt straps, which were about three-quarters of an inch thick, across the joints.

After that, bridge cranes that spanned the building ways would lift the sub-assemblies into place. These armor sub-assemblies were at about the limit of the crane's capacity. Once they were put in place, the pieces of armor were welded to the ship's structure itself, and the sub-assemblies were welded together with additional butt straps. What with all the heating from welding and cooling from the outside air, the steel incrementally forming the ship's structure would expand and contract, creating potential for misalignment. Every week an officer went out with a surveyor's transit to measure the alignment. Then corrective action was taken with judicious heating to keep things in line.[18]

In about 90 percent of the cases, the honor of selecting a battleship's sponsor belonged to the governor of the state for which the ship was named. Typically, the governors designated their wives or daughters to swing the bottle of champagne and christen the ship at the time of launching. An exception was made in the case of the *Missouri*. Several months before the hull was due to be launched, Senator Harry S Truman learned that the sponsor would be his daughter Mary Margaret, as she was then known. The senator had achieved quite a reputation by then as head of a powerful committee investigating war production. Senator Truman said the invitation from Secretary of the Navy Frank Knox "took me completely by surprise."[19]

Undoubtedly, a factor in the choice was that the incumbent governor of Missouri, Forrest C. Donnell, was a Republican, and President Franklin D. Roosevelt definitely was not. No sense wasting an opportunity of this sort on a member of the other party. And, as a writer for the *St. Louis Post-Dispatch* explained: "Realists in Washington point out that there is no question as to whose good graces are more essential to the Navy—those of Gov. Donnell in remote Jefferson City or those of the chairman of a powerful and dreaded investigating committee which in its time has raked the [Navy] department with more than one punishing broadside. It is added that Senator Truman is being widely discussed as a possible vice-presidential candidate in this year's national election."[20]

On January 6, 1944, only about three weeks before the planned launching of the *Missouri*'s hull in Brooklyn, Rear Admiral Monroe Kelly, the commandant of the New York Navy Yard, finally got around to inviting Governor and Mrs. Donnell to the ceremony. A week later

Senator Truman invited the governor's daughter, Mrs. Boyd Rogers, to serve as one of his daughter's attendants on the launching stand. The governor replied by saying that both he and his daughter had other plans for the day, but he did send a list of individuals he wished to be invited. Included was Branch Rickey, until recently the general manager of the St. Louis Cardinals baseball team and in 1944 serving in a similar capacity for the Brooklyn Dodgers.[21]

For nineteen-year-old Margaret Truman, a slim, blonde sophomore at George Washington University in Washington, christening the battleship named for her home state meant her first real trip to the city of New York. She was accompanied by two close friends, Drucie Snyder and Jane Lingo, who would serve as her maids of honor during the christening ceremony. The night before the launching the three of them went to see the popular musical *Oklahoma*, Margaret's first Broadway show. Afterward, as she wrote years later, "Drucie, Jane, and I were so excited we stayed up all night; we literally did not go to sleep for one second." They arrived glassy eyed at the navy yard the next day, the twenty-ninth, which was cold and overcast by haze and a layer of gray clouds—typical New York weather in January.[22]

Unlike the keel-laying in 1941 and the commissioning that would take place in June of

By New Year's Day 1944, four weeks prior to launching, the navy yard had erected a good deal of the superstructure. This picture was taken from the conning tower, looking aft. The circular openings on the starboard side are for 5-inch gun mounts, all of which were installed prior to the launching. (Bureau of Ships photo in the National Archives: 19-N-72971)

Right: Margaret Truman stands poised to christen the ship with a champagne bottle suspended by a long cord from the forecastle above. Pictured (*left to right*) are: Rear Admiral Monroe Kelly, commandant of the New York Navy Yard; Rear Admiral Sherman S. Kennedy, who had taken part in the keel-laying three years earlier; and U.S. Senator Harry S Truman. (U.S. Navy photo in the National Archives: 80-G-44891)

Below: Taken from alongside the hull, this picture shows the press platform at the head of the shipways. On the lower level are still photographers; on top are newsreel cameramen. Both types are ready to record the launching. (Bureau of Ships photo in the National Archives: 19-N-73072)

1944, the *Missouri*'s launching was a highly public affair. The Navy estimated the crowd at twenty to thirty thousand spectators. Dozens of reporters and cameramen were present to let the world know of the event. The ceremony even made television, then in its infancy, though the coverage was far from nationwide. Cameras sent pictures to workmen in General Electric plants in upstate Schenectady, New York, where much of the ship's propulsion machinery and electrical equipment had been manufactured.[23]

The bow of the dreadnought towered high above as workmen knocked away the wooden shores holding the ship in place. Speeches were timed to end so that Margaret would swing her

magnum of champagne, made from Missouri grapes, just as the ship began to move. In her view, the admirals on the schedule ahead of her dad were taking revenge for the humiliations he had visited upon them previously as part of his work on the investigating committee. They took longer than they were supposed to, leaving the senator only a scant opportunity before the optimum time for launching. As Margaret explained in a memoir: "When Dad finally got to the microphone, he had about three minutes to deliver a fifteen-minute speech. I never heard him talk so fast in my life."[24] One of the things he said during his brief remarks made Truman something of a prophet. "The time is surely coming when the people of Missouri can thrill with pride as the *Missouri* and her sister ships, with batteries blazing, sail into Tokyo Bay."[25]

The champagne bottle, encased in a silver jacket engraved with the ship's name, was suspended from the forecastle by a long cord. The silver container had holes cut in it so the champagne could escape when Margaret smashed it against a metal plate sticking out from the ship's bow. When Admiral Kelly gave her the signal, Margaret smashed the bottle against the metal plate and said, "I christen thee USS *Missouri*."

Men up on the forecastle had been instructed to pull up on the long cord as soon as the bottle made impact with the hull. They did so, contributing to a fiasco. It was the Treasury Department's responsibility to score bottles so they would break more readily during christening ceremonies, but the staff didn't do it right this time. The bottle broke on the bottom rather than the side, with the result that champagne showered down on Margaret and Admiral Kelly, who was standing next to her. The admiral was furious, whereupon Margaret reminded him, "You're not the only one getting wet." She was wearing a fur coat during the ceremony, and as she remembered years later, "I never got the smell of champagne out of that coat."[26]

Despite the fact that Senator Truman had been forced to cut his speech short in order to meet the launching schedule, the hull didn't begin to move when it was supposed to. So Margaret playfully reached out with her white-

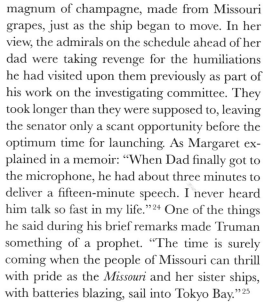

gloved hand and pushed on the battleship as if to get the hull started on its journey. A full minute later, at 1:05 P.M., it did begin to move, then picked up considerable speed during the journey down the inclined ways, and hit the East River with a splash. At that moment, the sun poked through the overcast, the only time all day it did so—a good omen to many present. Soon a flock of sixteen tug boats, blasting loudly on their whistles, converged on the hull so they could deliver it to an outfitting pier for the installation of turrets and the construction of the towering superstructure.[27]

Alas, for Governor Donnell, the Navy added insult to the injury it inflicted earlier when it bypassed his daughter. In an apologetic letter, Admiral Kelly explained that the plan had called for the ship to be launched at 1:10 in the afternoon. While Kelly was giving his own speech, however, the yard manager told him the launching would have to be moved up to 1:05 to accommodate the wind and tide. Kelly

During the time that the *Missouri* was being outfitted at the New York Navy Yard, various citizens of the state of Missouri were besieging Senator Truman's office with requests that they or their relatives be assigned to the brand-new battleship. Many of their letters are still on file at the Truman Library in Independence, Missouri. Word processors had not yet been invented, but the typewriters of the era churned out a standard boilerplate reply, indicating that the senator would love to help, but the personnel assignments were the prerogative of the Navy. In fact, that was the case, and it enabled Truman to say that he had tried to do something for his constituents, but the matter was out of his hands.

The senator still managed to pull a few strings in specific cases, though. One of the officers who joined the crew after completing Navy communication school at Harvard University was Lieutenant (j.g.) Leonard Chinn of Springfield, Missouri. His father, Hiram "Dig" Chinn, was a local restaurateur and strong Democrat who played poker with Truman whenever the senator visited Springfield in connection with political events. And so it was that the son got assigned to the *Missouri*.[30]

In addition to the requests that went to Truman's office, the Bureau of Naval Personnel was besieged as well. Some three thousand officers applied to be part of the battleship's initial crew, nearly thirty times as many as she could accommodate. The bureau chose Captain William M. Callaghan, more than a quarter century out of Annapolis, to be the first skipper. Tall and slender, Callaghan had gone to sea in an earlier battleship *Missouri* during a summer training cruise while he was a midshipman. He had graduated from the Naval Academy during World War I, commanded the destroyer *Reuben James* in the 1930s, served as an observer with the Royal Navy in the early days of the war, and had been on the OpNav staff in Washington. Most recently he had served on the Pacific Fleet staff of Admiral Chester Nimitz in Hawaii.

Once back on the mainland, Callaghan stopped at the Bureau of Personnel in Washington. The bureau chief suggested that the new

The hull of the *Missouri* enters the water for the first time. The clumps of anchor chain hanging down from the bow were put in place to provide drag, thus slowing the ship's momentum once she entered the East River. The Missouri state flag can be seen just to the left of the superstructure. (U.S. Navy photo courtesy of Allan E. Smith, Jr.)

reported that he had finished his own remarks and read a message from Admiral Ernest J. King, the chief of naval operations, but in order to leave time for Senator Truman to talk, Kelly had been forced to omit the speech that Governor Donnell had sent for the occasion.[28]

That evening—January 29—Margaret Truman and her friends felt the effects of their excitement-induced insomnia the night before. As they were being served dessert after dinner at the posh Waldorf-Astoria Hotel, they fell sound asleep sitting in their chairs. The waiters were amused. Senator Truman remained considerably *un*amused, however, as he reflected on the brief time allotted for his speech and the champagne bath for his daughter. Two years later, by which time he was president, he still wasn't forgiving those he felt had slighted him in January 1944. He suggested that they should have taken the advice of writer Josh Billings: "Always be nice to your pore relations—they may suddenly become rich someday and it will be hard to explain."[29]

skipper invite Senator Truman to make the principal speech at the upcoming commissioning ceremony in June. Truman demurred, saying that the state's senior senator, Bennett Champ Clark, should have the opportunity instead. Forty years earlier Clark had watched the launching of the *Missouri* in which Callaghan made his midshipman cruise.[31]

Enlisted men were also preparing for their roles on board the new battleship. Before reporting to Brooklyn, Seaman Walt Yucka received instruction on board a real relic, the gunnery training ship *Wyoming*. Originally commissioned as a battleship in September 1912, she was still at work thirty-two years later. Operating in the protected sanctuary of the Chesapeake Bay, she gave thousands and thousands of men hands-on experience with guns before they got to their own ships. He learned how to operate in a 5-inch/38 mount identical to the type on board the *Missouri*.[32]

Only a relatively small number of the ship's future crew members, the so-called nucleus crew, were at Brooklyn as the ship prepared to go into service. These were generally experienced men, primarily those destined for the engineering department. While at Brooklyn they helped with the installation of the propulsion plant and received training in its operation. Other future *Missouri* men in the shipyard were technicians who helped with the installation of electronic equipment and fire control gear. After his time in the *Wyoming*, Yucka arrived at the New York Navy Yard in March, three months prior to the commissioning of the *Missouri*. Work was still moving forward at a steady pace to complete the ship's construction. Yard workmen were welding metal seemingly continuously, which meant Yucka and many others had to stand fire watches, ready to respond with an extinguisher in the event something burst into flame.[33]

The remaining hundreds of future crewmen were at the naval training station in Newport, Rhode Island, where the ship's prospective executive officer, Commander Jacob "Jocko" Cooper, helped indoctrinate them in a myriad of shipboard practices. Lieutenant Jack Clancy, destined to be the assistant communications officer, thought that the strict Cooper overdid

Captain William M. Callaghan, first commanding officer of the battleship, poses in his cabin with the state seal of Missouri. (U.S. Navy photo in the National Archives: 80-G-K-46841)

it. For instance, Cooper demanded that all hands be punctilious about saluting officers even if they were on the other side of the street. As Clancy remembered later, "Cooper gave me hell the second I was there, because three sailors passed about twenty yards away from me and didn't salute." Clancy had just come in from sea duty, where there was more emphasis on getting the job done and less on exaggerated displays of military courtesy.[34]

Because many of the prospective crew members were from New York, New Jersey, and Connecticut, Rhode Island was especially handy after they completed recruit training at Camp Sampson in the scenic Finger Lakes region of upstate New York. The majority of these men had until recently been civilians, so few had any sea duty behind them. And, since they could contribute little before the *Missouri* got under way, the training period at Newport indoctrinated them in specific skills they would need once they reported to a division in the battleship. The future shipmates also learned about things that applied to men in any number of divisions: namely, the method of putting on a gas mask and handling a hose during firefighting drills.

Seaman Joe Vella, for instance, went through a course designed to prepare him to

Right: The guns of
turret three point
skyward during the
commissioning
ceremony at the New
York Navy Yard on June
11, 1944. Crew
members and families
were invited, but it was
not the public event
that the launching was.
(U.S. Navy photo in the
National Archives:
80-G-K-3858)

Below: The *Missouri* lies
moored at the New York
Navy Yard on June 27,
two weeks after
commissioning and two
weeks before getting
under way for the first
time. She is painted in a
"dazzle" camouflage
scheme (designated
Measure 32, Design
22D) of black, ocean
gray, and light gray.
Overhead is a
hammerhead crane.
(Bureau of Ships photo
in the National Archives:
19-N-72973)

be a crew member of a 20-mm antiaircraft gun.
Because he might have only an instant to make
a decision whether to fire, he learned aircraft
recognition by looking at silhouettes of U.S.
and Japanese planes flashed on a screen for
only a second or less. He practiced over and
over at taking a 20-mm gun apart and putting
it back together again so he could make battle
repairs if necessary.[35]

Another who was trained on 20-mm guns
was Seaman Herman Leibig. He put his shoulders into the half-moon supports that helped a
gunner steady himself as he fired. As a plane
towed target sleeves past, the object was to put
holes into it within twenty seconds. The sooner
a gunner could shoot down a plane, the less

danger to the ship. Leibig was so enthusiastic,
however, that he kept blasting away for more
than half a minute, whereupon a chief petty
officer whacked him on the back and asked,
"Can't you count?" The seaman was having
too much fun to count and shoot at the same
time.[36]

Not all systems are perfect, of course. When
Vella and Leibig reported to the *Missouri* herself, they were put into the fourth division,
which had the 5-inch mounts on the port side.
Thus, they had no opportunity to apply the
knowledge they had picked up about the 20-
mm guns. They had to learn all over again on
a new type of antiaircraft weapon.

Eventually, the training came to an end.
Some of the men went from Newport to New
York by train; others went by ship. One day in
early June the USS *Chilton*, an attack transport,
took aboard the *Missouri* men. The *Chilton* was
herself a training ship at Newport for men who
would be in the crews of attack transports. Now
she went farther afield than usual to deliver the
future battleship men down the Long Island
Sound and up the East River to the navy yard.
They walked from one ship to another and began an entirely new way of life.

Except for boot camp and the training period at Newport, seventeen-year-old Joe Vella,
who came from Enfield, Connecticut, had

hardly been away from home at all before he reported to the *Missouri*. As he stepped aboard the huge battleship one morning, he remembered something that had been drummed into him during recruit training. "You follow orders. You do what you're told." So he followed along as part of a group when a boatswain's mate took a draft of new men down to the ship's mess compartment on the second deck. He showed Vella a pair of hooks on bulkheads and told him to sling his hammock from them. Like all new men, Vella had been issued a hammock during training, and he carried it with him, wrapped around his seabag, whenever he was transferred.[37]

The petty officer said: "This is where you're sleeping. Until I come back and tell you what to do, you don't leave this spot." Even though he was reluctant to do so without authorization, the young seaman did go through the chow line at meal time, then quickly returned to his spot. He slept in the hammock that first night but still dutifully stayed nearby, waiting for whatever was to come next. Over the loudspeaker came the summons for the crew to muster at quarters. Even though his new shipmates urged him to accompany them, Vella didn't move, still recalling the order to stay put. On the third day, he finally succumbed and went to quarters. When the boatswain's mate saw him, he demanded, "Where the hell have you been?"

"I was down in the mess hall. You told me to stay there until you came for me."

"You mean to tell me you were down there this whole time?"

Meanwhile, the division officer was watching the exchange and wondering whether it had really happened or whether it was a ruse to cover an unauthorized liberty Vella had taken. Finally, Vella convinced them of the legitimacy of his story, and he was quickly given a bunk and better instructions than previously on what was expected of him.[38]

The afternoon of Sunday, June 11, was a bright, sunny one. Along with both Missouri senators, those in attendance at the *Missouri*'s commissioning included: the new Secretary of the Navy, James Forrestal; a number of admi-

rals; and relatives of the men who would form the crew of the gleaming new warship. The official act of commissioning fell to Admiral Kelly, who had been doused with champagne at the battleship's launching ceremony. Normally, a ship's deck log is written in the dullest of prose, just the facts with no editorializing. On this auspicious occasion, however, the log writer got caught up in the excitement of the event and wrote, "At 1522, after making a stirring speech to those present, the Commandant, Navy Yard, New York directed that the U.S.S. Missouri be placed in full Commission."[39]

Signalmen eagerly raised the national ensign and a commissioning pennant as symbols of the ship's new status. The first personal flag to go up was that of Secretary Forrestal, who had decided at the last minute to come to Brooklyn. He was understandably preoccupied with other things; the Allies had invaded Normandy just five days earlier, and four days later Marines would be stepping ashore at Saipan in the Pacific.[40]

For some of the crew members, such as Seaman Vella, the commissioning ceremony was "a pain in the neck." It meant they had to do a lot of standing around either at attention or parade rest while people they didn't know made speeches. He felt he was being used—a bit player in a show put on largely for the benefit of visitors, not for the crew. Part of the feeling stemmed from Vella's youth and inexperience. He hadn't been in the Navy long enough to understand the significance of the occasion. Half a century later, though, he relishes his status as one of the *Missouri*'s initial crew members. Others, such as Seaman Yucka, felt a mixture of excitement and pride: he got to show off the ship to his wife, who visited for the occasion. Mary Yucka was less than thrilled, however, when she had to use the trough-type head that was to become all-too-familiar to *Missouri* sailors in the months to come.[41]

At the conclusion of the commissioning ceremony, Captain Callaghan used a term from the old Navy in directing the executive officer to bring things to a close: "Pipe down, Commander Cooper." In naval parlance, that referred to a boatswain's pipe, used to signal vari-

ous events in the ship's routine. Essentially, the captain was telling the executive officer to have the boatswain's mate blow his pipe and thus end the ceremony. Members of the civilian audience, unaccustomed to the terminology, chuckled at the skipper's wording. In their frame of reference, Callaghan was telling Cooper to be quiet, and Cooper hadn't been saying a thing.[42]

Once the show was over the crew began to settle in and adjust to living in this new, crammed-together society that constituted a battleship. Privacy was a thing of the past. Nobody had his own room, as might have been the case back home. Men slept in bunks stacked several tiers high. They kept their uniforms and personal belongings in lockers that had to be artfully packed to fit everything in. From time to time the officers held locker inspections, again with no concern for privacy. When the enlisted men were out at quarters on deck, the officers used master keys to open up lockers and see that crew members weren't hiding liquor or other contraband items. If an individual had a combination lock on his locker instead of one that took a key, a master-at-arms would snip off the lock with a bolt cutter to permit inspection.[43]

With the huge crew on board the *Missouri*, not all of the enlisted men were able to get bunks in the berthing compartments. Some men slept in the turrets themselves; others lived in one of the powder-handling areas well below decks. The bunks in compartments went three or four high; they were even higher in the handling rooms. The space deep within the ship was somewhat cooler than the compartments in those days before air-conditioning.[44]

Reporting to the *Missouri* was a dramatic change in life-style for Seaman Al Circelli, whose previous ship was the old battleship *New York*, commissioned in April 1914. The size alone commanded his attention, as did the living accommodations. Now he had a bunk instead of having to sleep in a hammock, and he could unpack his seabag and stow a locker in his living compartment. In the *New York* his seabag was his closet, meaning he had to dig down into it whenever he wanted to wear a particular uniform item. The new ship had a laundry to wash his uniforms; he'd previously been washing them himself, using rationed water.[45]

Meals in the *Missouri* were served cafeteria style in a general mess that fed the entire enlisted crew. In the *New York* divisions ate in their sleeping compartments, served family style by mess cooks. It was also the job of mess cooks to pull down tables stowed in racks in the overhead between meals. With the tables thus out of the way, men could sling their hammocks. That wasn't necessary in the *Missouri*, where the tables could be left standing between meals. Off-duty crewmen could thus sit down as the opportunity permitted to have some coffee, smoke, chat with shipmates, and so forth.[46]

Even though Commander Cooper was tough, he earned the respect of many members of the crew. One who admired him was Circelli, who was used to the regulation-type Navy from his days in the *New York*. Once, while he was walking down the street in the shipyard, Circelli spotted the exec coming the other way on the opposite side of the street. He deliberately crossed the street so he could salute the ship's number-two officer.

On the other hand, Circelli wasn't above evading Cooper's regulations if it suited his interests. Cooper enforced the practice of

Left: Cooks mass-produce lemon pies in the galley, scooping the filling out of the vat in the foreground. (U.S. Navy photo in the National Archives: 80-G-K-4516)

Below: *Missouri* sailors receive their chow in the cafeteria-style serving line in the general mess. (U.S. Navy photo in the National Archives: 80-G-K-47246)

allowing only Navy-issue uniforms. Circelli and others in the crew, however, preferred the tailor-made blues, which fit more snugly and were generally more dashing in appearance. They also proved to be more appealing to the women that crew members met on liberty. Thus, when the ship was going to be in New York for a period of time, Circelli would go ashore wearing two uniforms—the regular jumper and trousers over the tailor-mades. Then he'd find a locker in which to store the regulation uniform while wearing only the fancier tailor-mades during his excursions about town.[47]

During June and July, while the navy yard was still putting the finishing touches on the *Missouri*, her crew members were preparing as well. By the dozens they were going to various schools so they could receive training in radar, the new Loran system for navigation, antiaircraft gunnery, operation and maintenance of

This view of the *Missouri* in dry dock at Bayonne, New Jersey, on July 23, emphasizes the bridge and fire control tower, equipped with both search and fire-control radars. (Bureau of Ships photo in the National Archives: 19-N-73026)

the big guns, among other duties. They also received training during shipboard drills while in the yard. Still another activity was loading the ship with the food, spare parts, and other supplies she would need during the months ahead. To Seaman Leibig—an available body, even if not a completely willing one—it seemed that he was summoned for one working party after another.[48]

Eighteen-year-old Fireman Bob Schwenk was a rarity in the commissioning crew of the *Missouri* in that he came from California rather than the East Coast. After going through boot training at San Diego, he had been slated as an alternate to go aboard a destroyer, later to an amphibious landing ship, but he wound up reporting to neither. Instead, he was part of a draft reporting to the newest battleship. During the training period his duty was in number-

three fireroom, as a talker on the JV sound-powered telephone circuit. Water Tender Second Class John DeGroff was in charge and was teaching Schwenk how to handle the circuit. He said a man in main control would give Schwenk messages, and then it was his job to pass them along to DeGroff. When Schwenk started receiving messages, DeGroff asked him, "What are they saying?"

"I don't know," Schwenk replied. "They're speaking in a foreign language, and I can't understand them."[49]

The "foreign language" turned out to be the accents of New York, New England, and New Jersey—the East Coast sailors to whom the Californian was completely unaccustomed. In those days before television and the homogenization of the language, regional accents were strange indeed to those whose upbringing had been confined to another part of the country.

As a junior enlisted man, Schwenk received a salary of a mere thirty-six dollars a month. He and his shipmates were fortunate that servicemen were treated generously by the civilian populace out of a feeling of gratitude for their service to the country. Thus it was that they fell into the practice of making "quarter liberties," as Schwenk called them. They would leave the navy yard in Brooklyn, walk down Sand Street to the subway, and get on the train without paying. They pretended to put a nickel in the coin slot, then vaulted over the turnstile. Once over in Manhattan, they attended such events as fights, ball games, and shows—free of charge to servicemen. Their Navy uniforms were the only tickets they needed to be able to walk into New York's Polo Grounds or Ebbets Field in Brooklyn. (Considering the subpar quality of wartime baseball, it was a fair price.) They also found their way to the Pepsi-Cola canteen, which dispensed all the free Pepsi they could drink. Hot dogs went for a nickel apiece, so each man ate five of them, thus spending the twenty-five cents that constituted the entire cost of the liberty.[50]

On July 10, the ship conducted dock trials in Brooklyn, then went out to an anchorage near the Statue of Liberty before proceeding across the harbor to Bayonne, New Jersey, for dry-docking. One of the chores that fell to Lieutenant Doug Plate of the gunnery department was that of going through her magazines to determine a stowage plan for 5-inch projectiles and powder charges. The experiences of the sisters in the *Iowa* class provided rough guidelines, but Plate still had considerable work to do on specifics. Part of the job depended on the expected missions of the ship and thus the various types of projectiles needed. Shore bombardment, for instance, called for one type; gunnery practice for another; antiaircraft, still a third. Antiaircraft rounds predominated because by that stage of the war the fast battleships had been relegated to that role in carrier task group screens.[51]

Next, the ship went to an anchorage in Gravesend Bay, part of New York harbor, to take aboard the 5-inch ammunition and the thousands of rounds of other sizes that would also fill her magazines. Just as in the old days, when coaling ship was an all-hands chore, so was the ammunition loading. Both officers and enlisted men, many stripped to the waist, worked for days to get everything aboard from barges alongside. Then the powder and projectiles had to be struck down below, put into magazines, and strapped into place so they wouldn't move around once the ship was at sea. Lieutenant Plate had a demanding night on the town just before the ammo loading; he found the strenuous work an effective way of sweating alcohol out of his system. On another night in New York, Plate had gone to a small club in Greenwich Village to listen to a skinny singer named Frank Sinatra.[52]

Once the loading was complete, the *Missouri* steamed out through New York's famous Am-

This view of the superstructure on July 23 shows SG surface-search radar antennas atop both mainmast and foremast. The circular antenna for the SK-2 air-search radar is on the foremast. (Bureau of Ships photo in the National Archives: 19-N-73031)

Right: Gunner's Mate Charles Hansen works on 40-mm mount number thirteen during the ship's shakedown. The tattoo on his right shoulder commemorates his shipmates killed in the sinking of the heavy cruiser *Vincennes* at Guadalcanal in August 1942. On his left shoulder is a record of the battles the cruiser was in prior to her loss. (U.S. Navy photo in the National Archives: 80-G-K-4510)

brose Channel to the ocean beyond. On the last day of July, the battleship began doing what she had been built for—shooting her guns. The purpose was structural testing, to see how well the hull and superstructure would withstand the blasts of gunfire. It started with the chattering of the 20- and 40-mm light antiaircraft guns. Then, at 1:48 in the afternoon, she unleashed a projectile from the right gun of turret one, followed later in the afternoon by the firing of the 5-inch/38 dual-purpose guns that could be used against both air and surface targets. The *Missouri* had lost her virginity.[53]

Then it was time to head out into the Atlantic, if only briefly, on the way to the Chesapeake Bay. In those enclosed waters, safe from enemy submarines, the *Missouri* would conduct some initial shipboard training for the crew. Years later Callaghan described the experience from the skipper's viewpoint. "What a sensation it was to have the responsibility and thrill of handling the ship in the open sea after we dropped the pilot at Sandy Hook lightship."[54]

Once inside the bay it was time to swing the ship around through the various headings on the compass to check the deviation between her electrically operated gyrocompass and her old-fashioned magnetic compass. The information was necessary in the event the gyro failed and the ship had to operate on the magnetic one. The chore was a demanding one, requiring the *Missouri* to come to a range of new courses and stay on each one long enough for the compass readings to be recorded. It was also distracting, with the result that the navigation team temporarily lost track of the ship's position in relation to the shoal-water areas plotted on the chart.

Captain Callaghan noticed that an ebb tide seemed to be pushing the battleship toward the Virginia shoreline. He quickly confirmed his suspicions by radar and rang up emergency full speed to take the ship into safer deep water. The skipper's Marine orderly, Private First Class Roland Couture, was standing nearby on the bridge. He observed that Callaghan remained characteristically calm throughout the incident.[55]

The captain's external demeanor didn't match his inner uneasiness. He was under-

standably concerned that the ship had scraped bottom—a real no-no as far as the Navy was concerned—when she strayed near the shoal area. His sense of apprehension was heightened when he received a report that evening that soundings in a forward water tank revealed two feet of water. As he recalled the incident, "I sweated through the night until the next morning when the tank was opened for inspection and we discovered the water had backed up from a leaking drain line."[56]

The *Missouri* spent a few days in Norfolk in August during a respite in her crew's training. One day Seaman Leibig, who had grown up in Pennsylvania, went out on liberty. He boarded a bus and happened to take a seat near the back, thinking nothing of it. He came face to face with a culture much different from what he had known. The bus driver screamed at him: "Hey, swabbie, you get up front. The niggers sit in the back." He found out that white sailors weren't all that welcome in some places in Norfolk either. With thousands of Navy men in and around the city at the mouth of the Chesapeake Bay, some of the locals had had more of them than they wanted.[57]

The tavern operators were more accommodating because the men from the battleship contributed so much to their livelihood. Leibig was served beer, even though he was only seventeen at the time. After he and several of his buddies had a few beers one day, they decided to get tattooed. He had seen men with large tattoos and concluded he wanted to take a much more modest approach. So the tattooist's needle stuck only a relatively small amount of blue ink under the skin on Leibig's right forearm—his name and the name *Missouri*. Half a century later, the color is still there, though the letters have largely run together, a lasting reminder of his first cruise in the "Mighty Mo."[58]

When Ensign Jack Barron reported aboard the *Missouri* that August, he discovered one of the disadvantages of having graduated from the Naval Academy. There to greet the self-described "red-ass ensign" was Lieutenant Clancy, the man who'd run afoul of the executive officer in Newport. Clancy had been with Barron in the V-7 reserve officer training program in 1940. Soon after Barron graduated from college in New York, he got an unexpected appointment to the Naval Academy. Clancy, without such an appointment, had gone ahead and gotten a reserve commission through the V-7 program, so he was gaining seniority as an officer while his friend Barron was putting in time as a midshipman in Annapolis. The reunion of the two friends was soon interrupted by Clancy's nemesis, Commander Cooper. He directed Clancy to knock off the small talk and get the new ensigns squared away.[59]

When Art Albert reported to the ship that same month, he was fresh out of boot camp at Sampson, New York. As in recruit training, he discovered anew that what he did was almost always the Navy's choice rather than his own. When Albert got to the *Missouri*, Commander Cooper asked him what he had done in civilian life. He replied that he had worked on a farm at home, near Syracuse, New York. There he had become familiar with tractors and other machinery. Cooper said, "All right, we'll make you a fireman."[60]

As Albert met other newcomers to the ship, he tried to explain his new job, saying naively, "I guess I've got to fight fires." He quickly found out, though, that he would keep the fires going, not put them out. Because of his mechanical background, he was put in training as a machinist's mate, operating equipment connected with the ship's boilers in one of the firerooms. That one quick conversation in the summer of 1944 had a considerable impact on Albert. More than twenty years later, he retired from the Navy as a machinist's mate first class.[61]

For her shakedown training the *Missouri* operated with the new large cruiser *Alaska*. She and her later sister *Guam* were the only U.S. warships built in World War II with 12-inch guns, a size mounted on battleships earlier in the century. Since the two new capital ships had been completed at the same time, they joined with destroyers for training in the Gulf of Paria off the coast of Venezuela. The landlocked gulf offered the same advantage for training that the Chesapeake Bay had—protection against

submarine threats—but it offered more room in which to roam and deeper water than the bay, a welcome relief for Callaghan after the near grounding earlier.[62]

Some in the crew probably qualified as alcoholics, because the Navy culture of the period generally accepted that some sailors drank prodigiously when they got ashore. These men had to make real adjustments when the *Missouri* got out into her training phase. Seaman Leibig observed one shipmate who bought bottles of after-shave lotion in the ship's store and chugalugged them when he felt the urge. It was a way of coping—albeit in unorthodox fashion—with an acquired addiction.[63]

The young crewmen of the *Missouri*, serious about their business, grew up in a hurry. Part of the learning process was aided by the presence of "mustang" officers; that is, former enlisted men who had a wealth of experience to share. The 16-inch turret crews, for example, learned from men who had been gunner's mates and turret captains before getting their warrants or commissions.[64] While the turret crews were shaking down, so were those assigned to smaller guns. Day after day the anti-aircraft gunners worked out against target sleeves towed by airplanes, including Army Air Forces bombers. The repetition made the crew increasingly capable for the job that would be its most important once the ship reached the Pacific and faced the enemy.[65]

The shakedown training was in more southerly latitudes than the crew had been accustomed to. The August sun was hotter than in New York, and the work was hard. Thus, the men sought to slake their thirsts when they had the opportunity. Those respites from training came when the ship stopped at Trinidad for liberty. The result, according to Joe Vella, was "one big drunk." Captain Callaghan was extremely strict in prohibiting liquor on board

Arthur Stratham of Commander Edward Steichen's famed photo unit captured this view during the shakedown in August 1944. Probably the most well-known picture of the *Missouri*'s pre-combat period, it shows the six projectiles from the forward turrets airborne at right. Notice the blast effect on the water. (U.S. Navy photo in the National Archives: 80-G-K-4515)

A leadsman casts the weighted sounding line—just as Mark Twain did on the Mississippi River—in order to determine the depth of water while piloting near shore. Next to him is a line holder, and the telephone talker is on deck to relay reports to the bridge. (U.S. Navy photo in the National Archives: 80-G-K-4542)

admiral and his staff during the training, so the newsmen bunked on cots in the future flag quarters on the 02 level. Ensign Barron and some of his newly arrived cohorts joined them in camping out because the junior officer berthing was crowded.[67]

The *Missouri* went to a navy yard annex in Bayonne after the training period ended. There the battleship settled in for a shipyard availability period to repair various items that had broken down during the initial at-sea period. The newspapermen went back to their offices, leaving the group of ensigns as the only occupants of flag quarters. Said Jack Barron with a laugh, "My claim to fame is that I slept in [Admiral William] Halsey's bed before he did." He had his own cabin, head, closet, dresser, and even the admiral's brass bed. His mother and sister lived in nearby New York, so he brought them aboard for a tour. When he showed them his accommodations, his mother asked, "Does everybody get a room like this?" All too soon the clock struck midnight, and Barron's magic coach turned into a pumpkin. When the ship got around to the West Coast, he had to move into the "ensign locker" where he was jammed into a bunkroom with seventeen other officers.[68]

While the ship was at Bayonne the officers had an enjoyable farewell-to-New York party in one of the city's fancy hotels. Ensign Barron was there with his girlfriend (and future wife), seventeen-year-old Elie McDonald. She soon developed as healthy a dislike for the executive officer as Barron had. While she was dancing with Commander Cooper, she said to him, "I hope you take good care of Jack."

Cooper put her down gruffly. "He has to take care of himself." Young and apprehensive, she was concerned that she had committed a faux pas that would get Ensign Barron into trouble.[69]

ship, but the command wanted to reward the men for their hard work. So during the training period they provided a beer party ashore—large G.I. cans filled with ice and canned beer. Many members of the *Missouri*'s crew were bombed by the time they'd drunk their fill and then ridden liberty launches to get back to the anchored battleship. They were unable to get aboard under their own power and had to be hauled up in cargo nets, a few men at a time.[66]

During the shakedown cruise the *Missouri* was loaded with newspaper reporters taking notes so they could file stories about this wondrous new battleship. The ship didn't carry an

Back when the *Missouri*'s men were going through the precommissioning training period, one of the instructors at Newport was Lieutenant James Starnes, who taught navigation to the crews of new ships. He had been commissioned in the first V-7 naval reserve officer training class in 1940. In fact, he had received his training on board the USS *Illinois,* a sort of floating barracks that had been built on the hull of the former battleship and served the naval reserve in New York City. After that, Starnes had been assistant navigator of the light cruiser *Boise,* which was involved in some of the savage night surface actions against the Japanese off Guadalcanal in late 1942. Once he was assigned to Newport, he thought he had found a splendid, peaceful place to serve out the remainder of the war.[70]

His enjoyable reverie came to an end suddenly in November 1944 when he received orders to report immediately to the *Missouri,* and he became the navigator. As such, Starnes was part of an experiment. Until then the battleship's navigator had been Commander Hylan B. Lyon, previously the skipper of the submarine *Gudgeon.* The Navy Department decided to use the *Missouri* as a test ship for an organization that would include an operations department, with navigation as one of the divisions. Starnes's experience in the *Boise* and as a navi-

Above: A chief petty officer serves as referee while two *Missouri* men hold a boxing match on the fantail. (U.S. Navy photo in the National Archives: 80-G-47251)

Left: Three OS2U floatplanes sit on the fantail: two on catapults and one on a dolly. The picture was taken while the ship was anchored at Hampton Roads, Virginia, during a break from shakedown training. The men are in ranks for captain's inspection. Notice the dazzle camouflage pattern visible on the teakwood covering the main deck. (U.S. Navy photo in the National Archives: 80-G-47220)

The barbershop does a steady business. Notice the two bunk bottoms triced up against the bulkhead at the left edge of the photo, next to the sink. The *Missouri* was so crowded during World War II that a number of men slept in their work spaces. (U.S. Navy photo in the National Archives: 80–47250)

gation instructor fitted him for the role. Right after Starnes reported, he just had time to check in before the *Missouri* left for distant duty.[71]

The rationale for this new shipboard organization was the need to adapt to the requirements posed by having radar and a combat information center. The operations department would process information from a variety of sources, including radio, radar, visual signals, lookouts, weather, intelligence, and navigation. Whereas communications, like navigation, had previously been an independent department, it was also amalgamated into the new ops department. In time, the experiment was pronounced a success and spread to ships throughout the Navy.[72]

Another new member of the crew that November was Seaman John C. Truman, son of Senator Truman's brother J. Vivian. The nephew, customarily known as J. C., had been a high school teacher in Independence, Missouri, from 1936 to 1941. Later he was a defense worker for the Remington Arms Com-

pany in Independence. At thirty-one years old when he joined the Navy in February 1944, he was married and had three children, different from the young single men who had flocked to the service early in the war. After boot camp Truman attended quartermaster school and then was assigned to a ship. He and the men with him did not make it to that ship in time, however, and thus wound up in the crew of the *Missouri* instead. It was apparently happenstance and not the result of any political influence. Seaman Truman was assigned to the battleship's navigation division and remained there throughout her wartime cruise.[73]

On November 10, 1944, the *Missouri* began the initial leg of the long journey that would take her to war. That first night brought disquieting news, however. Because of the possibility of submarines in the Atlantic, crewmen were standing watches topside on the guns. During the course of the evening, someone rotated a 40-mm gun mount without checking to see if anyone was in the way. As the guns swung around in the autumn darkness, Seaman Second Class Herbert A. Wunsch was evidently unaware of their movement and received a crushing blow to the lower chest. He went into severe shock, which Lieutenant Commander Thornton Scott of the ship's medical department tried to treat with plasma and morphine. Unfortunately, the treatment was not effective, and young Wunsch died shortly before eleven that night.[74]

The tragedy was compounded the following day when the ship stopped briefly in the Hampton Roads area for some personnel transfers, including sending Seaman Wunsch's body ashore by boat. The deck crew lowered the stretcher by hand because the new men were still unfamiliar with the electrically operated controls. When the stretcher had nearly reached the boat, Seaman First Class F. R. Rapasky apparently slipped and lost his grip on the hoisting machine's L-shaped handle, which then went spinning out of control. It struck him in the head and groin, resulting in a compound skull fracture, lacerated scalp, intracranial injury, and abrasion of his right thigh. The new battleship had not even gotten into combat for the first time, but she had already demonstrated that she was an inherently dangerous place in which to live and work. The silver lining for the crew, as Captain Callaghan observed, was that the accidents emphasized how raw the men were and how much they still had to learn.[75]

The newest battleship in the U.S. Navy had some interesting company as she began her voyage to the far Pacific. She was accompanied by the two oldest battleships in the fleet: the *Arkansas*, commissioned in 1912, and the *Texas*, commissioned in 1914. Earlier in the year, those two ships and the *Nevada* had provided naval gunfire support for the D-Day invasion

of Normandy in June and the landings in southern France in mid-August. Now, with the war in Europe having gone too far inland for naval guns, they were heading for the Pacific to add their bombardment support to the coming amphibious invasions of 1945. The third oldest battleship, the *New York*, commissioned in 1914, had spent most of the war as a training ship for midshipmen. Soon she too would be headed for the Pacific.[76]

In mid-November the *Missouri* went through the Panama Canal. The fit was so tight in the locks that the *Missouri*'s steel sides knocked off pieces of concrete that fell onto the main deck. The men then went on liberty. The permanent

An escort carrier is astern on November 22, 1944, as the *Missouri* steams from Panama to San Francisco. The battleship had just entered the Pacific Ocean for the first time a few days earlier. (U.S. Navy photo in the National Archives: 80-G-K-288333)

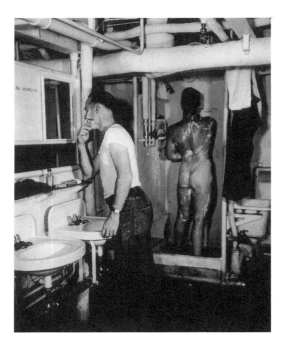

Fireman First Class Edward T. Hands shaves while a shipmate showers in the crew's head. (U.S. Navy photo in the National Archives: 80-G-K-4552)

shore patrolmen in Panama (as opposed to those supplied by individual ships) were hand-picked on the basis of experience in U.S. civilian police forces and a height exceeding six feet. The Army had its equivalents in the military police. The main thing was to keep fighting and disturbance of the peace to a minimum, and in that the service policemen were largely successful. The shore patrol also tried to steer sailors away from "blue-moon gals," a generic term for bar girls and hookers.[77]

On the other hand, sometimes the shore patrolmen were more cooperative. When Joe Rodrigues went ashore, he and two other shipmates got into a taxi. Rodrigues asked to go to the local USO, remembering good times he'd had in the one in New York. The driver took them right to the red-light district. There the military police said, "Go ahead, and hurry up."[78] Of course, even without the benefit of complaisant law-enforcement officials, the *Missouri* men concluded they didn't have much to lose in having a fling with women before going to the Pacific. A possible punishment was that they would be restricted to the ship, and that was going to happen anyway as soon as they reached the war zone.

Once in the Pacific the *Missouri* followed orders to head for the naval dry dock at Hunters

Point in San Francisco where she was to be fitted out as a fleet flagship. Her sister *New Jersey* had received such modifications earlier in the year at Pearl Harbor in order to accommodate Admiral William F. "Bull" Halsey and his Third Fleet staff. In anticipation of Halsey using the *Missouri* as flagship when the *New Jersey* was unavailable, the shipyard beefed up her radio equipment and made other alterations. The ship would have heavy communications requirements while carrying the top admiral and his staff.

The *Missouri* also required a different camouflage scheme. Throughout her period in the Atlantic she had been outfitted in an unusual "dazzle" pattern of black, white, and gray irregular shapes. Lieutenant Plate heard that it was a state-of-the-art camouflage design intended to make it difficult for men in submarines and other ships to discern the range and heading of the ship. It was largely a Pacific Fleet measure, although the *Missouri*'s differed in having rounded contours rather than the jagged edges seen on most ships. But that old scheme was being phased out. Thus, the shipyard workers at Hunters Point painted the ship in a scheme—called measure 22—that had been commonplace in the Atlantic Fleet. It was worn, for example, in the U.S. Navy ships that supported the invasion of Normandy earlier in the year. It featured a navy-blue hull from the main deck level downward; the area above that was painted haze gray. The decks were painted dark blue-gray so they would blend in with the sea when viewed from above.[79]

Still another change for the ship was a new complement of aircraft. Taking the place of the two-seat Vought OS2U Kingfishers were single-seat SC-1 Seahawks, built by Curtiss. The new plane had higher performance, although it lacked the advantage of a rear-seat man to help out with gunnery and to provide an extra pair of eyes during spotting and scouting. On the day before sailing, the ship conducted catapult tests, launching the new aircraft despite the lack of wind. The planes dipped noticeably downward after leaving the catapult track.[80]

All of the *Missouri*'s pilots had a lot of learning to do. The four of them had a total of only thirty-one hours of flight time among them in the SC-1, and most of those were in the land-based version outfitted with wheels. But, being naval aviators, they were determined to test the new machine's characteristics. One of them violated safety rules by flying under the Golden Gate Bridge.[81]

San Francisco afforded the crew one last opportunity for stateside liberty before heading west. Many of the crew members gravitated to USO canteens, which provided free refreshments and entertainment. Pretty girls showed up, including movie starlets at times. Seaman Leibig managed to dance with a young actress named Joan Leslie for about forty seconds before someone else cut in and took her away from him.[82]

About half a dozen *Missouri* sailors, including Seaman Circelli, went out as a group for a night on the town. They wound up in a large Italian restaurant just off Market Street. Because of his own Italian heritage, it was particularly appealing to Circelli. Blessed with the appetite of a young man, he ordered a whole chicken, baked lasagna, and several other items from the menu. The owner was suitably impressed when he heard about the order, so he came out to chat. In a spirit of patriotism, he told Circelli the meal was on the house and wished him good fortune in what lay ahead for his ship. The sailor gratefully ate everything his host brought him. It would be a long time before Circelli had an opportunity to eat a meal so delicious. The memory of it remains with

This photo captures a silhouette of the *Missouri* slicing through the Pacific on November 27, 1944, a day before reaching San Francisco. On the fantail she carries OS2Us, which will be replaced before she departs the West Coast for the war zone. (U.S. Navy photo in the National Archives: 80-G-288336)

him to this day, as does the trim figure he had as a young man.[83]

When she got under way for Hawaii, the *Missouri* carried a number of men as passengers in transit to other duties. And the after end of the ship was loaded with hundreds of mail sacks that had collected at the fleet post office in San Francisco and were heading west to Pearl Harbor for redistribution. When the *Missouri* reached Pearl Harbor, all hands stood at attention while passing the hulk of the shattered *Arizona*, immobile ever since she was bombed by the Japanese in 1941. After the *Missouri* moored, Seaman Ernest Zimmerman and many of his shipmates joined working parties to carry the mail bags ashore. Then they went on liberty, swimming and sunbathing at the beach. They also downed large quantities of the widely available pineapple juice, which was dispensed from spigots of the type then popular in soda fountains.[84]

Pearl Harbor was the next-to-last stop on the way to battle. The U.S. Fleet had undergone a remarkable transformation since the war began there. In December 1941 the battle line had been preeminent, the framework around which an offensive surge into the western Pacific was to be built. That strategy was shattered in a single day—7 December 1941. In its place came war-fighting doctrine built around aircraft carriers, submarines, and amphibious forces.

As 1944 ended, the *Missouri* was moored next to Ford Island at berth F-2, which had been unoccupied when the Japanese struck. Astern of it was F-3, which had held the Battle Force flagship *California*. There was no more Battle Force per se. Now the principal striking weapon was the fast carrier task force. When the *Missouri* joined it, her role would be as a support ship. Not once would she engage in the ship-to-ship surface gun battles for which she was designed and built.[85]

In January, accompanied by the prewar heavy cruiser *Tuscaloosa* and an escort of destroyers, the *Missouri* steamed still farther westward. The crew began standing dawn and dusk alert watches because those were likely times for Japanese submarines to approach. Lieutenant Plate compared the process to a farmer doing chores in the morning and evening, cutting into opportunities for relaxation and sleep. Fatigue began to set in for the crew, a harbinger of much more strained times in the weeks and months ahead.[86]

The remainder of the month of January was essentially an illustration of the old Navy saying, "Hurry up and wait." The ship had gone through a multitude of training, steamed thousands of miles, and then sat for a while in Ulithi Atoll as the Third Fleet prepared for the next station on the road to Tokyo, the invasion of Iwo Jima. In the meantime, officers and enlisted men went ashore to a recreation island called Mog Mog. They swam, got sun on parts of their bodies normally covered by uniforms, collected coral and sea shells, and drank at bars that had thatched roofs. In the evenings the crew watched movies on the fantail. One night they had to watch the new Otto Preminger suspense movie *Laura* in three installments because the film was interrupted by rain—one hazard of an open-air theater.[87]

Near the end of the month officers and crew got the welcome news that the overbearing executive officer, Jocko Cooper, was being detached from the *Missouri* and ordered to other duty. His replacement was Commander Louis "Molly" Malone, who moved up from his initial job as gunnery officer. He looked appealing immediately just because he was somebody else. Lieutenant Plate undoubtedly articulated the thoughts of many *Missouri* men when he wrote that, with the departure of Cooper, "things are slowly coming to an even keel."[88]

2 ❖ Victory in Combat

February–August 1945

Stretched across the vast lagoon at Ulithi lay a potent collection of naval power. Tethered by their anchor chains were heavy aircraft carriers; light carriers that had been converted from cruiser hulls; heavy cruisers, both of prewar and wartime construction; light cruisers with 6-inch main batteries; antiaircraft light cruisers with 5-inch guns; destroyers by the score; dozens of amphibious warfare ships; and various supply ships that would provide the combatants with food, fuel, and ammunition.

The lagoon also held battleships, both old and new. All the new fast battleships were present except for the *Iowa* and *Alabama*—both in overhaul on the West Coast. Since the first tentative offensive steps in early 1942, the U.S. Navy had been moving steadily west toward Japan. This armada had now gathered for the final miles of that long journey. Many of the ships already had long combat experience; the *Missouri* was about to get her first.

On the morning of February 10, 1945, Task Force 58 sortied from Ulithi. The day got off to a bad start for the *Missouri*. Soon after getting under way the ship catapulted off the three SC-1 Seahawk floatplanes carried on the fantail. Lieutenant Everett N. Frothingham's plane developed engine trouble almost immediately. He crashed some ten thousand yards from the ship; the plane trailed smoke as it made a steep glide into the sea. The Seahawk came down near the destroyer *Lewis Hancock* at a time when the seas were heavy and the wind was more than twenty knots.[1]

After the plane hit the water, the wind quickly capsized it; for a time the Seahawk remained afloat upside-down. Frothingham managed to get clear but had trouble keeping his head above water because he was injured and his Mae West life jacket was only partially inflated. The destroyer sent a swimmer into the water after him. The sailor secured a harness to the pilot, who was by then unconscious. As the destroyer was lifting him from the water, Frothingham slipped out of the harness and sank from view.[2]

On February 16, Task Force 58 launched the first carrier strikes against Tokyo since the Doolittle raid of April 1942. The *Missouri*'s role, as it would be for much of the next several months, was to provide antiaircraft defense for those carriers. Present in the protective screen—along with the battleships and cruisers—was a group of fuel-thirsty destroyers. Their role was to supply both antiair and antisubmarine defense for the big ships. But these little ships, the "tin cans" of the fleet, had only limited capacity for the heavy black oil that fueled them. Thus, part of the battleship's job was to refuel those small boys every few days. Lieutenant Doug Plate, one of the battleship's officers of the deck, sometimes looked down and saw that she had four destroyers alongside at once—two to port and two to starboard. Of course, the *Missouri*, at approximately fifty-eight thousand tons, required a considerable amount of oil herself. In the days and weeks that followed, when the battleship frequently steamed at speeds above twenty knots, her boilers burned approximately 180 gallons per mile.[3]

After the strikes on Japan's main island of Honshu, the ships of the task force turned their bows toward tiny Iwo Jima in the Bonin Islands. Iwo Jima has since become part of the legend of the Marine Corps, in part because of the dramatic flag-raising photo on Mount Suribachi. The U.S. objective was to seize a base at which damaged Army Air Forces bombers could land if they ran into trouble during bombing raids launched from the Marianas against the Japanese home islands. The island would also serve as a base from which Army fighter planes would be close enough to the target area so they could escort the bombers. In effect, Marine Corps lives were lost so that Army Air Forces lives could be saved.

The invasion was on February 19, and the fast carrier force supported it with air strikes. The only battleships doing shore bombardment at Iwo were the prewar veterans, which were too slow to steam with the fast carriers. As a result, they had specialized in shore bombardment from 1943 onward and had become better at it than the fast battleships, which had more varied duties. As part of Task Group

58.2, the *Missouri* was some sixty-five miles away from the island as the carriers launched their planes against it during morning sorties. Her closest point of approach was within thirty-seven miles of Iwo during the afternoon.[4]

That evening, the men of the *Missouri* opened fire for the first time against a Japanese plane. The twin-engine bomber was probably a "Helen," using the nickname that was part of a system the Allies adopted to avoid having to pronounce Japanese names. The plane came in from slightly forward of amidships on the port beam, flying at an altitude of about fifteen hundred feet. When it was approximately ninety-eight hundred yards away from the *Missouri*, the battleship took it under fire and knocked it down at 7:53 P.M. with the first few bursts of gunfire. It splashed at ninety-two hundred yards. The radar setup worked smoothly as the

While steaming as part of Task Group 58.4 in support of the Okinawa campaign on April 4, the *Missouri* and a destroyer put up numerous flak bursts as their antiaircraft guns fire at Japanese planes. The photo was taken by R. M. Colby of the aircraft carrier *Intrepid,* seen in the foreground. (U.S. Navy photo in the National Archives: 80-G-316697)

plane was tracked initially on search radars, then transferred to the fire control radars of the Mark 37 directors as soon as it came within range of the 5-inch guns.[5]

Two nights later the ship demonstrated the ability to shift targets among various 5-inch guns while steaming at high speed and making radical turns. Fire control radar and proximity fuzes made a dramatic difference over the old prewar systems of optical range finders and mechanical time fuzes. During the air attacks of February 21 the *Missouri* was firing at a target flying at twelve thousand feet, even though a solid overcast of clouds made the visible ceiling only five thousand feet above the ship. The SK-2 air-search radar, with its distinctive large round antenna atop the foremast, worked well in tracking both U.S. and Japanese planes. For example, men in the ship's combat information center were able to track groups of U.S. B-29 bombers at a range of 160 miles.[6]

Another enemy was the weather. Although the huge *Missouri* had such a deep draft that she didn't roll and pitch nearly so much as destroyers, there were compensating drawbacks. Since she plowed through the waves and swells rather than going up and over, she was susceptible to topside damage. On February 27, for instance, while bound for Tokyo, she took plenty of green water over the bow. The large waves carried away ready service boxes full of 20-mm ammunition, strewed 40-mm projectiles around the deck, and even washed a 20-mm magazine up to the top of turret one. Eventually, the planned strikes against Tokyo and Nagoya were cut dramatically short because the weather over the target area was so bad that the aircraft of Task Force 58 couldn't see to attack.[7]

At the beginning of March, as the *Missouri*'s first combat patrol wound down, she and the rest of the fast carrier task force headed back toward Ulithi and a break in the action. One of the destroyers in the *Missouri*'s task unit during the journey was the USS *Callaghan*. She was named for Rear Admiral Daniel J. Callaghan, who was killed in a night battle off Guadalcanal in November 1942. His younger brother William was now the commanding officer of the *Missouri*.[8]

In early March Commander Roland Faulk reported as the ship's senior chaplain, having held the same job for a few months in sister ship *New Jersey*. In making a change from one ship of the class to another, Faulk was able to compare their crews. He concluded that the *New Jersey* was a happy ship, while the *Missouri* was not. The *Missouri* had gone into commission more than a year after her sister, by which time the requirements from the armed forces had plunged more deeply into the U.S. manpower pool. He observed that the *Missouri*'s crew was made up of an unusually large number of older men who had either enlisted or been drafted. (Harry Truman's nephew was among the many examples.) Many of them had families, so for them military service called for even more of a sacrifice than for the younger sailors who had enlisted earlier in the war.[9]

Though the time at anchor in Ulithi provided a respite from the rigors of combat, the men of the *Missouri* weren't able to relax completely. On the night of March 12, while the crew was watching a movie, a Japanese kamikaze plane flew in low and plowed into the carrier *Randolph*, which was anchored nearby. Seaman Walt Yucka, on the stern of the *Missouri*, saw the flames that leaped up after the initial explosion.[10] Seaman Joe Vella heard the urgent call to general quarters as the *Missouri* reacted to the potential threat. He felt fear invading him as he hurried to his battle station in the after 5-inch mount on the port side.

In large part Vella's fear, along with that of his shipmates, grew out of their shortage of experience in combat. Vella didn't want his buddies to know he was frightened, so he put on something of a false front. But he didn't fool the men who had been through this sort of thing many times before. A kindly gunner's mate said to him, "Take it easy; don't get excited." The older man's words—and his calm, self-assured example—were reassuring to the teenage Vella.[11]

Fortunately, Ulithi offered calmer times too. Getting ashore on Mog Mog Island wasn't exactly a visit to paradise, but the men did get a chance to leave the confines of the ship and stretch their legs. Corporal John Dubensky of the *Missouri*'s Marine detachment sought a drink and found that the only available water was hot and stored in a canvas bag. Thus, even though he didn't really want a beer, that's what he went for as the sole cold drink on the island. The other pleasure for crewmen was the opportunity to meet people from other ships. For example, Dubensky enjoyed talking with a fellow from his hometown in Pennsylvania and comparing notes on what they'd been through.[12]

Soon it was time to go to sea again. The *Missouri* by now was in Task Group 58.4, which also included the *Wisconsin* and the large cruisers *Alaska* and *Guam*. All of those ships were assembled into the same group because they each could exceed thirty knots, a few knots faster than the battleships of the *North Carolina* and *South Dakota* classes. The *Missouri* seldom traveled at her top speed of thirty-three, but if called upon, she could keep up with the fastest.[13]

When the *Missouri* fulfilled her role as an antiaircraft ship, her crew had frequent reminders of the hazardous nature of the job. On March 18 a Japanese plane bombed the nearby carrier *Enterprise*. The *Missouri* fired on a plane that crashed and exploded near the *Intrepid*. Then came an even more dramatic event early on the morning of March 19 as the fast carrier force steamed near the island of Honshu to launch air strikes. The carrier *Franklin*, part of Task Group 58.2, was only a few miles away when a Japanese plane descended from low-hanging clouds and planted two bombs on her deck.[14]

Seaman Herb Leibig, whose battle station was on a gun mount on the *Missouri*'s port side, watched as one explosion after another ripped the *Franklin*. When he was in boot camp, he had asked for assignment to an aircraft carrier. Now he was just as glad that his wish had not been fulfilled.[15] Captain Callaghan, watching from the bridge of the battleship, years later remembered that the carrier "was soon engulfed in such a mass of flames that we wondered how anyone could survive such an inferno. That the ship did survive became one of the epic achievements of the war." Hundreds of men died on board the *Franklin*, but fire-fighting efforts succeeded, and the ship eventually

steamed back to the United States under her own power.[16]

Though the men of the *Missouri*—along with those in many other ships—were frightened during the Japanese air attacks, they managed to maintain a sense of humor. When the suicide planes were swarming around, they'd point elsewhere and say, "The carriers are over there." Actually, the battleship's men didn't need to do much pointing because the kamikazes were really seeking the carriers anyway. By smashing into ships with wooden flight decks and filled with volatile aviation gasoline, the Japanese had the potential for inflicting greater damage than by hitting the heavily armored battleships.[17]

The island of Okinawa was the next target for invasion because it was only 340 miles from the closest point in Japan. It would be the final stepping-stone on the path to the home islands. With the fast carriers having already begun attacking Okinawa from the air as a prelude to sending in troops, the fast battleships were called upon to conduct a shore bombardment. Crew members in the *Missouri* got a preview of the target's appearance by constructing a scale model of the terrain at the site on southeast Okinawa. The operation was to be a feint, deceiving the defenders as to the location of the intended landing beaches, which were on the island's west side. In making their model the battleship men glued together sheets of cardboard that they had cut out according to the shapes on a contour map of the island. When the model was put together, someone painted it with plaster of paris to make it smooth.[18]

For the bombardment itself, on March 24, the *Missouri* joined with the two other sister ships then in combat, the *New Jersey* and *Wisconsin*. The *Missouri* catapulted off her SC-1 Seahawk for spotting the fall of shot. She fired at distances beginning at 20,000 yards from the targets and closing to 17,500 yards. The *Missouri* used reduced-charge powder during the operation. Had she been trying to shoot at the same distances with full-service charges, the trajectory of the shells would have been relatively flat. With reduced charges, the 16-inch guns were elevated to a higher angle to achieve

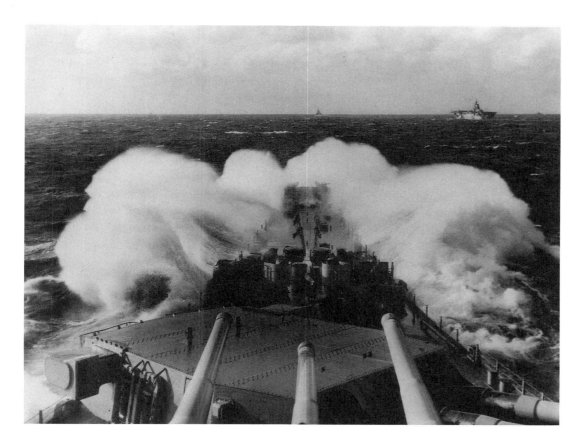

In early April, the *Missouri* ran into such rough seas that Seaman Second Class John Dwyer was washed overboard from the forecastle. (U.S. Navy photo in the National Archives: 80-G-316557)

the same range. That enabled the *Missouri* to shoot over the tops of slopes and also to achieve plunging fire as the bullets came down on top of enemy positions at a more nearly vertical angle.[19]

Seaman Tony Alessandro was the powder-hoist operator for the left gun of turret three during firing. His principal qualification was his size—5′6″, 138 pounds—because it enabled him to squeeze into the small space available. He sat on a seat and had a lever to control the movement of the powder hoist as it moved up and down between the gun room of the turret and the lower handling room several decks below. The hoist could best be described as a two-story elevator. The space in each story could house three cylindrical powder bags placed end to end. As soon as he received word on his headphones that the bags were loaded on below, Alessandro moved a lever to bring the hoist up. He stopped it at a point at which it was level with a door that opened onto a brass tray that lowered into position at the breech end of the 16-inch gun. Another man with a lever then pushed the bags onto the tray, where still other men would steady them.[20]

From his vantage point, where he could see the tray, Alessandro then raised the hoist another couple of feet, after which the other three powder bags went out onto the tray. As soon as the bags were out of the hoist, the rammerman pushed them in behind the projectile, which had already gone in ahead of them. As that was happening, Alessandro tripped a lever so that the hoist again descended to the depths of the ship to be reloaded. At the same time, the tray was folding up out of the way, and a primerman was putting a primer the size of a shotgun shell into the firing lock in the breech of the gun. Then the gun was fired, usually from one of the main battery plotting rooms.[21]

All told, the *Missouri* fired 180 rounds that day, shooting at coastal defense guns, antiaircraft installations, barracks, and an observation post. The shooting destroyed or damaged a number of the buildings and led to the explosion of a large ammunition dump. As the dreadnoughts steamed away from the island, they left behind a collection of Japanese buildings still afire. It was a rare use of the *Missouri*'s main battery during World War II; soon she was back with the carriers.[22] The men of the *Missouri* had enjoyed firing the ship's big guns as a contrast to the defensive antiaircraft role to which she was consigned most of the time. Navigator Jim Starnes said of the bombardment: "When the time came for us to act like the battleship we were, it was great. It was exhilarating—really a good feeling."[23]

On March 29 the fast-carrier force demonstrated its continuing mobility by making air strikes in the Kyushu area. Radar detected enemy planes in the early afternoon, and the men of the *Missouri* went to general quarters. One Japanese pilot closed the formation with two U.S. fighters of the combat air patrol following him down through the clouds in hot pursuit. Eighteen-year-old Seaman Second Class Julian Ganas was first loader on a 20-mm gun mount on the starboard side, near turret three. He watched as the Japanese plane approached, flying between the *Missouri* and the *Wisconsin*, which was several hundred yards away. The light antiaircraft guns on both ships sprayed out streams of bullets. Enough hit the Japanese plane that it splashed into the ocean.[24]

Suddenly, Seaman Ganas felt a pain—as if he'd been kicked in the midsection while playing football. He looked down and discovered a bullet hole near the base of his ribs. Then he saw that a 20-mm shell from the *Wisconsin* had lodged in the deck of the *Missouri*. The Japanese airplane had been flying parallel to the two ships, so any machine-gun bullet it fired would have gone forward, not into someone on the deck of the *Missouri*. Thus, the stray bullet had to be a "friendly" one. It passed all the way through the young man's stomach and, fortunately, did no permanent damage. Soon a party of stretcher bearers carried him to sick bay, where one of the ship's doctors sewed him back together. After he had recuperated for thirty days, Ganas was given a battle station in the aft fire control tower rather than having to go back to his exposed position on the 20-mm gun crew.[25]

Seaman Al Circelli served in a 5-inch mount in the *Missouri* during the air actions against the Japanese and considered it relatively easy compared with his previous duty in the battleship *New York*. In that ship, with an antiquated antiaircraft battery, fuze settings were done by hand. In the *Missouri*, outfitted with radar fire control, equipment in the gun mount automatically set the fuzes on the projectiles. What's more, the 5-inch guns were encased in a protective steel mount. Circelli gained great admiration for the men on the 40- and 20-mm guns. Not only were they subjected to the vicissitudes of wind and wave, they also had virtually no protection when enemy planes came boring in on the ship—as young Ganas had discovered.[26]

The ship's food, which had been okay when the *Missouri* was still near the United States, deteriorated once she got away from land and began operating on a steady basis. The sailors ate Spam cooked about every way imaginable, plus some commodities that had been dehydrated and then reconstituted. Included were "square eggs." The dehydrated eggs were mixed with water and then cooked in flat pans. The result was somewhat akin to scrambled eggs, which were then cut up into square pieces and distributed on the mess line. The crew did enjoy fresh-baked bread and pastries, and coffee was available in seemingly unlimited quantities.[27]

At times when the ship was at battle stations, the cooks passed out cardboard boxes containing K rations, and the men ate them in their gun mounts, engine rooms, and other places. This precluded the need for cooking during battle and also made it unnecessary for everybody to troop to the mess deck for meals. Generally, those meals included canned meat or cheese, some crackers, and a dessert item. Seaman Alessandro particularly enjoyed a tropical candy bar that some company had devised so that it wouldn't melt in warm climates. It was like a hard fudge and delicious—a term that could not be applied to the rest of the meal. Packed in with the various food items in the box were a few cigarettes, a commodity taken for granted at the time. Alessandro, who didn't smoke, found himself quite popular with shipmates because they could bum the cigarettes he didn't want.[28]

For the Okinawa invasion itself on April 1, Easter Sunday, the old, slow battleships did the shore bombardment. The *Missouri* was back in her customary spot in Task Group 58.4. Throughout the day of operation with the fast carriers, the ship's crew had no opportunity for the normal worship services expected on Easter. Eventually, though, came a respite at day's end. At nine that night Chaplain Faulk held a Protestant Easter service in the mess deck, which was packed. Speaking to the dog-tired crew of the *Missouri,* Faulk concluded that it was no time for sermonizing. Instead, he led the men in singing old hymns—which they did with great gusto—and saying prayers of thanksgiving for the successful beginning of the campaign to conquer the island of Okinawa.[29]

As for the Catholic sailors, Radioman Moose Conner was struck by Captain Callaghan's disappointment that so few of them went to Easter Mass. The skipper told them that their mothers were home praying for their safety, and they didn't even go to communion themselves. The crew greatly respected Captain Callaghan, who served as a father figure for the many still in their teens or early twenties. Even those who were punished at captain's mast felt they had been treated fairly. The skipper was willing to listen to explanations and mitigating circumstances, but he didn't like to hear excuses. When someone said he didn't get a particular job done because he didn't have time, Callaghan was likely to say, "Young man, you'll find out in this man's Navy that you make time."

Radioman Conner kept that in mind once when he and a few shipmates got into a squabble with some of the men in another division on board the *Missouri.* When Callaghan asked them about it, they all repeated, "No excuse, sir." The captain gave them ten hours' extra duty scrubbing the bulkheads on the mess deck. The ship got a little cleaner, and the men had a lesson by which to govern their future actions.[30]

During the continued operations of the carrier task group, the men of the *Missouri* received dramatic evidence of the power of the ocean. On April 3 Seaman Second Class John Dwyer of the second division was working on the forecastle with other members of the deck force. After one wave had subsided, a coxswain warned Dwyer, "Hold on again. Here comes the big one." Dwyer grabbed for the handles on a gear locker, but the water overpowered him. He and his shipmates were washed aft along the deck. He bounced painfully off the anchor chain and then over the side, unconscious. Fortunately, he was wearing a life jacket. Hitting the water woke him up, but he was dismayed to see the *Missouri* already some distance away. After he had been in the water for about an hour, the crew of the destroyer *Colahan* made several unsuccessful attempts before finally recovering him. He spent the night in the captain's cabin of the destroyer, then was returned to the *Missouri,* where he spent a week in sick bay recovering from a wrenched neck and leg.[31]

On April 7, carrier planes from Task Force 58 sank the giant battleship *Yamato,* armed with 18.1-inch guns. Her last voyage was essentially a suicide run in an attempt to inflict damage on the invading American forces at Okinawa. Neither the old prewar battleships nor the new fast battleships were close enough to engage in a gun duel with the *Yamato.* Thus, the great dreadnought slugging match that had been anticipated for years never came to pass.

On the afternoon of April 11, Chaplain Faulk was making his way up an inside ladder in the superstructure in order to get to the navigation bridge. Just as he reached a passageway at the top of a ladder, he was nearly trampled by men moving from the starboard side of the bridge to port.[32] Among those involved in the mad rush was Lieutenant Jim Starnes, who was the officer of the deck at general quarters because of his billet as navigator. He and others were trying to find shelter behind the massive armored conning tower because they saw a threat to the ship and themselves that was more compelling than anything in their previous experience on board the *Missouri.*[33]

A Japanese suicide pilot was coming in about a hundred feet above the water and ap-

At 2:43 P.M. on April 11, a Japanese "Zeke" fighter is shown at the moment of impact with the *Missouri*'s hull, just below the level of the main deck. Men of 40-mm gun crews and directors are in the foreground. (U.S. Navy photo in the National Archives: 80-G-315811)

parently headed for the bridge—at least in the expectation of those who were there. Men on a 40-mm gun mount got a good look at the plane and said the pilot looked like a jockey, squatting in his seat. At 2:43 P.M. the plane struck the hull of the *Missouri* on the starboard side, frame 169, about three feet below the level of the main deck. When the left wing tip hit, it deflected the nose of the plane into the hull. Fortunately, the bomb attached to the "Zeke" fighter did not explode.

The crash essentially cut the pilot in half. His head, chest, and torso landed on the main deck. His body hit with such force that it mangled a basket holding floater nets to be deployed in the event of a shipwreck. One ma-

chine gun impaled itself on a 40-mm gun. Parts of the engine, radio, canopy, and another machine gun landed on the deck. The rest of the plane, and the rest of the pilot's body, went into the water.[34]

As the kamikaze hit, the right wing sheared off on impact and was catapulted forward. It landed on the 01 deck in the superstructure, frame 102, near the center 5-inch gun mount on the starboard side. Gasoline stored in the wing spilled out onto the deck and ignited, producing a cloud of dark smoke. The heat and flames temporarily blocked access to intake vents that supplied air to an engine room and fireroom below. Smoke poured down into the engineering spaces. Men on duty there rigged gas masks with hoses connected to a low-pressure air line and thus were able to keep breathing in their smoke-filled compartments.[35]

During the airplane's approach, Seaman Len Schmidt was on the 02 level, about amidships, taking pictures of the air attack in progress. Despite the fear he felt for his personal safety, he managed to take a picture that has become a classic image of World War II. He clicked the shutter when the plane was just abreast of the hull, an instant before the impact of the wing against the hull began the disintegration of the aircraft. As soon as he had photographed that, Schmidt went down and got a shot of the "Zeke"'s machine gun impaled on the barrel of a 40-mm mount, as well as a picture of the Japanese pilot's remains. The young man's innards were hanging on the side of the floater net storage cage. Some parts of him had smacked against a bulkhead. *Missouri* sailors then began picking up pieces of the dead Japanese pilot and yelling triumphantly about having shot him down.[36]

Fireman Art Albert was assigned to a repair party with a battle station on the ship's 01 level. When the gasoline from the kamikaze landed there, Albert joined in extinguishing the blaze. The fire fighters were concerned that the wooden deck would catch fire from the burning gasoline, so they smothered the area with spray and fog foam. That, in turn, cut off the oxygen supply, and the fire went out within three

minutes after it started.[37] The crew salvaged aluminum from the airplane's wing and cut it up to save as souvenirs. Pieces of the plane's metal surfaced for months afterward, sometimes when crew members bought pieces of the plane from shipmates who'd been able to grab them.[38]

At the moment of impact from the plane, the ship had taken a jolt. Albert was climbing a ladder at the time to get to his battle station. He banged his knees against the ladder, felt some momentary pain, and then went on. The fireman was eighteen at the time and shrugged off the injury. But as a result of riding several destroyers subsequently in his naval career, his knees took a pounding that aggravated the 1945 injury. The result has been a series of operations, including one that fused the knee joint on one of Albert's legs so that it no longer bends at all.[39]

The day after the "Zeke" hit the ship, Chaplain Faulk conducted a military funeral for the young Japanese man—apparently only eighteen or nineteen years old—who had elected to die for his emperor. His half body wound up on a slab, attended by an honor guard. Some of the crew grumbled at the military honors rendered to an individual who had tried to kill

them. Others had a grudging respect for someone who would go to such lengths to serve his country. In his brief eulogy, Faulk reminded them of something else. "A dead Jap is no longer an enemy." Then members of the battleship's crew committed to the deep what remained of the young man who was alive and well only a day earlier.[40]

At eight o'clock on the morning of April 14, the signalman who raised the American flag on board the *Missouri* quickly lowered it to half-mast.[41] The gesture was one of mourning in honor of President Franklin D. Roosevelt, who had died in Warm Springs, Georgia, on April 12, which was April 13 in the Far East. The

Right: Seaman John C. Truman, from Missouri, was a quiet and unassuming member of the *Missouri*'s navigation gang, even after his uncle became president on April 12. The button over his shirt pocket bears the letter "N" to signify his division. Such buttons were part of the uniform for World War II crewmen. (U.S. Navy photo in the National Archives: 80-G-700670)

Below: Crew members from the state of Missouri pose in front of turret one. J. C. Truman is all the way at the left in the top row, right under the "X" on the gun bloomer. (R. E. Dillon photo in Harry S. Truman Library collection: 67-5156)

new president was a man little known to the nation at large but well known to the crew of the *Missouri*. Harry S Truman of Independence, Missouri, had been present for both the launching and commissioning of the ship named for his home state. His nephew J. C., a member of the ship's navigation division, expressed the thought held by many of his countrymen when he wrote to the White House two weeks later, in a handwritten note to "Uncle Harry," "I still find it difficult to realize you are the President."[42]

Seaman Truman's division officer was Lieutenant Jim Starnes, who was several years younger than the enlisted man. Starnes found Truman to be a quiet, unassuming sailor. He was polite to seniors, did his job, and tried to blend in with the crowd. If anything, observed Starnes, Truman seemed almost apologetic about his relationship with the president, because he didn't want other people to think he was asking for special favors. It was not a rela-

tionship that he in any way wanted to use for his own advantage.[43]

April 16 was the worst day of air attacks the *Missouri* endured throughout her World War II service. She was threatened for twelve hours, including being the target of another kamikaze pilot. Even though this "Zeke" fighter was hit numerous times by antiaircraft fire, it kept coming toward the stern in the pilot's desperate attempt to hit the battleship. The plane's wing clipped a guard rail at the top of the fantail airplane crane. Then the aircraft crashed in the *Missouri*'s wake, exploding violently and spraying the fantail with debris. Among other things, flying particles of metal tore the rubber gun bloomers on turret three. Two *Missouri* men, Seaman A. J. Palermo and Seaman D. J. Guiliano, were injured; one suffered a compound leg fracture and got shell fragments in his calf.[44]

One of the great advantages the American ships had in locating and shooting down the attacking Japanese was radar. Recognizing this, the Japanese tried to employ countermeasures during night air attacks, dropping aluminum chaff that would attract the radars' attention. Both the SK-2 air-search radar and the Mark 12 fire-control radar on board the *Missouri* were affected by the chaff, although the radarmen

were still able to track the planes. Another Japanese gambit was to drop dozens of radar reflectors that simulated planes when they showed up on U.S. radar scopes. The only apparent effect of both chaff and window was to deceive Americans into thinking the raids contained more planes than they actually did. The *Missouri* and other U.S. ships retaliated at times, jamming Japanese airborne radars. The only hitch was that the jamming sometimes caused interference to the *Missouri*'s radars on the Mark 37 directors used for controlling the 5-inch guns. In dealing with air attacks, the ship also used a Mark 57 director—one in each corner of the ship—to control a 5-inch mount and two 40-mm quad mounts.[45]

During the cruise, which lasted from mid-March to early May, the *Missouri* fired on sixteen enemy planes, claiming five kills, one probable, and six assists.[46] As the ship headed for a period of rest and relaxation at Ulithi, Captain Callaghan and many others on board the battleship enjoyed the opportunity to lead

Left: A machine gun from the "Zeke" kamikaze plane was impaled in the barrel of a 40-mm gun on the *Missouri*'s starboard quarter. (U.S. Navy photo in the National Archives: 80-G-331280)

Below: Members of a shipboard repair party stand on top of the Japanese plane's wing after the fire was extinguished. Pieces of aluminum from the wing became highly prized as souvenirs. (U.S. Navy photo in the National Archives: 80-G-273955)

Crew members prepare to bury the corpse of the kamikaze pilot at sea. It takes up only a portion of the wooden slab because the bottom half of the pilot went down with the airplane following impact. (U.S. Navy photo in the National Archives: 80-G-315822)

relatively normal lives. At least for a while the officers and men could relax the vigilance that had kept them on the alert for kamikazes day and night. As the skipper put it: "It is difficult, unless one has gone through it, to imagine the physical and mental strain of maintaining such a constant state of readiness. Retirement to a rear area for a replenishment of fuel, ammunition and food about every five days was a stupendous relief."[47]

Captain Callaghan got another kind of relief when Captain Stuart "Sunshine" Murray came aboard by high line from a fleet oiler so he could prepare to take command. He rode the *Missouri* to Ulithi, talking with Callaghan, who was a Naval Academy classmate and long-time friend. When the ship reached the large atoll, shipfitters from Service Squadron Ten came aboard to add still more bunks to the already crowded battleship. Admiral William F. Halsey would be embarking, bringing with him several dozen officers and about three hundred enlisted men of the Third Fleet staff.[48]

Many a nickname is ironic, such as the bald man known as "Curly," but in this case Sunshine fit the new skipper. Murray was a big bear of a man with a warm "gentle giant" sort of personality.[49] Because of his job as navigator, Lieutenant Starnes spent a great deal of time with Captain Murray. He attributed the skipper's down-to-earth quality to the many years Murray had spent in submarines. In the long-ago days before World War II, submarines were small and cramped, and the crews operated in an atmosphere of informality and togetherness. They were literally all in the same boat and virtually on top of each other. Murray's own innate personality was augmented by some of the mental outlook that he acquired in the pig boats, as those submarines were called.[50]

Starnes viewed Captain Callaghan as a "grand person" and true gentleman, but he had a different manner. He was aristocratic and quiet, whereas Murray had close human contact with the subordinates he dealt with on the bridge. Starnes had a sea cabin just aft of the bridge on the port side so he could be immediately on call if needed; the captain's sea cabin was in a similar position to starboard. The navigator thus had frequent physical proximity to both men. He viewed his relationship with Captain Callaghan as somewhat akin to that of a father and son. Captain Murray treated Starnes more as he would a younger brother.[51]

Once the bunk installers had done their work in preparation for the arrival of the staff, the *Missouri* headed to Guam to pick up her new passengers. On the way, Captain Murray asked the crew to test-fire the guns to see how accurate the pattern of 16-inch projectiles would be. The ship unleashed a salvo in which all of the projectiles landed in a circle about 150 yards in diameter. A tight pattern was the objective, but that was too tight to suit the new captain. He asked the gunnery officer, Commander Horace "Dickie" Bird, to create a five-hundred-yard circle and thus cover a few more possibilities with the shooting.[52]

On May 18 Admiral Halsey moved aboard the *Missouri* in preparation for assuming command of the Third Fleet. Halsey's choice of flagship was a pragmatic one. He was a late-in-life aviator who had commanded the aircraft carrier *Saratoga* in the 1930s and had his flag in the carrier *Enterprise* at the beginning of World War II. Though his emotional decision would have been to put the Third Fleet flag in a carrier, the thin-skinned flattops were vulnerable. Thus, he had gone to sea in the *New Jersey* in the summer of 1944, and he would have preferred that ship again in the spring of 1945, but she was in overhaul on the West Coast. The

Left: In May 1945, Captain Stuart S. "Sunshine" Murray became the second commanding officer of the *Missouri*. (Harry S. Truman Library collection: 70-4068)

Below: Flak bursts fill the sky as a Japanese plane crashes into the sea off the *Missouri*'s bow during task group operations in April. The picture was taken by Photographer's Mate J. E. Krueger of the *Intrepid*. (U.S. Navy photo in the National Archives: 80-G-316057)

Navy had anticipated the scheduled yard period and had therefore directed the *Missouri* to stop at San Francisco in December to become equipped as a fleet flagship.[53]

Halsey's chief of staff was Rear Admiral Robert B. "Mick" Carney, who would later serve as chief of naval operations from 1953 to 1955. Lieutenant Bob Balfour, a communications watch officer on the staff, offered a brief assessment of the two flag officers at the top of the Third Fleet organization. "I don't know that this is exactly true and fair to say, but, generally speaking, I think most of us felt that Halsey was the blood and guts but that Carney was the brains. . . . It's my feeling and the feeling of several that Admiral Carney was a force that was very, very important and probably more important than anybody would realize with the Third Fleet."[54]

Some members of his staff complained when three or four officers were jammed into a stateroom, but the ship was so crowded that there weren't really any alternatives. The ship's officers welcomed the prestige that came from having the fleet commander on board, but they didn't like the increased crowding any more than the staff people did. As events developed, the resentment might have had another source as well, because the Third Fleet staff did not have stations for general quarters. Lieutenant Balfour, for example, joined games of bridge in the wardroom if he didn't have a communications watch during a period when the ship's crew was at battle stations.[55]

During his first day on board the *Missouri*, Halsey walked around getting a feel for his new flagship. He was accompanied by a Marine orderly and preceded by a Navy chief master-at-arms who called crew members to attention. Members of the deck force, who had been swabbing down, stopped their work and snapped to attention. Halsey quickly sent the Marine orderly ahead and told the master-at-arms to knock it off, because it was interfering with the ship's work. That set the tone for his time on board. He wanted enlisted men to remain at their duties; on the other hand, he did expect the officers to stop and salute when he encountered them.[56]

Halsey thus quickly picked up a reputation on board the ship as a sailors' admiral. Radioman Moose Conner was intrigued by this, and so he asked the orderly if Halsey ever chewed out a sailor. The only time, said the Marine, had been once at Pearl Harbor when the admiral had come out of a building and collided with a young seaman. After they separated, the sailor began to walk away, whereupon Halsey asked, "Wouldn't it be customary to stop and salute an admiral just after you knocked him on his ass?"[57]

Soon the *Missouri* and her consorts were on their way to Okinawa. During the voyage, the ship received intelligence reports of massive kamikaze raids. Admiral Chester Nimitz, commander in chief of the Pacific Fleet, directed Halsey to join up with a replenishment group and go into a holding pattern several hundred miles away from the island until the threat had diminished. After the raids had calmed down, the *Missouri* proceeded to Okinawa for the turnover process between fleet commanders.[58]

As the *Missouri* prepared for the continuation of the Okinawa campaign, she would be officially part of a different organization, the Third Fleet, although the accompanying ships remained essentially the same as before. On May 26, Admiral Halsey met Admiral Raymond Spruance, commander Fifth Fleet, and at midnight of the twenty-seventh took over the ships that Spruance had commanded. The routine called for one fleet commander to be planning upcoming operations while the other was at sea and operating. Before too many more months had passed, the U.S. Navy's power in the Pacific became so strong that it had enough ships to put both the Third and Fifth fleets to sea simultaneously.

To effect the turnover, Admirals Halsey and Spruance had back-and-forth conferences on board each other's flagships, as the *Missouri* was anchored perhaps a mile offshore. While these high-level talks were going on, so were some lower-level negotiations. Dozens of landing craft came out from the beach at Okinawa, mostly loaded with soldiers, sometimes with a few Marines. They carried Japanese rifles, machine guns, pistols, and even ammunition, which they wanted to trade for food because it had been a long time since they'd had a regular meal. Soon the cooks were doing a brisk business, toting up pots of hot food, fresh fruit, fresh bread, and so forth. The *Missouri*'s officers had to step in because trading ship's food for personal souvenirs was not exactly kosher. Nor was it a good idea to have ammunition and guns spread throughout the ship. So after a while the weapons were confiscated and stored in the armory. Some wound up as personal souvenirs for *Missouri* crewmen.[59]

The *Missouri* got under way the afternoon of May 27, still officially part of the Fifth Fleet for a few more hours. The battleship unleashed both her 16-inch and 5-inch guns for nearly an hour in a bombardment of the southwestern coast of Okinawa, near Naha. The targets were the mouths of caves that might harbor high-speed attack boats. The psychological value of the shelling was explained by Halsey afterward. "I gave orders for her to drop some 16-inch

calling cards on the enemy's doorstep; I wanted him to know I was back."[60]

During the first week in June the *Missouri* went through a typhoon that damaged several ships of the fleet. In mid-December 1944, near the Philippines, Halsey—on board the *New Jersey*—and the Third Fleet had been caught by an earlier typhoon, which sank three destroyers. Now, nearly six months later, Halsey and the Third Fleet again tangled with a tropical storm, this one a few hundred miles south of Okinawa. On June 5 the center of the typhoon passed about twenty-five miles southwest of Task Group 38.4. Weathermen on board the *Missouri* measured winds of forty-eight knots and gusts up to eighty knots. The ship suffered only slight damage, though: some topside fittings and two motor whaleboats were smashed.[61]

Quartermaster Don Rouse, standing watch on the helm, described the process of trying to steer the *Missouri*. "It was just incredible the

In mid-May, the *Missouri* went to Guam to embark Admiral William F. Halsey, Jr., and his Third Fleet staff. Anchored in the background are escort carriers and a hospital ship. (U.S. Navy photo in the National Archives: 80-G-469991)

amount of rudder that you had to use to maintain any resemblance of a course. We were trying to go in one direction, but we went at a general direction because there were no compass headings. We just wallowed around out there like a ping-pong ball in a bathtub with a baby playing with it."[62] On occasion, Ensign Jack Barron went up into the superstructure and watched the *Missouri*'s long, narrow bow plunge down into the waves and sway vigorously from side to side. Crewmen were reluctant to sleep in the forward part of the ship during the storm.[63]

Captain Murray was fascinated to listen to reports coming in over voice radio. At one point he heard Captain Jack Redman, skipper of the *Massachusetts* and a Naval Academy classmate of his. Redman reported: "There's a dead calm in here, waves coming from everywhere, and the sun's shining. There is no wind. This is the eye of the storm, and our radar shows nothing except clear blank walls all around us." At other times, the voice radio would carry a message from a carrier, "We got our nose smashed." Murray didn't know quite what that meant until the ships joined up a day or so later. The flight deck on the *Hornet*, for example, had been pounded down at the front corners as if hit by a giant fist. In another case, a 104-foot section of the bow of the heavy cruiser *Pittsburgh* had been torn off by the ferocity of the storm.[64]

One of the demanding duties for a junior officer of the watch in the carrier task force formations was to execute the zigzag plans. Enemy submarines lurking nearby could presumably do a better job of getting into a setup position for firing torpedoes if the formation remained on the same course for a considerable period of time. On the other hand, if the ships zigzagged frequently, it would be more difficult for a submarine to anticipate their movements. The plan called for steaming on a course for a certain number of minutes, then turning in unison to the next leg. The *Missouri* was flagship, and Ensign Barron found it a real "pain in the rump" to run the zigzag plans over voice radio. It was particularly stressful at night and in bad weather.[65]

Fortunately, he had some help in station keeping from Captain Murray, a skilled sea-

man and ship handler. Murray habitually sat in his captain's chair on the starboard side at the front corner of the bridge. He advised Barron to pick out a spot on a bridge window and line it up with the formation guide. As long as the spot and guide were in line, the *Missouri* was on station.[66]

While the ship was at sea, one of Admiral Halsey's forms of recreation was to don a pair of khaki shorts and go out bare chested to play deck tennis with members of his staff. The game called for stretching a net across an expanse of teakwood deck. Rather than a tennis ball, the players used a ring perhaps four or five inches in diameter. The players caught the ring and then flipped it back and forth over the net. The object was to have the ring fall onto the deck on the opponents' side. Despite being in his sixties, Halsey was a vigorous competitor and played to win.[67] The consensus among *Missouri* officers was that the admiral bent the rules a little bit. For instance, when he was throwing the ring he would raise his arm higher than the rules specified, but who was going to tell him he couldn't?[68]

Admiral Halsey liked informality. He preferred the khaki uniform and wouldn't permit officers to wear the gray "bus-driver" uniforms that Admiral Ernest J. King, the chief of naval operations, had initiated in Washington. On one occasion when Lieutenant Doug Plate was officer of the deck, a destroyer came alongside the *Missouri* for refueling. Halsey looked across the water and saw that the destroyer officers, seeking to put on a good show for the fleet flagship, were wearing neckties. Halsey grabbed a megaphone and yelled over to them, "Take off your damn ties."[69]

In mid-June the Third Fleet dropped anchor at Leyte in the Philippines, closer to the action area than when at Ulithi. In typical fleet anchorages the hospital ships were normally placed far away from the combatant types. When the *Missouri* anchored at Leyte, however, a hospital ship soon anchored practically alongside. A flock of nurses from the hospital ship came aboard and went up to the flag mess for lunch with Admiral Halsey and members of his staff. Among the witnesses was Lieutenant

Plate, one of the officers from the battleship's gunnery department. He and others were intensely interested because it was the first time they'd seen American women since leaving Hawaii months earlier. He heard one of his shipmates expressing the thought of many, "God, they smell good."[70]

One day while the flagship was anchored, Lieutenant Balfour of the Third Fleet staff was in his stateroom when a Marine came to him and said, "Sir, I have a set of orders for you." Balfour thought he was finally headed back to the States after months in combat. Instead, the orders told him to board the admiral's barge that afternoon, proceed to the nearby hospital ship, and report to the wardroom. There he was to select a date from among a group of nurses under similar orders, and to report to the flag bar ashore "for one hell of a well-deserved party." As Balfour recounted the situation, even though he was married he had to follow orders.[71]

On July 1 the vast Third Fleet left Leyte for yet another thrust at the Japanese home islands. As they had done several times previously when the fleet sortied, the heavy surface units joined up for a few days of exercise, something notably missing before the big battles of 1944. When Task Force 34 assembled on July 2, it included eight of the Navy's ten fast battleships. The only ones missing were the *New Jersey* and *Washington,* which were at the Puget Sound Navy Yard for overhaul.

Ironically, though, with the *Yamato* having been sunk by aircraft in April, the fast battleships no longer had any real missions against counterparts in the Imperial Japanese Navy. After the few days of drilling, they rejoined the carrier forces for strikes against Japan. They faced the prospect of doing that for some time, until the planned invasion of Japan in November. In the meantime, though, Admiral Halsey felt a sense of frustration while watching events from flag plot or his chair on the *Missouri*'s flag bridge. He was an old battleship man himself, having served in the predreadnought *Missouri* in 1904–05, upon completing four years at the Naval Academy. So he sent a message to Vice Admiral John "Slew" McCain, commander Task Force 38, in the *Shangri-La* and asked him to give the battleships some battleship jobs.[72]

McCain turned to his operations section, which included Captain John S. Thach and Commander Noel Gayler, both of whom had also served in battleships before becoming naval aviators. Following Halsey's direction, they

From July 1 to August 27, 1945, the *Missouri* was under way continuously. She and the other ships of Task Force 38 were able to remain at sea because of the replenishment ships that kept them supplied. Here, the battleship approaches the oiler *Tappahannock,* which is already refueling the carrier *Yorktown,* flagship of Rear Admiral Arthur Radford. (U.S. Navy photo by Barrett Gallagher in the National Archives: 80-G-421844)

came up with missions. The morning of July 15, the *Missouri* joined the *Iowa* and *Wisconsin*, plus cruisers and destroyers, in a bombardment of steel works at Muroran, Hokkaido, the northernmost Japanese island. While steaming in coastal waters, the *Missouri*'s officers were concerned about mines. For one thing, they ordered paravanes rigged at the bow, although with some difficulty. These were whale-shaped metal objects, towed by chains leading from a pad eye on the bulbous bow. The chains were intended to deflect moored mines away from the sides of the ship. In addition, some of the ship's Marines were up in the bow, armed with rifles, in the event they had to blow up floating mines on the surface.[73]

This time, the *Missouri* used full powder charges with her 16-inch projectiles because she was firing at much longer ranges than at Okinawa. The shortest range was 29,660 yards, and the longest was 32,000. The American task unit encountered no hostile fire from the beach, but the battleships' spotter planes were under continuous antiaircraft fire. Accuracy was useful but not essential, because the prodigious amount of fire essentially saturated the target area. The *Missouri* alone fired 297 rounds, including three nine-gun salvos that were aimed at large hammerhead cranes. The shooting caused fires, explosions, and heavy damage to all the buildings in the iron works.[74]

Lieutenant Plate was main battery plotting room officer during the bombardment. He was surprised that the Japanese didn't react at all; the men of the *Missouri* fully expected retaliation. That they received none testifies to the depleted state of Japanese defenses by that late stage of the war.[75]

Ensign Barron watched the bombardment through a periscope from inside turret two. The sensation of firing was muted because he was encased in steel. He did see the results ashore when chimneys from the Japanese steel factory toppled over as 16-inch projectiles slammed home. Years afterward, Barron took his wife, Eleanor, to see the area, planning to show her the devastation that the *Missouri* and the other ships had wrought. "You wouldn't believe what we did to Muroran," he told her proudly. To his chagrin, the steel plant had long

since been repaired and returned to operation. She enjoyed the ensuing kidding she was able to inflict.[76]

Soon afterward, on the night of July 17–18, the *Iowa*-class ships were joined by the slightly older *Alabama* and *North Carolina* for a bombardment of industrial targets at Hitachi on the island of Honshu. Again the *Missouri* was firing at a range of approximately fifteen miles. This time she and the other ships did not have the benefits of daylight and good weather. Low overcast and heavy rain prevented spotting, so the ships were essentially firing blind, picking ranges and gun azimuths from their navigational tracks to the targets. Even that was difficult because the smooth coastline didn't offer distinctive features for radar navigation.[77]

During the course of the operation, the *Missouri*'s shell handlers inadvertently loaded an armor-piercing projectile in the hoist rather than the high-explosive round used for shore bombardment. Once it got up to the turret, however, someone ordered it to be fired anyway, so off it went. Not that it mattered; there weren't really any heavily armored ships to save it for. The *Missouri* didn't face any air opposition either, which was just as well. For one five-minute period the ship's SK-2 air-search radar was effectively jammed by American planes that were trying instead to jam enemy fire-control radars.[78]

Navigator Jim Starnes had to rely mostly on navigation information provided by the new Loran electronic navigation system during that night bombardment. The weather and the distance from the beach made visual navigation essentially out of the question. Starnes was particularly pleased by the confidence Captain Murray displayed in taking Starnes's recommendations as to when the *Missouri* should turn and come to a new course during the back-and-forth track off the enemy coast. On that dark and rainy night the people on the bridge could see little of the target. Starnes didn't even have that limited opportunity. As usual, he was in the charthouse aft of the bridge, plotting the ship's position on a chart and sending the information out to the conn by sound-powered telephone.[79]

By late July, the carrier planes were at-

Opposite page: In this picture taken from the *Yorktown*, the oiler in the foreground refuels the *Missouri*. Notice the bombs and drums of lube oil on the deck of the replenishment ship. (U.S. Navy photo in the National Archives: 80-G-376365)

At the beginning of July, the *Missouri*'s turrets got some firing practice while she was operating with the other fast battleships of the Third Fleet. In the middle of that month, the ships used their big guns for bombardments of the Japanese home islands of Hokkaido and Honshu. (U.S. Navy photo in the National Archives: 80-G-335781)

tacking Japan on a steady basis and continuing to encounter opposition from enemy aircraft. After concentrating largely on land targets, late in the month the carrier planes ranged over to the Inland Sea to attack shipping in the Kure-Miho-Kobe-Nagoya area. Among others, the battleship *Nagato*, once the flagship of Admiral Isoroku Yamamoto, was heavily damaged.[80]

One of the jobs of the ship's chaplain was to build the morale of the crew. His methods included evening prayers and the broadcasting of news over the public address system. Commander Faulk inherited the newscasting from his predecessor, Commander John R. Boslet, who had installed in his office three short-wave radio receivers that could pick up news from all

over the world. Each day Faulk and his assistants culled highlights from the news and then put together a twenty-minute summary to inform the crew. Naturally, as the war got closer and closer to Japan, this meant putting into a broader perspective the events that the men of the *Missouri* were seeing for themselves on a daily basis.

In early August, Faulk relayed an announcement that came from President Truman as he rode back to the United States on board the cruiser *Augusta* after attending the Potsdam conference in Germany. There, Truman and the Allied leaders had laid down the conditions for a Japanese unconditional surrender. In addition, as Faulk told his shipmates, an American B-29 bomber had dropped an

atomic bomb on Hiroshima, Japan, on August 6. He announced that the bomb had the explosive equivalent of twenty thousand tons of TNT. As he remembered years later: "When I read that news account, I was later viewed with some slight suspicion in the wardroom, as though I had lost my marbles. Later, when the bomb was used on Nagasaki, my reports were much more credible, for by that time it was obvious that the war was reaching a terminal climax."[81]

Even as the Army Air Forces was continuing its bombing campaign, so too was the carrier task force. On August 9, the day of the atomic bomb strike against Nagasaki, Task Force 38 was attacking northern Honshu and did so again the following day. On the ninth the Japanese staged what the *Missouri*'s action report described as the last kamikaze attack of the war. In this instance the arcs of fire for the Third Fleet flagship were limited because of her position in the center of the formation. In every direction were friendly ships at a time when unfriendly planes were approaching.[82]

As a Japanese suicide plane dived on the carrier *Wasp* nearby, the only *Missouri* guns unobstructed by U.S. ships were two 40-mm quad mounts. The battleship's gunners got off only two short bursts at 4:10 that afternoon because the suicide plane, known as a "Grace" in the shorthand Allied terminology, was closely pursued by a fighter plane from the combat air patrol. Witnesses observed the *Missouri*'s 40-mm tracers entering the plane as it passed within about thirty-five hundred yards of the battleship's stern while crossing from starboard to port. Riddled by bullets, it crashed into the wake of the *Wasp*.[83] When he described the incident in his Naval Institute oral history, Murray said, "Of course, everyone claims he hit him, and probably not more than about forty ships were shooting at him."[84]

On the evening of August 10, the ship received unofficial reports of Japan's offer to accept the terms of the Potsdam ultimatum, provided they did not compromise Emperor Hirohito's prerogatives as a sovereign ruler. The end was obviously near.[85] On August 11, various senior officers came aboard the *Missouri* for conferences with Admiral Halsey on what

their ships would be doing in connection with the upcoming occupation of Japan, which appeared to be imminent.

One of the thirty-seven ships alongside the *Missouri* that day was the fleet oiler *Sabine*. She was simultaneously refueling the *Missouri* on one side and the British battleship *King George V* on the other. That facilitated a conference between Admiral Halsey and Vice Admiral H. B. Rawlings, commander of the British carrier force in the Pacific. They discussed the incorporation of British warships into the occupation force going forward.[86]

Other, more junior, officers also went back and forth between ships. Each group had a good reason for making the trip. The Americans were interested in strong drink and the British in better food than they had been eating. It was quite an experience for men who had been at sea for weeks. As Ensign Barron of the *Missouri* put it, "Two drinks of Scotch, and you were bombed." He hardly recalled the trip back to the *Missouri* at all. Barron's main impression of the *King George V* was the dirt. She had been at war a long time and was not maintained to the same spit-and-polish standards as American battleships.[87]

At 4:13 on the morning of August 15, the first planes rose from the decks of Task Force 38 carriers, ready to head for the Tokyo plains

Commander Roland Faulk, the ship's senior chaplain, delivers a sermon to observe VJ Day on August 15, 1945. In the foreground, Seaman Second Class W. E. Britton serves as organist. On September 2, Faulk delivered the shipboard prayer as part of the surrender ceremony. (U.S. Navy photo by F. D. McGill in the National Archives: 80-G-337589)

area. A few hours later, Admiral Halsey was eating breakfast in the *Missouri*'s flag mess when Captain Doug Moulton, the fleet air operations officer, burst in with a message blank in hand. "Admiral, here she is!" he exclaimed and showed Halsey the transcript of President Truman's official announcement of the Japanese surrender. Halsey joyously shouted "Yippee!" and began slapping the backs of all those within range.[88]

Down in the *Missouri*'s communications center, where he was on watch, Radioman Moose Conner was monitoring an aircraft distress frequency. As he listened through a set of earphones, a message came down from flag communications. In Guam, Fleet Admiral Chester Nimitz's staff had sent out an urgent dispatch directing the recall of all American planes. Hal-

sey's people relayed it, and the *Missouri* radiomen sent it on down the line. As the various communicators sent out the message to cease hostilities and return to their ships, a reaction came in from an incredulous airman, "No shit?"[89]

Before the day was over, American fighter planes and antiaircraft gunnery had shot down eight Japanese planes whose pilots hadn't received the order to surrender. Admiral Halsey himself had anticipated that situation in a message that has been quoted many times since then. He sent out instructions to Task Force 38 on how to deal with the uninformed Japanese pilots. "Investigate and shoot down all snoopers—not vindictively, but in a friendly sort of way."[90]

3 ❖ The Surrender

August–September 1945

Admiral Halsey ordered an immediate celebration in reaction to the news of the end of hostilities. Among other things, he called for the *Missouri* to blow her steam whistle for one minute. The deep-throated sound began coming forth at 11:09 on the morning of August 15. But the whistle, which hadn't been sounded in months, wouldn't stop once it started. It stuck in the open position and blasted forth for two full minutes. The engineers finally silenced it by cutting off the supply of steam from deep within the ship.[1] Signalmen ran up a large American flag—battle colors—on a mainmast halyard, and they raised Admiral Halsey's blue-and-white four-star flag to a yardarm on the foremast. When the Japanese aviators, including kamikazes, were flying around in the preceding months, the men of the *Missouri* didn't want to advertise that this was the flagship for the highest-ranking U.S. admiral afloat in the Pacific.[2]

The joyous *Missouri* sailors had a quick response to the word that the war—which began three years, eight months, and seven days earlier at Pearl Harbor—had finally come to an end. They yelled, "Break out the beer." That prompted Captain Murray to get on the loud-speaker. He told the crew he understood their excitement, but he had to remind them that the Navy prohibited drinking on board ship. He did, however, promise them all the beer they wanted when the ship finally got to port.[3] Not everyone had to wait so long. Demonstrating the old saying that "rank hath its privileges," the officers in the *Missouri*'s flag mess broke out champagne and toasted the victory over a determined Japanese enemy. Admiral Halsey also sent out a message to Task Force 38: "Splice

the main brace," an old British term authorizing all hands to have a drink. The only hitch was that the admiral's message included a provision negating it for the three American task groups. It applied officially only to Task Group 37.2, the Royal Navy carrier group operating with Task Force 38. Doubtless, men in some U.S. ships ignored the "negat" part of the signal.[4]

Seaman Joe Vella had ridden the *Missouri* thousands of miles from the United States and had essentially resigned himself to the notion that he would never see Connecticut again. When he heard the news of peace on August 15, he looked over at a gunner's mate second class whom he knew well; the other man was crying out of his sense of relief. With an expression of wonder in his voice, Vella said to his shipmate, "Mac, I made it."

The other man, who had survived the torpedoing of another ship before reporting to the *Missouri*, said quietly, "Me too."[5]

On board the *Missouri*, Admiral William F. Halsey is exultant after receiving news of the Japanese decision to surrender. (U.S. Navy photo in the National Archives: 80-G-700703)

Despite the combination of exuberance and relief, the men of the *Missouri* were not in a position to relax right away. It was not until September 6, for example, that a message arrived from the headquarters of Fleet Admiral Chester Nimitz, commander in chief Pacific Fleet, authorizing warships to show running lights at night and to steam without zigzagging when they were under way. In the meantime, until the signatures were on the surrender documents, the Third Fleet ships remained ready for anything that might come along.[6]

U.S. strategy had called for invasion of the Japanese islands by force in late 1945 and early 1946. By late July, however, while Allied strategy talks were being held in Potsdam, Germany, it was apparent that the end was near. When the Americans received news that the Japanese were ready to accede to surrender terms outlined in the Potsdam declaration, Fleet Admiral William Leahy and General of the Army George Marshall, both members of the Joint Chiefs, asked President Truman where he wanted the formal surrender to take place. In his post-presidential memoirs, Truman wrote that he quickly responded by saying that the surrender should take place on board a naval vessel in Tokyo Bay. That would impress upon the Japanese people that they were defeated, and having it on board ship would minimize the opportunity for fanatical final attacks. Truman also reported that it was he who designated the *Missouri* to be the specific ship. It was an obvious choice for the president from Missouri.[7]

Truman's unequivocal statement in his book, however, is somewhat at odds with a letter he wrote to his nephew J. C. on board the *Missouri*. The president's letter, dated August 18, said, in part: "I hope you are entirely well and that you will not have to be shot at any more. There is a possibility that the big battleship you are on will be used for the surrender although that matter is entirely in the hands of the Allied Commander in Chief."[8] Perhaps the president was being coy and was actually referring to himself in the third person. In a syndicated newspaper article of August 13, shortly before the Japanese threw in the sponge, Washington insider David Lawrence was already reporting the *Missouri* as the surrender ship.

For several days after the fifteenth the *Missouri* and her consorts milled around south of Japan, waiting to learn what would happen next. During the interlude, bags of mail from the United States came aboard. On August 23, Captain Murray was in his cabin when a chief yeoman came dashing in with a letter from home. He exclaimed: "Captain, the *Missouri* is going to be the surrender ship. Here's a clipping from the Santa Barbara paper. My wife just sent it."

It was the first Murray had heard that the *Missouri* would be *the* ship. The news also came in a letter from Murray's own wife, who asked plaintively, "Why don't you tell me about these things instead of letting me read it in the newspaper?" Murray soon discovered that the news had raced throughout the ship once the mail arrived. He went to discuss the situation with Halsey's chief of staff, Rear Admiral Robert Carney, who told him that official notification had just arrived by radio message five minutes earlier. At that point the surrender was scheduled for August 31, although adverse weather later delayed it by two days.[9]

The men of the *Missouri* began cleaning and painting their ship to get her ready for the ceremony. Because of the potential fire hazard in battle, ships were supposed to leave their paint ashore. The battleship's boatswain soon produced cans of paint from a hidden cache, however, and then more paint came over from other ships willing to help improve the flagship's appearance. Plans also started taking shape for just where the ceremony would be held. It would be in the admiral's cabin in the event of rain, but the preferred location was the 01 veranda deck on the starboard side, abreast of turret two and just outside the captain's inport cabin.[10]

In Guam, Admiral Nimitz's staff had already developed a plan for peaceful occupation of Japan. When they were gathered at Potsdam, the Joint Chiefs of Staff approved the Nimitz concept for initial landings by Marines and Navy men of the Third Fleet. The plan directed the Third Fleet to seize the Japanese naval base at

Yokosuka, near Tokyo; to take over the naval air station at Atsugi; to operate Japanese naval facilities; and to help the Army occupy the Tokyo region. The occupying forces were to demilitarize the remaining Japanese capabilities to make war. Another important mission was to release and care for Allied prisoners of war held by the Japanese.[11]

To implement the plan quickly, the landing force included three naval landing battalions of approximately four hundred men each, drawn from ships of Task Force 38. Rear Admiral Oscar C. Badger, operating as a battleship division commander in the *Iowa,* was selected to head the expeditionary force. The light cruiser *San Diego* became his flagship. On August 20, the *Missouri* and *Iowa* maneuvered alongside so that the former could transfer two hundred men over for temporary duty with the Tokyo occupation force. The senior member of the *Missouri*'s contingent was the executive officer, Commander Malone. The ship's Marine de-

tachment was not included in the landing party; the Marines would have security duties to perform on board the *Missouri* herself.

Among the *Missouri* men selected for the landing force was Ensign Jack Barron, most junior of the three officers assigned to turret two. Now that the ship appeared to have no further combat assignment, he could be spared for the time being. He and his counterparts in the other turrets picked enlisted men to go with them.[12]

After going aboard the *Iowa* briefly, the men transferred to the transport *Monitor,* namesake of the revolutionary Civil War ironclad that was a forerunner of the Navy's later battleships. There the *Missouri* contingent joined counterparts from the *Indiana, Wisconsin, Massachusetts,* and *Alabama.* Barron and the other officers conducted marching practice on the decks of the *Monitor* because the sailors' skills in that area had atrophied after leaving boot camp. On August 30 the land-going sailors climbed into

On August 20, the *Missouri* (*left*) transfers crew members to her sister ship *Iowa* so they can form a bluejacket landing party to go ashore in Japan. (U.S. Navy photo in the National Archives: 80-G-421126 via Norman Polmar)

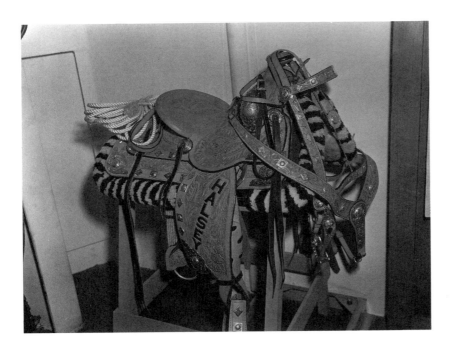

Reno, Nevada, sent this hand-tooled saddle for Admiral Halsey to use if he rode the emperor's horse. It is now in the Naval Academy museum in Annapolis. (U.S. Navy photo in the National Archives: 80-G-490400)

landing craft for the final leg of the journey. They went ashore at the Yokosuka naval base, the initial occupation of the Japanese home islands.[13] One drawback, as far as bragging rights were concerned, was that the *Missouri* men were not on board ship for the surrender ceremony on September 2. They didn't return to their seagoing home until shortly afterward.

As the *Missouri* men went ashore, the officers were armed with .45-caliber automatic pistols and the enlisted men with vintage Springfield rifles drawn from the ship's armory. They encountered no hostilities, only Japanese and American photographers taking pictures as they walked onto the soil of the former enemy. The landing party soon camped in the barracks of a former Japanese naval gunnery school near Yokosuka. One building housed a museum, filled with ship models in glass cases. When Ensign Barron walked into the building, he discovered that U.S. Marines brought in from Okinawa had been through ahead of him, and they had engaged in wanton destruction. They had used their rifle butts to smash the glass cases that held the models. Seeking an explanation, Barron learned that the Marines thought the ship models had gold anchors, and they wanted them as war prizes.[14]

One group from the landing party had the duty of demilitarizing the *Nagato,* which lay at anchor in the harbor at Yokosuka. The lone remaining Japanese battleship, she was long past her glory days. When she was completed in 1920, she and her sister *Mutsu* were the world's first battleships armed with 16-inch guns. Ensign Barron went aboard and found the old dreadnought deserted and desolate; her Japanese crew had gone elsewhere. He and his men took the bags of powder out of her magazines, carried them ashore, and destroyed them on the beach. Out in the open air, the grains of powder burned rather than exploded, although the fire flared up dramatically when sailors tossed on handfuls of black powder.[15]

Elsewhere ashore the Navy contingent found that the whole area of the naval base had been tunneled to produce caves, perhaps to guard the industrial facilities against aerial bombing. Inside the caves were extensive machine shops and supplies of food—saki and bagged rice. The machine tools were rusty because the American blockade had dried up the supply of fuel and lubricants needed to keep them running. Nearby were graving docks filled with row upon row of midget submarines. Dozens of them were there in various stages of construction; they were intended for a last-ditch defense against an anticipated invasion of Japan.[16]

Another duty for the landing force was to guard a warehouse filled with cruise boxes containing the effects of naval kamikaze pilots who had gone off to die. Jack Barron conceded that the men of the *Missouri* were not able to be very effective in their guard duties. A conqueror's mentality had taken hold of the Americans set loose in this alien nation, and they seemed compelled to seize whatever they could in the way of war souvenirs. The occupiers were taking samurai swords, daggers, and other items to be carried home as loot.[17]

At one point Barron was directed to accompany Lieutenant Commander R. J. "Matty" Matusek, the *Missouri*'s main battery officer, on a trip to carry a message to the naval air station at Atsugi. They used a weapons carrier as transportation. Throughout their journey ashore, particularly around the port city of Yokohama, nearly everything they saw had been flattened by American bombing. The few exceptions were buildings constructed of reinforced concrete. The windows in those had been shattered. Metal roofs that had once been atop buildings had been fashioned into crude shacks. Japanese children stood beside the roads and waved at the Americans, whereas women stood silently alongside the curbs, their backs turned toward the victors. No men were in evidence.[18]

Even as the landing party was beginning to do its job, dissident elements within Japan sought to defy the directive to surrender. At the Atsugi air station, near the naval base at Yokosuka, for example, pilots from the Imperial Japanese Navy continued to fly even after ordered to cease. And two thousand members of the special attack corps declared their intent to attack the *Missouri* when she was anchored in Tokyo Bay. The emperor, desiring that his people obey both the letter and spirit of the surrender, sent his younger brother, Prince Nobuhito Takamatsu, to Atsugi so he could dissuade the still-bellicose pilots. The Japanese fliers made the airfield available to the occupation forces on August 24, and the following day American planes began to appear in the sky overhead.[19]

On August 25 the high-speed transport *Gosselin* came alongside the *Missouri*'s port side to make an unusual high-line transfer. She was the final delivery vehicle for a fancy saddle that had been crafted in the United States and sent out as a personal gift for Admiral Halsey from the chamber of commerce in Reno, Nevada. It had his name tooled into the leather and was intended for a special purpose. The inspiration for the saddle and also for bales of hay that arrived on board the flagship was a remark the flag secretary, Commander Harold Stassen, had made when he was on a trip back to Washington shortly before. "It won't be long before Admiral Halsey is riding the Emperor's white horse." Evidently, a number of Americans were willing to help contribute to the victorious feeling evoked by that image.[20]

Finally, the American armada moved into Japanese waters and prepared to enter Sagami Wan, a bay separated from Tokyo Bay by the peninsula that includes Yokosuka. General of the Army Douglas MacArthur, newly desig-

nated as supreme commander Allied Powers, had originally scheduled the fleet arrival for August 25. Then he moved it back two days because a typhoon in the area threatened his airborne troops. Admiral Halsey didn't want his ships to have to wait at sea any longer than necessary in typhoon weather, so he requested and received permission to enter Sagami Wan on the twenty-sixth. The *Missouri* arrived off the Japanese coast at dawn that day and awaited the arrival of the destroyer *Hatsuzakura*, which carried a party of Japanese naval officers and navigation pilots. As per American instructions, the small ship's guns were depressed, their breeches open, and the torpedo tubes were empty.[21]

The forlorn destroyer threaded through the American formation, guns pointed at her as she steamed along. Altogether she had on board fourteen emissaries destined for various ships of the American task force. Initially, the *Hatsuzakura* transferred the men to the U.S. destroyer *Nicholas*, where they were searched and their weapons were confiscated. Then they came aboard the *Missouri* by high line.[22]

Suspicion was rife that the Japanese were going to pull something once on board the Third Fleet flagship. Attempting any sort of violence would have been suicidal, of course, but the Japanese had been wont to commit suicidal

Two members of the Marine detachment frisk a Japanese officer as he arrives aboard the *Missouri* on August 27. (U.S. Navy photo in the National Archives: 80-G-490398)

acts for months. Thus, even though the navigation group had already been checked for weapons on board the *Nicholas*, Corporal Joe Drumheller of the ship's Marine detachment gave the Japanese another thorough search once they reached the deck of the *Missouri*.[23] Lieutenant Doug Plate watched the treatment of the Japanese and their reaction as they were subjected to the humiliating treatment in front of hundreds of curious witnesses. Said Plate, "They were a frightened little bunch, I tell you."[24] All surrendered their swords and other weapons, which were placed on a table decorated with a small statue of a white horse.

After that, two Japanese captains and an ensign went under guard to Captain Murray's cabin for a navigation conference. Commander Gil Slonim, Japanese language officer on the Third Fleet staff, listened to the visitors converse among themselves. He concluded that the ensign must be part of the imperial family, because he spoke with a cultured accent and was condescending to the two captains. The Japanese soon found out who was boss. When one lit up a cigarette, Admiral Carney immediately made him put it out. When they asked to have their sidearms returned so they could be in full uniform, Carney refused, saying that the Americans would be prescribing the uniforms from now on.[25] As Carney described the scene: "There were no pleasantries or amenities exchanged, the atmosphere throughout being strictly cold and formal with every [phrase] and gesture intended to impress upon them that they were totally defeated, were in no bargaining position, and were strictly taking orders."[26]

Then it came time to enter Sagami Wan. The chief pilot, who spoke English, was on the bridge with Captain Murray, along with several other Japanese pilots. Their purpose was to keep the American ships out of mine fields. Murray passed the word to the chief pilot that he wanted the destroyer *Hatsuzakura* up ahead, as part of the screen with the American destroyers. His rationale was that the Japanese ship would—as a matter of self-preservation—steer clear of mines. Word came back from the Japanese destroyer that the skipper wanted to remain close by the *Missouri* so he would be

ready to respond to Captain Murray's orders. Murray again said that the ship should join the screen; the *Hatsuzakura* moved a little farther out, but still kept station on the *Missouri*.

At that point Murray directed the 40-mm mount atop turret two, as well as all ten 5-inch guns on the starboard side, to train on the destroyer. That action delivered the message, and the destroyer hustled off at high speed to her assigned station. Murray then directed the destroyer to ping with her sonar as a means of detecting any kamikaze submarines that might be lying in wait. The U.S. screen commander reported that the *Hatsuzakura* wasn't complying. Murray had the pilot send a message in Japanese to the destroyer, directing her to get with the program; still no action. So Murray ordered that the two forward turrets be pointed in the destroyer's direction. That did it. Soon the destroyer was pinging, and the force then proceeded into Sagami Wan. Astern of the *Missouri* were the *Iowa* and the British battleship *Duke of York*.[27]

By late afternoon many of the ships of the Third Fleet had moved in and anchored in an area, off Kamakura, which some called the Japanese Riviera. In the distance loomed snow-capped Fujiyama. That evening, from the *Missouri*'s vantage point in the fleet anchorage, the sun seemed to set directly into the crater of Japan's sacred mountain. The symbolism was striking.

About a week after hostilities ceased, Admiral Halsey had sent a dispatch to the Naval Academy Museum in Annapolis. A couple of months earlier, Captain Harry Baldridge, the

Opposite page: Hundreds of curious crew members look on as Japanese naval officers and harbor pilots are transferred from the destroyer *Nicholas* to the *Missouri* on August 27. Barely visible on the main deck, just above where the two lines at center reach the ship, is one of the Japanese. Marines converge to search the Japanese, part of the reason they weren't included in the landing party. (U.S. Navy photo in the National Archives: 80-G-490408)

Above: Swords, sabers, and daggers cover a table in Admiral Halsey's quarters after the Japanese were disarmed after coming aboard on August 27. In the center is a statue emblematic of the admiral's supposed boast to ride Emperor Hirohito's white horse. (U.S. Navy photo by F. D. McGill in the National Archives: 80-G-338143)

Japanese naval officers and harbor pilots go over charts for the Third Fleet's upcoming approach to Sagami Wan and Tokyo Bay. At left, in the baseball cap, is Rear Admiral Mick Carney, Third Fleet chief of staff. At right is Commander Gilven Slonim, Japanese language officer on the staff. (U.S. Navy photo in the National Archives: 80-G-490401)

museum's director, had suggested to the admiral that he could lend him a special flag to be used in connection with the Japanese surrender when the time came. It was a thirty-one star flag flown from the flagship of Commodore Matthew C. Perry when his squadron steamed into Edo Bay—as Tokyo Bay was then called—in 1853. Perry's purpose was to open up Japan to the West. Now Baldridge believed it was time for the flag to be used again in connection with another American naval enterprise in Japan. The surrender came much more quickly than expected. That accounted for the urgency of Halsey's message, which requested transportation of the flag by officer courier.

The museum director called for help from the Navy's Office of Public Information in Washington. The director, Rear Admiral Harold "Min" Miller, turned to Lieutenant John Bremyer for advice on getting the flag to the *Missouri* because Bremyer was in charge of the officer messenger mail center. Bremyer allowed that he'd be willing to undertake the chore and beat out several other applicants for the job. Flying in the propeller-driven airplanes of the era, he had top priority for transportation throughout the journey. The flag was in a box inside a bag, and it was Bremyer's constant companion during the one hundred hours it took him to travel through more than a dozen time zones. He had the flag with him when he ate, when he slept, and even when he went to the head.

The lieutenant's itinerary took him across the United States, thence to Hawaii, Johnston Island, Guam, and Iwo Jima. A PBY flying boat carried him the last lap to Sagami Wan, where he boarded a motor launch for the trip to the *Missouri*. He went aboard the giant battleship and presented his valuable cargo to Commander William Kitchell, Halsey's flag lieutenant. Once Kitchell and Bremyer opened the package, they found a letter from the Naval Academy curator saying that the flag was too fragile to be flown aloft. So Kitchell arranged to have it framed and put in a glass case. Curiously, it was framed backward, with the blue field and stars to the right.

Lieutenant Bremyer was made to feel at home in the *Missouri*'s flag quarters. Halsey greeted him warmly and asked for details of his long journey. Bremyer was struck by the admiral's bushy eyebrows and the fact that he seemed so relaxed with the coming of peace. When the visitor arrived, Halsey had his feet up on his old-fashioned roll-top desk as he read a book. He took great pride in showing off his new saddle, four bridles, and ten pairs of spurs. Admiral Carney, the chief of staff, was wearing a skivvy shirt without a khaki shirt, presumably because everyone knew who he was anyway. As he surveyed the scene in flag quarters, Bremyer later reported: "People were running in and out of there just like it was a pool hall or something, no aides to go through or anything. It was a very informal outfit." Someone asked the courier if he would be willing to stay for the surrender ceremony, and he pronounced himself delighted. Then he went to bed and slept for two days to recover from his journey two-thirds of the way around the world.[28]

On August 29 the *Missouri*'s crew was at general quarters when she and her accompanying armada entered Tokyo Bay, the destination toward which the U.S. Navy had been pointing since December 1941. Admiral Halsey was out on deck, wearing a long-billed cap of the sort customary for railroad engineers. He was chatting with various members of his staff when someone remarked about aircraft carriers. Halsey replied: "You know, I was writing a letter to my wife last night, and I told her, 'Well, dear, this is the day we have been looking forward to. I'm going into Tokyo Bay to accept the surrender terms of the Japs on board the *Missouri*. You know why I'm aboard the *Missouri?* That's President Truman's home state, and President Truman's daughter christened the *Missouri*. But, you know, you don't have anything to worry about, dear. You're doing all right because I only brought one aircraft carrier into Tokyo Bay with me. That's the *Cowpens*, and that's the one that our daughter christened.' "[29]

Indeed, in January 1943, Margaret Halsey Spruance had named the light carrier after a battle of the Revolutionary War. Halsey's daughter was married to a distant relative of Admiral Raymond Spruance, commander Fifth Fleet, who was then far away in Wakayama, Japan, on board his flagship *New Jersey*. He would not be present for the upcoming ceremony because an experienced senior admiral needed to be ready to command the reaction force in the event the Japanese did something untoward and wiped out the American command structure in Tokyo Bay. Similarly, nearly all of Task Force 38 was dozens of miles away from Tokyo Bay, remaining at the ready. Only the *Cowpens* would represent the Navy's air branch in celebrating a victory that aircraft carriers had done so much to bring about.

As the ships reached Tokyo Bay, the *Missouri* anchored in a spot quite near that of Commodore Perry's flagship ninety years earlier. The other ships arrayed themselves around the *Missouri*, putting her essentially in the center of the anchored formation.

When the news had reached the crew that the *Missouri* would be the surrender ship, Captain Murray's immediate reaction was that it would be an extremely formal affair, with the officers and enlisted men wearing dress whites, medals, polished swords, and so forth. Then the word came from Admiral Nimitz that the uniform of the day would be necktie-less khakis for the officers and chiefs, and it would be undress

white uniforms for the other enlisted men.[30]

In the days leading up to the ceremony, Commander Horace Bird, the gunnery officer, supervised as the men of the *Missouri* prepared. General MacArthur had specified that he wanted the Japanese delegates on the main deck only a brief time, then right up to the 01 deck for the ceremony. That meant numerous rehearsals to see just how long it would take the Japanese to climb the gangway steps, walk across the main deck, then up the ladder to the veranda deck where the signing would take place.

One sailor stuck a swab handle down his pantleg so he could simulate the slow walk of Mamoru Shigemitsu, the Japanese foreign minister. The Japanese envoy had a wooden left leg as the result of a bomb thrown at him by a Korean revolutionary in Shanghai, China,

The *Missouri* steams into Tokyo Bay for the surrender ceremony. Astern is the *Iowa*. (U.S. Navy photo in the National Archives: 80-G-700770)

Mount Fujiyama is visible over her two forward turrets as the *Missouri* rides at anchor in Tokyo Bay. (U.S. Navy photo in the National Archives: 80-G-338272)

in 1933. During the various rehearsals, the walk by the Shigemitsu substitute and his retinue generally took about ninety seconds. Captain Murray assumed that his young sailors were probably more energetic than the Japanese would be, so he calculated the walk would take three minutes. He thus planned for the boat to come alongside at 8:56, with the ceremony to start at nine.[31]

The big day, September 2, 1945, began even before dawn on board the flagship. At five o'clock the *Missouri*'s bugler blew reveille to rouse all hands except those who'd just come off the midwatch a little before four. As for the rest, they were soon up and out. The deck hands were out in force, scrubbing the quarterdeck and 01 veranda deck with fresh water. Like the other decks on board the *Missouri*, the veranda deck, where the signing would take place, was painted a dark blue-gray as part of the camouflage scheme. After a time the final cleaning was complete, and the crew moved to eat breakfast a little before six.[32]

Others were busy as well. Each member of the crew was permitted to send out five pieces of mail that would bear the ship's postmark and the surrender date. As a result, the post office canceled an estimated fifteen thousand pieces of mail that day. The postal clerks worked at the job from 5:30 in the morning until midnight. The *Missouri*'s print shop had been busy as well, turning out wallet cards designed by Chief Shipfitter Donald G. Droddy. They bore a red rising-sun insignia plus facsimile signatures of MacArthur, Nimitz, Halsey, and Murray. On each was a place for the name of the individual crew member. Hundreds of the men have held onto those cards for the past fifty years. Captain Murray specified there would be one card per man, and they would go only to those who were physically on board the ship that day. When Admiral Nimitz later asked for a few extra copies to pass out at Pacific Fleet headquarters, Murray politely declined.[33]

After he had eaten breakfast, Lieutenant Bob Mackey, the ship's disbursing officer, was out on deck talking to one of the men in his division. Then he went to the 01 level and saw the polished mahogany table sent over by the British battleship *King George V* for the signing. It was about forty inches square, little bigger than a card table. Mackey talked with Commander William Kitchell, Halsey's flag lieutenant, and they agreed that the table was clearly too small to accommodate both sets of surrender documents: the green leather-bound copies for the Americans and the black canvas-bound ones for the Japanese. Kitchell asked if the supply officer had any bigger tables on board. Mackey told him that one from the general mess would work. The tables there had spindly metal legs, however, and so he suggested that one could be made presentable by covering it with a green baize cloth of the type used on wardroom tables between meals. Kitchell directed Mackey to see what the American alternative would look like.[34]

Seaman Al Circelli was standing watch on the quarterdeck at the time. Mackey dispatched him and two of his shipmates to the second deck to get a mess table from the eating compartment. They were challenged by a mess cook, who wanted to know why they were filching one of his tables. After providing an explanation, they carried it topside to set it up.

The supply officer sent a steward's mate to the wardroom for a cloth, and when it was in place, Commander Kitchell pronounced the arrangement satisfactory.[35]

Shortly after seven o'clock the destroyer *Buchanan* came alongside to transfer 170 reporters, photographers, movie cameramen, and ra-

USS MISSOURI
Tokyo Bay   SEPTEMBER 2, 1945

CERTIFYING THE PRESENCE OF:

LIEUT. ROBERT L. BALFOUR USNR

at the formal surrender of the Japanese Forces to the Allied Powers.

S. S. Murray
Captain, U.S. Navy
Commanding Officer

Douglas MacArthur
General of the Army
Supreme Commander
Allied Powers

C. W. Nimitz
Fleet Admiral, US Navy
United States
Representative

W. F. Halsey
Admiral, US Navy
Commander
Third Fleet

Above: Each man on board the *Missouri* on the day of the ceremony received a card like this as a souvenir. Lieutenant Bob Balfour was a member of Halsey's Third Fleet staff. (U.S. Navy photo in the Naval Historical Center: NH 100856-KN)

Left: The *Missouri* is in the foreground in this collection of Allied ships in Tokyo Bay. At the center of the photo are the British battleships *Duke of York* and *King George V.* (U.S. Navy photo in the National Archives: 80-G-339381)

General of the Army Douglas MacArthur and Fleet Admiral Chester Nimitz stride toward the surrender table. Walking in front of them is Commander William Kitchell, Admiral Halsey's flag lieutenant. Bringing up the rear is Halsey himself. (U.S. Navy photo in the National Archives: 80-G-700776)

dio sound men to the *Missouri.* Then it was time for the victors to come aboard to observe the surrender of the vanquished. Lieutenant Commander Jim Starnes, by virtue of his position as navigator, had the honor of standing the forenoon watch on September 2. Among other things, that meant he had picked out the eight sideboys who stood on the quarterdeck—four to the left and four to the right—and saluted as visiting dignitaries came aboard. Following direction from above, Starnes had picked out eight men who were each more than six feet tall. It was still another gimmick in the psychological game with the Japanese. Just as the huge battleship was larger than the few remaining ships in the Imperial Japanese Navy, so too were the individual Americans larger than the Japanese emissaries.[36]

The junior officer of the deck was Lieuten-

ant Doug Plate. He was amused that the vice admirals, rear admirals, and captains—and their Army equivalents—did not rate eight sideboys. But they received salutes from that many anyway, so the watch team didn't have to shuffle bodies with each arrival. None of the visitors seemed to mind.[37]

The visitors were on hand when Chaplain Roland Faulk delivered a special prayer he had composed for the day of surrender. Faulk was mindful of all who had died since the day in December 1941 when destruction rained from the sky on the old battleships moored at Pearl Harbor. In part, the prayer included: "May we never forget those who have paid the cost of our victory and our peace. On this day of surrender we turn hopefully from war to peace, from destroying to building, from killing to saving."[38]

Fleet Admiral Nimitz boarded the *Missouri* shortly after eight. With a yank of a halyard, his five-star blue flag was opened up at the main truck, and Admiral Halsey's, bearing four stars, was hauled down. On board the nearby *Iowa,* signalmen raised a four-star flag. Even though he was physically in the *Missouri,* the *Iowa* was officially Halsey's flagship for about an hour and a half. General of the Army MacArthur arrived at 8:43, and his red five-star flag was unfurled on a metal bar so that it was side by side with Nimitz's, a rare case of two flying simultaneously. Nimitz's flag was to starboard, signifying seniority, since this was a Navy ship.

Shortly afterward, other signalmen ran up a special flag on the foremast, replacing the American flag that had been there. The one that went up had been flying over the U.S. Capitol in Washington on December 7, 1941. Just as the Commodore Perry flag symbolically tied this day back to a previous encounter with Japan, so also did the national ensign from Pearl Harbor day. Despite the ceremonial aspects, the men of the *Missouri* remained vigilant. At Captain Murray's direction, the ship's antiaircraft battery remained manned except for the guns on the starboard side, in the vicinity of the ceremony about to take place.[39]

One other contingent of visitors to the ceremony, in addition to the many dignitaries, was made up of released prisoners of war. Captain

Fitzhugh Lee was handling public information for Admiral Nimitz. He heard that General MacArthur would be bringing former Army POWs, so he made a call ashore by radiotelephone to request a group of naval prisoners. There Commander Stassen lined up several, including a Navy captain, a young pilot, and some enlisted men. They arrived at the *Missouri* by boat not long before the Japanese delegation. The pilot's face was already familiar to many Americans because he had been photographed for the documentary film *The Fighting Lady* before being captured. While he was in prison a Japanese guard had knocked out his teeth with a baseball bat. Even so, he arrived aboard the *Missouri*, said Lee, "cheerful and happy and smiling and almost crying" because he was so glad to be out of prison camp.[40]

Captain Murray was consumed with details on that morning. One had to do with the ship's position. The National Geographic Society had proposed sending representatives to the ceremony to establish the precise location of the *Missouri*. Murray concluded that he didn't need still more visiting firemen; the ship's own navigation team could do just as well. So he directed that at nine o'clock crew members on the bridge take bearings on six different objects ashore—twice the normal number—and establish a precise fix where the lines of bearing intersected. (Such a fix was necessary because the *Missouri* was swinging around on her anchor chain and not staying in a constant location.) As soon as the bearings were taken, the captain had ordered that electrical power to all of the ship's gyrocompasses be cut off so that no one could come along later and claim to have taken a more accurate position at the precise moment of signing. The position from the fix was subsequently enshrined in a plaque embedded in the deck. It was 35° 21′ 17″ north latitude, 139° 45′ 36″ east longitude.[41]

After the Japanese government finally came to the decision in mid-August to give up, it had to pick an official delegation to go to the *Missouri*. Toshikazu Kase, who became one member of the group, expressed the general attitude, "Nobody wanted to volunteer for the odious duty." The prime minister, Prince Higashikuni, wasn't

appropriate because he was Emperor Hirohito's uncle. Prince Fumimaro Konoye, the real power in the government, opted out. Finally, the principal obligation fell on Foreign Minister Shigemitsu. Kase reported afterward that Shigemitsu had worked to end the war and regarded the coming of peace as an opportunity to put his nation back together. As he wrote several years later, "If this day marked a journey's end, it must also signify a journey's beginning."[42]

All told, the delegation included eleven men: three each from the Foreign Office, the Army, and the Navy, and two from the Japanese government bureaucracy. On that September morning the eleven had made their way through the devastated lands that lined the road from Tokyo to Yokohama. They traveled in secrecy to prevent Japanese extremists from interfering with their mission. In the port city they boarded the destroyer *Lansdowne*, which had fought in the Pacific from Guadalcanal onward. The Japanese rode for an hour in the small ship until they arrived near the *Missouri*, which was anchored a few miles off Yokohama.[43]

The delegation then transferred to one of the *Missouri*'s motor launches for the final lap of the journey. Because of his wooden leg, Shigemitsu had to be lowered over the side of the *Lansdowne* in a boatswain's chair, rather than climbing down steel rungs welded to the side of the destroyer.[44] At 8:55 the *Missouri*'s boat let the first of the passengers off at the forward accommodation ladder—instead of having them come aboard at deck level as the Allied dignitaries had done from the destroyer. Moreover, these men who had come to the battleship would not have the luxury of surrendering in private as the German leaders had done earlier in the year in France.[45]

The *Missouri*'s decks were silent; the only sound that greeted the arriving Japanese was the trilling of a boatswain's pipe. Because of Shigemitsu's wooden leg—and perhaps because of the figurative pain involved in what he was about to do—his journey up the gangway to the quarterdeck was even slower than expected. Commander Bird extended a hand to the foreign minister. At first he disdained the

This bird's-eye view
shows the *Missouri*'s 01
veranda deck as it
appeared the morning of
September 2, 1945. The
turret was trained about
thirty degrees to
starboard to create a bit
more standing room for
the rows of spectators.

Sketch layout of Surrender Ceremony, 2 September 1945

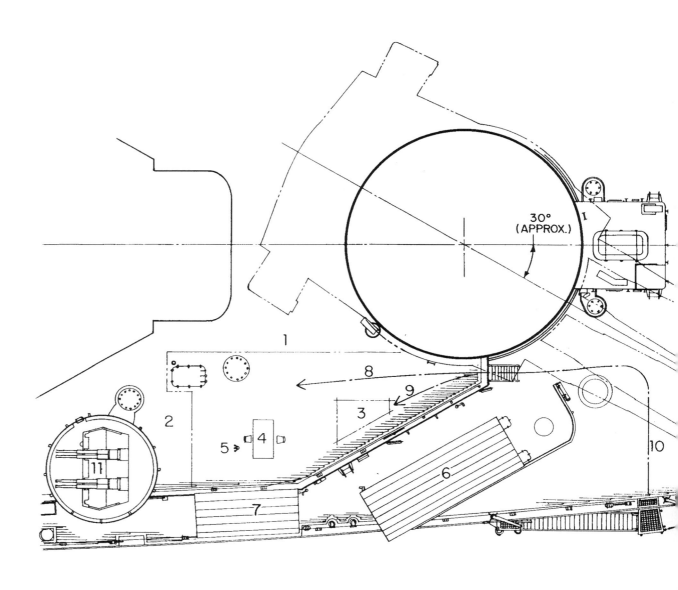

Drawings by Alan B. Chesley

1 UNITED STATES OFFICERS
2 ALLIED OFFICERS
3 JAPANESE DELEGATION
4 SURRENDER TABLE
5 THREE-HEAD MICROPHONE
6 STAGE FOR REPORTERS AND CORRESPONDENTS

7 STAGE FOR MOVIE CAMERAS AND PHOTOGRAPHERS
8 PATH OF NIMITZ AND MACARTHUR
9 PATH OF JAPANESE DELEGATION
10 JOINT PATH
11 QUAD FORTY (TRAINED AFT)

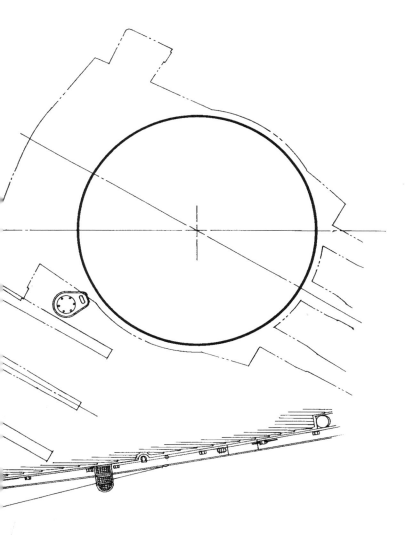

A *Missouri* boat approaches the ship's starboard accommodation ladder to bring the Japanese delegation aboard shortly before nine o'clock on the morning of September 2. Photographers are at left, radio technicians at right. (Courtesy Puget Sound Naval Shipyard: YV-3256)

help, then accepted it briefly.[46] Despite the rehearsals and the fudge factor Captain Murray had allowed, the Japanese delegation was late. MacArthur's plan was to step out of Admiral Halsey's cabin, on the 02 level, at precisely nine o'clock, make a grand entrance down a ladder, and begin the ceremony in the presence of the waiting Japanese. He didn't want to have to wait for them, but when he did emerge he saw Shigemitsu's black top hat just about at the level of the 01 deck. So he went back in to allow the Japanese to get themselves into position and then wait for him.[47]

Once on the veranda deck, the Japanese arranged themselves in three rows. They faced the surrender table and its green cloth cover. They stood looking stoic and mostly expressionless, disguising whatever thoughts they had at the time. The American officers in ranks were more animated. An observer noted hatred in the eyes of Chinese delegates; their country had suffered from Japanese aggression since 1937. General Joseph W. "Vinegar Joe" Stilwell, who had served heroically in the China-Burma-India theater, flexed his cheek muscles angrily. Lieutenant General George Kenney, who had done much to contribute to the success of the air war, curled his lips in contempt. When the Japanese did look to their right, they appeared apprehensive at the sight of Admiral Halsey.[48]

Correspondents and photographers were all around, frantically seeking the best view. Hundreds of sailors and Marines looked down on the scene. One of the Japanese, Toshikazu Kase, probably spoke for all of them when he wrote: "As we appeared on the scene, we were, I felt, being subjected to the torture of the pillory. A million eyes seemed to beat on us with the million shafts of a rattling storm of arrows barbed with fire. I felt them sink into my body with a sharp physical pain. Never had I realized that staring eyes could hurt so much."[49]

They felt somewhat like errant schoolboys, called up for a reckoning before a teacher. They had trouble maintaining their dignity, especially when they looked up at the *Missouri*'s bridge and saw painted there the eleven rising

Left: Sideboys salute as top-hatted Japanese Foreign Minister Mamoru Shigemitsu reaches the top of the accommodation ladder to come aboard. The ship's Marine detachment is at lower right. (U.S. Army photo in the National Archives: SC-329104)

Below: The Japanese representatives stand in rows as General MacArthur reads his speech. (U.S. Army photo in the National Archives: SC-210626S)

sun flags that signified Japanese aircraft the battleship had shot down on her kamikaze-riddled journey to Tokyo Bay. At 9:02—a little late despite all the meticulous planning and rehearsal—General MacArthur stepped to the microphone. He stood stiffly; his hands trembled as he began to read from the paper they were holding.[50]

> We are gathered here, representative of the major warring powers, to conclude a solemn agreement whereby peace may be restored. The issues, involving divergent ideals and ideologies, have been determined on the battlefields of the world and hence are not for our discussion or debate. Nor is it for us here to meet, representing as we do a majority of the peoples of the earth, in a spirit of distrust, malice or hatred.
>
> But rather it is for us, both victors and vanquished, to rise to that higher dignity which alone befits the sacred purposes we are about to serve, committing all our people unreservedly to faithful compliance with the understanding they are here formally to assume.
>
> It is my earnest hope and indeed the hope of all mankind that from this solemn occasion a better world shall emerge out of the blood and carnage of the past—a world founded upon faith and understanding—a world dedicated to the dignity of man and the fulfillment of his most cherished wish—for freedom, tolerance, and justice.
>
> The terms and conditions upon which the surrender of the Japanese Imperial Forces is here to be given and accepted are contained in the instrument of surrender now before you.
>
> As Supreme Commander for the Allied

Powers, I announce it my firm purpose, in the tradition of the countries I represent, to proceed in the discharge of my responsibilities with justice and tolerance, while taking all necessary dispositions to ensure that the terms of surrender are fully, promptly, and faithfully complied with.

Kase, a diplomat, spoke excellent English as a result of having studied at Amherst and Harvard. His mood changed as he listened to General MacArthur's statement, which he considered both eloquent and noble. Instead of announcing an impending regime of vengeance, the general called for justice, tolerance, and rebuilding. In the years ahead, MacArthur proved in Japan to be the instrument that would carry out those high-sounding words expressed on the deck of the *Missouri*.[51]

After MacArthur made his speech, he called for Foreign Minister Shigemitsu to come forward. As the leader of the Japanese delegation sat down, his wooden leg bounced off a tie rod that held up the spindly legs of the mess table. Captain Murray, one deck below on the quarterdeck, heard the sound of rattling metal and was concerned that the table might collapse, but it didn't. Shigemitsu took off his silk top hat and put it on the table, then removed a yellow glove from his right hand. He fumbled with watches and papers in his pocket before pulling out a pen. Then he seemed to hesitate a bit in finding the correct place on the surrender document, so General MacArthur called to his chief of staff, Lieutenant General Richard Sutherland, and said, "Sutherland, show him where to sign."[52]

The chief of staff came over from his posi-

Opposite Page: Men crowd every available perch in the superstructure in order to get a look. On the wing of the bridge are small Japanese flags representing the airplanes the *Missouri* shot down. In the lower right is the flag flown at Tokyo Bay by Commodore Matthew Perry in 1853. (U.S. Army photo in the National Archives: SC-210644S)

Right: General MacArthur reads the speech that struck his listeners as magnanimous. Arrayed behind him (*left to right*) are representatives of the various Allies that contributed to the victory: Admiral Chester W. Nimitz, General Hsu Yung-Chang, Admiral Sir Bruce Fraser, Lieutenant General Kuzma Derevyanko, General Sir Thomas Blamey, Colonel L. Moore Cosgrave, General Jacques LeClerc, Admiral C. E. L. Helfrich, and Air Vice Marshal Leonard Isitt. (U.S. Army photo in the National Archives: 111-SC-210644S)

Above: At 9:04 A.M. on September 2, Foreign Minister Mamoru Shigemitsu signs the surrender document on behalf of Japan. To his left is Toshikazu Kase, who subsequently wrote a book—titled *Journey to the* Missouri—about the Japanese viewpoint during the war. (U.S. Navy photo in the National Archives: 80-G-332699)

Right: General MacArthur signs for the Allies. Standing behind him are Lieutenant General Jonathan "Skinny" Wainwright and General Sir Archibald Percival. (U.S. Army photo in the National Archives: SC-210625S)

tion by turret two and pointed to the assigned spot on the document. Without saying a word, Shigemitsu signed the first surrender document. The line above his name included a space for the time of signing, so he looked up inquiringly at Kase, who was standing next to him. Kase consulted his wristwatch and told Shigemitsu it was four minutes past nine. History was satisfied as the foreign minister wrote on the document the precise time of the official

surrender. He then signed the Japanese copy as well.[53]

Without a word, General Yoshijiro Umezu, chief of the Imperial General Staff, nervously came forward and signed on behalf of the Japanese armed forces. He alone, of all that day's signers, disdained the chair and remained standing, leaning over to write his signature. Then General MacArthur sat down to sign, motioning for two gaunt, tired men to come stand beside him. One was Lieutenant General Jonathan "Skinny" Wainwright, who had been left behind on Corregidor when MacArthur and his family were evacuated in the spring of 1942. Also nearby was General Sir Archibald Percival, who had been captured at Singapore.

MacArthur signed at 9:08, using five pens for his two signatures. Of four black pens, he gave one each to Wainwright and Percival; the two others were destined for archives in Washington and West Point. The last one, red in color, was his wife's, and she would get it back as a souvenir. He used the red pen to sign the "Arthur" portion of his last name. That also happened to be the first name of both his father and his son.[54]

Next, Admiral Nimitz sat down at the green-covered table, pulled out a fountain pen, and signed his name to the surrender document at 9:12. Originally, State Department planners in Washington had called for General MacArthur to be the only individual to sign on behalf of the Allied powers. Vice Admiral Charles "Savvy" Cooke, an individual who had made a great contribution to the victory by his service as a planner on the staff of Fleet Admiral Ernest King, made another one in connection with the surrender. When he heard about the intent of the State Department committee, he was considerably upset because there was no recognition of the Navy's role in the Pacific victory. He called in Captain Robert Dennison, a member of the Joint War Plans Committee working for the Joint Chiefs of Staff, and told him to approach the committee planning the surrender and get a role for Admiral Nimitz. The upshot of the efforts of Dennison—and other individuals—was that Nimitz was designated to sign on behalf of the United States.[55]

Left: Admiral Nimitz signs for the United States. To the left of MacArthur are Admiral William F. Halsey and Rear Admiral Forrest P. Sherman. Sherman was the chief of naval operations when the *Missouri* went to war in Korea five years later. (U.S. Navy photo in the National Archives: 80-G-701293)

Below: Onlookers crane to see the Japanese emissaries on the 01 veranda deck. The formal rows seen earlier have been relaxed, indicating that the ceremony was near its end when this photo was taken. (U.S. Army photo in the National Archives: C-4626)

We, acting by command of and in behalf of the Emperor of Japan, the Japanese Government and the Japanese Imperial General Headquarters, hereby accept the provisions set forth in the declaration issued by the heads of the Governments of the United States, China and Great Britain on 26 July 1945, at Potsdam, and subsequently adhered to by the Union of Soviet Socialist Republics, which four powers are hereafter referred to as the Allied Powers.

We hereby proclaim the unconditional surrender to the Allied Powers of the Japanese Imperial General Headquarters and of all Japanese armed forces and all armed forces under Japanese control wherever situated.

We hereby command all Japanese forces wherever situated and the Japanese people to cease hostilities forthwith, to preserve and save from damage all ships, aircraft, and military and civil property and to comply with all requirements which may be imposed by the Supreme Commander for the Allied Powers or by agencies of the Japanese Government at his direction.

We hereby command the Japanese Imperial General Headquarters to issue at once orders to the Commanders of all Japanese forces and all forces under Japanese control wherever situated to surrender unconditionally themselves and all forces under their control.

We hereby command all civil, military and naval officials to obey and enforce all proclamations, orders and directives deemed by the Supreme Commander for the Allied Powers to be proper to effectuate this surrender and issued by him or under his authority and we direct all such officials to remain at their posts and to continue to perform their non-combatant duties unless specifically relieved by him or under his authority.

We hereby undertake for the Emperor, the Japanese Government and their successors to carry out the provisions of the Potsdam Declaration in good faith, and to issue whatever orders and take whatever action may be required by the Supreme Commander for the Allied Powers or by any other designated representative of the Allied Powers for the purpose of giving effect to that Declaration.

We hereby command the Japanese Imperial Government and the Japanese Imperial General Headquarters at once to liberate all allied prisoners of war and civilian internees now under Japanese control and to provide for their protection, care, maintenance and immediate transportation to places as directed.

The authority of the Emperor and the Japanese Government to rule the state shall be subject to the Supreme Commander for the Allied Powers who will take such steps as he deems proper to effectuate these terms of surrender.

Protocol then demanded that the officers from the other victorious nations sign as well, and so they did. The only hitch came when an aide to Shigemitsu discovered that some of the Allied signatures were on the wrong lines on the Japanese copy of the documents. Colonel L. Moore Cosgrave, the representative of Canada, started the process, and the three subsequent signers—on behalf of France, the Netherlands, and New Zealand—were thus forced out of place and also signed on incorrect lines. Once the miscue was pointed out, a brief conference followed, and then General Sutherland corrected the error with his pen.[56]

Photographers were crammed in all over the place, each trying to have the best vantage point from which to take pictures of the ceremony. Carl Mydans of *Life* magazine had been covering MacArthur for several years. On this occasion his access wasn't as free as he was ac-

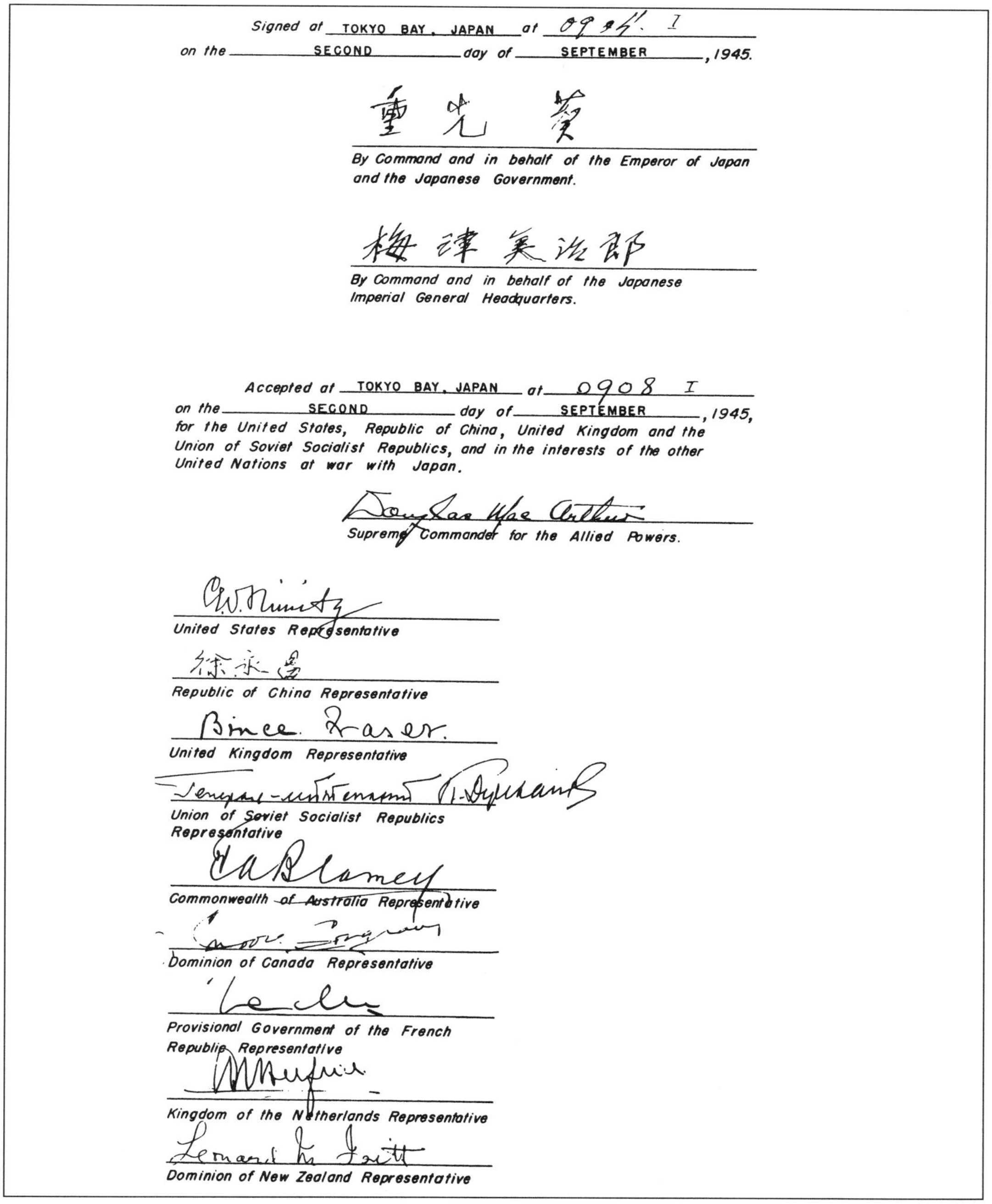

Signed at __TOKYO BAY, JAPAN__ at _0g94. I_
on the _____SECOND_____ day of ___SEPTEMBER___, 1945.

重光葵

By Command and in behalf of the Emperor of Japan
and the Japanese Government.

梅津美治郎

By Command and in behalf of the Japanese
Imperial General Headquarters.

Accepted at __TOKYO BAY, JAPAN__ at _0908 I_
on the_____SECOND_____ day of___SEPTEMBER___, 1945,
for the United States, Republic of China, United Kingdom and the
Union of Soviet Socialist Republics, and in the interests of the other
United Nations at war with Japan.

Supreme Commander for the Allied Powers.

United States Representative

Republic of China Representative

United Kingdom Representative

Union of Soviet Socialist Republics
Representative

Commonwealth of Australia Representative

Dominion of Canada Representative

Provisional Government of the French
Republic Representative

Kingdom of the Netherlands Representative

Dominion of New Zealand Representative

customed to—or as free as he wanted. His assigned post was in a 40-mm gun tub that was behind MacArthur as he spoke and as he signed. Mydans thus had face-on shots of the Japanese, but he was looking at the backs of the Americans and other Allies. During the brief interruption when the problem of Cosgrave's misplaced signature was being resolved, Mydans jumped out of the gun tub and ran over to the surrender table. He managed to click the shutter of his camera only once before a huge *Missouri* Marine lifted him up and carried him bodily back to the 40-mm mount. General MacArthur watched the brief episode unfold, his dignified posture a contrast to the indignity visited upon a noted *Life* photographer. As Mydans passed by the general, however, he noticed that MacArthur dropped his mask of solemnity for an instant—just long enough to wink at his friend.[57]

An army plane swooped in low over the bow of the *Missouri* to capture this view of the crew arrayed on deck during the surrender ceremony. (U. S. Army photo in the National Archives: SC-210649)

The Russian cameramen present for the ceremony were somewhat on the obnoxious side and paid particular attention to the portion of the ceremony that called for Lieutenant General Kuzma N. Derevyanko to accept the surrender on behalf of the Soviet Union. In fact, later photos reproduced in the U.S.S.R. tended to give the impression that this was a Soviet ceremony. In the meantime, though, one of the Russian photographers was not satisfied with his location on a wooden platform just forward of the 01 deck. He left his position and sought to climb up the ladder leading to the forward part of the veranda deck. His problem was that he walked right by Captain Murray and an equally large chief boatswain's mate.

The skipper nodded his head, whereupon he and the chief walked over and grabbed the Russian's legs just as he was going up the ladder. The man's suspenders weren't all that effective, with the result that his trousers drooped to around his knees. The captain and the boatswain's mate then carried the Russian several feet, holding him face down. They took him back to his platform and swung him up into his assigned position.[58]

The officer in charge of all the photography that day was Colonel Bert Kalisch, an Army officer, who wrote a fascinating article on the subject for the August 1955 issue of the U.S. Naval Institute's *Proceedings*. Kalisch had come to the *Missouri* through a background that well

Aircraft from the carriers of the Third Fleet fly over the *Missouri*'s forward turrets at the conclusion of the ceremony. (U.S. Navy photo by Barrett Gallagher in the National Archives: 80-G-472630)

suited him. More than twenty years earlier he was a midshipman at the Naval Academy, undergoing training with the class of 1924. He dropped out, though, after his third year and subsequently worked for some of the biggest newsreel companies of the day—Hearst Metrotone and Pathé News. He was recruited by the Army Signal Corps to make training films and eventually became General MacArthur's photo officer. It was Kalisch who made all the assignments as to where the dozens of photographers would stand on September 2. In his article he reported that his people moved the surrender table a few feet so it would be in focus for sideline photographers, and they moved the 1853 Perry flag so it would show up prominently over MacArthur's shoulder in the pictures.[59]

When the various signings were concluded, General MacArthur announced, "Let us pray that peace be now restored to the world and that God will preserve it always." Then he turned to the Japanese delegation and said, "These proceedings are now closed."

Back in the United States, where it was still Saturday evening, millions of Americans listened to a radio broadcast of the proceedings on board the *Missouri*. After the formal ceremony ended, President Truman spoke briefly from the White House, then shifted back to the battleship for statements from MacArthur and Nimitz. The general concluded his remarks by saying: "And so, my fellow countrymen, today I report to you that your sons and daughters have served you well and faithfully. . . . They are homeward bound. Take care of them."[60]

Just at the moment when the last Allied representative, Air Vice Marshal Leonard M. Isitt from New Zealand, had signed at 9:22, the overcast sky suddenly opened up. Up to then the day had been drab, with rolling clouds obscuring the sky in all directions. But now shafts of bright sunlight penetrated breaks in the clouds and danced on the surface of the water. Radioman Moose Conner, permitted by his division officer to watch from high in the superstructure, looked at the sun's rays and was reminded of the rising-sun insignia on the Japanese flag.[61]

Then came even more symbolism. Earlier, while Nimitz was signing, two naval officers stood with him. One was Rear Admiral Forrest Sherman, his war plans officer; the other was Admiral Halsey. As they stood there, MacArthur reached over, put his arm around Halsey's shoulders, and whispered, "Start 'em now!" With that a message went out to 450 carrier planes of Task Force 38 that had been orbiting nearby. Upon receiving the signal, they roared in over the anchorage at low altitude. After that a horde of B-29 bombers of the Army Air Forces flew over the fleet just as the Japanese were going down the accommodation ladder to depart the *Missouri*.[62]

The timing and coordination were beautiful, said Navigator Jim Starnes, who said the planes were so numerous that they "blackened the sky" for a time. Lieutenant Bob Balfour of the Third Fleet staff actually felt a sense of concern that the bombers were so low that they might clip the tops of some of the ships. Their engines were so loud that all conversation was impossible until they had passed by. It was a truly dramatic moment, demonstrating without any question the military power that had been spawned by the arsenal of America.[63]

As Gunner's Mate Walt Yucka looked up at the hundreds of airplanes flying in front of the sunburst, a thought passed through his mind: American power was blocking off the Japanese rising sun. Nearly a half century later, the memory was so emotional that it still gave him chills. He said simply: "That was the greatest thrill of my life. The war was over."[64]

4 ❖ Homecoming

September 1945–March 1946

After the surrender ceremony was over, Captain Murray called the ship's department heads to his cabin so they could compare their impressions of the morning's events. Murray would have preferred a couple of stiff drinks to help him unwind, but he settled for coffee. As the officers were talking, one of them said: "We'd better save that table and that cloth and those chairs. Somebody might want to give them to a museum." The comment struck a responsive chord, and soon the captain and department heads were rushing out to recover the everyday items that had suddenly been transformed into historic artifacts.[1]

They went out the door from Murray's cabin to the veranda deck, and the table was gone. The green cloth from the wardroom had been dumped up against a bulkhead, so someone picked it up and tossed it into the captain's cabin, along with the two British chairs that had been put there earlier. Then a search went out for the missing table. The party went down to the mess deck, where a mess cook was cheerfully setting up for lunch. The group of officers selected a table; they hoped it was the right one, although there was no way to tell for sure. Enlisted members of the crew who were in the mess deck that morning have expressed open skepticism that the retrieved table was the one on which the signing took place. Once the *Missouri* got back to the East Coast, the whole collection of artifacts, including Halsey's saddle, was turned over to the Naval Academy museum in Annapolis, where they remain to this day.[2]

To celebrate the successful conclusion of the ceremony, the ship's officers and some of the visiting dignitaries went to the wardroom for a buffet lunch of sliced beef, ham, pork, turkey, and trimmings such as potato salad.[3] On the mess deck the enlisted men of the *Missouri* enjoyed a holiday-type turkey dinner. In the days after that, though, they returned to their canned, dehydrated, run-of-the-mill food. It inspired a cruel joke among some crew members.

Did you hear about the prisoners of war that were guests at the surrender?
No, I didn't hear about that.
Well, they came down and took one look at our chow and said, "The hell with you. We're going back to prison camp. We got fed better there."[4]

On September 3 Lieutenant Bob Balfour and two other members of Admiral Halsey's staff caught a train to Tokyo. Balfour had a newspaper background before joining the Navy, so he went to visit an English-language newspaper in the Japanese capital. He asked to see the editor, who explained that he had learned English while going to a small college in Michigan. By coincidence, Balfour had attended the same college for two years before heading off to journalism school at the University of Missouri. So the two fellow alums hit it off right away, and the Japanese editor took Balfour and his friends on an escorted tour all over Tokyo.[5]

In looking back on the reception they received, Balfour observed, "I don't think Americans could possibly have accepted the Japanese the way the Japanese accepted us." He reasoned that the Japanese felt such a profound sense of relief that the war was over, they were willing to endure whatever came with the end of that war. From what the three officers saw

A few weeks before, the 01 veranda deck had been filled with dignitaries. Here, as the *Missouri* steams toward Hawaii, sailors use holystones to grind away the dark blue-gray paint that covered the teakwood for camouflage purposes during the war. (U.S. Navy photo in the National Archives: 80-G-351246)

during their tour, Balfour felt a sense of regret that the United States dropped atomic bombs at war's end. The city was just leveled, leading him to conclude years later: "I think the Japs were within a week of quitting without any atomic bomb. . . . I don't feel it had to be dropped."[6] That conclusion, of course, is far from universally shared. The question of the American use of the two atomic bombs has been debated vigorously since 1945.

On the morning of September 5 the battleship *South Dakota* moved in alongside the *Missouri* so Admiral Halsey's staff could transfer files and luggage from one ship to the other. The *South Dakota* would be carrying Halsey and his people to a Navy Day ceremony in San Francisco. At 5:02 on the morning of the sixth, the *Missouri* weighed anchor and moved away from the spot in Tokyo Bay where she had made history. In company with the destroyer *Kimberly* she set out for Guam on the first leg of a long journey. For a good many on board it would not be until years later that the significance of their pres-

ence in the crew of the surrender ship would really sink in. For the moment, their overriding interest was in getting home.[7]

One night during the voyage to Guam, Chaplain Faulk was lying in his bunk, unable to sleep. He got up and had what he later remembered as "kind of a mystic experience." His cabin was in the forward part of the ship, so he went out onto the main deck and walked up alongside turret one. It was a gorgeous, moonlit night. The only sound was the swish of waves along the sides of the ship. Faulk was overcome with the feeling that he was part of God's universe. It was an experience that moved him many times in subsequent years as his mind went back to that wondrous night of moon, sea, and the sound of waves against the hull of the *Missouri*.[8]

The other chaplain on board was Lieutenant (j.g.) Paul O'Connor, a Jesuit priest, who had reported for duty in the *Missouri* shortly before the surrender ceremony. From time to time, Radioman Moose Conner went to Chaplain O'Connor for confession, which didn't have the privacy booths customary in churches ashore. On board ship the Catholic penitents had to kneel down at the priest's feet and look him in the eye. Still, their confessions were limited in scope, since there wasn't a whole lot of sin to commit at sea with no booze and no girls around. It took some imagination, but Conner was able to come up with a few sins, such as admitting that he had cursed from time to time, but that was about it. So O'Connor would ask, "Do any gambling, son?"

"Oh, yeah, I played a little cards and shook a little craps."

"Well, you know you're not supposed to do that. The captain forbids that aboard ship, and so that's disrespectful to your Father. Say twenty rosaries." Later, in the living compartment, Conner would look around, and his shipmates would be making tick marks to record the rosaries they were saying as penance for whatever they had done.[9]

Once the ship reached Guam, Captain Murray redeemed the promise he made when hostilities ceased. The various watch sections went over onto a recreation beach and drank their fill of beer, although some of the younger crew members preferred less potent refreshments.[10] During her stay, the *Missouri* took aboard a number of veterans who had enough discharge points to be released from the service as soon as they reached the States. Murray remembered years later that the battleship took aboard about fifteen hundred servicemen, swelling the

During the homeward journey, the ship operated her floatplanes a fair amount to keep the deck crews and flight crews in training. This photo shows the fantail crane lowering the SC-1 Seahawk onto the starboard catapult. (U.S. Navy photo in the National Archives: 80-G-353397)

total population to about four thousand souls. Many of the homeward-bound passengers were sleeping in the mess deck or wherever else they could find room, but they didn't seem to mind.[11]

Before the trip back to the United States, a number of officers and enlisted men had already left. Lieutenant Doug Plate became senior watch officer, but he had to work under the handicap that several of the officers trained to stand deck watches had been detached. So it was his duty to train a new crew of officers of the deck and junior officers of the deck for the transit home. All told, the *Missouri* picked up about twenty-five green ensigns when she was in Tokyo Bay and Guam. Fortunately, the watches were a good deal less demanding than those in wartime had been. No longer was it necessary to steer zigzag courses to avoid submarines; no longer was it necessary to ward off enemy air attacks; no longer was it necessary to maintain station in a huge carrier formation. The only real duty was to get from point A to point B without running aground or colliding with another ship.[12]

During the ride home to the States, the ship decided to put on some entertainment now that the pressures of war were past. Part of that entertainment included a nightly series of boxing matches. It was essentially a tournament to see who the best boxer was in each weight category. Fireman Bob Schwenk had joined the Navy to avoid being drafted, and as a result he had to pass up some college football scholarships that were offered. Instead, he used his athletic ability on board the *Missouri* as a boxer, participating in the various smokers held on the fantail. The inducement came one day when he saw the ship's fighters eating a meal of steak and eggs.

The first time he fought a match, it was against a boatswain's mate named Johnny Beaton, who really clobbered him. As Schwenk put it, "He hit me in the jaw so hard I couldn't eat my steak that night." He also cut Schwenk's eye during the course of administering a beating. For the most part, the lopsided outcome of the fight was the result of Schwenk's inexperience. He could throw a punch but didn't yet know

how to protect himself. As time went on Schwenk improved steadily. Eventually, during the voyage home to Norfolk, he was involved in the ship's heavyweight championship fight against Beaton. Beaton proposed that they take it easy, but Schwenk would have none of it, saying: "I've hated your guts for months. That first fight I ever had, you hit me in the jaw so hard I couldn't eat my steak. I'm going to kick your ass tonight." And Schwenk did, with a knockout, then proceeded to eat one of the most delicious steak dinners of his life.[13]

As the *Missouri* approached Pearl Harbor, she was officially designated flagship of the Pacific Fleet. Accordingly, Fleet Admiral Chester Nimitz held a fancy reception on her deck while she was at Ten-Ten Dock, the mooring for a previous fleet flagship, the USS *Pennsylvania,* in the months before the war. Most of the crew, however, had other things on their minds during the Hawaiian interlude. The officers and men had their most delicious taste of life— both literally and figuratively—since leaving Oahu months earlier. The parents of one of the junior officers lived on the island of Oahu, and they were fairly well-to-do people. They had a substantial home, where they threw a party for all the officers in the ship's wardroom. Included on the menu were fresh milk, fresh fruit, fresh vegetables, and fresh bread. Case after case of cold milk—obtained for the Navy men despite a strike by truckers—disappeared down the throats of the officers. It was mixed in some cases with alcohol to make the treat even stronger.[14]

The days of the lousy chow were also over for the enlisted men. Gunner's Mate Walt Yucka reveled in the opportunity to eat steak for breakfast. They also got a chance to drink—more than the two cans of beer available at Mog Mog Island. Some stayed overnight at the plush Royal Hawaiian on Waikiki Beach. Included were Bob Schwenk and some of his shipmates from the engineering department. The hotel provided a great change of pace from the shipboard routine. They got to stay in the shower as long as they wanted, eat all they wanted, and sleep as late as they wanted. Then they began sharing a bottle of

whiskey and headed to town, already liberated by the drink from the inhibitions that normally serve to moderate behavior. One of the shipmates was in such bad shape that Schwenk tried to get some food in him as a first step toward sobriety; then he planned to take him back to the hotel. Alas, his condition did not improve, so Schwenk took him to the alley to try to walk him around and clear his head.[15]

Along came four shore patrolmen—the "Gestapo," in Schwenk's approach to life. They demanded to know what was going on. Schwenk told them to leave the *Missouri* men alone because they were already on their way and didn't need to be harassed. But the shore patrolmen threatened to throw Schwenk's buddy in jail and put a billy club up as a token

of power. Schwenk, the boxer, unloaded with his right hand, and one shore patrolman fell to the pavement. Then the others jumped on Schwenk, hit him behind the ear, and down he went.[16]

When he woke up he was in a jail in Honolulu. Schwenk was subsequently transported to the brig at Pearl Harbor and after that back to the *Missouri* in handcuffs and leg irons. At that point he had no hat, no belt, no neckerchief, no shoestrings, and his whites were a shambles. The shore patrol directed the watch standers on board the battleship: "Put this man down there in the cross-bar hotel," as the ship's brig was called. Later, when the ship was proceeding from Hawaii to Panama, Captain Murray had a long series of captain's mast hearings to

Artists in the crew pose with a map of the *Missouri*'s travels, painted onto the forward bulkhead in the officers' wardroom. Seen (*left to right*) are: Petty Officers Jose de la Torre, Jr., and Gerald Parker, and Lieutenant (j.g.) Reichart Muncie, Jr. In the 1980s, after the ship had extended her reach to the Persian Gulf, new artists extended and updated the painting. (U.S. Navy photo in the National Archives: 80-G-353425)

deal with misbehavior ashore. As Schwenk showed up for his case, the captain said, "Now, this is a very serious charge against you, so I'd like to hear your story."[17]

"Well, Captain," said Schwenke, "I went out to buy some souvenirs, and I had a whole bunch of souvenirs in my hand. We were standing in this long line to get a drink, and some guy started mouthing off about this ship and that ship. He asked us what ship we was on, and we said, 'The *Missouri*.'

"He said, 'Ah, that bucket of bolts. It has a bunch of fairies on there.'

"I said, 'Watch your mouth.' So, anyhow, we got into a little fight, and he took a swing at me. He sort of hit me on the side. I dropped all my packages, and I swung at him. And he must have ducked, and I hit the shore patrol by mistake."

Captain Murray said, "You know, that's a pretty good story." Then, turning to the chief engineer, Lieutenant Commander Tom Doyle,

the skipper asked, "What kind of man is Schwenk down there in the fireroom?"

Doyle replied, "He's the best man I have down there; I'm real proud of him."

Murray then said: "That's about the best story I've ever heard. I'm going to restrict you for one liberty." Schwenk's buddy, the fellow who had been the initial cause of the altercation, was reduced in rate. His only crime was that he had gotten drunk and passed out—normally a good deal lower on the punishment scale than attacking a member of the shore patrol.[18]

Once she reached Panama, the *Missouri* scraped concrete all the way through the canal.

In one set of locks the ship broke off a pretty good-sized hunk. As the battleship squeezed through the Pedro Miguel locks, Radioman Moose Conner was awestruck by the thousands of Army coast artillerymen who had gathered to watch the surrender ship. They wore khaki-colored baseball-type fatigue caps. Sailors on deck swapped their white sailor hats for the soldiers' caps. Conner joined in by offering to trade his to an Army man standing ashore. Once the other man agreed, each threw his hat to the other. Then they struck up a conversation about their hometowns. When Conner announced that he was from Streetor, Illinois, the soldier, Bill Lowns, responded, "So am I." Then Lowns pushed his way to the edge of the lock so they could shake hands. Lowns has since died, but fifty years after that meeting in Panama, his daughter still has Conner's Navy white hat as a keepsake.[19]

The ship's last stop before New York was Norfolk, where a good many crew members were released to go back to the civilian world. They had enough points to rate discharge, and they were ready to get on with the rest of their lives. One who left was Seaman J. C. Truman. Though he might have stayed around to see his uncle, he made another choice. As he wrote to the president, "I could have postponed applying for discharge until after I arrived in New York, but I did not know how long that would delay me, and I am certain you understand I want to get home as quickly as possible." The nephew had a wife and children at home; the president could wait.[20]

One of the big events during the stop in Norfolk was the installation in the 01 veranda deck of a bronze plaque to commemorate the surrender signing. Upon arrival, the commandant of the Norfolk Navy Yard offered Captain Murray a choice of three different plaques. One was designed by the Norfolk yard, one by the Bureau of Ships, and a third by an artists' group. Murray picked the one that had been cast in the shipyard's foundry because it had the most substantial lettering and was likely to last the longest.[21] It bore the essential information about the surrender and was soon to be an object of great attention on the part of visitors.

Far left: A *Missouri* seaman receives a warm reception at Norfolk. The sailor at right (white hat cocked down over one eye) appears envious. (U.S. Navy photo in the National Archives: 80-G-353387)

Left: While the ship was at Norfolk, workmen installed this bronze plaque in the spot on the 01 deck where the surrender table had stood during the signing ceremony. (U.S. Navy photo in the National Archives: 80-G-437905)

Below: Personnel stand in ranks for inspection during the homeward voyage. (U.S. Navy photo in the National Archives: 80-G-353429)

planned to be on board the *Missouri* for the Navy Day celebration in New York. When Murray met him in Washington, though, Nimitz had just come from a meeting with Secretary of the Navy Forrestal. The secretary told him that he would instead have to take part in the Navy Day observance on the West Coast, since he was still in command of the Pacific Fleet. Murray observed that it was about as disappointed as he'd ever seen Nimitz. Said the

The plaque marked the spot where the table holding the documents had been sitting. As workmen from the naval shipyard chipped out wood to make room for the installation of the recessed plaque, *Missouri* Marines stood guard to prevent the workers from gathering up souvenirs. The chips were regarded as property of the ship's crew and subsequently passed out to those serving on board. Lieutenant Commander Plate, for instance, was officer of the deck during the cutting of the deck and came away with a shaving bored out by a workman's drill.[22]

While the ship was in Norfolk, Captain Murray took a few days' leave and went to Washington, D. C., so he could find where he would be headed as soon as he was relieved of command of the battleship. During the course of his time there he encountered Admiral Nimitz. When they were previously together in Pearl Harbor, the admiral mentioned that he

Below: An amidships view of the *Missouri* moored in the Hudson River. The ships had their names painted on their sides—the only time in her career this was the case for the *Missouri*—so spectators ashore could identify them. (James C. Fahey collection, U.S. Naval Institute)

Opposite page: This magnificent photo shows some of the ships moored in the Hudson River on October 27 for Navy Day. The *Missouri* is in the center, to the left of the blimp. In the foreground (*bottom to top*) are the *Augusta, Midway,* and *Enterprise.* (Harry S. Truman Library collection: 71-3163)

skipper, "I think he rated this opportunity to lead the fleet into New York City."[23]

In late October the ship completed the last leg of the long journey to the city where she was built. After milling around outside Ambrose Channel while waiting for a heavy fog to lift, the *Missouri* finally made her triumphal entry on October 23. After a brief time pierside, she joined a long line of warships moored in the Hudson River, on the city's west side, for a naval review.

One of the chores for the officers in the duty section was to provide escorts for congressmen, high-ranking military officers, and other VIPs who came to visit. Ensign Cecil Hartson drew the duty one day while the ship was moored in the Hudson. An Army general and his daughter came aboard for a tour. The young woman was about eighteen and had the sort of figure that would attract a Navy man's attention. She wanted to see the inside of a 16-inch turret, so Hartson took her to number two. As she was climbing the small ladder through the hatch at the turret's rear overhang, a gust of wind came

and put her skirt around her neck. She apologized demurely for the breach in ladylike decorum, but she was undaunted.[24]

Next she wanted to see the enlisted men's living quarters. Ensign Hartson told the general he didn't think that was a good idea, in part because it was an invasion of the crew members' privacy. But his daughter wanted to go anyway, and the group did. As they passed a shower, two *Missouri* men came out—naked, naturally, and in a playful mood. They were snapping their wet towels, trying to hit each other in the bare rear ends. The daughter was giggling, and Hartson was apologetic. The general said, "Forget it; she wanted it." Meanwhile, the two enlisted men were extremely discomfited by the presence of not only a woman and one of their ship's officers but a general as well. Hands and towels were flying around as the men sought to cover themselves and to come to a semblance of attention in the presence of a senior officer. As Hartson put it, "If you've ever seen four hands going crazy, you should have seen those guys."[25]

Soon it was time for Navy Day, which was

then celebrated on October 27 because it was the birthday of President Teddy Roosevelt, a big-navy advocate. Now another president, Harry Truman, was coming to applaud the achievements of the big Navy that had just won the war. After his arrival by train from Washington, Truman began the day by participating in the commissioning of a large new aircraft carrier. She had been launched on April 29 as the *Coral Sea.* Two weeks later the name of the ship was changed to *Franklin D. Roosevelt,* and now Roosevelt's successor was present as she joined the fleet. Also in attendance were the widows of both Franklin Roosevelt and Woodrow Wilson, the presidents during the two great wars of the twentieth century.

From the naval shipyard, the president rode through the city in an open car, waving to thousands along the route and being showered with paper dropped from office windows. He also stopped for a visit at New York's city hall and later made a twelve-point speech in Central Park on the subject of postwar foreign policy. The speech presaged his strong stance toward the Soviet Union in the months to come.

In the afternoon he came by boat to the *Missouri.* The battleship fired three, twenty-one-gun salutes that day: one when he boarded the ship, one when he left, and one at the conclusion of the day's activities. They were the first gun salutes the ship fired after the war; indeed, she didn't even have a saluting battery because antiaircraft guns had much higher priority during the hostilities. To prepare for the ceremonial firing, workmen made some saluting rounds the night before at a little ammunition depot called Iona Island in New York harbor. Normally, the blank cartridges used for salutes are about the size of 40-mm projectiles. These new ones were special charges made up to be fired by the 5-inch guns. When they went off, they rattled windows up and down Riverside Drive on Manhattan's west side. (Afterward the ship received a number of complaints, all of which were ignored.)[26]

During the firing of the first salute, Fleet Admiral William Leahy, the president's chief of staff, was standing on the quarterdeck next to Lieutenant Commander Plate, the officer of the deck. As one round after another was fired and the noise hurried off into the distance, Leahy said not a word. He had been through this experience hundreds of times in a naval career that stretched back more than fifty years. Right after the firing of the final round, the old admiral snapped at Plate, "Twenty-one; that's enough." The lieutenant commander, who was already uneasy about having his actions scrutinized so closely by the nation's top-ranking military officer, was jarred by the sudden outburst.[27]

Once he stepped aboard, Truman inspected the crew and then took a tour of the mammoth warship that had so many personal connections for him. On the veranda deck he leaned over to look at the newly installed bronze plaque. For a time he sat at the surrender table

The *Missouri* fires a salute with one of her 5-inch guns, rattling windows on Manhattan's west side. Alongside is the destroyer *Renshaw.* (Harry S. Truman Library collection: 70-4109)

(or its twin brother, depending on whether the right one was retrieved) and wrote his name in the ship's guest register. As he did so, he exclaimed, "This is the happiest day of my life."[28]

After that the president went in through the door to Captain Murray's cabin. Previously, Commodore James Vardaman, a St. Louis reservist who served as Truman's naval aide, told Murray that the president wanted to have a drink when he was on board. Murray thus obtained two bottles of bourbon. When Truman came in, he raised his hand and declared: "By virtue of the fact that I'm President of the United States and commander in chief of the Navy, I hereby declare the captain's cabin of the USS *Missouri* to be wet for one hour. Vardaman, where did you hide that whiskey?" Murray removed the bottles from his safe, and Truman and his companions drank. The president explained that he was clearing out the dust that had collected in his throat during all the riding around in open cars he'd done that day. When the bourbon was all gone, Truman declared the captain's cabin dry again.[29]

After that, Truman joined a collection of people for lunch in the admiral's quarters. Admiral Jonas Ingram, commander in chief Atlantic Fleet, had temporarily embarked. Thus, the *Missouri*, which had carried the flag of Pacific Fleet Commander in Chief Nimitz the previous month, now spent a few days as Atlantic Fleet flagship. Margaret Truman had the pleasure of dining in a room decorated with a picture of herself taken during the previous year's launching ceremony. The special meal, prepared by local caterers rather than *Missouri* cooks, included a few dishes with names not featured in the customary Navy recipe books: "Chicken Curry Tokyo," "Virginia Smoked Ham Tojo," "Baked Beans Missouri," "Ice Cream à la Pacific with Cakes," and "Demi-Tasse Atlantic."[30]

One of the guests at lunch was Lieutenant Commander George Elsey, a reserve officer who had been a member of the White House staff since early in the war. He had served President Roosevelt, gone on temporary duty to Normandy for the D-Day operation, accompanied Truman to Potsdam, and now was with

him on board the *Missouri*. Among his contributions—along with helping devise postwar foreign policy—was that he had helped design and issue a new presidential flag that made its debut on Navy Day. In place of the four stars of the old flag was now a circle of forty-eight, one for each state in the union. Moreover, in a change to heraldry, the eagle depicted in the seal in the center of the presidential flag now had its eye turned toward the olive branch of peace, rather than the arrows of war.[31]

At mid-afternoon Truman's party went aboard the *Fletcher*-class destroyer *Renshaw*, which was briefly alongside. She had been designated as the Hudson River taxicab for the VIPs as they reviewed an impressive array of forty-some ships moored or anchored in the river between Manhattan and New Jersey. All told, the procession of warships stretched for seven miles. Directly astern of the battleship was the carrier *Enterprise*, which had contributed mightily to the victory in the Pacific. Aft of the *Enterprise* was the new *Midway*, sister of the carrier commissioned that morning in Brooklyn.[32]

To accommodate the visitors to the *Renshaw* during her Navy Day role, the New York Navy Yard had made a couple of modifications. The

President Truman stands on the quarterdeck after boarding the *Missouri*. Next to him is Governor Thomas Dewey of New York. In 1948, Truman defeated Dewey in the presidential election. (Courtesy Vice Admiral Douglas Plate)

Sailors line the decks of both the *Missouri* and *Renshaw* while side by side for the transfer of President Truman. This view from a blimp overhead gives an idea of the amount of antiaircraft guns a Japanese plane had to deal with when making an attack run on the battleship. (Bettmann Archive: U1027704INP)

cabin itself was also spruced up. Commander George Cairnes, the destroyer's skipper, made it clear to everyone that no one else was to use that head during the president's visit. More than that, they were to ensure that Truman used that particular head if he used any at all.[33]

Once he was on board the *Renshaw*, Truman climbed up the special ladder to the flying bridge, which was protected that day by wind-screens that reached waist high. Even so, it was well that the guests were bundled up because a strong breeze was blowing the shipboard flags stiffly horizontal. The temperature was in the low forties during the trip, which lasted more than two hours, and the windchill factor doubtless made it feel a good deal colder.

On board both the battleship and destroyer, Navy men in blue uniforms manned the rails, standing an arm's length apart. Even to honor the president, it was an unpleasant duty, because the sailors had no protection from the wind, nor the opportunity to move around to get warm. And the same was true on board ship after ship as the *Renshaw* pulled away and

Above: President Truman signs the ship's guest book set up on the surrender table on the 01 deck. As he did so, he exclaimed, "This is the happiest day of my life." Flanking him are Admiral Jonas Ingram and Fleet Admiral William Leahy. (Courtesy Vice Admiral Douglas Plate)

Right: The *Renshaw* pulls away from the *Missouri* to begin her journey up and down the Hudson River. Flying from the battleship's port signal halyard is the new presidential flag that made its debut that day. (Courtesy John W. Hird II)

yard put in a special ladder leading up to the flying bridge and also installed a glistening new head—for the president's use only—in the unit commander's cabin on the main deck. The

headed north toward the George Washington Bridge. At the northern end of the swing, the destroyer turned south, headed down the New Jersey shore, and went to the Battery at the tip of Manhattan.[34]

As the *Renshaw* moved along, Lieutenant Jack Hird, one of the officers on board, tried to keep moving—a luxury the sailors didn't enjoy. He saw Margaret Truman walking around in the cold. At one point the president's daughter tried to negotiate her way down a ladder as a gust of wind swirled about. He noticed that she was doing well at keeping her skirt under control, although he averted his eyes to ensure that he wouldn't see too much. Margaret appeared to take it all in good humor.[35] What she didn't like nearly so well were the infernal saluting guns that sent out one ear-cracking blast after another. Each time the *Renshaw* passed another warship, here came another twenty-one guns. One of the admirals on board the destroyer said: "My dear Miss Truman, why are you holding your fingers in your ears? All you have to do is open your mouth, and it won't bother you in the least."

She tried it once—unsuccessfully—then turned to him and said, "Admiral, don't ever con me like that again."[36]

After a time, Jack Hird went below to the *Renshaw*'s wardroom in order to get a cup of coffee and go to the head. He was wearing a Navy raincoat, which carried no indication of his rank on it. Just as he was about to go back up the ladder, he encountered Commodore Vardaman, the officer who had ensured that Truman had bourbon available on board the *Missouri*. The officious naval aide, festooned with the gold "chicken guts" denoting his position, came barreling down the ladder and demanded of Hird, "Where's the head, sonny?"[37]

After nearly three years of war, Hird didn't care for the "sonny." Even so, he remained polite and said, "Just around the corner here, Commodore."

Vardaman then turned and said, "This way, Mr. President." Hird knew that he was supposed to direct Truman to the wonderful new head refurbished just for him, but he couldn't react quickly enough. Truman himself, unaware of the advance preparation, went to the

regular officers' head. As he passed Hird, he beamed, patted him on the shoulder, and said, "Thank you, son." He then proceeded into the officers' head. Hird enjoyed the presidential greeting much more than the contemptuous treatment from Vardaman. Only later did the lieutenant confess sheepishly to the *Renshaw*'s captain that the president had not used the gorgeous new facilities upon which the taxpayers' money had been spent.[38]

Finally, after all the chilly winds and the gun salutes, the destroyer deposited the presidential party ashore. They rode to the train station and then headed for home in Washington. It had been a glorious Navy Day.

The following day, the *Missouri* left her mooring in the river and headed for pier ninety on the west side of Manhattan. Being pierside was an

Truman waves to the crowd from the bridge of the *Renshaw*. The officer with aigulettes on his right shoulder is the president's naval aide, Commodore James Vardaman. The *Missouri* is in the background. (U.S. Navy photo in the National Archives: 80-G-K-15861)

Opposite page: The *Missouri* was jammed with visitors when she went to a pierside berth following Navy Day. (U.S. Navy photo in the National Archives: 80-G-353681)

Right: The *Renshaw* (*left*) carries the president upriver in the late afternoon. Forward of the *Missouri*'s forecastle is the old battleship *New York*. (Harry S. Truman Library collection: 71-3165)

Below: Navy ships put on a searchlight display from the Hudson River on the night of October 27. This picture was taken from the Empire State Building. (Harry S. Truman Library collection: 70-4075)

advantage to the hordes of citizens who wanted to come aboard because it removed the necessity of running boats back and forth. And come they did: nearly three-quarters of a million the week and a half the ship was there. Brows were installed fore and aft, and they provided the way for a mass of humanity. People could do little but walk forward on the starboard side, aft down the port, then off again, but at least they could say they had been there.

Some were not content to stay on the assigned tour route, though. For instance, one boy managed to slip away and set off the general alarm from the navigation bridge. That caused consternation for a while as it sent crew members to their battle stations.[39] Another boy pushed a lever that released a heavy life raft and sent it crashing to the deck below. Fortunately, it didn't injure anyone during its fall, but the youngster lost a finger in the process.

So eager were some visitors for something from the famous ship that they used their fingernails to scrape grease out of gun barrels. Others ripped plastic or metal identification plates off various pieces of equipment. Some tried to pry up the surrender plaque. Others scratched the paint of the 16-inch guns to such an extent that the barrels had to be elevated to get them out of the visitors' reach.[40] Hands reached in through the portholes to Captain Murray's cabin and stole things off his desk, including one of his officer caps with gold decorations on the visor.[41]

The tourists in New York left behind what would today be called graffiti. In addition to all the souvenirs they lifted to take with them, they used pencils and lipstick to write their names, telephone numbers, and various sentiments on different parts of the ship.[42] To Ensign Hartson, the hordes of people resembled the inhabitants of a giant ant colony; they were everywhere. Months later, when the ship was in the Mediterranean, the *Missouri* had no such problems. Hartson attributed the difference to the moral structure of the people involved. In Europe the people had been through a devastating war and were respectful of the battleship as a symbol of American might. The Americans, as he put it, "just wanted to grub and grab." They felt a smug sense of confidence and wanted tan-

gible souvenirs of the victory so recently achieved.[43]

One day of the New York visit, October 29, was set aside for visits by the family. Seaman Len Schmidt's parents and siblings came down from upstate New York to tour the ship. They didn't have to brave the huge crowds of other days. As one of the ship's photographers, Schmidt was able to get pictures of the family members on their tour, including a shot of his sister climbing up the side of a gun turret. Schmidt's father took great pride in what his son had accomplished—going out into the big war and coming back as part of the victorious fleet.[44]

Ten days after the Navy Day celebration with the president on board, the battleship's command changed. The new skipper was someone Truman thoroughly approved of because Captain Roscoe Hillenkoetter had lived

in St. Louis before entering the Naval Academy thirty years earlier. In fact, he had worked briefly as an office boy for the St. Louis Browns baseball team. He had been an intelligence sub-specialist at various times during his career and was executive officer of the battleship *West Virginia* when the Japanese struck in 1941.[45]

Hillenkoetter spent thirty-two months on wartime duty in the Pacific and thus was well seasoned by the time the Bureau of Naval Personnel nominated him for the command. He believed the bureau may have picked a Missouri man to keep in the new president's good graces. In any event, Hillenkoetter was overjoyed when he received the news that he would become the skipper. When he got to New York to begin briefings with Captain Murray, the *Missouri* was back alongside a pier, and the swarm of visitors was immediately apparent to the new man. "It's not as bad as it looks,"

A brief interruption of the hordes of people that descended on the ship came on October 29, when the ship was moored at a pier at the end of West 50th Street in Manhattan. The only visitors allowed that day were the families of crewmen, shown here on the fantail. (Bettmann Archive: U776211ACME)

Murray reassured him. Hillenkoetter and Murray had known each other for years and were good friends, so the turnover process went smoothly.[46]

Finally, the ship and her crew got a break. After months filled with activity—Iwo Jima, Okinawa, raids on the Japanese home islands, the surrender, and Navy Day—the *Missouri* headed to the New York Navy Yard for an overhaul. Her crew had shrunk considerably because of the many men released for discharge. Still others went on leave as the holiday period approached. And a few new men were coming as well. Chief Quartermaster Clarence "Bud" Johnson reported to the crew of the *Missouri* in mid-December, when she was in dry dock at Brooklyn. He stepped aboard, saluted the colors at the fantail, and dropped his gear on the quarterdeck. Then, having just come from duty in a destroyer escort, he looked forward at the towering superstructure and massive turrets and asked himself, "What the hell am I doing here?" Fortunately for his peace of mind, the chief master-at-arms took him to chiefs' quarters, shook his hand, and made him feel instantly welcome.

The new *Missouri* man was a "Tojo chief" and thus personified a wartime phenomenon. Before World War II, because advancement was so slow during the Great Depression, enlisted men remained stagnated in their pay grades for years at a time. Then came the war, with a dramatic expansion in the size of the fleet and the number of personnel needed to man it. Because of the conflict in which Japanese Prime Minister Hideki Tojo played such a large part, men shot up through the enlisted rates at a pace unimaginable only a few years before. Johnson, for example, had enlisted in the Navy in 1939, when he was seventeen. He became a chief quartermaster in 1944, only five years later. So here he was on board the *Missouri* as a twenty-three-year old chief petty officer, entitled to all the privileges of the rate and also expected to perform at that level.

Chief Johnson enjoyed moving into the chiefs' mess in the stern of the ship. It housed eighty-some chief petty officers. Their seniority was determined by when their particular rating had been established in the Navy's long history. Quartermaster was right near the top, so Johnson had no problems, despite his age. Nor were the older chiefs inclined to haze new men, because they respected professional expertise. When he first arrived, Johnson observed that the old-timers were mostly long-time battleship men. In the prewar Navy, petty officers often served for years at a time in the same ship, almost like a civilian job. As time passed during Johnson's tour on board the *Missouri,* the old battleship men departed, replaced by more young chiefs such as himself. And because battleships were relatively few in the wartime Navy, most of the chiefs had made their marks in smaller ships. Johnson, for example, had served in destroyers, a minesweeper, a tugboat, and a destroyer escort before reporting to the *Missouri.* It was a different Navy from the one he had joined only six years earlier.[47]

While the *Missouri* was in the shipyard, the St. Joseph Lead Company of Missouri made a proposal through its New York office. In the course of mining its lead, the company came up with small amounts of silver and proposed to make a sculpture of the great seal of the state of Missouri and present it to the ship. In due course the company produced the plaque, and a delegation from the ship went to Missouri in early January 1946 to receive it. Included were the captain and exec, as well as Chaplain Faulk and the members of the crew who hailed from the state.

The junket started with a party hosted by the St. Louis council of B'nai B'rith at the Chase Hotel, one of the city's most posh. Among the crew members who came from the ship was a black steward whose home was in Missouri. A member of the hotel management said to Captain Hillenkoetter, "We can't let the nigger in. He'll have to leave the hotel."[48]

At that point the skipper earned the considerable esteem of Chaplain Faulk by announcing: "He's a member of the crew of the *Missouri.* If he doesn't come, we don't come." That threw things into an uproar temporarily, but the management relented, saying, "He can come to dinner, but he can't dance." The steward said he had no plans to dance anyway, so peace was restored. Each side could claim a partial victory.[49]

From St. Louis the group went by train to the lead company's headquarters in Flat River, a town in southeastern Missouri. There, on January 6, Governor Phil M. Donnelly presented the thirty-pound silver plaque to the ship's representatives. After being displayed for a time at New York's Metropolitan Museum of Art, it was later mounted to a stanchion in the battleship's wardroom.[50]

Soon after the traveling party returned from Missouri to the *Missouri*, the ship ended her recuperative period in the naval shipyard. The Brooklyn Bridge and Manhattan Bridge had been built a long time before the *Missouri*, with the result that the ship was too tall to get underneath them when heading either to or from the shipyard. So crew members had to unfasten the large parabolic SK-2 radar antenna from its pedestal and lower it out of the way to permit the ship to get under the bridge. Also, the navigation team had to time the tides so the ship would make the East River trips at low water. Even at that, the margin was narrow.[51]

On one of the trips, Ensign Hartson went up to the 011 level so he could judge the clearance for himself. As he and other crew members stood there, they noticed that men were painting the bottom of one of the bridges under which the *Missouri* would pass. They were so close that Hartson felt he could almost reach up and shake the hands of the men working from scaffolds on the bridge. Once the battleship had cleared the East River, she went across the harbor to the shipyard annex at Bayonne, New Jersey. There the SK-2 antenna was put into place so it would be ready during the ship's operations.[52]

While the ship was at Bayonne, she was open for visitors from the New Jersey side of the harbor. One day while both civilians and visiting naval personnel were on board, a thief or thieves added to the toll of larceny racked up while the *Missouri* was in New York. Someone got into the ship's photo lab on the 02 level and made off with a movie camera, a 35-mm still camera, and twenty-six 4x5-inch photo negatives taken during the surrender ceremony in Tokyo Bay. A battleship represented strength and might, but the *Missouri*'s very popularity seemed to make her vulnerable.[53]

Running the *Missouri* was difficult with a crew badly depleted by the massive demobilization that took place in the months following the end of the war. The result was a burden on those who remained and had to stand watches twelve hours out of every twenty-four. Many functions were still essential even when the number of men to perform them had been reduced. She went down to Guantánamo Bay, Cuba, so the fleet training group could work with the remaining crew members and rebuild their readiness after the layoff in New York.[54]

While the ship was in Cuba, Chaplain Faulk wrote a letter of protest to the Navy Department because of the ship's response to the prostitution rife in Caimanera, across the bay from the naval base. Rather than making it off-limits, the ship tacitly condoned it by loading up a liberty boat and sending it to Caimanera along with prophylactics to be distributed to the crew. Faulk never received a reply to his letter, leading him to believe that it had been sidetracked by the ship's executive officer, Commander Art Spring. At the same time, Faulk sought a constructive remedy to the situation by setting up a dance on board the ship for the benefit of the crew. He worked with a USO-type organization to invite respectable girls from Cuban families in the region. After the dance on the *Missouri*'s fantail, the girls were to be served dinner in the wardroom.[55]

The dance was held as scheduled. During the course of it, one of the ship's black stewards asked one of the white Cuban girls to dance, and she refused rather strenuously. So he went to the stewards' living quarters and told his shipmates what had happened. When it came time for the dinner in the wardroom, the stewards refused to serve the girls who had come for the dance. They reasoned that the girls wouldn't dance with them, so they didn't feel like doing anything for the girls. One of the leaders of the protest was the steward who had accompanied the ship's delegation to Missouri for the plaque presentation.[56]

The dinner was postponed until Commander Spring returned to the ship from the

In early January 1946, Captain Roscoe Hillenkoetter, a former St. Louisan, went to his home state to receive a silver sculpture of the state seal from Governor Phil M. Donnelly. (*St. Louis Globe-Democrat* photo in the St. Louis Mercantile Library)

officers' club ashore. He called the stewards out on deck and had them muster by turret one. Feeling the effects of his time ashore, he was unconvincing. Thus it fell to Chaplain Faulk to appeal to the protesters. He told them he didn't approve of the girl's action, but the men shouldn't let down the ship by foiling the dinner party. That defused the situation, and the dinner was served, but the black men had made their point.[57]

Many other crewmen were going on liberty in Cuba, oblivious to the racial situation involving some of their shipmates. When the *Missouri* sent off liberty parties, the crew was still so large, even after demobilization, that there might easily be hundreds of men going ashore and living it up. Ensign Hartson had ways of maintaining decorum at the after quarterdeck when crew members came back in liberty launches, often the worse for wear.

Since Hartson was the assistant damage control officer, he had an effective weapon available. When he had the duty, he would commandeer a master-at-arms and energize a fire hose near the quarterdeck, putting pressure

on the nozzle so that it required only an opening of the handle to unleash a powerful column of water. The master-at-arms used a stick to tap the ankles of the returning men. If the stick clanked against a bottle of contraband liquor, the master-at-arms confiscated it, broke the bottle, and threw the shards over the side. In the case of men who were drunk and seemed likely to raise some hell, Ensign Hartson lined them up against one of the airplane catapults at the stern. He persuaded them to go below quietly without causing any trouble, because, he told them, the alternative was the fire hose. The threat worked in most cases. The actual alternative was that the truly boisterous men were escorted to the ship's brig to sleep it off.[58]

The maneuvers in the Caribbean went on for weeks, going through such drills as antiaircraft firing, surface tracking drills against other ships, damage control drills, battle problems, shore bombardment at Culebra, ship handling, and formation steaming. The experienced personnel were gradually breaking in new crew members, much as the original crew had gone through shakedown in the Gulf of Paria in the

Captain Harry A. Baldridge, director of the U.S. Naval Academy Museum, poses with the surrender table (perhaps) and the surrender table cloth (unquestionably) in early 1946, after they were delivered to Annapolis. Embedded in the floor in front of the table is a replica of the surrender plaque. (Courtesy Naval Academy Museum)

summer of 1944. Now a good many of those plank owners had departed the *Missouri* and gone their separate ways.[59]

Among those who left when the *Missouri* returned to Bayonne in March was Seaman Joe Vella, who'd been on the ship's fantail during the commissioning ceremony in June 1944. Now his time was up, so he received his discharge. For months he had looked forward to getting back to Connecticut, but now he experienced a sense of letdown. Perhaps without his even realizing it, the *Missouri* had become a home. He had made friends with these men who had shared excitement and danger together. He and his shipmates had developed a bond different from the relationships in a quiet Connecticut community. Once he was back in the town he'd left only two years earlier, it was not nearly so enjoyable as he imagined it would be. As he explained, "I missed the guys. I missed being aboard ship."[60]

5 ❖ Postwar Diplomat

March 1946–September 1947

While the *Missouri*'s primary claim to lasting fame grew out of her role as the surrender ship in 1945, that was largely a ceremonial event. The following spring the battleship made a trip to Europe that contributed to more substantial and long-lasting effects: stability in the Mediterranean, a U.S. national strategy of containment of the Soviet Union, and the impetus for the subsequent creation of the deployed U.S. Sixth Fleet. The reason the *Missouri* was able to be so effective as a postwar diplomatic tool was precisely because of the worldwide attention she had received as the surrender site.

Immediately following the end of World War II, the U.S. Navy was a service in search of a mission. It had been so successful in helping sweep potential enemies from the seas that, in effect, it had no one left to fight. The top naval leaders of the time projected that the fleet would be operated primarily in the Pacific, as it had been for much of the time between the two World Wars. But Japan, the threat during the twenties and thirties, no longer had a navy. The biggest potential threat came from the Soviet Union, which was a major land power but not a naval one. At the same time, the Truman administration and the State Department were taking a close look at the Soviet Union, which they suspected of planning to establish considerable sway in eastern and southern Europe.

In early 1946, as Robert Fisher argued in a superb master's thesis for San Diego State University, naval and diplomatic policy began to converge. The Navy concluded that it might be able to play an effective role by demonstrating power and thus influencing nations on the rim of the Mediterranean—Turkey, Italy, and Greece—and Iran on the Persian Gulf. That Communist regimes could take over those areas was a definite possibility. The naval influence could help bolster the anti-Communist governments and that, in turn, would provide a viable mission for the service.

After-the-fact mythology suggested that the United States intended from the beginning to send the *Missouri* to the Mediterranean and then needed to create a pretext for doing so. The mission supposedly created for the surrender ship was to return to his homeland the remains of former Turkish ambassador Mehmet Munir Ertegun. He had died in Washington on November 11, 1944. Since then his body had rested in a sealed crypt at the national cemetery in Arlington, Virginia. In fact, the *Missouri*'s participation in the mission, which became significant in hindsight, was almost accidental at the time.

Tradition had it that a cruiser be used for such a diplomatic purpose, but in early 1946 the U.S. Navy's cruiser force was occupied elsewhere. Those in the Atlantic were either decommissioned in the rapid postwar demobilization or else involved as "Magic Carpet" ships bringing home servicemen from overseas.[1] The Atlantic Fleet had no cruisers readily available for the transport of Ertegun's body, so on February 7, Rear Admiral John McCrea of the Navy Department notified the State Department that it planned to use the light cruiser *Providence*. She was to steam from the Mediterranean to the United States, pick up the ambassador's body, and then go to Turkey.[2]

Two days later the Navy Department sent a message indicating that, rather than have the *Providence* make a round trip, it was considering a battleship instead. The choice at that point was the *Missouri*'s sister ship *Wisconsin*. Finally, on February 14—because no cruisers were available, because the *Wisconsin* was due to start a yard overhaul on April 1, and because the *Missouri* had recently completed an overhaul—the commander in chief Atlantic Fleet recommended using the *Missouri* for the mission. The following day Vice Admiral Forrest Sherman, deputy chief of naval operations for operations, directed that the *Missouri* be the ship.[3]

In late February Secretary of the Navy James Forrestal talked with Secretary of State James Byrnes about sending a sizable task force of warships along with the *Missouri* to the Mediterranean. On February 28 Byrnes made a hard-line speech in New York, and he gave Forrestal preliminary approval to send along the two newest carriers, *Midway* and *Franklin D. Roosevelt*, as well as support ships. This would indeed be a formidable task force to parade before the Soviet Union as well as any nations that might be wavering.[4]

Secretary Byrnes was initially receptive, but on March 18 military correspondent Hanson

W. Baldwin reported in *The New York Times* that the *Missouri* would be going it alone. He said that since the battleship was a larger-than-normal ship for the mission, the State Department was concerned that the addition of the aircraft carriers might provoke the Soviet Union. The article by Baldwin, a former naval officer who was well plugged into the government, essentially represented the conventional wisdom that has come down through history. In his thesis Robert Fisher suggests the real reason was something else—that Baldwin was probably covering up for the Navy, perhaps to avoid exposing weaknesses in the national defense. Admiral Marc Mitscher, commander Eighth Fleet, had taken the two new carriers out for exercises in the Atlantic and found that their crews simply didn't have sufficient training or experience to carry out the planned mission to the Mediterranean.[5]

Months later, in the wake of the *Missouri*'s historic voyage, U.S. naval strength in the Mediterranean began to grow. In June, the position

On March 21, 1946, an honor guard of sailors carries the flag-draped coffin of Ambassador Munir Ertegun on the *Missouri*'s quarterdeck. The quartermaster of the watch, standing next to the lifelines with a long glass under his arm, is Bud Johnson, who became a "Tojo chief" during World War II. On the dock beyond is the Navy hearse that delivered Ertegun's body to Bayonne. (Courtesy Ralph A. Barry)

of commander, U.S. Naval Forces Mediterranean, was upgraded from rear admiral to vice admiral. Two more cruisers and several more destroyers arrived, beefing up the substance of the American commitment. Meanwhile, Admiral Mitscher and his chief of staff, Captain Arleigh Burke, had initiated a vigorous training program in the Atlantic, with the result that the *Franklin D. Roosevelt* was able to deploy to the Mediterranean in the fall.

The U.S. Navy was moving ever closer to the ability to establish a continuous presence in the eastern Mediterranean. In January 1947, Admiral Sherman presented to President Truman the new U.S. naval strategy in which the Mediterranean was preeminent, thus shifting the focus away from the Pacific. In March of that year, the president issued the Truman Doctrine, committing the United States to support democracies in the region and to contain the Soviet Union. The shift started with the battleship *Missouri*.[6]

On March 21, 1946, the *Missouri* was moored to a concrete peninsula, a pier that extended into New York harbor from Bayonne, New Jersey. That afternoon a train transported the body of Ambassador Ertegun from Washington to New York. At Pennsylvania Station in Manhattan a Navy hearse took the body aboard and drove—with a police escort—through the Lincoln Tunnel to Bayonne. Accompanied by protocol and ceremony, an honor guard of sailors brought the casket aboard the battleship and boosted it up to the 02 level, where it would ride under Marine guard during the upcoming trip.[7]

When the *Missouri* reached Gibraltar, a number of dignitaries came aboard, including Admiral H. Kent Hewitt, who had been a successful amphibious commander during the war just past. Now he was commander U.S. Naval Forces Europe and commander Twelfth Fleet. Actually, calling it a fleet was rather grandiose, given the scarcity of U.S. warships in the European theater. Others who joined were Alexander Weddell, U.S. ambassador to Turkey, and M. Kadri Rizan, Turkey's minister of protocol.

Keeping in mind Rizan's Moslem religion and its dietary strictures, Captain Hillenkoetter

made a point of telling his steward not to serve pork while the minister was eating in the captain's mess. One afternoon, shortly before dinnertime, the skipper returned after being on the bridge and noticed the unmistakable aroma of pork permeating his cabin. He immediately began berating the mess steward for violating his directive. Just then, Rizan emerged from a chair where he'd been sitting, out of the captain's view. He quickly explained the situation to Hillenkoetter. "I asked the steward to cook me pork. I love it, but I can't eat it at home."[8]

On the afternoon of April 4, the American formation—the *Missouri*, *Providence*, and destroyer *Power*—picked up still more company in the form of three Turkish destroyers. Early on the following morning, when the procession

Left: Captain Hillenkoetter kibitzes a game of cards in the admiral's quarters during the journey to Istanbul. Seated (*left to right*) are: Alexander Weddell, U.S. ambassador to Turkey; Admiral H. Kent Hewitt, commander, U.S. Naval Forces Europe; M. Kadri Rizan, Turkish minister of protocol. (U.S. Navy photo in the National Archives: 80-G-365725)

Below: The Marine detachment is at right and officers at left as a seaman guard salutes the coffin of Ambassador Ertegun. It is attached to a lifting bridle so the boom at right can lower the coffin into a boat for the trip ashore in Istanbul. (U.S. Navy photo by Lieutenant Commander Dewey Wrigley in the National Archives: 80-G-376894)

Turkey issued souvenir postage stamps in honor of the battleship's arrival on April 5, 1946. (U.S. Navy photo in the National Archives: 80-G-703679)

arrived in Istanbul, thousands of spectators lined the shore; the show of protocol was impressive, including an exchange of twenty-one-gun national salutes. The *Missouri* traversed the Dardanelles and the Sea of Marmara, then anchored in the Bosporus, off the Dolmabahce Palace. It was not an easy trip, even for as expert a ship handler as Captain Hillenkoetter. Years later he recalled that the Bosporus was crowded with sightseers and ferry boats. The current was running swiftly from the Black Sea into the Mediterranean, and he didn't have the benefit of tugboats.[9]

An hour later, after the *Missouri* had anchored, she fired a nineteen-gun salute, denoting the ambassadorial rank of Ertegun. The salute was returned by the Turkish battle cruiser *Yavuz Sultan Selim*, a relic indeed. Originally completed in 1912 as the German *Goeben*, armed with ten 11-inch guns, she and the cruiser *Breslau* outran ships of the Royal Navy in August 1914 in order to reach Turkey and induce that nation to enter World War I on the side of the Central Powers. Although she performed little active service after her encounter with the *Missouri* in 1946, the *Yavuz* continued to survive as a physical entity until being scrapped in 1971, more than sixty years after her keel was laid in 1909.

Ambassador Ertegun's body was taken ashore amid pomp and ceremony that exceeded its arrival back in Bayonne. With American diplomatic and military leaders on hand, the body was put onto a four-wheeled gun carriage and drawn through the streets of the city by seven black horses. The funeral was held in a heavily carpeted mosque, at which American visitors were obliged to remove their shoes upon entering.[10]

Throughout the battleship's visit, the Turks were enthusiastic in their displays of celebration. A harbor lighthouse bore a huge sign, "Welcome *Missouri*." The name and image of the ship appeared on souvenir cigarettes, scarves, and postage stamps.[11]

As part of its hospitality in preparation for the Americans, the Turkish government spruced up two city blocks in the red-light district. Working parties cleaned and painted the houses of prostitution to ensure that they were in tip-top condition. They also checked the women to ensure that they were free of disease and then set them up in the newly decorated houses. It was something akin to the Good Housekeeping seal of approval, and the hospitality was further enhanced when the *Missouri* sailors were welcome to enjoy sex with the women without having to pay for it. (Captain

Hillenkoetter called it "free love.") American shore patrolmen and Turkish military personnel patrolled the intersections in the area so that only U.S. Navy and Marine personnel were allowed in those blocks. Out of curiosity, Ensign Cecil Hartson went to survey the scene. "When you looked," he said, "there was a sea of white hats. It was there for the boys."[12]

Among the many forms of entertainment was a series of banquets, and the Turks obviously went all out to be hospitable. One such fete was at the Dolmabahce Palace. All the important people of Istanbul were there, and the Turks put out a lavish spread of food.[13] Another, for the *Missouri*'s officers, was at a hotel in Istanbul. To guarantee a good time for the Americans, the Turkish navy went so far as to assign its own officers as individual escorts. The program of entertainment included a group of Turkish belly dancers who danced to "The Missouri Waltz." The dancers, who were generally short and chubby, wore gauzy outfits. As Ensign Hartson described the scene: "All of us were just sitting there dying, because we couldn't break out laughing. We couldn't say anything, because every one of us had a Turkish naval officer with us." The Turks considered it the height of hospitality, and so the Americans had to stifle themselves to avoid embarrassing their hosts.[14]

The *Missouri*'s sailors were objects of great curiosity when they went ashore in Istanbul. To Photographer's Mate Len Schmidt it seemed as if they were treated like men from Mars, completely different from anything the local citizens had experienced. If a sailor stopped to tie his shoe, for example, a crowd would form to watch him do it.[15] The Turks watched the *Missouri* men eat in their restaurants, bound to make one self-conscious about chowing down in public. One English-speaking family invited Seaman Tony Alessandro to its house for refreshments so family members could make conversation and observe him. They offered him a demitasse of coffee, which was strong and bitter. When the host proffered a refill, Alessandro knew he didn't want any more, but all he could think to say was that he was "full." Right away he realized "the stupidity of the remark after the tiny cup of liquid I had taken aboard," but the family was gracious about it.[16]

During one liberty in Istanbul, Alessandro and three of his buddies began with some shopping at a bazaar. They were impressed by the

Dolmabahce Mosque dominates the foreground as the *Missouri* lies anchored in the Bosporus off Istanbul. At left is the destroyer *Power;* at right is the World War I–vintage battle cruiser *Yavuz.* (Courtesy Ralph A. Barry)

Above: Lieutenant Paul O'Connor, the *Missouri*'s Catholic chaplain, shows a scrapbook to Pope Pius XII when crewmen made a visit to the Vatican from Naples, Italy. Captain Hillenkoetter is at right. (Courtesy Ralph A. Barry)

Below: Motor launches line the starboard side to take liberty parties ashore while the *Missouri* is anchored at Piraeus, Greece. The hull of the battleship, which was dark blue when she reached New York for Navy Day, had been painted a dark gray by the time of the Mediterranean cruise. (U.S. Navy photo in the National Archives: 80-G-K-9343)

swords they saw, so they bought some, including both the straight-blade type and scimitars with curved blades. These were not toys but substantial pieces of metal, two to three feet long. After making their purchases, the foursome happened to pass by a movie theater and saw that an American romance film was playing.[17]

The sailors expected the dialogue would be spoken in English with Turkish subtitles printed on the screen for the benefit of the local audience. It didn't take them long to realize, however, that Turkish voices had been dubbed in, so the American actors were speaking in words that were literally foreign to them. The *Missouri* men were bored, so the four of them picked up their newly bought swords and started dueling in the balcony. The Turks were captivated by the live sword-fighting Americans and lost interest in the images on the screen. After a while the activity subsided, the sailors de-

parted, and the audience finally returned its attention to the screen.[18]

Radioman Moose Conner found that the American sailors wore out their welcome after only about three days in Istanbul. Their wages were far above those of the Turkish soldiers and sailors, and they flaunted it. They stole the girls away from the Turkish men, which certainly did not endear the Americans to the locals. Some fights and pushing matches ensued, although nothing serious. Conner explained, "That was booze talking, mostly, on our side."[19]

Finally it was time for the *Missouri* to leave, despite the tumultuous reception in Turkey. She had other ports to visit, other nations to impress with American power. As he had done during the arrival, the captain had to contend with the current. The ship's bow was headed upstream, toward the Black Sea, so he had to twist her around in order to make his exit. While he was in the process, he heard the word passed, "Captain, the admiral's on the bridge."

Hillenkoetter may have had a moment of uncertainty about doing the maneuver with the big boss looking over his shoulder. Hewitt quickly reassured him with: "I'm not going to say a word, no matter what. I've never been on a ship this big. I just want to see how you do it." Hewitt's own major command had been in the 1930s, when he had the heavy cruiser *Indianapolis*, perhaps two-thirds the length of the *Missouri*. He was probably just as glad to leave the driving to the battleship's skipper.[20]

Next on the agenda was Greece, about

which Moose Conner recalled: "My fondest memory of Piraeus was going through a champagne distillery and getting bombed out of my gourd. I've never been so sick in my life." His division officer added insult to injury by assigning him some extra duty. During his more lucid moments in Greece, Conner took a tour of the Acropolis and nearby ruins at Athens. It reminded him of some of the history lessons he had studied in high school just a couple of years earlier.[21]

When the ship was in Naples, Italy, during Holy Week, the *Missouri*'s Catholic chaplain, Lieutenant Paul O'Connor, arranged trips to Rome for each of the three duty sections—Wednesday, Good Friday, and Easter Sunday. This contrasted vividly with Easter a year ear-

lier when the ship was off Okinawa on the day of invasion. Fireman Art Albert was among those who visited Vatican City during his section's tour. He and his shipmates exchanged greetings with the pope in English. Albert and others purchased beads from a local merchant and got Pope Pius XII to bless them. When the sailor returned home later, he presented them to his appreciative Catholic grandfather.[22]

Another man along on the tour was Ensign Harry Upthegrove, who served as the ship's photography officer on a collateral-duty basis. A few months earlier, as he got talking with Photographer's Mate Len Schmidt about his new duty, Upthegrove confided that all he knew about photography was that one clicked the shutter and then turned in the film to a

Captain Hillenkoetter holds flowers presented to him by women of the Greek-American Society during the ship's visit to Piraeus. (U.S. Navy photo by Lieutenant Commander Dewey Wrigley in the National Archives: 80-G-376882)

drugstore to have it developed. So the officer made a bargain with Schmidt. In return for Schmidt teaching him about photography, Upthegrove would see to it that Schmidt didn't have to stand watches and that he would be included in special events.[23]

One such event was the trip to see the pope. As the pontiff went down the row of *Missouri* men, shaking hands as he went, Schmidt was off to the side so he could get individual shots. When the pope reached his spot, he hurriedly handed the camera to Ensign Upthegrove to take a picture of him. Unfortunately, Schmidt hadn't taught the officer as well as he might have. Instead of positioning himself to the side, so that he would capture the faces of both Schmidt and the pope, Upthegrove shot it from the rear. Schmidt still has the photo all these years later—the smiling Pope Pius XII and the back of Schmidt's head.[24]

Captain Hillenkoetter won some admirers for his ship handling when the *Missouri* was in

Above: The 5-inch guns of the destroyer *William R. Rush* frame the *Missouri* as she fires shore bombardment practice at the island of Culebra in the Caribbean on May 21, 1946. (U.S. Navy photo in the National Archives: 80-G-702697)

Right: The catapult crew launches the SC-1 Seahawk during the course of training exercises. (Courtesy Ralph A. Barry)

Algiers, the next stop. When mooring to a pier, the typical process is to put the ship's length alongside, parallel to the pier. In a so-called Med moor, however, the practice is to moor perpendicular to the pier, putting out an anchor forward, then backing in and mooring the stern to the pier. Though it was a hairy operation, Hillenkoetter backed the giant dreadnought in smoothly with the aid of a French pilot.[25]

The battleship went on to Tangier, Spanish Morocco, near the end of her Mediterranean venture. One of the individuals who shared the ride was Seaman Second Class Ed Wiernik, who had been in the commissioning crew of the light cruiser *Providence* in May 1945. Now that his enlistment was about to expire, he had the opportunity to ride the *Missouri* back to the United States for discharge. While the ship was in Tangier, Wiernik was struck by how exotic the African city was—men wearing red fezzes, a man with a collection of snakes around his neck and shoulders—in contrast to his native land. The atmosphere reminded him of the Humphrey Bogart movie *Casablanca*, filmed a few years earlier in Hollywood but set in French Morocco.[26]

When the ship reached Norfolk at the end of her journey, she had a new home port. She had essentially been based in New York City from commissioning onward. The sprawling naval base at the mouth of the Chesapeake Bay would be home now that she moved into the postwar period. She had a new postwar crew as well. Many of the plank owners, the members of the original commissioning crew from 1944, had departed soon after the ship returned to the United States the previous autumn. Some had remained on board for the trip to Europe, and then still more were detached. The size of the crew had shrunk dramatically in the process. In particular, the ship no longer had such an intense need for antiair gunnery as when she had been facing kamikazes in the spring of 1945. Lieutenant Commander Bob Merritt, the new communications officer, observed that by early 1946 he had so few electronics technicians that it was not easy to maintain the radio and radar equipment.

The ship could no longer communicate as well as she could when in combat. What a difference a year made.[27]

Among the new crew members reporting at Norfolk was Seaman Dick Klug. Unlike most of the ship's enlisted men, who had received their initial military training at a Navy boot camp, Klug had been a machine gunner in the infantry in Europe during World War II. After being discharged he found he had difficulty readjusting to civilian life. Back in Pennsylvania he tried working for a railroad, but the cold days outside reminded him too much of the brutal Battle of the Bulge. Then he chatted with a buddy who had been in the Navy and told him of the steam heat, clean bunks, hot meals, and so forth on board ship. Klug asked, rather incredulously, "This was war?" Navy life sounded appealing, so he enlisted and was made a seaman first class on the basis of his prior service. Because she, like so many other ships, was undermanned, the *Missouri* had a place for a willing, battle-experienced man such as Dick Klug.[28]

Captain Murray had commanded the *Missouri* for six eventful months, and that proved to be true for Captain Hillenkoetter as well. When the ship was in New York for Memorial Day,

One of the fantail catapults is in the foreground as the Seahawk hooks up to the stern crane to be lifted back aboard. The ship's name is painted in an arc over the national insignia on the aircraft's fuselage. Use of ship names on floatplanes was a practice followed before and after World War II, but not during. (Courtesy Ralph A. Barry)

Hillenkoetter was relieved by Captain Tom (not Thomas) B. Hill, an experienced black-shoe officer. Hill had spent much of the war on Admiral Chester Nimitz's Pacific Fleet staff. For a time he was fleet gunnery officer and later was combat readiness officer. In the latter capacity he was on board the *Missouri* during the surrender ceremony. Included in the new skipper's background was service as the first gunnery officer of the Navy's first fast battleship, the *North Carolina*, which was commissioned in 1941. Just before reporting to the *Missouri*, he had been commanding officer of the USS *Wyoming*, a former battleship that served as a gunnery training ship.[29]

Not surprisingly, observed Commander Merritt, Captain Hill spent more time talking with members of the battleship's gunnery de-

partment than any of the others. In the months to come, Merritt came to know the skipper better than almost any other crew member. They lived near each other in Norfolk, and Hill often gave the communicator a ride to work. Merritt found the skipper to be a friendly, sociable man with a good sense of humor. These social skills, like those of Captain Hillenkoetter, came in handy because of all the time the *Missouri* spent entertaining dignitaries. Also like Hillenkoetter, the new man was a good ship handler.[30]

Soon after her New York visit, the *Missouri* was back into the peacetime training routine, preparing to battle against an enemy if the need should arise. Then she headed off to spend the summer in cool, comfortable Maine. Fireman Bob Schwenk (the *Missouri*'s heavyweight boxing champ) decided to go swimming. Having grown up on the beaches of California, he was in for a rude awakening when he discovered that the water of Old Orchard Beach, Maine, was more akin to that in the Arctic. Looking for other diversions, he and one of his shipmates spotted a pair of young women in bathing suits. Schwenk did a dramatic belly slide on the beach, splashing chilly water onto Dorothy Ohman, who was outfitted in a two-piece bathing suit. Soon the foursome struck up a conversation, and the sailors helped take up space on the women's beach blanket.

When the *Missouri* men then went to retrieve their uniforms, which they had stashed while swimming, their new acquaintances discovered they were in the Navy and said, "We don't like sailors." The sailors were persistent, though, and ultimately persuaded the women to go to a movie that night at a local theater. The ship's schedule included operations during the week and liberty on weekends. In Schwenk's case, he was able to swing seventy-two-hour weekend liberties in return for putting on boxing exhibitions for the crew. As a result, he and Dorothy were able to spend quite a bit of time together. They had a number of dates, exploring the local attractions, eating clams, and drinking beer. In November 1947 they were married, and they've been together ever since.[31]

The summer wound down, and on September 2, half a world away from the momentous

Captain Tom B. Hill, an officer with a great deal of experience in battleship gunnery, took command of the *Missouri* in May 1946. Here, he poses in his in-port cabin. (Courtesy of Mrs. Emma West)

ceremony ending the war, a much quieter one was held to commemorate the first anniversary. Fleet Admiral Nimitz was now chief of naval operations. He journeyed to Boston to speak to a crowd assembled for the occasion. The following month, the *Missouri* was in New York for Navy Day, just as she had been in 1945. The ship was bedecked with flags at her berth at pier ninety. She had been subject to a swarm of visitors a year earlier, and now she was again. Crew members tallied 17,691 guests during the course of the day.[32]

In late November, the *Missouri*, the carrier *Kearsarge*, the light cruiser *Little Rock*, and some destroyers journeyed north to Davis Strait, near Greenland, to conduct cold-weather tests. Much of what a Navy does in peacetime is to prepare for a vast array of potential scenarios that probably will never come to pass. In this

case, with the Soviet Union installed as the most likely enemy in the event of wartime, the Navy wanted to test itself for the possibility of a naval action in cold weather.

The task group conducted a variety of war games, but the trip north to Greenland was a disappointment because the weather wasn't as cold as expected. In fact, it was actually warmer than the weather in New York and Boston at the time. Another anomaly had to do with radio communications, which can be affected by atmospheric conditions. Commander Merritt discovered there were times when the ship could reach Guam but couldn't get Boston, which was much, much closer.[33]

Far worse than the weather was an incident on the evening of December 3, when the *Missouri* took station sixty-five hundred yards on the port beam of the *Little Rock* for a star-shell

A year after her 1945 Navy Day visit to New York City, the *Missouri* was back again. This view is from October 25, 1946, as she and the Cunard liner *Queen Elizabeth* lie moored on the city's Hudson River side. The British ship was on her maiden voyage as a commercial passenger ship, following wartime service as a troop transport. (Bettmann Archive: U1052435)

duel. The specific scenario was a night surface battle, and the star shells could be useful in illuminating an enemy ship to facilitate gunfire. In years past, the illumination had been done with thirty-six-inch searchlights, but they were far from ideal. Their bright beams provided a point of aim for the guns of enemy ships. The star shells were 5-inch projectiles with pyrotechnic "warheads" attached to small parachutes. Once they were fired into the air, the flares would ignite and provide a bright light as the star shells drifted slowly down over the target. Star-shell duels were a feature of war games as each ship tried to suspend the flares over the top of the target ship.

On this evening, however, something went horribly wrong. At 7:25 a star shell from the *Little Rock,* intended to hang over the *Missouri,* hit the battleship instead. The bearing was correct but the altitude far too low. It struck on the 01 level on the starboard side, penetrating the wood and steel of the deck. Then it was deflected upward, destroying an acetylene bottle stored in a rack for use in welding. It went to the 02 level, where it finally came to rest with the illuminant and the parachute still intact. The tragedy was magnified considerably by the projectile's chance encounter with the acetylene bottle. The gas burst into flame and damaged partitions, furniture, wiring, and plumbing. Four men were injured; they sustained contusions, electrical shock, kidney compression, and burns.[34]

The most serious of the casualties was Coxswain Robert Fountain, who had been in the superstructure near the acetylene bottles. He sustained second-degree burns to the torso, arms, neck, and head and was in agony. Messman Eddie Fletcher saw the injured coxswain and heard him begging his shipmates to throw him overboard, which they would not do. He died the next day. His body was put into one of the ship's refrigerators and brought back for burial ashore. Fountain was a victim of cold-weather preparations for the Cold War that was gathering momentum in the first year of peace.[35]

At the beginning of 1947, the *Missouri* followed the same winter routine she did in most of the postwar years—steaming to the Caribbean for maneuvers with other ships of the fleet. The warm weather provided a welcome respite from the cold farther north, and it gave the ship an opportunity to train the crew.

During the trip, the *Missouri* went to Puerto Rico. Quartermaster Bevan Travis was amused by the conditions he found. There was no port per se, so members of the liberty party had to catch a train that ran about five miles to the little town of Ponce, which was only a few blocks long. The crowd of battleship sailors was undoubtedly a boon to the local economy. The first day, Travis found that a dollar would buy a fifth of rum, six Cokes, a bowl of ice, and some limes. By the second day, the enterprising merchants had hiked the price to twenty-five dollars. Other businesses also had special "sale" prices. In the manner of discounters who mark through one price and put in a lower one, so also did the Puerto Rican merchants, but in their case the substitute prices were substantially higher than the regular ones.[36]

In late January, a new occupant moved into the *Missouri*'s flag quarters. Vice Admiral William H. P. Blandy, commander Second Fleet, embarked so that he could direct training maneuvers about to take place. About a week later, on February 4, the *Missouri* hauled down Blandy's three-star flag and raised a new one with four stars. He had just been promoted to full admiral and become commander in chief Atlantic Fleet, following the death a day earlier of his predecessor, Admiral Marc Mitscher. Mitscher was commander Task Force 58 when the *Missouri* first reported for combat in February 1945. The gallant carrier admiral had expended his strength in the successful campaigns against Japan. Two years later he was dead. Because of the circumstances, Blandy had the unusual postwar distinction, albeit brief, of commanding the Atlantic Fleet from a seagoing flagship rather than a headquarters ashore. In early March, Vice Admiral Arthur Radford came aboard the *Missouri* as commander Second Fleet, and Blandy went ashore.[37]

Chief of Naval Operations Nimitz looked forward to the Navy of the postwar world. He wanted the service to have a politico-military division so that the Navy would have closer liaison with the State Department than in the past and take an appropriate role in carrying out national policy. Nimitz turned to Captain Robert Dennison (a brilliant officer who would eventually become a four-star admiral and commander in chief Atlantic Fleet) to draft the charter for the new organization. Dennison considered his job done when he finished that draft and sought to go back to sea, having been in Washington since 1943. Instead, Nimitz tapped him to head the new division he had recommended. The CNO said to him: "I want you not to mention the subject [of sea duty] to me again for a year. Get organized and get going."[38]

Captain Dennison did as ordered and essen-

An HO3S helicopter operates from the *Missouri*'s turret one in the spring of 1947. Because of the catapults on the fantail, there wasn't enough room for the helicopter to operate safely there. This helo is still so new to the fleet that it carries the name of the manufacturer, Sikorsky, on the side rather than Navy markings. (U.S. Navy photo in the National Archives: 80-G-704030)

tially became the political-military adviser to Secretary of the Navy Forrestal. A year to the day after Nimitz gave Dennison his mandate, he sent for the captain again and told him to pack his suitcase because he was going to sea. Dennison thanked the admiral, and then, as he was about to leave the CNO's office, asked, "By the way, where am I going?"

"You're going to command the *Missouri*," said the smiling admiral.[39]

In mid-April 1947, two weeks after he had taken command, the *Missouri* made another of her periodic visits to New York City. During his years in Washington, Dennison had gotten to know John D. Rockefeller III, scion of the Standard Oil family. Rockefeller had provided valuable help to Dennison in setting up the political-military affairs office. Based on their friendship, Dennison sent a telegram to Rockefeller and invited him to lunch on board the *Missouri*. He told Rockefeller that he was welcome to bring his wife, children, and anyone else he might want to. They did indeed come for lunch, but even before that, Dennison was handed a message when the ship reached New York: "Dear Captain Dennison, I am the telegraph operator who handled your message to Mr. Rockefeller. I just want to tell you that if you're having trouble filling your table, I would be delighted to come."

The amused Dennison replied, "I'm very grateful to you for your offer, but my table is filled. If you will present this letter to the officer of the deck at any time you wish to visit the ship, he will be glad to see that you're shown around."[40]

Shortly after Dennison took command, he received a letter from Admiral Nimitz. The CNO said he would like to assign a black officer to the *Missouri* and wanted to get Dennison's reaction. Dennison wrote back and said he would welcome any officer ordered to the *Missouri* but felt that sending a black would be perceived as artificial because of the publicity spotlight that followed the ship. Since the Navy had only a handful of black officers at that point, and such officers were not at all representative of the service at large, it would appear phony. Moreover, said the captain, the CNO would run out of maneuvering room with such

an assignment. By starting such an individual out in a top-of-the-line ship, there would be no place else for him to go. Instead, recommended the battleship's skipper, a black officer should start his sea duty in a smaller ship and work his way up. Nimitz chose not to force the issue, and no black officers were sent to the *Missouri* on Dennison's watch.[41]

The battleship did have black enlisted men in the crew. Integration was beginning to reach the combatant ships of the fleet in the immediate postwar period, but the result was a de facto segregation by occupation. Men of the various divisions lived with others of their own rating—whether engineers, storekeepers, radiomen, gunner's mates, and so forth. Since the stewards were black, their presence in one division had them living together as well. Only gradually did some of the stewards receive training that enabled them to strike for the general service ratings. When they did move to other types of jobs, they naturally moved to the appropriate living spaces. It took some adjustment for both the black and white sailors to adapt to the new conditions.

A number of the stewards were angry and unsatisfied with their lot because the migration to other types of jobs was slow and difficult. Some chafed at the restrictions that essentially made them servants for the ship's white officers. Despite their frustrations, remembered Messman Eddie Fletcher, a wardroom steward, they prepared and served the officers' food because the alternatives were slow to come along. As Fletcher put it: "You did what you had to do. . . . A lot of us didn't particularly like it, but you had said that you would do it."

There were some ameliorating factors. One was the pride in the ship; another was the opportunity to travel to places such as the Mediterranean that were well beyond the previous experiences of most crew members—black or white. Fletcher had come from Alabama before joining the Navy, and certainly the treatment he received in places such as Turkey, France, and Brazil was better than what he remembered from the segregated South. What's more, he had good relationships with his shipmates. If any did feel hostility toward him, they kept it to themselves.[42]

At the beginning of July the *Missouri* arrived at the Norfolk Naval Shipyard to begin an overhaul period. Equipment was removed from the battleship and taken to shops ashore so it could be repaired. Soon after the overhaul began, Captain Dennison received a telephone call telling him that the ship would be heading to South America to bring President Truman and his family back from an international conference in September. That meant reversing the initial stages of the overhaul, bringing equipment back aboard, repainting the ship, and making special preparations for the president's stay on board. Included in the yard work was a job order to install air-conditioning in the flag cabin where Truman would be staying.[43]

On August 30, 1947, the *Missouri* arrived at Rio de Janeiro on the eve of the Inter-American Conference for Maintenance of Hemisphere Peace and Security. Typically, the skipper and exec shared the ship-handling duties, and on this particular day the chore fell to the executive officer, Commander John B. Colwell. As the ship made her way into the spectacular harbor, the local pilot put his finger down on the navigation chart and said of their approach to the anchorage, "You can put it down in there wherever you like."

Colwell hesitated, noticing a ferryboat crossing and a great many merchant ships in the area that the pilot kept pointing to.

"Shouldn't we choose another spot?" he asked.

"No, you go ahead and put your ship where you want it. They'll move."[44]

And move they did. As they saw the battleship approaching, the merchantmen hoisted anchor and got out of the way. Just like the apocryphal two-ton gorilla, the *Missouri* could sit wherever she wanted to.

Once the ship settled into an in-port routine, her liberty parties began fanning out ashore to enjoy the pleasures of Rio. Sight-seeing attracted many in the crew. For instance, Machinist's Mate Art Albert joined some of his buddies in catching a taxi to the top of Sugar Loaf Mountain. It was a chore for the cab, which had to stop several times en route because the engine overheated. The trip was worth it, though, because Albert and his ship-mates were afforded a spectacular view of the harbor. Others, such as Dick Klug, enjoyed sunbathing on Rio's fabulous beaches. Klug took care to order several drinks in advance of noon so he wouldn't be caught short when the bartenders left for their daily siestas.[45] The night life was particularly appealing to Messman Eddie Fletcher. He enjoyed going out to nightclubs, listening to the Brazilian music, dancing, meeting local people, and having a few beers. It was an exotic, appealing life-style, even if only a brief interlude in the shipboard routine of cramped living quarters and early reveille.[46]

Earlier, on August 31, President Truman, his family, and some of his staff assistants left Washington in his new DC-6, named the *Independence* after his hometown in Missouri. After the plane landed on Governor's Island in Rio,

Harry S Truman, the common-man president, is outfitted in unusual garb, including top hat and swallow-tail coat, during formal ceremonies on board the *Missouri* at Rio de Janeiro. Standing next to him and saluting is Captain Dennison, the skipper. (Courtesy Richard Klug)

Truman and his family crossed the harbor in a luxurious launch in order to reach the mainland. As they did so, the *Missouri* and the Brazilian battleship *Minas Gerais* boomed out twenty-one-gun salutes. (The latter, which was the first dreadnought for a South American nation, was built in Britain, 1907–10.) As at the Navy Day celebration in New York two years earlier, Pres-

ident Truman enjoyed the sound of gunfire; daughter Margaret definitely did not.[47]

Part of the occasion for the conference in Brazil was a celebration of the 125th anniversary of the country's independence. Because it was an official state visit, all sorts of social festivities were the order of the day. Officers and men from the *Missouri* were welcomed hospitably ashore, and a number of them received decorations from the Brazilian navy. To reciprocate, the battleship threw a reception for more than six hundred persons on September 2, the second anniversary of the surrender ceremony. Years later, when he was a retired captain, Bob Merritt said he had attended dozens of wonderful receptions during the course of his naval career, but the one on board the *Missouri* at Rio de Janeiro was the finest of them all.[48]

The conference was highlighted by the signing of the Treaty of Rio de Janeiro, a mutual-defense agreement involving nineteen nations of the Western Hemisphere. After a week of all sorts of festivities and official business in Rio, President Truman, his family, and his entourage came aboard the *Missouri* on September 7. The Trumans were assigned to the flag quarters. Truman had the cabin that Admiral Halsey had occupied during the waning months of World War II, while Mrs. Truman and Margaret were in twin beds that the ship's crew had installed in the chief of staff's cabin, just aft of the flag mess area, before the ship left the States. The twelve-day trip back to the United States was the first real vacation the president had had since taking office more than two years earlier.

The trip northward was made in uncommonly beautiful weather, balmy and not a hint of motion in the giant battleship. It was a blessing for the large contingent of landlubbers who had come aboard to join the cruise for the trip back to the States.[49] It was an entertaining time as well, including morning calisthenics led by an enthusiastic president, who was wearing a T-shirt emblazoned with "Truman Athletic Club." As daughter Margaret pointed out, however, it was "enjoyment for him, but not for everybody else." She got some of her enjoyment taking sun baths during the balmy

weather. Clad in a white halter top and skirt, the twenty-three-year-old Margaret soaked up rays while lying on the surrender deck. Curious crew members peered down from the signal bridge and from behind gun mounts.[50]

One day President Truman sent word that at a certain time he wanted to listen to a speech by George Marshall, the secretary of state. Commander Merritt ran the ship's communications operation, so it was he who was selected to tune the console model radio in Truman's quarters. When he arrived, Merritt found Truman and some of his friends sitting around playing poker. As Merritt moved over to the radio, he hesitated, because Margaret was taking a nap on a nearby couch, and he didn't want to disturb her. Truman happened to glance up and notice Merritt's reluctance. Once the *Missouri* officer explained the problem, Truman said: "Oh, don't bother. I know what he's going to say anyway." Merritt served in the ship during a period when many of the great and famous came aboard. He observed that President

Above: Bess and Harry Truman push their trays through the starboard mess line. (Harry S. Truman Library collection: 66-1252)

Left: Margaret Truman, the *Missouri*'s sponsor, told Captain Dennison she knew more about the crew than he did because she ate meals with them. (Harry S. Truman Library collection: 66-1258)

Truman greets sailors in ranks during an inspection on the fantail. (Harry S. Truman Library collection: 66-1341)

only people on board the *Missouri* who held the code were a member of the communications department and Captain Dennison. The messages arrived through the Navy's communications circuit and, once decoded, were brought to Dennison, who then carried them to the president.

Nearly every evening, Margaret Truman watched movies with the officers in the wardroom. Her father, meanwhile, did something that cut into that routine. The navigation division each day gave him a drawing that showed the *Missouri* in the center and the relative positions of the various constellations of stars that would appear overhead that night. The president was enthusiastic on the subject, so he would drag his daughter around the main deck so they could locate and identify the various groupings. Despite her reluctance, he suggested she look up and learn. Lo and behold, she saw the Southern Cross, and it dawned on her that this was a constellation she could see only because the ship was south of the equator.[53]

From time to time during the cruise, Margaret took to teasing Captain Dennison. She would say, for instance: "This isn't your ship. This is my ship, because I christened her." Another time, referring to the fact that the captain had a separate mess, she said, "I know more about this ship than you do, because I eat with the officers and crew, and you don't." She knocked off the kidding when she realized that Dennison wasn't taking it in the same playful spirit in which it was being offered. Here was a man who normally was the absolute ruler on board the *Missouri*. Now, however, he had to put up with the president, senior officers, a large press corps, and a mischievous presidential daughter, so his sense of humor may have been a bit strained. A few years later, when Dennison was serving in the White House, he and Margaret developed a much more friendly relationship.[54]

The highlight of the entire trip came with the equator-crossing ceremony. Obviously, the ship had crossed the equator already in order to get to Brazil, but the captain had deliberately delayed the ceremony so it could take

Truman was less trouble than any of them; he was undemanding and totally unpretentious.[51]

President Truman also did some work during the course of the voyage, including ordering James Forrestal, the first secretary of defense, to be sworn in ahead of schedule because of the world situation. He also authorized relief efforts after a hurricane hit southern Florida. Two special communications teams were on board to handle White House messages and the dispatches emanating from embarked members of the press. All told, the ship's communication center averaged some fifty-two thousand words of messages a day.[52] Fortunately, by that time teletypes were coming more into play, replacing the Morse code keys that had been the norm during the war. By prearrangement, a special code was used for messages sent from Washington to Truman. The

Truman—earlier seen with a silk top hat—here wears a baker's hat for his encounter with Neptunus Rex. Left of him is Fleet Admiral William Leahy, who first crossed the equator in 1898; on the other side is Captain Robert Dennison, commanding officer of the *Missouri*. (Franklin D. Roosevelt Library: NPX58–607[12])

place when the president and his party were embarked.[55] In preparing for the festivities, Captain Dennison sought to find out who on board the *Missouri* was the senior shellback. He made various inquiries, including one to Fleet Admiral William Leahy, who was berthed in Dennison's in-port cabin while Dennison was living in the sea cabin aft of the bridge.

Leahy patiently put up with the skipper's inquiry, then replied, "Well, in 1898, aboard the USS *Oregon*, we came around the Cape [Horn] to get into the Battle of Santiago." Leahy, who had graduated from the Naval Academy in 1897, held the rank of passed midshipman a year later. He was involved with the engineers operating the *Oregon*'s coal-fired boilers during her long, pre-Panama Canal journey to take part in the Spanish-American War. Leahy did confide, though, that he hadn't really gone through the initiation ceremony back then. Following the custom of the time, he had bought off the shellbacks with a keg of beer and thus escaped the usual punishments.[56]

On the day itself, September 11, the ship

Crewmen sport the customary outlandish outfits in connection with the crossing-the-equator ceremony in September 1947. (Courtesy Richard Klug)

tions. Davy Jones arrived near sunset, heralded by five ruffles and flourishes from the bugler—one more than the president himself rated. Truman, garbed in a sport shirt and baker's hat, watched the proceedings from the superstructure. When Jones approached Captain Dennison, he said, "I have on good authority you have on board the number one pollywog of your country, Captain."[58]

Dennison then introduced the president to Davy Jones, portrayed by Chief Petty Officer Robert Zeller, who was so flustered by the experience that he forgot his lines. After that the ceremonies wound down, and the crew went off to their bunks to rest and—in the case of the newly initiated—to recover from the pounding they had received. Before going to sleep, Margaret Truman wrote in her diary: "Grown men have to act like boys now and then, I suppose. I haven't seen anything like it since I was in junior high school, and even then we weren't so silly."[59]

The silliness continued the following morning with the arrival of King Neptune, Chief Warrant Officer S. C. Harrington, outfitted in a green robe and fake beard. The Jolly Roger flag of skull and crossbones went up on a halyard to signify the king's presence. Admiral Leahy sat in a place of honor next to Neptune's throne; over the throne was a banner that said, "Expect No Justice."[60]

In keeping with custom, pollywogs were accused of all manner of crimes, real and imagined. When the president was summoned before the throne he was charged with insulting Neptune by using a "despicable and unnatural means of travel," an airplane, during his trip south from the States. Truman, in the spirit of the event, pleaded guilty, explaining that he had to do this sort of thing from time to time. King Neptune cut him some slack, sentencing the president to provide the "royal court" with autographed cards and a bountiful supply of cigars. Mrs. Truman got off scot-free, and daughter Margaret had merely to lead a band of six pollywog ensigns in singing a dubious rendition of "Anchors Aweigh."[61]

Alas, things did not go so well for others in the president's entourage. They suffered many of the same indignities visited upon pollywog

went through a number of the traditional rituals of pollywog initiation. Costumes for those who hadn't crossed the equator before included clothes on backward and leggings above bare feet. Shellbacks hit many a rear end with energetically swung shillelaghs. Afterward, the ship's medical department had to provide treatment for sixteen injured men, including the CIC officer, Lieutenant Commander C. S. Jacobs, who had a broken toe.[57]

Tables on deck contained a variety of instruments of torture, including leg irons, saws, knives, and whips. President Truman was amused by the whole spectacle, although the pollywogs were more circumspect in their reac-

crew members. Most of them were put onto the royal operating table, where they took their medicine. Grinning shellbacks poured down the pollywogs' throats a mixture that included alum, mustard, quinine, and epsom salts. Then they were jabbed with electrified pitchforks, smeared with grease, flipped backward into a tank of water, and finally forced to go through a double line of shellbacks who pounded them on their bottoms.[62]

Each day during the northward cruise, Truman got up early and walked the main deck, just as he customarily took early-morning walks when he was in Washington. Messman Fletcher was among the many crew members who gathered in spots along the deck so they could see the president as he passed by. He smiled at them when he saw them, giving Fletcher the impression that he was enjoying himself.[63] Seaman Klug noticed that Truman

showed a genuine interest in the men of the crew during his walks. When they brought out their cameras to take pictures of him, for instance, he would show an interest in the cameras and ask if he could take a few pictures. Naturally, the sailors were thrilled.[64]

Klug had a chat with Truman himself when the president inspected the crew. As the president came upon the seaman in ranks, he asked him where he got his Purple Heart, because few men in the *Missouri*'s crew had been wounded in combat. Klug explained that he had been in the Army during World War II and was wounded at Saint-Lô in the Normandy campaign. They also chatted good-naturedly about their favorite baseball teams. Klug, a man from Brooklyn, touted the Dodgers, while Missourian Truman spoke up on behalf of the Dodgers' great rival, the St. Louis Cardinals. St. Louis had won the National League pennant the year before, and Brooklyn went on to

Tugboats nudge the ship in alongside the familiar pier seven in Norfolk. With their journey from South America at last complete, President Truman and his family will soon leave the *Missouri* to return to Washington. (Courtesy of Ernest Arroyo)

A chief boatswain's mate leans on a lifeline as he supervises the mooring of the *Missouri* after her arrival at Norfolk. At lower right, a heavy mooring line, with a light messenger line attached, has just passed through a chock at deck level. Sailors on deck prepare to feed out the line so it can be attached to a bollard ashore. (U. S. Navy photo in the National Archives: 80-G-387414)

win it in 1947. Klug found the president to be extremely pleasant and "a man's man." As an example of his democratic spirit, Truman on one occasion during the voyage went to the ship's barber shop and patiently waited in line for his turn.[65]

Several times during the course of the cruise President Truman went up to the charthouse aft of the bridge once he had completed his morning walks. There he would drink some coffee and chat with Quartermaster Third Class Bevan Travis. Years later Travis doubtless spoke for a good many *Missouri* men when he provided an assessment of the president: "He was a very down-to-earth person, very practical. He didn't stand on ceremony too much. . . . He would sit there and talk to you about things that really mattered. . . . He worried about the little guy, the problems he was having. You really felt like he cared when he talked to you."[66]

6 ❖ Training Ship

September 1947–December 1949

Once the *Missouri* returned to Norfolk, she disembarked her famous passengers, who then walked across the pier to board the presidential yacht *Williamsburg* for the voyage to Washington. As for the battleship, she lingered in her home port for just a few days before heading for the New York Naval Shipyard. There she would receive the overhaul that had been planned for the summer but postponed practically as soon as it started because of the mission to South America.

The last few months of 1947 were essentially anticlimactic. The *Missouri* was flooded with yard workers, whose presence and requirements upset the routine that the crewmen were accustomed to. The ship was filled with noise and dirt; hoses snaked from compartment to compartment to provide compressed air and other services. Perhaps the principal redeeming feature for the crew was that they had the opportunity for frequent liberty. But even that was diminished by the low wages of enlisted men in the era.

On January 23, 1948, less than a year after he had taken command, Captain Dennison suddenly departed as the *Missouri*'s skipper. President Truman had picked Captain James Foskett as his naval aide after observing the job he did in command of the heavy cruiser *Augusta* in 1945 during his historic trip to Potsdam, Germany, to work out terms for the ending of the war. Now it was time for Foskett to be relieved. Truman asked the Bureau of Naval Personnel for a list of names of potential successors. When Dennison's appeared on it, Truman picked him because he had been impressed with him during the trip from Brazil. The Bureau of Naval Personnel ordered Dennison to turn the *Missouri* over to his executive officer right away and report for duty at the White House. Dennison continued as naval aide for nearly five years, the remainder of Truman's presidency.[1]

Thanks to the sudden change, Commander John Colwell, less than seventeen years out of the Naval Academy at that point, became commanding officer of the world's most famous battleship. Once the turnover ceremony had been completed, Colwell sent out the traditional message to tell the chain of command that he had the job. Since the surprise order from Washington hadn't yet filtered down, his message provoked some interesting reactions, especially at Atlantic Fleet headquarters in Norfolk, where someone asked, "What in the world has happened to Dennison, and who in the hell is Colwell?"[2]

A month later, Captain James Thach arrived to take over as the full-fledged skipper. He was the older brother of Captain John S. Thach, a noted fighter pilot and inventor of the famous "Thach Weave" to combat Japanese Zeros. The younger brother had been dubbed "Jimmy" at the Naval Academy in the early 1920s by those who had known his older brother. Ironically, though both were top-notch naval officers, the real Jimmy Thach was considerably less well known than the brother widely referred to by that name. The *Missouri*'s new skipper had served in the battleship *Texas* and cruiser *Concord* as a junior officer and later was gunnery officer of the new light cruiser *Brooklyn*. Among the other credentials in his service record were duty as an instructor in English and history at the Naval Academy in the mid-1930s and command of the attack transport *Montour* in 1944–45.[3]

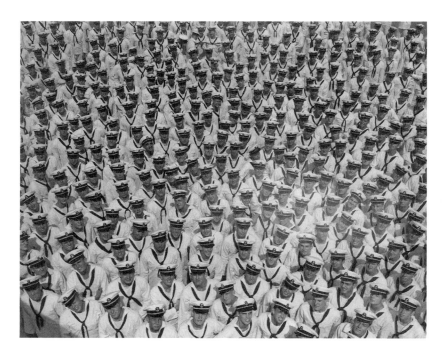

Because her crew had been reduced considerably from its wartime high near three thousand, the *Missouri* had room to embark all these midshipmen—and more—for the summer cruise in 1948. (U.S. Navy photo in the National Archives: 80-G-365725)

One of the challenges Captain Thach confronted was the understrength crew. In a continuing game of robbing Peter to pay Paul, the Navy shuffled bodies from ship to ship to enable them to meet operating schedules. During the overhaul in Brooklyn, the *Missouri*'s crew had dwindled to only about eight- or nine-hundred men. The ship was particularly bereft of engineering personnel and would have been hard-pressed to go to sea. Gradually, as the end of the overhaul approached, new men began to report.[4]

Captain Thach had a personal demonstration of the obstacles involved in training the inexperienced men, many of whom had reported right from boot camp. One day during the first week the new skipper was on board, a young seaman was directed to deliver a message to Thach's cabin. Although a Marine orderly was standing guard outside the door, the seaman barged right past him. He approached the skipper, who was at his desk, and announced, "Excuse me, sir, I'm looking for Captain Tack."

The captain, whose name rhymed with "hatch," replied, "I am Captain Thach, if that is whom you are looking for." Again, the young man said he had a message for "Captain Tack." The skipper decided that he might as well go through all the steps in getting the new

man squared away, so he asked him to walk over to the cabin door, where the Marine sentry was standing at attention. He explained that when the seaman had a message for the captain, he was supposed to deliver it to the Marine, who, in turn, would pass it on to the captain.

The seaman looked at the Marine, then at Thach, then back at the Marine, and finally said, "Shucks, Captain, I'm here now, so I'll give it to you myself."[5]

In March 1948, the *Missouri* got back into the operating routine, including training exercises off the Virginia Capes and also in the Caribbean operating areas. Her catapult planes got frequent workouts during the training period. During the previous summer, the *Missouri*'s detachment of aircraft, pilots, and enlisted support personnel shifted for a time to the *Wisconsin* to make that summer's midshipman cruise to Europe. Presumably, with not enough detachments to go around, the planes were sent to the ships that would give them more operational work with the fleet than would the *Missouri*'s point-to-point transit to South America.[6]

Lieutenant Alan Lee was the senior aviator in the *Missouri*'s detachment. He and four other pilots rotated in flying the three Curtiss Seahawks assigned to the ship. They flew each airplane about thirty to thirty-five hours a month. The SC-2 had both advantages and disadvantages in comparison with the OS2U Kingfisher that had originally outfitted the *Missouri* in 1944. During World War II the Kingfisher had operated near land, both when spotting and when picking up downed aviators. Its slow rate of climb handicapped it in attempts to escape from enemy antiaircraft fire, so the subsequent SC was designed to have better rate-of-climb performance. But it had thick wings and was certainly not as fast or as maneuverable as a fighter. Its cruising speed was a mere 105 to 110 knots.[7]

Lee concluded that the SC was rushed into service to overcome the OS2U's slow climbing, but in the process, the Navy came up with a plane that was not the result of a careful, well-considered design. For one thing, the Seahawk's rate of descent was erratic and produced a number of accidents. Thus, the SC-1 had serious restrictions in being able to fly at night. Another shortcoming was the SC's limited fuel capacity, good for only about two hours of flight time on its wing tanks. Whereas that could be doubled by using tanks in the pontoon, Lieutenant Lee had flown for more than ten hours on just the internal tanks of the OS2U. The Seahawk's capacity to fly out only about a hundred miles before coming back substantially limited its usefulness for scouting.[8]

The *Missouri* aviators' primary mission was observation for gunfire: spotting the fall of 16-inch projectiles in relation to a target and sending back corrections to the plotting rooms by radio. The planes could carry small bombs or depth charges on the float instead of an extra supply of gasoline. Wing racks were also available for mounting either bombs or depth charges. The planes had one .50-caliber machine gun installed inside each wing and the capability to mount additional ones under the wings, but Lieutenant Lee well knew that the Seahawk was "not a fighter aircraft under any condition." The internal guns were intended strictly for self-defense if the plane encountered fighters. The add-on guns could give the plane a capability for strafing if a mission called for it.[9]

Still another role, which tied in with the depth bombs, was antisubmarine warfare. The SC-2 had an APS-4 radar that enabled the plane to spot surfaced submarines on the water. As a result of either visual or radar detection, the Seahawk could then attack a submarine with depth bombs. Lieutenant Lee found during exercises that the floatplanes had an advantage over the carrier-based ASW planes:

Left: Captain James H. Thach, Jr., became the new skipper when Captain Robert Dennison was summoned to Washington to become President Truman's naval aide. Thach's younger brother, John, was a well-known naval aviator. (Courtesy James H. Thach III)

Below: Barefooted midshipmen have spelled out the word "NAVY" in the cleaning solution on the teakwood during the course of holystoning the deck. (U.S. Navy photo in the National Archives: 80-G-705883)

their pilots could keep their mouths shut. The carrier pilots chatted on their radios a lot, alerting the submarines and enabling them to take cover as the planes approached. The floatplane pilots sneaked in quietly and nailed several submarines in mock attacks.[10]

One of the enlisted men in the *Missouri*'s floatplane detachment was Seaman L. F. Barker, who specialized in aviation ordnance. He and his enlisted shipmates had a particularly high regard for Lieutenant Lee, the Naval Academy man who served as their division officer. One night Lee walked back and forth on the deck with Seaman Barker in an effort to get him to reenlist in the Navy. It was something the officer did with a number of them to try to combat the severe personnel shortage

that still lingered more than two years after the postwar demobilization.[11]

After the refresher training in the Caribbean, the *Missouri* headed off in the summer of 1948 for a delightful midshipman training cruise to the Mediterranean. Seaman John Williams, who was in the fire control division, observed the midshipmen and mentally divided them into two categories. In one group were those who struck him as hardworking and eager to learn as much as they could about the ship. In the other were the ones who knew they had to go through the experience but wanted to exert a minimum of effort. They knew they would be officers in either one year or three years and were just trying to get by until then. The ones

The *Missouri* lies at anchor in the small, picturesque harbor of Villefranche on the French Riviera in early July. (U.S. Navy photo in the National Archives: 80-G-705978)

in the latter group treated junior enlisted men as if they didn't know anything and thus wouldn't listen to them.[12]

Because he had studied Portuguese at the Naval Academy, Midshipman Leonard Seagren found himself in a most fortunate position when the *Missouri* arrived in Lisbon at the outset of the cruise. Seagren and his like-speaking shipmates chatted with all sorts of people, from the line handlers who helped moor the *Missouri* to families whom they encountered during their travels about the country. The generous Portuguese were eager to talk with their visitors and thus wouldn't let the midshipmen spend their own money.[13]

The main topic the Portuguese wanted to discuss was the election coming up that fall

in the United States. President Truman faced challenges from Republican Thomas Dewey and also from South Carolina's Governor Strom Thurmond, who was the standard-bearer for disaffected southerners known as "Dixiecrats." Because the midshipmen were on board the *Missouri*, the Portuguese assumed they were loyal to Truman. Actually, remembered Seagren, many of the midshipmen, coming from fairly well-to-do families, were likely to have Republican leanings. Seagren, who was from Nebraska, fit that category himself. "Out there," he quipped, "we considered Calvin Coolidge a dangerous liberal." The midshipmen confidently predicted a Dewey victory and later—after Truman was reelected—they had to write to their new

Viewed from a nearby aircraft carrier, the *Missouri* buries her long, narrow bow in the spray-topped sea. (Courtesy James H. Thach III.)

Midshipmen chow down during the 1948 summer cruise. (U.S. Navy photo in the National Archives: 80-G-706090)

vented military men in uniform from gambling in the famous casino at Monte Carlo. Considering the relatively low pay of both midshipmen and enlisted men, the prohibition probably served well for their own protection. Rainier impressed Midshipman Seagren with his amiability and with his command of English, including colloquialisms, jokes, and expressions familiar to Americans.[16]

After that came a short trip across the Mediterranean to Algiers. Midshipman Third Class Bob Dunn had never been prone to motion sickness, but the ocean was tossing the battleship around sufficiently that he felt a bit queasy as he stood watch down in one of the engineering spaces. A midshipman first class came along and asked, "Feeling sick?"

"Yeah, I feel a little bit ill," said Dunn.

"Why don't you sit down on that valve there and watch the water slosh back and forth in the bilges. That'll make you feel better." Of course, such a "remedy" was likely to have the opposite effect, so Dunn didn't believe the senior midshipman had his best interests at heart.[17]

When the ship got to the Caribbean, Midshipman Seagren had a battle station in the forward main battery director, up at the 011 level. He was there during night-firing shore bombardment exercises on the Navy's perennial target—the island of Culebra, near Puerto Rico. At that level, the noise of a nine-gun salvo amounted to a loud whoosh, not as intense as that heard on the bridge. The ship was enveloped up to his 011 level in a tremendous cloud of burning gases and powder, which he described as "reddish orange and incandescent-like." The sea breezes quickly blew away the burning cloud, and then Seagren saw the nine 16-inch projectiles soaring off through the night sky. They traced a parabolic arc as they headed toward their target some twenty miles distant. The bases of the projectiles glowed a cherry red, so they stood out distinctly against the blackness of a Caribbean night. They reminded him of the color of molten steel in a blast furnace.[18]

When the ship was shooting, Seaman Williams of the fire control division operated the optical range finder in turret two. The range finder consisted of a long horizontal tube, per-

Portuguese friends and explain that they had been wrong.[14]

Another stop on that Mediterranean cruise was the port of Villefranche, on the Riviera of southern France. The French government provided bus service to take crewmen and midshipmen over the mountains to Nice. As Seagren remembered, "Nice was very nice." Bikini bathing suits were new at the time, and the Americans saw them in abundance on the beach. Seagren observed that the French women were "stunning," "had the bodies to go with" the new outfits, and were well tanned.[15] Sailors in the duty section made "long-glass liberty," using binoculars or telescopes to scan the beaches.

The midshipmen also got an escorted tour of Monaco and met Prince Rainier, then in his early twenties. He was still a highly eligible bachelor at that point; he didn't marry American actress Grace Kelly until 1956. The *Missouri* welcomed Rainier aboard with full honors. The prince met the midshipmen at a reception and apologized that regulations prehaps two feet in diameter, extending all the way across the inside of the turret. The eyepieces were at the two ends, which looked out from the "ears" on either side of the turret. The device worked on a stereoscopic principle. With a coincidence-type range finder, the idea was to match up the images from the prism-type eyepieces on each side. The image was split until gradually brought together by twisting dials,

similar to the focusing device in a single-lens reflex camera. When the two coincided, the operator read off the range, and that figure was used in setting the elevation—and thus the range—at which the 16-inch guns would fire.[19]

In addition to the optics in the turrets, the *Missouri* also had range finders in Spot One and Spot Two, the forward and aft fire control directors. They had the advantage of height over

Crew and midshipmen alike sunbathe on the "splinter beach" of the fantail. The picture was taken from the airplane crane at the stern. In the foreground are wings of the two Seahawk floatplanes on the catapults. (U.S. Navy photo in the National Archives: 80-G-705943)

Hands-on training was part of the program during the 1948 cruise. Boiler Tender First Class Hans Jacobs of the *Missouri*'s crew provides training to two Naval Academy midshipmen. Kneeling in the foreground as he prepares to light off a boiler is Charles Bivenour, class of 1951; standing is William B. Anderson, Jr., class of 1949. (U.S. Navy photo in the National Archives: 80-G-705881)

the turret range finders, and thus the ability to see targets farther away from the ship. But the disadvantage was that the two eyepieces were closer together and didn't provide as much magnification. Sometimes Williams stood his watches up in one of the directors during gunnery drills. The dummy projectiles used for target practice were filled with sand so they would have approximately the same weight as the explosive variety. He would know the expected time of flight and would peer through the range finder and get a good look at the projectiles as they neared the end of their flight. As he watched the point of impact, Williams sometimes saw the shells bounce as many as five times after hitting the water. He compared the experience to skipping a stone off the surface of

a pond. The regular service projectiles exploded on impact—rather than bouncing—at the end of the flight.[20]

One member of the FM division, Fire Controlman Second Class Bill Dixon, was extremely good in operating the optical range finder. He could line up the diamond patterns in his eyepiece and make accurate determinations of how far away a given target was. Bob Eichenlaub, another member of the division, tried it and just didn't have the needed skills. So Eichenlaub wound up operating the Mark 13 fire-control radar. He found its greatest usefulness to be during surface fire against a sea target, such as a towed sled. When the *Missouri* unleashed her 16-inch battery, Eichenlaub watched the images on the radar scope, which

Until the floatplane catapults were removed in the spring of 1949, the *Missouri* still had to operate helicopters from atop turret one, as she is doing here during the 1948 summer cruise. By this time, the HO3S has Navy markings rather than those of the manufacturer. Notice the life rafts and floater nets stored atop turret two. (U.S. Navy photo in the National Archives: 80-G-706093)

was perhaps four or five inches in diameter. He could see the target itself and the splashes in the water as the projectiles landed nearby. He then provided corrections in range and deflection to bring succeeding shots onto the target.[21]

For some on board the *Missouri* that summer—including Captain Roland Smoot—the enjoyment was considerably subdued. He was there as chief of staff to Rear Admiral Heber "Tex" McLean, an old-time submariner who was commander Cruiser Division Two. For this particular operation McLean was serving as commander Task Force 84. Smoot found the admiral a difficult man to deal with and the whole experience something of a nightmare that "could drive a normal person nuts."[22]

The only redeeming feature, Smoot observed, was the amount of patience he learned from the experience. For instance, in the vari-

ous ports the *Missouri* visited, the admiral sent Smoot to represent him at evening functions such as diplomatic receptions and official parties. In the European style, the dinners often didn't begin until ten o'clock in the evening and didn't end until the wee hours of the next morning. McLean then hazed the chief of staff by setting his alarm clock for five o'clock, waking up and summoning Smoot for a report on the previous evening's activities. Naturally, it just wouldn't do for Smoot to make the reports in his pajamas. Even though he might have gotten to bed only a couple of hours earlier, he had to don his full uniform, then deliver a detailed report while standing in the admiral's doorway. The admiral himself remained in bed.[23]

Seaman Dick Klug, one of the ship's postal clerks, enjoyed the happiness that he brought to shipmates with the delivery of mail when they were away from home port. These were

Commander Lawrence D. Earle, the battleship's gunnery officer, gives midshipmen a chalk talk on the organization of his department. In the lower right corner of the photo is the top of a 5-inch gun mount. (U.S. Navy photo in the National Archives: 80-G-396326)

men who became almost like children in their delight over receiving letters and packages. When mail came aboard, Klug couldn't sort it quickly enough to suit the crew. Representatives would come by and pick up the mail for the various divisions. Klug performed other services as well. For example, gambling often followed payday, and the fortunate players would come to see him to convert their winnings into postal money orders they could send home. Getting the funds off the ship right away prevented loss of the money in subsequent games of chance. Klug's shipmates took care of him in return—a "one hand washes the other" philosophy. For instance, he could drop by the mess deck and get early chow from cooks he had helped. Or he got special delivery service on clean uniforms from laundrymen for whom he had done favors.[24]

In late September and early October, with the midshipman cruise completed, the *Missouri* was

called upon for a two-week reserve training cruise to Cuba and Panama. Hundreds of men received orders from their reserve training centers in various parts of the country and converged upon Norfolk. One of these men was eighteen-year-old Apprentice Seaman Robert Graham of Cleveland, Ohio. Even though he was on board the famous battleship for only two weeks, the experience planted a vivid series of images in his memory.

The dreadnought was moored at Norfolk Naval Station's pier seven when Graham went aboard. He stowed his gear below and then went topside to watch her get under way. As a tugboat eased over toward the battleship, a crewman unleashed a heaving line that would serve as an advance messenger for the heavier mooring line to come. To give some thrust to the heaving line, the end of it was knotted into a ball known throughout the Navy as a monkey's fist. When that knotted fist landed on the *Missouri*'s deck, it hit right at Graham's feet. Feeling like a hero during his first day on board, he began reeling in the attached line, bringing it over the top of the deck-edge lifelines. Unfortunately, the proper procedure was to move the monkey's fist below the lifelines and then thread it in through a chock, a metal opening just above deck level.

A scruffy-looking sailor on a nearby submarine shouted, "No. No. No. Fucking reservist." Graham, startled, froze in his tracks, completely unaware of what the problem was. Then a member of the *Missouri*'s regular crew, who obviously knew what to do, stepped forward and deftly pulled the end of the line down and through the chock. In humiliation, Graham faded into the shadows.

Soon, however, he began learning his way around this seagoing behemoth. He knew he had to master the basic locations—bunk, head, mess deck, and battle station. Whatever came in addition to those was a bonus. Some people didn't even do *that* well. One young reservist was from Minneapolis, and during his first day in the ship he wasn't able to find his way to his battle station. Rather than admit his ignorance on subsequent occasions, he found places to hide whenever general quarters drills were held during the remainder of the cruise.

After the *Missouri* left Norfolk, rough weather accompanied her to Guantánamo, which was intended as one of the liberty stops. The ship anchored, and the boatswain's mates laboriously rigged out the standard in-port equipment, including boat booms, accommodation ladders, boats in the water, and so forth. The water was so choppy, however, that boating was suspended. The next morning the crew got up at an ungodly hour, and the deck force went out on deck and undid all the rigging it had done the day before. Then the *Missouri* was off for Panama.

The weather brightened, and Graham thoroughly enjoyed himself as the days passed. When he drank from a water cooler, the distilled water produced by the evaporators tasted much better than what he was used to at home. He couldn't get enough of it. The lemonade, made from real lemons, was delicious. The cooks made it in huge vats in the galley, tubs so big that a man could take a bath in one. After the lemons had been squeezed, the cooks threw the rinds into a large pan, maybe three feet in diameter. Then two of them carried it up to the fantail and dumped the contents into the Atlantic. As Graham gazed seaward, he saw a yellow streak as the lemon peels danced atop the water and gradually drifted away toward the horizon. "The splash of color was eye-catching," he remembered.

Another time, Graham was lounging on the teakwood deck of the fantail in a rest period after lunch. As he soaked up the Caribbean sun, he heard an announcement over the loudspeaker: "Prepare for thirty-two knots." Gradually, the propellers turned faster and faster, transmitting ever greater levels of vibration through the decks above them. The sensation reached Graham directly as he felt his head start bouncing up and down on the deck. At that point, he got up, and, looking aft, saw what sailors call a rooster tail of white water. The propellers were scooping the water up so high that it was almost level with the main deck. It reminded Graham of being at Niagara Falls a few years earlier, except this time the waterfall was horizontal.

Graham's battle station was on one of the shell decks inside the barbette for turret three.

On one occasion he missed his chance to be in the barbette when the ship fired her 16-inch guns. About the time the alarm sounded, Graham felt the need to go to the head. Normal access routes were blocked because watertight doors had been closed. By the time he got to the appropriate barbette, the armored hatch was closed and he couldn't get in. He then decided to go to the galley and wait out the drill. What he heard when the 16-inch guns fired wasn't a bang or a boom but a roar. The ship shuddered from the impact of it. The pots and pans in the galley shook and banged together. As he contemplated the experience he had been through, Graham remembered an expression he had heard in pirate movies set on board wooden ships of old: "Shiver my timbers."

Going into Panama was a real thrill, in part because of the opportunity to get away from the ship and then to look back at her graceful contours with admiration. As soon as the sailors got off the ship, they ran into young boys

During personnel inspection forward of turret three, Captain Thach passes through a double row made up of both midshipmen and *Missouri* crew members. At right is the circular shield from which the 40-mm gun mount has been removed to save on manpower. Guns were later reinstalled in the position when the ship went to Korea. (U.S. Navy photo in the National Archives: 80-G-396323)

offering their sisters or mothers for entertainment. The saying was: "I take you my mother. She cherry."

The land itself held an attraction. The vegetation was lush, and the flowers had a fragrant smell. Coffee shops and other places added their aromas. At one point Bob Graham played checkers with a Dutch sailor whose ship was in port. They had no common language, but the game of checkers needs none. The Dutchman won.

After Panama, the *Missouri* was under way again, headed home to Norfolk. On the morning of October 1, the ship launched her Seahawk floatplanes off the catapults. What happened next was reminiscent of the fate of Lieutenant Frothingham when the ship began her first combat sortie in 1945. In this instance, Ensign Robert L. Friedlein was in the plane

fired off from the starboard catapult. Those on deck thought they heard the engine miss, so CIC was directed to query Friedlein by radio; he said the engine was functioning normally. But the plane made a steep climb as if the pilot had just yanked the stick back. It went up and around in a circle, back down, and crashed into the water about fifteen hundred yards astern of the ship. It flew apart on impact and sank almost immediately, taking Ensign Friedlein with it. The ship maneuvered to get back to the spot, then put a motor whaleboat into the water. The only thing left of what had been a complete airplane just minutes before was a piece of wing float.[25]

The *Missouri* stayed on the scene until all hope for the pilot's recovery was obviously lost, then resumed her northward journey. Soon she was back in Norfolk, and Bob Graham was on

While the midshipman task force was en route from the Mediterranean to Cuba, the various ships stopped in mid-ocean for swim call. Cargo nets were dropped over the side of the battleship to facilitate climbing back aboard. (U.S. Navy photo in the National Archives: 80-G-705792)

his way home to Ohio. He left the *Missouri* long ago, but the memory of his two eventful weeks on board has never left him.[26]

Later that year, as she had in late 1946, the *Missouri* participated in cold-weather exercises around Greenland. In this instance, she was again the flagship for commander Second Fleet, as she had been when Admiral Blandy and Admiral Radford were embarked in early 1947. This time the fleet commander was Vice Admiral Donald "Wu" Duncan, who would later become vice chief of naval operations in the 1950s. The weather around Davis Strait wasn't all that cold, but the ships did run into heavy snow showers on occasion. Task Force 28, which also included three aircraft carriers and two cruisers, conducted a number of exercises. The various ships were split up into opposing groups and played war games for nearly a week. During the midpoint in the scenario, the *Missouri* conducted a simulated bombardment of Argentia, Newfoundland. In late November, the battleship returned to Norfolk.

President Truman, a man with a vested interest in the *Missouri*, came to visit on December 4. The occasion was the state's presentation of a formal silver service. Going back to the turn of the century, such gifts of silver had been traditional with U.S. battleships. The state of Missouri had made no presentation at the time of commissioning because of the war in progress. In 1947, the state legislature in Jefferson City appropriated ten thousand dollars to purchase the silver as a gift to the ship. In due time the 281-piece collection was manufactured by the Goldman Jewelry Company of Kansas City. The company scrupulously submitted a bill for $9,976.50, just under the amount appropriated. Now the president was on hand for the ceremony at which Governor Phil M. Donnelly presented the gift to Captain Thach.[27]

After the ceremony, Truman walked over to a group of reporters covering the event. He was responding to a story that had appeared in *The Washington Post* to the effect that the Navy might decommission its last battleship if the service didn't get a sufficiently large budget. The president's response was characteristic. "Some smart aleck who poses as a spokesman for the Navy said the *Missouri* is going to be taken out of commission. The *Missouri* will not be taken

In mid-November 1948, the *Missouri* and other ships traveled to Davis Strait, near Greenland, for cold-weather training in Operation Frigid. Here, the battleship maneuvers on November 13 with the destroyer *Stormes* and hospital ship *Consolation*. (U.S. Navy photo in the National Archives: 80-G-397519)

Right: When this picture was taken on November 24, 1948, the *Missouri* was just returning to Norfolk from exercises off Newfoundland. Outbound after an eight-day stay in the port was HMS *Duke of York*, which had been with the *Missouri* at Tokyo Bay in 1945. (Bettmann Archive: U887528ACME)

Below: President Truman boarded the *Missouri* at Norfolk on December 4, 1948, as the state of Missouri presented a silver service to the ship. At left is Secretary of the Navy John Sullivan. To the right of Captain Thach is Phil M. Donnelly, governor of Missouri, who had earlier presented the silver state seal to Captain Hillenkoetter. (Bettmann Archive photo in the Harry S. Truman Library collection: 77–785)

out of commission. I want to make that as strong as I can make it, and I am speaking as the president of the United States." One of the reporters explained to his readers that Truman sought to underscore his words by giving permission to quote them. In these days of televised presidential press conferences and numerous sound bites, it seems quaint to realize that in 1948 newspapers could not use the actual words of a presidential interview unless specifically authorized.[28]

Truman's sense of indignation arose in the context of the steady drawdown in the size of the fleet following the cessation of hostilities in 1945. With the decommissioning of the *New Jersey* and *Wisconsin* in mid-1948, the *Missouri* was the only remaining battleship in the Atlantic Fleet. The *Iowa*, then in the Pacific, would follow her sisters into mothballs in early 1949. Although she still bore the name and physical manifestation of a battleship, the *Missouri* was no longer one in function. Her role in the waning months of the 1940s was as a training platform. It was a good deal less than the purpose intended for her when her keel was laid seven years earlier, but it was a good deal more of a mission than the mothballed battleships were experiencing.

The new year of 1949 began with the battleship in her home port of Norfolk, and then later in January she began the annual winter training pilgrimage to the south. Far too soon to suit Captain Thach, his tour in command came to an end.[29] Captain Harold Page Smith got the job in February 1949 because he wasn't bashful. Even though he'd had a major command as a destroyer squadron commodore in World War II, he concluded that he needed a cruiser to be competitive for possible selection to flag rank. So he pestered the Bureau of Naval Personnel for a cruiser and did even better than that; he was nominated to command the Navy's only active battleship. There was one intermediate step. He was invited to Washington for cocktails at the home of Admiral Dennison, by then the president's naval aide. Truman was there as well to check out Smith and see whether he was up to being the skipper of the ship that the president regarded as his own. Smith passed the test.

In late 1948, when Captain Smith knew

Far left: A portion of the silver service is arrayed on a table in the flag quarters of the *Missouri*. On the bulkhead is a photo of Admiral Chester Nimitz signing the surrender document in 1945. (U.S. Navy photo in the National Archives: 80-G-343185)

Left: In late March, Captain Page Smith (*right*), the new skipper of the *Missouri*, went to the White House office of Rear Admiral Robert Dennison, one of his predecessors in command of the ship. Dennison presented a Missouri mule trophy to Smith on behalf of the state division of the Veterans of Foreign Wars. It was subsequently awarded annually to the top-performing division in the ship. (U.S. Navy photo in the National Archives: 80-G-707075)

where he was destined, he was talking with Rear Admiral Felix Johnson, whom he had known for some time. Johnson was due to become commander Destroyers Atlantic Fleet, and asked Smith to be his chief of staff. Smith said he didn't want to lose his major command. Johnson said, "You serve me as chief of staff, and I'll see that you get it."

Smith replied: "My mother told me that when they pass the blueberry pie, you take the biggest piece because it may not come around again. So I've got to take this ship."[30]

In his relationships with the crew, Smith demonstrated himself to be a skipper from the old school. He made the rounds of the *Missouri* to learn what was going on, but the members of the crew knew that they could not jump the chain of command and present their concerns to him personally. As he put it: "I was just a bit autocratic maybe. . . . We were run differently in those days if you did it right. You couldn't play bosom pal with the crew; not in my day you couldn't. . . . You've got to know whether you're the buddy-buddy type or whether you're going to be just a bit dignified. I think I had to be the latter."[31]

As for maneuvering the ship, Smith discovered she was an absolute pleasure to handle. The *Missouri* was sluggish in shallow water but extremely responsive to rudder and engines when in the open sea. During his quarter century since graduation from the Naval Academy, he had served in the *Idaho, Arizona,* and *Nevada.* They were slow, lumbering craft—"big tubs," he called them—but he found the *Missouri* to be an enlarged version of a destroyer in terms of maneuvering.[32]

A few weeks after he took command, Smith also became enamored of her gunnery. The *Missouri* was in the Caribbean during amphibious exercises to practice gunfire support on the island of Vieques, near Puerto Rico. Umpires were assessing the way the war games were going, and some of the judges thought the Marines among their number were giving the *Missouri* credit for too much accuracy. So they asked for a demonstration. The *Missouri* would lie five thousand yards off the beach and attempt to hit the junction of sand and water with a 16-inch projectile. The first projectile kicked up sand; the second kicked up mostly water; the third threw up both sand and water—right at the junction. Among other things, the ships involved in the amphibious exercises worked the still-new nuclear weapons into their scenarios. Aircraft dropped flares to simulate an atomic bomb attack. The ships then executed a prescribed dispersal plan.[33]

That training sojourn in early 1949 was the last use of floatplanes in the battleship Navy, ending an era that went back nearly three decades. In fact, right after World War I, U.S. battleships began using fixed-wing aircraft that flew from turret tops to spot the fall of shot for a ship's guns. In the early 1920s, floatplanes replaced the wheeled variety.

The new aircraft were launched from catapults, as had been the case in the *Missouri* her-

Below: The *Missouri* launches a target drone for gunnery practice near Vieques in March 1949. Steaming on the port quarter is the light cruiser *Juneau*. (U.S. Navy photo in the National Archives: 80-G-399536)

self from 1944 onward. Now the utility of the catapult planes had passed, primarily because of the advent of helicopters to perform the spotting function and carry out dozens of errands such as transferring personnel, mail, and spare parts. Landing a helo on a ship's deck didn't pose as much hazard as being recovered at sea with the stern crane.

And so, while the *Missouri* was in the naval shipyard at Norfolk for a brief period in May 1949, yard workers took off the fantail catapults and installed additional wooden deck planking where the catapults had been.

Each year, June Week brought to a climax the four-year career of the graduating class at the Naval Academy. In 1949, the ship made her way up to Annapolis to pick up another load of third-class and first-class midshipmen as soon as the graduation ceremony was over. (The new second classmen had a separate training program for the summer.) As the *Missouri* then headed eastward on the way to Europe, Navy planes flew out from a naval air station and made mock attacks on the formation. Midshipman Wayne Hughes climbed up to the ship's 011 level for one of the demonstrations. He watched as a flight of F8F Bearcats came in to attack, flying perpendicular to the ship's course. The Bearcat was the hottest propeller-driven fighter the Navy had—before or since—and the planes particularly impressed Hughes when he had to look down to see them because they were approaching below the level of the battleship's top hamper.[34]

At one point in the cruise Midshipman Hughes went up and looked at the bronze plaque on the surrender deck. As he put it later, "It was a big ho hum for me." He did favorably observe, however, that the enlisted men were proud of the *Missouri;* a number of them had served in the ship for quite a time. For them it was a home; for the midshipmen it was just a temporary stop along the way. In fact, recalls Hughes: "If there was a corporate attitude among the midshipmen, it was that we were screwed because we had to go on the battleship. Everybody was told—and believed—that destroyers were where you really learned about the Navy."[35]

Whereas a passenger ship could make the crossing of the Atlantic in half the time, the *Missouri* and her escorts took a leisurely ten days because they were involved in a series of war games and training maneuvers en route. Things became hectic as the American ships approached the British coast. The battleship encountered heavy traffic in the English Channel. When the *Missouri* passed Plymouth in the late afternoon, Captain Smith found himself in the middle of a yacht race between England and France. In effect, he put on the brake lights and came to a stop until the sailing ships had passed by. They didn't have as much control as a powered vessel would have, and the *Missouri* was a large, imposing target.

Smith anchored for a time at Spithead, where he encountered a swift-running current. Then he was up much of the night as the *Missouri* made her final approach to Portsmouth, where she arrived on June 17. After the arrival, the battleship's officers and crew went through welcoming ceremonies that included Admiral of the Fleet Sir Algernon Willis. Once the pomp and circumstance were over, Captain Smith retired to the captain's cabin to go

In late April, tugboats ease the *Missouri* into a berth at Cristobal, Panama Canal Zone, during the course of a naval reserve training cruise. The Seahawk floatplanes have already been removed from the battleship's fantail, and shortly thereafter catapults would be as well. (U.S. Navy photo in the National Archives: 80-G-413184)

through the mail that had arrived from Washington. Soon after he sat down, his Marine orderly came in and said, "A lady wants to see you."

Smith replied, "Ask her to see the watch duty officer or the executive officer."

"She specifically asked to see you," the orderly persisted. Smith consented, and in came a short Englishwoman who was carrying a tiny plate, obviously her prize possession. She told the skipper that she wanted to present it to him as an expression of thanks from the English people for all that the Americans had done during World War II. Smith graciously accepted her gift and invited her to have a cup of

tea. They chatted for a bit, and then she went on her way. Forty years later, after retiring as a four-star admiral, Smith had the plate on display in a cabinet in his home—a reminder of an Englishwoman who had displayed a genuine sense of gratitude.[36]

The officers and men of the *Missouri* and other ships of her task force had stocked up in anticipation of essentially playing summertime Santa Claus for large numbers of British children. Among the many letters that came to the ship afterward was one from an orphan who thanked his battleship hosts for the "comical films which made us giggle inside." The child added that "the tea was a very lovely one. It

These two photos (*right and opposite*) taken on July 14, 1945, and August 8, 1949, respectively, show the difference in the *Missouri*'s fantail with catapults and without. Floatplanes can be seen in the photo on this page, a helo in the photo on the opposite page. (U.S. Navy photos in the National Archives: 80-G-407103 and 80-G-407104)

consisted of cakes, tubs of strawberry ice cream and an apple." The party was quite a treat for a new generation of children who had grown up during the era of wartime deprivation. The battleship held a lottery and gave away prizes to Britons who held programs with lucky numbers on them. One young lad won a canned ham. He didn't seem to be with his parents, so an officer from the *Missouri* followed him to make sure he was all right. Soon the boy joined his mother, and the officer said, "I was wondering if anyone was looking after him."

The boy's mother replied, "Yes, this is the first ham he has ever seen in his life, and I have to let him carry it."[37]

The embarked flag officer, Rear Admiral Allan E. Smith, wanted to thank Portsmouth for the enthusiastic welcome the townspeople had accorded the ship. That was particularly the case because it was a port with a storied naval tradition: Lord Horatio Nelson's flagship *Victory* was there. Smith decided to hold a big reception on board the *Missouri* and invite everyone of any note. It was quite a show, tables laden with the finest prime rib, members of the mess staff outfitted with chef hats to do the serving. Some of the ship's officers thought it

Left: Admiral of the Fleet Sir Algernon Willis, commander in chief Portsmouth, welcomes Rear Admiral Allan E. Smith, commander of the midshipman task force, to Portsmouth. In the background is HMS *Victory,* Lord Horatio Nelson's flagship in the Battle of Trafalgar. (Courtesy Allan E. Smith, Jr.)

was a bit excessive, sort of like showing off when the poor cousins come to call. The British visitors were grateful, however, going for the food with great enthusiasm.[38]

Commander Jack Fisher, the supply officer,

English children visit the *Missouri* at Portsmouth, England, during the midshipman cruise. Fireman Marvin James signs an autograph for a local boy. (U.S. Navy photo in the National Archives: 80-G-406060)

was among the ship's officers invited to a ball at the Admiralty in London. There he received an exceptionally warm welcome, he remembered with a smile years later, because of his name. Admiral Jackie Fisher had been First Sea Lord during World War I and earlier, during the construction of HMS *Dreadnought*. That ship was the prototype all-big-gun battleship that gave her name as a generic label to all succeeding generations of battleships in the world's navies. After several belts of Scotch, Fisher opined that yes, indeed, he probably was related to the old admiral.[39]

During his trip to London, the supply officer went shopping to find some buttons for his wife and children to wear on their clothes. He came across a company that had been supplying buttons to the British royal family since about the seventeenth century. It was a marvelous little store, filled with oaken trays lined with velvet. The *Missouri* officer bought enthusiastically, getting gold buttons, silver buttons, and others that caught his eye. Altogether, he bought perhaps twenty pounds' worth of the notions, approximately one hundred dollars in the exchange rate of the day.[40]

The proprietor noted Fisher's uniform and commented on his being a visitor from the U.S. Navy. Then he added: "I have something here that may be of interest to you. My great-

grandfather was an interesting man, and somehow he got the contract when you were having your Civil War." With that he pulled out perhaps fifty gold buttons that the company had made nearly a century earlier. They were decorated with crossed cannons that had the initials CSN on them for Confederate States Navy. Fisher bought one and gave it to the *Missouri*'s skipper, Captain Smith, who came from Alabama and had had an ancestor in the Confederate Navy. Smith was delighted, and from then on he wore the Confederate button in the top buttonhole of his white service uniform.[41]

One of the sailors who went from Portsmouth to London was Seaman Rob Jones from Wisconsin. He had been in the British capital in 1944 in connection with the invasion of continental Europe. Now, five years later, he tried to track down a girl he'd met back then. He wasn't able to locate her, but he wound up with female companionship anyway. Jones explained to a London newspaperman, "I didn't have her address, and the telephone number I had was wrong—so I made a date with the telephone operator."[42]

Many midshipmen went to London also. One of the groups from the Naval Academy included four classmates: Harry Anderson, Roger Freeman, Bill Dombrowski, and Lee Royal. They had been to England on a midshipman cruise two years earlier and felt they had seen most of the standard tourist attractions. Then Lee Royal suggested that it would be interesting to go shake the hand of Winston Churchill, who at that time was living in temporary retirement between his two periods as prime minister.

Anderson was the editor of the Naval Academy yearbook, and he knew that a naval uniform shop on Bond Street in London had bought an ad in the book for many years. So, at his suggestion, the group went to the store, where Anderson expressed gratitude for the company's patronage. In the course of the visit, the midshipmen asked where Churchill lived. One of the men in the store pulled out a large Who's Who–type book and gave them an address in London. They rode over in a taxi and knocked on the door. A frightened cleaning woman, decked out in white apron and hat, told them: "Mr. Churchill is not here. He's in the country, at Chartwell, and won't be back for a few days."

The enterprising midshipmen had also written down the country address when they were in the uniform shop, so three of the four got on a train and headed for the country. Midshipman Freeman decided the scheme had become too harebrained for his taste, so he dropped out at that point.

It was a beautiful sunny day when the others arrived, a taxi having taken them the last lap. Unbeknownst to the Americans, the taxi driver had excused himself long enough to call Churchill's security man and warn him that he was bringing uninvited visitors. The head of security at Chartwell was Scotland Yard's Detective-Sergeant E. A. "Bish" Davies, so nicknamed because his bearing tended to be as pontifical as that of an Episcopal bishop. Davies explained that Churchill was then asleep because he worked odd hours and was in the process of taking a nap.

The midshipmen, who were already apprehensive, volunteered that it would be a good time for them to leave, but Davies invited them to sit down and visit for a while. After chatting for a bit on a grassy spot, he invited the three of them to join him and Churchill's two secretaries, Jo Sturdee and Elizabeth Gilliatt, for dinner that evening in the nearby town. That having gone well, Davies and the secretaries took the midshipmen pubbing in the English countryside. Then the Navy men spent the night at an inn in the town. Ever undaunted, Harry Anderson proposed that they try again to see Churchill, so again they took a taxi to Chartwell. This time Detective-Sergeant Davies said he would go talk with Churchill and see what he could arrange.

Pretty soon Churchill emerged, wearing a broad-brimmed white hat ornamented with a huge white turkey feather. In one hand he held a large, brand-new cigar. As the great man approached, Lee Royal's knees turned to jelly. But the former prime minister couldn't have been more gracious. He introduced himself to each of them in turn, and they told him who they were. Just as they were about to turn and leave, having accomplished their mission, Churchill asked the three if they would like to join him for a walk through his gardens. They made a long jaunt.

The three Americans took turns walking be-

After three intrepid midshipmen went to Winston Churchill's country estate in June 1949, three members of his staff paid a visit to the *Missouri.* Seen (*left to right*) are: Midshipman Lee Royal, secretary Jo Sturdee, Detective-Sergeant Bish Davies of Scotland Yard, Midshipman Bill Dombrowski, secretary Elizabeth Gilliatt, and Midshipman Harry Anderson. (Courtesy Lee Royal)

side Churchill. When it was Royal's turn, he told his host that he was from Texas. So Churchill told him of some rich Texas friends he had, including one who sent four live turkeys as a gift shortly before Thanksgiving. That not being an English holiday, Churchill had donated them to the London zoo. He told Royal the zoo was as delighted to get them as he was to get rid of them.

The talk also turned to the midshipmen's summer home, the *Missouri*. Churchill struck Royal as being "amazingly well informed" on the ship's characteristics, particularly her main battery of 16-inch guns. Then he grew reflective and said: "You know, in the 1930s we considered 16-inch guns, but in those days we were trying to show everyone what a peace-loving people we were. So we chose 14-inch guns, and they're just not as good as 16-inch guns." Churchill himself was out of power when the British *King George V* class was conceived, so when the war came the Royal Navy had to fight with less capable ships than it might have had.

Back at the house, he asked, "I say, do you young gentlemen drink?" (He invariably referred to the group as "you young gentlemen.") They allowed as how they did, and he said he didn't want to do anything wrong, because he knew the U.S. Navy was dry. He asked if they knew who had made it dry, and they said they didn't. Churchill explained that it was Josephus Daniels, secretary of the Navy during World War I. Churchill had been Daniels's British counterpart at the time, serving as First Lord of the Admiralty. With a sly look on his face, Churchill then said, "Good friend of mine, but we did have our differences."

Along with wine, Churchill offered the visitors cigars, small ones to smoke then and large ones as souvenirs. Royal had had some unpleasant encounters with cigars previously, so he put his into his pocket and still has them nearly a half century later. Then the former Prime Minister, who was also an author, went out and came back with three books he had written. He inscribed and autographed one for each of the three midshipmen. Finally, after a visit that had lasted more than two hours, he had Detective-Sergeant Davies take the Americans and the secretaries to town for lunch. As

they ate, Davies said to them: "I have seen some of the great people come and just get ushered out the door. He treated you like I've never seen anyone treated. The only reason I can think for his hospitality is that he likes Americans, he likes young people, and he likes the Navy. You embodied all three of those."[43]

After the *Missouri* and her accompanying warships left England, they headed south, threading their way through some of the Azores on the way to Cuba. During the long journey they engaged in a war game reminiscent of actual battles involving German battleships in the early years of World War II—the *Graf Spee* in 1939 and the *Bismarck* in 1941. In each case the battleship was damaged from initial contact with the British and then pursued by smaller ships. To simulate damage in the *Missouri*, her speed was limited to fifteen knots, and her ammunition allowance was cut in half.[44]

In this exercise in the summer of 1949, the nine destroyers went out to a distance of one hundred miles from the battleship and then began making their approach to attack her during the night. Each ship had umpires, linked by a radio circuit, to determine how effective the attacks were. Even with only half her ammunition available, the *Missouri* had an enormous advantage in the much longer range of her guns. Over the course of forty-five minutes, the umpires ruled that she essentially sank five destroyers and damaged two others. Admiral Smith wrote of the engagement, "It was an unequal contest and came out just the reverse of both the *Bismarck* fight and the *Graf Spee* fight." It was a moot point, because the day of the surface gun battle was over.[45]

As the ship proceeded toward the warmer climes of the Caribbean, the crew watched evening movies, which were social events, done with dignity. Boatswain's mates rigged a screen so that it hung down from the hook on the airplane crane at the stern. Officers had chairs, and enlisted men sat on the deck. When it was nearly time for the show to begin, the skipper, Captain Smith, walked to the fantail with a retinue of senior officers, and they took their seats. Midshipman Wayne Hughes, who later became a captain and a ship skipper himself, observed that the movie provided a bonding experience, a relaxation of the normal officer-enlisted relationship that prevailed during the work day. Here, men of all positions in the rank and rate structure were enjoying entertainment in the same place at the same time. "I always thought we lost something," Hughes observed years later, "when the officers started watching in the wardroom and the chiefs watched in chiefs' quarters and everybody watched some-place segregated."[46]

During the ship's stay in Cuba, crew members got to go ashore. Buses took Navy men from the fleet landing to Guantánamo City. For Hughes it was his first exposure to the poverty found in many places in Latin America, and it was quite an eye-opener for a young man who

had grown up in the cornfields of Illinois. The streets were dusty, the city treeless and dry, the walls made of adobe—a far cry from the culture and glitter of Havana on the other end of the island. In the notebook he kept during the cruise, Hughes wrote of Guantánamo City, "It was a place to not miss but to see only once." In that regard it resembled Subic Bay's Olongapo City, which he visited as a naval officer in later years.[47]

The *Missouri's* second midshipman cruise that summer was to Cherbourg, France. On the way, Rear Admiral Allan Smith arranged a special ceremony on September 2 to commemorate the fourth anniversary of the Japanese surrender. When the battleship arrived there, her

Midshipmen and crew members encircle the surrender plaque during a ceremony at sea on September 2, 1949, to mark the fourth anniversary of the Japanese signing. (U.S. Navy photo in the National Archives: 80-G-707344, via Norman Polmar)

crew observed that the French port was still pretty well torn up from World War II. Seaman John Williams saw the British liners *Queen Mary* and *Queen Elizabeth* come in at separate times, but they weren't able to go alongside a dock as the liners had prior to the war. They had to anchor out—just as the *Missouri* did—and send passengers ashore in boats.[48] The *Missouri* was able to swing around on her anchor chain as the tidal currents ebbed and flowed, but the harbor was so congested that the passenger ships didn't have that luxury. Captain Smith observed that the liners had to be tended by tugboats to keep them from swinging into the battleship.[49]

While the battleship was in Cherbourg, the crew and the midshipmen went out on liberty. They visited some of the wartime sites such as the D-Day landing beaches in Normandy. They also enjoyed the various French cafés because France at that time was better stocked with food than England. The mayor of Cherbourg served a nine-course dinner in the town hall for the benefit of his American guests. The French people were extremely friendly, showing their gratitude for the liberation that had taken place five years earlier.[50]

Many of the battleship's crew members and midshipmen took trains to Paris for liberty and tours. Ensign Fred Koch drew the unfortunate assignment of serving as shore patrol officer. He didn't have to pay money for his Paris trip, but he paid in exasperation because the men on the train were so unruly. The midshipmen, in particular, were like men freed from prison. They had been cloistered in the Naval Academy for months and then sent to a ship, where a new regimen awaited them. Now they were sent out into the great big world at large. A number of them hung out the open windows to buy wine as French men and women walked alongside selling it before the train left Cherbourg. The midshipmen then became drunk and boisterous as the train rolled along the rails toward Paris. They threw the empty bottles out through open windows into farmers' fields.

The midshipmen broke at least one window in their exuberant scuffling.[51]

Soon after she had returned to the States and dropped off her load of midshipmen, the *Missouri* went into the naval shipyard at Portsmouth, Virginia, for the last few months of 1949. She was winding up the year similar to the way she had two years earlier when she came home from the presidential cruise with the Truman family embarked. In the course of two years, various equipment went through the usual wear and tear, and the ongoing process of installing new equipment would keep the ship up to date technologically.

Among the many jobs during the yard period was one performed by the *Missouri*'s lighting shop. Electrician's Mate Third Class Leonard Dolan and a shipmate were assigned to install fluorescent light fixtures in the captain's cabin and flag quarters. Up to then, the illumination was provided by light bulbs. The skipper was ashore at the time, and no flag officer was embarked in the battleship during the yard period, so the two young enlisted men pretty much had the run of both places. They started in the skipper's cabin and concluded it was pretty plush. Then they went to the admiral's quarters and decided those were even a little bit fancier. As they went about their job of installing the new fixtures, they noticed a framed scroll on a bulkhead outside the admiral's head. It contained perhaps eighteen to twenty autographs of the great and famous who had been there during the five eventful years the ship had been in commission.

Petty Officer Dolan contemplated pilfering the scroll but concluded he and his fellow electrician would be the prime suspects. He also thought about adding his own signature, but then people would be sure to ask, "Who is this guy Dolan?" Finally, Dolan decided that he would use the head for its intended purpose, explaining years afterward, "My claim to fame was that I used the same head as Harry Truman and General MacArthur."[52]

7 ❖ Aground

December 1949–May 1950

As the shipyard period was winding down for the *Missouri*, so was Captain Smith's tenure as skipper. He had enjoyed commanding the ship during the 1949 training cruises for reservists and midshipmen, but now it was time to move on. The prize command went to Captain William D. Brown, who was tall, slim, forty-seven years old, and a quarter century out of the Naval Academy. In the period before World War II it was common for some blackshoe officers to spend a period of time in submarines, then return to surface ships. That was the case with Brown, who went to submarine school in 1926, when he was two years out of the Naval Academy. He then served in a number of boats, culminating in command of the *S-38* in the mid-1930s, but he did not return to submarines after teaching at the Naval Academy in the late thirties.[1]

Except for one year of wartime staff duty in Washington, D. C., Brown spent much of the period from 1939 through 1945 at sea. He was briefly chief of staff for a cruiser division commander in the middle of World War II, but most of his time he was in destroyer types—as executive officer of the *Selfridge*, commanding officer of the *Gregory* and *Nicholas*, and squadron commander for destroyers in the screen of the fast carrier task force. He compiled a distinguished war record but then went into a period when he was not in position to exercise his seagoing skills. At the time he relieved Captain Smith on board the *Missouri* on December 10, 1949, Captain Brown had not had active sea duty in nearly four years. Since September 1947 he had been in command of a naval mine countermeasures station in Florida.[2]

In late December, the battleship shook off the shackles that had bound her to the shipyard in Portsmouth for the previous few months and went out for two days of sea trials. When she returned to port the day before Christmas Eve, she moored again at the shipyard. Around that time the ship's executive officer, Commander George Peckham, approached the new skipper with some suggestions to improve navigational procedures. Captain Brown dismissed him brusquely: "George, I know the advice you gave me this morning was well meant and was the result of your experience on the *Missouri*. However, I am the captain and you are the executive officer and administrator. I expect the operations officer and navigator to keep me advised on navigational matters. Do we understand each other?"[3] Peckham passed on the results of his encounter to the department heads. The supply officer, Commander Jack Fisher, for one, got the impression from his dealings with Brown that the new captain was an individual who tried to master details himself rather than delegating.[4]

In early January, the ship moved to her familiar pier-seven berth at the Norfolk Naval Station, there to take on her load of ammunition and prepare for the annual ritual of training maneuvers near Guantánamo Bay, Cuba. On Friday the thirteenth, the officer of the deck handed Captain Brown a package sent by the Naval Ordnance Laboratory. It contained a letter and a chart with markings for a special range the lab wanted the ship to run when she got under way the following week. The range was just beyond Old Point Comfort, an outcropping of land on the north side of the entrance channel to Norfolk. The lab wanted to use some acoustic cables to record the sounds

Strong-jawed Captain William D. Brown poses with the state seal in his in-port cabin on board the *Missouri*. (U.S. Navy photo in the National Archives: 80-G-413652)

the ship made with her propellers, part of an effort to detect and identify warships by their characteristic noises.[5]

Captain Brown gave only brief attention to the letter in the package, entirely overlooking the paragraph indicating that the test run was optional. It was an oversight he came to regret. While in the process of preparing the ship for her first sea assignment under his command, Brown had many items of business to attend to, so he delegated this one to the appropriate department head. He passed on the letter and accompanying chart to the ship's operations officer, Commander John R. Millett. Under the operations department concept that had been pioneered by the *Missouri* in 1944–45, Millett's department, including the navigation division, would be taking the assignment for action when the ship got under way for Cuba on January 17.[6]

Millett passed the package on to the ship's navigator, Lieutenant Commander Frank G. Morris, whose background in the V-7 naval reserve training program was similar to that of Jim Starnes, the *Missouri*'s wartime navigator. Morris reported to the ship just prior to the brief pre-Christmas sea trials. Captain Brown had had misgivings about Morris's performance on that occasion, but he hadn't said anything about them to either Millett or Morris.

The project was in Morris's hands. On January 14 Brown held a conference with Millett and Morris to discuss the upcoming voyage. The navigator had learned that three of the five buoys used to mark the acoustic range had been removed, but they were still on the chart because he had received no authorization to delete them. Brown and Millett were under the impression that there would still be five buoys in place to mark the one-mile range because five still showed on the chart.[7]

On the morning of Tuesday, January 17, the navigation team gathered. Captain Brown and Commander Morris were on the 08-level conning station, which was high enough off the deck to afford views of both bow and stern. In that regard it was superior to the 04-level navigation bridge used for normal steaming. The massive superstructure limited the view aft from that level. Captain Brown looked at Morris's chart; to the left of the proposed track and the acoustical range were red markings to indicate shoal water—too shallow to accommodate the *Missouri*'s draft of nearly thirty-seven feet. Also on the 08 conning station were the ship's executive officer, Commander Peckham, who had served in the *Missouri* for some time, and Captain R. B. McCoy, a civilian employed by the Navy as a harbor pilot.[8]

The officer who would be plotting the *Missouri*'s course through the water was the assistant navigator, twenty-three-year-old Ensign E. R. Harris. Like the navigator and the captain, Ensign Harris was new to his job. His only previous experience in plotting the ship's movements had come during the brief sea trial in December. Neither Harris, his enlisted bearing takers, nor Commander Peckham knew of the plan to run the acoustic range on behalf of the Naval Ordnance Laboratory. Peckham finally learned of it while talking with Brown in the chartroom aft of the conning station.[9]

At 7:25 A.M. the last mooring line was tossed off from pier seven. A blast of the battleship's whistle indicated that she was under way, and she began turning to head seaward. A collection of tugboats was linked to the *Missouri* to aid in the process. The weather and visibility were excellent. At 7:49 Captain McCoy, who had been conning the ship—that is, providing course and speed orders for the *Missouri*—turned the conn over to Captain Brown. McCoy left the ship.[10]

Shortly after eight o'clock the captain mentioned the acoustic range to the offgoing and oncoming officers of the deck, neither of whom had been informed previously. He sent them scurrying to the chartroom to find out, complicating the inexperienced Ensign Harris's problem in trying to figure out what was happening. Commander Peckham prepared to go below to the 04 navigation bridge, the normal underway station, so the watch could be shifted there as soon as the *Missouri* had run the prescribed range. Before leaving the 08 level, the executive officer went into the crowded chartroom. He noticed that the ship's track was approaching the red marks on the chart that indicated dangerously shallow water and gave a warning to navigator Morris.[11]

At 8:12 Captain Brown ordered a speed of fifteen knots. He concluded that the *Missouri* would be more responsive to the rudders at that speed than at a slower, more cautious one. As the *Missouri* began to accelerate, the officer of the deck, Lieutenant Ed Arnold, reported to the captain that he had seen a small orange-and-white buoy. His subsequent report that it carried the letter B didn't reach the skipper. In fact, it marked the left, or north, edge of the acoustic range the ship was due to run. The ship should have kept the buoy to port. Instead, Millett and Arnold advised Captain Brown that it would be safe to pass to the left of the buoy, and thus he ordered a course of 053°, putting the buoy on the *Missouri*'s starboard bow.[12]

As they looked out ahead, Brown, Millett, and Arnold spotted two small spar buoys that marked a fourteen-foot-deep channel for fishing boats. The skipper mistakenly assumed these were the exit buoys for the acoustic range—even though the previous exit buoys, farther to the south, had been removed. The captain expressed a question as to whether the buoys he saw were the exit buoys for the range. He addressed his query to no one in particular, and no one answered, so the *Missouri* kept plunging onward on a course headed directly for shoal water.

Down on the 04 level, Commander Peckham was sending up urgent warnings that the ship was standing into danger, but Captain Brown did not heed them. (Subsequent testimony demonstrated some of the bridge telephone talkers to be poorly qualified for their roles, so Brown may not have heard the warnings.) Commander Morris, on the 08 level, twice suggested to Captain Brown that the ship come right. Brown said to the operations officer, "I don't believe the navigator knows where we are; go find out." Both Morris and Millett went into the charthouse.[13]

Forging one more link in the unfortunate chain of circumstances that morning was the nonperformance of the watch team down in the combat information center on the fourth deck. The men on duty there were using radar scopes to monitor the *Missouri*'s progress out of port. The CIC officer, Lieutenant John Carr, concluded that the radar equipment wasn't operating correctly, because it showed that the battleship was venturing toward dangerous waters. The CIC team kept its conclusions to itself, both as to the condition of the equipment and the ship's position. Carr later explained that "the standard practice on board the ship did not call for radar advice to the bridge in the absence of specific requests." The fathometer, designed to report the depth of water under the

These four individuals had key roles in the events of January 17. They are (*left to right*): Lieutenant Commander Frank G. Morris, Captain William D. Brown, Commander George Peckham, and Lieutenant Ed Arnold. (U.S. Navy photo in the National Archives: 80-G-413651)

Quartermaster Second Class Bevan E. Travis is shown at the helm on the *Missouri*'s 08-level primary conning station. He had been in the crew of the battleship for nearly four years by January 1950 and tried unsuccessfully to warn Captain Brown he was heading toward shoal water. (Bettmann Archive: U1133626INP)

keel, wasn't working, but the man assigned to it didn't provide that information—also because no one asked.[14]

The petty officer following the captain's rudder orders that fateful morning was Quartermaster Bevan Travis, who had been standing helm watches in the *Missouri* since 1946. (In 1947 he had shared coffee with the president when Truman stopped by the charthouse on his morning rounds of the ship.) Now, as the *Missouri* headed on the wrong side of the buoy that marked the acoustic range, Travis was concerned for several reasons. For one thing, she soon became sluggish in answering the helm; for another, she appeared to be slowing down even though there had been no order to the engines to reduce speed. Finally, in desperation, Captain Brown ordered the rudder right ten degrees.

By then it was too late. At 8:17, the *Missouri*'s bow hit sand, and her speed, which had

reached about 12.5 knots on the way to the intended 15, provided sufficient momentum that she just kept right on going—three ship lengths (about twenty-five hundred feet) onto a mud flat. A minute later a phone talker on the fantail reported seeing mud stirred up. During this process, Captain Brown finally realized the seriousness of the situation and ordered right full rudder and the engines into reverse. By then, however, the engines were no longer functioning.[15]

When the battleship did slide up onto the mud bank, Quartermaster Travis was not surprised. He had already concluded that the *Missouri* was too far to the left, based on her position in relation to the Thimble Shoal Light. As he put it, "I knew that harbor in my sleep, for God's sakes, knew where we were supposed to go." Years later he told an interviewer that he twice questioned Captain Brown's order to turn left when the skipper ordered the course of 053°. The captain repeated it, so Travis did as directed, even though he knew it was wrong. He did express a measure of sympathy for Captain Brown, in that he was new on the job and didn't seem to be getting much help from his bridge team in a confused, hectic situation. As the helmsman put it: "I felt a little bad about it, because I wasn't a little more assertive, I guess. But I did question him twice, and when I questioned him the second time, he stuck his head in and got pretty sarcastic about doing what I was told, so I said, 'Yes, sir.'"[16]

While all this was happening topside, two ensigns from the engineering department, Fred Koch and Bob Walters, were in the A division office on the port side of the main deck. As they chatted, they had a sensation that something wasn't right. An individual gets used to the motion of a ship, and when he realizes that a change has taken place, he reacts. They had not heard or felt the scraping of the ship moving across the bottom. Said Koch: "[The ship] slid up as smooth as silk. It might have been paved with banana peels." In this case, the two went out onto the weather deck and looked over the side. They saw so much black boot topping exposed that they realized the ship was aground. They beat a quick path to main control, the spot in number-three engine room

This bow-on view of the ship, taken shortly after she went aground, shows how much black boot topping was exposed by the trip into shoal water. (U.S. Navy photo in the National Archives: 80-G-413643)

from which the entire propulsion system was controlled. They knew that the engineering plant would be in trouble if the condensers that normally pulled in sea water to cool steam were not able to get their regular supply.

Once there, they encountered Lieutenant Jim Forehan, the engineering officer of the watch, who said: "Koch, you go forward. Walters, you go aft. Wrap them up." As quickly as they could, they ordered the shutting of the valves sending fuel into the boilers. In the wake of the grounding, the engineers were commended for their quick reaction.[17]

The condensers operated as scoops, in this case ingesting large quantities of sand and mud that were then packed solidly into the condenser tubes because of the force imparted by the ship's momentum. The Missouri's emergency diesel generators came on briefly to keep electrical power going throughout the ship, but then they also went blinking off as their condensers filled up. The inside of the Missouri became silent and dark except for the shouts of men and the lighting of battle lanterns and flashlights. Of most immediate concern was the ship's ability to fight fire if it broke out. Said Koch, "We didn't have a prayer if anything started to burn." All the pumps on the firemain system had gone out during the power failure. As quickly as it could be arranged, smaller vessels came alongside and used fire hoses to hook into the Missouri's external fire hydrants and restore water pressure in the fire and flushing system.[18]

One of the oft-quoted aphorisms of the naval service is, "There's always that 10 percent who don't get the word." Perhaps 10 percent is an exaggeration, but there's a kernel of truth in it. That morning, while hundreds of members of the Missouri crew had the unfortunate experience of seeing or feeling their ship go aground, some men slept blissfully through the experience. During a normal sea detail assignment, which certainly would have no gunnery involved, there was no call for the talents of the fire control specialists in the FM division. As a result, those in secondary main battery plot, back near turret three, turned off the lights as their ship headed out Thimble Shoal Channel. Some slouched down in their chairs to nap,

others curled up on the deck. It was only sometime afterward that an outsider came in and told them that their ship was stuck in the mud.[19]

Soon, however, the entire world would know. It proved to be one of the most embarrassing incidents to confront the Navy during the period between World War II and the Korean War. Members of the other services heaped scorn on the Navy and made fun of the Missouri for months. The grounding gave ammunition to those who argued that the day of the battleship was over.

As the Navy's only active battleship at the time, the Missouri belonged to a type command known as Cruisers Atlantic Fleet. Previously, the word battleships had also been part of the title. In January 1950, the type commander was Rear Admiral Allan Smith, the same officer who had been on board the Missouri in the summer of 1949 for the midshipman cruises to England and France. His headquarters were in an office building in the Norfolk naval complex. His flag lieutenant, newly reported that month, was Lieutenant Joe Drachnik. It happened that Drachnik had the duty on the night of January 16 and thus the following morning as well. He was tending to his chores while the admiral, chief of staff, and other officers were attending their morning meeting.

Around 8:30 the duty quartermaster approached Drachnik with the news that the tugboat office had just called with a question, asking why the Missouri had requested all tugboats in the area to assemble at her position off Thimble Shoal. Since he was new and didn't know quite how to react, Lieutenant Drachnik decided to interrupt the staff conference. As he entered and passed on the query, all heads turned toward him. Admiral Smith rushed to a group of second-floor windows in the headquarters building. He reported later that his eyes saw something that his mind "momentarily refused to believe." He then turned to his staff and remarked, "Gentlemen, USS Missouri has just gone half a mile inland." Later that same day, Admiral Smith and a number of officers from the staff, including Drachnik, moved aboard the Missouri in order to supervise her return to navigable waters.[20]

Earlier that month, Captain Roland Smoot had reported as chief of staff to Admiral Smith. Smoot had been in the ship before, serving with the demanding Tex McLean during the midshipman cruise of 1948. Smoot was part of the staff contingent that moved aboard the *Missouri*. They left only a skeleton staff ashore to handle routine duties involving the type command. Smith was determined that the job would be accomplished by the Navy, not commercial salvage firms. A few pieces of good news glimmered in the situation. One was that the ship was in protected waters, not subject to pounding by the sea; another was that she was near a great collection of Navy salvage equipment. The official report on the salvage later concluded, "In fact, if a ship of the Navy had to go aground, it could not have chosen a more convenient place."[21]

The chores that faced the staff were manifold, including keeping meticulous records of everything that was done, recruiting all sorts of assistance, answering frequent inquiries from the news media, and putting up with an avalanche of mail. The attention was magnified by the circumstances of the grounding and the fact that she was regarded as the president's ship.[22]

Captain Smoot estimated that close to ten thousand letters came in, from all over the world, proffering advice on how to refloat the battleship. A special unit within the staff was set up to handle the mail. Every letter was answered, although nearly all those who wrote in got a canned reply, something along the lines of: "Thank you for your interest. The matter will be looked into, and we'll see if we can get it." Some of the suggestions were memorable because of their offbeat nature. One letter writer advised consulting a person with false teeth, because such an individual would be an expert on suction. Another counseled the use of fans mounted on barges to blow water into the vicinity of the ship and thus enable her to float. Some of the suggestions did make good sense, however. In fact, a number of the actions had already been taken by the time the letters arrived.[23]

A few individuals had a more selfish approach in mind. For instance, a marine contractor named Thomas F. Little of Norfolk sent a telegram to the White House on January 18, the day after the grounding. He talked about the *Missouri*'s disgraceful predicament and said that unless the Navy ceased the salvage methods it was using, it would have another disaster comparable to when the former French liner *Normandie* burned and capsized in New York early in World War II. Naturally, in his efforts to save the Navy from such embar-

Tugboats gather around the ship on January 17, in the wake of the grounding. (U.S. Navy photo in the National Archives: 80-G-707570)

rassment, Little had a solution. With the aid of only two Navy tugs—and two hundred thousand dollars of Navy money—he promised to refloat the beleaguered battleship and return her to base in Norfolk. Considering the amount of time and effort that the salvage ultimately required, Little's offer was unduly optimistic.[24]

An individual with a far more practical approach was Rear Admiral Homer N. Wallin, commander of the Norfolk Naval Shipyard. This was a man with considerable salvage experience: he had played an important role in raising damaged battleships from the mud of Pearl Harbor following the Japanese attack in 1941. Now he was in Norfolk—the right man in the right place. Admiral Smith wisely gave him technical direction of the salvage operation. The basic salvage plan had five parts, as Smith later recounted in a book he wrote about the *Missouri*. First, remove as much weight as

possible; second, lift the ship by means such as pontoons; third, remove hard-packed sand from around the ship; fourth, use sheer force from pulling tugboats to get the battleship moving; fifth, provide a dredged channel so the ship could return to deep water once free from the mud. The target date was an unusually high tide that would come on February 2.[25]

Lieutenant Commander Tom Weschler, the gunnery officer on the type commander's staff, did not have a background in salvage. Thus, he marveled at all the resources that Admiral Smith was able to draw together for the chore of refloating the *Missouri*. Included were submarine rescue ships and specialized salvage ships, divers to blow mud away from the underwater hull, and even giant pontoons that had been used for refloating the sunken submarines *S-4* in 1927 and the *Squalus* in 1939. The pontoons were to provide some added buoyancy to

Ammunition lighters are moored on the starboard side. Some tanks of 16-inch powder charges are already on the forward barge. Notice that the optical range finder ears have been removed from turret one during the late 1949 shipyard overhaul. (Fifth Naval District photo courtesy of the Naval Historical Center)

aid the tugboats and rescue vessels that were digging in with anchors and exerting hundreds of tons of pulling power.[26]

Wallin was almost invariably present at the morning staff meetings in Admiral Smith's cabin on board the *Missouri*. Commander Weschler got an example of Wallin's technical competence during one of those meetings. As part of the overall process to take weight off the ship, the two heavy anchors and anchor chains at the bow had gone the way of the ammunition, fuel, and so forth—off the ship. One morning, though, Wallin announced that he planned to put one of the anchors back on. Weschler's initial reaction, which he judiciously kept to himself, was that the admiral must have made a rare mistake. But then Wallin explained: "There is a fulcrum effect. The ship has really taken the bottom somewhere aft of that point, and it's very hard aground for the width behind it." The thrust of his analysis was that returning the anchor to the narrow bow would add little to the drag up forward, but it would help the ship teeter forward just a bit, slightly reducing the friction aft where the ship was wide. It made perfect sense to Weschler once the shipyard commander explained it.[27]

Adding to all the bad luck that had already accumulated on January 17, it happened that the *Missouri* had run aground at the crest of an unusually high tide. The attempts to refloat the behemoth had begun almost immediately but had little effect. One of the many maneuvers that the *Missouri*'s own command tried was a technique inherited from the Age of Sail—sally ship. Hundreds of sailors were ordered up on deck, remembered Electronics Technician Angelo Goffredo. They started on the starboard side, and at the sound of a whistle, they ran over to the port side. It was all to no avail.[28]

Working during the high tide that day, sixteen tugboats pulled mightily, but without success. January 17 was also the day when the weight removal began. Two fleet oilers, the *Chemung* and *Pawcatuck,* came alongside to transfer the *Missouri*'s load of fuel to their tanks. At the time the transfer started, Fire Controlman Warren Lee stood on the main

deck of the battleship and looked up at the deck of one of the oilers. The following day, when the pumping had sent hundreds of thousands of gallons from one ship to the other, Lee now looked down to see the deck of the oiler. The *Missouri* had not moved— she was still aground—but the oiler was drawing a lot more water than before.[29]

On January 19, the Army dredge *Comber* came down the Chesapeake Bay to begin the process of sucking out mud from around the ship and to create a channel through which she might proceed to the main ship channel. Three days later, the civilian dredge *Washington* joined in. Ammunition was removed as well, and it was a disquieting job because the water was a bit choppy, and the barge alongside the ship was rolling. It was a chore to get the 16-inch projectiles wedged into place to keep them from moving around inside the barge. Sometimes, though, the barge would roll before a projectile could be secured into place, and Lee had to jump out of the way a few times when the loose projectiles were coming after him.[30]

Still another part of the off-loading job was to take the food out of the ship's storerooms. Lo and behold, as the working party was doing its

A diver with a tunneling hose prepares to go below to blow away sand from around the battleship's hull. (U.S. Navy photo in the Naval Institute collection)

job, cases of pineapple juice came up from below. Warren Lee concluded that this must be a delicacy reserved for the officers' mess, because he and his enlisted shipmates hadn't had the opportunity to drink pineapple juice. So they liberated some of the juice by dropping the cartons, which then broke open. They spirited away the cans of juice, hid them under deck plates in the plotting room, and then drank their fill whenever they got a chance. With considerable exaggeration, Lee joked, "I guess I urinated pineapple juice for a month after that."[31]

While all these things were happening on board ship, the members of both the ship's crew and the embarked type commander's staff were as separated from their wives ashore as if the ship had been at sea. Given the shameful nature of the situation and the fact that mistakes had clearly been made, the women back home also felt a strain. Some of their husbands faced the likelihood of courts-martial and possibly ruined careers. The wives weren't able to be with their husbands to offer comfort, advice,

and possibly a shoulder to cry on. Nor were the husbands able to allay the concerns of the wives. Communication, to the extent possible, was extremely important in the situation, and the chore fell largely on Sally Smoot, wife of the chief of staff. Years later, her husband credited her with an excellent job of keeping in touch with the various wives of *Missouri* men and trying to minimize the stress and uncertainty they were feeling.[32]

Meanwhile, life went on at some semblance of normality. Submarine rescue ships alongside were providing electricity, fresh water, and fire-main pressure. Seaman John Williams was operated on to repair a hernia during the period while the ship was stranded. During the surgery the electricity went out in the operating room in the sick bay. Williams had only a spinal anesthetic, so he was conscious throughout and observed that the rest of the surgery was performed under battle lanterns. He finally completed his convalescence and got up and about the day after the ship was refloated.[33]

Thousands of 5-inch projectiles were removed from magazines to help lighten the ship. (Fifth Naval District photo in the Naval Institute collection)

As mortifying and unpleasant as the grounding was for the Navy—the surface Navy in particular—the incident nevertheless provided a few moments of levity. For years, surface officers had been chiding naval aviators for their poor seamanship, saying they couldn't learn as much about ship handling in airplane cockpits as the surface types had while standing watches on the bridges of ships. Now there was an opportunity for revenge.

Helicopter Squadron Two was a pioneer outfit, then the only helo squadron in the Atlantic Fleet. It had a variety of duties, including training fixed-wing pilots to operate helicopters and supplying helo detachments to large combatant ships. The main part of the squadron was based at Lakehurst, New Jersey, but it maintained a detachment of three Sikorsky HO3S planes at Norfolk in order to provide immediate response to unplanned fleet requirements. The commanding officer of the squadron was Commander Francis Drake Foley. As Foley remembered years afterward, "Mischievous naval aviators in my Norfolk unit concluded that the grounding of the *Missouri*

fitted perfectly into their assigned mission, challenged their ingenuity, and provided a golden opportunity to have some professional fun with their surface contemporaries."[34]

Without divulging their intent beforehand, pilots flew their three Sikorsky helos to the vi-

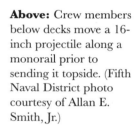

Above: Crew members below decks move a 16-inch projectile along a monorail prior to sending it topside. (Fifth Naval District photo courtesy of Allan E. Smith, Jr.)

Left: A floating crane takes an ammunition-handling truck crane off the ship after all the powder and projectiles have been removed from the *Missouri*. (U.S. Navy photo in the Naval Institute collection)

cinity of the *Missouri*. One hovered over the ship's bow, one over the stern, and the third stood by abeam to photograph what was about to happen. The ones over bow and stern payed out hoisting lines to the ship's deck, providing a gag photo that made it appear as if the tiny helos were trying to hoist the huge battleship off the shoal. The resulting picture caused roars of laughter at the Norfolk Naval Air Station and subsequent embarrassment when the Norfolk newspaper obtained a copy and published it prominently.

Foley recalled: "The photographic escapade of my boys evoked heavy wrath from above. We were all in it." Felix Stump, the crusty vice admiral who commanded Air Force Atlantic Fleet, lowered the boom on the squadron. Foley mused: "Immediate execution of all involved, including me, was somehow averted, probably by the persuasive intervention of my good friend, Jimmy Flatley [Stump's] Chief-of-Staff! When 'Mighty Mo' was eventually freed, so were we, amen."[35]

The salvage technique involved keeping a steady pull on the *Missouri* with tugs so that she could be towed off when she was able to break free from the bottom. The use of the battleship's own deck winches multiplied the pulling force from the tugboats. Beach gear was installed in the form of anchors from the tugboats and salvage ships, giving them great purchase. It would be analogous to the advantage someone would have in a tug of war if his feet were anchored to the ground to keep him from slipping. Simultaneously, divers worked underwater with lances that attacked the sand around and under the ship with water under high pressure. The idea was to dig a channel around the hull and back out to deeper water. The high-pressure water softened the sand.

The Bureau of Ships provided invaluable assistance in the project, not only with technical advice but in making available salvage experts, both military and civilian. The whole experience was extremely wearing on those involved, not permitting the participants much sleep. In an interview more than twenty years after the event, sixty-nine-year-old Vice Admiral Smoot said of the period after the grounding, "I was never so tired in my life."[36]

The first big pull was on January 31, when the efforts of all the tugboats and salvage ships were coordinated. The *Missouri* did not move from her berth of two weeks, despite the strain. Cables made from two-inch wire rope broke during the pull. The problem was an unexpected obstacle. An anchor from an old wreck had punctured the ship's bottom and was stuck there. In addition to clearing out the anchor, the remedy was still more lightening of the ship (including the anchors and chains being taken off again), addition of two more pontoons, and an expectation that an even higher tide the next day would help.

Contingency plans that might have been used were also drawn up. One was the use of a barge that was available at the naval shipyard. It could have served as a small floating dry dock. In fact, a wooden crib was constructed to fit the *Missouri*'s stern. The idea was to submerge part of the barge at the aft end of the *Missouri*, pump it out, and gradually raise the stern in the process. Photos of the barge and a detailed description of the entire salvage procedure appear in an excellent report published by the Navy's Bureau of Ships a few months after the grounding.[37]

The end of the ordeal came on the morning of February 1. The greatest effort was planned for the morning high tide. The tugs had tried the previous morning to no avail. Captain Smoot was on the *Missouri*'s bridge when success came at last. With the tugs applying maximum strain, the mighty battleship, in Smoot's words, "broke very nicely, sort of easy and with grace." It was a joy for those on board to feel movement under their feet once again.[38] The bad news was that the moving dreadnought headed toward the *Windlass*, one of the salvage ships, and wiped out part of her side railing. Commander Weschler observed that the smaller ship suffered insignificant damage, but he was convinced that Admiral Smith wouldn't have stopped the operation even if the banging had been more serious. The *Missouri* was moving at last, and Admiral Smith wasn't about to stop her.[39]

That morning Electronics Technician Goffredo set up a radio transmitter on the 02 level for WNOR, one of the Norfolk radio stations. As he looked astern, the petty officer could see a tower at the Norfolk Naval Air Station with a blinking red light on top. Tugs to port were pulling; tugs to starboard were pulling; tugs were pulling from astern. About seven in the morning Goffredo saw some movement as he lined up the ship's stern crane and the tower ashore. The radio announcer told the listeners ashore, "The *Missouri* is finally moving after fifteen days on the mud." The ship was fully afloat by 7:09.[40]

To celebrate the moment of liberation, the ship's band played the "Missouri Waltz," "Anchors Aweigh," and "Nobody Knows the Trouble I've Seen." Signalmen hoisted the largest battle colors fore and aft, and they put up on halyards signal flags that carried a message, "Reporting for Duty." The ship's navigator handled traversing the way to the Norfolk Naval Shipyard; the actual rudder and engine orders came from one of the Norfolk harbor pilots. With many, many people watching, the job was done with extreme care.[41] Among those witnessing the ceremony were those attending a change-of-command ceremony as Admiral William Fechteler relieved Admiral Blandy as commander in chief Atlantic Fleet. The outgoing admiral was able to report to his successor that the *Missouri* was once again afloat.[42]

In the wake of the grounding, it was time for the postmortems and the inevitable questions of "Who shot John?" Rear Admiral Milton E. Miles headed the court of inquiry. One of the witnesses was Quartermaster Travis, the helmsman on the day of the grounding. Not surprisingly, his testimony while in uniform was more polite toward Captain Brown than his oral history years later. He omitted references to the captain's sarcasm when he told the court that he knew the ship was going to go aground but did not tell Captain Brown so because: "It is not my place to give the captain orders. It is my place to take orders, and besides, the captain was quite busy at the time."[43]

Opposite Page:
Tugboats churn away during one of the unsuccessful pull-off attempts that preceded the ultimately successful effort on February 1. (U.S. Navy photo in the National Archives: 80-G-707570)

Captain Brown's expression is probably indicative of his mood as he listens to testimony during the court of inquiry into the grounding. (Norfolk Public Library)

On February 18, Captain Brown himself appeared before the inquiry. His initial approach, which was not well received in naval circles, was to put the blame on his subordinates. As he spoke of the morning of January 17, he said that he felt "utterly alone as far as assistance from my team of officers was concerned." In particular, he said he had developed a distrust of the navigator, Commander Morris, on the basis of the brief sea trials in December and because he didn't get adequate instructions for course changes from Morris until just before the "agitated" directions that preceded the grounding.[44]

In a later session, on February 20, Brown talked about the two spar buoys that he believed marked the entrance to the acoustic range. "When I commented that they must be the entrance buoys, none of the officers around me said anything to the contrary. I took it for granted I was right in my assumption, or they would have said something."[45]

After the court of inquiry had met for seventeen days, Captain Brown did a dramatic about-face on February 28 and accepted the blame he had until then been putting on others. In a statement about the grounding, Brown said, "I and I alone bear the sole responsibility." He added: "As captain of the ship, it was

my duty to keep her safe and secure. I didn't do it."[46]

Essentially, Captain Brown was restating a principle that has been handed down throughout the history of the U.S. Navy—the idea that the commanding officer is ultimately responsible for the actions—both positive and negative—of his subordinates. Reading from a prepared statement, Brown said, "I feel, and I feel it strongly, that despite all of the numerous shortcomings of others which have been revealed in this courtroom, I could have, and should have, kept the ship in deep water." He conceded that it was he, "in an overzealousness to complete the job I had started" (namely, running the acoustic range), who had not given enough concern to "the far more important job of safely navigating the ship. I cannot now, nor will I ever, be able to explain this lapse of judgment."[47]

Brown was one of four officers courtmartialed as a result of the incident. The president of the court in Brown's case was Rear Admiral Sunshine Murray, who five years earlier had been the *Missouri*'s skipper. On March 30, at his court-martial, Captain Brown pleaded guilty to charges of neglect of duty and negligence and placed himself at the mercy of the court. His sentencing included being reduced by 250 numbers on the Navy's lineal list of captains. The result was that he was not selected for flag rank during the remainder of his active naval career, which he spent on shore duty in Florida. In June 1955, at the time of retirement, he received a "tombstone promotion" to rear admiral on the basis of his combat service in World War II. It was essentially an honorary promotion that brought no additional pay.

Of the others court-martialed, Lieutenant Carr of the combat information center received a letter of reprimand. Commander Morris, the navigator, was reduced on the lineal list, as was Commander Millett, the operations officer. Commander Peckham, the executive officer, was not court-martialed. He had tried to warn Captain Brown the ship was standing into danger, but his advice was not heeded.[48]

Captain Smoot, as chief of staff for Cruiser Force Atlantic Fleet, had some useful perspectives to offer, in addition to those handed down by the judicial process. In the late 1940s he had been involved in making duty assignments for captains while in the Bureau of Personnel, and he also had the perspective of big-ship command, having been the first skipper of the new heavy cruiser *Newport News*. He observed that Captain Brown was a most capable officer—flamboyant and smart. But during his previous command experience, all of it in relatively small ships, Brown had been used to piloting largely by seaman's eye, observing buoys and other landmarks. It just wasn't possible to do business that way in the *Missouri*, though, because of the size of the ship and her inability to respond to her rudders and engines nearly so quickly as in smaller vessels.

A battleship skipper needed to rely on the navigation team for frequent fixes and for advice on courses and turn times. Instead, said Smoot, Captain Brown tried to eyeball it and got confused by the crowd of buoys at the spot in Thimble Shoal Channel where the ship was supposed to turn. The problem was compounded by his unfamiliarity with the ship. Rather than being willing to listen to those who were more experienced, however, he insisted on doing things himself, and he paid dearly for that insistence.[49]

As the damaged *Missouri* sat on keel blocks in the dry dock, before the judicial proceedings, Commander Peckham relieved Captain Brown and took temporary command on February 3. As for the new commanding officer, the Navy chose Brown's predecessor, Captain Harold

The *Missouri* sits in dry dock on the night of February 1, prior to its being pumped out so the ship's bottom can be inspected and repaired. To make room for the *Missouri* in the dock, the hull of her never-completed sister ship *Kentucky* was towed out. (Bettmann Archive photo by Charles Gossett: U1133753INP)

Above (left): A dramatic bow-on view in dry dock on February 2. (Norfolk Naval Shipyard photo courtesy of Samuel Loring Morison)

Above (right): Rear Admiral Homer N. Wallin, the shipyard commander who played an important role in freeing the ship, points to the damage to her hull. (Norfolk Naval Shipyard photo courtesy of Samuel Loring Morison)

Page Smith. By then Smith was chief of staff to Rear Admiral E. T. Wooldridge, commander Destroyer Force Atlantic Fleet. One day while Wooldridge and Smith were having lunch on board the flagship at Newport, the admiral received a telephone call from Admiral Fechteler. He told the admiral that Captain Smith was to report to Norfolk immediately and take over the *Missouri*. Wooldridge passed on the news to Smith, whose first reaction was: "Admiral, this is entirely wrong to send me, of all people, back down there. The Navy should know that any captain can take that ship. He should be prepared to do it and love it. I think it's wrong." His concern was that it would create the perception that the Navy didn't have many trained captains capable of handling the job. But orders were orders, so he left right away for Norfolk.[50]

During that period in dry dock, the engineers had the chore of cleaning out the condensers that had been packed solidly with debris, including sand mixed with a variety of marine life, parts of lobster traps, and other impediments that had settled to the bottom. First, the engineers had to take the heads off the condensers, an operation performed only rarely. Then they used long rods to break up the compacted mess, finally blasting it out with fire hoses once it was loose.[51]

Despite the magnitude of her public travail, the physical damage to the ship was relatively minor, confined mostly to some tanks damaged by the impaled anchor and bending of the tips of the propellers. Repairs were effected in one week at a cost of less than fifty thousand dollars.[52]

The grounding affected the supply department as well. Commander Fisher had seen the in-port time in late 1949 as an opportunity to get his storerooms in good order. They hadn't really been cleaned out and repainted since the ship went into commission in 1944. In addition, he enhanced the ship's store by adding stainless-steel display cases, Plexiglas, and indirect lighting. He worked with a young ship's superintendent and used a couple of hundred pounds of coffee in a procedure known universally in the Navy as "cumshaw." In essence, it's a system whereby individuals pay for work with merchandise rather than through the normal shipyard financial systems. When the ship left

Norfolk in mid-January, the supply department spaces were sparkling.[53]

After the grounding, the supply people had to go through the whole drill of unloading the storerooms again as part of the overall effort to lighten the ship. While the *Missouri* was in dry dock, the yard people worked long shifts to get her ready to go again, and the storekeepers refilled the storerooms again. Commander Fisher, who had expected to be enjoying the relatively easy at-sea routine by this time, was instead supervising the wholesale relocation of supplies.[54]

Then it was time to flood the dry dock and refloat the ship. Fisher got a frantic call from one of the men he had stationed in the storerooms. The report was that water was rising in the compartment. They found that some of the plates forming the storeroom had been unbolted and not put back into place properly. Breakfast cereal, among other things, was kept in the storeroom, and Fisher was appalled to see cornflakes and raisin bran floating on the surface of the water that had leaked in. All the cereal had to go over the side. Another room was filled with tin cans, whose labels soaked off. Fortunately, the Navy had developed a tin can manual that decoded the letters stamped on

each can and thus revealed what was inside. The cans of food, unlike the cereal, could be salvaged, but then the storerooms had to be drained, dried out with fans, and restocked yet *another* time.[55]

Captain Smith reported aboard on February 7, as the dry dock was being flooded to refloat the ship. He went to the bridge and told a surprised Peckham that he was taking over command again. Peckham gave him an "Aye, aye, sir," and they shook hands. Once the ship was back alongside the dock, she took on tens of thousands of gallons of fuel during the night. She had, after all, been pumped dry during the

Left: Seaweed extends down from the inlets for the main condensers, which scooped up a good deal of sand and mud from the bottom. At the lower edge of the photo are the keel blocks that supported the *Missouri* while in dry dock. (Norfolk Naval Shipyard photo courtesy of Samuel Loring Morison)

Below: This view at the turn of the bilge shows the beginning of the scrape caused by an underwater obstruction, perhaps an anchor. The tear in the hull started at frame 99 and went aft. At left is the starboard bilge keel. Inside the damaged area were fuel oil tanks. (Norfolk Naval Shipyard photo courtesy of Samuel Loring Morison)

Captain Page Smith spent his second command tenure grandstanding with the *Missouri* so he could rebuild the confidence of the officers and crew. (U.S. Navy photo in the National Archives: 80-G-708285)

time on the mud flat. The next day, the *Missouri* went out for post-repair engineering trials, which proved satisfactory. The skipper noticed that boats followed the ship with movie cameras grinding away, perhaps in the hope of seeing another grounding. If so, the cameramen were disappointed because the departure and subsequent return were routine, as so many of them had been prior to January 17.[56]

As soon as he had the chance, Captain Smith took stock of the situation. What he found quickly convinced him that the decision to send him back to the battleship was the correct one. In walking around the *Missouri* and talking with people, he came to realize that the officers and enlisted men had been shocked and deeply demoralized by the grounding. It had badly shaken their confidence—particularly the officers of the deck. Because they had confidence in Page Smith, however, his actions during the ensuing weeks would enable them to rebuild their confidence in themselves.

One of Captain Smith's regrets was that he knew Commander Peckham had been scarred by the grounding even though he had tried hard to prevent Captain Brown from following the wrong course. Peckham was later promoted to captain but was not selected for flag rank. As was the case with Brown, Peckham subsequently received a tombstone promotion to rear admiral upon retirement.[57]

Following the brief period for trials, the *Mis-*

souri pulled in at Norfolk to reload her depleted magazines and projectile decks with ammunition. One day during the loading, Admiral Fechteler, the new commander in chief of the fleet, came aboard as a light rain was falling. Captain Smith soon joined him, and the two of them circumnavigated the ship twice, going all the way around the main deck and then making a circuit of the 01 level as well. Afterward, the skipper invited the admiral to his cabin for a cup of coffee and said: "Admiral, I want to tell you how much I appreciate what you've done. You've shown your interest in this ship to a lot of sailors that need it."

"Oh, Christ," said the four-star admiral who would become chief of naval operations the following year, "an admiral ought to be worth something."[58]

The crew finished the ammunition job, and then it was time to head south for Guantánamo, the planned destination that the ship hadn't reached a month earlier. On February 15, the day the *Missouri* began her delayed voyage, cost-conscious Secretary of Defense Louis Johnson made an announcement in Washington. The *Missouri* would be turned into a school ship to train midshipmen and naval reservists. Doing so, he said, would cut in half the battleship's annual operating cost of 6.7 million dollars. Part of the savings would come in the form of a reduced operating schedule, part by reducing the crew from eighteen hundred men to fifteen hundred.[59]

Although Johnson's announcement seemed to add insult to the injury suffered in the humiliating grounding, it was not that dramatic a change of status. Despite having made high-visibility trips to the Mediterranean in 1946 and South America in 1947, the battleship had spent much of the time since then in a training role—for her crew, for midshipmen, and for reservists.

Johnson's announcement really amounted to a compromise position. Representative Carl Vinson, long-time chairman of the House Armed Services Committee, had wanted to get rid of the *Missouri* entirely and use the money instead to activate another aircraft carrier. Truman's adamant support for the ship removed that from the list of options. There were also some naval reasons for the action: the size of the ship provided considerable opportunity for gunnery training; she offered more substantial shore-bombardment capability than cruisers and destroyers; and she was a large, stable platform from which to fire antiaircraft guided missiles, clearly the wave of the future in antiair defense.[60]

When guided missiles did enter the fleet in the mid-1950s it was on board converted heavy cruisers. By then the *Missouri* was in temporary retirement in mothballs, but her achievements in the meantime had demonstrated the wisdom of keeping her in service.

In the two months that his second command tour lasted, Captain Smith decided that the best remedy was to do some grandstanding with the *Missouri,* running her at high speed when the opportunity permitted and maneuvering her with panache. Despite the Navy's attempts to economize on the ship, he conceded that he burned a lot more fuel than he needed to, but he believed it was worth it. His approach served two purposes. On the one hand, it helped with the process of rebuilding the crew's confidence and pride in their ship. On the other, it told the rest of the Navy—and the world beyond as well—that the *Missouri* was back in service and none the worse for her un-

Marine gunners fire twin 20-mm antiaircraft guns at a radio-controlled drone target during an exercise in the Caribbean in March 1950. (U.S. Navy photo in the National Archives: 80-G-413312)

On April 19, 1950, Captain Irving T. Duke reads his orders while taking command of the *Missouri*. At center is Captain Page Smith, outgoing skipper; at left is Captain Roland Smoot, chief of staff for the type commander. (U.S. Navy photo in the National Archives: 80-G-414591)

fortunate experience in the mud. The gibes and sarcasm about the grounding would persist for some time, but she was, in fact, operational again. As he assessed the effect of his approach, Smith said, "It was exactly what I wanted—a first-class ship again." He had served the purpose for which he was returned to command, and on April 17 his second tour as skipper of the *Missouri* came to an end.[61]

His relief was Captain Irving T. Duke, an officer with a solid seagoing background. Like Brown, he had spent time in both submarines and destroyers. Nearly a decade earlier, as skipper of the destroyer *Mayo*, he had earned the Navy and Marine Corps Medal for taking his ship alongside the burning transport *Wakefield*

and rescuing 247 passengers. But Duke also had big-ship experience. He was gunnery officer of the light cruiser *Helena* prior to World War II and had been serving as captain of the heavy cruiser *Rochester* since November 1949.

The battleship was some two hundred feet longer and forty feet wider than the *Rochester*. Shortly after he had taken command of the *Missouri*, Captain Duke was on the bridge with Lieutenant (j.g.) Don Giles. As the two were looking aft, contemplating the hundreds of feet of ship stretching toward the fantail, the captain posed a mixed-gender question when he exclaimed, "She's a big son-of-a-bitch, isn't she?"[62]

8 ❖ The Korean War Begins

June 1950–April 1951

On June 25, 1950, the North Koreans staged a sudden, overwhelming invasion of South Korea. When it happened, the Navy's only battleship was on the first midshipman cruise of her new official role as a training ship. As part of the economy measures that called for a downgrading of the *Missouri*'s status, her cruise was on the East Coast rather than overseas as in previous years. She went first to Boston, then to New York, and finally headed south. The initial bulletins on the Korean War came shortly before the *Missouri* pulled into Panama. The merchants there were abuzz with the idea that the ship was in position to head directly out to the Pacific to enter combat. It wasn't to be—at least not for a while yet.

One night soon after the start of the war, Midshipman Wes Hammond was standing watch on the bridge of the *Missouri*, near where Captain Duke was sitting in his chair on the starboard side. The skipper was wistful as he spoke about the tides of fortune that had removed him from command of the cruiser *Rochester*, which was part of the Seventh Fleet and preparing to go into action in the first strikes of the Korean War. Instead, he was far away, hauling around a cargo of midshipmen.[1]

Another of those midshipmen was Bill Lawrence, president of the Naval Academy's class of 1951. Some thirty years later, he himself served as the superintendent of the academy. During this summer of training, Lawrence detected an air of tension on the battleship's bridge, as if Captain Duke was keeping a tight rein on things to ensure there wouldn't be a repeat of the ignominious grounding in January. Lawrence and other first classmen received limited opportunities to give orders to the helm and thus practice at being junior officers. The command did not seem to exert such control over the training program, which gave Lawrence and his midshipmen staff considerable latitude in its administration. One interesting diversion came during the stop in Panama, where Lawrence made a ceremonial presentation to that nation's president. He wrote and memorized a speech in Spanish, then practiced it over and over so he was able to deliver it smoothly during the actual ceremony on the surrender deck.[2]

The second training cruise of the summer was for the benefit of midshipmen from the Naval Academy and NROTC units, as well as fifty cadets from the Military Academy at West Point. The first stop was Halifax, Nova Scotia. On the way south the *Missouri* engaged in exercises at Narragansett Bay, then continued on to

Midshipman Bill Lawrence, president of the Naval Academy's class of 1951, presents a plaque to President Arnulfo Arias of Panama during a ceremony on the surrender deck in June 1950. At left is Rear Admiral Fred Kirtland, commander of the midshipman training squadron. At right is Midshipman William W. Sullivan, class of 1953. (U.S. Navy photo in the National Archives: 80-G-416218)

New York City. There the battleship moored at pier eighty-eight, a former French Line pier that had been the New York home of the glamorous liner *Normandie* during her heyday in the 1930s.

One of the battleship's newly reported officers was Ensign Lee Royal, a member of the group of three midshipmen who visited Churchill during the summer cruise a year earlier. He had a girlfriend in New York, and one evening the two of them went to see a Broadway musical called *Where's Charlie?* After he had taken her home, Royal got back to the *Missouri* around one o'clock in the morning. The duty officer on the forward quarterdeck asked, "Did you have a good time?"[3]

"Yeah," said the ensign, in a happy mood after a pleasant evening.

"Good, because that's the last one you're going to have for some time. Go down to the wardroom. The exec wants you down there."

Despite the late hour, the wardroom was fully lighted, and people with clipboards in hand were running back and forth. They were making lists of items the *Missouri* would need for a deployment and sending them by message to Norfolk. She had just been ordered to leave at first light. Instead of going to Guantánamo for the scheduled conclusion of the training cruise, the *Missouri* was to head directly back to her home port. There she would off-load the midshipmen and take aboard ammunition and supplies for a voyage to the Pacific.[4]

What the crew didn't know yet, because of security restrictions, was that the Navy wanted the *Missouri* to provide gunfire support for General Douglas MacArthur's planned behind-the-lines amphibious invasion of Inchon, a city on the west coast of Korea. As soon as the brows went over to connect the ship with the shore at Norfolk, the midshipmen left and went right into waiting buses. For the next five days and nights the battleship took aboard railroad-car loads of supplies. Lighters came alongside so the ship could off-load her dummy training ammunition and take aboard the real kind, the projectiles that exploded when they reached their targets.[5]

On the dock, waiting to go aboard the battleship, was a large contingent of sailors. When she became a training ship, the *Missouri*'s crew had been reduced in size, in part because shortages in manpower could be made up by midshipmen and reservists to carry out some of the duties that crew members would otherwise do. Now she took aboard an additional 36 officers and 952 enlisted men to bring the crew to a total of 114 officers and 2,070 enlisted. Some of the men reporting for duty were castoffs and thus a mixed blessing. Lieutenant (j.g.) Don Giles observed that many of the ships in the Norfolk area had simply sent their undesirables to the *Missouri* when asked to provide men. A number of the bad apples had to be court-martialed for a variety of misdeeds by the time the ship arrived in the Far East.[6]

Unlike the men who had been tried and found wanting elsewhere, some of the new crew members were reporting to sea duty for the first time. One of them was Fireman Tom O'Malley, an eighteen-year-old naval reservist. His father was a district attorney in the Scranton, Pennsylvania, area and tied in with the Democratic Party political apparatus. He knew a retired Navy warrant officer who told him that the battleship would offer the best protection for his son in a wartime situation. Telephone calls went to the appropriate places within the Navy Department, and young Tom O'Malley became part of the crew of the Navy's only battleship.[7]

The requirement to get over to Korea was so urgent that the *Missouri* departed for Panama on Saturday morning, August 19, after only a few days in port. Some crew members complained, wondering why they couldn't at least have had one weekend in home port before departure. Worse than that, the battleship encountered rough seas soon after getting under way. As the ship proceeded south, Ensign Royal was standing watch in the combat information center. As he looked at a radar scope, it showed the unmistakable whirling pattern of an approaching hurricane.

Captain Duke was running the *Missouri* southeast at twenty-five knots, planning to turn southwest off Cape Fear, North Carolina, in order to maneuver into the storm's safer semicircle. But the hurricane didn't follow the predicted track, so Duke had to continue on a

southeasterly course, keeping the winds and seas on the starboard side. Despite her great bulk and deep draft, the *Missouri* moved about considerably in the storm. It was particularly disconcerting when she leaned over in a roll and hung there for what seemed far too long. Then she would slowly roll back upright and on over to the other side—then hang there for a time.[8]

One of the *Missouri*'s junior officers, Ensign Fred Koch, was in a turret shell deck during some of the worst of the rolling. As he felt a roll coming on, he reached up to the overhead and grabbed an I-beam for support as his legs moved out from under him.[9]

The worst of the weather hit the battleship between 1:30 and 2:30 on the morning of Au-

gust 20. The eye of the storm passed about 170 miles to the west of her. The wind gauge at one point registered a speed of sixty-eight knots. As the winds howled and the waves surged around the *Missouri*, they made a considerable mess. The seas turned the motor whaleboat on the starboard side into kindling. Larger boats on the fantail were in dollies, attached to pad eyes in the deck with chains and turnbuckles. The moorings broke loose, and the laden dollies became battering rams, smashing into the two HO3S helicopters on the stern and sending them overboard to port.[10]

The boat dollies careened to port as well. The wheels on the bottom became lodged in the waterway between the edge of the teakwood deck and the edge of the ship, so they

On August 19, 1950, the *Missouri* backs away from her familiar pier-seven berth at Norfolk to begin the long journey to Korea. At left is the aircraft carrier *Coral Sea*. The battleship's forward 40-mm gun tubs are empty. (Courtesy Donald T. Giles, Jr.)

A view of the fantail on August 20 shows the various boat-loaded dollies crowded over to the port side after the action of the previous night's heavy seas. (Courtesy Donald T. Giles, Jr.)

helmsman dutifully replied, "Right standard rudder, aye, sir." The captain and pilot, looking forward, saw the bow begin to swing slowly to the left. Suddenly, voices came clamoring in through the slots in the barbette: "*Right* full rudder! *Right* full rudder!" The quartermaster immediately realized that he had unwittingly said one direction but turned the helm in the other. He began frantically spinning the wheel in the other direction. Gradually, the swing to port was arrested, then the bow began moving right, and the ship went on to make her approach to the locks.[12]

Ensign Lee Royal, the junior officer of the deck, observed that the color drained from Captain Duke's face when the skipper saw the bow of the ship head toward shoal water on the port side. Because of the circumstances under which he had come to the *Missouri*, Duke's number-one job was to keep from running the battleship aground. Now he appeared visibly shaken because his helmsman had made a rare mistake that threatened to put the ship aground for the second time in the same year. As soon as the situation was under control, Duke said, "Relieve that man." The erring quartermaster left the bridge, and Travis was recalled to duty. After that, when it was time to stand his watches, the quartermaster who turned the wheel the wrong way was prevented from doing it again. He went to after steering, far away from the bridge, and stood his watches there the rest of the time Irving Duke was in command.[13]

After passing through the canal, the *Missouri* turned her bow west toward Hawaii. During that transit the ship had to divert off her intended track for two days to avoid a storm in the Pacific. Part of the work in the shipyard at Pearl Harbor involved repairing the hurricane damage from the Atlantic, and part was to beef up her armament. The yard replaced one 40-mm mount mangled by the storm and added four more to empty gun tubs. In addition, the ship received fourteen 20-mm dual mounts for possible use against aircraft. The guns had been removed for reasons of economy; they were put back for combat-readiness reasons.[14]

The *Missouri* then went out to shoot at the island of Kahoolawe to give her shore-

remained on board, though damaged beyond repair. A searchlight on the flag bridge was ripped loose, watertight doors sprung, vent ducts sheared off at deck edge, and numerous electrical circuits shorted out or grounded. A 40-mm mount was smashed so badly that it had to be replaced. If ever an illustration were needed of the old proverb, "Haste makes waste," this was it. Despite the order to proceed to Korea at best possible speed, the *Missouri* wound up spending nearly a week in Pearl Harbor for voyage repairs. Captain Duke's superiors in the chain of command declined to take any punitive action, considering the damage regrettable but understandable under the situation. He was in a no-win situation, ordered to steam into dangerous weather because of an urgent military requirement. It was a calculated risk, and the ship paid for it.[11]

During the course of her trip through the Panama Canal on August 23, the *Missouri* crossed the fresh-water Gatun Lake between sets of locks. As the ship was approaching the next locks, Quartermaster Bevan Travis—the man who was at the wheel during the grounding in January—had just left the bridge after several hours on the helm. Soon after Travis's relief took over, the canal pilot ordered right standard rudder. From his spot behind the 18-inch armor of the conning-tower barbette, the

bombardment team some practice. Ensign Royal was in Spot Two, the main battery fire control director at the aft end of the superstructure. He was supposed to observe the fall of shot ashore, although he felt a bit reluctant because he had only book knowledge of the technique, no practical experience. The plan called for the ship to start at five thousand yards and then gradually increase the range. It was a beautiful sunny day as Royal trained the director's range finder toward the target on the beach. In his inexperience, he was wondering just how to phrase the necessary corrections to get the guns on target. His task was made even more difficult when he saw no indication at all that any projectiles landed. As he wondered what to do next, he heard the voice of Commander Harry Seymour, the ship's gunnery officer, over the sound-powered telephones he was wearing: "Kee-rist, we've missed the island!"[15]

The phone circuit was soon filled with a good deal of extraneous noise, and then gradually an explanation emerged. Someone in the main battery plotting room, deep within the ship, had accidentally left a switch on the mechanical fire-control computer in the wrong position. The result was that the order on how high to elevate the guns was a constant, rather than varying with the ship's distance from the target, as it was supposed to. Consequently, when the gun was fired, it was on the correct bearing but at the range determined by the switch, not the actual range to the target. The projectile had roared all the way over the island. The next thing Ensign Royal overheard on the telephones was from Commander Seymour, "I want a five-hundred-word theme on my desk by supper on how you can miss an island with a 16-inch gun at five thousand yards."[16]

The *Missouri* headed on to the west and threaded her way through the Philippine Islands. As the ship approached Japan from the south, another ugly storm threatened, Typhoon Kezia. Winds approached forty knots during the storm, and the swells were large. Captain Duke took a more deliberate approach this time because he didn't want to lose any more helicopters. The giant battleship essen-

Captain Irving Duke had a colorful personality that left lasting impressions in the memories of many men who served under him in the *Missouri*. (U.S. Navy photo in the National Archives: 80-G-427587)

tially tacked back and forth, keeping on relatively gentle courses and gradually making her way toward the objective. Her original destination had been Sasebo, but there wasn't time for that; she was to rendezvous with two destroyers and then head right to Korea.[17]

While this maneuvering was in progress, all officers not on watch were summoned to the wardroom. Captain Duke uncovered a map of Korea that was set up on an easel. It showed the peninsula on which the North Korean forces had been so successful that the U.N.–controlled area had been compressed to a tiny area in the south, the Pusan perimeter. It was dramatic evidence to the *Missouri*'s officers of how poorly the war had gone for U. N. forces in the first two and a half months. Duke said he didn't know whether the battleship was going to help American forces fight their way back up the peninsula or perhaps cover a withdrawal from Korea. The captain suggested the retreat might be comparable to that at Dunkirk, France, ten years earlier. The mention of Dunkirk shot through the room like electricity. Ensign Royal, sitting at the back of the room because he was so junior, had thoughts that probably echoed those of some of his shipmates. "Going to war is bad, but going to war and getting your ass whipped is really bad."[18]

In retrospect, one can observe that security for the Inchon invasion was so tight that not even the captain of the *Missouri* knew it was coming up. What makes the situation even more intriguing was that the very reason the ship was rushed around from the east coast was so that her 16-inch guns—with their much greater range than those of cruisers and destroyers—could be used to interdict the roads leading to Inchon and prevent enemy reinforcements once the invasion started. Only when the *Missouri* joined up with the U.S. task force on the east coast of Korea the next day did those on board the ship learn about the invasion about to take place on the west coast at Inchon. The hurricanes had cost her the opportunity to be present for the landings.[19]

As if the ship hadn't been through enough hassles in trying to prepare for the upcoming action in Korea, one more came up on the eve of combat. The *Missouri* was to be part of a U. N. fighting force, but she didn't have the flag of the United Nations. So on September 14 the chief quartermaster and his subordinates had to go around gathering up material and getting information on the design of the U. N. flag. With the help of some men in the boatswain's locker and their sewing machine, the *Missouri*'s crew put together a homemade flag showing a blue background with a white design of the globe and various nations on it. Disbursing Clerk Joe Debenedetto was topside the following morning and watched as the new flag went up for the first time.[20]

Commander William H. Hoffman, one of the *Missouri*'s chaplains, holds a service on the fantail prior to the ship beginning her bombardment operations in mid-September. (U.S. Navy photo in the National Archives: 80-G-420321)

An inspection party from the heavy cruiser *Helena* looks over a crater at Pohang, Korea, caused by the explosion of one of the *Missouri*'s 16-inch projectiles. (U.S. Navy photo in the National Archives: 80-G-710035)

On September 15—one month and one day and eleven thousand miles after she had left her mooring at pier eighty-eight in New York's North River—the *Missouri* entered her second war. On Korea's east coast, South Korean guerrillas mounted a small landing at Changsa-dong, ostensibly to tie down North Korean troops. A day earlier, the cruiser *Helena* and destroyers *Brush* and *Maddox* had bombarded Samchok on Korea's east coast. Now the *Missouri* beefed up the group considerably. With a helicopter for spotting, her 16-inch guns fired for an hour and a half at Samchok. All told, the *Missouri* unleashed fifty-two high-capacity projectiles that first day, destroying one railroad bridge and damaging another.[21]

A day later, she fired at Pohang. On September 17, Army Lieutenant Colonel Rollins Emmerich, operating with a South Korean division, asked for some naval gunfire to harass a position held by many North Koreans. His corporal sent a call-fire radio message to the *Helena* offshore, but he was interrupted by a reply from

someone on board the *Missouri:* "Hello, Cliff-dweller, this is Battleax. We will take that mission." Evocative voice call signs such as "Battleax" have long since disappeared from the Navy's lexicon; their very familiarity reduced their effectiveness from the standpoint of communications security. On the other hand, the soldiers ashore felt a security of another sort from the knowledge that the Navy's only battleship was nearby. On September 20 Emmerich was so confident of the ship's shooting that he called for her gunners to fire projectiles at positions a mere three hundred yards from where he was spotting. He reported that the rounds shook the countryside when they exploded.[22]

After the brief flurry of shooting on the east coast, the *Missouri* went to Sasebo, Japan, on the island of Kyushu. This naval port would be the battleship's home away from home during much of her two Korean War deployments. It was near the Korea Strait and just a short run to the east coast of the peninsula. When the *Missouri* first reached the Japanese port, the

Japanese civilians there were still recovering from World War II. Lieutenant Giles saw many people pulling carts of building materials behind them as they made their way through the streets. Motor vehicles were rare, so many people were on bicycles or in pedicabs. A few unhappy-looking men were still wearing their wartime military uniforms. By and large, though, the Japanese people, especially the merchants, were friendly toward Americans. The change in attitude over the years since 1945 probably had a lot to do with the influence of General MacArthur, who was essentially a potentate in the postwar years. Giles recalled that MacArthur was revered in Japan at the time: "They loved him when we were out there. His name was godlike."[23]

Within a few days the *Missouri* left Japan and steamed around to the west coast of Korea. She

General Douglas MacArthur salutes as the boatswain's mate pipes him aboard at Inchon on September 21. The slender officer at lower right is the junior officer of the deck, Ensign Lee Royal. A year earlier, Royal was one of three midshipmen who went to see Winston Churchill. (Courtesy Lee Royal)

anchored in the Inchon Channel, south of Wolmi-do Island, which had been a key during the invasion on September 15. The North Korean forces that had been so successful during the first several weeks of the war had been completely surprised by MacArthur's brilliant landing. They were in full flight northward, with U. N. forces in pursuit. The various surface ships on the scene used their guns to support the effort; the *Missouri*, for instance, fired at concentrations of enemy troops on the road north from Suwon to Seoul, capital of South Korea.[24]

Although she was back in action and demonstrating the power of her 16-inch guns, the battleship had her troubles. Firing off Korea demonstrated that some of the 16-inch projectiles loaded aboard at Norfolk had faulty fuzes. They had no effect against the enemy because they never got that far; instead, they exploded within a second or so after leaving the gun barrels. Crew members had a dramatic demonstration of the effect of the explosive charge within a projectile; it shattered the heavy molded steel into sharp-edged shards. Most of the fragments dropped harmlessly into the ocean, but a few fell onto the deck of the *Missouri* herself.[25]

General MacArthur himself came to visit the ship on September 21 while she was anchored at Inchon. As he stood on the quarterdeck at rigid attention, the general saluted during the playing of ruffles and flourishes that were part of the honors rendered to him. While he was doing so, the junior officer of the deck, Ensign Lee Royal, was struck by the trembling of the general's right hand. At seventy, MacArthur was old to be a fighting man.[26]

In the days just before that, MacArthur had been the subject of some rather irreverent discussions from Marines on board the *Missouri*. The long-standing references to "Dugout Doug," the glory hound, were thrown back and forth. An eager participant in the discussions was Captain Lawrence E. Kindred, the commanding officer of the ship's Marine detachment. For some years, members of the Marine Corps had taken a jaundiced view of the theatrical Army general. And now he was about to return to the ship on whose deck he had accepted the Japanese surrender just over five years earlier.[27]

The *Missouri*'s Marine detachment was lined up on the quarterdeck as the general strode aboard through two lines of saluting sideboys. He shook hands with Captain Duke and then moved in close to Captain Kindred as he prepared to inspect the Marine honor guard. Then, in an impressive voice, sounding as if it were emanating from God himself, the general said something close to the following: "Captain, I have just returned from the far north, where your comrades-in-arms are in close combat with the enemy. And I wish to report to you that there is not a finer group of fighting men in the world than the U.S. Marines." The general's words rocketed through the ship, endlessly repeated, and Captain Kindred's fellow officers began riding him mercilessly, asking him what he now thought of "Dugout Doug." The captain, who had been completely won over by the general's two sentences, was now a MacArthur fan and defender.[28]

In early October the *Missouri* became a fleet flagship, as she had been during World War II. On October 7 the flag quarters received a new resident, Vice Admiral Arthur D. Struble, who had presided over the recent landing at Inchon in his capacity as commander, Seventh Fleet, and commander, Joint Task Force Seven. Struble was an old hand at such things: in 1944 he was chief of staff for the invasion of Normandy in June and then went to the Pacific for the landings in the Philippines that autumn. Now, in the autumn of 1950, the objective was a landing at the port of Wonsan, on North Korea's east coast. But Rear Admiral Allan E. Smith, the man who supervised the *Missouri*'s salvage earlier in the year at Norfolk, discovered that the U. N. forces did not have command of the sea. Naval mines, which were age-old weapons, were holding up the process of getting ships and landing craft into the harbor.

On October 12, while waiting for the mines to be cleared at Wonsan, a task group of gun ships headed up the east coast to lay a bombardment on the port city of Chongjin, North Korea, merely thirty-four miles south of the Manchurian border. In an operation reminis-

MacArthur talks with Captain Lawrence Kindred, commanding officer of the *Missouri*'s Marine detachment. Captain Duke is between the two men. (Courtesy Donald T. Giles, Jr.)

cent of the shore bombardments right at the end of World War II, the *Missouri* now trained her 16-inch rifles on the Mitsubishi Iron Works, starting fires and creating piles of rubble. In just under an hour the battleship fired off ninety-six rounds from her big guns. Later the ship worked over a warehouse and dock area in the port city.[29]

The following day the *Missouri* bombarded the port of Tanchon, south of Chongjin. Writing in a book published a couple of years later, three Navy authors concluded, "The battleship was still more useful for coastal bombardment than, as had been contemplated, a conference site for General MacArthur and President Truman, who were to meet soon at some point in the Western Pacific."[30]

It's fascinating to consider the possibility of a meeting between the two men on board the ship, since both of them had previously made history in connection with the *Missouri*. Instead, the meeting was held at Wake Island. At this point the general and the president disagreed on the strategy for winning the Korean War. During their meeting at Wake, they were able to patch up their differences—temporarily.

On October 16 the *Missouri* and heavy cruiser *Rochester* headed to Wonsan to conduct a bombardment, but the mission was canceled

The *Missouri* is at right, along with other Seventh Fleet ships moored at Sasebo, Japan, during an early-October respite from Korean operations. The carrier next in line astern of the battleship is the *Valley Forge;* aft of her is the *Philippine Sea.* (U.S. Navy photo in the Naval Institute collection)

One of the most famous U.S. Navy photos of the Korean War shows the *Missouri* in October 1950 as she fires turret two during a bombardment of Chongjin, North Korea, less than forty miles south of the Soviet border. (U.S. Navy photo in the National Archives: 80-G-421049)

because the weather hampered visibility. So the battleship rested beyond the swept channel while waiting for an opportunity to shoot. That night she received a flash report that four unidentified contacts had been detected on radar. They were nearly eighty miles away and headed toward the American ships at a speed of about forty knots—probably enemy torpedo boats. The *Missouri* and three destroyers began heading toward the contacts to intercept them. As the ships steamed onward, radar picked up more and more of the high-speed intruders. Finally, human eyes identified the approaching "enemy" as low-flying geese, and the naval formation headed back to Wonsan.[31]

At dawn on October 26, with the mine-sweeping chores accomplished, the amphibious landing began in the port of Wonsan. The *Missouri*, with Admiral Struble on board, was nearby. Even though she had been contributing her 16-inch projectiles to the United Nations's war effort, the battleship's misadventure at Norfolk earlier in the year was difficult to shake. As the attack transport *Pickaway* steamed past the *Missouri* on her way to off-load Marines, one of those Marines yelled out: "Hey, Mudbank, how'd you get out here? This is deep water."[32]

One individual who served in the *Missouri* during the early stages of the war was not part of the crew; Lieutenant Commander Frank Man-

son was assigned to the Seventh Fleet staff as a historian in uniform. Admiral Struble, the Seventh Fleet commander, provided Manson with invaluable access to official action reports, as well as daily interviews on the fleet's operations. Manson observed that Struble was conscious of his own place in history and thus eager to share his viewpoints with someone who would be writing that history. Manson got twenty minutes a day with Struble, twenty minutes with Marine Corps Major General Oliver P. Smith, and "as long as I wanted with Major General [Edward M.] Almond," commander of the Army's X Corps and previously chief of staff for the publicity-conscious General MacArthur.

With the Seventh Fleet staff embarked in the *Missouri*, staterooms and offices were at a premium. As a result, Manson set up shop in the ladies' powder room, just forward of the wardroom and across the passageway from the executive officer's cabin on the main deck. The room was so small that it couldn't accommodate a desk, so the author and his yeoman put a board across a sink to hold a typewriter. The rough drafts of the eventual book took shape as Manson consulted his notebooks and dictated material to the yeoman for typing. Having survived kamikaze attacks on the thin-skinned destroyer *Laffey* a few years earlier, Commander Manson felt quite secure as he wrote history inside the fortress-like battleship.[33]

Because of the intense interest in the States concerning the Navy's only battleship being back in combat, she was the target of a number of news correspondents and public information officers. One day that autumn a camera team showed up from the movie newsreels to do a story about the role of the *Missouri* in support of the Korean War. The idea was to show the sequence of events in a gunfire mission, putting together film footage of the various elements involved. From a helicopter, a cameraman photographed aerial shots of the ship steaming along, then a view of the guns training out, and also one with the guns erupting in flame and smoke. Other views showed the movement of powder bags in a handling room, as well as the hoisting of projectiles from the shell deck to the turret. Still other images were filmed inside a

turret as the breech was opened and the projectile and powder rammed in.[34]

One sequence took place in the main battery plotting room, where Fire Controlman Warren Lee was operating the analog computer that controlled the aiming and firing of the guns. The film showed the fire control officer raising his hand and ordering "Shoot." Then the camera focused on Lee pulling the trigger to send a salvo on its way to the target. When the various pieces of film were edited together, people in movie theaters got an idea of the different elements involved in gunfire support by the *Missouri*. Warren Lee received letters from his family members who had seen

This Navy recruiting poster was based on the photo of the *Missouri* firing at Chongjin. (U.S. Naval Institute collection)

Right: Fire Controlman Warren Lee poses with his left hand on the salvo alarm and right hand on the firing key in one of the main battery plotting rooms. He and other *Missouri* men were the subjects of both still photos and movie footage released in the United States to show the ship in operation. (U.S. Navy photo in the National Archives: 80-G-421179)

Below: Chief Gunner's Mate W. L. Stull (*left*) and Ensign R. H. Sprince relay an order to load all guns of turret one during a bombardment of Korea. (U.S. Navy photo in the National Archives: 80-G-421187)

him on the screen in their movie theater—this in an era before television news became commonplace. The following year Hollywood put out a feature film on the Korean War, *Retreat, Hell*, starring Frank Lovejoy and Richard Carlson. The producer took the *Missouri*'s firing sequence out of the newsreel and spliced it in among the scenes that included the movie

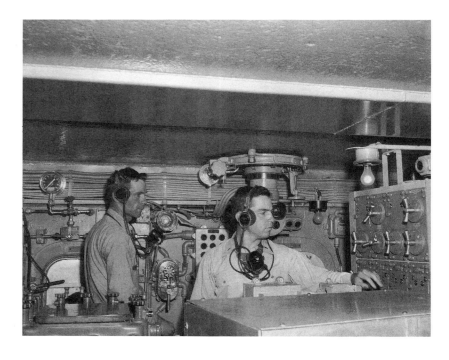

actors. Lee received still more letters after that.[35]

All of that publicity in the various media produced a boost in the ship's effectiveness. Commander Charles Cassel, the ship's operations officer, talked to some of the naval intelligence people at the headquarters of commander, Naval Forces Far East, in Tokyo. They told him that every time the *Missouri* moved up the east coast of Korea, the enemy made a notable movement inland to get beyond the range of her 16-inch guns. On the other hand, the ammo was relatively scarce; the *Missouri* carried the only load of 16-inch powder and projectiles in the Pacific. On one occasion, Lieutenant Giles heard a radio conversation between Captain Duke and an aerial spotter. The spotter was lavish in his praise for the *Missouri*'s shooting and kept calling for more and more rounds. Finally, Duke asked him what the target was, and the spotter said he was using the 16-inch rounds to chase a truck going down a road. With that, Duke checked fire rather than waste ammunition.[36]

Comedian Bob Hope was generous with his time when he and Marilyn Maxwell visited the ship for Navy Day in late October. As he was approaching the *Missouri* by helicopter, he sent a radio message that he was about to come aboard "Admiral Struble's floating hotel." Once on board, he put on a masterful performance as he stood on a fantail platform while a cold Korean wind blew across the ship. He delivered one zinger after another for perhaps half an hour. His stories were filled with double entendres, suggestive of sex without becoming raunchy. The sailors, who had been away from home for more than two months, ate it up, laughing uproariously.[37]

After the outdoor show, Hope went to the wardroom, where he did an abbreviated show for the ship's officers. Still later, when he heard that some of the crew had been on watch and missed the first show, he did still another for their benefit. Perhaps more than anything, the presence of Hope and his troupe reinforced an idea engendered by the frequent news coverage: The people back home in the States cared about the ship and her crew.[38]

By the time of Hope's visit, cold weather was descending on the war zone. For crewmen who had been accustomed to midshipman cruises to Europe in the summer and training in the Caribbean in the winter, the Korean War brought a dramatic change of climate. In the winter of 1950–51, as the *Missouri* steamed off the barren coast of Korea, her crew members stayed inside the skin of the ship as much as they could. It was bitterly cold outside at times, and for some of the men, it was the only time in their lives that they saw snow falling at sea.[39]

One day Ensign Royal, who was standing junior officer of the deck watches on the bridge, went to a locker and asked the proprietor for a foul-weather jacket. The man in charge of the locker smirked as he went to get a jacket. The entrance to the locker was guarded by a Dutch door, the top half of which was open. The man put a jacket on the counter atop the lower half of the door. As he did so, he asked, "You're not superstitious, are you?" The reason for the question became apparent when Royal looked down and saw the name patch on the jacket— "Captain W. D. Brown, USN." It was the jacket the skipper had left behind when he was relieved of command after running the *Missouri* aground.[40]

Royal replied: "I'm not superstitious, but I'd just as soon not have that one. How about another one?" When he gave the subject some more thought, the ensign came to the conclu-

Crewmen laugh as comedian Bob Hope presents a Navy Day show on the *Missouri*'s fantail. Foul-weather jackets abound because of the cool autumn nights in Korean waters. (Courtesy Donald T. Giles, Jr.)

sion that the man in the locker probably got his jollies by offering the captain's old jacket to everybody who came to the door and asked for one. So far he hadn't had any takers.[41]

Lieutenant Koch, the boiler division officer, normally stood his underway watches in main control. One of his collateral duties was that of fueling officer, whether the ship was receiving black oil from a fleet oiler or dispensing it to the thirsty destroyers that came alongside about every three days. At times, four ships of the task force steamed together on parallel courses. As the *Missouri* was taking on fuel from alongside the oiler, both the oiler and the battleship were simultaneously fueling destroyers outboard of them. Koch manned a sound-powered telephone so he could keep in touch with the oil king below deck. The oil king was an enlisted man who kept track of the amount of fuel in each of the ship's many tanks. Koch directed where incoming fuel was to be distributed and from where outgoing fuel was to be taken.[42]

During good weather, the refueling assignment got Koch out of main control and topside to enjoy the sun. The job was obviously a good deal less enjoyable during the winter months off Korea. Visits from stewards bearing hot chocolate were most welcome, but on one occasion in particular even that seemed hardly enough. The sea was choppy, with spray flying up and onto the superstructure deck where Koch stood with his phone. The movement of the ship sent him into contact with a bulkhead, and to his chagrin he discovered that the cold air had frozen his ice-encrusted foul-weather jacket to the cold gray steel.[43]

Lieutenant Giles stood bridge watches for four hours at a time throughout those bitter cold months. During one of the night watches, he looked over to the starboard side of the bridge and saw Captain Duke sitting in his chair. Through the darkness, interrupted only by the glow of radar repeaters and the red lights to illuminate charts, Giles heard the voice of the skipper. In his youth, before going to the Naval Academy, Duke had worked in a bank in Richmond, Virginia. All these years later, off chilly Korea, Duke demonstrated the sense of

Included among the ammunition the *Missouri* took to Korea were several faulty 16-inch projectiles. This one detonated shortly after being fired by the ship, producing a black cloud and showering the water below with shell fragments. (Courtesy Donald T. Giles, Jr.)

humor that made him popular with the crew. "Just think," he said, "I gave up a good job as the head teller of the First National Bank of Richmond, Virginia, for this." This, of course, was the same Captain Duke who the previous summer had lamented that he was training midshipmen rather than commanding a ship off Korea. His wish for a combat command had come true.[44]

While the ship was at sea, Captain Duke often came out onto the bridge during the wee small hours of the morning, perhaps because he had trouble sleeping in his sea cabin. The men on watch could smell him before they saw him because the odor of his cigar wafted forward. Then they saw the glowing orange end of the cigar and finally the dark outlines of the man himself, clad in bathrobe and slippers. He didn't interfere, just pleasantly exchanged a few words with them and asked how things were going.[45]

The crew of the *Missouri* liked and respected Irving Duke, but he did institute one practice

at captain's mast that struck many of the men as strange. After seeing some of the same faces over and over at nonjudicial punishment proceedings, the skipper decided he would try a bit of psychology to see if he could induce better behavior. Duke sentenced some of the repeat offenders to be "passengers" for a while rather than crew members. They were relieved of all their duties, didn't have to get up at reveille, and had their pictures posted in the mess deck, where they got head-of-the-line treatment for chow and reserved seats at the movies.

Evidently, the captain hoped that these men would be treated as outcasts and slackers by their fellow crew members and would perform better in order to get back into the good graces of their shipmates. Fire Controlman Bob Eichenlaub of the FM division observed of the captain: "He probably thought he was putting them to shame. I don't know about the other men, but the two men in my division enjoyed it. . . . They loved being passengers."[46] Duke apparently had more success with men in some of the other divisions. Lieutenant Giles observed that peer pressure was quite effective in some cases, so much so that some individuals were practically begging to be restored to the duty list.[47]

After U. N. successes in the months following the landings at Inchon and Wonsan, the tide turned late in the year as the Red Chinese entered the conflict on the side of the North Koreans. Once again, American forces were heading south to escape the onslaught. As the Marines retreated from Chosin Reservoir and elsewhere, they converged on the port of Hungnam shortly before Christmas to be evacuated in the face of the advancing Chinese army. The *Missouri* received orders to proceed to the area, anchor, and take specific coordinates under fire.

Other gunfire support ships were there as well. Included was Task Group 90.8 under Rear Admiral Roscoe Hillenkoetter, who had been third commanding officer of the *Missouri*. Now he was embarked in the cruiser *St. Paul*. The battleship's mission during this operation was to lay down a curtain of fire as the Marines' perimeter contracted. It would protect their rear as they moved into the port. While the battleship was anchored, her crew saw a flotilla of amphibious ships and landing craft moving

Right: Tattooed Commissaryman Ratha Hancock digs out a frozen turkey in preparation for Christmas dinner on board the battleship. (U.S. Navy photo in the National Archives: 80-G-424642)

Below: Turret one fires a projectile toward the advancing enemy at Hungnam shortly before Christmas of 1950. The arcs of fire at upper left are from rocket-equipped landing ships (LSMRs) near the Korean coast. (Courtesy of Lee Royal)

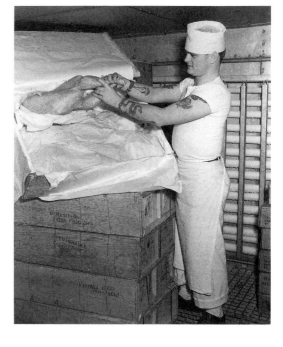

to seaward after they had loaded up with American fighting men, Korean civilians, goats, chickens—"the damnedest collection of things you ever saw," according to one witness. Their next stop was the port of Pusan, which was still controlled by U. N. forces.[48]

At Hungnam the *Missouri* was firing over cruisers, destroyers, and inshore rocket-launching ships known as LSMRs. Fire Controlman Warren Lee was impressed, saying later, "I have never seen such a perimeter of fire as the one set up to protect that particular evacuation." Since the shooting was at night, it provided a spectacular contrast to the surrounding darkness.[49]

Finally, the evacuation had been completed. It was a relatively pleasant day as Ensign Royal stood on the forecastle as part of the special sea and anchor detail. The *Missouri* raised her port anchor and prepared to leave the Hungnam harbor. As the forecastle detail was securing the anchor in the hawsepipe and putting on chain stoppers and pelican hooks, they felt a strange shaking sensation, as if the earth were erupting beneath them. It was momentarily frightening. Then they turned around and looked toward the waterfront area. As Royal saw it: "The whole damn city of Hungnam was about two hundred feet in the air. They blew that place wide open." The last of the U. N. soldiers had blown up ammunition caches to keep the place from being of any use to the advancing enemy.

The mobile *Missouri,* which had been steaming off and on throughout the fall with the fast carriers of Task Force 77, rejoined them once again now that she had completed the shore bombardment. On December 25 the ship held a Christmas service. One of the replenishment ships supplied Christmas trees and turkeys for the benefit of the battleship's crew.[50]

The ship also began receiving a considerable amount of mail. Lieutenant Giles had sent a letter to the *Baltimore Sun* complaining about what the paper was printing. His wife had told him of the paper's coverage of debutante balls and other things while American servicemen were serving in Korea with little recognition from the newspaper. Giles's letter appeared under the headline, "Bitter Blast from Korea." The result was an outpouring of mail addressed to the ship in support of those who were serving. In particular, the letter inspired a man with the local VFW; he began bombarding Giles with mail. When the bags of mail showed up, the officer took them down to the mess deck and distributed the contents, which included a lot of magazines and newspapers so crew members could catch up on what was happening back home.[51]

The initial months of the ship's deployment to Korea—up to the end of 1950—had been filled with exciting and unusual events: the tussles with the storms; support of the aftermath of the Inchon invasion; the landings at Wonsan; Bob Hope's visit; and the coverage of the withdrawal from Hungnam. With the coming of 1951, the ship fell into a fairly routine pattern wherein four major components were regularly repeated: shore bombardments, mostly on the east coast; operations with Task Force 77; at-sea replenishment; and journeys to Sasebo, Japan, for resupply. With few exceptions, the ship followed that routine until it was time to head home in the spring.[52]

Task Force 77 was built around aircraft carriers. As an indication of the decline in naval strength in the five years since the end of World War II, the entire task force was smaller than one of the component task groups that had made up Task Force 38/58 at the end of the previous war. The threat, of course, was much less by this time because North Korea was not a naval power. Even so, there was a concern about the air threat, and thus the *Missouri* and cruisers were part of the task force to lend their antiaircraft capabilities. Also a concern—perhaps farfetched—was a possible Chinese submarine threat, so the ships of the task force typically went to general quarters for an hour each at dawn and dusk, just as the carrier force had in World War II. It would have been a great feather in the cap of the Communist forces to launch a successful attack against the "Mighty Mo."[53]

The U.S. Navy's three newest carriers, those of the *Midway* class, operated with the Sixth

Missouri men decorate a Christmas tree in the mess deck. Kneeling is Seaman Edwin Pawlak; Seaman Enoch Smith stands at right; and Marine Private First Class Charles McConnell is at the rear. (U.S. Navy photo in the National Archives: 80-G-424640)

Right: The South Korean national flag flies from a halyard on the *Missouri*'s mainmast to honor a visit by President Syngman Rhee on February 3, 1951. (Courtesy Donald T. Giles, Jr.)

Below: Crewmen stack empty 5-inch powder cans following a bombardment of Kansong in February 1951. (U.S. Navy photo in the National Archives: 80-G-426472)

Fleet in the Mediterranean throughout the 1950s. That meant Task Force 77 off the east coast of Korea was comprised of the older *Essex*-class ships that had been the workhorses in World War II. The difference was that they were now operating jet fighters, such as F9F Cougars, in addition to their propeller-driven AD Skyraiders. They delivered ton after ton of ordnance on targets in North Korea.[54]

It's probably just as well that the North Koreans and Red Chinese did not challenge the task force with jet fighters in that period, because the *Missouri*'s guns and fire control systems were geared to deal with the slower propeller-driven aircraft of World War II. Fire Controlman Amory Houghton stood watch in the Mark 37 directors that controlled the 5-inch mounts. At times, he tried to track some of the American jets the *Missouri* was operating with, but he just wasn't able to keep up. The speed of the new planes was beyond the technical capability of the equipment. Of course, the other side of the coin was that the best defense is a good offense. The jet fighters of Task Force 77 dealt with enemy aircraft over land, before they ever came close to threatening the ships at sea.[55]

Typically, Task Force 77 operated in a race-track holding pattern several dozen miles off the Korean coast. Because of the need for wind over the carriers' decks for launching and recovery of aircraft, the task force steamed into the wind at about twenty-five knots during those operations. Then, when the planes were in the air or back on deck, the ships would turn and go downwind, reducing speed to perhaps ten knots while steaming in that direction. The great mobility that the fast carriers had demonstrated one war earlier wasn't needed. Off Korea—as off Vietnam a decade later—the target was stationary.[56]

Breaks in the operating routine did come, at which time about one-third of the ships would go off from the task force and rendezvous with a replenishment group to take aboard food, fuel, ammunition, and mail. The ships to receive supplies would line up and take various items in sequence, proceeding from one delivery ship to another down the row. It was almost like going through a cafeteria. One hitch,

though, was the delivery of 16-inch ammunition at sea. After a few experiments proved difficult, the 16-inch rearming was done subsequently when the *Missouri* went off line for a while and made quick trips to Sasebo.

There was little rest for the weary. A lighter full of projectiles came along one side of the battleship and a lighter full of projectiles along the other. Then the crew set to work on the around-the-clock process of manhandling the heavy ammunition down below. After the ship had done a substantial amount of shooting since the last replenishment, the reloading process could take three or four days of hard physical work. Ensign Royal was usually either on watch or supervising the loading. After a while, he became a sleepwalker whenever the ship was in Sasebo.[57]

Because of her draft the *Missouri* had to anchor well away from the fleet landing when she went to the Japanese port. And that's when she paid dearly for the boats that had been damaged during the various storms the ship had encountered on the way to the Far East. Her boat crews were obliged to operate hand-me-down boats drawn from the local boat pool. Typically, they had standing water in the bottom, which immediately drenched the shoes of the

members of the liberty party.[58]

Moreover, recreational facilities in Sasebo were not luxurious. The officers had a Quonset hut in which to do their drinking. Then they would climb a hill to have dinner at a nice officers' club run by the Eighth Army. One night several of the *Missouri*'s junior officers had a number of drinks and decided to have a rickshaw race on the way back down the hill to the boat landing. The Japanese drivers were lined up with their rickshaws, but the naval officers asked the Japanese to get in and be the passengers. The Americans did the pulling, at a breakneck pace, down the hill. Surprisingly, no one was hurt, although the regular drivers concluded this was an adventure they preferred not to repeat.[59]

In early March the *Missouri* went to the large naval base at Yokosuka, Japan, on the island of Honshu. It was not at all far from where the ship anchored for the surrender in 1945. During the battleship's time in port, Captain George C. Wright relieved Captain Duke of command. Wright was the younger brother of Rear Admiral Carleton H. Wright, commander of a cruiser force in the Battle of Tassafaronga, off Guadalcanal, in late 1942. The new skipper, unlike other *Missouri* captains of

The *Missouri* steams into Hawaii in April 1951 on her way home from Korea. (Courtesy Donald T. Giles, Jr.)

that era, had not made a side trip into submarines. He served in the battleships *New York* and *Pennsylvania* as a junior officer and later commanded the destroyers *Bernadou* and *McDougal*. During the invasion of southern France in August 1944 he was a destroyer division commander and later commanded a destroyer squadron. In personality, he was a good deal less colorful than the unpredictable Captain Duke. The impressions of Wright that remain in the minds of his crew are much blander.[60]

While the ship was at Yokosuka, crew members had a chance to get out and find their pleasures as they chose. Some, such as Fire Controlman Houghton, opted for sight-seeing and souvenir buying. He went to the cities of Tokyo and Yokohama, which had been rebuilt in the years following the war and were by now bustling metropolises again. He took colored slides of the countryside he saw. He toured factories where Japanese workers made pottery, pearl necklaces, and other items.

The Japanese he encountered appeared to

harbor no ill will, although his range of contacts was essentially limited. As he put it, "Most of the people we were exposed to, quite frankly, were trying to earn a buck, either by prostituting themselves or selling you gimmicks or booze." He didn't really have a chance to engage in dialogue with members of the middle class and learn their true feelings about the American-aided revival of their country. He did discover, however, that the label "made in Japan" had a negative ring to it in that era, so he was more inclined to do his shopping in the military exchanges or ship's store than on the Japanese economy.[61]

In mid-March the *Missouri* shot her final shore bombardment of the campaign. During her first deployment to Korea the battleship fired 2,895 16-inch rounds and 8,043 rounds of 5-inch. As the ship wound up her war cruise, the amount of metal extruded from the interiors of her gun barrels provided mute evidence of the support the *Missouri* had provided to the

U. N. effort in that far-off land. Ensign Royal, who served as a junior officer in turret two, observed that seven-eighths of an inch of liner extended beyond the end of each outer barrel. The shooting itself had extruded that much of the liner beyond its previous limits.[62]

In late March, Admiral Struble's tenure as commander, Seventh Fleet, ended. He traded jobs with Vice Admiral Harold M. "Beauty" Martin, who was just coming out from the West Coast, where he had served as commander, First Fleet. Admiral Struble remained on board for the *Missouri*'s upcoming trip to the West Coast, so the ship became the First Fleet flagship for about two weeks. Martin had his flag in a cruiser while awaiting the arrival of the *Missouri*'s sister ship *New Jersey*, which had

been reactivated from mothballs soon after the onset of the Korean War. Because the *Missouri*'s tour in the Far East had lasted more than six months already, she began the journey home before her relief's arrival.

When the *Missouri* stopped at Pearl Harbor on the way home, Lieutenant Giles and another officer, George Lengren, wanted to treat themselves to a night at the Royal Hawaiian Hotel. That had been a pleasant stopover for a number of *Missouri* sailors during the ship's homeward-bound voyage in 1945. There was one big difference, however. During the war the Navy had taken over the plush hotel as a rest camp for officers and enlisted men. Now the guests—both military and civilian—had to pay. When Giles and Lengren discovered how

On April 27, 1951, tugs ease the *Missouri* in toward her berth at Norfolk. (U.S. Navy photo in the National Archives: 80-G-428359)

expensive the rooms were in 1951, they beat a hasty retreat.[63]

The *Missouri* was on her way home from the deployment, about two hundred miles from Long Beach, when President Truman fired General MacArthur on April 10, 1951. MacArthur wanted to take the war across the Yalu River into Red China. President Truman wanted to keep the war limited and not risk still another world war. As the disagreement came to a boil, the president fired MacArthur, who was an insubordinate subordinate. The news raced through the crew of the battleship that the general had visited at Inchon just a few months earlier. At first, men were shocked, then many were bothered. In the dispute between MacArthur and President Truman from Missouri, the men of the *Missouri* sided with the general.[64]

Two days later, on April 12, the *Missouri* arrived at Long Beach, California, her first stop in the United States since the previous summer. She was the first major ship back from Korea, so her arrival in California was quite an event. A television camera was mounted on a crane to provide live coverage of the battleship's arrival and mooring. In the ship's wardroom was a television set, still quite a novelty in the United States at the time. The officers took turns walking up to the forecastle, where they could get on camera while their shipmates watched them from the wardroom. When crew members from the battleship went out on the town in Los Angeles, they were feted by their fellow citizens. Spotlights were shown on them when they visited nightclubs.[65]

Then it was time to go back to sea for the final leg in the long journey home. Admiral

Opposite page: Sailors gather on the starboard side of the *Missouri*, waiting to go ashore after the long trip home from Korea. (U.S. Navy photo in the National Archives: 80-G-428360, via Ernest Arroyo)

Left: Across the pier at Norfolk (*right to left*) are the heavy cruisers *Albany* and *Macon*. (U.S. Navy photo in the National Archives: 80-G-428357)

Struble left to join another flagship, and the *Missouri* shoved off for Panama (where she had a brief encounter with the *New Jersey* on the twenty-second), and then the last lap to her home port. The whole city of Norfolk turned out on April 27 for the *Missouri*'s return to her familiar berth at pier seven of the naval station. One nice touch during the homecoming was the greeting from a biplane, swooping overhead as the long gray ship approached land. The plane was of the sky-writing variety common in those days—equipped with a smoke generator so it could send out a white trail astern and spell out messages. In this case the aircraft also towed a banner that carried a greeting for the men below: "WELCOME HOME MIGHTY MO."[66]

9 ❖ Midshipmen and More Korea

June 1951–May 1953

During the first few weeks of recovery from the taxing Korea deployment, the *Missouri*'s crew fell into a routine of liberty, time with families, repairs to equipment, working parties to replenish supplies, and dealing with the local shore establishment in Norfolk. It was also time for many of those who had made the cruise to move on—either to other duty stations or back to civilian life. New men reported aboard as well, similar to the ship's experience when she returned from overseas in 1945.

Among the arrivals was a new ship's band, which comprised about thirty men, nearly all of whom had been musicians in civilian life. They enlisted in that capacity and then attended the Navy music school in Anacostia, D. C. The band was thus different from virtually every other division on board the *Missouri*. In areas such as gunnery, deck, operations, and engineering, the Navy began with essentially untrained men and then taught them to operate various equipment and systems. They became a unit only after they reached the battleship. In the case of the ship's band, the Navy presented it to the ship as a developed unit. The group's repertoire during the Korean War was based mostly on the popular tunes of the 1940s, such numbers as "Begin the Beguine," "Stompin' at the Savoy," and "The Continental."[1]

When the bandsmen reported to the *Missouri*, the other sailors were initially aloof because they were still strangers. That changed quickly, though, as the other men got to know the newcomers and to appreciate their music. After a while, men from other divisions were helping the band members lug their gear around and get set up for their gigs. It even became a point of pride. When *Missouri* men talked to the crews of other ships, they would boast, "Our band is better than your band."[2]

Soon enough, the bandsmen had an opportunity to use their musical abilities, for they would play often during the summer's midshipman training cruises. The first one began at the end of May, just a little longer than a month after the ship returned from the Pacific. The *Missouri* journeyed to Annapolis to take on a load of Naval Academy men and then picked up a group of NROTC men at Norfolk. One of the latter was Jim Hessman, a midshipman third class from Holy Cross College in Worcester, Massachusetts.

One of the phenomena Hessman encountered as the ship headed toward Oslo, Norway, was the practice of rotating midshipmen among different watch and general quarters stations in order to vary their training. As a consequence, Hessman got locked into an arduous routine for about a week. His normal underway watch station was in the after-steering compartment, all the way aft and a couple of decks below the main deck. At least once a day, as part of the training program, the *Missouri* held general quarters drills. Hessman's station for that was as a surface lookout on the 011 level.[3]

When the bong-bong-bong of the general alarm was sounded, Hessman had to shed his sound-powered telephones, climb vertical ladders to get topside to the weather deck, hustle forward on the starboard side, and then climb eleven flights of stairs to the lookouts' perch well above the bridge. During general quarters, the ship was buttoned up for watertight integrity, meaning he couldn't get back inside the skin of the ship once he had gone more than a hundred yards forward. So he climbed up external ladders, including a trip past the flag bridge, where the task force commander, Rear Admiral James L. Holloway, Jr., was standing during these drills. Once he got all the way up to the top, Hessman was invariably winded. Fortunately, he was young and energetic, and—after all this climbing for a week—he was in the best shape of his life.[4]

As the *Missouri* approached Oslo, she came up a beautiful fjord, the mountains rising on each side. Once the ship anchored, the crew members and midshipmen rode landing craft into port and began the process of exploring. One of their concerns was the lack of public restrooms. Hessman and the other midshipmen learned that they were welcome to use the restroom in one of the hotels downtown. The only catch was that it was a dual-gender arrangement. Hessman and his fellow Holy Cross midshipman, Jerry Heavey, did their

business quickly and encountered some Norwegian girls entering just as they were leaving. Others entered without realizing the setup and thought they had stumbled into the wrong restroom by mistake. Still others found themselves interrupted while at the urinals by the friendly greetings of unself-conscious local girls.[5]

Fire Controlman Amory Houghton also came to the conclusion that Norwegians were not as uptight about sex and nudity as the Americans. The locals were more inclined to change clothes on the beach, for example, rather than looking for total privacy, as the visitors would. One of the members of the FA division, accustomed to working with the optical range finders, discovered one day "a very well-proportioned woman who sunbathed in the nude on the beach." Soon crew members were training all sorts of battleship optical equip-

ment on that particular portion of the beach. Houghton happened to be looking through the range finder when the woman picked up a pair of binoculars. She took one look at the *Missouri*, saw what an audience she had, and disappeared.[6]

Many of the *Missouri*'s crew members were struck by the friendliness of the Norwegians and their command of the English language. One afternoon the American Embassy held a dance for the visiting midshipmen. A few officers attended as well, partly in the role of chaperones, but the enlisted men from the various ships in the task force were not welcome. Much more so than today, a considerable gulf existed between officers and enlisted men, so joint socializing ashore was not part of the program. The embassy did a wonderful job of lining up English-speaking local girls who ranged in age from perhaps seventeen to the early twenties. Typically, observed Hessman, almost all were "pretty, friendly, very healthy-looking people."[7]

On the afternoon of the *Missouri*'s last day in Oslo, the midshipmen and sailors had to catch liberty boats before evening came so they could get back to the ship. As the Americans looked up from their launch, they saw hundreds of attractive, friendly Norwegian girls on the pier. A lot of them were crying. As the Navy men looked back, one of the midshipmen said, "They're not the only ones crying."[8]

The next stop on the cruise, a few days later, was Cherbourg, France. The real treat for the midshipmen and crew was the opportunity to take a train to Paris. As the midshipmen descended on the French capital, they checked into hotels. During the daytime Hessman and Heavey did the usual sight-seeing: the Eiffel Tower, the Place Invalides, and the tomb of Napoleon. They also stayed up until the wee small hours because no one was enforcing taps as had been the case on board the *Missouri*. During their nocturnal walks the midshipmen avoided the Parisian ladies of the evening, in part because of a midshipman's low pay, in part because of a fear about consequences, and in part because these fellows were young and mostly innocent.[9]

One night Hessman and Heavey struck up

A gunner's mate provides instruction to midshipmen gathered on the 40-mm mount atop turret two. (U.S. Navy photo in the National Archives: 80-G-431119)

an acquaintance of a different sort as they walked along one of Paris's brightly lit boulevards. A man approached and inquired about all the naval officers he saw. Hessman explained that they were midshipmen, briefly in the city during the course of their training. The man was a genial sort, explaining that he was an American who lived in Paris and worked for the European edition of the *New York Herald Tribune*. Hessman asked if there were any reasonably priced nightclubs they might visit.[10]

The American invited them to come along with him to a place he knew. They didn't know how they would be able to pay for anything, but the man asked them to state their preferences, and they did. Hessman ordered Rhine wine with ginger ale and settled back to relax and enjoy himself, especially when it became

The Norwegian flag flies from the mainmast, and the crew mans the rail in honor of a visit by Crown Prince Olav at Oslo on June 20, 1951. (Courtesy of Ernest Arroyo)

Rear Admiral James L. Holloway, Jr. (*left*), commander of the midshipman training task force, welcomes Norway's Crown Prince Olav to the *Missouri*'s quarterdeck on June 20. (U.S. Navy photo in the National Archives: 80-G-430836)

apparent that he and his friend were guests. The host explained that he had written quite a bit about this bar, so the place was happy to extend hospitality to the visitors. Half an hour later, the man left, telling the midshipmen that they could stay and enjoy themselves free of charge. Three hours later, the young Americans walked out, having experienced a truly enjoyable evening.[11]

Many years later, after he had served as a naval officer and then gone into civilian life as a journalist, Hessman was at a Gridiron Club dinner in Washington, D. C. There, among the gathered crowd, he spotted the very man who had been so kind to him and his friend when they were in France in July 1951. Hessman shook hands and introduced himself, reminding the man of that wonderful night when he had taken them to the Parisian bar. Yes, said the man, he recalled that incident himself. Their benefactor had been a World War II Marine, later a newspaperman, still later an internationally renowned humorist and columnist—Art Buchwald.[12]

All too soon it was time to go back to sea again. Later, after the *Missouri* had been to Cuba and finally returned to Norfolk to disgorge her load of passengers, Midshipman Hessman reflected on what he had been

through. He'd had a wonderful time in the overseas ports. He had been impressed by all the detailed planning that had gone into an extended cruise for a task force of different types of ships. He got a sense of the power built into these ships. Above all, the experience of living in a crowded compartment with thirty other young men from a variety of places had drawn them all closer together. Much more than when he had been sitting in naval classes back at Holy Cross, he had become part of the brotherhood of men who live and serve at sea.[13]

After the ship returned to Norfolk from the cruise, Ensign Lawrence "Ace" Treadwell was one of the 1951 Naval Academy graduates who reported to the *Missouri* for duty. He was recently married, and one Sunday afternoon he and his bride Ellen went to pay a call at the home of Captain Wright and his wife, Estelle. Following World War II, such calls were still a part of the protocol for naval officers, especially those in large ships. They permitted juniors and seniors to get to know each other in a setting different from that on board ship.[14] When the newcomers arrived, they put their calling cards on a silver tray by the front door. They and their hosts then exchanged pleasantries, perhaps for about fifteen minutes. As a result of this contact and further interaction on board the ship, Treadwell came to view Wright as "a real gentleman of the old school." He later watched Wright in action on the bridge and observed him to be imperturbable, even in trying conditions.[15]

In his introduction to the battleship, Treadwell also encountered a group of salty reserve officers who had served in World War II and then been recalled to active duty for Korea. They had a good deal of hard-bought naval experience, and they weren't particularly happy about having been uprooted from the civilian lives they had established following World War II. The fact that the ensign was from the Naval Academy didn't seem to impress them. They expected him to learn, expected him to do his job, and stayed on his case to make sure he did. To him it was almost like a repeat of his plebe year at Annapolis.[16]

Still another individual that Ensign Treadwell came into contact with when he reported aboard was his division officer, Lieutenant (j.g.) Charles Brooks. Brooks, who was involved in the battleship's communications, apparently was the first black officer to serve in the *Missouri*. Ellen Treadwell, who came from Virginia and was a member of the Daughters of the American Revolution, asked her new husband, "How can you do this?"[17]

He responded, "What the hell am I supposed to do?" He had to do his duty as ordered, which proved not to be a problem. Brooks treated Treadwell just fine, but the situation took some getting used to because the ensign had never previously worked for a black man.[18]

Soon it was time for the second training cruise of the summer, and it proved to be much less glamorous than the first one. This one was entirely in the western Atlantic. After a few days of initial training exercises in the Virginia Capes operating area, the *Missouri* went to New York City, as she had the summer before, just before she was sent on her hurried mission to Korea. Fire Controlman Bob Eichenlaub went on liberty Saturday afternoon, August 11. He took the subway up to Harlem, where he watched a baseball game at the Polo Grounds, home of the New York Giants. Pitcher Robin Roberts of the visiting Philadelphia Phillies pitched a 4–0 shutout for the victory. It was the last time the Giants lost before embarking on a sixteen-game winning streak. The team's successes led eventually to a playoff against the Brooklyn Dodgers and Bobby Thomson's celebrated home run that put the Giants into the World Series.[19]

Eichenlaub observed that some of his shipmates were particularly eager to go on liberty in New York because it offered other opportunities more exciting than baseball. Several of the men traded duty days in other ports so they could have maximum time in New York and even sold their blood in local blood banks to increase their supply of spending money. One man returned to the ship and then passed out in an alcohol-induced stupor as soon as he reached his bunk. The abstemious Eichenlaub

Midshipman Charles Reichmuth and his Norwegian date receive refreshments during a tea dance on board the *Missouri* at Oslo. (U.S. Navy photo in the National Archives: 80-G-430926)

was appalled to see the man the next morning because he was covered with dried vomit—in his ears and down his neck. Undaunted, however, the sailor got up the next day, took a shower, and headed off for yet another round of good times.[20]

In a few days, the *Missouri* was on her way again. After the cruise concluded with trips to Panama and Cuba, the battleship spent much of the remainder of the year in her home port, either at the naval station or at the naval shipyard in Portsmouth. On October 18, Captain John Sylvester relieved Captain Wright as commanding officer, but the former skipper didn't go far. He moved from the *Missouri*'s sumptuous in-port captain's quarters to the considerably less elegant stateroom for the admiral's chief of staff. In this case the commander of the midshipman task force, Admiral Holloway, had remained on board in his capacity as type commander. Since Wright had been ordered to be Holloway's chief of staff, he was still on board as well. A few months later, in early January, Holloway, Wright, and the rest of the staff moved to the cruiser *Albany*.[21]

That autumn, the ship underwent her first overhaul since late 1949, the one that had preceded the notorious grounding of January 1950. The autumn of 1951 was an unpleasant time for the crew because of all the interruptions to normal routines. Ensign Treadwell had the quarterdeck watch one cold night in dry dock as the yard workmen banged away during the graveyard shift. Around two in the morning, some of the chief petty officers came up from below with complaints that the crew members couldn't sleep because of all the noise. So Treadwell had to wrangle with the shipyard duty officer over the competing priorities—getting the work done in timely fashion, on the one hand, and letting the crew get some sleep on the other.[22]

Because of such conditions, crewmen sought to get away as much as they could. One who did was Interior Communications Electrician Dick Reisig, from Long Island. He and a few other New Yorkers from the ship's E division pooled their resources and bought a station wagon. They generally went north with seven or eight men in the car, picking up a little extra money from the passengers to help amortize their investment. In those days before the construction of the network of interstate highways, the *Missouri* men headed north on the two-lane roads in Virginia, Maryland, and Delaware before finally reaching the New Jersey Turnpike.

The trip took about ten to eleven hours each way, which didn't leave much time for socializing at home. The group left after work on Friday afternoons and got home in the early hours of Saturday. Then they had to leave Sunday evening after dinner and drive through the wee hours of Monday. The big challenge was getting back to the ship in time to make muster on Monday mornings. The current Hampton Roads bridge-tunnel had not yet been built, so the sailors had to catch the 5:00 A.M. ferryboat to cross from the Newport News side over to Norfolk. A few times they missed the ferry and had to explain themselves at captain's mast.[23]

Early in 1952 the *Missouri* repeated her prior wintertime practices as she went to Guantánamo for training. She fell into an operating routine that the crew abbreviated as "BBF— Be Back Friday." She would get under way on Monday mornings for a week of exercises, then get back into port to enable sailors a weekend of liberty. They frequented the on-base clubs for officers and enlisted men and also went out drinking in nearby Guantánamo City.[24]

While on a brief side trip to Haiti in March, the ship anchored out, and crew members had to take boats to get ashore on liberty. During one such venture the boat went past the corpse of a man who had been killed recently and thrown into the harbor. Musician Norm Clem observed that the locals were seemingly unconcerned about recovering the body and giving it a proper burial. When Clem went to a restaurant for a meal, live chickens were running around in the place. Flies abounded.[25]

Amory Houghton was struck by the contrasts of both luxury and poverty in Haiti. He and some of his shipmates went to a luxury hotel, where they ate a wonderful meal, then went to a nightclub, and finally to a place where they watched a cock fight. On the way back to the ship afterward, the group of sailors passed near some woods where a funeral or some sort of ceremony was in progress. Included were flickering fires, the banging of drums, and what he presumed to be some sort of voodoo ritual. Evidence of poverty was everywhere, including children who came out in boats and dove into the water to retrieve coins that *Missouri* crew members pitched over the side of the ship for their amusement.[26]

That spring, following her return from the Caribbean, the *Missouri* did more training in the Virginia Capes area, including taking aboard a load of naval reservists. In May, she went to New York to host visitors for Armed Forces Day. Nearly eleven thousand came aboard to see the ship's various attractions. Toward the end of the day, while Ensign Treadwell was standing quarterdeck watch, yet another batch of visitors arrived, asking to see the famous surrender plaque. Treadwell turned to the messenger of the watch and asked him to escort the group to the surrender deck, whereupon the young sailor asked, "Where is it?" In this case, the visitors knew more about it than the man who lived there. He learned his lesson on the spot.[27]

In a few weeks it was time for Admiral Holloway to return aboard so he and his staff could command the midshipman training cruise for the second summer in a row. The task force was an impressive one, including two battleships, two heavy cruisers, an aircraft carrier, and an appropriate complement of escorts.[28]

During the trip across the Atlantic, Ace Treadwell was impressed by the tactical sagacity of Captain Sylvester, who had ranked number one of the 456 graduates in the Naval Academy class of 1926. Now, twenty-six years later, he maneuvered the *Missouri* with ease as she and the other ships took various stations within the steaming formation. The highly regarded Sylvester, who later became a vice admiral, had had a good deal of staff duty on his way to command of the battleship. In the late 1930s, for example, he was flag lieutenant for Admiral Harry Yarnell, commander in chief Asiatic Fleet, during the tense period when Japan started a war against China. Sylvester also married Admiral Yarnell's daughter. For nearly two years during World War II, Sylvester was

executive officer of the cruiser *Columbia*. After the war he commanded a destroyer squadron and served as operations and plans officer on the Second Fleet staff.[29]

The big advantage of the summer training cruise, of course, was that it gave the midshipmen an opportunity to apply lessons they had learned in the classroom. What formerly had been only abstract now became real. A good example was navigation, in which mids had worked dozens of canned problems out of books. Now they had to take the star sights of celestial navigation, had to plot the visual bearings during a piloting exercise. Midshipman Staser Holcomb glowed with pride when he

On the eve of the 1952 midshipman cruise to Europe, the major combatants lie in their berths at the Norfolk Naval Station. Lined up (*top to bottom*) are: the *Missouri, Wisconsin, Saipan, Des Moines,* and *Macon.* (U.S. Navy photo in the National Archives: 80-G-442623)

Captain John Sylvester took command of the *Missouri* in October 1951. He stood number one in the Naval Academy class of 1926. (U.S. Navy photo in the National Archives: 80-G-641305)

came up with an excellent series of fixes during one exercise, particularly because Admiral Holloway wrote a complimentary note on Holcomb's booklet.[30]

Holloway was right at home on such a cruise because he had previously served as superintendent of the Naval Academy. He believed in passing along to the new generation his reverence for the traditions of the service. Included was a ringing speech to the midshipmen on the sea as "the natural habitat of the men who wear this blue suit." He was meticulous and precise about naval matters and, in a sense, old-fashioned in his insistence on doing things in time-honored ways.[31]

To some, the admiral's conservatism came across as stiffness. During the summer cruise a year earlier, for instance, Admiral Holloway had dictated that the *Missouri*'s officers wear hats with their civilian clothes whenever they went ashore. It was not a popular decree with the young Americans. When he rode the admiral's barge ashore in Norway in 1952, Holloway donned a boat cloak, a seldom-used part of the naval uniform. President Franklin D. Roosevelt had worn a similar cloak during vis-

its to the fleet in the thirties and forties.[32]

One of the midshipmen first class who made the 1952 cruise in the *Missouri* was Ross Perot. If anything, his Texas twang at the time was even more noticeable than it is these forty years later. He was president of the Naval Academy's class of 1953 and in 1992 ran for president of the United States. One of his classmates was Staser Holcomb, who observed that Midshipman Perot was "Mr. Energy" and "Mr. Enthusiasm." He was a leader, motivator, deeply loyal Navy man, and "go-for-it kind of a guy." According to Holcomb, Perot stood out from the beginning of their Naval Academy experience as one with leadership talents. It came as a great surprise to classmates when Perot later resigned his commission and chose to make his way in the business world.[33]

The first stop on the *Missouri*'s overseas itinerary was Bergen, Norway. There the visiting Americans discovered that temperature is a relative thing. Boats ferried young women from the city out to the battleship for a dance with midshipmen and crew members. Musician Arthur Nau, a member of the ship's band, was among those who provided music for the dance. He and his shipmates were wearing dress blues with turtleneck sweaters as protection against the chilly air in that northern latitude. Meanwhile, some of the Norwegian women were clad in strapless gowns. For them, it was a summer evening.[34]

One of the interesting aspects about Bergen for the visitors was the evidence of its role in World War II. The *Missouri* crewmen could still see the U-boat pens the Germans had built there during the war. Electronics Technician Lew Travis heard about a new, much different kind of threat. He drew shore patrol duty and heard the warnings passed out that certain bars and restaurants in town were under the influence of Communists. Thus, crew members were supposed to avoid those. Explained Travis: "Well, you know what happens when you tell sailors that. The adventuresome ones go check them out." So it was Travis's duty to go into these places and roust out the U.S. sailors.[35]

From Norway the traveling Americans went

to Portland, England. When Musician Marty Thumudo, who grew up in Massachusetts, went ashore, he gained a new appreciation for why his region of the United States is known as New England. He noted many similarities, including names of towns identical to those he had encountered back home. He enjoyed playing darts in an English pub but was not as happy with the decidedly un-American custom of drinking warm beer. When he went aboard the last British battleship, HMS *Vanguard,* he enjoyed a spot of rum. In those days the Royal Navy still handed out grog to its ratings on a regular basis. Thumudo was struck by the fact that the *Vanguard* was not as clean as the *Missouri* was habitually kept. It was reminiscent of Ensign Jack Barron's impression when he went aboard the *King George V* off Japan in the summer of 1945.[36]

One group of midshipmen that went out sight-seeing included Staser Holcomb. The most fascinating thing they were invited to do was attend a luncheon along with the keeper of Queen Elizabeth's swans. The swans lived in the beautiful green countryside of southern England. To Holcomb, the pastoral tranquility of the area made it look as if things were still the way they had been for centuries. The mids also made their way to London on tour and enjoyed cut-rate admissions to West End shows. Mealtimes, on the other hand, were austere because the nation's food supply had not yet recovered from wartime. The best meal to hope for might be a piece of fish with sauce on it and some boiled potatoes.[37]

Part of the training regimen on board the battleship called for the midshipmen first class to shadow officers in the crew as a means of learning from them. For one-third of the cruise, for instance, Holcomb was the midshipman gunnery officer, the counterpart of the *Missouri*'s full-time gunnery officer, Commander Oscar Gray. Holcomb was responsible for training midshipman gun crews to prepare them for firing various mounts and turrets on board the ship. Initially, the midshipmen had dry runs for a few weeks, moving powder around and moving dummy projectiles in order to become familiar with the procedures. The payoff came

in using the midshipman crews during target practice as a means of measuring how well they had learned.[38]

When the *Missouri* and *Wisconsin* fired at targets near Guantánamo, Holcomb was in the armored gun control station on the 05 level. He stood side by side with Commander Gray as the two battleships fired their projectiles. Holcomb recalled of the *Missouri*'s gun boss: "What I saw of him was the very model of a wiry, competent, quiet professional. I hadn't been around people of his seniority very much as a midshipman. To watch a guy with that responsibility be as cool as he was, and delegate as well as he did, was a really good object lesson for me."[39]

All told, about three times as many third class midshipmen were on board as first classmen. The latter shadowed the *Missouri*'s

During the 1952 summer cruise, the *Missouri* carried West Point cadets along with the naval midshipmen. At left is Cadet E. L. Gallup; at right is Midshipman Frederick C. Andrews. (U.S. Navy photo in the National Archives: 80-G-444577)

officers and learned from them. They, in turn, supervised and helped train the third classmen. Holcomb concluded that the mids from the Naval Academy were considerably better prepared for the cruise experience than were their counterparts from civilian universities. When a given drill came up, the Annapolis men had a better idea of what to expect and how to cope with the challenges—primarily because they lived with naval subject matter seven days a week in Annapolis. The NROTC men were studying the Navy as one of several subjects in a broader curriculum.[40]

At times, the youthful midshipmen demonstrated a degree of immaturity. On one occasion, Electrician Dick Reisig had to do some repair work in one of the turret barbettes, working on a servo switch used to control the motions of the turret. He had one of the midshipmen stand by a DC controller panel near "Broadway" on the third deck. He told the midshipman to make sure that no one cut in any electricity on the panel while Reisig was working in the barbette. All of a sudden the electrician felt a strong shock as a shot of 440-volt DC power jolted him. Reisig discovered that the midshipman had turned on the electrical switch and left the control panel unattended. Reisig demanded an explanation from the midshipman, who said he had gotten tired of the chore and so went to get some coffee. Reisig, who had been hit by a surge of power, then proceeded to hit the inattentive midshipman himself, literally short-circuiting the official disciplinary chain of command.[41]

When he wasn't dealing with miscreant midshipmen, Reisig and others in the interior communications gang performed a variety of maintenance duties for equipment throughout the ship. They took care of the gyrocompasses and the circuits that connected the main gyros to the repeaters in various parts of the ship: the bridge, captain's sea cabin, combat information center, plotting rooms, directors, and so forth. They took care of the sound-powered telephones that were operated as the name implies. There was no external electrical source; rather, the impulse of an individual's voice activated contacts inside the mouthpiece to generate the necessary power. The ship had numerous sound-powered circuits and squawk boxes in addition to the regular dial telephone system. The IC electricians also maintained such diverse equipment as the anemometer cups topside that measured wind direction and speed, as well as salinity indicators that measured the percentage of salt in the boiler feedwater.[42]

After the training cruise was completed, the Missouri spent some time in the Norfolk Naval Shipyard, getting a final tune-up before a return engagement in Korea. By now all three of her Iowa-class sisters had been reactivated from the reserve fleet and went in rotation to the war zone. Soon it would be the Missouri's turn again, and she would have a new commanding officer when she went. On September 4, a bright, sunny day in Norfolk, Captain Warner Edsall relieved Captain Sylvester. The forty-eight-year-old Edsall brought a background in submarines, destroyers, and staff duty to the Missouri. He commanded the submarine S-34 before World War II; during the war he was skipper of the destroyer Melvin when she sank two Japanese submarines and a troop transport. He was Atlantic Fleet operations officer in the late 1940s, and just prior to joining the Missouri was on the joint staff that served the Joint Chiefs of Staff in Washington.[43]

A week after the change of command, the Missouri began her second deployment to Korea. On board for the leg that carried the ship to California were a number of guests of the secretary of the Navy. Included was a man from Springfield, Missouri, Ralph E. Truman, a cousin of the president. After she passed through the Panama Canal, the battleship steamed in company with the carrier Shangri-La during part of the voyage to Long Beach. She also put on a full-power run, cranking the main engines up to 32.4 knots.[44]

As the ship steamed westward, Ensign Treadwell was part of the rotation of officers who stood watch on the bridge. During one of those watches he heard Captain Edsall say, "It's great to be back to sea." This was somewhat difficult to understand for Treadwell, a young officer who was eager to be back home with his wife. Obviously, the perspective was different for someone of Edsall's seniority, especially after shore duty in Washington. There, an officer had to navigate a sea of paperwork; here, the skipper could give commands and feel the satisfaction of instant response.[45]

One of the quaint titles perpetuated on board the *Missouri* was that of the Marine Corps bugler. Corporal Harry Smith was known as a "field music." He joined the crew during the ship's brief visit to Long Beach and thereafter shared the bugling duties with a Navy enlisted man. Each had the duty for a twenty-four-hour period, every other day. The two of them stood their watches on the bridge while under way and on the quarterdeck in port. It was up to them to play the variety of calls that signaled events in the day's routine: reveille, call to colors, attention, chow call, commence ship's work, secure, taps, and a number of others. Probably the most dramatic was the call to battle stations—an urgent, attention-arresting melody that even now would be instantly recognized by a battleship man of that era.[46]

When Smith joined the ship's Marine detachment, he observed that some of the members were draftees and less than thrilled about serving on active duty. One small group of disaffected Marines, largely from New York, New Jersey, Pennsylvania, and New England, formed a clique. These men were inclined to start trouble—both verbal and physical—with their shipmates, especially the sailors. Part of their problem was that several of them seemed to be stuck at the private first class level and were disgruntled over not advancing more quickly. Essentially, the men had chips on their shoulders and were ready to take issue with those who were doing better than they were. The unhappy ones were relatively few, however; for the most part, the members of the detachment got along well with each other.[47]

The Marines and the rest of the ship's company proceeded to Hawaii, first for a stop at Pearl Harbor and then for some shore-bombardment refresher training, shooting at the island of Kahoolawe. In late October, the

Missouri arrived in Japan. Chief Gunner's Mate Jack McCarron was fortunate that a chief with whom he'd served previously was then on shore duty at Yokosuka. The other chief had a car, which was available for them to use in sightseeing around the country, including Tokyo and various other places.[48]

Visiting Japan was an interesting experience for McCarron, who, on December 7, 1941, had been manning a 5-inch/25-caliber antiaircraft gun on the battleship *Arizona*. An explosion blew him over the side, leaving him badly burned. Now, nearly a dozen years later, he was controlling a battery of 5-inch/38-caliber dual-purpose guns in another battleship. Unlike a number of Pearl Harbor survivors who have harbored a sense of bitterness to this day, McCarron felt no hatred toward the Japanese. He was interested in meeting them and seeing their country and was, in fact, impressed by how quickly Tokyo had been rebuilt in the years since the war ended.[49]

All told, Chief McCarron stayed in the *Mis-*

Captain Warner Edsall, seen here at the desk in his in-port cabin, took command of the *Missouri* shortly before her second deployment to Korea. (U.S. Navy photo in the National Archives: 80-G-641309)

souri for about five years—from 1949 until shortly before she was decommissioned. Part of the reason for the long tour of duty was that he was comfortable with both the ship and his fellow residents in the chiefs' mess. Nearly one hundred men lived there and developed a genuine camaraderie. McCarron concluded that the *Missouri* had the best chiefs' mess in the Navy in terms of food. They had a talented cook who fed them as well as guests in the finest hotels.

After dinner the chiefs played pinochle, watched movies, and talked. The talk was the kind that develops among friends who have gotten to know each other well through long association, knowing each others' habits, quirks, families, and interests. The conversations were on a professional level as well, discussing the events in the life of the ship, problems in dealing with personnel, equipment, or the operational situation. For men such as Jack McCarron, the niche in the chiefs' quarters was a comfortable one, and thus he was happy to stay in it year after year.[50]

While the *Missouri* was in Yokosuka, she was moored alongside the *Iowa* so the Seventh Fleet staff could move from one flagship to the other. The latest resident in the flag quarters was Vice Admiral Joseph J. "Jocko" Clark, who had demonstrated considerable aggressiveness as a carrier task group commander in World War II. He exercised that same aggressiveness in Korea, getting the ship into action on numerous occasions once she reached the war zone. As in 1950–51, the *Missouri* divided her time between formation steaming with Task Force 77 and shore bombardment operations. The latter by now were known as "Cobra strikes." For the next several months, primarily off Korea's east coast, the fleet flagship bombarded such places as Tanchon, Wonsan, Chongjin, Songjin, Chaho, Hamhung, Hungnam, and Kojo. In between were regular visits to Sasebo, Japan, primarily to rearm with the 16-inch ammunition that was not readily transferred at sea.

The ship was moored to a buoy at Sasebo on November 10, the Marine Corps' birthday. Instead of having to go through the regular chow line, the members of the Marine detachment got a special dinner in a side room off the mess compartment. Captain Edsall joined the

The *Missouri* (*left*) and the *Iowa* lie moored to a buoy at Yokosuka, Japan, in October 1952 to facilitate the transfer of the Seventh Fleet commander and staff. The *Missouri*, which originally had a wraparound shield for the 20-mm guns on her bow, by this time had a different design from her sister. She also still had small hull numbers, which were replaced by the larger ones soon after she began Seventh Fleet operations. (U.S. Navy photo in the National Archives: 80-G-447941)

Marines for the steak dinner. Meanwhile, the sailors had to pass by the doorway to that room as they were getting their own chow, which wasn't as glamorous as the Marines' birthday fare. That didn't sit too well with the Navy men. That night First Lieutenant Robert Dern, commanding officer of the detachment, arranged for a birthday ball ashore in Sasebo.[51]

Afterward, everyone gathered at the fleet landing for the return to the ship. There were probably three times as many sailors as Marines. The sailors were still unhappy about what they perceived as special treatment for the Marines, and a scuffle erupted. The fighting then moved into the landing craft that was taking the men back to the ship. The ensign in charge of the boat fired his .45 pistol into the air in an unsuccessful attempt to restore order. Once the unhappy men reached the ship, duty masters-at-arms were waiting for them and quickly shoved them off in the direction of their respective berthing compartments.[52]

Others went touring while the *Missouri* was in the Japanese port, taking a bus trip over to Nagasaki. That had been the site of an American atomic bomb dropped on August 9, 1945. Corporal Smith and his *Missouri* shipmates were there seven years after the bomb had hit and found a good deal of devastation still unrepaired. They saw craters and some buildings that were standing, but they were just shells. Electronics Technician John McHugh found a church that had statues next to it. Each statue was two colors: the side facing the direction of the atomic bomb had turned white; the other side was the original gray. Many of the Japanese had little smiles on their faces as they contemplated the visiting Americans. Corporal Smith wondered what thoughts lay behind those smiles.[53]

Musician Second Class Tom Allen was a member of the *Missouri*'s band. During his trips ashore in Sasebo, he enjoyed going to bars and nightclubs. He was used to the old dime-a-dance routine in the United States in which a man bought a string of tickets and then used them one at a time to line up dances with the girls who worked in the place. One night he was particularly enamored of a beautiful Japanese girl and handed her a large number of tickets so he could essentially stake his claim to her companionship for longer than a single dance.[54]

Allen, who was with a shipmate and that man's girl, was having a great time until three Japanese men walked in—two large and one small. Allen's date immediately got up and left to join the three Japanese men. Allen was understandably unhappy, because he hadn't yet received his money's worth for all the tickets he had turned over to the beautiful girl. He was about to retrieve her when the other girl at the table restrained him, suggesting that the small Japanese man was a local gangster, essentially the Al Capone of Sasebo—not someone to mess with. Allen left the nightclub and never went back.[55]

Another liberty port was Pusan, South Korea, where Electronics Technician McHugh found an enjoyable reception ashore. While in town he met some of the Army men stationed there. As soon as they learned he was from the *Missouri,* they sought to find ways to express their gratitude for what the ship had done on the battle front. The soldiers' outfit was pinned down by North Korean shelling, and then the battleship arrived on the scene. At the time of the action, McHugh had heard no feedback on the effects of the *Missouri*'s shooting. The generous reaction of these soldiers told him it had been most effective. They broke out steaks and drinks and even shared the contents of goody packages their mothers had sent from home.[56]

On November 20, during the visit to Pusan, the ship's crew manned the rail in honor of President Syngman Rhee of South Korea. It was a three-ring-circus event for the individuals who specialized in honors and ceremonies, including the navigator, officer of the deck, ship's band, and the Marine bugler, Harry Smith. Admirals, generals, and diplomats—every dignitary within miles—came aboard the ship that day, both to see and to be seen. Some arrived at the quarterdeck via the accommodation ladder, which was abreast the surrender deck forward. Others landed on the fantail by helicopter.

The *Missouri*'s welcoming party had to rush back and forth. When an individual or group stepped onto the deck, Corporal Smith blew

the racks mounted on the inside of the cylindrical metal shield surrounding the quadruple mount. He then handed the projectiles to the first loader, who used two hands to drop the clip into the breech of the gun itself. The inside of the gun tub was kept stocked with projectiles so the guns would be ready to go at a moment's notice. This was necessary for the 40-mm guns because, unlike the 16-inch and 5-inch guns, there was no direct link to the magazines for a steady supply of ammunition.[59]

One of the fascinating experiences for Thumudo came during night watches while the ship was operating around Wonsan. He saw carrier planes come in and drop tanks of jellied gasoline, known as napalm. The darkness lit up with a flash of orange flame. Woe betide any enemy soldiers unfortunate enough to be showered with that fiery hell. For the *Missouri* men, safe on board their fortress-like ship, it was an interesting diversion from their routine. In fact, because of the virtual absence of an air threat, the routine produced little real use for the 40-mm gunners. Thus, it was particularly frustrating to stand such watches during the Korean winter, especially when a steady mist fell and produced icicles on the equipment.[60]

That kind of weather—along with the fatiguing routine of dawn-and-dusk alerts when the *Missouri* was at sea—did not agree with Ensign Treadwell's respiratory system. He had to stand bridge watches day after day in the cold wind; to him Korea was "the coldest place in the world" during the winter. For months during the deployment he had a cold he just couldn't shake off. The ship's store sold handkerchiefs, and he went through about three dozen of them as the weeks passed.[61]

The *Missouri* had a firing mission near Taedol-li, Korea, on December 21. The ship's Marine detachment had a new executive officer, First Lieutenant Rex Ellison, who had been on board only a few days. Normally, the skipper of the detachment and a noncommissioned officer would go up with a Navy pilot to do the spotting for the main battery from an HO3S helicopter. On this day, the commanding officer of the detachment, Lieutenant Dern, wanted to take his new exec up for indoctrina-

On November 20, 1952, the crew manned the rail while at Pusan, South Korea, for a visit by that nation's president, Syngman Rhee.
(U.S. Navy photo in the National Archives: 80-G-449191)

"attention" on the bugle, and the band followed up with the appropriate number of ruffles and flourishes. National anthems were part of it as well. After tours of the ship, the whole sequence had to be done in reverse.[57] Musician Marty Thumudo, who alternated between a saxophone and clarinet while playing with the ship's band, was less than enthusiastic about these honors and ceremonies, particularly as the days got colder. The reed on his instrument almost froze to his mouth at times because of the temperature.[58]

Thumudo had a much different job whenever the *Missouri*'s guns were manned at sea. He was a first loader on the 40-mm gun mount atop turret two. The job of the second loader was to take the clips of four projectiles out of

tion. After the ship had fired a salvo, the men in the helo radioed a message to say that they were going in for a damage assessment. Corporal Smith heard the helo's transmission as it arrived on the *Missouri*'s bridge. The next thing he heard was static, because the helicopter was down. Further attempts to contact the craft were futile.[62]

The HO3S had crashed about five hundred yards from the shore, in the vicinity of a railroad tunnel. The cause of the crash was not ascertained. No enemy antiaircraft batteries were known to be in the area. Once the contact was lost, the *Missouri* launched a second helo to fly to the scene. The pilot, Lieutenant W. P. Jensen, saw a seat cushion and rotor blade on the water. And he saw the body of the first helicopter's pilot, recently married Ensign Robert Mayhew. Later, the destroyer *Harry E. Hubbard* sent out a motor whaleboat to look for the bodies of the two passengers. The boat crew used grappling hooks to drag the bottom but couldn't find the Marines' bodies. The mission ended when the boat was subjected to enemy small-arms fire from ashore.[63]

While Jensen's helicopter was at the scene, a member of the crew tied a line around Mayhew's body and he was hoisted up. The men in the helo were not able to pull the body all the way into the fuselage, so Mayhew was suspended from the plane as it returned to the *Missouri*. Corporal Smith had a sickened feeling as he watched the HO3S come back aboard with the corpse of one of his shipmates hanging below it. Electronics Technician Lew Travis, who happened to be on the bridge, noticed that Captain Edsall was crying.[64]

At that point, all of the ship's Marines were called below and ordered to put on their packs, helmets, bayonets, and the rest of their combat gear. They were issued ammunition for their rifles and were ready to engage the enemy. The *Missouri* prepared to lower away boats to send the Marine landing party ashore. As Harry Smith reported later, Admiral Clark received information that sending in the detachment would be essentially suicidal, so he called it off. Sergeant Major J. D. Briscoe, who was the senior surviving member of the detachment, was angry and frustrated. He was "cussing a blue streak" as he paced up and down in front of the formation of Marines gathered before him on the ship's deck.[65]

The loss of the three men had an emotional impact on the rest of the crew as well. The war produced thousands of casualties on the ground in Korea, but the *Missouri* herself was insulated from such dangers because of her position offshore, out of reach of the enemy. Lieutenant (j.g.) Jack Zeldes stood watches as lookout officer on the 011 level and up to that time had been nonchalant because he knew the North Koreans had no air force to speak of. Fear had not been a part of the crew's mindset. But now death had visited the helicopter, which was an extension of the ship, and the ship's crew felt the hurt.[66]

During the times when the *Missouri* operated with Task Force 77, Chief Jack McCarron was impressed by the performance of the carrier aviators, especially when the seas were rough and the weather was cold. The planes had to find their way back to the carriers and land on decks that were pitching and rolling with the action of the waves. McCarron stood watches in Sky Three, a Mark 37 director that con-

Saluting on the battleship's fantail during the rendering of honors are Lieutenant General Maxwell Taylor, commanding general, Eighth Army, and Vice Admiral Jocko Clark, commander, Seventh Fleet. Later, during the Kennedy administration, Taylor served as chairman of the Joint Chiefs of Staff. (U.S. Navy photo in the National Archives: 80-G-641293)

Turret two unleashes a projectile while at Wonsan, North Korea. (U.S. Navy photo in the Naval Institute collection)

trolled the 5-inch guns on the starboard side. He remembered watching the pilots approach those heaving decks. "I'd be looking through the binoculars, and I'd be saying a prayer for them—and with them, probably—with my fingers crossed, looking at them landing on the carrier."[67]

Watches seemed awfully long during the cold winter days and nights off Korea. Despite the low probability of an attack that would necessitate use of the *Missouri*'s 5-inch guns, part of the battery had to be manned during condition watches. That meant McCarron was in a chilly director, trying to keep warm, trying to keep awake, and trying to keep men prepared for action if need be. Fortunately, a kind soul deep in the ship was helping everyone pass the long, slow hours of watchful waiting. Often the

sound that went through the sound-powered telephones was entertaining music—perhaps a song by Doris Day or another popular vocalist of the day. Someone in a plotting room or the interior communications shop or elsewhere in the *Missouri* was playing records for his shipmates.[68]

During those hitches with the carrier task force, the practice was for some of the department heads to stand command duty officer watch on the bridge. Essentially, the department heads were stand-ins for the captain so they could provide senior-officer supervision to the officers of the deck without the necessity for Captain Edsall to be on the bridge all the time. Lieutenant (j.g.) Ace Treadwell found Commander Gray, the *Missouri*'s gunnery officer, to be something of a bully when he was in the command duty role. The situation was challenging enough as it was: steaming around in formation at twenty-five knots; looking frequently at the radar scope to maintain station because the ships operated at night with no lights showing; and listening to radio transmissions that combined static with a variety of messages from various sources, including Task Force 77 and the Seventh Fleet staff. Years later Treadwell remembered that these were "hairy operations."[69]

Gray added to Treadwell's information overload by peppering him with frequent comments and questions. One day the *Missouri* was turning as part of the overall formation, and Gray was heckling the officer of the deck about the amount of rudder he was using. Treadwell finally responded: "Commander, I'm doing the best I can with what I've got. I wish you'd get off my back." From that point on, Gray no longer bothered him.[70]

On January 20, 1953, Dwight D. Eisenhower took the oath as president, replacing the *Missouri*'s friend, Harry S Truman. The ship was much too far away for him to say good-bye personally. His successor, an Army general in World War II, had pledged to end the war in Korea as soon as possible.

On February 13, the *Missouri* got a new executive officer in the person of Commander

James R. "Bob" North. The previous exec, Commander James E. Smith, was a genial type. His successor was a demanding individual, much closer to the stereotype of an executive officer. One of North's practices, for example, was to get up at reveille and go out on deck to ensure that the deck was being swept and swabbed. Soon he directed his subordinate officers from the gunnery department to be up and out there with him, earlier than they were probably used to getting up.[71]

The firing missions continued as the new year progressed. On a number of occasions during the deployment, the *Missouri* and other warships went into the large harbor at Wonsan, which was an important industrial and transportation center. They sent thousands of projectiles ashore as part of the effort to disrupt support of the North Korean war effort. On March 5, as the battleship was turning around to come back out of the harbor, her gun batteries were almost completely masked—both of the forward turrets and all the 5-inch mounts. The only guns that could bear on targets ashore were those of turret three. At that moment, when the *Missouri* had the least ability to respond, North Korean shore battery fire started coming at her.

The enemy projectiles were fuzed to burst in the air. The result was that some shrapnel fell onto the main deck aft, although the ship did not receive a direct hit, nor was she damaged. On the bridge Corporal Smith and several others hit the deck, lest something hit them. It was the first time during the war that the ship had been under enemy fire. The *Missouri* continued turning so she could unmask her entire broadside gun battery, and then she unleashed salvos at the shore batteries. The ship estimated the enemy guns to have been 76-mm and 105-mm artillery pieces; they fired twelve rounds, all told.[72]

At the time of the shooting, Lieutenant (j.g.) Art Ward was down in the aft secondary battery plotting room, the one near turret three. He heard the explosions, which were separated from him by several steel decks. Some crew members went out to harvest pieces of the shrapnel, somewhat in the manner that their

predecessors had when the kamikaze hit the ship in 1945. In this case the souvenir hunters were admonished, because they would have been vulnerable to subsequent rounds.[73]

On March 10, also at Wonsan, the *Missouri* was again fired upon from shore. This time there were seventeen rounds from three North Korean positions, probably from 105-mm guns. As before, Lieutenant Ward was in the secondary battery plot. He had been frustrated on previous trips into the cul-de-sac harbor because the 5-inch batteries were often muzzled. The distance to the targets ashore was considered too great for their effective range, which was in the neighborhood of fifteen- to sixteen-thousand yards—less than half of that for the big guns.

Empty 5-inch shell casings litter the deck after heavy firing at Wonsan in March 1953. On March 10, the 5-inch battery fired just two rounds short of one thousand as part of the retaliation for gunfire directed at the *Missouri* by North Korean shore batteries. (U.S. Navy photo in the National Archives: 80-G-480989)

But Ward and his people had been tracking possible targets anyway. The fire-control radars were locked on, and the range keepers were generating fire-control solutions. Permission to open fire came just as the ship was fired upon. The gun control officer complimented the secondary battery for the alacrity of its response. The 5-inchers put on quite a show that day, pumping out 998 rounds. In the entire deployment, the second most prolific day for the 5-inch guns was January 31—a far-distant second at 307.[74]

Lieutenant Jack Zeldes was the ship's public information officer during the deployment to Korea. One of his duties was editing *The Mo News*, a small daily newspaper compiled from wire-service reports. The paper reached the crew each morning at breakfast. One issue—of which Zeldes was particularly proud—reported an event that occurred in early March in Moscow, the death of Soviet dictator Joseph Stalin. Using the best tabloid style in presenting the obituary, Zeldes composed a pithy headline: "RED HEAD DEAD."[75]

Zeldes was also editor of the cruisebook, although his assistant, Ensign Robin Westbrook, did most of the hands-on work. One of the book's highlights was an aerial photo, in color, that showed turret one firing a three-gun salvo. That was about a ten-thousand-dollar photo, considering the price of powder and projectiles at the time. In all, the book was filled with excellent photographic coverage of the Far East deployment but skimpy on narrative and photo captions. The rationale was that the crew members had lived through these things, so they knew what the photos depicted. More than forty years after the fact, though, Zeldes expressed some regret that the text hadn't been more thorough. The memories that were so fresh in 1953 have now faded considerably.[76]

It happened that Zeldes did have one memory problem at that time as well. He was given leave from the ship to take a suitcase containing the photos and layouts to the printing company in Tokyo. He carried everything with him on board a Japanese train but then blithely forgot the suitcase when he got off. He had a terrible sinking feeling as he stood on the railroad platform and realized that he was empty-handed. With a combination of gestures and pidgin English, he was able to communicate his problem to the Japanese railroad officials. They then called ahead to the next station and had the material rescued. It was an interesting reaction for a people whose surrender was depicted in the historical section of the book Zeldes and his staff had created.[77]

On 9:45 on the morning of March 25, the *Missouri* completed her final gunfire mission of the war. She bombarded targets in the vicinity of Kojo, a short distance south of Wonsan on the east coast of North Korea. Her tally for that final day of shooting was 102 rounds of 16-inch and 61 rounds of 5-inch. That day's output brought the total of rounds expended in gunfire missions during the second Korean deployment to 3,861 for the big guns and 4,379 for the smaller ones. As mentioned in the previous chapter, the *Missouri*'s totals for the first deployment to Korea were 2,895 of 16-inch and 8,043 of 5-inch. The numbers for 1952–53 reflected Captain Edsall's philosophy that the big guns had the far greater potential for effectiveness than the 5-inch, particularly against the targets that were farther away and on the reverse slopes of hillsides. Wonsan was one of the few places where the 5-inch could get close enough, and even then nearly one-fourth of all the 5-inch projectiles for the entire deployment were fired in one day, March 10, when the battleship was responding to shore batteries.[78]

After the last bombardment, the *Missouri* headed back to Sasebo one final time so she could pick up her boats, which had been offloaded there for the duration of the operations off Korea. On the morning of March 26, the *Missouri* approached Sasebo harbor. Captain Edsall was on the 04-level bridge, binoculars strapped around his neck as he gave orders for course and speed. The harbor entrance was guarded by antisubmarine nets, and the opening through which the battleship was to pass was relatively narrow. The problem was further complicated by a good deal of traffic, as fishing boats darted to and fro.

Lieutenant Ward had observed previously that the captain got excited by all these maneuvers and was not his usual calm self as he tried to avoid the smaller vessels. The course to go through the opening in the nets required a large turn. At 7:21 A.M., just after the skipper had given the order to the helm, he grasped the arm of Commander Bob North, the executive officer, and collapsed to the deck—no longer breathing. North quickly took over the conn. As North was maneuvering the *Missouri* to her mooring buoy, medical personnel were summoned. At 7:30 they pronounced Captain Edsall dead of a heart attack.[79]

Throughout the crew of the huge battleship the reaction was one of shock. Lew Travis was struck by how downcast his shipmates were at the news of the skipper's death. Edsall was actually a remote individual to almost all of them; their contacts with the captain were fleeting, if at all. But he was the father figure, the man who spoke to them over the general announcing system, who conned the ship and set the

Left: Captain Warner Edsall died on the bridge of the *Missouri* the day after the ship completed her final firing mission of the Korean War. (U.S. Navy photo in the National Archives: 80-G-641289)

Below: The crew of the *Missouri* gathers on the fantail to attend a memorial service for Captain Edsall at Sasebo on March 26, 1953, the day of his death. (U.S. Navy photo in the National Archives: 80-G-641294)

Chief petty officers carry Edsall's corpse in a Stokes stretcher as they proceed down an accommodation ladder that will take the body ashore, thence by air to Yokosuka. (U.S. Navy photo in the National Archives: 80-G-641295)

overall tone for the battleship *Missouri*. They had grown accustomed to his leadership, and now he was gone. That afternoon the men of the *Missouri* held a memorial service on the fantail for their dead skipper.[80]

Once the service was over, a group of chief petty officers served as pallbearers to carry Captain Edsall's body down the accommodation ladder to a waiting boat. Lieutenant Ward then escorted the body from Sasebo to Yokosuka. It was a chilly flight in a Navy flying boat. His duties concluded when he turned the body over to the naval hospital at Yokosuka, whence it was flown back to the United States for burial.[81]

Commander North took the ship to Yokosuka, where she moored to a buoy and awaited

the arrival of sister ship *New Jersey* to come alongside and take Admiral Clark and his Seventh Fleet staff aboard. The *Missouri* was also waiting for a new commanding officer to fill the void left by Edsall's passing. Captain Robert Brodie, Jr., took command on April 4. Lieutenant Ward was a Naval Academy classmate of Captain Brodie's son. He had learned, probably through that connection, that the new captain had always wanted to serve as skipper of a battleship. Edsall's death presented that opportunity.

Brodie was on duty in the office of the deputy chief of naval operations for operations in Washington, D. C., when the news came. In less than a week, he had been relieved and was on his way to the Far East to take over. Brodie, who came equipped with a walrus-style mustache, had a long career in destroyers. He had earned the Navy Cross for his exploits as skipper of the four-piper *Dallas* during the occupation of French Morocco in November 1942. Later, he commanded the destroyers *Ordronaux* and *Haynsworth* and Destroyer Squadron Eleven.[82]

There was to be no combat for the *Missouri* under Captain Brodie's direction. The last firing mission under Edsall had been the last one scheduled for the ship on that deployment. Thus, the *Missouri* ended her participation in a second war, not that far removed geographically from the one in which she had fought in 1945. During the first six months—the summer and fall of 1950—the Korean War was one of movement. After that it had settled into a frustrating stalemate. In July 1953, a few months after the *Missouri* got back home to Norfolk, an armistice was concluded in far-off Panmunjom, Korea. The line of demarcation dividing North Korea from South Korea was not all that far from the 38th parallel of latitude that had been the division before the war started. The armistice settlement essentially maintained the antebellum status quo.

President Truman's two main objectives at the outset of the war had been fulfilled. The sovereignty of South Korea had been preserved, and the war had been contained within the Korean peninsula. Truman had not per-

On April 4, Captain Robert Brodie, Jr., reads his orders while taking command of the *Missouri* at Yokosuka, Japan. At left is Vice Admiral Joseph J. "Jocko" Clark, commander Seventh Fleet. (U.S. Navy photo in the National Archives: 80-G-641298)

mitted offensive action to extend into Red China because he did not want the conflict to become a tinderbox for the outbreak of World War III. If anything, the Korean War ended in a draw. The U. S. battleships had made useful contributions, but they had not participated in a decisive victory of the kind experienced in World War II.

Fire Controlman Amory Houghton, who was a member of the crew during the *Missouri*'s first cruise to Korea, probably spoke for many when he said: "There was a certain amount of John Wayne-ism that was created in all of us. . . . Hence, there were certain frustrations that we did not take greater action. . . . I don't think we had the frustrations of the Vietnam War, in terms of the massive opposition to us, or the attitudes of the public. . . . I think there was a lot of benign neglect as far as Korea was concerned. We came back, went home, and that was it."[83]

The *Missouri* and *New Jersey* lie moored together at Yokosuka in early April while Vice Admiral Clark transfers his flag to the latter. (U.S. Navy photo in the National Archives: 80-G-645099)

10 ❖ The Long Farewell

June 1953–February 1955

On the first Saturday in June 1953, Annapolis Roads had some unaccustomed visitors. Normally, merchant ships going between Norfolk and Baltimore plied the deep waters of the Chesapeake Bay off Annapolis. Sailboats and power boats also frequented the area. On this particular morning the gray shapes of men-of-war accompanied those pleasure boats: the battleships *Missouri* and *Wisconsin*, the heavy cruisers *Macon* and *Albany*, and destroyers. Landing craft made trips back and forth from the ships to the seawall bordering the U.S. Naval Academy.[1]

Ashore, hundreds of midshipmen were gathered near the mast of the old coastal battleship *Maine*, a monument at one end of the seawall. An explosion had sunk her in Havana harbor in 1898, precipitating the Spanish-American War. Her mast was about all that remained. After stealing a few last-minute kisses

with girlfriends, the midshipmen embarked for the ride out to the warships of a modern generation. The young men were joined by cargo nets full of seabags, lifted into the landing craft by a diesel-powered crane. The Naval Academy band serenaded the departing mids with tunes that evoked the destination of those gray ships in the roadstead: "Brazil" and "The Carioca." Girlfriends waved from the seawall until the boats were too far away for them to recognize their men.

Once the men and cargo were loaded on board, the ships weighed anchor and headed south to Norfolk to meet up with the aircraft carrier *Saipan*, fleet oilers, a submarine, and the tin cans that would comprise the rest of the midshipman squadron. Then they were off to South America.[2]

As the *Missouri* and the ships in company headed south, the temperature became in-

While the *Missouri* lies anchored off Annapolis in June 1953, engineers below decks blow boiler tubes and send black smoke skyward. The ship loads midshipmen from a landing craft alongside. (U.S. Navy photo in the National Archives: 80-G-626645)

creasingly warmer. Crew members and midshipmen went out on deck to sunbathe and get their tans ready for the Brazilian beaches. Sometimes they got beet red as a result. Berthing compartments were not air-conditioned, so at night men slept clad only in skivvy shorts and sweat. While many slept, others were standing watches through the night—on the bridge, in radio central, in the combat information center, down in the engineering spaces. Sometimes the men of the A division, in charge of maintaining auxiliary equipment throughout the ship, ate supplemental meals during the night to break the monotony. Since they were in charge of the ship's ice-making machines and refrigeration equipment, they had keys and access to the food supply.[3]

As the *Missouri* approached the equator, the shellbacks on board prepared to dish it out to the pollywogs, just as a previous crew had done during the 1947 trip to Rio de Janeiro. In this case merely three hundred of the twenty-two hundred men on board had been initiated previously. With their six-to-one numerical advantage, the pollywogs launched a preemptive strike the night before. When they spotted shellbacks topside, they doused them with fire hoses. Below decks they stuck them in cold showers, uniforms and all. The shellbacks, of course, got the last laughs and the last whacks on the day of initiation. They used two-foot-

long shillelaghs, made from canvas and stuffed with rags. It was a typical line-crossing initiation made unusual by the size of the midshipman training task force. All told, the formation included twenty-six ships, and all killed their engines and lay dead in the water as the games proceeded.[4]

On the morning of June 27, midshipmen and ship's crew members went topside for the arrival at Rio de Janeiro. They were dressed in blue uniforms because it was winter in the Southern Hemisphere. The men on deck looked with appreciation as they swept past Copacabana Beach, art-deco apartment buildings, Sugar Loaf Mountain (which looked to Midshipman Bob Rogers like "a gigantic, granite-gray potato jammed into a verdant point of land"), and the impressive mountaintop Christ of the Andes statue with its outstretched arms. The women of Rio knew that the *Missouri* had arrived. Division officers talked to their men at quarters, advising them what to do and not to do when ashore. Among other things, they warned the midshipmen and crew that this wasn't like the United States. In Brazil, the respectable girls would be bringing their chaperones along on dates. That led one man to blurt out, "Who wants a respectable girl anyway?"[5]

Bob Rogers and Jay Smith were two midshipmen engaged to girls back in the States, so they weren't on the prowl when they began exploring Rio. Their uniforms attracted attention from those ashore, and they happily accepted an invitation to visit a Brazilian home. It was not that much different from one they would find in the United States, except that the bathroom was equipped with a bidet in addition to the usual toilet. It was a seatless, porcelain bowl with three valves at the rear. Rogers had heard that such contraptions were popular in Europe and decided to see how it worked. He turned on one of the faucets and set off a geyser of water that sprayed his forehead, the ceiling, and the walls before he could get it shut off. It took a while for Rogers and Smith to get the mess dried up, leading the hosts to wonder why North Americans needed twenty minutes in the bathroom.[6]

South American beef was one of the great

An LCM landing craft from the attack transport *Botetourt* lies alongside as its human cargo climb aboard the *Missouri* for the summer's midshipman cruise. (U.S. Navy photo in the National Archives: 80-G-482673)

attractions in Rio, and the men of the *Missouri* indulged themselves. In one restaurant Corporal Harry Smith ordered steak and eggs. The waiter brought a large platter: a big steak covered one half and a huge egg the other. It was an ostrich egg, which tasted to him about the same as a chicken's.[7]

Electrician's Mate Tom O'Malley had a special advantage in Rio de Janeiro. He had a cousin who was married to a Brazilian man, and they put him up in their apartment. They also had a friend who supplied him with a tuxedo for his stay in the city. Thus it was that O'Malley had something to wear when he crashed a military ball in Brazil's principal port. The ball was for the officers and midshipmen of the visiting American task force, not the enlisted men. O'Malley pretended to have congressional connections in order to get a ticket. During his stay in the city, O'Malley took some leave and had a great time living in his cousin's apartment, dating airline stewardesses, and driving around the city in a borrowed car.

When the last night came, the *Missouri*'s crew members were—like Cinderella—due back on board by midnight. O'Malley announced that he was enjoying Brazil too much to leave. Wearing his tuxedo and filled with liquid cheer, O'Malley went down to the officers' landing to say good-bye to Lieutenant (j.g.) Tony Suraci, an officer in the *Missouri*'s gunnery department. Both were from Scranton, Pennsylvania, and Suraci was dating O'Malley's sister, so they had become friends. O'Malley shook hands with Suraci as he was saying good-bye.[8]

When the officer took hold of the enlisted man's hand, he yanked on it and pulled him into the boat, then ordered the coxswain to head for the *Missouri*. He had shanghaied O'Malley to keep him from getting into serious trouble for missing the ship's departure. Suraci was acting in his friend's best interests by keeping him from doing something stupid. Once O'Malley got back aboard, his shipmates helped him down to his berthing compartment. Word of the electrician's mate's attempted defection never got to the executive officer or captain, but he did scrub quite a few garbage cans to make up for his misdeeds. Had the ship left

Rear Admiral E. T. Wooldridge (*right*) makes a speech to the crew of the *Missouri* in connection with the equator-crossing ceremony en route to Brazil. In the center is Captain Robert Brodie, the battleship's skipper. (Courtesy of Robert Brodie III)

without him, the punishment would have been far worse.[9]

The task group of ships began heading north to make the long journey home. The *Missouri* stopped for a time in Panama, where both midshipmen and crew members were able to observe the workings of the canal. Then they went on to the vicinity of Cuba for more gunnery practice. One fillip this time was a break in the shipboard routine for the members of the *Missouri*'s Marine detachment. They went ashore on Cuba with their field packs and weapons to do some land-warfare training. In fact, the objective of the maneuvers was to conduct a mock battle with the Marine detachment from the *Wisconsin*. Corporal Smith concluded that the training hadn't really accomplished a great deal, but presumably it amounted to checking off a box on someone's master plan.[10]

On August 2, the ships of the training squadron were on the final leg of their journey home, just two days before ending the cruise. That afternoon the destroyer escort *Thaddeus Parker* steamed alongside the *Missouri* to starboard for a high-line transfer. The battleship's band was gathered on deck, and it appeared to Midshipman Rogers that this was not a routine transfer. Among the other spectators was Rear Admiral E. T. Wooldridge, embarked in the

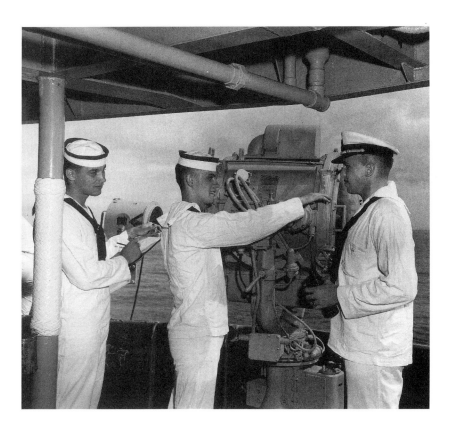

Midshipmen use a twenty-four-inch light for signaling practice during the 1953 cruise. Pictured (*left to right*) are: Peter W. Sandusky, Edward H. Browne, and Robert F. Rigling. (U.S. Navy photo in the National Archives: 80-G-633588)

Finally, the crews on board both ships got the lines under control. The soaked civilian official returned to the *Missouri* and went to sick bay for repairs. He soon sported a head bandage because of an abrasion on his forehead, and he had a sprained right shoulder as well. Admiral Wooldridge, who had, naturally, wanted to make a good impression on the visiting dignitary, was horrified by the turn of events. He was profuse in his apologies to the assistant secretary. Nash had been a naval reserve officer in World War II, reaching the rank of captain, so he undoubtedly understood that these things sometimes happened. Soon afterward, the *Missouri* pulled in at Norfolk, and the cruise was over. Secretary Nash walked ashore to complete his brief journey.[12]

A few months after the dunking incident, Lieutenant Jack Zeldes wrote a letter to the *Missouri*'s skipper. Captain Brodie had asked Zeldes for his assessments of the ship and her personnel as he left for civilian life. The twenty-three-year-old reservist could afford to be candid because he wasn't concerned about future promotions. In part, he wrote, "After eighteen months in public information work in the Navy, I've come to the conclusion that the PI function should be eliminated from the naval establishment." His contention was that the Navy was using taxpayers' money to advertise the Navy to those same taxpayers. It released "the news of which we are proud" but didn't bother to report on such embarrassments as giving an unexpected bath to an assistant secretary of defense.[13]

Missouri in his capacity as type commander and head of the training task group. Assistant Secretary of Defense Frank C. Nash had come aboard in Cuba, and he was to be transferred to the smaller ship for an inspection and a chance to visit with the crew. He donned an orange life jacket over his pressed suit. As Nash was sent out in a cage-like transfer chair from the side of the *Missouri*, he was suspended in midair between the two ships.[11]

Some of the devilish sailors on board the battleship secretly hoped that the secretary would get his shiny shoes wet. They got even more than they bargained for. The *Parker* sheered in to port, moving closer to the battleship. That caused the high line to droop. The line handlers on deck didn't take out the slack quickly enough, and the secretary was dunked into the sea. Admiral Wooldridge leaped immediately into action, barking orders at the line handlers down on deck. They overreacted, pulling back hard to take the slack out of the line. As they did so, the *Parker* moved back the other way, sending the secretary and the chair shooting upward as if shot from a bow.

That summer, after the cruise concluded, Lieutenant (j.g.) Dan Williams of the Navy's medical service corps reported to the *Missouri*. As part of the check-in process, Williams met Captain Brodie and found that the skipper liked to toss a question at newly arrived officers during his welcome-aboard interviews. Along with getting to know the newcomers, Brodie would point at the Latin motto on the Missouri state seal: *Salus Populi Suprema Lex Esto*. Brodie asked the new officer to translate the state's motto into English, which few could. It meant, "The welfare of the people shall be the supreme law." Those who could translate it correctly made points with the skipper, whom Williams found to be a quiet, studious man. He was friendly, easygoing, and not so forceful as other officers whom Williams encountered.[14]

In August and September, the *Missouri* spent some time pierside in Norfolk and also went out to the Virginia Capes operating area for training exercises. That October the *Missouri* steamed to the Caribbean in company with other ships to participate in a training exercise known as Operation Springboard. By then she had a new admiral on board. Admiral Wooldridge had transferred to the *Albany*, and one of his subordinates boarded the *Missouri*. He was Rear Admiral Clark Green, commander Battleship Division Two, which was made up of the four ships of the *Iowa* class.

During her career the *Missouri* had served as the flagship of numerous commanders: for both the Atlantic and Pacific Fleets; in combat for the Third, Fifth, and Seventh Fleets; for the First and Second Fleets off the coasts of the United States and the Twelfth Fleet in the Mediterranean; for the battleship and cruiser type command in the Atlantic Fleet; and for many special task forces, particularly for midshipman training. This exercise in the fall of 1953 was among the very few times she had been flagship of a battleship division, one of the basic administrative units in the fleet for decades, going back to the beginning of the century.

Many of the members of the Korean War crew had left by then, so the training period was an indoctrination for their replacements. Having completed the exercises around Cuba and the Virginia Capes, the *Missouri* entered the Norfolk Naval Shipyard in late November. She began undergoing an extended overhaul that included replacing the barrels of her 16-inch guns. A considerable amount of metal had been lost during the firing at Korea. The ends of the barrel liners had pushed out beyond the ends of the barrels themselves, then the excess metal was shaved off.

As the overhaul progressed during the new year of 1954, rumors floated around the ship that she was going to be decommissioned and put into the reserve fleet. Then came a request from the Bureau of Naval Personnel for officers

to fill out preference cards for change of duty, and decisions had to be made on who would leave soon and who would remain on board for the remaining months of the *Missouri*'s time in service.[15]

The *Missouri* wrapped up her overhaul and departed the shipyard on March 24, 1954. Four days later, though the Navy Department was saying nothing officially, *The New York Times*

Left: Captain Brodie and executive officer Bob North pose together next to the surrender plaque. Both the officers and the deck are wet, suggesting they were hit by sea spray shortly before. (Courtesy Mrs. Sybil-Carmen North)

Below: In January 1954, workmen use slings to remove the 120-ton center gun from turret three. The replacement gun barrels inserted that year were still in place during Desert Storm in 1991. (U.S. Navy photo courtesy Kermit Bonner)

The right gun of turret two is missing during the replacement of barrels in January 1954. The change in guns was part of an overhaul at the Norfolk Naval Shipyard. (U.S. Navy photo via Vince Falso)

carried reports from unnamed sources indicating that the *Missouri*—then the only U.S. battleship never to have been decommissioned—was about to undergo that fate. Her recently completed overhaul had put her into good material condition, and in the fall she would go to the Puget Sound Naval Shipyard at Bremerton, Washington, to begin the second phase—the actual mothballing process. The newspaper report stated that the Navy Department had put out two inactivation feelers to President Truman. He was so possessive about the ship, though, that he had squelched the idea whenever it came up, arguing that the *Missouri* was a symbol of national might.[16]

By 1954, however, Truman was in retirement in Independence, Missouri, and the Korean War, to which the *Missouri* had contributed thousands of rounds of shore bombardment, was over. Thus, about a year into the presidency of Truman's successor, Dwight D. Eisenhower, the decision was reached. The Navy would soon commission its first supercarriers, the *Forrestal* and *Saratoga*, and it was looking to save money where it could.[17]

Soon the *Missouri* got a new skipper in the person of Captain Taylor Keith, an experienced

destroyer man. Among other things, he had commanded the USS *Nicholas* and USS *Herbert J. Thomas* in World War II. Keith had also been commander of two destroyer divisions and a destroyer squadron. In the early 1950s, he was secretary of the academic board at the Naval Academy, and he served as chief of staff to the commander of the Atlantic Fleet Destroyer Force.

Captain Keith was already slated to return to duty in Annapolis as commandant of midshipmen when his brief tenure in command of the *Missouri* was concluded. The new skipper thus went into the job with his eyes wide open when he took command on April 1. He knew that she was a lame-duck battleship. The good news was that successful command of an *Iowa*-class battleship in that era almost assured selection for rear admiral.

All of Captain Keith's predecessors made it except three. The unfortunate Captain Brown, of course, was removed from flag consideration by the court-martial sentence following the 1950 grounding of the *Missouri*. Captain Edsall died while he was still in command. Captain Brodie's failure to be selected was not so clearcut. It could well be that he was a victim of a youth movement initiated in the mid-1950s by Secretary of the Navy Charles Thomas. Right around the time Brodie was up for consideration, Thomas encouraged the deep selection of younger flag officers than previously. The primary beneficiary was Arleigh Burke, who was promoted over dozens of more senior officers to become chief of naval operations in 1955. Possibly victimized by the trend were Brodie and Captain John C. Atkeson, his 1927 classmate at the Naval Academy. Like Brodie, Atkeson had a Navy Cross for his World War II destroyer exploits. He was skipper of the *New Jersey* when Brodie had the *Missouri*. Both completed their active service as captains.

Following the change-of-command ceremony, Captain Keith met all of the ship's officers when they lined up in the wardroom. He shook hands with everybody, said hello, and heard the name of each man in turn. That evening the wardroom officers held a reception for the new skipper, and Lieutenant Willard Clark observed that Keith knew every officer by name. Such a facility with names and faces was a remarkable gift.[18]

On the day following the change of command, Keith prepared to get the *Missouri* under way from an anchorage in Hampton Roads. He had to turn the huge battleship to get her headed in the direction of the open sea, so he began twisting the ship with her engines. He ordered the starboard screws ahead one-third, port back one-third until she was swinging in the right direction. Then, in order to move out smartly in destroyer fashion, he increased the power to full, and the ship went into irons, unable to move farther.[19]

At that point, Commander Bob North, who had been handling the ship since the days of Captain Edsall, asked, "Captain, why did you do that?" Keith explained that he'd read a book by a British admiral who had tried the same maneuver when he took over command of a battleship. Unfortunately, the British skipper had put his ship into irons, and Keith hadn't learned from the other man's mistake. As Commander North patiently explained, in shallow water with a mud bottom, the increased revolutions kicked up so much mud that they canceled out the turning movement. It was lesson number one in the education of a new skipper.[20]

The *Missouri* was in and around Guantánamo Bay, Cuba, during much of April. When Seaman Dave Roth joined the crew of the *Missouri* that spring, he ran into an old-timer who told him, "You know, in later years you'll only remember the good times." In thinking about those experiences nearly forty years afterward, Roth found that to be the case. Images that stuck in his memory were of ice cream sundaes from the gedunk stand, lying on the deck for sunbathing, and going over for liberty when the ship was at Guantánamo. The pleasure there was partly a matter of appreciating what he had in coming from the culture in the United States. He took a train to Guantánamo City and saw the living conditions in pre-Castro Cuba—including poverty and run-down areas. When Castro came along a few years later, sailors had to make their liberties on the Ameri-

Commander J. R. North, as exec, was president of the wardroom mess. Here, he sits at the head of the senior officers' table during the ship's cruise from Guantánamo to Norfolk in mid-May 1954. At the table are two civilian guests of the secretary of the Navy. On the bulkhead beyond North is a map of the ship's travels. (Courtesy Mrs. Eleanor Keith)

canized base rather than going into Cuba itself.[21]

In early June, it was time for yet another midshipman training cruise, the *Missouri*'s last real operation before beginning a long farewell cruise to Puget Sound. All told, Task Group 40.1 was made up of sixteen warships that had a total of some three thousand midshipmen on board. The *Missouri* was the flagship, as she had been for the previous year's cruise. Rear Admiral Ruthven Libby, who had relieved Admiral Wooldridge as commander Battleship Cruiser Force Atlantic Fleet, was in overall command. Second in seniority was Rear Admiral Arleigh Burke, commander Cruiser Division Six, who was embarked in the USS *Macon*.

Before the *Missouri* headed for Europe, she and her three sisters of the *Iowa* class rendezvoused briefly off Norfolk on June 7 and did a few maneuvers. It was the only time all four ships of the class steamed together in formation. It hadn't been possible previously because of their combat assignments in World War II and Korea, nor would it be possible much longer because the *Missouri* was soon to head for the Pacific. Fireman Herb Fahr stood topside on the *Missouri* and took in the sight of the huge dreadnoughts. Up above, a photographer in an airplane was capturing pictures of the formation steaming. In the years to come, whenever he saw one of the photos, Fahr remembered with pride that he was present for the occasion.[22]

This aerial view of the *Missouri* under way in the Atlantic was taken in June 1954, during the midshipman cruise. (U.S. Navy photo in the National Archives: 80-G-645102)

Even though many in the crew would disappear rapidly once the ship began the inactivation process, her battle readiness was already inadequate when she made the summer training cruise because many of the Korean War veterans were gone. In the secondary battery plotting rooms, for example, Lieutenant Clark didn't have enough enlisted crew members to run all of the computers at the same time during firing exercises. Men had to move from one piece of equipment to another as an exercise progressed. The Mark 37 directors for the 5-inch guns were manned, but only one of the four director officers had sufficient experience to do the job well. The enlisted fire control personnel were just barely qualified as operators. On top of that, the very fact that the crew members knew the ship was going out of commission robbed them of a considerable degree of incentive for learning how to run the equipment.[23]

At one point during the cruise across the Atlantic, the *Missouri* launched a drone aircraft for an antiaircraft gunnery drill. The drone flew up one side, and all of the battleship's 5-inch guns fired and missed. Then the drone flew down the other side, where the 5-inch guns there missed as well. Finally, a destroyer escort fired her 3-inch gun and hit the target.[24]

In addition to the problems with the 5-inch, Clark didn't have sufficient personnel to maintain the Mark 56 and Mark 63 directors for the 40-mm guns. That compounded the problem of the directors' obsolescence. They were marginal for use against the aircraft of the mid-fifties, and they required an excessive amount of manpower to maintain in the best of circumstances. With the undermanned crew, these were far from the ship's best circumstances.[25]

While the midshipman task force was making its way eastward, Journalist Third Class Tom Koenninger and a photographer were on board the *Missouri* on a temporary basis to cover the activities of the midshipmen. The pair was regularly moved by high line to and from the destroyers and destroyer escorts of the

The *Missouri* had eight hundred midshipmen on board during the summer training cruise in 1954. Twenty-four of them gather near the surrender plaque to form the numeral 10 in honor of the tenth anniversary of the ship's commissioning on June 11, 1944. (U.S. Navy photo courtesy of Jacob Zeldes)

task force so they could put together stories about the training. As the ships plodded eastward, Koenninger was, for a time, on board a destroyer escort that was rolling heavily—more than forty degrees to each side—and throwing men and equipment all over the place. He had occasion to look back at the *Missouri* and saw her steaming majestically along, solid as a rock and largely unaffected by the waves. Her bow pitched slowly forward into the sea, then rose up gracefully as succeeding swells came along.[26]

When the time came to take a high-line ride back to the battleship, Koenninger was eager to return to the more comfortable ship. He learned that the crew of the *Missouri* was still embarrassed over the previous summer's incident of dunking the assistant secretary of defense, and as a result, they took extra care during high-line operations in the summer of 1954. As the first leg of the voyage neared its end, Koenninger went out onto the battleship's 01 deck for the arrival at Lisbon, Portugal, on the morning of June 19. The sun was just coming up, painting the sky in hues of orange and purple. The tranquility of the scene was a welcome contrast to the stormy seas through which the task group had steamed over the previous several days.[27]

When it came time to go ashore on liberty, Koenninger showed up on the quarterdeck in a white uniform that he had "pressed" by putting it under his mattress at night. The officer of the deck took a look at the whites that bore the cross-hatch marks of wire framework that held up the mattress. He told the journalist that the whites weren't up to *Missouri* standards, so he had to go below and find an iron to press them before he could embark in a liberty boat. The officer wanted pride in ship to be reflected in the men's appearance when they were ashore.[28]

Once he did get onto dry land, Koenninger was pleased by the degree to which the local populace welcomed the American sailors. A group of the Navy men went up the coast to Estoril for some gambling, and they also went to a bullfight. The midshipmen and crew members were introduced to the crowd at the bullfight. Each place the Americans went, the Por-

Captain Taylor Keith and Rear Admiral Ruthven Libby pose together on the *Missouri*'s flag bridge during the summer training cruise of 1954. Libby, the battleship-cruiser type commander, also had command of the training task group. (Courtesy Mrs. Eleanor Keith)

tuguese went out of their way to greet the visitors and help them overcome language difficulties. If they wanted to ride a train, for example, someone would provide useful guidance on schedules and getting aboard.[29]

At that time, the United States and Red China had no economic relations at all. Portugal, however, had much more of a reputation as a neutral and did not share the U.S. compunction against commerce. Fireman Fahr was struck by seeing products from mainland China in shop windows as he walked the streets of Lisbon on liberty.[30]

The next stop was Cherbourg. As the warships in company approached France via the English Channel, Admiral Libby demonstrated amazing mental prowess. Libby had tactical command, which he exercised from the *Missouri*'s flag plot. He had the sixteen ships of the task group in a circular formation, then put them into a column to go through the channel at night. Typically, a commander in that situation leaves it to individual ships to maneuver on their own to avoid other shipping. Libby, however, kept the stick himself. Captain Keith observed that the admiral did the whole thing from the radar scope. As he saw contacts that could possibly come near, he anticipated sufficiently far in advance that he could make necessary course changes to the formation to keep all his ships clear. At other times, he demonstrated the same skill when directing ships in formation to take new stations.[31]

The *Missouri* went to Cherbourg as part of the celebration of the tenth anniversary of that city's liberation. Following the invasion of Normandy on D-Day in 1944, the Allied forces had fought northward along the Cotentin peninsula until finally recapturing the port city during the last week in June. Also on hand for the occasion was the huge liner *Queen Elizabeth*, which had just arrived from the United States with Prime Minister Winston Churchill on board. Captain Keith sent a letter over to the liner, to be delivered to the "former naval person." In part, the skipper wrote, "As this historic ship nears its September inactivation date, it is our great privilege to assist in the education of our prospective officers in the greatest of all schools— experience at sea." A few days later, Churchill sent a gracious response from 10 Downing Street in London.[32]

In keeping with the anniversary of wartime victory, many visitors came aboard the ship for tours. At the same time, some of the *Missouri* sailors, such as Herb Fahr, went to visit a French fort that had been recaptured from the Germans a few weeks after D-Day. By 1954 it contained a museum depicting events of World War II. Fahr's liberty was largely limited to walking around to see the sights, taking pictures, and eating a few ham sandwiches on French bread. Having just the meager pay of a nonrated enlisted man, he couldn't afford to join his shipmates who took tours to Paris. Even so, it was a wonderful adventure for a German immigrant's son who had grown up in New York during the latter years of the Great Depression. Back then, being able to visit France had been far beyond realistic expectations.[33]

Because of the drawdown in the crew, Lieutenant Williams of the medical service corps was the legal officer as well. He spent some of his time in France as a foreign claims coordinator for the visiting American task group. He operated out of a local police station. If the Navy men caused damage ashore, Williams and the local police would determine who was at fault and, if necessary, see that the local citizens received an appropriate settlement.[34]

One day—July 9—while Williams was in this capacity, members of a French gang cornered and mugged a *Missouri* sailor, Seaman W. K. Bonura. The thugs savagely knifed the seaman and left him bleeding. His chest was punctured on the right side, and he had lacerations on his face, neck, lower chest, abdomen, right arm, and right leg. Williams happened to be nearby when someone said, "One of your sailors is being attacked." He rushed to the scene and, with the help of some civilian bystanders, succeeded in driving away the attackers.[35]

Bonura was fortunate that the man on duty was a shipmate, particularly a shipmate with a medical background. Williams provided first aid on the spot to stop the bleeding of Bonura's chest; then he commandeered a car to transport Bonura to the battleship's operating room for surgery. Lieutenant Norm Cooley of the *Missouri* and Commander Charles Longnecker from the *New Jersey* performed hours of surgery to sew the young man back together and stabilize his condition. All told, the doctors used hundreds of stitches to close all the wounds. To Lieutenant Williams, it appeared that the muggers had done an almost methodical job of cutting the Navy man. Bonura's *Missouri* shipmates lined up that night to provide blood transfusions. Once Bonura had been sufficiently patched up, he was sent to a medical facility ashore for further treatment and recovery. Captain Keith officially commended Lieutenant Williams for his actions on Bonura's behalf.[36]

During the stay in Cherbourg, Journalist Gerald Renner promoted a marvelous boondoggle for himself. He persuaded the public information officer to let him go to Paris with a type of camera used by newspaper photographers. He stationed himself near the Louvre, the famous French art museum, and took pictures of *Missouri* midshipmen as they stopped by during their tours of the city. He posed them by the well-known statue titled "Winged Victory." In a few cases, the midshipmen were with French women and waved Renner away rather than having photos made, but usually they were cooperative.[37]

Each time he took a picture, Renner dutifully wrote down the names and hometowns of the midshipmen. Then, after he had developed and printed the pictures, he sent them to the Navy fleet's hometown news center in Great Lakes, Illinois. From there the pictures and captions went to the hometown papers of the midshipmen and gave them a nice local angle on the cruise of the *Missouri*. It was good for the morale of the midshipmen to be recognized back home, and it was great for Renner to be able to catch some liberty in Paris when he wasn't taking pictures.[38]

All too soon it was time to go to sea again, headed once more for Cuba. On the evening of July 17, the *Missouri* had to transfer Boilerman Third Class Howard Evans by high line to sister ship *New Jersey* for surgery. Thus Evans, already hurting from appendicitis, had to endure the boatswain's chair ritual as well. The men of the *New Jersey* were gathered on their ship's fantail that night for an evening of entertainment, including music, jokes, mimics, and even a boatswain's pipe contest. As the two ships steamed along, Captain Keith brought the *Missouri* alongside smartly and dropped her into position with only one order to the engines. When the bows and sterns of both ships were lined up for the transfer, the band of the *New Jersey* temporarily departed from its planned program for the evening and broke into a rendition of "The Missouri Waltz."[39]

Captain Keith concluded that the whole thing was quite a show for the midshipmen of both ships. He would see them all again soon because of his orders to Annapolis as soon as he delivered the *Missouri* safely to Bremerton, Washington, for mothballing. A few weeks later, as the midshipmen were leaving the *Missouri*, one of them wrote a long, humorous poem mentioning various divisions within the ship. Included was a stanza for the skipper: "To Captain Keith, our thanks abound. Your ship is really cool. Now, how about more weekends when you take over at our school?"[40]

Captain Keith was an officer who liked to keep involved with the crew of the *Missouri*. At one point during the cruise, for example, a feed pump needed to be repaired to enable the ship to make the necessary speed the following day.

The skipper wanted to know how things were going, but he figured that if he asked the quartermaster to summon him at, say, 2:30 A.M., the word would be all over the ship. The chief master-at-arms would show up to escort him, perhaps the engineer officer as well. The captain would become part of a parade down through "Broadway," the extended longitudinal passageway connecting the engineering spaces.

To avoid that kind of showmanship, Keith set his alarm clock for half past two, got up and pulled on his uniform, then went to the fireroom by himself. There he had a cup of coffee with the men repairing the pump and let them know how important their work was in enabling him to do his own job as skipper.[41] In more recent times, such behavior has come to be called "management by walking around."

Another part of the engineering plant was emergency diesel, designed to provide temporary electrical power if the steam-driven generators were unable to perform their customary duties. One of the men who stood watches in the after emergency diesel plant, down in the bowels of the ship, was Fireman Fahr. Only the triple bottoms and voids separated the deck plates from the ocean below. As Fahr and other engineers went about their duties, they had to duck under the propeller shafts that passed through the compartment while connecting the propellers themselves with the reduction gears and engines that ran them.[42]

As the men moved about the compartment, they could see how fast the shafts were turning and get a pretty good idea what speed the *Missouri* was making at the time. By going through the reduction gears, the speed of the shafts had been slowed considerably from the revolutions per minute of the turbines. Thus, the shafts didn't present a particular safety hazard; they turned slowly enough that a man could hold his hand on one of them as it made its revolutions. The shafts were about three feet in diameter, so large that no one could completely encircle them with his arms. The man in A division who had the longest arms gave it a try, and still his fingertips were about a foot apart as he reached around.[43]

Throughout the summer of 1954, even as

the *Missouri* was cruising and training midshipmen, her executive officer, newly promoted Captain Bob North, was leading the planning team for the inactivation to come. Using guidance from the shipyard at Bremerton, the exec was laying out what each division would have to do to prepare the battleship for her coming hibernation in mothballs.[44] Planning also took place in connection with the personnel. As the ship returned to Norfolk in early August to conclude the midshipman cruise, the command put out the word that those who wished to go to the West Coast were welcome to stay aboard. Those who wanted to stay in the East could seek swaps with counterparts in other ships or else stand in line for normal transfers or discharges. By the time all the changes had been made, the *Missouri* had little more than a skeleton crew left on board. All they had to do was get her to Bremerton; she had no more combat responsibilities.

The *Missouri* was moored at pier seven of the Norfolk Naval Station for one last time. At midmonth Admiral Libby, the type commander, shifted his flag to the *Iowa*, which was moored

across the pier. Even before the *Missouri* began her long voyage from Norfolk, the crew began gradually closing her down. They got rid of a lot of material, emptying storerooms, taking off gear that could be used by other ships.[45]

One night during this period in August, Journalist Renner was, to use his description, "really tanked" when he returned from liberty on the town. He climbed the brow to the after quarterdeck, requested permission to come aboard, and then made his way to the berthing compartment. To his surprise, when he got to his bunk, he found another man in it. Renner pulled him out, and the other man came out fighting mad—an understandable reaction from a person so rudely awakened. Renner fought back, and the other man wound up on the deck during the altercation. When Renner looked down at his opponent, he saw a gleaming shine on the metal, evidently produced by the vigorous use of steel wool.[46]

At that point, the *Missouri* journalist said to himself, "Oh, shit. I'm on the wrong ship," for the deck in his berthing compartment in the *Missouri* was dull. This shiny deck was in the

After having made her home port at Norfolk since the spring of 1946, the *Missouri* pulls away from pier seven for the last time on August 23, 1954. Across the pier is sister ship *Iowa*. (Courtesy Mrs. Eleanor Keith)

GOOD BYE MIGHTY MO

virtually identical sister ship *Iowa*. By that time the *Iowa*'s master-at-arms force had converged on the scene and gotten Renner under control. He sheepishly explained his predicament, and the masters-at-arms got him up to the quarterdeck. The *Iowa*'s officer of the deck took him into protective custody and delivered him back to the correct floating home.[47]

On August 23, the *Missouri* left Norfolk for the last time. Families and well-wishers gathered on the pier for a departure ceremony that included dancing girls and speeches by the mayor of Norfolk, Admiral Libby, and Captain Keith. Libby was unduly optimistic when he said, "She is a fine ship and will be back on the active list before long." Barbara Pharo, Miss Norfolk, made a tour around the deck but politely declined Captain Keith's impish invitation to make the cruise to California. A band on the pier played "California, Here I Come" and "Anchors Aweigh."

When it was time to get under way, four *Missouri* officers who had just been detached from the ship pulled the final mooring line off

Tugs ease the *Missouri* away from pier seven in this aerial view of her Norfolk departure. At left is the *Iowa;* at right is the light carrier *Saipan,* built on the hull of a *Baltimore*-class cruiser. (U.S. Navy photo in the National Archives: 80-G-645685)

its bollard and tossed it into the water. The tugs pulled the battleship out into the channel and then gradually fell away as she moved out under her own power. As she got farther and farther away, those watching from the pier saw what a newspaperman called "a shimmering farewell salute." It was the sun reflecting off the fifty-some automobiles parked on the fantail so crew members would have the use of them when they reached the West Coast.[48]

Near Cuba, Rear Admiral George R. Cooper, who had succeeded Clark Green as the commander of Battleship Division Two, visited by helo. He was among thousands of admirers who wished the Mighty Mo well on her sentimental last journey. Within a few days, the *Missouri* reached Panama. While the ship was going through the Panama Canal, Lieutenant Williams and the ship's damage control officer, Lieutenant (j.g.) D. D. Vacca, looked in through the wardroom portholes from the weather deck. They noticed that the executive officer was sitting by himself at a table, drinking a cup of coffee and eating coffee cake. As a lark, Williams decided to play a prank on Captain North. Some of the local Panamanians were on the deck of the *Missouri* to handle lines and fenders. One had a particularly scruffy look: he was wearing a straw hat with a hole in it, a dirty shirt, and gaudy red-white-and-blue-striped pants. Williams suggested to the Panamanian that he go in and help himself to some of the coffee cake.[49]

North, who was reading while he ate, glanced up and was startled by what he saw. There was the Panamanian, stuffing a piece of cake into his mouth and other pieces into his shirt and trousers. North ordered him to leave the wardroom immediately. Meanwhile, Williams and Vacca were enjoying the scene through the porthole as they watched North's discomfiture. Shortly thereafter, the general announcing system called for all officers not on watch to report to the wardroom. North demanded, "Who did it? Who did it?" Since the exec didn't specify what had been done, Williams didn't volunteer any information initially.[50]

Then he reasoned that since he was head of both the medical and legal departments, his services would be needed soon and he wouldn't receive much of a punishment. So Williams confessed, and Captain North called him into his cabin and dressed him down for violating the dignity of the *Missouri*'s wardroom. Then North suspended him from duty—threw him "in hack," as the Navy terms it. That meant Williams had to go to his stateroom and contemplate his misdeed. He could leave only to eat meals and go to the head. The next day, as Williams expected, he was needed to perform his duties, and the suspension ended.[51]

The next stop on the journey was Long Beach, California, where traffic created an incredible jam as the local citizens fought to get aboard for a tour. So many people flocked to visit the ship that sailors who were not in the duty section often stayed on board for a while rather than heading ashore right after liberty call. Being on board the *Missouri* enabled them to scout the young women coming aboard as tourists and thus to make dates with the appealing prospects. A number of movie stars came aboard as well; included was Jimmy Stewart, who had appeared that year in the Alfred Hitchcock thriller *Rear Window*.[52]

After a few days in southern California, the *Missouri* headed to San Francisco. The Golden Gate Bridge was lined with hundreds of people waving to the battleship and her crew as she went under it. This was the first time the *Missouri* had been to the port since 1944, when she was on her way to the war zone for the first time. As the ship approached a pier at the naval shipyard at Hunters Point, the harbor pilot who came on board turned out to be an old friend of Captain Keith. In fact, Keith had met him in the mid-1930s when he was serving in the ammunition ship *Nitro* that went in and out of San Francisco frequently. As he prepared to take the *Missouri* to her berth, the pilot mentioned that the Mighty Mo would be his final job because he was due to retire the next day. Indeed, it was quite an honor, for he hadn't handled a battleship since the immediate aftermath of the war, nine years earlier.[53]

Alas, the pilot had missed the desired tide by about ten minutes, so as the ship headed toward the pier, the outgoing tidal current caught the *Missouri*'s stern and began pushing it. The

pilot used the engines and tugboats to try to compensate, but he wasn't succeeding to the satisfaction of Captain Keith. The skipper was responsible for the handling of the ship, regardless of the fact that the pilot had the conn. So Keith asserted himself, ordered all engines to back at emergency power, and stopped the ship. Once he had her under control, he turned the conn back to the pilot to make the final approach. The *Missouri* then moved in alongside, and line handlers moored her to the pier. When Keith stepped ashore, a friend greeted him by saying: "I thought you had won yourself a pier. You were five feet from it when you stopped."[54]

The one-day record for visitors during the time at Long Beach had been 16,900; on September 13, at San Francisco, more than 20,100 people boarded the ship for one last look. The ship even extended the visiting hours that day but didn't begin to accommodate all who wanted to come aboard. One who didn't have to wait in line was Fleet Admiral Chester Nimitz, who came aboard in uniform to see again the ship upon which he had signed the surrender documents nine years earlier. Captain Keith escorted the admiral to the surrender deck for a look at the plaque. While they were there, three uniformed cub scouts stepped forward and gave Nimitz a snappy salute. Following the cub scout style, each used only two fin-

Above: Tourists wander the decks of the *Missouri* as she lies moored dockside at Balboa, Panama Canal Zone. (Courtesy Mrs. Eleanor Keith)

Opposite (top): C. S. Townsend, senior Panama Canal pilot, is shown in the white shirt as he gives orders from the 08-level conning station during the *Missouri*'s canal transit on August 28, 1954. At left is a close-up of the fire-control radar on one of the Mark 37 directors. (U.S. Navy photo in the National Archives: 80-G-645162)

Opposite (bottom): Sightseers gather on the starboard side to get a close look at the tight clearance between the side of the ship and the wall of the lock. (U.S. Navy photo in the National Archives: 80-G-645164)

them a guided tour, much more thorough than they would have received by standing in line. When it ended, the family reciprocated by inviting Williams to their home for a drink. It was a pleasant afternoon for all concerned.[56]

After a run north up the coast, the *Missouri* arrived at Seattle on the rainy morning of September 15. She poked her way through a heavy fog and moored at pier ninety-one to facilitate still more general visiting. Can-can girls, standing on the pier amidst orange and blue streamers that had been tossed in celebration, waved their rain-sodden skirts and petticoats at the crew members on board ship. Thousands of local citizens braved the rain to get a look at the famous ship. Among them was the local Seafair queen, Carol Christensen, outfitted in tiara and strapless gown. She planted a kiss on the cheek of the grinning Captain Keith. He was so distracted by the gesture that he spilled a sack of symbolic mothballs that someone had handed him.[57]

The next stop was at Bangor, Washington, on Puget Sound. There the crew off-loaded the *Missouri*'s supply of ammunition before going to Bremerton. Ammo handling requires a lot of manpower in any situation, and in this case it took essentially all hands—both officers and enlisted—because the ship was so badly undermanned. Keith didn't sit quietly by in his office. He was down with the men, offering encouragement orally and by his very presence. One of those who was involved physically in the unloading was Lieutenant Williams. This instance was one of the many reasons Williams considered the skipper a forceful, dynamic person—a true leader. He had what Williams viewed as a commanding presence. Eventually, Keith became a three-star admiral and served in the early 1960s as commander First Fleet.[58]

Still more crew members were detached as soon as the *Missouri* arrived in Bremerton to begin the inactivation process. After that the size of the crew of the ship declined progressively in the months leading up to decommissioning.[59] Among those departing was Keith himself. On September 18, Captain North relieved him as commanding officer. North had been out of the Naval Academy nearly twenty years by that point. After his graduation in 1935, he had

gers of his right hand. Nimitz returned their salute, using two fingers instead of four.

To protect his privacy during the onslaught that day, Captain Keith closed the curtains on the portholes of his cabin, those leading out to the 01 surrender deck on the starboard side. He didn't want all the pedestrians to look in on him. One visitor was completely undaunted, however. He opened the door from the weather deck and walked right in on the skipper, announcing: "I'm from Missouri, and I know old Harry. He's from my hometown, and I knew he would want me to see the whole ship, so I just came on in." As Keith observed, it takes all kinds.[55]

As Lieutenant Williams was leaving the ship on that day for a brief period on liberty, he saw a boy—perhaps seven or eight years old—standing at the end of the visitors' waiting line with his parents. He was very enthusiastic and got the attention of the battleship officer by saluting him. Williams had a few souvenirs with him, small medallions that were replicas of the famous surrender plaque. He gave one to the boy and began chatting with him and his parents. One thing led to another, and so Williams took the family aboard the *Missouri* and gave

served six years in the battleship *California*. During World War II he was the gunnery officer of two aircraft carriers, the *Monterey* and *Lexington*, and later became gunnery officer and navigator on the staff of Vice Admiral Marc Mitscher, commander Task Force 58. After the war, North commanded the destroyer *Duncan*. As part of the changes, Commander Bill Davis, the engineer, took over as executive officer. Davis had a major role in the inactivation process.[60]

Within a few days of her arrival at Bremerton, the *Missouri* was shepherded into a large stone graving dock. Men with surveying transits lined her up so she was right over the keel blocks that would support her once the water was pumped out of the dry dock. Herb Fahr was up on deck during the process and observed that shipyard workers were going down the stone stairs at various places on the inside of the dock. Fahr concluded that they must have some duties to perform once all the water was gone. Soon he realized that their real purpose was to collect the hundreds of salmon that had been trapped in dock when the caisson was put into place to seal off the open end. Now the salmon were on the floor of the dock, and fishing couldn't have been easier. The yard workers carried them out by the armload.[61]

Crew members had a variety of duties during the inactivation process of the ensuing months. Down in the after diesel plant, for example, Fireman Fahr and others took practically all the machinery apart. Worn bearings were replaced with new ones. Pieces of gear were cleaned and preservative poured into the interior of different pieces of equipment. The purpose was to provide a protective coating that would ward off rust in the years to come. Once the job was done, the men assigned to the after diesel got a piece of sheet brass, stamped the letters of their names into it, and riveted it to a stanchion.[62]

The goal of the crew during the inactivation period was to preserve the ship well so that she could be reactivated in a brief time. (After the *New Jersey* had been in the mothball fleet for two years, 1948–50, for instance, she was brought back for the Korean War in a matter of a few months.) One of the chores was off-

Left: On September 18, 1954, the day the *Missouri* arrived at Bremerton, Washington, for inactivation, Captain Bob North relieved Captain Keith of command. North had previously been temporary skipper for a brief period after Captain Edsall's death in March 1953. (Courtesy Mrs. Sybil-Carmen North)

Right: On November 11, 1954, the United States observed Veterans Day for the first time. Up to then, the holiday had been called Armistice Day in honor of the end of hostilities in France in World War I. On this occasion, federal court was held on board a battleship—an event that had never occurred before. The judge is at the table, presiding over the naturalization of the immigrants seated in the foreground. (Courtesy Mrs. Sybil-Carmen North)

Opposite (top): Seaman Lynn Jex stands by as Seaman Carl DeWese lowers the national ensign near the end of the decommissioning ceremony at Bremerton. (U.S. Navy photo in the National Archives: 80-G-659071)

loading the many supplies that were in the *Missouri*'s storerooms. Dan Williams supervised the recycling of medicines and other supplies that were perishable and needed to be used elsewhere rather than sitting on board the battleship during the years to come.[63]

In the process of wrapping up the medical areas of the ship, Williams and his enlisted men wrote out directions on how to operate the various pieces of equipment. They also recorded standard operating procedures for handling various kinds of problems that might come up. More than thirty years later, when he was a retired commander, Williams visited the by-then-recommissioned *Missouri* and went down to the medical spaces. The current crew had found the instructions and notes his men had left for their future successors. Few of the new men in 1986 had much sea duty experience at that point and thus welcomed the pointers.[64]

After five months of off-loading, mothballing, repairing, and inventorying, the shipyard workers and ship's crew had the battleship *Missouri* essentially buttoned up. More and more

crewmen had departed with each passing month. The final act was on February 26, 1955. The day was a dismal one on Puget Sound—overcast, temperature around freezing, intermittent rain and snow. Because of the conditions, the decommissioning ceremony was held in the wardroom. The only *Missouri* crewmen remaining were 25 officers and 176 enlisted men.[65]

Among those who joined the crew in the wardroom was Rear Admiral Homer N. Wallin, commander of the Puget Sound Naval Shipyard. Wallin was the officer who had provided the technical expertise five years earlier when the *Missouri* escaped the mudbank after her grounding at Norfolk. At 10:12 on the morning of the twenty-sixth, Captain North ordered, "Mr. navigator, will you haul down the ensign, the jack, and the commissioning pennant." The message went to the bridge, where someone gave a signal to half-frozen Carl DeWese, standing at the flagstaff on the stern. He lowered the stars and stripes slowly, in part because his hands were cold and in part because the wind was whipping the flag around.[66]

Elsewhere, others received signals and took down the union jack from the bow and the commissioning pennant from the mast. At 10:14, North directed Commander Davis, the executive officer, to secure the final watch. The *Missouri* was no longer part of the fleet. Custody passed to Captain Karl Poehlmann, commander of the Bremerton group of the Pacific Reserve Fleet. She still belonged to the Navy, so his first action was to establish a security watch.[67]

Moods varied among those on board that day. Lieutenant Willard Clark, the fire control officer, was among the unsentimental. As he put it: "The battleships at that point were on their way out, and we all knew it. They had some future for shore bombardment and so forth, but that hadn't really amounted to an awful lot." Clark had orders to report to the Naval Academy to teach in the mathematics department. He was eager for the decommissioning to be over so he and his wife could get into their car and drive down the coast to San Francisco as the beginning of the long trip across country to Annapolis.[68]

Lieutenant Dan Williams, on the other hand, was sorry to be going. His gloomy outlook coincided with the Bremerton weather that day. Years later, Williams remembered: "It was tremendously nostalgic. . . . I'm sort of Irish emotional anyway. It was very hard for me. I got choked up, because there's really an attachment [to your ship]. It's part of you."[69]

Below: Captain Karl Poehlmann, commander of the Bremerton group of the Pacific Reserve Fleet, accepts custody of the *Missouri* at the decommissioning ceremonies on February 26, 1955, in the ship's wardroom. Captain North, next to the stanchion, holds the commissioning pennant in his hand. At left is Commander William Davis, the executive officer. Next to him is Rear Admiral Homer Wallin, commander of the Puget Sound Naval Shipyard. (U.S. Navy photo in the National Archives: 80-G-659069)

A view from the forecastle on February 26, 1955, the *Missouri*'s last day in commission and first day of her mothball existence. The aluminum "igloos" cover the 40-mm gun mounts and connect them to the dehumidification system. (U.S. Navy photo in the National Archives: 80-G-659070)

11 ❖ Mothballs

February 1955–May 1984

The evergreen-clad hills lining Puget Sound provided an aesthetic backdrop as the *Missouri* began a new phase of her existence, one that would last for nearly thirty years. Upon decommissioning, she replaced the mothballed battleship *Indiana* as the accommodation ship for the Bremerton group of the Pacific Reserve Fleet. It would be grandiose to call her a flagship, since decommissioned warships no longer fly the national ensign. In function, however, she was essentially that. Captain Poehlmann, who had accepted the battleship during the decommissioning ceremony on February 26, afterward moved aboard with his staff. He set up his office in what had been the captain's in-port cabin. On the bulkhead hung framed replicas of the surrender documents of a decade earlier.

In her new role, some of the ship's messing and berthing facilities were still used, although they served far fewer men than when the *Missouri* was still in active service. Whereas the inactive fleet at Bremerton is now administered from office buildings ashore, at that time the offices on board the battleship served the purpose. She was sort of a station ship for the collection of mothballed warships gathered at the Puget Sound Naval Shipyard. In addition, the *Missouri*'s machine shop and other shops were used to make and repair parts for inactive ships that needed them. Obviously, the shipyard itself could have taken care of the chore, but this was handier and essentially meant the mothball fleet could take care of itself as far as minor repairs were concerned.[1]

Prior to World War II, when the Navy put a ship out of commission for possible future use, the preservation and maintenance program was often minimal. Skeleton crews, if that, were assigned to attend to essential housekeeping chores. After the war, the Navy became much more scientific about it, particularly by installing dehumidification equipment to prevent rust and corrosion. The system had proved successful when dozens of ships were reactivated during the Korean War and sent back into service. The *Missouri* received this sort of treatment when she reached Bremerton. The most noticeable external manifestation of the preservation program was the installation of aluminum "igloos" over the 40-mm gun mounts. These were connected by piping to dehumidification machines that kept the air at a low-humidity level—in the ship's interior and in the gun mounts as well.[2]

Inside the ship, a layer of preservative covered some metal surfaces. In addition, the underwater hull was coated with a protective plastic. Bags of silica gel were put in some places to absorb moisture. Much of the equipment was left in place. Other items were moved and marked with tags indicating where they should go. Gauges throughout the ship measured the humidity level; whenever it rose above 30 percent, the dehumidification machines automatically kicked on.[3]

Nearby were three dozen other ships that had received the same treatment. Some *Essex*-class carriers, such as the *Lexington* and *Princeton*, had been pulled out of the reserve fleet and returned to active service. The *Bunker Hill* remained behind, too badly damaged by a kamikaze in 1945 to be considered worth upgrading. The fast battleships *Indiana* and *Alabama* were there, along with some of pre-World War II vintage: the sister ships *Colorado*,

Opposite page: Accompanied by Boatswain's Mate Elmer Lewis as a security guard, two Puyallup Indians inspect the *Missouri* from a small boat in the spring of 1964. The Indians expressed the desire to use the battleship as a bargaining weapon in their fight with the state of Washington over fishing rights. This trip did get the boaters the publicity they sought for their cause. (Bremerton *Sun* photo courtesy of the Naval Historical Center)

Maryland, and *West Virginia*. The latter was the sole battleship that had been present both when the Japanese attacked Pearl Harbor in 1941 and when they surrendered at Tokyo Bay in 1945.[4]

Soon the *Missouri* became the foremost tourist attraction for Bremerton. Visitors came by the thousands, stopping to have a look at the big guns and the surrender deck.[5]

Because President Truman had been so adamant about keeping the *Missouri* in commission while he was in office, he was particularly rankled by her decommissioning in faraway Bremerton soon after Dwight Eisenhower took over. Finally, Eisenhower's eight years as president came to an end. In August 1961, a few months after John F. Kennedy's arrival, the seventy-seven-year-old Truman wrote to the new secretary of the Navy, John Connally. In typical blunt fashion, he stated, "I don't know whether you understand it or not, but the objective of the people who were in command from 1953 until the new President came in in

1961, has been to cover up almost everything that was done in the Administration between 1945 and 1953 [Truman's term in office]." To rectify these slights, the former president proposed that the Navy move the *Missouri* to the New York Naval Shipyard, where she had been built twenty years earlier, so she would be readily available for visiting by the public. Secretary Connally did not act on the suggestion.[6]

Truman considered the ship's banishment to remote Bremerton an effort to get her out of the public eye. In January 1963, after various proposals had been made to move the ship, the *Seattle Post-Intelligencer* asked Truman for a comment. Not surprisingly, he fired back strongly, "I don't want to appear to be too persistent in this matter, but it seems to me that if Eisenhower wanted to place it in a closet, he couldn't have found a better place than the Bremerton Navy Yard." Truman said his first preference would have been to bring the ship up the Mississippi River to St. Louis, but that wouldn't work because the ship draws too much water, and her superstructure could not have passed

under various bridges across the river. Instead, the former president proposed that the ship be put on display in a coastal population center.[7]

Ironically, at least in the short term, Truman's blast stirred up such controversy that more tourists made their way to Bremerton to see her. To illustrate, in December 1962, 2,072 tourists took the bus tour of the shipyard, including a half-hour stop to allow people to walk the decks of the *Missouri* and get a look at the surrender plaque. In January 1963, the month when Truman made his remark about the ship being in a closet, attendance jumped to 3,825 and nearly doubled the month after that. Indeed, the battleship became so popular with visitors that local politicians stoutly resisted any proposals to have her placed elsewhere.[8]

Even though the Navy welcomed those who visited the *Missouri* on the bus tours, it was much more picky when it came to those who tried the do-it-yourself approach. In the summer of 1963, for example, a mustang naval officer named Oree C. Weller went out for a boat cruise with his wife and another couple. Weller was no ordinary naval officer: in December 1941, as a young enlisted man, his battle station was in the maintop of the USS *Arizona* when she was blown up by a Japanese bomb. Weller took a swim in the oily waters of Pearl Harbor that day but survived and was later commissioned. In 1963, he and his companions decided to take their boat past the long line of mothballed ships at Bremerton and get some pictures of the *Missouri*.

As they passed the *Missouri*'s starboard quar-

ter, they took a couple of snapshots of the surrender deck area. Then they circled the stern to get another shot. As they did so, they saw a gray Navy truck, complete with flashing police light on top, roar down an adjacent pier. Men got out of the truck and waved at the boaters. Another truck arrived, with more men. A group of sailors got into a landing craft and went out to accost Weller and his party. They said that picture taking was not authorized, so the film would have to be destroyed. Weller reluctantly opened his camera and threw the offending film over the side. He protested that the *Missouri* was a tourist attraction that the public could see readily. His accuser said that was not the case, and they would have to leave. So they did.

Afterward, Weller complained publicly about the incident, and with considerable justification, because it's difficult to see what could be classified about a row of mothballed ships. Weller concluded his letter to a Seattle newspaper by saying that the heavy-handed Navy approach "only reinforces Mr. Truman's 'closet' theory." He then gleefully sent a clipping of the letter to the former president.[9]

On a couple of occasions during her long tenure in mothballs, the *Missouri* was a prop for

movie-making. In the mid-1970s, she was used for a reenactment of the surrender scene in a Universal Studios movie called *MacArthur,* which starred Gregory Peck. In that era, prior to her 1980s modernization, her outward appearance was little changed from 1945, so she was well able to portray herself. The film company paid for the costs of moving the ship away from the pier and getting her into shape. That included taking the aluminum igloos and dehumidification piping off the 40-mm mounts that appeared within the view of the cameras. The gun barrels, which had been removed from the mounts so the igloos could fit over them, were stored below decks. They had to be retrieved and put back in place. The producers did an excellent job of recreating the look of 1945, including outfitting both Japanese and Americans in appropriate dress. On the bulkhead in the captain's cabin was an enlarged copy of the first issue of *The Missourian,* the ship's newspaper. Published in 1944, it had Captain Callaghan's photo on the front page. It was a nice touch.[10]

In the early 1980s, the *Missouri* was extremely versatile while being filmed by Paramount for the television miniseries *Winds of War.* The drama was based on Herman Wouk's novel of the period leading up to the U.S. entry

Left: Two pigeons perch on a chain stopper for one of the anchor chains on the *Missouri*'s forecastle in March 1970. (U.S. Navy photo in the National Archives: 80-G-1143671)

Below: This view from September 1975 shows the ship's typical appearance during her long stint in the reserve fleet. (Courtesy Puget Sound Naval Shipyard)

Right: Actors are outfitted in 1945-era uniforms for the 1976 reenactment of the surrender ceremony in *MacArthur.* (Courtesy Puget Sound Naval Shipyard)

Below: Actor Gregory Peck, as General MacArthur, watches with a cold gaze as a Japanese actor signs at the table. (Courtesy Puget Sound Naval Shipyard)

into World War II. The series featured Ralph Bellamy as President Franklin Roosevelt and Robert Mitchum as his fictitious naval aide, Pug Henry.

During one episode, the *Missouri* portrayed three different warships. In a scene set in March 1941, she was the *Texas,* flagship of the Atlantic Fleet. For the Atlantic Charter summit in August of that year, the *Missouri* portrayed the heavy cruiser *Augusta,* which took President Roosevelt to Argentia, Newfoundland, for his first-ever face-to-face meeting with Winston Churchill. Then the *Missouri,* painted in places with North Atlantic camouflage, became the British battleship *Prince of Wales,* which had brought Churchill across the Atlantic to Argentia. It's unlikely that many viewers noticed that the hull number "63" popped up on the stern of both the *Augusta* and *Prince of Wales* when barges were bringing officers alongside. The video of the episode is worth watching because it includes interior views of the *Missouri*'s flag quarters, which were still intact during the filming but were wiped out when the ship was reactivated a few years later.[11]

Through the remainder of the 1960s, the *Missouri* was chained to a pier in the reserve fleet. In 1969, she received the company of sister ship *New Jersey,* which was mothballed at Bremerton that autumn following a brief period of active service in the Vietnam War. At the time, I was serving in the crew of the *New Jersey.* One afternoon in late September, I joined several other officers from the ship and went on a tour of the *Missouri.* We roamed through her from the fourth deck to the 010 level and from the anchor windlass room to the mess deck. Not surprisingly, my knowledge of the *New Jersey* greatly facilitated getting around in the other battleship.

Probably the most fascinating aspect of the tour—since the basic structure of both ships was obviously quite similar—was the extent to which the *Missouri* was a time capsule. We saw repeated evidence that life on board had essentially ceased to exist in the 1950s. On a bulletin board, for example, was a picture poster depicting events that occurred in 1955—the last year the *Missouri* was in commission. We saw plans of the day and a copy of the *Navy Times* newspaper dated 1959, this from the period when she was the headquarters ship for the reserve fleet.[12]

In the captain's and admiral's quarters were console-type radios that probably dated from the forties or fifties. One of them may even have been in President Truman's quarters in 1947 when he directed Commander Merritt, the communications officer, not to turn it on because daughter Margaret was sleeping. The beds in both quarters were large metal ones

The ship is reflected in the still waters of the shipyard during filming of the movie *MacArthur* in August 1976. (U.S. Navy photo: USN 1168177)

Above: This picture of the *Missouri* in mothballs shows two still-visible dents where the Japanese "Zeke" slammed into the starboard side of the hull in April 1945. The fainter impression at left is where the wing hit; the smaller, deeper one is where the propeller hub hit the ship's steel side. (Courtesy Richard A. Landgraff)

Opposite (top): This is one of the fourth-deck magazines for storage of 16-inch powder, photographed during the mothball period. The tray at right was for passing bags to the other side of the magazine, beyond the hatch. At left is a dumbwaiter for lowering bags to the fifth deck, thence to the powder flats and access to the hoists that carried bags up to the turrets. (Pam Lama photo via Robert Sumrall)

with lattice-work headboards. In the wardroom I saw the silver bas-relief plaque that Governor Donnelly presented to Captain Hillenkoetter in 1946 and that Captain Brodie used in 1953 when he was quizzing new officers about the state's Latin motto. On the bulkhead was the mural map painted in 1945 as the ship returned home from World War II.[13]

Not surprisingly, after her fourteen years in the mothball fleet, I saw signs that the *Missouri* needed repairs, painting, and preservation. Despite the best efforts of the men of the inactive fleet, they were not able to keep her in nearly the shape that our *New Jersey* crew did in the course of maintaining a ship on a daily basis. An exception was the engineering plant, which was in beautiful condition. As I emerged from the interior of the *Missouri*—returning to the real world of 1969, as it were—I discovered that my mouth and nose had dried out. It was vivid evidence of the effectiveness of the dehumidification equipment on board. In a way, the machines made the empty ship symbolic: a dried-up vestige of her former self.[14]

Though the *Missouri* remained a constant, some ships left Bremerton when their time was up and new ones came in. The *Maryland, West Virginia,* and *Colorado* were scrapped in the early sixties. Later in that decade, the *Indiana* went to

the breakers, and the *Alabama* went to the state for which she was named so she could be a memorial. The *Bunker Hill* was scrapped in the early 1970s. By then, many of the World War II–built ships, including heavy cruisers, light cruisers, destroyers, and amphibious warfare ships, reached the age of thirty and went off to be recycled into all sorts of metal products. The *Missouri* herself continued to be at the last pier in a row of inactive ships, available for tours by the public.

One of the custodians assigned to the Bremerton facility in the late 1970s was Senior Chief Hull Technician Larry Kohrt. He figured that the dehumidification machines would take care of the potential problem of rust; his main concern was flooding. The ships contained blocks of Styrofoam in the bilges and voids, and those blocks were outfitted with mercury switches. Each was designed so that rising water would tip over the block and set off the alarm. An indicator board reported the location of the problem, alerting the maintenance facility people to a flooding situation before it became serious.[15]

The solidly built *Missouri* didn't have any problems with flooding, but on one occasion the system served a different purpose on board another ship. A member of the caretaker force failed to follow the two-man rule, which specifies that no one should go in alone when inspecting the interior of a mothballed ship. In this case, a man went alone and got locked inside a ship with the lights off. He made his way to a void, knocked over a Styrofoam block, and the resulting alarm brought someone to his rescue.[16]

In addition to the normal security measures connected with the mothballed ships, Senior Chief Kohrt was involved in another project on the *Missouri*. He and others had to go aboard the battleship and remove round buttons, each about the size of a quarter. They were designed to give off a dull green glow in the dark—similar to a watch with a radium dial—and therefore help orient people if they were caught down inside the ship when the electrical power went off. The buttons were posted near ladders, telephone jacks, and other such places so people could get an idea what was nearby.[17] By the late 1970s, however, health concerns dictated that the radioactive buttons be removed from the ships. Kohrt and the men working with him took out hundreds of them.[18]

Another thing that came off the battleship in those mothball years was fuel oil. In the mid-1970s, as a result of war in the Middle East, the United States had been subjected to gasoline price hikes and lines at the pumps. The *Missouri*'s supply of heavy black fuel oil had been sitting in her tanks for more than twenty years by that time, doing no one any good. Tank trucks showed up at the Bremerton piers around 1978, and pumps delivered an amazing amount of oil to them from out of the reserve fleet ships. The Navy special fuel used at the time had a consistency close to that of tar, so it had to be thinned out by applications of steam to facilitate the pumping process. The *Missouri* also had a large supply of diesel fuel in her tanks, and for years, that was the fuel source for operating the landing craft used as utility boats by the maintenance force.[19]

During the first fifteen or so years that the *Missouri* was in mothballs, visitors were permitted to walk the entire length of the main deck and climb to the 01 level to view the surrender plaque. They were not permitted to go inside the skin of the ship. By the late 1970s, though, that had changed. Fences were erected on the main deck, just aft of the wardroom, so that visitors could no longer go to the fantail, thus reducing the number of security people needed to keep an eye on all the tourists. Sometimes, visitors would try to climb the fence to get aft, and they had to be apprehended by the security force. The main concerns were the potential for vandalism and accidents to visitors.[20]

For the benefit of those interested in the ship's history, the wardroom was opened up, and displays featured photos from the *Missouri*'s past. One of the pictures showed the men of the battleship looking down from the ship's superstructure as the surrender ceremony was taking place on the 01 deck. Larry Kohrt discovered that more than just *Missouri* men were pictured in the photo. One day, while looking closely, the hull technician found the face of his

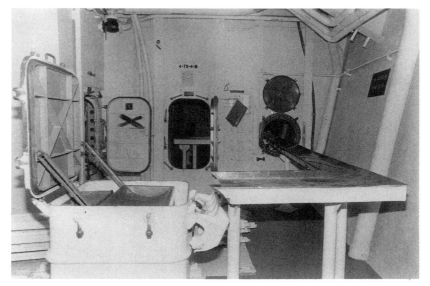

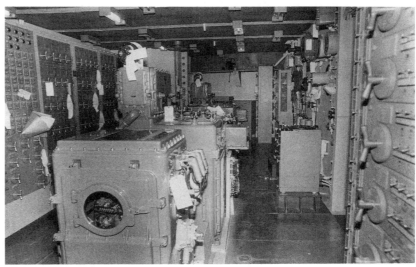

brother Arnold. In 1945, his brother was in the crew of the submarine tender *Proteus* and had been lucky enough to get to go aboard the *Missouri* to see the ceremony.[21]

Just forward of the wardroom, on the starboard side, is the executive officers' cabin. As part of the exhibits for tourists, the inactive fleet crew took off the watertight door that provided access from the weather deck to the cabin. In its place they put a big piece of clear plastic so tourists could peer in. There they could see the office area where the exec worked, a commander's cap and uniform blouse hanging up, and some magazines laid out to provide the atmosphere of bygone days. The hands of the clock on the bulkhead were set at 9:02 A.M., the

Above: This secondary battery plotting room has tags on various equipment to provide information to reactivation crews. In the left foreground is a stable element with the handles for the firing keys visible on the right side. On the bulkheads are selector switches to set up various combinations of directors and gun mounts. (Pam Lama photo via Robert Sumrall)

A view of the forecastle, looking down from the superstructure. This picture was taken in the spring of 1984, shortly before the *Missouri* was towed from Bremerton to Long Beach. (Photo in DoD Still Media Records Center: DN-SC-93-00822)

time the surrender ceremony began on September 2, 1945.[22]

One requirement involved with keeping the *Missouri* in shape for daily visitors was a good deal more cosmetic work than she received during her later reserve-fleet stint in the 1990s, when the only interest was in preservation for possible reactivation. Harry Ehlert, an electrician, was in the maintenance crew in the late 1970s, as he was again fifteen years later. He observed that those assigned to the mothball fleet in the visiting years had to do painting and preservation work frequently, although not to the degree that the crew of an active ship would have to. Back then, paint was touched up more often, decks cleaned, brass shined, and so forth.[23]

During that period when the ship was a tourist attraction, the maintenance facility kept a guest log on the quarterdeck so visitors could write down where they came from. A majority of the people who stepped aboard the decks of the *Missouri* had come a long way. Obviously, the local people who were interested had long since been aboard to see what was what. Ehlert observed that many of the visitors in the late 1970s were Japanese. They evinced great curiosity in the ship, looking at everything possible, including the guns, the surrender deck, and the displays that had been prepared concerning the ship's history. A few of the visitors were former *Missouri* crew members who wanted another look at their old home.[24]

After years and years, when the workers at the Naval Inactive Ships Maintenance Facility had run the dehumidification machines and done all the other things needed to preserve the *Missouri* for potential future use, the word finally came in early 1984 that the ship was going to be towed to Long Beach for reactivation and modernization. As the Navy's industrial complex prepared to turn potential into reality, swarms of visitors from the Naval Sea Systems Command in Washington, D. C., made the trip across country to ascertain the material condition for themselves.[25]

The visitors looked at the records the facility in Bremerton had maintained, and they also had the plans that had been developed for the modernization of the *Iowa* class as a whole. NavSea commended the mothball maintenance facility for the overall condition of the ship, which was better than headquarters personnel had expected. The 16-inch guns had been relined in 1954 and had now only to be reactivated. The engineering plant had undergone overhaul as well. Even so, twenty-nine years is a long time for a warship to remain out of service and then return to full-fledged service in the fleet.[26]

As the ship prepared to depart, the dehumidification system was shut off, but its machinery remained on board and was later removed at the Long Beach Naval Shipyard. The main thing the men in Bremerton had to do was rig the ship for the trip, putting on a towing bridle and installing an alarm system. The system could let the riding crew on board know if anything in the battleship was amiss during the long transit. Another addition was a portable generator to supply power to the wardroom for the benefit of the riding crew. Alas, the fire and flushing system was not activated until after the ship got to Long Beach, so the riding crew had to use portable toilets brought aboard for the trip. The ship riders were essentially campers.[27]

The day of departure was May 14. The *Missouri* was still a dead ship as the tugboats pulled her away from the pier that had the decommissioned guided missile cruisers *Chicago* and *Oklahoma City* on the other side. It was an exciting moment as the battleship left for her encounter with a new generation of shipyard workers in far-off Long Beach. They were prepared to breathe life once again into the mountain of steel that had been dormant for so long. Although she was covered with temporary age spots, the long gray ship still had her sleek lines. As the tugs moved her past the piers of the na-

val shipyard and out toward the open waters of Puget Sound, the reaction was mixed. Bremerton civic officials hated to see the city lose her as a tourist attraction. On the other hand, men such as Harry Ehlert felt great satisfaction. All of their efforts at preserving the ship would be repaid by her ability to return to active service.[28]

The Navy salvage ship *Beaufort* had the job

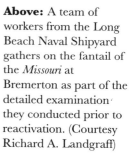

Above: A team of workers from the Long Beach Naval Shipyard gathers on the fantail of the *Missouri* at Bremerton as part of the detailed examination they conducted prior to reactivation. (Courtesy Richard A. Landgraff)

Left: In early 1984, the *Missouri* lies moored at the last pier of the reserve fleet berthing. The space across the pier had previously been occupied by the *New Jersey* until she was towed away in 1981 for reactivation. Shown here are two guided missile cruisers—the *Chicago*, next to the pier, and the *Oklahoma City*, outboard. (Pam Lama photo via Robert Sumrall)

On May 14, 1984, tugboats guide the *Missouri* as she begins the long tow to Long Beach. (DoD Still Media Depository: DN-SN-84-10587)

of towing the dreadnought south toward Long Beach. Included in the riding crew of twenty was Chief Petty Officer Don Heath. At night he liked to go to the narrow forecastle and look up at the stars as the ship moved slowly through the Pacific. The ship riders, who had a microwave oven in which to cook their meals, had their pick of staterooms on board. They just plopped their sleeping bags down in whatever bunks looked appealing. Among the group was a nineteen-year-old woman, Seaman Beverly Stokes, who said of the trip: "It was cold out there in the middle of the night. I'd bundle up in my sleeping bag with a cup of hot chocolate and think warm thoughts."[29]

12 ❖ Around the World

May 1984–December 1986

After eleven days at sea, the *Missouri* arrived in Long Beach on May 25, escorted by a fireboat that sent out arcing streams of water. More than five hundred Navy personnel and shipyard workers gathered for a brief welcoming ceremony. Captain George Fink, the shipyard commander, had a receptive audience when he explained the effect that the modernization job would have on the local economy. The yard's workload had dropped off recently, and this meant a real boost in terms of employment. It was expected to save at least five hundred threatened jobs and create, at least for a time, another three to four hundred new ones.[1]

When the ship came into Long Beach that day, former crew member Tom O'Malley was one of the first to step aboard. He was there for a sentimental visit and also had a pragmatic reason for coming back. O'Malley had smuggled some liquor onto the *Missouri* in 1953 when she was in Japan but hadn't been able to smuggle it back off when she returned to the United States. He had put the bottles into a wooden crate and hid it in a void area. A welder had put in a false bulkhead to cover up the liquid treasure. Upon his return in 1984, O'Malley found that the false bulkhead had been removed during the ship's long stay at Bremerton. The hiding place had disappeared and so had the cargo he had waited so long to reclaim.[2]

One of the things the crew had gone through during the inactivation period in 1954 was closing down each individual space. In the electrical shop O'Malley was frustrated by a rotating fan that wouldn't work. After some effort, he finally got it back into operating condition. When he went aboard thirty years later,

O'Malley made a point of going to that same shop. He put in some fuses, and the fan that he had repaired in 1954 worked once again. It was, he observed, a literal demonstration of the expression "the man meeting the boy." He had left the shop in his early twenties; he returned in his fifties. Being in the same place again swamped him with feelings of nostalgia for the youth that had long since departed.[3]

Just about a month prior to the *Missouri*'s arrival, the *Iowa* was recommissioned; the *New Jersey* had been recommissioned in 1982. The *Missouri* would be the third of her class to rejoin

A view from astern as the *Missouri* arrives in Long Beach to end her long journey on May 25, 1984. (Photo by Lawrence Foster in DoD Still Media Records Center: DN-SN-84-10420)

the fleet. These three ships (and later, the *Wisconsin*) were part of a program spearheaded by Secretary of the Navy John Lehman, who took office in 1981. The country had been stung by a series of events in the mid-to-late 1970s, including Soviet adventurism in places such as Angola and Afghanistan and the seizure of the American Embassy in Teheran, Iran. All this served to create a perception that the United States was weak. In addition, the Navy had fallen off in training readiness, ammunition supplies, and manning levels for ships. The energetic Lehman set out to reverse that situation and announced a goal to build to a six-hundred-ship fleet. Reactivating the four *Iowa*-class battleships was a way of symbolizing the resurgence.[4]

The administration and Congress had approved the battleship program for political reasons. Gradually, the Navy put together a doctrine to spell out missions for the ships. As part of the business of selling the forty-year-old ships, Lehman emphasized their new batteries of Tomahawk and Harpoon missiles, both capable of long-range strikes. No longer would the ships' reach be limited to the range of their 16-inch guns. Now they would again have an offensive role, as they had had when originally conceived. Among the various other missions for the dreadnoughts were naval presence as a

means of influencing events ashore, beefing up aircraft carrier battle groups in high-threat areas, and serving as centerpieces of battleship battle groups in low-threat areas. The missions dearest to the Marine Corps revolved around those 16-inch guns. The *Missouri* could provide shore bombardment during amphibious assaults and then gunfire support for troops once ashore.[5]

All told, the *Missouri*'s reactivation and modernization package cost about 475 million dollars; her original cost in World War II had been in the neighborhood of 100 million. The *Missouri* was essentially reactivated to the configuration designed for the *Iowa*. The *New Jersey* had been a special case because she had been modernized for her brief Vietnam stint, and the designers did not need to make as many changes with her as with the other three when she came back in the 1980s.

The shipyard set to work soon after the *Missouri* arrived, putting her into dry dock and beginning the rip-out phase: that is, taking off old equipment that would be replaced during the modernization. In January 1985, Captain Andrew Fahy, the prospective executive officer, reported to the Fleet Training Center at San Diego to head the ship's precommissioning unit. This was analogous to the situation in

Opposite page: A great deal of scaffolding is already in place on the stacks as a crane lifts off the tripod after mast that had been on board the *Missouri* since the early 1950s. The picture was taken in June 1984, during the rip-out phase of the yard period. (Long Beach Naval Shipyard)

Left: By August 1984, the top of the forward fire control tower was bare. Both the optical range finder and the 011 level had been removed to facilitate reconstruction in the area. (Long Beach Naval Shipyard)

1944. The difference this time was that the program was starting more than a year ahead of time, rather than just a few months early. By the 1980s, the Navy had a well-established program of "pipeline" training for men reporting to ships. By the summer of 1985, the training was in progress at several locations, including Tomahawk missile school at Dam Neck, Virginia. One of the main items emphasized among all personnel was damage control, either as a refresher for veterans or a first-time experience for new men.[6]

In March, Captain Lee Kaiss reported as the prospective commanding officer. He was the first *Missouri* skipper who was not a Naval Academy alumnus. Kaiss had joined the Navy after graduating from the University of Maryland in 1962 and had served in a variety of destroyer-type ships. He commanded the destroyer *Paul F. Foster* and the guided-missile cruiser *William H. Standley* but had no big-ship experience. As part of his pipeline training, he went to a commercial school in Toledo, Ohio, to learn how merchant captains conned large tankers. He later went to sea in the *New Jersey*, where Captain Rich Milligan gave him some pointers.[7]

When he arrived at the shipyard in Long Beach, Kaiss met up with a nucleus crew that

comprised five chief petty officers and about fifty lower-rated men. The *Missouri* was hardly glamorous at the time; she was still in the rip-out phase. The ship was sitting in dry dock and had about eighty holes in the bottom as work progressed on void spaces. Topside hatches were open, so when he went into one of the berthing compartments, Kaiss found three inches of standing water. He cleared that up during a conference with Captain Fink, the shipyard commander. Kaiss soon developed a fine working relationship with him and with Ray Richetti, the shipyard's civilian project manager for the *Missouri*.[8]

Machinist's Mate First Class Bill Holland reported to San Diego for training in July and moved aboard a living barge—essentially a boxy-looking floating building. To identify it for new men, it had a banner on the brow that bore the legend "USS *Missouri* BB-63." As he approached the barge one day, he came up behind two young sailors who had just come from boot camp and had orders to report to the precommissioning crew of the battleship. He overheard one of them say: "So that's the *Missouri*.

Right: Scaffolding encases the forward fire control tower as the modernization work proceeds in February 1985. The bridge is at bottom, and above that is a Mark 37 director. The 08 level is at the center of the picture. (Photo by Randy Hayes in DoD Still Media Records Center: DN-ST-85-08817)

Below: This boxy-looking structure is a floating barracks barge in which crew members lived before moving aboard the *Missouri* in late 1985. (Courtesy Robert Sumrall)

My God, I thought it would be bigger." Machinist's Mate Holland, with considerable sea duty under his belt, couldn't help but chuckle at the newcomers and then give them the straight scoop.[9]

When Electrician's Mate Robert Webber arrived at Long Beach that autumn, he went down to the engine rooms and found them to be like dungeons in appearance. They still had the old light fixtures that used incandescent bulbs, probably no more than seventy-five watts. It was the same as in 1955 and made Webber wonder how the machinist's mates could do their jobs back then. The answer, of course, was that they didn't have any alternatives. One of his tasks during the modernization was to help install fluorescent lighting in the engineering spaces. On the other hand, the generator setup in the ship was still the same as in 1944; it required no modifications. The ship had enormous capacity in that regard in order to operate all the electrical equipment on board. Each turret, including all of the associated motors and so forth, inside, drew more than seventeen hundred amps. The ship didn't have as many guns as in 1944, but now she had

more electronic gear, and missile systems were being added as well.[10]

In 1984 and early 1985, Yeoman John Lewis had served in the *New Jersey*. In that ship he worked for Lieutenant Commander John Jones, the main propulsion assistant. Then Lewis developed an interest in serving in the *Missouri* when she came along because he came from the small town of Palmyra, Missouri, not far from Mark Twain's home at Hannibal. So he contacted Jones, who by then was a commander and prospective chief engineer of the *Missouri*. Jones made a few telephone calls, and Lewis got his wish, transferring to the *Missouri* in August 1985.[11]

Having served in the *New Jersey*'s engineering log room, Lewis went down to the corresponding space on the second deck of the *Missouri* and found quite a contrast to the vibrant office he'd left in the sister ship. Here he saw only a single light bulb suspended from the overhead; it reminded him of police interrogation scenes depicted in crime movies. The bulkheads had been stripped down to bare metal. The paint of thirty years ago had partly flaked off in the dry mothball-fleet atmosphere, and the rest had been removed deliberately. Indeed, few signs indicated that this had once been the work space for dozens of human beings. Part of Lewis's job—and one that gave him great

Left: In early 1985, Captain Lee Kaiss reported as prospective commanding officer of the *Missouri*. (U.S. Navy photo courtesy of Walter Urban)

Below: The propeller is removed from the number-three shaft with the ship in dry dock in February 1985. (DoD Still Media Records Center: DN-SN-93-00828)

A workman repaints the name "MISSOURI" on the stern in February 1985. It was in vain. Prior to the recommissioning the following year, the shipyard installed an opening for the towed AN/SLQ-25 NIXIE decoy, designed to distract acoustic homing torpedoes from the ship. That necessitated the raising—and repainting—of the ship's name. (Photo by Kenneth D. Mehl in DoD Still Media Records Center: DN-SC-86-00753)

satisfaction—was to help make the logroom functional and ready for occupants.[12]

The assignment of Commander Jones, a black man, as a department head demonstrated how much the U.S. Navy's personnel situation had changed since the *Missouri* was last in commission. By 1985, blacks were at nearly all levels of the ship's rank structure and in a variety of occupational specialties as well. Not surprisingly, Yeoman Lewis had developed a high degree of loyalty to Commander Jones, a former enlisted man who had worked his way up to the commissioned ranks. It was reciprocated. Some of the new *Missouri* engineers were put off a bit by Jones, not because of his race but because of his frequent references to how things were done in the *New Jersey*. For them it was probably similar to the parental statement, "Now, when I was your age . . ."[13]

The main propulsion assistant as the *Missouri*'s engineering plant came back together was Lieutenant Commander Geoff Calabrese. He also was a former enlisted man and, like Jones, he later became the *Missouri*'s chief engineer. The testimonials by his shipmates to Calabrese's competence are legion. His firsthand experience gave him a minutely detailed

knowledge of the ship's engineering plant. During the reassembly and eventual operation of the boilers, engines, reduction gears, generators, pumps, and all the rest, he was in the spaces constantly to ensure that things were working properly. Some mustangs aren't able to withdraw from the desire for hands-on involvement, and Calabrese was one such officer. As Bill Holland put it, "God help you if he knew more about your plant than you did."[14]

In order to accommodate all of the computers and other electronic gear that went with the ship's missile systems, shipyard workmen gutted the old flag quarters on the 02 level. Included were the office, mess, and berthing spaces in which President Truman lived during the 1947 cruise from Brazil. For the earlier modernization of the *New Jersey*, the shipyard at Long Beach installed a layer of armored steel over the forward bulkhead in the wardroom. This was a means of providing additional protection to the cable and piping trunks that were installed to run up to the new combat engagement center that filled the spaces previously occupied by the flag quarters.[15]

There would have been a problem of historical preservation if the same change had been instituted in the *Missouri*. Dick Landgraff worked in the design section of the Long Beach Naval Shipyard, and he was concerned because that particular bulkhead in the *Missouri* was covered with a mural map of the ship's travels. As he put it, "I vowed that there was nothing on this green earth powerful enough to stop me from redesigning that armor in such a way that the mural would remain totally intact." And so he came up with an alternative scheme that put the armor on the other side of the bulkhead, attached only to stiffeners, not the bulkhead itself.[16]

Alas, when it came time to install the change, Murphy's Law struck. One night during the swing shift a welder who hadn't gotten the word attached the new armor directly to the back side of the bulkhead. The heat of the welding arc burned through and created ugly two-inch-wide vertical streaks that marred the mural. Landgraff was fit to be tied. Fortunately, experts from the Los Angeles County Museum of Art were able to recommend appropriate repairs. A shipyard employee who was an artist then repainted the damaged areas so skillfully that the mural became good as new.[17]

Another historic relic was the surrender plaque. The shipyard workmen removed it when the ship arrived and stored it in a vault for safekeeping. Chris Plambeck of the design shop then came up with a new Plexiglas dome to protect the plaque from the elements, rather than leaving it exposed as in the past. Much of the teak planking on the ship, including all on the surrender deck, was replaced during the yard period. All that remained of the historic area was the steel deck beneath the wood.[18]

One of the most notable differences in the reactivation packages installed in the *New Jersey* and *Missouri* was in the electronic countermeasures equipment room on the 010 level in the superstructure. When the *New Jersey* was modernized for Vietnam, the Philadelphia Naval Shipyard built protruding deckhouses from either side to accommodate the ULQ-6 electronic warfare gear. That same structure was used for the installation of the more modern

SLQ-32s in the 1980s. For the other three ships of the class, including the *Missouri*, a wraparound deckhouse was built. The yard removed the old 011 perch to put the new structure in place.[19]

Still another difference between the ships had to do with a "spook room," an electronic intelligence-gathering space adjacent to the combat engagement center. The initial installation for the *New Jersey* was done on a hush-hush basis that did not take into consideration all of the requirements for adequate power, ventilation, and air-conditioning support. For the *Missouri*, the Long Beach shipyard was given the opportunity to incorporate the spook room into its designs and therefore support it properly.[20]

One of the problems with reactivating an old ship is that many of the items of equipment are no longer manufactured. Besides the "cannibalization" of mothballed ships, the Navy combed storerooms in three memorial battleships—the *North Carolina, Massachusetts,* and *Alabama*—to come up with parts that could be incorporated in the four *Iowa*-class ships. All told, the scavengers uncovered hundreds of tons of battleship items that could be used in the ones

A close-up of the bridge shortly before recommissioning at San Francisco in May 1986. At the top of the photo is the new wraparound deckhouse built to support electronic warfare equipment. (Photo by Michael D. P. Flynn in DoD Still Media Records Center: DN-SN-86-07026)

going back into service. As Landgraff pointed out, the *North Carolina,* which was intended to lie on the river bottom at Wilmington, North Carolina, lost so much gear that she actually came afloat again.[21]

Sometimes the removals were *from* the *Missouri.* Four of the ten 5-inch twin mounts came off, for example, to make room for Tomahawk launchers amidships. They were sent to the naval weapons station at Crane, Indiana, to be refurbished for possible future use. And all of the 40-mm quad mounts came off as well, after having been preserved under dehumidified igloos for all those years. The shipyard took care to do one-piece removals of the gun mounts and shields from atop turrets two and three so they could be preserved for shipment to museums rather than being cut up. A number of the 40-mms also went to Crane, although there was little chance of their being recycled.[22]

An important milestone in the reactivation came when the first crew members moved onto the ship on September 12, 1985. They went aboard in stages, taking a week or so to complete the move. Because of his insistence on damage control readiness, Captain Kaiss required that the crew members pass a test. They had to don blindfolds and then make their way topside from their berthing spaces. If they could learn the route well enough in a non-threatening environment, they would be better able to do it if visibility was poor because of smoke or electrical failure.[23]

Finally, the men of the *Missouri* left the berthing barges behind. Now they could get their hands on the ship's own equipment, not just mock-ups and paper diagrams. The crewmen also began to come under the supervision of their shipboard leaders rather than instructors ashore. Those assigned to the 16-inch guns benefited in particular from *Iowa* and *New Jersey* veterans who had reported aboard. Chief Gunner's Mate Wayne Evans, for instance, had previously served in a light cruiser and the *Iowa,* and now he was helping the *Missouri*'s turret three prepare to shoot. The turret had a ways to go because various components such as the breechblocks had been removed so they could be refurbished in shops ashore.[24]

At the same time, shipyard workers were on board every day by the hundreds. The crew members had a mixed reaction to them. Some workmen provided superb assistance; others appeared less motivated. The *Missouri* men felt possessive about their ship, so they were understandably itchy to cut the umbilical cord. The yard workers' presence symbolized that it would still be a while before that could happen.[25]

In the early stages of work in the engineering spaces, the deck gratings and deck plates had been taken up to facilitate access to piping systems, so men had to walk around on 2x10-inch wooden planks. Gradually, as the shipyard workers finished reactivating the propulsion plant spaces, they turned them over to the ship's crew one at a time. The first time each boiler was lighted off marked a real progress point, assisted considerably by a team from the Long Beach shipyard. The initial light off was for boiler number eight on June 24, 1985. As things began operating, crewmen discovered that a good many leaks manifested themselves when fuel and water began running through the plant.[26]

In addition, there was still a great deal to learn because so few crew members had experience with the system. One remedy was that the *New Jersey* took the *Missouri*'s prospective engineers to sea in late 1985 to give them specific training on the equipment. It was necessary because shipboard propulsion plants that steamed at six hundred pounds of pressure per square inch were rare in the U.S. Navy of the mid-1980s, and the ones in the *Iowa* class were even rarer. The technology in the *Missouri*'s engineering plant went back to the 1930s. It had amazing capability for cross-connection and thus redundancy in battle. She was built to keep operating despite punishment from enemy battleships.[27]

Other men throughout the *Missouri* also looked forward to the time when they could take over custody of specific spaces from the shipyard workers. As the work was completed, the crew began to feel a pride of ownership. Part of the *Missouri* men's pride was reflected in bumper stickers that began showing up on their cars and various places in the shipyard—cranes, trucks, buildings, and so forth. This was in an era of double-entendre bumper stickers that told how people in various occupations "do it." The most popular one among the ship's men was, "Battleship Sailors Do It with 16-inchers." The shipyard commander objected, whereupon Captain Kaiss reportedly answered, "My boys have got spirit."

Kaiss himself did much to build that spirit. During his meetings with new crewmen, he emphasized the ship's history. Morale took care of itself, particularly with Kaiss telling his men that *Missouri* sailors walked six inches taller than anyone else.[28]

The *Missouri* got under way on her own power for the first time on January 28, 1986, the same day the space shuttle *Challenger* blew up in Florida. The battleship was still only partway to completion. For example, because some of the shipyard scaffolding had been in the way, the crew had not yet painted her completely in haze gray. The ship still had some pea-green undercoating primer showing in places such as the 01-level bulkheads and one of the turret tops. Going to sea the first time was nevertheless a major achievement. Yeoman Lewis heard a cheer go up in the engine rooms when the ship pulled away from the pier and word came down over the general announcing system: "Underway. Shift colors." Steam surged through the turbines, but initially the orders called for only minimal speed as the captain and pilot eased the great battleship away from her pier. While the *Missouri* was either leaving a pier or arriving at one, the engines provided the fore-and-aft movement; tugboats moved the ship sideways.[29]

Testing the engineering plant demonstrated where bugs still needed to be worked out. By the time the *Missouri* reached Long Beach's outer breakwater on her way to sea, the engineers had shut down three of her four shafts for a time. The packing around them was too tight, and they were starting to smoke. Rain began falling during the time at sea, and the skipper had to halt the trials temporarily to seal holes in the superstructure so the electronic gear inside wouldn't be damaged.[30]

Captain Kaiss picked up some ship-handling experience along with testing the en-

Captain Lee Kaiss introduces Mayor Dianne Feinstein upon the ship's arrival at San Francisco on May 6. Feinstein strongly supported the effort to make her city the *Missouri*'s home port. (DoD Still Media Records Center: DN-SN-86-06997)

gines. As the *Missouri* was going back into port afterward, he hadn't anticipated the amount of momentum she could develop, despite the fact that she didn't have a full load of fuel and ammunition. She had made a full-power run and was cruising back in at twenty knots. As she approached the outer breakwater, Kaiss gave an order for five knots and was amazed at how long she took to slow down. All told, the first sea trials went remarkably well for the engineering plant, especially in view of the age of the equipment and the length of time since the ship had last operated.[31]

During the trials, the *Missouri*'s propulsion plant was burning a new fuel. As part of the modernization process, she had been converted from the tarlike Navy special fuel oil to DFM, a lighter distillate. One beneficial by-product was an almost negligible buildup of soot in the boiler tubes. A ritual in the black-oil days was the engineers' need to blow tubes, sending air to blow out the black debris. DFM also produced much less residue on brickwork in the boilers and much less maintenance for the boilers as a whole. One drawback of DFM was that it was more volatile and thus more

likely to produce boiler explosions. Another
was that the more fluid distillate could seep
through small holes in the fuel-oil service lines
and riveted tanks, whereas the black oil was so
thick it was almost self-sealing in terms of leaks.
Even so, the advantages outweighed the added
precautions necessary to deal with DFM's
problems.[32]

The ship's second sea trials, in early March,
marked the first firing of her guns since the
1950s. Safety was paramount. After the
16-inch guns were loaded, the turret gun
booths were cleared, and the manning down
below was at a minimum as well. All went off
without incident—another milestone passed.
The successful firing bred confidence, and after
that there was no sense of apprehension.[33]

While at sea the men on the *Missouri*'s bridge
spotted sister ship *New Jersey*, which was also out
on maneuvers. And so began a rivalry that
went on until the *New Jersey* was decommissioned five years later. Captain Kaiss wanted
smart operation on the part of the *Missouri* but
particularly so when the men of the *New Jersey*
were looking on. A little good-natured ribbing

went out by message to the slightly older sister,
"Do you want to race with a real battleship?"[34]

Among those on board as the *Missouri*
worked up toward rejoining the active fleet was
Master Chief Boatswain's Mate John Davidson, who later became command master
chief—in effect, the senior enlisted adviser to
both the captain and the crew. As a seaman
first class, Davidson was in the crew of the *Missouri* when she steamed to Istanbul in 1946. In
the years since then, he had been a much-
traveled sailor and sported visual souvenirs of
his experience in the form of tattoos injected
while he was in such places as Norfolk, Hong
Kong, Pearl Harbor, and Yokohama. When the
Missouri was approved for recommissioning,
Davidson received a telephone call from Washington asking if he would like to be in the crew.
Even though he had been eligible for retirement for some time, he said of the opportunity,
"I told them I'd pay them to let me serve." The
beauty of the situation was that the Navy would
continue to pay him.[35]

While all of the technical changes were being
made, political developments were proceeding
likewise. The *New Jersey* had been recommissioned at Long Beach, and the initial expectation was that the *Missouri* would be too. But
Mayor Dianne Feinstein saw considerable economic advantage to having the battleship
home ported in her city. She waged a spirited
campaign that dovetailed nicely with Secretary
Lehman's program of strategic home porting:
that is, distributing warships among various
ports. The stated rationale was that it reduced
the vulnerability of having too many eggs in too
few baskets. It also had the advantage of building support for Lehman's six-hundred-ship
Navy. Feinstein's campaign succeeded. The
Missouri was slated to make San Francisco her
home port and would be recommissioned there
as well. May 10, 1986, was set as the date.[36]

As the recommissioning approached, the
prospective crew of the *Missouri* went through
one rehearsal after another to ensure that the
ceremony would be as nearly perfect as possible. On one occasion Yeoman Lewis and
Lieutenant Jerry Miller, both from the state of

Missouri, cornered Captain Kaiss when he visited the engineering logroom. They told him: "The way you pronounce the name of this ship is Ma-zour-ah, not Ma-zour-ee. If Margaret Truman comes on board and hears you say Ma-zour-ee, you're going to be in trouble." Kaiss also took another step to bond ship and state. He decided that those standing the first quarterdeck watch upon recommissioning were to be from Missouri. Miller was the officer of the deck, and Lewis was petty officer of the watch. It was a proud moment for both.[37]

In early May, freshly painted and much changed from when she had arrived at Long Beach two years earlier, the *Missouri* steamed to San Francisco. The sky above was a bright blue when the ship was recommissioned on a glorious spring Saturday. The ceremony was held at pier thirty-two, just inside the Oakland Bay Bridge, the one that suffered earthquake damage three years later. Some twelve thousand people were seated on the pier to watch, and the crew was lined up in ranks alongside the ship. On the surrender deck were the captain and a number of politicians who had made themselves part of the event.

Two politicians who were not particularly cordial to each other during the recommissioning were Secretary of the Navy Lehman and Governor John Ashcroft of Missouri. The state had presented the ship with a silver service in 1948, and it had remained on board until the ship was decommissioned. At that time, the Navy sent the silver to the state capital, Jefferson City, specifying that it was on loan until such time as the ship might go back into commission. That time arrived in 1986, but Missouri had become so fond of the silver that it was reluctant to return it to the ship. Negotiations had gone on for some time until the silver finally returned to the *Missouri* the night before the recommissioning.[38] If the state had not relinquished the silver service, a federal marshal was prepared to take custody of it on behalf of the Navy.

Secretary of Defense Caspar Weinberger made the principal address during the May 10 ceremony and put the ship into commission. Captain Kaiss then accepted the command and began to speak. During the weeks leading up to that day, Kaiss had asked the public affairs office to draft a speech for him. Journalist First Class Bill Egan was assigned the task but received no guidance at all from the skip-

The sleek, newly modernized *Missouri* steams past the waterfront at San Francisco on May 6, 1986, as she arrives for recommissioning. (Photo by Steve Grzezdzinski in DoD Still Media Records Center: DN-SC-86-06960)

per. He wrote a speech that incorporated his own feelings for the ship, turned it in, and heard nary a word of feedback. Egan thus assumed that Kaiss had asked someone in Washington or elsewhere to put together a speech for him. But as he stood with other crewmen alongside the ship, Egan heard the words he himself had written. Included in the message that Captain Kaiss put forth to the audience was this opening: "On October 27, 1945, when President Harry S Truman stepped aboard USS *Missouri*, he said, 'This is the happiest day of my life.' Ladies and gentlemen, I know exactly how he felt."[39]

Egan had a special inspiration in writing that speech because he also had seen the battleship *Missouri* during that 1945 Navy Day celebration in New York. Egan was four years old at the time and had already started collecting newspaper pictures of the famous ship. Then his parents took him and his brother to see the fleet. His father parked the family car on the

New Jersey palisades, giving them a great view of the broad sweep of the Hudson River and the seven miles of warships anchored there. He told his dad that day he wanted to be a sailor on the "Big Mo." Forty years later—after having become a civilian newspaperman and then

joining the naval reserve in 1979—that dream came true for Bill Egan.[40]

After Kaiss's speech, an order from the surrender deck sent hundreds of *Missouri* crewmen running aboard from the pier. They moved up double brows, and many disappeared inside the skin of the ship. They raced up interior ladders and then began reappearing in rows on the various decks of the superstructure. Others manned the rail on the main deck. Once the crew members were in place topside, the *Missouri*'s weapons started moving simultaneously, further dramatizing the ship's symbolic return to life. The long barrels of the 16-inch guns turned to point toward the audience and then were raised to maximum elevation. The mounts of the Vulcan/Phalanx close-in weapon system began rotating and bobbing up and down. The 5-inch mounts turned their guns off the beam and elevated them as well. The armored box launchers for the Tomahawk missiles climbed to their firing position. The *Missouri* was back.[41]

Protesters demonstrated against the ship during the ceremony. Afterward, Machinist's Mate Holland went on liberty with a few shipmates. He overheard someone indicating that he didn't want nuclear-powered ships operating from the port. Holland asked him, "What are you talking about?"

"The nuclear power on the *Missouri*."

Holland replied: "There isn't any nuclear power. It's forty-year-old, six-hundred-pound steam." The protester probably figured the battleship petty officer was giving him a phony cover story. The ship had no nuclear weapons on board at the time either, although in that area Holland scrupulously adhered to the Navy policy of neither confirming nor denying their presence.[42]

That evening the state of Missouri sponsored a gala music-and-fireworks reception in San Francisco's city hall. Afterward, the state treated the crew members and their families to a sit-down dinner. Margaret Truman Daniel—who had that name since her marriage in 1956 to an editor for *The New York Times*—spoke to the crew, as she had during the daytime ceremony. She provided some brief recollections of

the launching, and she imparted a sense of the ship's history and what it meant to her. Then she turned to the skipper and said something that stuck in the minds of the officers and enlisted men who were there. "Captain Kaiss and the men of the *Missouri*, there's one other thing I want to say to you. Please take good care of my baby." As Lieutenant Mike McDermott observed, "The crew went nuts." They rose and gave the *Missouri*'s sponsor a standing ovation.[43]

A close-up of the superstructure during an at-sea evaluation period off southern California on July 25, 1986. (Photo by Thomas M. Hensley in DoD Still Media Records Center: DN-SC-87-09288)

Two ships with hull number 63—the *Missouri* and the carrier *Kitty Hawk*—refuel from the oiler *Kawishiwi* off the California coast in the summer of 1986. (U.S. Navy photo by Thomas M. Hensley)

On June 12, when the *Missouri* was back in Long Beach, two hundred former members of the crew returned aboard for old-timers' day. The format was particularly appealing because each veteran was paired with a counterpart from the modern crew who did the same job he once had. The current crew member gave the veteran a tour of the entire ship, ate lunch with him, and brought him up to date on the specific work space that was common to both. It was fascinating for the sailors of previous times to see what had changed and what was still the same. The pleasures of being back on familiar territory were manifold, but there were a few drawbacks as well. Herb Fahr had served in the A division back in the mid-1950s. When he came back more than thirty years later, it

was a struggle to squeeze his expanded girth through the hatch that led down into the after emergency diesel compartment. As he remembered, "I didn't realize you had such a small hole to go through."[44]

One benefit of the special day was to reinforce a sense of history among the new crew members. By talking with their counterparts, they got a sense of what life had been like decades earlier. As a machinery repairman from World War II talked with his successors in the ship's machine shop, for example, one of the new men asked the purpose of the hooks welded to the overhead. That's where he put up his hammock, he told them; the ship was so crowded that some men had to sleep in their work spaces. Another man went back to a for-

ward pump room where he had been on watch when the kamikaze hit in 1945. His sound-powered telephones went dead as the plane struck the ship; he was alone and had no one to talk with. When he went back to that same room in 1986, tears came to his eyes as he remembered the terrible sense of isolation he felt so many years earlier.[45]

The special day that Captain Kaiss had arranged came near the end of his time in command. Medical tests had revealed that he had heart trouble and needed to go ashore in a limited-duty status. At the time, Captain James A. "Al" Carney had nearly completed the training pipeline to command the Aegis cruiser *Thomas S. Gates*. He was taking a course in Newport, Rhode Island, when he received a telephone call from Vice Admiral Joe Metcalf, deputy chief of naval operations for surface warfare. Metcalf asked him if he would be willing to command the *Missouri* instead of the cruiser. As Carney recalled later, "It took me about a microsecond to say, 'Yes, sir, I'll do that.'"[46]

Carney had been commissioned through officer candidate school in 1961 and then got some big-ship experience in his initial duty assignment. He served in the amphibious assault ship *Princeton*, a converted *Essex*-class carrier. After that he had several tours in destroyers, including three years as the first skipper of the USS *Leftwich*. What probably helped considerably in his selection to command the *Missouri* was the visibility he gained in the Pentagon during duty as head of the branch of the CNO staff that oversaw the Aegis program.[47]

The crewmen were truly surprised when they learned that Captain Kaiss was leaving for health reasons. There had been no rumors to that effect, and they received very little advance notice of the change, which took place June 20. The men of the *Missouri* were sorry to see Captain Kaiss go because they had developed a strong relationship with him while working together to get the ship back into the fleet. He was a hard act for Carney to follow. Yeoman Lewis observed that it would have been a difficult position for any successor to step into. "Everybody was measuring him against Captain Kaiss, and that wasn't fair."[48]

Captain Carney, though friendly, was not so

Captain Carney, in his chair on the starboard side of the bridge, talks with one of the ship's officers. (Photo by Rich Pedroncelli)

gregarious as Captain Kaiss and not so inclined to interact with the crew at large. For example, he was less likely to move around the ship or use the general announcing system to stay in touch. He struck many in the crew as a soft-spoken, low-key officer and a nice guy—a fatherly figure, one who chided gently rather than loudly. During an underway replenishment sometime after Carney took over, Lieutenant McDermott was officer of the deck. He was slow in realizing how close he was to the oiler because he was still running through his checkoff list. Carney asked, "Are you going to start your approach now?" There was no shouting, no reprimand, just a quiet way of getting the conning officer's attention focused.[49]

In late July, about a month after the new skipper's arrival, the ship underwent naval gunfire support qualification at San Clemente Island, off the coast of southern California. The 16-inch firing was impressive. In one of her initial salvos, the ship scored a direct hit on the hulk of a bus being used as a target. The range master soon asked the *Missouri* to use an offset when firing: that is, deliberately aim to miss by a certain amount, because it was expensive to drag in more broken-down buses.[50]

The first time the ship fired a nine-gun broadside, Captain Carney was on the 05-level gun control station, right above the bridge. Initially, he was alarmed, wondering if something had gone wrong. Even with double protection—ear plugs and "Mickey Mouse" ears—the sensation was intense. As he explained: "When you fire a broadside and you're standing up there, the concussion gets inside your chest cavity and just kind of rolls around in there. It kind of feels like your heart stops."[51]

With the first real shooting accomplished, the *Missouri* was ready for her shakedown cruise. She would steam all the way around the world on a goodwill mission that would capitalize on her storied past. Not long before the cruise began, Secretary of the Navy Lehman relaxed the prohibition against drinking on board Navy ships. Since 1914 it had been absolute. Lehman modified the regulation to permit the serving of beer, wine, and sherry in connection with social events such as receptions. Captain Carney concluded that the *Missouri*'s com-

ing voyage was the stimulus for the decision because of all the public relations stops she would be making during the tour. In fact, Admiral James A. "Ace" Lyons, who was commander in chief Pacific Fleet at the time, allocated twenty-eight thousand dollars to the ship as an entertainment fund.[52]

The cruise began on September 10, when the *Missouri* left Long Beach for Pearl Harbor. She had an engineering problem the first day; an inspection plate fell into the reduction gears for number-one main engine and damaged gear teeth as it passed through. The shaft was locked initially to prevent damage. Then it was on to Hawaii, the first time there for many in the battleship's crew.

As the *Missouri* left Pearl Harbor after a brief stay, she steamed near the *Arizona* Memorial for a wreath-laying ceremony in honor of her long-ago predecessor. The ship then proceeded to the island of Molokai to reenact a 1908 salute that the previous battleship *Missouri* participated in during the voyage of the Great White

Gas-ejection air blows out the remnants of firing as the *Missouri* unleashes a fifteen-gun broadside prior to her arrival at Sydney, Australia. (U.S. Navy photo courtesy of Helen Devine)

Fleet. Back then President Theodore Roosevelt sent the fleet around the world as a means of demonstrating U.S. naval might. While the fleet was en route, he received a request from Brother Joseph Dutton, a patriotic Civil War veteran who was the spiritual and community leader of the leper colony on Molokai. Roosevelt directed that the fleet, including the old *Missouri*, divert from its course and salute those living there. As the later *Missouri* steamed past in 1986, her crew stood at the rail and saluted, and the ship dipped her flag as a sign of respect.[53]

While the *Missouri* was at Pearl Harbor, the engineering team had unlocked the number-one propeller shaft; consequently, it freewheeled during the voyage to Australia. Had it remained locked, it would have caused a drag and added to the ship's fuel consumption. There wasn't time to fix it in the meantime and still make the schedule for reaching Australia. Even so, on three shafts the ship achieved a speed of advance of about twenty-two knots, well within the capability of the engineering plant even on two shafts. With the number-one

shaft unlocked, the ship's force—having only minor help from an outside technical representative—was able to repair the reduction-gear damage. Lieutenant Commander Calabrese, with his hands-on approach, played a major role in smoothing the damaged gear teeth with a grinder. The *Missouri* later left Sydney on four engines.[54]

While on her way to Sydney, the *Missouri* crossed the equator at the international dateline, giving her crew members the distinction of becoming golden shellbacks. As in most such initiation ceremonies, the pollywogs had to crawl around the deck on their hands and knees, go through a garbage-filled chute, and get dunked in a pool of water. The character of King Neptune was assumed by Master Chief Davidson, who had been on board when President Truman crossed the equator in the *Missouri* in 1947.[55]

Lieutenant Bob Anderson was a member of the Seventh Fleet public affairs staff. The *Missouri*'s visit to Sydney was scheduled to coincide with the seventy-fifth anniversary of the Royal Australian Navy, so Anderson was sent to Australia and then aboard the battleship to provide public affairs support. Part of the publicity plan included the firing of a fifteen-gun broadside—all nine 16-inch guns, plus the six 5-inch guns

Left: Members of the Marine detachment man the rail as the battleship enters Sydney, Australia. (Photo by Ron Bayles in DoD Still Media Records Center: DN-SN-89-04942)

Below: Peace demonstrators float past the bow of the anchored *Missouri* at Sydney. (Photo by Ron Bayles in DoD Still Media Records Center: DN-SN-89-04947)

Right: A gunner's mate cleans one of the barrels of the Vulcan/Phalanx Gatling gun-type close-in weapon system. (Photo by Bob Lindel in DoD Still Media Records Center: DN-SN-87-02515)

Below: Dozens of small craft escort the *Missouri* as she arrives at Sydney to observe the seventy-fifth anniversary of the Royal Australian Navy. (Photo by Royal Australian Navy)

on the starboard side—the day before arrival. When the ship unleashed her massive salvo, Anderson was on the signal bridge. He was awed by a huge flash that temporarily obscured everything else in his field of vision. The heat from the combined fifteen guns was overpowering as well, and it was accompanied by great noise—albeit muffled by the ear protection. The heat lingered on Anderson's skin for a while after the guns were fired.[56]

On the starboard side, every steel hatch had been closed and dogged down except for one inadvertently left open. It led into a head on the main deck, about amidships. The pressure blast from the firing of fifteen guns tore off the aluminum joiner door that provided access to the head; it was ripped from its hinges. A sink and toilet were torn loose from their attachments and thrown against the inner bulkhead, leaving imprints of where they smashed into the metal. Water—no longer restrained by the plumbing fixtures—was everywhere in the head. Such was the power of 16-inch guns.[57]

People lined the shoreline for miles as the *Missouri* made her entrance into Sydney's spectacular harbor on October 1. She was the showpiece, the final ship in an international column of arriving warships. Kayaks and sailboats—emblazoned with peace signs and the logo of Greenpeace—were waiting for them. The ship just in front of the *Missouri* was a French corvette. Her conning officer saw all the protesters' boats coming, so he put the ship's rudder over and made a racetrack circle in the

water. That allowed her to come in astern of the massive dreadnought and thereby gain some protection. Australian police boats, equipped with nozzles to shoot water against burning vessels, were escorting the column of ships into the harbor. Without being too obvious about it, the police boats made subtle course changes so that the spray from their water cannons went into the protesters' boats and drove them away. None of them got even close to the *Missouri* or any of the other warships.[58]

The Australian people reacted to the *Missouri* with incredible enthusiasm. All told, perhaps a quarter of a million people showed up on the day specified for general visiting. The crowd apparently far exceeded all estimates, and it also far exceeded the ship's capacity to accommodate. After only about an hour and a half, the ship's command duty officer decided to cut off the visiting, because the situation was unsafe. Part of the problem was that there hadn't been a gradual, orderly buildup. The horde of people seemed to gather shortly before the visiting was due to start, and they couldn't be managed.[59]

The crush of humanity was such that about a dozen women fainted. Because of the glut of people, the women had to be raised overhead and passed from hand to hand to get them to the ship and into the wardroom so the *Missouri*'s doctors could attend to them. One of the women was pregnant and appeared about to deliver, which raised some interesting legal questions. Captain Carney and others wondered whether the baby would be an American citizen if born on board the *Missouri*. As it happened, the immediate treatment was successful, and the baby was not delivered on board after all.[60]

The *Missouri* crew members had a tough time working their way through the horde on the dock to go on liberty. As Electrician's Mate Webber experienced the crush, he felt he was trying to swim against a current. It was worth the effort, though, because *Missouri* sailors were instant celebrities. They seldom made it back to the ship with their hats: many of the local people wanted them as souvenirs. Australians were practically pulling the men into bars to

buy them drinks. In fact, that phenomenon became so evident that men from other ships began sewing *Missouri* patches onto their uniforms so they could cash in on the hospitality.[61]

One facet of the Royal Australian Navy's anniversary celebration was a fireworks display. As the *Missouri* sat at anchor, her men were on deck to watch the show. It turned out that the lights in the sky were not the entire show. Hundreds of small boats dotted the harbor, and the men on deck at times sent the roving beam of a spotlight through the boats to spot the Australian women in them. Some were in various stages of undress, which made the game more enjoyable for the sailors on deck.[62]

Left: Surrounded by fire bricks, boiler technicians service the boiler system in the *Missouri* in preparation for an operational propulsion plant examination (OPPE) that kept the ship's engineers busy throughout the long cruise. (Photo by Bob Lindel in DoD Still Media Records Center: DN-ST-87-00664)

Below: The *Missouri* puts up her dress-ship signal flags at Sydney to help observe the Royal Australian Navy's anniversary. The admiral at the lower right is Britain's Prince Philip, the Duke of Edinburgh. (Courtesy USS *Missouri*)

Above: A CH-53E Super Stallion helicopter lands on the new flight deck aft to deliver members of the Italian news media as the *Missouri* approaches Naples, Italy, in November 1986. The fantail has been covered with nonskid material, surrounded by a raised lip to prevent spilled fuel from spreading. (Photo by Bob Lindel in DoD Still Media Records Center: DN-ST-87-02536)

Right: Captain Al Carney speaks at a press conference during the ship's visit to Naples in November 1986. Standing beside him is Vice Admiral Kendall Moranville, commander, Sixth Fleet. (Photo by Andrew J. Brown in DoD Still Media Records Center: DN-SN-87-02554)

One of the visitors who was able to get aboard in Sydney was Dr. Mary Bertram, a pioneer in women's rights in Australia. She was a cousin of the Royal Navy's Lord Fraser, who had been on board the battleship in September 1945 to accept the Japanese surrender on behalf of Great Britain. The admiral had written to Dr. Bertram shortly after the surrender and described the ceremony to her. She brought the letter along when she visited the ship in Sydney. As she climbed the ladder to the 01 veranda deck where the surrender had taken place, she said, "I feel as if I should get down on my knees and kiss this deck." That was the sentiment of many Aussies old enough to remember World War II and the threat they had faced from a possible Japanese invasion of their country. Dr. Bertram and others with long memories treated the *Missouri* more as a shrine than a warship.[63]

Following Sydney, the *Missouri* visited Perth, in western Australia, during the America's Cup race. At that time Australia had the cup, and Dennis Connor was in the midst of his eventually successful effort to reclaim it for the United States. The battleship was anchored near the racecourse, so the crew got a good view of the competition. After that, the battleship headed west across the Indian Ocean toward the Red Sea and Suez.[64]

The Red Sea was extremely crowded when the *Missouri* moved through it. To Lieutenant McDermott, it appeared that the rules of the road were not always observed by the locals. The *Missouri* didn't want to get into the position of steering all over the place to avoid small craft, so she just cranked on the knots and roared on through, leaving it to the others to stay out of her way. They did. The transit of the Suez Canal was an all-day affair, tiring to the bridge watch team, which was essentially on a port-and-starboard basis. Some U.S. diplomatic personnel and their families were on board for the canal run and particularly enjoyed the *Missouri*'s chow. The stick-to-their-ribs fare was evidently a contrast to what they habitually ate in the Middle East.[65]

A "Krivak"-class Soviet "tattle-tail" destroyer began trailing the *Missouri* as the battleship arrived in the Mediterranean Sea. The battleship was unsuccessful in the attempt to shake her pursuer. The Soviet warship stayed close until the *Missouri* reached the Dardanelles en route to Istanbul, Turkey. That port was deliberately part of the schedule because of the battleship's history-making visit there forty years earlier.[66]

Vice Admiral Kendall Moranville, com-

mander Sixth Fleet, embarked for the transit of the Dardanelles, Sea of Marmara, and Bosporus on the way to Istanbul. The ship held a couple of receptions while anchored at the Turkish capital. Among the visitors were the children of Ambassador Ertegun, whose body the *Missouri* had transported to Istanbul for burial. The Erteguns, who had settled in the United States following their father's death, flew to Turkey for the occasion. Ahmet Munir Ertegun, the ambassador's son, was one of those who made the trip. He received a bache-

lor's degree from St. John's College, Annapolis, Maryland, in 1944 and later did graduate work at Georgetown. In 1947, he became co-founder of Atlantic Records in New York. He still heads the company.[67]

Other guests at the social events were prominent local citizens, one of whom brought along some of the postage stamps issued to honor the ship during her 1946 trip to the city. That individual apparently was the exception. When he went ashore, Lieutenant McDermott found the Turks to be friendly, but few seemed to have a great deal of awareness about the battleship's visit. That was in great contrast to the overwhelming welcome given the ship the first time.[68]

During the ship's stay in Istanbul, Captain Carney went to the local Hilton Hotel, which rests atop a hill overlooking the area. As he was sitting and having a drink, he looked through a large plate-glass window at an impressive view of the Bosporus, as well as the anchored *Missouri*. For a while Carney read a newspaper, and the next time he looked out the window, the ship was gone. The only indication of her whereabouts was a view of the top of the mast sticking up above some trees. Carney was filled with alarm—that the anchor had slipped and the ship had run aground.[69]

Spurred by his sinking feeling, Carney paid his bill, ran out, and got into a taxi. He raced down to the pier and discovered that the *Missouri* was doing fine; she was still anchored, just headed in the opposite direction. Because of the landmass in the area, about once a week changing currents produced a little whirlpool there. This had been spelled out in the sailing directions the skipper read on the way into Istanbul. When he saw that the ship was safe and sound, his memory was refreshed, and he breathed considerably easier.[70]

After that, the *Missouri* was on her way again, with still more port visits to make. Unfortunately, the engineers couldn't take full advantage of the schedule. Many of them had to spend considerable time on board because they were preparing the ship for an OPPE, operational propulsion plant examination. The ship was required to pass it in order to be able to keep steaming. That the *New Jersey* had failed hers the first time further motivated the Navy Department to ensure that both the physical equipment and personnel training were at a high level. One of the engineers put up a sign that expressed the feeling of a number of his below-decks shipmates, "If you're not in engineering, you're just along for the liberty." The work paid off, because the *Missouri* subsequently passed her OPPE.[71]

As she had in 1946, the *Missouri* went to Naples, Italy, then resumed her westward voyage. Because of Admiral Moranville's presence

This photo provides a silhouette view of the *Missouri* as she steams off the coast of Turkey in November 1986. Gone is the fantail aircraft crane that was a distinctive feature of her profile during her earlier period of service. (Photo by Don Koralewski in DoD Still Media Records Center: DN-ST-87-06691)

The *Missouri* enters one of the Gatun locks on December 9, 1986—the last time the ship ever passed through the Panama Canal. (Photo by Carlos Drake in DoD Still Media Records Center: DN-SC-87-10974)

on board, the rumor went through the battle-ship that she would have an opportunity to cross the "line of death" into the Gulf of Sidra off Libya. U.S. naval forces had been doing that during freedom-of-navigation exercises in previous months. The result had been the shooting down of Libyan aircraft brazen (or foolish) enough to challenge the Americans. The crew was excited about the prospect, so the *Missouri*'s officers raised the question with the admiral when he joined them for dinner in the wardroom. He said he wouldn't permit it because it would be too embarrassing if a Libyan plane flew a successful suicide mission against the ship. He said he probably would if he had a *Ticonderoga*-class cruiser to provide antiair protection, but none was available. The *Missouri* was no longer capable of providing her own air defense as she had when facing Japanese kamikazes in 1945.[72]

More liberty lay ahead in Portugal and the

island of Mallorca, then it was on to Gibraltar and the *Missouri*'s first venture into the Atlantic Ocean since the summer of 1954. When the ship went into the set of locks on the Pacific side of the Panama Canal, the tugs pulled her in a little bit cockeyed, and so she scraped a good deal of concrete. Captain Carney described the experience: "It sounded—magnified by ten thousand times—like fingers going down a blackboard. It was awful, the loudest screeching you ever heard in your life." Mike McDermott was struck by the sight of the aged locomotives that tugged and tugged when pulling the huge ship into locks. When it came time for them to climb an incline along the side of the lock, they were kicking back onto two wheels because they had to pull so energetically. To some on the deck of the battleship, it appeared that the locomotives might flip over backward.[73]

After that, the *Missouri* hurried home. Part

As the ship approaches her berth at Long Beach on December 19, Religious Program Specialist Second Class Angel Acosta stands atop turret two, dressed as Santa Claus. (Courtesy Terry Cosgrove)

of the impetus for using so much speed from port to port was to get back in time for Christmas. As the ship approached her berth at pier six of the Long Beach Naval Station, Religious Program Specialist Second Class Angel Acosta stood atop turret two, playing the role of Santa Claus. Welcoming signs and banners appeared in profusion. Among them were three placards, held by women, that read, "G'day/Paul/Leo." The crewmen had dated two of them while the ship was in Sydney, and the women had decided to surprise their newfound American friends by flying to the United States to see them again. One of the sailors' wives, knowing

nothing of what had happened in Australia, was standing next to the sign holders. Other crew members, whose wives had had babies during the cruise, rushed off to see their children for the first time.[74]

And so the *Missouri* came to the end of the first operation of her second period in commission. She had just completed the first around-the-world cruise by a U.S. battleship since the Great White Fleet made the journey between 1907 and 1909. (As it turned out, this was also the last ever.) The ship had been enthusiastically received wherever she went. As Captain Carney described the fast-paced voyage, "We were really working for the State Department . . . instead of the U.S. Navy." The average reception had been for eight hundred guests. Carney had been told beforehand that normally only about 75 percent of those invited to such affairs would show up. The *Missouri* was obviously special. As the cruise unfolded, she had a 100 percent response rate to the invitations, and even more people than those on the embassy lists demanded to come aboard.[75]

It had been a treat for the crew as well. In fact, the happy arrival in Long Beach gave them the best of both worlds, because the crowd on pier six welcomed the ship as enthusiastically as if she were just back from a grueling combat deployment. It had been, rather, in the words of Lieutenant McDermott, "a one-hundred-day party cruise, as far as we were concerned."[76]

13 ✦ With the Fleet Again

January 1987–June 1990

During the first few months of 1987, as the smog that blanketed southern California was accompanied by what passes for winter there, the *Missouri* was in the Long Beach Naval Shipyard. This was a chance to modernize her further and to repair equipment that had problems during the shakedown cruise. Among other things, the *Missouri* received a new fire-fighting system in the emergency diesel generator spaces and upgrades to her steering system. The time in port also gave the crew members an opportunity to relax and be with their families.[1]

Some of the enlisted men from the *Missouri* and *New Jersey* spent their off-duty hours as extras for the filming of the TV miniseries *War and Remembrance*, a sequel to Herman Wouk's *Winds of War*. They were costumed as officers, ranging from ensign to captain, at a lawn party filmed at a southern California estate. The film's producers sought crew members as extras, figuring they would be familiar with Navy practices. The men also had short hair, something many aspiring actors did not. Lance Corporal Darrell Landry of the *Missouri*'s Marine detachment particularly enjoyed portraying a 1944 Marine officer, explaining, "It even gave a little feeling of power while on the movie set."[2]

That spring, a year after the recommissioning, some of the *Missouri*'s plank owners were leaving for other duty. Among them was Yeoman Second Class John Lewis, who departed reluctantly after having served tours in the two West Coast battleships. He wanted to stay at sea, but he had orders to go ashore. Upon reflection, however, it turned out not to be all bad for the man from northeast Missouri. He was assigned to the Navy's recruiting district in St. Louis. As he later mused: "A hundred miles from home—Cardinal baseball, White Castle burgers, and Anheuser-Busch brewery. That's God's country."[3]

Once the yard period was over, the *Missouri* went through sea trials in May and gunfire requalification in June. She was preparing to become part of the fleet again after her extraordinary solo cruise around the world. On one occasion, the battleship went out for some surface gunnery, firing at a target sled towed by a tugboat. One of the turrets fired prematurely, before the gun had been raised to the proper elevation. The dummy projectile skipped off the water, bouncing along in a low, essentially horizontal trajectory. When it came down the third time, it was between the tug and the target. After hitting the surface of the ocean, it threw up a column of water, then deflected up and over the towline. That was too close for the tug master, who quickly made his departure. Fortunately, such a misadventure was a rarity in the battleship's shooting.[4]

Actor Robert Mitchum starred as Captain Pug Henry, President Roosevelt's fictitious naval aide, in the television miniseries *War and Remembrance*. Here, he poses in front of the *Missouri*'s forward turrets during a break from filming a Navy recruiting commercial. (Courtesy Terry Cosgrove)

In late June, the men of the battleship learned that their training was about to be used in an operational mission, not just more of the show-the-flag routine. The Department of Defense directed the Navy to send the *Missouri* to the North Arabian Sea. Iran and Iraq had been at war with each other since September 1980. As a means of going after Iran's revenue source, Iraq in 1981 had begun attacking oil tankers going to and from Iranian ports in the northern part of the Persian Gulf. In 1984, Iran also began attacking tankers. The number of attacks increased dramatically in 1986 and 1987. In May 1987, while the frigate USS *Stark* was on patrol in the gulf, she was badly damaged by two Exocet missiles fired by an Iraqi aircraft; thirty-seven crewmen were killed.

As a means of expressing its concern and keeping the oil flowing, the United States arranged for several Kuwaiti tankers to be shifted to the U.S. flag. This would enable the U.S. Navy to escort the ships as they moved up and down the Persian Gulf. The operation was dubbed Earnest Will, an expression of American resolve in the region. On July 24, during the first convoy under U.S. protection, the four-hundred-thousand-ton tanker *Bridgeton* hit an Iranian mine that ripped a large hole in her hull.[5]

In the four weeks before the *Missouri*'s deployment, the ship engaged in more of her goodwill program. As she had the previous

year, she went to northern California in anticipation of the planned home porting at San Francisco. She was in that city for the Fourth of July; among those who came aboard during the port call was U.S. Senator John Glenn. In 1962, while in the Marine Corps, he became the first American astronaut to orbit the earth. Twenty-five years later, he was touring the ship in his legislative capacity. Lieutenant Mike Mc-Dermott of the battleship's crew accompanied the entourage and could overhear people talking as they recognized the former astronaut. In a voice so clear that the senator couldn't have avoided hearing her, a not-very-diplomatic tourist said, "He looks so old."[6] The ship also sent some sailors to visit her honorary home port of Burney, California, and later went to Monterey to celebrate fleet week.

When the ship was back in Long Beach, the Navy tried to beef up the *Missouri* in preparation for her upcoming trip. Remotely piloted vehicles were then being developed as a means of providing gunfire spotting for the *Iowa*-class

Right: Boatswain's Mate Tony Austin examines a heaving line used as an advance messenger for a much larger mooring line. Hanging down from his right hand is the knotted ball known as a "monkey's fist." It gives the end of the line some momentum as it travels through the air. (Photo by Rich Pedroncelli)

Below: A color guard is atop turret two as the battleship approaches the Golden Gate Bridge during her visit to San Francisco in the summer of 1987. (Photo by Rich Pedroncelli)

Close-up of a Vulcan/ Phalanx antiair weapon, sometimes known as R2D2 after the *Star Wars* character. On the white top are hashmarks indicating the mount has shot down two exercise missiles. (Photo by Rich Pedroncelli)

Right: Marine Corps pride is reflected in this shot of a mount 51, a 5-inch twin mount emblazoned with the Corps insignia and manned by members of the ship's detachment. (Photo by Rich Pedroncelli)

Below: A chaplain holds the remains of a deceased Navy man during a burial-at-sea ceremony on the fantail. (Photo by Rich Pedroncelli)

removed what they had installed. It thus fell to the *Iowa* to do a good deal of the testing for the class during her subsequent deployment in the Middle East. The technology ultimately proved successful during the Persian Gulf War in 1991.[7]

The *Missouri* left Long Beach on July 25, setting out on her long westward journey. En route, the crew members rehearsed at great length for the threats they might encounter. While the ship was in the Hawaii area, for instance, she took part in exercises against a surface target. The *Missouri* coordinated Harpoon missile strikes by two P-3 aircraft. Using both 5-inch and 16-inch guns, she also practiced tactics for use against small boats. During the rehearsals, the ship fired a salvo of nine 16-inch projectiles fuzed for air burst—to shower boats with jagged fragments of metal—at a range of about fifteen miles from the ship. Captain Carney watched one such practice and observed: "The

battleships. A week before the *Missouri*'s scheduled departure, technicians descended en masse and began installing equipment and fittings in an attempt to give her an RPV capability. The day before the ship was to go, the workers realized they couldn't finish in time, so they

The breech end of this 16-inch gun is adorned with a sign calling it "Mad Max." A sailor has left a cleaning rag on the "mushroom" pad of the breech plug. The interrupted screw threads align with similar ones inside the barrel itself. When the breechblock is closed, the threads align, and a partial rotation of the block forms a gas-tight seal at the rear end of the barrel. Thus, all of the explosive force goes forward, out the muzzle end. (Photo by Rich Pedroncelli)

ocean just erupts below those things when they all go off. . . . It is damned impressive." After that, the battleship closed the target, peppered it with the secondary battery, and left it in flames.[8]

In late 1986, the type commander, Surface Force, Pacific Fleet, had asked the commanding officers of the *Missouri* and *New Jersey* if they would agree to the removal of the remaining six 5-inch mounts from each ship. The goal was to reduce the heavy manpower requirements for operating the labor-intensive battleships. Captain Carney did not agree to the proposal because of the potential degradation of the *Missouri*'s self-defense capability. Now, as his ship headed for the troubled Middle East, Carney was glad that he still had the 5-inch guns available, particularly because he did not have much confidence in the effectiveness of the 25-mm chain guns that had been hastily installed to protect against enemy small craft.[9]

The mining of the *Bridgeton* had given the

Missouri's journey an even greater sense of urgency than when the orders had originally come through in late June. Though she trained near Hawaii, she didn't stop at Pearl Harbor. The battleship headed for the Middle East at a brisk pace, spending only a few days in Subic Bay. On September 1, in the Arabian Sea, she and her escorts joined up with the carrier *Ranger* and her battle group, producing a large combined force. For the next several weeks, however, the *Missouri* just steamed around with the other ships of the battle group, engaged in no convoy escort work. The crew grew restless, wondering why they had been rushed to the scene.[10]

As a means of keeping crews occupied during the lull, the various ships in the area conducted war games nicknamed "Roadrunner." The ships were divided into teams, and—as in the cartoon series—the idea was to try to intercept ships on the other team as they sped past. Still, it was a desultory existence, exacerbated

Battle Group Sierra steams in the North Arabian Sea during the autumn of 1987. The *Missouri* leads the formation. In column behind her are the carrier *Ranger* and cruiser *Long Beach*. (Courtesy USS *Missouri*)

by the extremely hot weather of the region. The enlisted men wore cut-off dungaree shorts and gym shoes. Officers donned khaki cutoffs and docksider shoes.[11]

During the first week in October, the *Missouri* and some of the escorts anchored near Masirah Island, off Oman, for an upkeep period. With her machine shop and other repair capabilities, the ship essentially acted as a tender for the smaller ships in company. This was a role for which she had been designed back in the 1930s. For example, if a frigate needed a pump overhauled or a piece of electronic gear repaired, a boat brought it to the battleship, and her technicians did the work. The *Missouri* had a great deal of talent among the members of her crew, and sometimes her repair personnel did the work on board the smaller ship. As she left the anchorage on October 7, the *Missouri* marked her forty-fifth consecutive day without a port call. Under a Navy policy that had grown out of the long deployments to the region earlier in the decade, after forty-five days, each man was authorized two cans of beer. Crewmen drank them during a "steel-beach picnic" held on the fantail flight deck.[12]

During that autumn of 1987, newly reported Seaman Gary Price was assigned mess-cooking duties. He and his cohorts found it the kind of job they could hate together. They worked long hours: from five in the morning, when they began preparing for breakfast, until eight in the evening, when they finished cleaning up after the last meal of the day. Price, who worked in the scullery, developed dish-pan hands, and he found that the odors of food permeated his clothes and his person. "Even after you showered three or four times, you just had that food stench about you." The mess cooks came from the various divisions throughout the ship and then returned to them once they had served their time.[13]

Finally, on the night of October 11–12, the *Missouri* ran her first Earnest Will convoy escort mission. As the lumbering, essentially defenseless tankers went into the Strait of Hormuz at the southern end of the Persian Gulf, they were accompanied by guided-missile frigates and

other destroyer-type ships that would stay with them as they made their transit northward up the gulf. The battleship ventured no farther than the winding strait. Once the tankers and their immediate escorts were in the gulf itself and through the area of vulnerability for Silkworm missiles, the *Missouri*'s role was complete. She then went back out into the Gulf of Oman. The arrival of so significant a warship constituted an escalation of the U.S. naval presence. Lieutenant Mark Walker, the ship's public affairs officer, observed, "We knew we were sending a very powerful political signal by sending the battleship up there, and that wasn't lost on anybody."[14]

During the upcoming missions, the battleship would be escorted by an Aegis cruiser, whose missile system could provide protection against missiles in flight. The *Missouri*'s potential for devastating retaliation would serve as a deterrent to keep the missiles from being fired in the first place. Through intelligence sources, the crew of the *Missouri* knew where the Silkworm sites were along the Strait of Hormuz and had gunfire solutions ready if called upon.

Clad in relaxed garb, Secretary of the Navy James Webb chats with three *Missouri* enlisted men during a visit to the ship in mid-September in the North Arabian Sea. Webb, a decorated Marine Corps officer in the Vietnam War, was later a novelist and government official. Photographer's Mate Terry Cosgrove, who contributed a number of the pictures in this book, is on the ladder leading up to the surrender deck. (Courtesy Terry Cosgrove)

Above (left): Sailors draw their chow at the same starboard mess line used by the Trumans during the 1947 cruise north from Brazil. (Photo by Rich Pedroncelli)

Above (right): Marine Michael Heller enjoys a snack while at a four-man mess table in the mess deck. It is a much more substantial piece of furniture than the spindly-legged tables men used in World War II. (Photo by Rich Pedroncelli)

Right: The *Missouri* takes on fuel from a replenishment oiler during her Earnest Will support operations in the fall of 1987. Reading from left to right, the names on the sterns of the ships spell out "*Kansas City, Missouri.*" (Courtesy Terry Cosgrove)

Part of the reason for the convoys going through at night was that the Silkworm had a bright exhaust tail, making it easier to spot against a background of darkness.[15]

The crew members were tense the first time the *Missouri* prepared to go into the Strait of Hormuz. After they had had a chance to catch some sleep in the afternoon, the ship began her transit around dusk, and it lasted all night long. By the time the battleship dropped off the convoy, turned around, and headed out through the strait again, it was around eight o'clock the next morning.

That first night, Machinist's Mate Bill Holland had a battle station in the shaft alley on the port side. He had heard that if the Iranians decided to attack, they would try to disable the ship. A good way to do so would be to fire at the propellers and their shafts. As he stood his

watch in the shaft alley, Holland was surrounded by fuel on one side and gunpowder on the other. He concluded that that was not the best place to be, but he had no real choice in the matter. Nevertheless, most of the crew felt that if they had to be where they were, they were on board the right ship.[16]

The Iranians had two main Silkworm sites. That first night, there were indications of activity at one of them, so the crew members went back inside the skin of the ship. Lieutenant Walker was on the 08-level bridge with a combat camera team during the voyage. He and his men were garbed in flak jackets and helmets, but they had an advantage that many of the *Missouri*'s men did not: they could see what was happening during the course of the mission. The visual image that stuck most firmly in Walker's mind from that night was the string of lights of the column of convoy ships, just like ducks in a row.[17]

When the ship was in the close quarters of the Strait of Hormuz during that and subsequent missions, Captain Carney sent his bridge watch team, including the officer of the deck, inside the conning tower barbette on the 04 level. The vaultlike door on one side was closed, and Carney then remained out on the bridge proper to conn the ship while she was in the danger zone. He felt the safety of the ship required his presence there. During those missions, the *Missouri*'s electronic warfare systems indicated that the Iranian missile batteries were tracking the ship and sometimes lit off their fire-control radars. But the rules of engagement did not permit the ship to shoot unless fired upon, and the Iranians chose not to fire.[18]

The Strait of Hormuz provides virtually no aids to navigation, especially at night. The ship had to use radar to navigate. Even that was hampered by a coastline so smooth and devoid of distinguishable points that fixes were difficult. That was particularly challenging because gunfire support requires precise knowledge of the ship's position. Fortunately, the *Missouri* had installed a relatively inexpensive commercial global-positioning satellite system to provide latitude and longitude readouts. After practicing with that for a while during the trip to the Middle East, the *Missouri*'s greatest error on ini-

tial salvo was a mere 150 yards at 20 miles, the maximum effective range of the guns.[19]

One of the first tankers the *Missouri* escorted as part of Earnest Will was the *Sea Isle City*. After she was safely through the strait, she proceeded north to Kuwait and was hit there the next morning by a Silkworm. On a Sunday afternoon soon after that, the *Missouri* was in the North Arabian Sea, and the crew had an opportunity for some holiday routine. They were surprised to see two destroyers, the *Leftwich* and

Left: Front and center is the nose—including point-detonating fuze—of a high-explosive projectile, the type used against shore targets. The men are gathered around the articulated loading tray, which unfolds into a horizontal position so the projectile can be rammed into the breech of the 16-inch gun. (Courtesy Terry Cosgrove)

Below: "Broadway" connects the entrances to the *Missouri*'s four engine rooms and four firerooms. Running from turret two to turret three on the third deck, it is the longest passageway in the ship. (Photo by Rich Pedroncelli)

Above: Three petty officers—Mike Kinnis, Bill Allen, and James Hough—stand among the 16-inch projectiles in one of the turret shell decks. At left are armor-piercing projectiles; those with rounded caps are high-explosive. Metal restraints hold the shells in place against the inside of the barbette. (Photo by Rich Pedroncelli)

Right: A sailor leans up against a projectile as he writes a letter home during the long deployment. (Courtesy Terry Cosgrove)

Hoel, conducting gunnery practice and taking on ammunition. It was an odd time for it.

The explanation came the following day, October 19, when those destroyers and two others bombarded an Iranian oil platform in the gulf as retaliation for the missile attack on the *Sea Isle City*. Lieutenant Walker observed that the men of the *Missouri* were eager for their own ship to take a more active role. Americans had perceived Iranians as bad guys ever since the overthrow of the Shah and the Ayatollah Khomeini's rise to power in 1979. But the mission of the U.S. naval forces was to protect the American tankers, not to become involved as an active combatant in the Iran-Iraq War.[20]

In the weeks ahead, six more of the long, sleepless convoy missions followed, but after a while they became pretty much routine as one convoy after another went through the strait without being attacked. The men of the *Missouri* grew in confidence, and their sense of concern diminished. They concluded that the Iranians probably were not going to attack

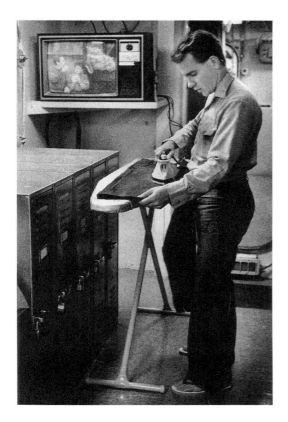

because they would face such a considerable potential for retaliation.[21]

One of the chores that fell to the public affairs staff during the deployment was to put out daily newspapers to keep men up to date on world events. Even more appealing were tapes of television programs from the United States. This was possible because, on the island of Diego Garcia in the Indian Ocean, the Navy had a facility that made copies of videotapes. The tapes were then flown to the aircraft carrier *Ranger* and distributed to ships in company by helicopter. The *Missouri*'s public affairs people showed the tapes on the ship's closed-circuit TV system. Particularly popular were sports tapes, such as the games from that year's World Series between the St. Louis Cardinals and the Minnesota Twins and the weekly contests involving teams in the National Football League. The crew got to see the tapes about two weeks after the games had taken place. Television sets dispersed throughout the ship had replaced the evening movies shown, during the previous period in commission, on the fantail, in the mess deck, wardroom, and chiefs' quarters.[22]

All told, the *Missouri* went more than one hundred straight days without touching port. The heat in the region didn't help the situation. Air-conditioning provided some relief, but it put a strain on the *Missouri*'s electrical plant, so its use had to be limited. A second beer day on November 20 was also welcome. Even so, near the end of the long time at sea Chief Electrician's Mate Webber saw tempers flare up, per-

Left: A crewman presses a pair of dungaree trousers in his living compartment. The television set in the background was one of hundreds throughout the ship, installed during the modernization. They enabled crew members to watch movies and other programs and replaced the movie showings on the mess deck or fantail in the ship's first incarnation. (Photo by Rich Pedroncelli)

Below: Captain Carney listens at right as a chief petty officer briefs Admiral Carlisle Trost (in sunglasses) on a chain gun installed for use again small boats. Trost, the chief of naval operations, visited the ship and spoke to the crew on November 9, 1987. (Photo by Terry Cosgrove in DoD Still Media Records Center: DN-SN-88-03112)

haps a symptom of something akin to cabin fever. The routine had become monotonous, and distractions were few. Part of it was a sense of isolation as well: they were a long way from anything familiar. As Webber said of the experience: "I hope I never have to do it again. . . . Three months of your life is just gone, and all you saw was water and sun. Every day was the same."[23]

Finally, the mission came to an end. The carrier *Midway* and her battle group arrived to relieve the *Missouri* on Earnest Will. The battleship had been promised a port visit in Australia as a reward for the crew. She began the first leg of her homeward journey on November 24. During the six-day voyage to the island of Diego Garcia, the men of the battleship saw rain for the first time since leaving the Philippines on August 21.[24]

The *Missouri*'s appearance had slipped during the long time at sea because she hadn't had

a chance for shoreside maintenance and upkeep. Consequently, when she arrived in Diego Garcia, crew members had to spend all day chipping and painting to get her in shape for her forthcoming visit to Australia. The schedule for the visit called for them to get liberty in the late afternoon and then go to a Quonset hut to hear a USO show put on by singer Wayne Newton. The public affairs officer concluded that many in the crew probably would have preferred to have a few beers first rather than having to sit through a singing performance for two hours.[25]

It turned out that something besides beer and Wayne Newton was waiting for the *Missouri* at Diego Garcia. Back in September, Bill Egan mentioned to Lieutenant Walker that a good many crew members didn't receive any mail. It was disheartening, especially for those sailors who wrote home and received virtually no letters in return. In an attempt to promote

The proprietor mans the snack shop, much enlarged from the old days but still known as the gedunk. (Photo by Rich Pedroncelli)

Crew members pose inside a gun room of one of the 16-inch turrets. Notice the maze of hydraulic lines behind them. (Courtesy Terry Cosgrove)

some mail for his shipmates, Egan wrote a letter to the "Dear Abby" newspaper advice column. Abigail Van Buren then suggested to her readers that they could make the men of the *Missouri* happy by writing to the ship.[26]

When the battleship pulled into her pier at Diego Garcia the last day of November, four tractor-trailers with "U.S. Mail" painted on their sides were waiting for her. The crew was flabbergasted by the number of bags that came aboard. When the bags were opened, it became apparent that this bonanza had resulted from Abby's brief mention in her column. The downside was that the ship's postal clerks were disgruntled by the sheer volume they had to deal with, but the contents of those bags produced tremendous pleasure among a lot of crew members.[27]

The mail included more than just letters: three Christmas trees came wrapped in wet burlap and plastic. Johnny Cash and Carol Burnett sent tapes for the ship's radio station. Schoolchildren wrote by the thousands. Some

schools sent boxes of Christmas cards, some sent tapes of Christmas carols. The VFW auxiliary in Burney, California, a community that had adopted the *Missouri* as its own, baked hundreds of chocolate-chip cookies. Bill Egan overdosed on the cookies to such an extent that he gave them up for a couple of years after that.[28]

The postal avalanche lasted for weeks, and there were no more mail-less sailors or Marines. For a while the ship held mail call about six times a day. Finally, the postal clerks gave up and began transferring the mailbags to the public affairs office after they found out that Egan was responsible for it all. Crew members then volunteered to help with the distribution. One Marine sorted mail from chow time one evening until about three o'clock the next morning. He explained that he had received only one letter the whole deployment prior to the Dear Abby column. On the morning of December 24, when the ship was in Australia, a young sailor arrived at the public affairs office even before it opened and asked for fifty letters.

Egan jokingly asked if the crewman was going to answer all of them. "Yes," he said, "these people are going to be my family, because my family forgot me."[29]

The stay at Diego Garcia was brief, and then the battleship was on her way to Australia. After a stop in Fremantle, the *Missouri* proceeded across the "bight" at the southern part of the large island-continent in order to get to Sydney. In those southern waters, looking toward Antarctica, the seas were roiled. Because of the waves breaking on deck, men stayed inside the ship. Mark Walker went up to a position high in the superstructure and looked forward. He watched in fascination as the bow at times would dig into a swell and be submerged for several seconds before reappearing again.[30]

As the ship approached Sydney, the initial planning called for a reprise of the previous year's firepower demonstration, including a gunnery broadside. Then someone concluded that such a fire-belching show was not exactly in keeping with the Christmas message of peace and goodwill, so it was canceled. Because the ship had been in Sydney only a little more than a year earlier, some of the crew members were able to look up girlfriends they'd met on that occasion.

During her modernization, the *Missouri* was equipped with "coffin racks," each outfitted with a reading light and privacy curtain. Jim Waldes is seen here reading in his. (Photo by Rich Pedroncelli)

The ship had made a tremendous impact during the 1986 visit, and the local citizens were again highly enthusiastic in 1987. There were so many requests for individual crewmen to come visit homes that the ship had to make specific assignments, telling the sailors and Marines that they would go to a particular home on Christmas Eve and another one on Christmas Day. The Australians who offered their hospitality didn't want to take "no" for an answer. In the southern hemisphere, of course, Christmas falls in early summer, so the holiday fare was made up of sandwiches and beer in many cases.[31]

After leaving Australia, the ship went to Pearl Harbor, arriving on January 10, 1988. During the transit from Hawaii back to California, the *Missouri* unexpectedly ran into gale-force winds that stirred up the ocean and played havoc with topside areas. Ladders and fittings were damaged or destroyed, as were some of the ship's boats. On board for the trip were male relatives of crew members, making a "tiger cruise" so they could experience the life- and work-styles of the *Missouri* men. They had trouble sleeping during the heavy rolling, as did a number of the ship's own crewmen. The frigate *Curts*, which was in company with the *Missouri*, rolled more than fifty degrees on occasion during the trip.

As she neared the end of her long journey, the *Missouri* passed in the vicinity of offshore Catalina Island, where the *New Jersey* was holding maneuvers. The sister battleship used her 16-inch guns to fire a salute to the returning warrior.[32]

Among the many *Missouri* men happy to be back in Long Beach was Robert Webber. But when he arrived home, he found that he had to adjust his mental picture of his family to the reality he encountered. When the chief petty officer was gone from his daughters, Jennifer and Melissa, time had stopped in terms of his physical presence in the relationships. When he returned home, he found his children taller and halfway through another year of school. Their vocabularies were better developed. Because he was divorced, his mother was taking care of the house, and he found that she had changed it in various ways. He was a bit of a stranger for a little while until he and the rest of the family readjusted to his presence.[33]

For more than a month, the ship went through a stand-down period in Long Beach to give the crew a break following the deployment. A sign at the head of pier six, where the *Missouri* typically moored, declared it to be "Battleship Country." One day some workmen from the nearby naval shipyard came aboard and removed three of four pressure gauges from one of the *Missouri*'s engine rooms. The gauges were designed to monitor vacuum in the main condenser. After getting started in one engine room, they came to another—number two main—to remove the ones there as well. Machinist's Mate Bill Holland said he wasn't aware of the need for such work, so the workers explained that they had job orders to take the gauges out to be calibrated. Once they pulled out the work order and looked at it, they discovered that they were supposed to be removing the gauges from the *New Jersey*, which was moored on the other side of the pier. Somewhat sheepishly, the workers put back the three gauges they had taken out and then went across the pier to do the job they were supposed to do.[34]

In the spring of 1988, the ship visited Vancouver, British Columbia, the first time a battleship had been in that port for many years. It was also the first time the *Missouri* had ever been in a port on Canada's west coast. Her only previous visit to the nation was to Halifax, Nova Scotia, on a midshipman cruise just before she went to Korea in 1950. In the latter part of May, the ship went out for weapons tests, including the Vulcan/Phalanx close-in weapon system and the 16-inch and 5-inch guns. On May 25, the *Missouri* fired a Tomahawk missile for the first time, testing one of the major capabilities added during the modernization program. Hundreds of crewmen were gathered on the flight deck aft to watch the test.[35]

In mid-June the ship left to participate in Exercise RimPac '88, which Lieutenant Walker considered "probably the biggest boondoggle in *Missouri*'s history." The ship did go out and

exercise with ships of other nations, but she also spent considerable periods in port at Pearl Harbor, during which time crew members went to luaus and saw the sights of the island of Oahu. They also hosted thousands and thousands of visitors.[36]

That exercise marked the end of a long career for Master Chief Boatswain's Mate John Davidson, the command master chief. He had first gone to sea in the *Missouri* in 1946; now he finished up with a retirement ceremony on the surrender deck on July 20. Davidson was replaced by Master Chief Personnelman Charles Fleeks, a black petty officer with a quarter cen-

Boiler technician Guy Burford monitors a boiler pressure gauge. In his right hand is a burner. The faster the ship needs to go, the more burners are inserted into the boiler. (Photo by Rich Pedroncelli)

Two sailors chat near the rear end of a four-cell armored box launcher for Tomahawk missiles. (Photo by Rich Pedroncelli)

tury of service behind him. The racial climate in the *Missouri* had changed dramatically since Davidson's initial service on board the ship forty-two years earlier.[37]

The *Missouri* had a new skipper as well, Captain John Chernesky. As with his two immediate predecessors, he was not a Naval Academy graduate. He received his commission through the NROTC program at Miami University of Ohio, then became a diesel submariner. He served in the *Tench, Wahoo, Blueback,* and *Bonefish.* When diesels were phased out in favor of nuclear-powered submarines, he moved into the surface community, where he was executive officer of the cruiser *Dale,* skipper of the frigate *Patterson,* and executive officer of the *Iowa.* Just before reporting to the *Missouri* he was in the Navy's Office of Legislative Affairs in Washington.[38]

Probably unlike several of his predecessors as captain of the *Missouri,* Chernesky had done nothing to bring about the assignment and actually would have preferred not to do it. Because of his service in the *Iowa,* he had already checked off the battleship experience box. He had specifically expressed a preference to command an Aegis cruiser in order to become ac-

quainted with the newest technology in the surface fleet. In fact, he had received advance notice that he would be commanding the Aegis cruiser *Ticonderoga.* The officer tentatively slated for the *Missouri* was Captain Fred Moosally, who later commanded the *Iowa* when she had a turret explosion. The chief of naval personnel, Vice Admiral Dudley Carlson, called Chernesky in and told him that because of his battleship experience, he would be a better fit for the *Missouri* at that point. Chernesky resisted but was ordered to the *Missouri* anyway.[39]

By the time he arrived at the ship, Chernesky had decided the *Missouri* would be his last tour of duty; he was not bucking for promotion. Self-described as irreverent, he planned to enjoy the command and serve the best interests of ship and crew. Despite the fact that the job was accompanied by considerable pressure, he did, in fact, derive great enjoyment from commanding the *Missouri.* It worked out that the change of command was on his forty-fourth birthday—July 6, 1988—a beautiful, sunny day in Hawaii. As he conned the ship out of Pearl three days later, he recognized the wisdom of Admiral Carlson's decision. Because of his previous service in the *Iowa,* Chernesky felt a sense of confidence that he wouldn't have had starting out in the *Ticonderoga*. He also found, to his considerable delight, that Captain Carney had left the ship in great shape for him in terms of both physical condition and training of the crew.[40]

The *Missouri*'s sailors soon discovered that the flamboyant, charismatic Chernesky had a much different personality than his predecessor. The crew perceived Carney as a nice, fair-minded, professionally competent man, but he was not the sort who communicated frequently with the crew via television or the general announcing system. He relied on his executive officer and the chain of command. During the long periods at sea in the North Arabian Sea, Carney left it to the chief petty officers and division officers to pass the word to their men. Chernesky was anything but reserved.[41]

Part of Chernesky's appeal stemmed from his age—he was a few years younger than both of his predecessors—and his mind-set. He listened to rock music that was akin to the tastes of the crew. He came across as hip and with it. In contrast to the low-key, business-like Carney, Chernesky's emotions—positive or negative—

were always at or near the surface. He reacted both promptly and demonstratively to events on board ship.

The general rule for leaders in dealing with subordinates is praise in public, reprimand in private. But Chernesky was not hesitant about chewing out men in front of their shipmates. It

Above: Master Chief Boatswain's Mate John Davidson first served in the *Missouri* in 1946. He eventually wound up his career as the ship's command master chief in 1988. (Photo by Rich Pedroncelli)

Left: The *Missouri* fires her first Tomahawk missile on May 24, 1988. This was also the last missile firing until the Gulf War in January 1991. (U.S. Navy photo by Terry Cosgrove)

got their attention. Journalist Gary Price, the victim of one of those chewing outs, said of the skipper, "He was one of those guys that if you screwed up, he was right there in your face." All in all, though, Price considered Chernesky his favorite of the three *Missouri* skippers under whom he served because of the personal interest he took. When the captain ran into Price and his wife, Betty, ashore, for instance, he instantly greeted them both by name. Considering that he had sixteen hundred shipmates, Price was impressed.[42]

In his talks with the officers in the wardroom, Captain Chernesky made it clear that his expectations for them were high. Fierce loyalty—both up and down the chain of command—was expected. The skipper demanded top-notch performance. He used the term "spine-ripper" to describe his approach to those who disappointed him.[43]

One day during a general quarters drill, the captain made the rounds of the ship. In the course of it, he talked to a young enlisted man who was a member of a repair party. Chernesky discovered that the man didn't know his duties. Lieutenant Mark Walker happened to be a fly on the wall in Chernesky's cabin when the captain called in the officer in charge of the repair party to discuss the incident. Quietly,

unemotionally—but with no doubt that he meant business—Chernesky made it clear that the sailor's lack of knowledge could endanger his shipmates. Furthermore, the sailor's ignorance was the result of the lieutenant's failure to carry out his training responsibilities properly. As strong as the impression was on Walker, it was even stronger on the repair party officer. His face was ashen as he left the captain's presence.[44]

During the latter part of 1988, the *Missouri* spent much of her time in and around the Long Beach area in various types of training, both at sea and in port. During that period, the ship's public affairs office began publishing a magazine called *Broadside* that went home to crew members' families. It was a successor to what had previously been the ship's family-gram. The magazine was attractive in design and informative in content. Seen in retrospect, the copies provide a valuable pictorial history of the ship's last few years in commission. The photography was excellent. Photographer's Mate Terry Cosgrove, who edited the magazine and took many of the pictures, was so highly regarded that he was subsequently assigned to the office of the secretary of the Navy. Initially, *Broadside* was a monthly, later a quar-

Opposite (left): On November 21, 1988, Captain Rose Mofford, governor of Arizona, presented the USS *Arizona* Memorial Trophy to Captain Chernesky. It was awarded to the *Missouri* for having the highest readiness among battleships during the previous eighteen-month competitive period. It stands more than three feet tall and weighs 150 pounds. (U.S. Navy photo by Terry Cosgrove)

Opposite (far right): Canister launchers are designed to fire the Harpoon antiship missiles installed during the modernization period. (Photo by Rich Pedroncelli)

Right: Family members cover their ears as the 16-inch guns fire during a dependents' day cruise off southern California in August 1988. (Photo by Thomas Milne in DoD Still Media Records Center: DN-SN-89-04586)

terly. Produced entirely on board ship, it was recognized with a Navy-wide award for its quality.[45]

The home porting of the *Missouri* in San Francisco was an on-again, off-again affair. In December 1987, San Franciscans elected Art Agnos as mayor. Unlike his predecessor, Dianne Feinstein, Agnos was not enthusiastic about selecting San Francisco as the *Missouri*'s home port. He said that the Navy, of course, could base the ship wherever it wanted, but he was unwilling to put up the city money that the Navy was seeking to improve the area around the old Hunters Point shipyard where the ship was to be based. Despite his opposition, local voters approved a two-million-dollar package in November 1988. The following month, the federal government's Commission on Base Closing and Realignment recommended to Congress that the *Missouri* be based in Hawaii instead. At a time when the government was trying to close down long-standing military bases to save money, the commission did not want to approve the idea of reopening an old one at Hunters Point. The *Missouri* remained at Long Beach.[46]

The political winds were unquestionably

blowing in a different direction than they had been in 1981, when the battleship reactivation program began. In addition to the local opposition from Agnos, another factor inhibiting the *Missouri*'s move to San Francisco was the departure of John Lehman as secretary of the Navy in 1987. He had been the strongest proponent of the strategic home-porting plan that would have distributed the Navy's ships more widely than before. With the passage of the Gramm-Rudman deficit-reduction law, the handwriting began to appear on the wall to say that Lehman's cherished goal of a six-hundred-ship fleet would not be realized. The momentum that had built up the Navy in the early years of the Reagan administration had unquestionably slowed as the president's tenure wound down.

At the beginning of 1989, the *Missouri* began an extended shipyard period at Long Beach. Included was a dry-docking to sandblast the hull and apply a preservative coating to the underwater portion. The yard also installed an improved cathodic preservation system to minimize hull deterioration, and it replaced the fire bricks in four of the ship's eight boilers. The bricks had a tendency to come loose during the firing of the 16-inch guns, so a new retaining system was used to try to minimize the problem.[47]

Another addition during the yard period embraced environmental concerns. Crewmen drank a whopping amount of soda from aluminum cans. Once the cans were empty, *Missouri* men typically threw them in the trash or into the ocean. Then one of the crew members submitted an idea to the captain's suggestion box. Why not recycle the thousands of cans, thus permitting their reuse and cutting down on trash quantity? The suggestion became an action item for Lieutenant (j.g.) Kent Davis of the supply department. He made numerous calls to try to find recycling companies but had no luck. Then one day he saw a can-recycling machine in front of a grocery store. He wrote down the telephone number from the machine, called it, and the *Missouri* wound up with two machines on board. An immediate benefit from the program was that the money realized from selling the cans to recyclers went into the ship's welfare and recreation fund.[48]

While the *Missouri* was in dry dock, the command organized a strong intramural sports program to keep the crew occupied during off-hours. To spur competition, the teams were seeking to win the captain's cup in basketball, volleyball, softball, racquetball, and bowling. The crewmen also held a five-kilometer run out on the earthen mole that extended to seaward from the Long Beach Naval Station. The winner, with a time of fifteen minutes and thirty-eight seconds, was Chief Signalman Walter Hearvey. The ship's deck department accumulated the most points during the various competitions and won the captain's cup.[49]

A substantial addition during the yard period was the installation of a new shipwide computer hookup. Initially, it was made up of about three dozen personal computers and was known as MONET, for *Missouri* Network. With tongues in cheeks, the ship's personnel pronounced it Mo-NAY, after the long-dead French artist. Fleet ships had been outfitted with personal computers for several years, but the business of tying them together throughout a ship was a pioneering effort. MONET was the brainchild of Lieutenant Commander Jim Bancroft, the battleship's meteorologist and a dedicated computer enthusiast. Linking the in-

The under-hull tunnel formed by the skegs leading back to the two inboard screws. This photo was made while the ship was in dry dock at Long Beach in February 1989. (Photo by Bob Lindel in DoD Still Media Records Center: DN-ST-92-01576)

dividual machines together was not easy in a ship built half a century earlier. Both the compartmentation and the armor were obstacles in running the various connecting cables from stem to stern. But the advantages to doing so were manifest because people in a variety of offices could now send E-mail messages to each other. Captain Chernesky found that the system improved efficiency. No longer did department heads and other individuals have to waste their time standing outside his door while waiting to see him. Although MONET certainly did not eliminate face-to-face contact, now these men could send him information electronically, at their convenience, and he could reply at his.[50]

Master Chief Personnelman Timothy Hofman reported to the *Missouri* in January 1989 to run the ship's personnel office. He and his men used MONET to fashion a data base from information in the crew members' individual personnel records. It was a labor-intensive job for some of the personnelmen to enter the data into the computer system, but the payoff came in terms of retrieval. For instance, the system could print out alphabetical lists of the crew, lists by divisions, lists by projected rotation dates, and so forth. And, with the use of passwords, appropriate individuals in the ship could use the system to draw out personnel information without going to the personnel office.[51]

Another application of MONET was for outgoing radio messages. In years past, messages were often drafted by hand, then typed in the smooth on a typewriter with characters that could be read by an optical scanner. If changes were made as the message went up the chain of command, the message had to be retyped. With MONET, the individuals in the chain could make their inputs on the computer screen without retyping the whole thing. Once the captain or executive officer released the message, the system sent it electronically to radio central, and it was then transmitted to a communication station ashore. This was a far cry from World War II, when the *Missouri*'s radiomen sent out messages by Morse code key.[52]

The *Missouri* got a new executive officer that spring. Captain Chernesky brought in Commander Joe Lee Frank, who had been operations officer of the *Iowa* when Chernesky was the executive officer. Like the captain, the new exec made an impression with his strong, distinctive personality. The crew came to have several nicknames for Frank, among them, "the man with no last name." He was hard on the people who came up before him at executive officer's screening. If they had problems that they needed help with, he would help them. If they needed a slap on the wrist or a kick in the rear, they got that. And if they would best serve the Navy by going home to become civilians again, Frank did what he could to arrange that also. He was not inclined to accept excuses, but if he was demonstrated to be wrong, he admitted it and apologized. He was not patient with the inabilities or mistakes of others.[53]

Among other things, Commander Frank had a fetish about cleanliness on board the *Missouri*. In fact, he declared a shipwide "war on dirt." Included were operation orders and fake messages from "CinCDirtPac." One of the ship's enlisted men, Eric Thibidoux, satirized Frank in a cartoon that showed him with hands on hips, a swagger stick in one hand and a pistol in the other. The cartoon version of Frank was saying: "War is hell, men. God, how I love it so!" Meanwhile, a voice off to the side declared, "All brooms manned and ready, sir."[54]

One of the *Missouri*'s junior officers observed that Commander Frank administered the wardroom mess "in a great traditional battleship fashion." Lunch and breakfast were generally informal; people would eat whenever they came in and then go back to work. Evening meals were at a set time, structured and formal. Perhaps five minutes before the appointed time, the officers went in and stood behind their chairs. The mustangs—former enlisted men—usually sat at their own table, and they'd invite a college officer to sit with them. It was a privilege to be so invited, because the conversations were fun and spirited. As president of the mess, Captain Frank demanded quality food. The mess caterer, Lieutenant Verlyn Hays, made sure the officers got it.[55]

Captain Joe Lee Frank (*left*) briefs Rear Admiral Daniel P. March during a visit to the after secondary battery plotting room in October 1989. (Photo by Terry Cosgrove in DoD Still Media Records Center: DN-SN-93-04053)

Junior officers didn't dare sit in the wardroom during working hours or even before eight o'clock in the evening. That was because of a practice known as "XO bowling." Captain Frank often went into the wardroom lounge, which was adjacent to his cabin. If he saw JOs sitting there watching TV or reading books, he'd clear them all out with what one lieutenant observed was "a great amount of sound and fury." He'd tell them to get back to work, study for their surface warfare qualifications, or whatever. After eight o'clock, the exec apparently concluded that the junior officers did deserve a break and was less likely to interrupt their relaxation.[56]

One day in the spring of 1989, the *Missouri* received an information copy of a message that actress/singer Cher wanted to film a music video on board a Navy ship. The song to be filmed was "If I Could Turn Back Time." The idea was to show something of a throwback to the World War II era. A battleship obviously represented such a motif. So, after the proposal

was approved by the Navy's Office of Information in Washington, production people came to visit the sister ships *Missouri* and *New Jersey*, both pierside in Long Beach. The Navy had pretty well decided at that point to make the video on board the *New Jersey* because the *Missouri* was scheduled to be at sea during the time planned for filming. The producer talked to Lieutenant Walker, the *Missouri*'s public affairs officer, who boasted: "You don't want to do it on the *New Jersey*. We're the most historic battleship in the world. This is where World War II ended. You want to do it on here." That convinced the producer, who decided to film on board the *Missouri*, regardless of the date. Cher's date of availability was changed as a result.[57]

The production crew did its shooting over the Fourth of July weekend. Both Captain Chernesky and Commander Frank were off the ship at the time. The production people did a spectacular job of rigging the ship with lights. The *Missouri* became a dramatic stage for the mod video. The original script called for Cher to come out wearing a jumpsuit and do her number. A stage would be set up, and members of the crew would cheer for Cher. When she rehearsed, she was indeed wearing a jumpsuit. The actual filming was about eleven o'clock on the night of July 4. At that time, however, Cher was wearing a costume that was unquestionably skimpy. Made up of mesh and leather straps, it was not what the agreement called for. The result was that her tattooed bottom—and a number of other portions of her body—was essentially bare. The crew loved it. Lieutenant Walker felt uncomfortable with the setup, but he knew it would be fruitless to protest. It would appear to be censorship.[58]

Walker got no unfavorable feedback on board the *Missouri* itself, although he did run into it a few months afterward when he reported for duty in the Office of Information in the Pentagon. Syndicated newspaper columnist Jack Anderson wrote a critical article, including the line, "If battleships could blush, the USS Missouri would be bright red." The Navy had to field a lot of letters that had been forwarded from congressmen. Their constituents complained in considerable numbers that Cher's costume was not appropriate. A number of World War II veterans indicated it was heresy for something of that sort to happen on board a battleship. Walker defended the result, saying that it enabled the Navy to reach a potential pool of recruits with an appealing message at a time when advertising dollars for that purpose were scarce. Perhaps some of the potential recruits really thought this was typical of a Navy ship. If so, they were in for a considerable awakening when they got to boot camp for training by a chief petty officer who was not a bit like Cher.[59]

Captain Chernesky later offered the opinion that if he had been on the deck of the *Missouri* when Cher showed up in her outfit and demanded that the cameras stop, he could have been fired for failing to carry out the Navy's direction to cooperate with the production company. In his view, he was in a no-win situation. The crew was very enthusiastic about the experience and the way the video turned out. Captain Chernesky then directed that Cher's song, "If I Could Turn Back Time," be played when the *Missouri* was subsequently involved in

underway replenishments with other ships.[60]

Another event on board the *Missouri* that summer also involved turning back time. Back around 1987, the *Missouri* Association, comprised of former crew members, began working on a replacement for the surrender plaque that had been on the 01 deck since 1945. The lettering on the old one had been gradually worn down by the hundreds of polishings administered over the years.

As a step toward the replacement, the association asked each member to send in a penny. Small pie-shaped pieces were cut out of the pennies so the slivers of metal could be part of the metal used in casting the new plaque. The penny-clipping operation took place on board ship, and altogether perhaps fifteen hundred to

Cher's jacket covers up part of her sparse costume as she sings "If I Could Turn Back Time" during her infamous filming session in July 1989. During her performance she also sat astride a 16-inch gun, an obvious phallic symbol. (Courtesy Master Chief James Roswell)

two thousand coins were cut up. A foundry in South Carolina made the new plaque, using the original 1945 mold. After the new plaque was poured, it was sent to the ship, where some additional work was done in the machine shop to smooth the rough edges on a lathe. Subsequently, the association presented the plaque to the ship, and on August 21 it was mounted on the surrender deck with due ceremony.[61]

Back in April 1989, when the ship was still in dry dock at Long Beach, Lieutenant Walker heard the grim news that a turret had exploded on board the *Missouri*'s sister battleship *Iowa*. He went to the captain's cabin to tell Chernesky and found that the skipper already knew. In fact, the skipper had schematic drawings of the ship spread out in front of him and was talking with various officers from the ship's weapons department. Chernesky was particularly troubled because of his own previous service on board the *Iowa*. As he sat and looked, he solemnly shook his head and said, "I just don't understand how this could happen."[62] The *Missouri*'s crew conducted a thorough examination of their ship, procedures, and training after the *Iowa* disaster. The Navy, meanwhile, was conducting an investigation into the tragedy. Until the results were complete, the office of the chief of naval operations implemented a moratorium on the firing of 16-inch guns by all four *Iowa*-class battleships.[63]

One of the hypotheses concerning the *Iowa*'s turret explosion had been that powder bags were accidentally over-rammed. As a remedy, the Navy directed that a pin be installed in the rammers that shoved the projectiles and powder into the gun barrels. The alterations ensured slow ramming speed for the powder. In previous years, turret captains such as Chief Gunner's Mate Carl Farmer typically taught the rammermen to do it slowly; this mechanical change made sure of it. Farmer also trained his individual gun captains to monitor the ramming process closely and use hand signals to make sure the powder was rammed far enough into a gun's breech, but not too far.[64]

The results of the investigation into the *Iowa*'s turret explosion were released in early September. Its disputed conclusion was that a member of the crew had deliberately caused the explosion, killing himself in the process. The moratorium on 16-inch firing was lifted. The next challenge was to get back to work with gun crews that had not fired the *Missouri*'s big guns in nearly eight months. One of the first concerns was to assign an adequate number of men to each turret, because in the *Iowa* situation, her problem stemmed in part from an insufficient number of trained men.

The minimum manning level specified for a turret—from top to bottom—was seventy-seven men. After the long layoff, many weren't as familiar with the equipment as they needed to be. The gunner's mates were okay, but men from the deck force and other departments who helped fill out the turret crews needed to be trained or retrained, as the case called for. There had been considerable turnover in the men other than gunner's mates, so they were essentially starting from scratch. Included in the new men was the gunnery officer, Lieutenant Commander Eric Taylor, who was still on board his previous ship when the moratorium was imposed.[65]

The moratorium ended just about the time the *Missouri* was embarking on a Pacific training exercise. Taylor explained the mind-set on board ship as the first firing exercise approached. "The thing that was weighing on everybody's mind [was that] the last time a battleship had attempted to fire a 16-inch gun, they'd had a disaster happen." So the new people felt apprehensive going in, which required some confidence building on the part of the more senior people. Captain Chernesky reassured the crew over both the closed-circuit TV and the general announcing system. During the initial shooting on September 21, Chernesky himself fired the center gun in turret two, the one that had blown up in the *Iowa*. He was in the turret itself, which was in local control. The firing was uneventful. It was the first time many of the turret personnel had been inside during a firing exercise, and it broke the ice for them.[66]

The *Missouri* had embarked on a long, involved at-sea exercise, PacEx '89, even before firing was permitted. All told, dozens of warships were involved in the exercise, which moved up the West Coast of the United States and Canada, then to the Aleutians, the Okinawa area, and down toward Korea. On October 14, the *Missouri* and *New Jersey* were together 112 miles off Okinawa so they could put on a firepower demonstration for the Japanese and ships from some of the allied nations in the area.[67]

The commander of the exercise specified a five-minute demonstration. In that time the *Missouri*, shooting essentially continuously, fired 263 rounds of 5-inch and 45 16-inch. The *New Jersey* got off considerably fewer. Master Chief Timothy Hofman, watching from the 08-level bridge, was buffeted by the repeated concussions. The one-word message that came to the ship from Captain Ron Tucker, skipper of the *New Jersey*, was "Awesome."[68]

A likely explanation for the disparity in the number of rounds fired was that the *Missouri* had practiced a good deal more than the *New Jersey*. The *Missouri*'s main battery had fired practically every day once the ban was lifted. Though some accused the *Missouri* of grandstanding, Captain Chernesky dismissed the charge. He argued that the point of the exercise was to put out as many rounds as possible in the allotted time. The question, he said, shouldn't have been why the *Missouri* fired so many but why the *New Jersey* fired so few.[69]

In addition to exercising the main battery, Captain Chernesky required the Tomahawk crew to simulate a missile launch during every watch while under way. He wanted the team to be ready at any time and well rehearsed during all the steps in the sequence. Despite the frequent drilling, the *Missouri* did not fire a single Tomahawk missile during his two-year tenure in command. The missiles cost more than a million dollars a copy, far more than the 16-inch projectiles that the ship shot often. But the real knowledge was in all the steps that the electronics and computer programs had to go through. The missile itself didn't need to fly off into the air for the crew to know how to make one go. The payoff, according to Chernesky, was the success of the actual firings later, in the Persian Gulf, after the crew had been so thoroughly trained previously.[70]

Though the *Missouri* fired no missiles during Captain Chernesky's command tour, he ensured that she fired the 16-inch guns often, sometimes on a daily basis. (Courtesy USS *Missouri*)

As the exercise wound up, the *Missouri* went into Pusan, South Korea. It was the first time a battleship had been there since the Korean War. As the ship approached the pier, Captain Frank, the exec, told Captain Chernesky that the flat wooden camels, floating against the pier, were not large enough for the *Missouri*. The dock master assured the bridge team by radio that there was plenty of water to accommodate the ship's draft, but evidently that didn't take into account the silting that had taken place since the last time the area was dredged. When the *Missouri* was about three hundred yards short of the pier, the Korean pilot said to Joe Lee Frank: "I quit. You tell me what you want." The ship was just too big for him to handle. He was willing to translate and pass orders to the tugboats in Korean, but he was not going to give any more orders himself.

Frank asked someone to go get the captain and bring him to the starboard side of the bridge. At that point, Frank informed the skipper that the pilot had resigned his duties. Chernesky said, "Aw, come on. Quit screwing around." [71]

"He quit," repeated Frank. "Ask him." The pilot nodded to indicate that he had indeed stopped carrying out his function. So the cap-tain said he would take care of the engines, and the exec could give the orders to the tugs. After a while, even though Frank had both tugs pushing against the side of the ship, she was no longer moving at all. The *Missouri* had run up against the silt bank that extended out from the side of the pier. So she had to sit there until some other tugboats brought out bigger camels that would allow the ship to be sufficiently far away from the pier to have enough water. The ship subsequently sent in a report to higher authority that mentioned a "shouldering" rather than a grounding. When the ship was dry-docked some six months later, the only effect discovered was a slight bending of a bilge keel. [72]

Afterward, the *Missouri* and her escorts made the long trip home to California. The previous year, the battleship had visited Canada; now it was time to extend the good-neighbor role southward. In December, the *Missouri* made a port visit to Mazatlán, Mexico, the first and only time the ship visited that nation during her long career. Many members of the crew participated in Project Handclasp, providing medical and dental aid to local residents. As in many of her port visits, the ship hosted general visiting. In the months that fol-

The *Missouri* steams as part of a battle group formation during PacEx '89 in October of 1989. The *New Jersey* is at left; the carrier *Enterprise* is just beyond the *Missouri*'s foremast. Though Long Beach was home port to both throughout the late eighties, this was one of the few times they operated together. (Courtesy USS *Enterprise*)

lowed, the *Missouri* was in or near her home port, sometimes conducting training exercises, at other times for crew liberty.[73]

For the most part, the enlisted men who populated the *Missouri* during that period pretty much fit a mold. They were generally young—in their late teens or early twenties—and unmarried. They had graduated from high school and were in either their first or second hitch of active service. Some planned to make a career of the Navy, while many others were using their service time as a period of maturation, training, or accumulation of savings as they prepared for the rest of their lives. One petty officer who assuredly did not fit that mold was Boatswain's Mate Second Class Warrick Woodard, who was about fifty years old when he reported to the *Missouri*.

He had enlisted for the first time in July 1958, served initially as a cook at Bainbridge, Maryland, and later became a boatswain's mate while in the crew of the destroyer tender *Tidewater*. He left active duty in the early 1960s when his first enlistment ended, then went into the naval reserve and civilian work. He reenlisted in the Navy in 1981 because of a shortage of experienced petty officers at that time. A year later, he joined the crew of the newly recommissioned *New Jersey*. He went on that battleship's year-long cruise to the Far East, Central America, and ultimately Lebanon during the crisis there in 1983–84.

Since he was a battleship sailor and doing something he enjoyed, Woodard reenlisted on the *Arizona* Memorial when the *New Jersey* was in Hawaii. After leaving the battleship, he served on shore duty in Norfolk and later on the West Coast. After two years of handling boats at Port Hueneme, California, he was assigned to the *Missouri* in 1989. Based on his experience, he was put in the *Missouri*'s fifth division. He and his men were responsible for the upkeep and operation of boats, as well as taking care of the sides of the ship and the maintenance of the boat davits. It was a natural for an experienced boatswain's mate.

Woodard sometimes had a generation-gap problem with some of the junior men in the crew of the *Missouri*. He was twenty-five or

thirty years older than most of the men working for him. But the difference in ages was a minor matter compared with one other factor. Warrick Woodard had a distinction not only among his *Missouri* shipmates but among all the citizens of California: he was the only person who made the state lottery's "big spin" three times. He was extraordinarily lucky during a seven-month period in 1989 and 1990; three of the tickets he bought in that time sent him to a televised spinning of a wheel. During the second of his three spins, he hit a million-dollar treasure chest. He received smaller payoffs on the other two spins, although he just missed a second million during his final spin and settled for fifty thousand dollars.

The million-dollar jackpot produces annuity payments of fifty thousand dollars, but that didn't lead Woodard to leave the *Missouri* until he had to at the time of her decommissioning in 1992. He enjoyed Navy life, he enjoyed the battleship, and he wanted to keep on serving as long as he could. He did, however, have to make it clear to his shipmates that he was neither a bail bondsman nor a banker. The money was his, not theirs for the asking.

He also found himself besieged by requests from people all over the United States and elsewhere in the world—asking for loans and handouts. He uniformly pitched the requests into a wastebasket, but he did begin making generous donations to legitimate charities. One of the recipients of his generosity was the USS *Missouri*. When he didn't think the Navy supply system was providing prompt enough support to maintain the captain's gig—such things as power sanders or replacements for vent covers blown off by gunfire concussion—he pitched in to buy the items with his own money. Charity, after all, begins at home.[74]

In early 1989, the ship had inaugurated its computer network. A year later, more technology came aboard when the *Missouri* installed four automatic teller machines. It was a far cry from the ship's first time in commission. Back then a disbursing officer and disbursing clerk set up shop on payday and dealt with long lines of men. They had boxes of cash in front of them and dutifully counted out the amount

Seaman Conroy Wilson sends the flashing-light message "G-G-G-G" from the *Missouri* to signify the firing of her 16-inch guns during the battle problem phase of Exercise RimPac '90. (Photo by Thomas P. Milne in DoD Still Media Records Center: DN-ST-94-00419)

from main control to tell him that another leak had occurred.

Once he got the call, he'd go down to the space where the fuel was leaking into the bilge. The engineers quickly shut valves and rerouted fuel so the offending section of piping was isolated and out of the loop. Then they pumped fog foam into the bilges to cut off the oxygen supply and ensure that the fuel wouldn't burst into flame. Once the danger was past, they pumped the mixture of foam and fuel into a holding tank, where it would be stored until they could unload it during the next time in port. Some of the piping, which was approximately a foot in diameter, was replaced with new sections manufactured from nickel steel in the machine shop on board. In other cases the replacements were accomplished during a shipyard period. Through a combination of those efforts, probably 75 to 80 percent of the *Missouri*'s fuel piping had been replaced by the time she went out of commission in 1992.[76]

In the spring, following her time in Long Beach, the *Missouri* went to Hawaii to join in RimPac '90, another multinational naval training exercise. During the exercise, the *Missouri*'s job at one point was to go break up the amphibious task force that was invading one of the islands in the Hawaiian chain. The *Missouri* left her task force in the middle of the night. The *Independence* battle group went looking for her. The *Missouri* changed her lighting patterns in order to resemble a tanker; she also steamed on steady course and speed as a tanker would. The *Missouri* was not emitting any electronic energy. As a result, the "enemy" Navy planes flew right over without recognizing her. When she finally revealed herself, the *Missouri* made her approach at twenty knots, with her main battery trained on the amphibious warfare ships. The battleship's flashing lights were sending the letter G over and over in Morse code, signifying gunfire. The amphibs were taken completely by surprise.[77]

due each man. The crew member then signed a pay chit and put on his fingerprint as well. The procedure served as a precaution against forgery or claims that someone didn't receive his money. During the long period the ship was in mothballs, the Navy went to paychecks. With the arrival of the 1990s, the *Missouri* emulated the civilian banking world. Each payday, the disbursing clerks made an electronic deposit to each man's account. Crewmen thus had twenty-four-hour-a-day access to their money, being able to withdraw it in five-dollar increments up to the total earned through the last pay period. They were also relieved of the concern about possible thievery and storing quantities of money in their lockers. They withdrew it only as needed.[75]

Even while the ship was being updated in such areas, she was showing her nearly half century of age in others. A particular concern was the fuel-oil piping, especially because it had been installed to handle the tarlike black oil of an earlier generation. Now it was carrying the much lighter Navy distillate fuel, more akin to that used in jet airplanes. The result was a multitude of leaks. The main propulsion assistant, Lieutenant Ross Mobilia, joked that he routinely set his alarm clock for two o'clock in the morning so he'd have time to wake up and be alert for the inevitable call

While the *Missouri* was lying in wait as the "stealth battleship," she anchored for a time. During the wait, a yacht came by with some young lovelies on board. One of them took off the top of her bathing suit as the yacht motored close aboard the battleship. The entire crew in

The hull of the battleship is covered with primer paint during a period in dry dock at Long Beach in January 1990. (Photo by Terry Cosgrove in DoD Still Media Records Center: DN-ST-92-00737)

position to do so moved toward that side of the ship to get a better view. Over the general announcing system came the voice of Captain Chernesky, "From the officers and crew of the battleship *Missouri,* bless you!"[78]

In one respite from the at-sea time, the *Missouri* was moored at the fueling pier at Merry Point in Pearl Harbor, right next to the inner harbor. The *Arizona* Memorial was off to the port side, perfectly framed between the back of turret two and the front of the superstructure. Captain Chernesky was responding to a request for a media visit, talking with about thirty journalists from Japan. The first question in the press conference was, "Captain, could you comment on the significance of the battleship *Missouri?*"

Chernesky took his trademark cigar out of his mouth, pointed to the *Arizona,* and replied, "World War II started for the United States

right over there." Gesturing downward, he said, "It ended right here."

As Joe Lee Frank observed, that comment nearly ended the press conference; little more could be said after that. He concluded that the Japanese took Chernesky's remark in the spirit in which it was offered and were politely amused by it.[79]

When she returned to Long Beach, the *Missouri* was moored across pier six from the *New Jersey,* as she was many times during the late 1980s. A healthy rivalry existed between the two ships, and one of the manifestations was that the men of the *New Jersey* referred to theirs as "the battleship" and her slightly younger sister as "the other battleship." For instance, the men of the *New Jersey* thought they shot better, their ship looked better, their Marine guards were more professional, and so forth. Such relationships

Photographer's Mate Terry Cosgrove took this magnificent shot of a 16-inch projectile emerging through the fireball during Operation RimPac '90. (Courtesy USS *Missouri*)

Left: A close-up of the 16-inch guns as the *Missouri* steams with other warships near Hawaii during Operation RimPac '90 in March of that year. (Photo by Brad Dillon in DoD Still Media Records Center: DN-ST-91-07903)

Below: The cigar was a trademark of Captain Chernesky, as was his unconventional manner. This picture was made on the *Missouri*'s bridge during Operation RimPac '90. (Courtesy Terry Cosgrove)

between ships' crews have gone on for years. One beneficial result is that the competition spurs both crews to perform better in their efforts to outdo each other. Attempts at one-upsmanship also occur at times.

That spring a group of junior officers from the *New Jersey* decided to play a joke on the battleship sitting across the pier. They noticed the attention their ship was getting as a possible tourist attraction in the state of New Jersey. The cost factor frequently came up in the discussion. So a group of them, led by Lieutenant (j.g.) Hoot Gibson, decided to bait the *Missouri*'s executive officer. They bought a classified ad in the local newspaper, the *Long Beach Press-Telegram*. It was essentially along the following lines: "For sale. National monument. Built 1944, very low mileage. For more information, contact Joe Lee Frank." The telephone number for the *Missouri*'s executive officer was included, and it produced a few phone calls.

Missouri men in life jackets pull hard to keep the slack out of a support line as a crewman from the Australian frigate *Darwin* is transferred to the battleship during RimPac '90. (Photo by Brad Dillon in DoD Still Media Records Center: Dn-ST-93-02570)

Captain Ron Tucker, skipper of the *New Jersey*, found out about the prank and applied some heat to Gibson and his co-conspirators. He made them go over to the *Missouri* and confess to Frank. The exec, of course, had been a junior officer himself a number of years earlier and remembered the inventiveness and mischief JOs are prone to. So he got a laugh out of it—sort of.[80]

Captain Chernesky had spent nearly two years in command. It was time for him to pass on the job to someone else, which he did in June. He left a legacy of readiness, training, and high professional standards among the crew members who operated the battleship in the months to come, including the Middle East war of 1991. He also left behind memories of his unpredictability and sense of humor. Among the things for which he is best remembered were the underway replenishments.

As the *Missouri* would pull alongside the ship that was going to deliver or receive fuel, Captain Chernesky liked to get on the speaker system, easily audible on board the ship steaming on a parallel course nearby. He started with: "Welcome alongside *Missouri*. Due to the unusual way in which we deliver our shot lines, we suggest all topside hands take DEEP cover." Turret two would then train around so that the guns pointed at the other ship. Meanwhile, a gunner's mate armed with a line-throwing gun was inside the center barrel of the turret. The gunner's mate fired the gun, and the line landed on the deck of the ship alongside. Since the 16-inch barrels were each about sixty-five feet long, they extended over the side of the battleship. The shot line didn't have all that far to travel to reach the other ship. It was typical Chernesky showmanship. As Machinist's Mate Bill Holland put it: "I'd never seen anything like it. He definitely had a style all his own."[81]

14 ❖ Desert Storm

June 1990–May 1991

The officer who relieved Captain Chernesky on the *Missouri*'s forecastle on June 13, 1990, was already familiar with the ship. The new skipper was the old skipper—Captain Kaiss. (For those inclined to collect trivia, three different men served twice each as commanding officer of the *Missouri:* Harold Page Smith, James Robert North, and Albert Lee Kaiss.) After Kaiss's sudden departure because of heart trouble in June 1986, he had gone into limited-duty status. He was grateful when Vice Admiral George Davis found a spot for him on his Surface Force Pacific Fleet staff at San Diego. There Kaiss served as assistant chief of staff for warfare and tactics while awaiting a medical disability retirement. Before the Navy could muster him out, though, he underwent experimental heart surgery that completely cured his problem.[1]

Timing and availability played a part in his return in 1990, just as they had when Kaiss was first picked for the *Missouri* in 1984. When the Navy learned that it needed to replace Chernesky on fairly short notice because of his intention to retire, Kaiss was nearby. He didn't need to go through the long pre-command training pipeline that other captains would. Moreover, he had handled battleship matters during his duty in San Diego. Part of the enjoyment for Kaiss in stepping back aboard was to find out that Carney and Chernesky had carried out a number of the objectives he'd had in mind in 1986. In fact, he discovered that they had improved on the programs he planned. He also found out that the knowledge he brought with him from four years earlier gave him immediate acceptance with the crew.[2]

* * *

In May 1990, the Navy initiated additional precautions in connection with the firing of 16-inch guns by the *Iowa*-class battleships. Congress had been skeptical of the suicide verdict as the cause of the *Iowa* explosion and had directed the Sandia National Laboratory in New Mexico to conduct tests to ascertain whether the *Iowa* explosion could have been accidental. The lab had caused gunpowder pellets of the type used in the battleship bags to blow up by dropping a weight on them. The *Missouri* had to check out the powder in her magazines and recertify the training of her turret crews before resuming firing. She did naval gunfire support training her first time at sea after Kaiss's return. On June 21, during the course of a readiness exercise off the coast of southern California, the *Missouri* fired a Harpoon antiship missile for the first time. As with the Tomahawk, the firing of the expensive weapon was extremely infrequent. The missile scored a direct hit on its target.[3]

In early July, the *Missouri* made her traditional midsummer visit to San Francisco. Late in the month, she went to the Seal Beach Naval Weapons Station, part of the large Los Angeles harbor, to exchange some of her 16-inch powder. The Navy had ascertained that powder bags with a certain number of pellets in the trim layer were slightly safer. It was better to be safe than sorry, so the crew had to examine all powder bags; the questionable ones were replaced.

That autumn, the *Missouri* went to Seal Beach twice more for powder exchanges—all accomplished with much manual labor. During the final one, in November, the ship took on a completely new load of powder shipped out from Crane, Indiana. It had been reworked, tested, and certified as completely safe.[4]

Once the ship was back home in Long Beach, Captain Kaiss went to San Diego to attend briefings for one of the battle groups that would be deploying to the Western Pacific at the same time as the *Missouri*. The battleship was scheduled to leave shortly on a three-and-a-half-month cruise that would include liberty ports in Japan, Korea, and the Philippines. On the final Friday in July, Kaiss received a telephone call from an officer on the staff of the type commander. The officer told Kaiss that the Pentagon would announce that weekend that it was considering inactivation and decommissioning of the ship.[5]

The *New Jersey*, which was across the pier from the *Missouri*, was already beginning the inactivation process; on the East Coast, the *Iowa* was nearly ready for decommissioning. This would obviously be big news for the *Missouri*'s crew so Kaiss received authorization to tell them in advance of the official announcement.

Once he returned to the ship, he appeared on the internal television system to report that the ship would probably begin inactivation after she completed her coming deployment. One enterprising crew member leaked the information to the local newspaper. A few days later, however, the situation changed dramatically.[6]

On August 2, in the faraway Persian Gulf region, President Saddam Hussein of Iraq sent three of his country's army divisions across the border into neighboring Kuwait and soon took it over. The conquest was easy because the victimized seaport nation is about one-tenth the area of the state of Missouri and its population one-ninth that of Iraq. Of immediate concern was the possibility that Iraqi forces would also move into Kuwait's southern neighbor, Saudi Arabia. The United States immediately sent naval forces to the region and then began a mobilization effort given the name Operation Desert Shield. At the same time, President George Bush began building political strength, seeking U. N. resolutions and economic sanctions. He was also forging an international coalition of

On June 21, 1990, the *Missouri* fires a Harpoon antiship missile for the first time. The event was part of a readiness exercise off the coast of southern California, soon after Captain Kaiss took command for the second time. (Courtesy Terry Cosgrove)

forces that would be ready to take military action, if necessary.

As soon as the Iraqi invasion took place, plans for the *Missouri*'s inactivation were put into abeyance. The ship now went on twenty-four-hour standby to leave for the Persian Gulf. After a bit, the warning time changed to seventy-two hours, and then it became indefinite. Remarkably, Saddam missed his opportunity to strike while the iron was hot. He dawdled, which gave the Coalition forces time to mount a massive buildup of men and material in Saudi Arabia. It also gave the *Missouri* more time.

The ship initiated many preparations for possible war service, including bringing aboard large amounts of supplies. In October, the *Missouri* went to San Diego, and the ship essentially served as a hotel while her crew members went off to receive training at Navy schools in the area. Protection against chemical weapons was strongly emphasized. Included was a stint in a gas chamber filled with a foul-smelling but harmless gas. The men thus became conditioned to how helpful it was to get their protective masks on as quickly as possible. And they learned how to inject themselves with anti-

dotes, if necessary. News reports carried Saddam's threats to use chemical weapons, so the crew was well motivated to prepare for the worst.[7]

Still another item of emphasis was 16-inch gunnery because of the lingering shadow of the *Iowa* tragedy. The Navy sought to take all reasonable precautions to prevent a repeat. In 1990, it substantially increased the requirement for the number of turret crewmen who had graduated from school on the 16-inch system. The *Missouri* was given the opportunity to send more men to the school but still not enough to meet the newly increased require-

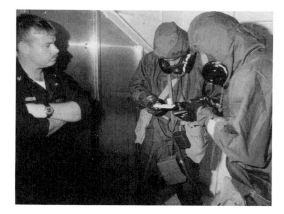

Left: As the *Missouri* prepares for the Persian Gulf, crew members practice donning protective suits and gas masks because of the possible use of chemical weapons by Iraq. (Courtesy Terry Cosgrove)

Below: In this twilight-of-the-battleships scene, the *Missouri* (*left*) and *New Jersey* are moored to their pier-six berth at the Long Beach Naval Station in the summer of 1990. The *New Jersey* is headed for inactivation and the *Missouri* for the Persian Gulf. (Courtesy Terry Cosgrove)

ment. Instead, the instructors moved aboard the ship and conducted the course in the turrets. The training began while the ship was in San Diego and finished while the *Missouri* was en route to the Persian Gulf. The last of the instructors left the ship at Pearl Harbor.[8]

In early November, the *Missouri*'s crew was augmented by the arrival of two specialized detachments that would play important roles in the fight against Iraq. One of them operated a group of remotely piloted vehicles (RPVs), which were small, pilotless airplanes. The RPV weighed about four hundred pounds and had computerized controls, a wingspan of seventeen feet, and a nose-to-tail length of fourteen feet. The wooden propeller was powered by a noisy two-cycle engine similar to those used in snowmobiles. Because the ship couldn't provide sufficient room for the RPV to make rolling takeoffs, a rocket was strapped to the side of the plane for launching. The rocket took the vehicle to seventy knots of speed and two hundred feet of altitude in less than two seconds. The recovery system involved a large net strung up on poles on the fantail. The aircraft flew into the net and dangled there until it was retrieved by the fantail crew. A detachment of twenty-two men came aboard the *Missouri* to run the operation.[9]

Right: The RPV "lands" by colliding with something akin to a volleyball net on the fantail and then dangling there until retrieved by the flight deck crew. (Courtesy Terry Cosgrove)

Below: The remotely piloted vehicle played a substantial role in the Gulf War through its ability to send live television and infrared images back to the ship during firing missions. (U.S. Navy photo by John Bouvia)

The controls that guided the aircraft's course and altitude via signal were housed on board the *Missouri*. The antennas were located inside two spherical structures, one at the front of the after stack, and one on the front of the forward fire control tower, above the primary conning station on the 08 level. The aircraft itself also had an antenna; it looked like a tin can on a stick. The signals told the aircraft how much to use its rudder and ailerons, and the instruments on the plane sent back reports of what it was doing.[10]

The "pilot" sat in the ground control station on the 03 level, inside the *Missouri*'s superstructure. Looking at a TV monitor, he had to visualize himself on board the remote vehicle and give directions accordingly. When the plane was within visual range of the ship, it was controlled by external pilots—also on the 03 level, but standing outside, right above turret three. They were armed with a control box of the sort used by model airplane enthusiasts.[11]

The other group that boarded the *Missouri* that November was an explosive ordnance disposal team; Lieutenant Steve Wilson was officer in charge. The team also comprised four enlisted men: Master Chief Engineman Jeff Crozier and three more junior petty officers with a few years in the program. Lieutenant Wilson took some kidding in the wardroom: his fellow officers teased him because he was getting a lot of sleep, while many of them were standing watches day and night. Captain Kaiss heard about the bantering and said: "There are two people I want to have plenty of rest on this ship, because if they have plenty of rest, it means they don't have a job to do. That's the medical officer and the EOD officer." That silenced the critics.[12]

Finally, after Coalition forces in Saudi Arabia had built their strength over a three-month period, it was time for the *Missouri* to go and join them. When the ship departed on November 13, many of the crew members' families were on hand. Lieutenant Commander Steve Chesser, public affairs officer for Naval Surface Group, Long Beach, observed that the "media crush was like I'd never seen before." Timing was one factor. A few days earlier the Department of Defense had made the official announcement about the planned decommissioning of the *Missouri* and *Wisconsin*. The *Wisconsin* was already in the Persian Gulf and due to come back before the *Missouri*. So it appeared that this deployment would be the last hurrah for the last battleship. Symptomatic of the media blanket that covers the Los Angeles area, the day of departure drew camera crews from fourteen local television stations, three radio stations, five newspapers, and three news services. The Cable News Network (CNN) covered the event live. At one point, nine helicopters were in the air over the ship as she pulled away from the pier, heading for the breakwater and seas far beyond.[13]

On her way west, the *Missouri* stopped at Pearl Harbor and Subic Bay. A subsequent port call at Pattaya Beach, Thailand, shortly before Christmas offered some opportunities for shopping, though the reactions were sometimes mixed. Ensign Ed Stockton explained, "My wife was kind of upset when she got the Visa bill, but when she saw the jewelry that I picked up, that kind of lessened the sticker shock." Bartering was popular as well. Baseball caps, T-shirts, and cigarette lighters bearing the ship's name and logo could be swapped for such things as ivory, tailor-made suits, and so forth. Thailand also provided the last chance for a real liberty before the Persian Gulf.[14]

The port city, with its gaudy neon lights, was tourist oriented. For example, it had lots of girlie bars that would appeal to visiting sailors. For those with other interests, a side trip to Bangkok was offered. Journalist Gary Price and his buddy Robert Evans (a hull technician)

went there on a sight-seeing tour. During their stay in Thailand, they and many of their shipmates ate in restaurants with familiar names from America—Hardee's and Pizza Hut—because it gave them a touch of home. The Pattaya Beach Pizza Hut offered squid as one of the toppings.[15]

Under way again, the ship spent Christmas in the Strait of Malacca. On Christmas Eve, the crew gathered in the mess deck, and one of the chiefs dressed up as Santa Claus. Members of the crew formed a choir to sing carols. Christmas Day was marked by a holiday dinner, a cookout, basketball games, and a talent show. The objective of all the activities was to keep men busy and involved so they wouldn't focus so much on what they were missing. While steaks were grilling during the "steel-beach picnic" on the fantail, some crew members formed a rock band that blared out the Rolling Stones' song "I Can't Get No Satisfaction." Considering how far the men of the *Missouri* were from wives and girlfriends, a good many of them could identify with Mick Jagger's lament of sexual frustration.[16]

The new year of 1991 began, and on January 3, the *Missouri* went through the Strait of Hormuz and into the Persian Gulf. As a result of political correctness—or whatever it might be in deference to an ally—the ship's deck logs

The *Missouri*'s cooks dish up Christmas dinner en route to the Persian Gulf in December 1990. (Courtesy Terry Cosgrove)

dutifully noted that she was now steaming in the Arabian Gulf, as the Persian Gulf is also known. After sending an assistance team to put out a fire on board the merchant ship *Tabuk* on January 4, the *Missouri* pulled in the following day to anchor off the island of Bahrain, her home away from home for the next two months.[17]

Mines were a great concern from the time of the ship's entrance into the gulf. The Iraqis didn't have to be physically present to do harm to the ship because the mines could act on their behalf. On January 9, the *Missouri*'s EOD team went after its first mine, which had been located by a helicopter from the frigate *Curts*. Two members of the ship's disposal team, Lieutenant Wilson and Interior Communications Electrician Bo Jones, went out in a motor whaleboat. They were outfitted in wet suits, masks, fins, and snorkels. Part of the reason for the rubber suits was to protect them against the sea snakes prevalent in the gulf.

The two men went into the water with an explosive charge and an initiator. The mine they encountered was about two feet high, three feet in diameter, and looked like a globe that had been squashed in at the top and bottom. It had three contact horns on it as detonators. The mine, which was floating free on the surface, was later identified as being Iraqi in origin, not something supplied by one of the major powers.[18]

Wilson and Jones attached an explosive charge with a fifteen-minute igniter, which they put on a piece of plastic bubble wrap to keep it afloat until it did its job. The task was complicated by the fact that the mine was bobbing up and down in the waters of the gulf. To activate the igniter, Wilson pulled out the safety pin at the end, cocked it, and then turned the spring-loaded firing pin. It fired into a pyrotechnic charge that set the fuse to work.[19]

Despite their training and experience, the men of the EOD detachment were obviously human: during that first mission Wilson thought to himself, "I don't want to be here doing this right now." But that was why he had rested so well en route to the Persian Gulf. It was a happy moment when the system worked as designed. The first explosion shot a column of black smoke and pieces of mine two to three hundred feet into the air.[20]

All had been anticipation—perhaps apprehension—up to this point. Now, at long last, the *Missouri*'s men could focus on something real instead of the variety of imaginings they had carried in their heads. The young men in the crew, many of whom had been in no confrontation more violent than a high school football game, came face to face with something far more dangerous. As Gunner's Mate Leon Tucker, a Vietnam veteran, put it, "That mine woke up the entire crew: those of us that remembered and those of us that didn't." The pace quickened from then on, and the crew's alertness level climbed dramatically.[21]

During the buildup to the start of the war, the joint task force commander, General Norman Schwarzkopf, in Saudi Arabia, sent direction as to the specific targets to be hit in Iraq if war came. Then the Tomahawk coordination team, headed by Captain David Bill, commanding officer of the *Wisconsin*, planned a number of different mission scenarios, a step comparable to assembling a playbook for a football team. A few days before the deadline for the war to start, Captain Bill designated specific missions for the ships in the gulf, a step comparable to a football game plan. Then the missile-firing teams rehearsed those specific plans with their individual ships' equipment.

The first success for the *Missouri*'s explosive ordnance disposal team came when this mine exploded on January 9. In the background is the frigate *Curts,* whose helicopter spotted the floating mine. (Brad Dillon photo courtesy Captain Joe Lee Frank)

When the time came, Captain Bill would be the firing coordinator for the approximately half dozen Tomahawk ships under his control. Among other things, this would ensure proper separation between ships and prevent one ship's antiair defense system from shooting down a Tomahawk fired by a nearby U.S. warship.[22]

Since the beginning of January, the air of expectation had become palpable. President Bush had given Iraq an ultimatum: leave Kuwait by January 15, or the Coalition nations would take steps to remove the Iraqi soldiers by force. On January 16, the president's deadline passed at eight o'clock in the morning, Persian Gulf time. It was time for the buildup phase, Desert Shield, to be transformed to the combat phase, Desert Storm. The *Missouri* had been at anchor at Bahrain for just a few hours that day when she was directed to get under way in the late afternoon. She then proceeded to her pre-designated area for firing Tomahawk missiles. Taps went at eight o'clock that evening on board the *Missouri*. Some men probably didn't sleep at all.[23]

About midnight at the beginning of the sev-

enteenth, Captain Kaiss called for reveille and told the crewmen they had time for a head call. Over the public address system he soberly announced: "In approximately ten minutes we will be going to general quarters, and we will be going to general quarters for real. We are currently in receipt of a strike order, and we are making preparations to launch Tomahawks in

Above: Two of the *Missouri*'s EOD personnel prepare to attach a detonator to the mine in the background on January 12. At left is Interior Communications Electrician Bo Jones; at right is Master Chief Jeff Crozier. In the fashion of the Bo Jackson TV commercials popular at the time, *Missouri* crew members declared, "Bo knows mines." (Brad Dillon photo courtesy Captain Joe Lee Frank)

Left: An Iraqi mine floats on the surface as the *Missouri* steams in the background on January 12. (U.S. Navy photo by Brad Dillon)

the next hour."[24] The ship's navigator, Lieutenant Commander Mike Finn, was one of many on board who felt a great sense of unease. Sending off those Tomahawks was an act of war, and the Americans could justifiably expect that the Iraqis would retaliate energetically.[25]

The officer of the deck was Lieutenant Wes Carey, who didn't believe the ship would actually fire her missiles. But then came the countdown, and at 1:40 A.M. a ball of flame erupted from one of the armored box launchers in the superstructure. The first missile flew away into the night—toward Baghdad. Recalled Carey: "I realized then that we were at war. There was no way you could bring it back." About thirty seconds later, Lieutenant (j.g.) Joe Raskin saw another missile soar off, this one launched by a cruiser or destroyer with a vertical-launch capability. Subsequently, one bright blast after another illuminated the area around the *Missouri* as she fired a half dozen Tomahawk missiles into enemy territory.[26]

The dread felt by many in the battleship proved unwarranted because the Iraqis were so overwhelmed that they were unable to send retaliatory strikes. In retrospect, decided Commander Finn, it was not so surprising, because

the Coalition forces had large numbers of planes in the air and effectively controlled the air space in the vicinity of the ships at sea. After all the anticipation and individual fears that had developed over a period of weeks and months, the crew suddenly felt a sense of relief. They had done their jobs, and they were unharmed.[27]

After the mission, the crew secured from general quarters and went to breakfast. About three in the morning the news began coming in on the shipboard television sets. The screen showed merely color bars, no picture. The sound was the audio portion of CNN's live presentation, which the ship received throughout the war. As they listened, the men could sense the pandemonium in the Iraqi capital, communicated through the voices of correspondents Bernard Shaw, John Holliman, and Peter Arnett. "It's a shame we missed Peter Arnett," joked one *Missouri* officer as he reflected a few years later on the newsman's role in the war. The crew perceived Arnett to be a conduit for Iraqi propaganda and reports of civilian casualties.[28]

The following night, the *Missouri* fired thirteen more Tomahawk missiles; only one failed

Opposite page: One of the armored box launchers fires a Tomahawk toward Iraq on January 17, the first day of combat for the *Missouri* during the Gulf War. She had previously fired some Tomahawks during the early-morning hours. (U.S. Navy photo by Brad Dillon)

Right: The *Missouri* and *Wisconsin* replenish simultaneously from the fast combat support ship *Sacramento* on January 14, 1991, in the Persian Gulf. This was one of the few times the *Missouri* operated with one of her sister ships after her recommissioning in 1986. (Brad Dillon photo courtesy Captain Joe Lee Frank)

A Tomahawk emerges from its launcher on January 17. (Brad Dillon photo courtesy Captain Joe Lee Frank)

to work as scheduled. A backup missile went off forty-five minutes later to complete the mission. In the days immediately after that, the *Missouri* shot off three more to bring the total to twenty-eight missiles by January 20.[29]

At the same time news was coming aboard the *Missouri*, the battleship was making news—and history—herself. The preponderance of media attention, however, was on her sister ship *Wisconsin*, which had the film crews and reporters on board. That was indeed a source of unhappiness for some *Missouri* crew members, who felt the newsmen should have been collecting stories in their ship instead. This was a change from 1950, say, when the *Missouri* went into combat off Korea. At that time she was sought after by the media because of her continuing fame and, in part, because of the desire by the chief of naval operations and others to foster such coverage as a way of reversing the negative image from her grounding. In fact, the absence of newspeople was the result of a decision on Captain Kaiss's part. He considered the ship's mission to be fighting the war, and he didn't want any potential distractions from fulfilling that mission and taking care of the crew.[30]

Following the Tomahawk strikes, the pace slowed. The ship moved back into a planning mode until the Khafji incident at the beginning of February. The Iraqis had taken that deserted

coastal town at the northern edge of Saudi Arabia, so the Coalition command decided to bring in the battleship to ensure that Iraqi ground forces there did not receive any further reinforcements.

As part of the division of labor that made Captain Bill of the *Wisconsin* the Tomahawk coordinator in the gulf, Captain Kaiss of the *Missouri* was designated the fire-support unit coordinator. (This was abbreviated FSUC and on board ship was pronounced, not surprisingly, "f-suck.") The *Missouri* was assigned the task of developing a system to coordinate the fire of all gunships in the area, including tracking their supplies of fuel and ammunition. Lieutenant Verlyn Hays of the *Missouri*'s supply department developed a computer program that kept track of these levels for all the ships and thus was able to predict when they were available for missions and when they needed replenishment. Hays had what might be called a "non-traditional battle station." During the Gulf War he often spent eighteen hours a day in front of a computer or television screen, sometimes on logistics matters, sometimes giving the line officers a break in tracking the RPV targeting pictures.[31]

The FSUC was set up in the former combat information center on the fourth deck. Adjacent to the forward main battery plot, it provided the locale for the planning, plotting, and execution of gunnery missions. Missile missions were run from the combat engagement center in the former flag quarters on the 02 level. The tactical action officer stood his watches there and had control of missile missions, electronic warfare, and the Vulcan/Phalanx close-in weapon system. Up on the bridge the captain and executive officer stood port-and-starboard watches to exercise control over all the combat functions. They had the authority to release the weapons and also served as visual observers for the firing.[32]

On February 3, at Khafji, the *Missouri* fired her 16-inch guns in anger for the first time since March 25, 1953, in Korea. The targets were concrete command-and-control bunkers. Because of the offshore beach gradient, the target areas were more distant from the ship than in Korea. That required the battleship to move

in much closer to shoal water than was comfortable for navigator Mike Finn. The fathometer sometimes measured as little as three feet of water under the keel, which was cutting it awfully close. American-trained Saudi coastal pilots assisted with the navigation, the *Missouri* weaving in and out of oil wells as she went in. They were happy to be serving with Americans because this was important for the defense of their own nation.[33]

On this mission, the RPV was used for the first time for spotting in combat. The unmanned aircraft had two payloads: a black-and-white television camera for daytime use and an infrared sensing system that sent back a high-resolution video at night. One thing that aided the RPV in its surveillance missions was its small size: it generally could not be seen from the ground by naked eye, nor could it be heard.

In the desert war, some of the best reconnaissance was done at night because the system could detect such things as trenches and tank tracks from their heat signatures. When the sig-

nal came from the RPV, it appeared on a TV screen in the 03-level control room. The operator could see where the explosion was and then use an electronic "doughnut" on the screen to measure the correction needed to put subsequent rounds on target. He then called the plotting room, where fire controlmen entered the necessary corrections into the computer.[34]

When the big guns cut loose, the turret crews needed leadership, both by word and example. Gunner's Mate First Class Leon Tucker, who had come over from the *New Jersey* just before the cruise, counseled and practiced calmness. He and his men were in a powder handling room, below the waterline and without a view of what was happening topside. They were encased in a steel barbette, and it was there that Tucker answered the inevitable questions born of uncertainty and inexperience: "Where do I go? Is this what I put on? How many of these do I need? Are you sure that's the right kind of powder we're supposed to break out? Do you want to use this scuttle or that scuttle?" Sometimes young sailors for-

The view from atop turret one shows the *Missouri* and *Wisconsin* operating together on January 27. (U.S. Navy photo by Brad Dillon)

got the things they had learned, and so it was that they had to be reminded of the routine they had practiced time and again.[35]

Higher up in the ship, Lieutenant Armin Dreier stood his watches in the combat engagement center, on the 02 level. Whenever turret two blasted forth at Khafji, the whole space shook, not particularly welcome for either the electronic gear inside or for the men who were operating it. At the same time, the men on watch were breathing in air that was filled with a sulfur smell from the oil wells burning nearby.[36]

The second Khafji mission was the following night. The Iraqis were stealthy about digging in and camouflaging themselves. The only movement the RPV detected as it flew around was a truck. Master Chief Fire Controlman Mark Snedeker was in main-battery plot and decided to have the RPV and its infrared sensor follow the truck as it went down the Iraq-Kuwait highway. It took a circuitous route, probably to avoid land mines. It turned out to be a chow truck (a "roach coach," to the Missouri crew) bringing food to Iraqi soldiers. The picture transmitted back to the ship showed the driver getting out at various spots, and then people would materialize from their hiding places to receive the food.

The tracking went on for about two hours, with the position of each feeding stop being noted on board the battleship. Then it was time for the Missouri to let go with her guns and blast those positions, one after the other. Said the ship's gunnery officer, Lieutenant Commander Eric Taylor, "I'm sure it totally surprised the truck driver when the rounds started falling on him."[37]

The ship fired a third day, February 5, and quieted an Iraqi artillery position. During the three-day firing stint, the Missouri shot 112 rounds of 16-inch. On February 6, the Wisconsin relieved her at Khafji. Less than a week later, the Missouri was back for more firing at Khafji, this time sixty rounds during nine fire-support missions. She shot at infantry battalions, a mechanized unit, an artillery battery, and a command bunker. While the ship was bombarding Khafji, the Iraqis fired some rounds—perhaps 40-mm—toward the Mis-

souri. They landed near the bow, and although they didn't hit the battleship, they definitely attracted the attention of the crew members who saw them.[38]

When the Missouri was shooting initially, the visual pictures from the unmanned aircraft were available on TV monitors in only three shipboard locations: the RPV control room, the combat engagement center, and the main-battery plotting rooms. It soon became apparent that it would be useful to have the picture in other places as well, including the fire-support unit commander's space and on the bridge. The technology was available to pipe the RPV pictures there via the ship's closed-circuit television system, so it was soon available on the hundreds of sets situated throughout the huge Missouri.

Captain Kaiss and Commander Ken Jordan, who took over as exec when Captain Joe Lee Frank left in early February, were initially concerned about what crew members would see while watching signals sent back from the RPVs. During the Vietnam War, televised pictures of violence and death had had a great impact in American living rooms, personalizing the destruction of war to a greater extent than previous news reports. The officers at the top of the Missouri's command structure wondered what the effect would be if crew members saw specifically the destruction their efforts were producing ashore.[39]

One thing that lessened the impact was that the drone was fifteen hundred to two thousand feet above the ground. Even though people could see bodies, they couldn't see close-ups of faces. Moreover, enemy troops were not the primary targets: for the most part, the ship was firing at installations. In fact, the change proved to be a boon to the morale of the Missouri's crew members. The advantage of making the RPV pictures available on all TV sets was that it gave the entire crew a greater sense of participation in the overall mission. It was no longer just a vicarious thing that they heard about; now they could see with their own eyes what was happening when rounds fell on enemy territory.

As the Gulf War moved along, a new practice developed. During firing missions, off-duty crew members often watched movies or other

The battleship shoots a projectile toward Khafji, in northern Saudi Arabia, on February 12. (Photo by Brad Dillon in DoD Still Media Records Center: DN-SN-91-08056)

programs on the closed-circuit TVs. When they heard the sound of the 16-inch guns firing, they'd wait sixty seconds, the approximate time of flight for a projectile, then switch to the RPV's target channel to watch the impact.[40]

After a while the sixteen hundred crewmen settled into a fatiguing routine of waking and sleeping, standing watches, and carrying out firing missions when directed. Because of their duties, some men didn't have time during the Gulf War to go to their bunks for sleep. Instead, they grabbed forty winks whenever and wherever they could. Master Chief Machinist's Mate Jim Roswell, for example, was in his office one time when four other chiefs from the engineering department were with him. They were nodding off as they sat in chairs that they leaned back in and propped against a bulkhead. When men were at general quarters in repair lockers or other places that didn't require constant action, the scene leaders had the option of allowing some of them to sleep where they were and thus keep from getting worn out. Those who were awake passed the time by playing cards or using hand-held video games. Nintendo's Game Boy did much to help the

men fight off boredom during those long hours of watchful waiting.[41]

Mail was a welcome diversion. Lieutenant Commander Hank Marchese, a former enlisted man, had been on the verge of retiring when the opportunity to serve in the *Missouri* came along. He had first met his future wife, Theresa, in 1968, at the beginning of his enlisted service. In 1990, as war loomed, she had urged him to apply for the ship, knowing he would be unhappy if he missed the opportunity. When he was in the Persian Gulf in 1991, he found just how supportive Terry was. After the ship had been bombarding at Khafji, he received a letter from her that read: "I miss you, and I really do wish you were here with me. But I know you're where you're supposed to be. You're finally doing what you've been trained to do. If you were home here with me, your mind and your heart would be out there. That's where you belong."[42]

Leon Tucker heard from people he knew, and he received letters from people who were complete strangers, those who had written to express their support. In the process, those strangers raised the morale of many *Missouri* men. The feeling was especially heartening for

Commander Jim Nickols, senior chaplain in the ship, holds a service during the war. (Photo by Terry Cosgrove in DoD Still Media Records Center: DN-ST-94-00428)

Vietnam veterans such as Tucker, because he remembered a time when the American people seemed to have forgotten the servicemen who were facing the enemy half a world away in Southeast Asia. Now the public and the sailors were on the same team again.[43]

As during the convoy-protection deployment in 1987, much of the mail that flooded in came from people who had no family connection. The outpouring was so huge that the crew couldn't possibly answer all the letters, but they did reply to many of them. Chief Gunner's Mate Carl Farmer, for instance, established a correspondence with a sixth-grade class from his home area in Harlan County, Kentucky. He sent letters, ship's patches, and other souvenirs, and the children responded with photos, drawings, and other slices of life from middle America.[44]

Journalist Gary Price and many other members of the crew kept in touch with their families via audiotapes to supplement the written mail. Price had radio and television experience because of his Navy occupational specialty and used that in making tapes for his wife, Betty. Armed with a boom box, he was like a disc jockey, putting together tapes that combined both music and his frequent reminders that he missed her. A favorite for both of them was "The Power of Love," the song played for the first dance of their recent marriage. During the periods when the ship was in port at Bahrain, Price "spent megabucks calling home. I think our highest phone bill [for one month] was nearly eight hundred dollars. . . . I can't put a monetary value on talking to my wife."[45]

Commander Jim Nickols, the senior chaplain, noticed that chapel attendance was better during the Gulf War than at other times. The crew also seemed more unified than usual, putting aside petty grievances and respecting each other. For the most part, men were focused on their jobs. When they did have time for reflection, they thought about the effect on those at home if they themselves didn't make it back.[46]

Men were more cooperative and shared with each other more than usual. Selfishness diminished. Ship's Serviceman Gregory Green observed that if a man had a problem with a supervisor, the supervisor was willing to talk it

Postal Clerk Jamie Hughes sorts mail into division bins prior to distribution to the crew. (Photo by Terry Cosgrove in DoD Still Media Records Center: DN-ST-94-00429)

through and work to find common ground. In the ship's first war, nearly a half century earlier, the black and white members of the *Missouri*'s crew were rigidly segregated. Now they were all serving together. Green, a black man, didn't find race to be a problem during his time on board.[47]

In his talks with the crew during the war, Chaplain Nickols found most of the men to be in favor of the *Missouri*'s effort. A few raised the question of why the United States should be there to help the Kuwaitis regain their supply of oil. Nickols sought to turn it around, concentrating not on the materialistic aspect but more on the humanitarian role of stopping evil. He reminded them that the *Missouri* and the rest of the U.S. forces were there to restore the country to people who had been evicted from their homeland.[48]

On February 13, the *Missouri* was joined by ships of the mine countermeasures force as she headed north to provide bombardment support for a possible amphibious raid on Faylakah Island. Occupied by Iraqis, the island was just off the harbor mouth for Kuwait City. It had an obviously commanding position for dealing with any potential amphibious assault on the city itself. As the battleship moved to the northern end of the gulf, she was traveling through well-mined waters.

Shortly before that, Captain Peter Bulkeley had taken command of Destroyer Squadron Twenty-Two. His tactical designation was commander Task Group 151.11. All told, he commanded a force of thirty-one ships—U.S., British, and Saudi—in the northern gulf. Even though Bulkeley was junior to both Captain Bill of the *Wisconsin* and Captain Kaiss of the *Missouri*, there was no awkwardness in the command relationships. Each of the skippers had plenty to do as it was, so it was helpful to have a unit commander available to direct the group of ships carrying out the operation. For communications purposes, Bulkeley was embarked in the amphibious assault ship *Tripoli*.[49]

For nearly a month, Coalition air forces had been bombing in great numbers to soften up the Iraqis for the coming ground war. How well that land war went would dictate whether it was necessary to mount an amphibious assault. Even if the Marines did not have to land—as proved the case—they tied down several Iraqi ground divisions and kept them out of the fight with Coalition forces coming in from the west.[50]

On the morning of February 18, while steaming near the *Missouri*, Bulkeley's flagship *Tripoli* struck a moored contact mine. A few hours later the cruiser *Princeton* triggered a couple of influence mines on the bottom. The *Missouri* turned away three thousand yards before she would have entered the mine field herself. The communications in the *Tripoli* were severely damaged so Bulkeley called Captain Kaiss in the *Missouri* and transferred tactical command of the group of ships to him for a few hours. Later that day, the *Missouri*'s embarked explosives experts destroyed two more enemy mines, bringing their total to ten.

It took five days for the mine countermeasures forces to clear a lane six miles long and one thousand yards wide so that the battleship could get in close enough to fire at Kuwait. Helicopters went in first for drag sweeping with their sleds. Then the British mine hunters went in to check out the area. The minesweeping commander had a confidence factor of 80 percent that the "box" was mine free.

On February 23, on the eve of still more shooting, the *Missouri* steamed in next to the damaged *Tripoli*, and Bulkeley and his staff moved to the battleship.[51]

As the *Missouri* got in close to the Kuwaiti coast, chemical alarms went off, and so the task group commander directed the ships to go to MOPP level four. The crew was at various MOPP levels during the Gulf War. That stood for mission-oriented protective posture and, in part, had to do with the degree of anti-chemical precautions. Level four included full chemical suits and gas masks. It was an arduous process and took the crew about two hours to get completely outfitted.

Several battleship sailors had problems as they tried to open the metal cans that contained charcoal elements for their gas mask air filters. Being of the younger generation, some didn't know how to use the type of key found on a can of sardines or Spam. Several cut themselves as the lengthening ribbons of metal unwound and bit into their fingers. One man thought the can had a pop top and sat on deck crying when it wouldn't come open. Some were scared by the thought of a gas attack; others were alarmed when they opened up their protective suits and found they had two tops and no bottom.[52]

The purpose in sending the *Missouri* so close to Kuwait itself was to let the Iraqis think that she was there to support an invasion over the beaches of Kuwait. At 11:15 on the night of February 23, as part of creating that impression, Captain Bulkeley directed the ship to fire on Faylakah Island as soon as she got within range and targets began appearing. The island itself wasn't part of the diversion, but as Bulkeley explained afterward: "Enemy troops [were] on there. . . . My job was to attack the enemy, and I did. Simple as that." (Part of the task group commander's aggressiveness may have been genetic. In World War II, his father, Lieutenant Commander John D. Bulkeley, received the Medal of Honor from FDR for his command of PT boats around the Philippines.)

The bombardment efforts by the *Missouri* were successful. The intelligence reports coming aboard to Bulkeley's embarked staff indicated that the Iraqis were moving corps-level artillery support to the Kuwaiti coast and the offshore island of Bubiyan—ready to repel the expected invasion.[53]

The land targets assigned to the *Missouri* forced her to the western edge of her fire support area in order to reach them with the 16-inch guns at maximum effective range. The combination of shoal water and distance to the targets gave the ship an operating box only about one mile long. That meant frequent changes of course to stay in the box, but the problem was complicated by the fact that the ship had to be steadied up on a particular course in order to allow the fire control equipment to calculate the bearings to the targets and generate firing solutions.[54]

To shoot the mission, the fire-control radars would lock on a fixed position as a reference point. In the northern area off Kuwait this was sometimes an island, sometimes an oil derrick. The ship's electronic navigation systems, including the global positioning satellite, enabled the navigation team to fix the *Missouri*'s position with great accuracy. Working from that known position, the World War II–era computers in the plotting room calculated the gun target lines—range and bearing to the target—and transmitted the appropriate orders to the turrets. The results were excellent, putting rounds on or near targets on initial salvos.

Throughout a mission, the navigator, plotting room, and combat engagement center compared their navigation fixes. The criterion for firing was that the gun target lines generated in the specific spaces had to be within three degrees and three hundred yards of one another. They were consistently better than that, usually within one degree and one hundred yards.[55]

Sometimes, depending on the direction the ship was heading, the *Missouri* had to fire over-the-shoulder rounds. The forward turrets trained as far aft as they would go before firing. This was a real problem for those standing watch on the bridge, such as the officer of the deck, Lieutenant Wes Carey. The windows had to be rolled down so they wouldn't shatter; the bridge people had to duck down so the blast

A boatswain's mate of the watch passes the word over the 1MC general announcing system. (Photo by Terry Cosgrove in DoD Still Media Records Center: DN-ST-94-00427)

coming in the windows wouldn't get to them. Ducking was an inconvenience when trying to answer the telephone or radio or carry on the other business of a watch. As he crouched, Carey saw billows of fire come in through the bridge windows over his head. During the Korean War, Captain Warner Edsall had prohibited the two forward turrets from firing aft of the beam. This time, because of the small area in which she could steam, the *Missouri* had to do it at times.[56]

When the ship was in the mineswept box, she was making legs along the diagonal of the box with merely a mile and a half of steaming room before having to turn around. Lieutenant (j.g.) Joe Raskin gave the orders to the helmsman. Previously, the conning officers thought that three knots was the minimum speed needed to maintain steerageway, but an even slower speed was preferable because that would give the *Missouri* more time to stay on the leg before reversing course. Boatswain's Mate Third Class Ronald Ladd was a superb helmsman, and he was able to keep the ship on course when the speed was down around one knot—sometimes as low as four revolutions per minute by the propellers. That allowed the ship to remain on the diagonal leg for about an hour at a time.[57]

On February 24, Coalition forces began their long-awaited ground war to recapture Kuwait. At five in the morning, the *Missouri* began firing into the occupied country to support the ground assault. The following day, the battleship was directed to be the centerpiece of an amphibious feint on Kuwait. General Schwarzkopf really would have preferred to have two battleships shooting instead of just the *Missouri*. That would have given the Iraqis even more reason to believe a landing was coming. Captain Bulkeley thus told Captain Kaiss that the *Missouri* would have to pretend she was two battleships—a pretense on top of a pretense.[58]

The *Missouri*'s bombardment opened up at three o'clock in the morning. The battleship began by firing one 16-inch round every fifteen seconds, using the nine barrels in rotation. With the average reload time per barrel just under a minute, that was no problem. Kaiss was amused when he got a call from Bulkeley saying: "It's too fast. Slow down." So the ship slowed down twice more. She was doing a great job of being two battleships but shooting off ammo that might be needed later for something else. At the end of the bombardment, the *Missouri* was getting off a round every forty-five seconds. All told, she put out 133 rounds of 16-inch in a two-hour period.[59]

The turrets were firing in numerical sequence that night. At one point, turret two had just completed firing, and those on the starboard wing of the bridge were looking aft to await the projectiles to come out of turret three. Navigator Mike Finn was there with the skipper and the weapons officer. As he looked toward shore, Finn saw dozens of fires in the distance because of the oil wells set ablaze by the Iraqis. Then, as he was looking somewhat aft of the beam, he saw a steady orange glow, like the tip of a lighted cigarette, growing larger and larger as it drew nearer the ship.[60]

Lieutenant Wes Carey was the officer of the deck. The former boatswain's mate had been in the Navy for nearly thirty years by the time of the war, and he had concluded that the captain of any ship, because of the onus of responsibility, was always the best lookout on board. So it was that night. When the orange fireball appeared, Captain Kaiss declared: "That's a missile. It's in-bound. Everyone hit the deck." Carey had been seeing flashes on the water for three days, so he was skeptical. After more observation he realized that the captain was right. Carey rushed into the pilothouse to pass the word over the general announcing system about the missile. As he went inside, he tripped over some of his horizontal shipmates and spilled a cup of hot coffee on a quartermaster lying there. Finally, he got to the microphone and warned all hands below decks to brace for shock.[61]

As the Iraqi Silkworm came ever closer, Kaiss concluded that it would probably head for turret two or the smokestacks. The stacks were particularly likely targets for a missile with a heat-seeking head. He thought the missile had liquid fuel, and so it would be best for everyone topside to take cover. Kaiss went into the pilothouse, inside the armored citadel, to talk briefly with Wes Carey. He saw "an awful lot of people down on the deck." Back out on the wing of the bridge, he could see the missile start to drift to the right. Then he was down on the deck himself.[62]

Among the many who felt fear when the Silkworm was streaking toward the *Missouri* was Ship's Serviceman Green. His mind contemplated a number of possibilities, including damage to the ship, abandoning ship, being captured as a prisoner of war, and even wondering what the Iraqis would feed him if they did capture him. He had no access to electronic gear or defensive weapons. The weapon he wielded in that circumstance was hope—as if to will away the Silkworm. He had hundreds of helpers in sending out such messages. One thing that helped many of them was the calmness of Lieutenant Carey as he put out the warning from the bridge. Just as panic can be contagious, so can a sense of confidence.[63]

Ensign Ed Stockton was the officer in charge of repair party five aft in the ship. The *Missouri* had been at general quarters for a while, and the men of the repair party had fallen into a sort of half-drowsy state, with their minds in neutral. They really had nothing to do unless the ship was damaged. Then, when the missile warning came in, Stockton and those around him instantly snapped awake. He warned them to brace for shock, and then they waited—as if for the other shoe to drop. Remembering later, he asserted, "That was probably about the longest two minutes of my life." His mouth went dry. When he tried to swallow, his throat wouldn't cooperate. Stockton and the repair party leader looked at each other and lamented, "This isn't fun anymore."[64]

The embarked task group commander, Captain Pete Bulkeley, was in the combat engagement center. As the missile approached, he observed that the operators of the Vulcan/Phalanx system were "as smooth and cool as could be." Chaff rockets—designed to decoy a radar seeker in the missile—were being fired in considerable numbers by various ships.[65]

Lieutenant Horace Rhoden was on the bridge as surface evaluator. He saw the Silkworm's fireball roar past astern of the ship, crossing from starboard to port at a range of perhaps half a mile. Then it appeared to be heading up the *Missouri*'s port side. At that point, he saw what he described as "two lightning bolts coming from the HMS *Gloucester*. The fireball just exploded." The British frigate, patrolling near the *Missouri*, had sent up two Sea Dart antiair missiles. One of them knocked down the offending Silkworm. "It looked like the world's largest flashbulb going off," Captain Kaiss recalled later. "It was really a big white light." The after lookout, on the *Missouri*'s fantail, saw the Sea Darts fired and thought the *Gloucester* herself had exploded.[66]

Navy combat artist John Roach, whose work goes back to the Vietnam War, captured the scene as two Sea Dart missiles leapt up from HMS *Gloucester* to intercept the incoming Iraqi Silkworm early on the morning of February 25. (Courtesy Navy Art collection)

The *Missouri*'s conning officer, Lieutenant Raskin, was on the port side of the bridge. Quite a bit of wind was blowing that night, and between that, his double ear protection, and the bridge windows being rolled down to prevent them from being shattered by the turrets' concussion, Raskin did not hear the warnings about the in-bound missile. He had been looking down at the instruments on the bridge. When he looked up again, he saw two missiles approaching from over the horizon, roughly off the port bow, from the direction of Faylakah Island. With both Carey and Kaiss on the starboard wing of the bridge, Raskin said to himself, "This is worth stopping what I'm doing and going to tell them."[67]

When he got to the starboard side, his eyes were as big as saucers. He saw that everyone was on the deck but decided to deliver his message to the skipper anyway. "Sir, we just had missiles fired at us."[68]

From somewhere in the sprawl of bodies came the response, "No shit." When he later returned to his position, Raskin reconstructed things and realized that what he had seen were the missiles from the *Gloucester*. The Silkworm had come from the other direction, the Kuwaiti coast.[69]

Lieutenant Rhoden also did a little reflection afterward. While the missile was in-bound, he felt no fear, just did his job. Five minutes later, however, his mind began replaying what he had just lived through. At that point, he explained: "Fear began to sneak in. I was very happy that it was a dark night out and that no one could see my legs shaking."[70]

The interval between the first sighting of the Silkworm missile and the explosion at the end of its mission was only thirty to forty-five seconds. Postattack analysis revealed that the *Missouri*'s Vulcan/Phalanx close-in weapon system had locked on and was tracking the Silkworm, but the missile didn't meet the threat profile that would activate the Gatling guns on that weapon system. Therefore, the system concluded that the Silkworm was going to pass safely astern of the battleship. Nor did the missile show up on the *Missouri*'s electronic warfare detectors, indicating that it did not have an active radar seeker head to guide it to the target. It could have had an infrared guidance system, a passive-type seeker, but that was probably not working either, or else it could scarcely have missed homing on the smokestacks and 16-inch guns as heat sources.[71]

Probably the most likely explanation is that the Iraqis fired on a compass bearing toward the Coalition ships and hoped they would hit something. Indeed, it may not have been a bona fide threat, but the *Gloucester*'s intervention provided a welcome margin of safety. Later intelligence revealed that the Iraqis had actually launched two missiles toward the *Missouri*, one that fell into the sea en route and the one that the British ship took out.[72]

After the missile exploded in midair, Captain Bulkeley directed the RPV team to send a drone back down the bearing from which the Silkworm had come. It went that way and found a burned-out abandoned missile site. A thousand yards south of it was a new Silkworm battery, including launching rails and camouflage right on the beach. A control truck was on a hill overlooking the site. Bulkeley then told Captain Kaiss to use the *Missouri*'s guns to engage the site. The first 16-inch round was correct in bearing, perhaps a hundred yards short of the battery in range. The second round was about two hundred yards long. After just a few more rounds, the RPV's camera showed that the men who had been operating the missile site were running for their lives. The battleship poured in about fifty rounds at a range of twenty miles and neutralized the battery.[73]

The men of the *Missouri* watched the dawn that day as they completed the long fire mission and thought about what they had lived through. Later in the day, about six in the evening, someone on board one of the British mine hunters saw a flare. Thinking it was another inbound missile, the individual sent out a warning by radio. As they had the night before, the various warships began sending up clouds of chaff to try to fool the radar on the presumed missile. The frigate *Jarrett* was only about a thousand yards away from the *Missouri*, and her Vulcan/Phalanx system was in a fully automatic operating mode.

Triggered by the *Missouri*'s chaff, the *Jarrett*'s Gatling guns poured forth a stream of 20-mm bullets and sprayed the side of the battleship in the process. Some came in through an officers' head. At the time, the mess management specialist assigned to the staff of Captain Bulkeley was leading a repair team through the interior of the battleship. One of the bullets missed his head by a mere six inches. The bullet exploded against a steam line, rupturing it, and sending out a piece of slag that hit the man in the ear. He was the only man on board the *Missouri* to be wounded during the entire war, and it was by friendly fire.[74]

During the final period in close to the coast of Kuwait, Captain Bulkeley had led with the battleships because he was more concerned by the threat from mines than enemy missiles. He concluded that the *Missouri* could far better withstand a mine hit than could an Aegis cruiser; the damage to the thin-skinned *Princeton* had already demonstrated the problem in that regard. Actually, even though the *Missouri* stayed in her safe box, it turned out

that she was already through the mine field and could have gone on to Kuwait. A further irony is that the biggest threat had, in fact, turned out to be from an enemy missile.[75]

While the ground war was in progress, U.S. forces were moving inland so rapidly that the demarcation line for firing was changing hour by hour. In other words, the safety line beyond which the *Missouri* had to fire in order to avoid hitting friendly troops advanced much more quickly than the war planning had anticipated. That ruled out some planned targets because shooting at them would have endangered allied ground forces. So the *Missouri* then had to shift her fire to targets farther up the coast.[76]

In one four-hour period of firing up north, Gunner's Mate Tucker and his men entirely emptied a large magazine—located so as to serve both of the forward turrets—of its 16-inch powder charges. The tall cans that stored three bags of powder apiece also contained a quantity of ether to serve as a preservative. With all the activity of opening cans and mov-

Captain Peter Bulkeley, a destroyer squadron commander embarked in the *Missouri* during the bombardment of Kuwait, poses on February 26 with two high-explosive shells. On them he has chalked messages of revenge for two ships of his task group, the *Tripoli* and *Princeton*, which were damaged by Iraqi mines. (Courtesy Captain Peter Bulkeley)

Stenciled artwork on this turret proclaims that it fired 289 rounds during the Gulf War. The map shows Kuwait and the northern part of Saudi Arabia. The southern star represents fire missions at Khafji; the top star is Kuwait City. The offshore island with the palm tree in it is Faylakah. (Photo by John Bouvia in DoD Still Media Records Center: DN-SC-92-02872)

ing bags, the odor of ether permeated the magazine; it even formed a mist that was visible in the air of the magazine.[77]

The impulse of the mission kept men going, even though the job of lugging around 110-pound bags of powder was physically demanding. The situation served as a shield against fatigue. As Tucker explained, "The adrenaline was flowing in the right direction." Finally, the respite came. The weary men climbed up and out of the barbette and went to the mess deck for hot food and relaxation. Playing on the television sets was a tape from the RPV showing the results of the shooting. This was a chance for men to see what their physical exertions had helped accomplish.[78]

Once during the shore bombardment, a *Missouri* RPV was shot down by ground fire. Via television the men on board the battleship could see the antiaircraft batteries on the ground and the tracer rounds coming upward toward the TV camera in the drone. It then fell to the ground, out of the war. It was a relatively cheap loss in comparison to the cost in both money and human life if a manned aircraft had been similarly destroyed. On board the battle-

ship it just called for sending up another remotely piloted vehicle and resuming the mission.[79]

Part of the RPV's time was spent on scouting missions, comparable to the role for the old battleship floatplanes in the period before World War II. When the men in the *Missouri*'s plotting rooms saw a likely target in the TV pictures coming back from the drone, crewmen talked by radio with Marines ashore to ensure that the target was indeed legitimate. If so, the battleship let go with her 16-inch guns. If it was a mobile target, the main information the Marines could provide was whether it was friend or foe.[80] In one instance, the RPV spotted a column of Iraqi tanks headed toward American troops. The men on board the *Missouri* passed the information out to the chain of command. Then they listened to radio reports as A-10 attack planes and Apache helicopters had a field day in going after the armored units.[81]

As the war went on and the Coalition forces made dramatic advances, Captain Bulkeley began to feel a sense of concern for the Iraqi troops. Earlier, he had ordered the firing of the *Missouri*'s guns at Faylakah Island because the enemy was there; now he concluded that they were stuck in a bad position. He didn't want the ship to fire indiscriminately against targets that did not count. The targets that counted were ammunition dumps, missile batteries, and antiaircraft sites.[82]

During the four-day period of the land war, the crew of the *Missouri* was at general quarters much of the time, as one mission followed another. Consequently, Lieutenant Commander John Finn, the navigator, had difficulty afterward recalling just what happened when. One particular mission stood out, though, as a highlight. It was a night shoot against an enemy ammunition bunker. When the first round went out, it scored a direct hit on the bunker and produced results that were visible on board the ship. The RPV wasn't up for spotting at the time, but it wasn't really necessary because the repeated secondary explosions bespoke success. The flashes of light in the distance provided a spectacular contrast to the blackness around them.[83]

All told, the battleship fired 611 rounds of

16-inch projectiles during a sixty-hour period ending on February 27. That brought her total for the war to 759 rounds. As the *Missouri* drew short on ammunition, Captain Bulkeley shifted his task group flag to the *Wisconsin* and she took over as the duty gunship. She did some firing to cover the surrender of Faylakah Island. The *Missouri* then moved out a few miles, dropped anchor, and sent the crew to bed. The day after that, the *Missouri* went out to reload her depleted magazines and projectile decks.[84]

By virtue of the ten or so rounds that the *Wisconsin* fired on the last day, bringing her total to 324 for the war, she became the last battleship to fire her big guns in anger. Throughout the time the two battleships were in the gulf, there was some sense of rivalry between the crews. The men of the *Missouri* were pleased that their ship was the first to fire at Khafji and also that the *Wisconsin* was out of it for much of the land war, which ended in victory for the Coalition forces on February 28.[85]

It was an extraordinary period for the battleship *Missouri,* and it was an extraordinary experience for the men of the crew. Being able to perform effectively for four straight days with essentially no sleep is beyond usual human capability. Navigator Finn attributed the work that he and many others did to the functioning of adrenaline within their bodies. It gave them phenomenal endurance. Finn described it as "incredible," adding, "There's no way I could ever be up that high without getting any sleep, but for those four days I was."[86]

The Coalition forces had been so dramatically successful in their war of mobility, slashing across the desert and outflanking their foes, that Kuwait was liberated and the *Missouri* was out of a job. Once the ship had taken on ammunition, she had no more targets for those one-ton bullets. She retired to Bahrain soon afterward. Once the situation was calm, Captain Kaiss requested permission for the ship to depart, and she was released to head for Australia. On March 21, the battleship went through the Strait of Hormuz and out of the Persian Gulf. The *Missouri*'s third war was over.[87]

Fate had dealt Captain Lee Kaiss an interesting hand. In 1985 and 1986 he had gone through a great deal to bring the ship and crew together for the recommissioning. Then his health denied him the opportunity to take the ship around the world and operate her with the fleet. It may also have robbed him of the chance for flag rank, because he was in restricted-duty status during prime time for selection. But in 1991, he did something even more significant than an around-the-world cruise. As he put it: "No one likes to go to war. But . . . I think that one of the most magnificent things that I've ever done in my life is [that] . . . I stood on the bridge . . . on a battleship in combat and directed it. There's no feeling like that in the world."[88]

During her subsequent passage through the Indian Ocean, the *Missouri* crossed the equator and held yet another round of initiations on March 27. A special target for the shellbacks was Lieutenant Commander Hank Marchese, the fire control officer. The former enlisted man made it a point to go counter to all the pre-initiation rules. Among other things, he called particular attention to himself by joking around about the festivities. Thus, he was singled out for special treatment. This was one of the few times the enlisted men got a legitimate opportunity to take shots at their officer.[89]

Unlike the old days, the *Missouri*'s shellbacks did not beat the pollywogs physically. Someone had gotten hurt during an initiation in one of Captain Kaiss's previous commands. He didn't want a repetition, so he kept a pretty tight rein on what happened. Some men brandished shillelaghs, made by cutting fire hoses down to size. Men were smacking them against the deck to make noise, but didn't hit the pollywogs with them.[90]

Along with the equator festivities, the *Missouri*'s crew spent part of the time restoring the ship to her prewar condition. Sailors shined brass, holystoned and swabbed decks, and put on a new coat of haze-gray paint. Captain Kaiss directed that the ship be turned back into a sparkling jewel in appearance. To maintain her appearance during the war itself was virtually impossible; the crew couldn't do much more than clean the decks then. They couldn't paint because most of the paint had been off-loaded as a fire hazard.[91]

As he went out on deck during that ride back, Chaplain Jim Nickols had a feeling similar to the one experienced by his predecessor of long ago, Commander Roland Faulk, when the *Missouri* was steaming home from Tokyo Bay in 1945. For Faulk the ship was new; for Nickols there was a reaching back to Faulk's era and those that followed. Nickols reminisced: "When you see the ship gliding through the water under the moonlight, on a quiet sea in the Pacific, you think back and remember the sailors who worked those decks and manned those guns, stood in the conning tower and the watch. I don't know how you can describe it; it's a spiritual event that connects you with those people. . . . It was almost a sense of a time warp in all of that." [92]

The ship received a warm reception in Australia, as she had during the previous stops in 1986 and 1987. Incredible lines of people waited to tour the ship. As before, the Australians were picking up the tab whenever the men of the *Missouri* went out for drinks. The beer was aw-fully potent. "I don't recommend it on an empty stomach," recalled Ross Mobilia. In Perth one day, Mobilia was sitting in a restaurant when a man—with his wife and two children—came up to him. He invited the American to his nearby home for tea and biscuits. Mobilia had a good time talking with the family and answering their "millions of questions" about the ship and the Gulf War. [93]

Timothy Hofman, the command master chief, was amused by the curiosity of the Australian tourists about the *Missouri*. Many wanted to know details about Desert Storm, but many others evinced even more curiosity about Cher—what gun she sat on, her costume, and so forth. They had seen the video that had caused so much indigestion in Washington. The answer to their question was that she sat on the center gun of turret one. [94]

During the various port visits, Master Chief Machinist's Mate Jim Roswell used to play a game with Commander Larry Doong, the *Missouri*'s chief engineer. The contest was to see who could find the visiting child who appeared

During her stop in Hawaii on the way home from the Persian Gulf, the *Missouri* displays the dark gray hull numbers she sported while in the war zone. The dark numbers were directed by the Pacific Fleet Surface Force to make visual detection at night more difficult. The *Wisconsin*, which had arrived in the theater earlier from the Atlantic, had white numbers throughout the war. (Photo by John Bouvia in DoD Still Media Records Center: DN-SC-92-02875)

With a huge wreath around her bow, the *Missouri* arrives back at her familiar pier-six berth in Long Beach on May 13, 1991. The throng of well-wishers was behind the photographer who took the picture; they were restrained from coming onto this small pier to avoid interfering with line handlers. (Photo by Robert Wilson in DoD Still Media Records Center: DN-ST-93-01482)

to need the most. The tip-off was an expression of unhappiness during what should have been a pleasant occasion. In Perth, for example, Doong ran into a kid who was celebrating his birthday while the battleship was there. His parents appeared to be people of modest means, so the boy's present was a special tour of the battleship, guided by the chief engineer. When the ship was in Hobart, Tasmania, Roswell found a boy who was doing well in school, but his mother couldn't afford to reward him for his efforts. Captain Kaiss let the boy have a ride in his gig, plus a tour of the ship and a *Missouri* ball cap. Still another child arrived too late for visiting hours, but he wound up with a special tour anyway. The main prize in the contest between the engineers was the sense of satisfaction that came from making the youngsters happy.[95]

When the ship stopped in Pearl Harbor, Journalist Gary Price went to the *Arizona* Memorial visitors' center to see the relics of the memorialized battleship. Some of the docents at the memorial were survivors of the Japanese attack. Price struck up a conversation with a man named Dick Fiske, who had been a Marine bugler on board the battleship *West Virginia* in

December 1941. He told Price he had had two buddies who were serving in the *Arizona* at the time of the attack. He said to Price: "You know, this being Good Friday, I might go out and see them, because I just don't think of them as gone. I think I'm going to go out today and say hello." Behind his sunglasses, Price felt tears forming in his eyes.[96]

After all they had been through, the crew of the ship had an additional pleasure as the *Missouri* traversed the final leg home from Pearl Harbor to Long Beach. It was a tiger cruise, in which male relatives of the crew got to ride along. Lieutenant Commander Mike Finn was joined by his eight-year-old son, Brian. Brian had heard the war reports back home and had mostly to use his imagination to visualize what things were like. Now he could see for himself and receive a firsthand recounting. On May 9, during that homeward journey, the *Missouri* put on a firepower demonstration with her main battery, secondary battery, and close-in weapon system. It was the last time the ship ever fired her 16-inch guns.[97]

Along with running the *Missouri*'s laundry and helping the ship fight in Desert Storm, Gregory Green had spent the deployment working toward his enlisted surface warfare qualification. He finally made it on May 12, the next-to-last day of the deployment. It was a rare achievement for a man in his rating because there are no specific warfare skills in washing clothes, cutting hair, or running the ship's store. He had been spurred in part by his wife's suggestion that he needed a personal goal during the long trip.[98]

As the battleship approached her home port on May 13—six months to the day since she had departed Long Beach—Green was so excited that he got up at five o'clock in the morning. He donned the brightest white uniform the laundry could produce and shined the silver surface warfare pin that went over the left pocket of his shirt. As he looked down at the pier from his spot on board ship, he saw a mass of humanity, balloons, animals, former *Missouri* crew members, a band, Los Angeles Raiders cheerleaders, and girls who had received letters from crewmen during the deployment. But the only people he was really looking for were his wife, Anita, and their children.[99]

The *Missouri*'s arrival home was the most dramatic of all the ships that returned to Long Beach after the Gulf War. The crowds on the pier had to stay back as the ship came in so they wouldn't interfere with the line handlers. Sailors were standing with their arms linked and their backs to the crowd. Still the crowds surged forward, trying to reach the ship and their men. The frenzy of emotion reminded Lieutenant Commander Steve Chesser of *Triumph of the Will,* Leni Riefenstahl's tour de force

documentary about Hitler and Nazism. Meanwhile, the TV cameras were capturing the atmosphere and interspersing the live views with black-and-white photos that depicted the ship's historical role during World War II. At times, it seemed that the *Missouri* was almost treated as an icon, in part because of the brief patriotic high the nation was going through in the wake of the victory over Iraq.[100]

Weeks before, the skipper's wife, Veronica Kaiss, sent her husband a letter suggesting that the new babies be the first aboard the ship once the *Missouri* was pierside at Long Beach. All told, fifty-some children had been born to the wives of *Missouri* men during the deployment. The captain coordinated from the ship and his wife from the shore to make sure that the new mothers and their children were, in fact, the first to get aboard that happy day.[101]

Just walking on the pier was a challenge for members of the families. They had to weave their way through a tangle of strollers and children, wives, parents, brothers and sisters. Finally, the flood gates were opened. Families surged aboard ship; crew members greeted them enthusiastically and then went off to their private celebrations of reunion. Among the many reunited were Gary and Betty Price. He described what happened when they left the ship and returned to their home: "The first thing I did was call in a Domino's pizza, and everything after that you can't print in your book."[102]

15 ❖ The Last Battleship

May 1991–Summer 1995

Once the *Missouri*'s crew settled into a workaday routine following the return to home port, they could enjoy the fruits of their wartime deployment. For instance, Disneyland and Universal Studios donated tickets so that crewmen and their families could get in without charge. Another source of enjoyable benefits was the welfare and recreation fund, which had grown to considerable proportions because of the surpluses generated in the ship's store. It amounted to an allowance of forty dollars per man per month that could be used for movie tickets, sporting events, and other attractions in the Long Beach–Los Angeles area.[1]

In that summer of 1991, especially with the ship's planned inactivation only months away, the *Missouri* was flooded with tourists. Thirty thousand came aboard the first weekend of July, during the last spasm of general visiting in Long Beach. The men of the *Missouri* enjoyed showing off their ship. Lieutenant Ross Mobilia, for example, guided a man who billed himself as the "undertaker to the stars." To reciprocate, the visitor later invited Mobilia to a country club for an enjoyable round of golf. For the naval officer it was an eye-opener. He and his companions came upon a telephone at the ninth hole. Alongside was a menu so they could phone in their orders for beer and sandwiches. At the next hole, a man came out and handed them a tray with their refreshments. After that welcome respite, they resumed their play. The nineteenth hole was sumptuous as well, leading Mobilia to conclude, "It's good to be rich."[2]

Master Chief Journalist John Caffey of the ship's public affairs office considers the number-one factor in the dreadnought's appeal to be her status as the surrender ship. Being re-cently returned from a successful war was another, and, finally, there was the timeless allure of being the last of the breed known as battleship. When new crew members reported for duty in the *Missouri*, Captain Kaiss told them, as part of their indoctrination, that they were expected to learn the ship quickly and then be able to give tours for the benefit of visitors.[3]

Now that the ship was back in southern California, her crewmen were subject to a number of temptations that just hadn't been available during the long days and weeks of operation at sea. One of the concerns for the command throughout the *Missouri*'s second tour of duty was alcohol and drug use on the part of crew members. Drugs had been a big problem for the Navy of the seventies, but that situation was largely turned around by the adoption of a zero-tolerance policy throughout the service. With few exceptions, a crewman who used drugs was transferred off the ship and was probably on his way to civilian life.

Alcohol was a much more difficult problem to handle because it had become ingrained in the Navy culture over the centuries. When the *Missouri* was in service in the 1940s and 1950s, drinking was expected and usually tolerated. As long as a man could get back to the ship and get up the next day to do his job, he was left alone. He incurred disciplinary sanctions only for such things as fighting, property damage, and failure to do his duty.

By the 1980s and 1990s, the *Missouri* was part of a Navy-wide effort to discourage drinking and to provide programs designed to lead men toward sobriety. Among other things, that included promoting recreational activities such as sports competitions and the entertainment allowance for tickets. The ship also took advan-

tage of Navy alcohol rehabilitation programs, including the *Missouri*'s own chapter of Alcoholics Anonymous. Recovering alcoholics among the crew—generally senior petty officers—led chapter meetings, counseled shipmates, and referred men to Navy rehab programs and AA meetings in the ship's home port. In a closed community such as a ship's crew, of course, anonymity wasn't possible. In essence, the men were forfeiting the nameless approach that is a hallmark of AA. They recognized that motivation was a key to success in rehabilitation efforts and were willing to describe their own experiences with alcohol as part of supplying that motivation.[4]

Back in late 1990, about the time the *Missouri* was leaving for the Persian Gulf, Master Chief Personnelman Timothy Hofman, who had been the *Missouri*'s personnel officer, stepped up to become the ship's command master chief. With the return to Long Beach, he had to deal with a great many situations that had taken a backseat during the war. He counseled men on problems with wives, girlfriends, finances, alcohol, and so forth, that were separate from the men's military duties. One example concerned an enlisted man of about twenty. In California, he had a thirty-year-old girlfriend with children. In his hometown, he had a girlfriend, about the same age as he, whom he had impregnated. He had promised both that he would marry them. When Hofman questioned the man, he said he didn't really love either of the girlfriends. Hofman counseled the man to take care of his obligation to the pregnant girlfriend. Otherwise, he should back off from both relationships in order to prevent bad situations from becoming worse.[5]

During the *Missouri*'s final years in commission, about half the enlisted crew was married. If couples qualified, Hofman suggested that they avail themselves of food stamps. The proliferation of marriages also presented a challenge for the captain in administering discipline. If he fined a young married sailor for misbehavior, he was really punishing the man's wife and children, who would have to get by with less income.[6]

In handling problems, Hofman often put men in touch with the information or people they needed. If, for example, a crew member and his wife were questioning whether to keep their marriage going, Hofman referred them either to the chaplain on board or to the family services center on base at Long Beach. If the problem was amenable to a short-term solution, the center handled it; if not, it went to counselors in the civilian medical community. Sometimes a man's problem was a combination of loneliness, immaturity, and homesickness. In that case the master chief had a sympathetic ear to offer and helped the youngster formulate some goals to shoot for.[7]

The demise of the *Wisconsin*, whose home port was Norfolk, had been particularly rapid. She returned from the Persian Gulf in March, made a final East Coast cruise that summer, and then began the mothballing process. She was decommissioned at the end of September. Because of her historical status, the *Missouri* had a somewhat longer lease on life. Back when she was heading from the Persian Gulf to Australia, information reaching the battleship made it fairly evident that she would be at Pearl Harbor in December to take part in the fiftieth anniversary observation of the Japanese attack. At that point, Captain Kaiss and Commander Jordan, the executive officer, began their planning for the ship's role. They also concluded that the ship had about another year in commission, rather than having to begin the inactivation process that summer.[8]

The decommissioning of the *Missouri* and her sisters was a combination of economics and politics. The international situation had changed dramatically from a decade earlier, when the four battleships were reactivated as a symbol of American resolve during the Cold War. By 1991, the Cold War was over and the perpetual threat, the Soviet Union, had self-destructed. American taxpayers were looking for something elusive known as a "peace dividend," and the battleships were an obvious target. They had been designed and built when manpower was a relatively inexpensive commodity.

In World War II, for instance, a seaman first class drew fifty-four dollars a month in base pay. By 1991, a seaman's base pay was around nine hundred to a thousand dollars a month, depending on his years of service. In addition, higher-rated crew members were drawing sea pay, and the Navy was also paying housing allowances to many more men with families than in 1944. In 1991, the crew's payroll alone was about a million dollars a payday, twice a month. Compare that with the situation in the late 1940s, when the total annual operating cost for the ship was less than seven million.[9]

In addition to salaries, it took a good deal to feed the crew. While at sea, the ship served the equivalent of six thousand meals a day, including the traditional breakfast, lunch, and dinner, plus midnight rations for watchstanders and supplements for those with extra-healthy appetites. Because she was a half-century old, the *Missouri* didn't have the internal cargo-moving capabilities of more modern warships. When food came aboard, either at sea or in port, it typically required a hundred-man working party about once a week to move things to freezers, chill boxes, dry storerooms, and so forth—five decks down. Canned sodas were heavy to lug down all that distance. *Missouri* men typically drank between fifty and a hundred thousand cans a month. And that was on top of the mess-deck soda-dispensing machines that served drinks to be consumed with meals.[10]

In the autumn of 1991, the *Missouri* made a farewell tour along the West Coast, one last go-

A forklift tractor carries away a pallet of 5-inch powder cans while at Seal Beach. (Photo by Brad Dillon in DoD Still Media Records Center: DN-SN-93-01496)

Close-up views (*above and below*) of the superstructure during the *Missouri*'s visit to San Francisco in October 1991. The two spherical objects—in front of the fire control tower and on the after stack—cover the antennas for the remotely piloted vehicles. (Photos by Dr. Giorgio Arra via Norman Polmar)

pression by members of American society, he said he had a hard time taking seriously people who had painted their lips black to add one more touch to their mourning costumes.[11]

At the other end of the political spectrum were citizens living in high-rise condominiums and hotels a few hundred yards from the spot where the ship was moored. Each morning and evening, the *Missouri*'s Marine detachment went out to hold colors, using bugle calls as they raised and lowered the flag at the stern. After the first morning, people came out onto their balconies to observe the ceremonies, in effect taking part in the colors ritual right along with the ship's Marines.[12]

The ship also took part in fleet week in San Francisco that autumn. She was moored at her usual berth near the Oakland Bay Bridge. During the first night or two, the local authorities specified that Navy men and Marines on liberty had to be dressed in uniform rather than in the civilian clothes customarily worn. With that many servicemen released on the city, it was, said Mobilia, "a flashback to 1944. The town was just covered with blue uniforms." The visiting servicemen rode taxis and trolleys free of charge and soaked up the generous hos-

around for the old warhorse. At SeaFair in Seattle she was the main attraction, and long lines of people came aboard. A few unfriendly visitors showed up too. Greenpeace members protested the ship's presence, although they didn't seek to interfere with crew members going ashore on liberty. Lieutenant Ross Mobilia took a cynical view of the protest movement. Although acknowledging the right of free ex-

pitality of the cosmopolitan city by the bay.[13]

One of the *Missouri*'s crew members had a far different attitude at that point from the feelings of most of his shipmates. Soon after reporting to the *Missouri* in May 1990, Fire Controlman Third Class Larry Alpert had experienced a catharsis as a result of reading the writings of Martin Luther King, Mohandas Gandhi, Leo Tolstoy, and others. He observed the obvious—that the ship's purpose was to destroy—and he decided he did not want to contribute to that purpose. After he communicated his feelings to his superiors in the *Missouri*'s chain of command, Alpert was relieved of his fire control duties and assigned to work in the areas of damage control and cleaning the ship.[14]

During the Gulf War, Alpert watched the television pictures transmitted from the RPVs and saw the results of the *Missouri*'s bombardment. Unlike many of his shipmates, he was saddened by what he saw.[15] After the war ended, the ship returned to the United States, and Alpert filed an official petition for conscientious objector status. As it was forwarded up the line, he was removed from the weapons department and sent to work in the office of the first lieutenant. His enlistment ended in March 1992, the same month the *Missouri* was decommissioned. When he was finally freed from her, she no longer had the destructive mission that had caused him so much disquiet.[16]

While the ship was in Long Beach that autumn, action-adventure movie actor Steven Seagal and his wife came aboard for a tour of the ship. He was preparing for a starring role in a movie to be called *Under Siege*. The pair was accompanied by a producer and a naval reserve captain who provided liaison with the Navy's Office of Information. The visitors asked about the plausibility of the planned scenario, which called for a band of terrorists to seize control of the battleship. Commander Ken Jordan, the exec, explained that it would be a challenge because of the Marines on board and the various patrols. He indicated, among other things, that the perpetrators would do well to work around a big event, as a distraction, and would need an inside man

among the chain of command to prepare the way for the terrorists who stormed the ship.

The *Missouri* was filmed from the air as she steamed away from Long Beach at the end of November. Those scenes in the finished film were aesthetically pleasing, including the nice touch of showing dolphins leaping ahead of the battleship's bow as she steamed westward. Because of the nature of the plot, however, the Navy's cooperation with the production was limited. The dozens of action scenes in the film were actually shot on board the memorial battleship *Alabama* at Mobile. In a scene filmed ashore, the *Missouri*'s first lieutenant, Wes Carey, had a speaking role as he portrayed an aide to the character who was the chief of naval operations. Commander Jordan was not at all pleased when he later saw in the completed film that the plot specified the *Missouri*'s executive officer as the inside man who helped in the takeover. Jordan's one-sentence review of the film: "It's not exactly one of my favorite movies."[17]

That trip to Hawaii provided some of the worst weather most of the crew members encountered during their time on board. By one estimate, the seas were fifteen to twenty feet high. The captain secured the weather decks below the 04 level, except for essential personnel. Lots of water came cascading aboard topside. Waves badly damaged three boats: the admiral's barge for commander Third Fleet—on

Missouri's Governor John Ashcroft is at right as his son Andrew makes throttle corrections in main control. Giving directions is Master Chief Machinist's Mate Jim Roswell. The Ashcrofts were on board for the cruise from San Francisco to Long Beach in October 1991. (Courtesy Jim Roswell)

the fantail—and the captain's gig and motor whaleboat—stored in davits to starboard. When the ship reached Pearl Harbor on the morning of December 5, she had to anchor for a while near the *Arizona* Memorial to off-load the damaged boats before the ship went pierside.

Ensign Ed Stockton was the *Missouri*'s technical officer responsible for the maintenance and operation of the main engines and the electrical generators and associated equipment. During that final voyage in late 1991, he addressed the persistent myth that the *Missouri* had been under a speed restriction because of damage during the grounding at Thimble Shoal in 1950. It was simply not true, he said. The only restrictions near the end of the ship's second period in commission were slight ones on number one and number four main engines as a result of damage to the reduction gears after the ship was recommissioned in the 1980s.[18]

The problem with number-one engine during the around-the-world cruise in 1986 has been mentioned previously. Then, in 1991, following the return from the Persian Gulf, some washers dropped into number-four reduction gear when one of the inspection covers fell apart during an inspection. As a result of the damage to the two reduction gears, the *Missouri* was limited to about thirty knots during her last full-power run. That compared, said Ensign Stockton, with 34.5 knots for a full-power run shortly after the ship was recommissioned in 1986. He emphasized that the figures were probably from pit log readings because of the difficult logistics involved in setting up calibrated runs over a measured-mile course.[19]

Several media representatives were on board for the voyage to Hawaii, including television crews and newspaper reporters from both Los Angeles and St. Louis. Among them was Harry Levins, the military writer for the *St. Louis Post-Dispatch*. He later wrote a day-by-day account of the journey for his paper to capture the atmosphere of life on board. Each day's report included an example about the food to demonstrate, as he put it, that "the Navy really *does* eat well." He also told of all the chipping, painting, waxing, cleaning, and polishing

that crewmen were doing in order to prepare for the upcoming visit from President and Mrs. Bush. "If it wasn't for the honor of the thing," quipped Levins, "they'd rather see their commander-in-chief visit some other ship."[20]

In preparing for the appearance, Lieutenant Carey had his deck crews using a water-based paint to conform to California environmental laws, and it worked well. The vapors from regular oil-based paint contributed to the depletion of the earth's ozone layer, something that was seriously threatened already by the pollution in the southern California area. Surprisingly, Carey found that the new paint maintained its shine and color better than oil paint.[21]

One of the men Levins interviewed in the course of his time on board was Yeoman Second Class John Lewis of Palmyra, Missouri, up the Mississippi River from St. Louis. Lewis had been a member of the recommissioning crew in 1986 and had been invited back by Captain Kaiss to make one last ride in the ship. As he sat at a table in one of the berthing compartments, Lewis talked of the upcoming decommissioning. "I'm losing a member of my family. It's really hard to accept and understand. . . . There are only two kinds of sailors in the Navy. Those who have been on a battleship and those who wish they could."[22]

On December 3, after the seas had calmed, an honor guard of sailors and Marines gathered on the fantail flight deck to pay their final respects to a battleship sailor. Captain Kaiss and Chaplain Jim Nickols presided during a burial at sea for Signalman First Class Merle J. Jones, who had served in the USS *South Dakota* in World War II. His family had requested that his ashes be distributed from the deck of the Navy's last battleship. By then the sun was out again, and both sea and sky were a bright blue as the ashes drifted out onto the broad Pacific. That long-ago sailor's last voyage was over.[23]

Two days later, just at sunup on the morning of December 5, the *Missouri* pushed her bow in through the entrance channel of the place with an evocative name, Pearl Harbor. Overhead, the roar of jet engines announced the arrival of a Japan Airlines 747 making its final approach on nearby Honolulu airport. How different from the arrival of Japanese planes fifty years

Two boiler technicians stand watch in one of the ship's firerooms during her last voyage in December 1991. (Photo by Brad Dillon in DoD Still Media Records Center: DN-ST-94-00422)

The last active battleship sweeps in past the *Arizona* Memorial on the morning of December 5, 1991. (U.S. Navy photo by G. Montgomery)

ri's flight deck. The *Missouri* moored near the supply pier, opposite the *Arizona* Memorial. The memorial could not accommodate all the people who wanted to be there, so those with sufficient clout watched things from on board another battleship.

As the commemoration ceremonies unfolded on that bright Saturday morning, Ross Mobilia was struck by the atmosphere of serenity. The whole harbor was quiet. At 7:55 A.M.—fifty years to the minute after the Japanese came roaring in—the silence was a deliberate contrast. Then the Aegis cruiser *Chosin* steamed slowly down from around Ford Island, blowing her ship's whistle at intervals. It was a moment of reverence and reflection on a world turned upside down half a century earlier. After President Bush had taken part in the ceremonies at the *Arizona* Memorial, he came over by the pier where the *Missouri* was moored. He made a speech from the pier, then came aboard. It was the first time in Mobilia's career he ever heard eight bells and the announcement, "United States—arriving."[25]

Bush did a television interview from the surrender deck. While that was in progress, Captain Kaiss was host to Mrs. Bush. He said of her afterward, "She struck me as everybody's mother." Kaiss got the impression it had already been a long day for her. She preferred to sit and relax in the captain's cabin rather than going on a planned tour of the galley. She said that what she really wanted to do was drink some iced tea and watch the Army-Navy football game on television. The president took a brief tour of the ship after his TV appearance. Mrs. Bush joined her husband when he got to the surrender deck. Chaplain Jim Nickols observed that many in the crew would have preferred more of a personal exposure to President Bush than they were able to have. The visit was a relatively brief one, so he didn't wade in, shake hands, and talk with individuals as Harry Truman had done back when he was on board in the forties.[26]

About two minutes before the Bushes arrived, the Secret Service called the ship to say that General Colin Powell, chairman of the Joint Chiefs of Staff, wanted to come aboard for a tour. That was not in the original sched-

earlier. The *Missouri*'s arrival was nowhere near so routine as that of the airliner. This was the last time ever that a battleship would enter the famed port. Harry Levins described it thusly: "The *Missouri* curves gracefully to starboard, and we're gliding into the channel, entering Pearl Harbor. Now we know what it's like to be Princess Diana gliding into a ballroom. Everybody—*everybody*—stops to gawk at you."[24] (For both Diana and the *Missouri*, the glory has faded considerably since 1991.)

Reveille for the crew occurred at four in the morning on December 7. Two hours later, some twelve hundred guests arrived to watch the anniversary ceremony from the *Missou-*

Members of the Marine detachment stand in ranks on the 01 deck as the ship arrives at Pearl Harbor. The surrender plaque itself is in storage during the ship's underway period. (*St. Louis Post-Dispatch* photo by Harry Levins)

Above: As the *Missouri* moves toward her mooring, the bow passes the *Arizona* Memorial. (U.S. Navy photo by G. Montgomery)

Below: A barge bearing the presidential party moves past the stern of the *Missouri* in order to deliver President George Bush aboard on December 7, 1991. (Photo by Brad Dillon in DoD Still Media Records Center: DN-SC-92-06658)

ule, so Commander Ken Jordan, the exec, was relieved of looking after Mrs. Bush and sent to show the general and his wife around. By the time Jordan reached him, Powell had started his own tour. He had already gone in and begun to look at turret two; then they went to look at the flag bridge, Admiral Halsey's old roost. As they looked down on the surrender deck, Jordan regaled the couple with lore from the 1945 ceremony, including the story of the table

and table cloth. After that Powell went back to the fantail and was swamped by *Missouri* crew members, Pearl Harbor survivors, and others gathered there. He went out of his way to shake the hands of sailors. In the process, he received a number of kisses from women visitors.[27]

On the evening of December 7, Admiral Charles Larson, commander in chief Pacific, hosted a reception for various dignitaries in the *Missouri*'s wardroom. Guests included some of the members of the last crew of the *Arizona*. They had survived not only the Japanese attack in 1941 but also the events of the ensuing fifty years. Among the visitors was Franklin Van Valkenburgh, Jr. His father, the captain of the *Arizona*, was killed when the forward part of the ship erupted into a tower of flame. Captain Van Valkenburgh was awarded a posthumous Medal of Honor. The *Missouri*'s officers and chief petty officers joined the reception that evening. It was a friendly, informal gathering and so enjoyable that the conversations between the old sailors and the current ones went on for some time past the scheduled end of the affair.[28]

The *Missouri* did not stay long in Hawaii. A few days after the anniversary, she began the return leg to southern California. After all the

President and Mrs. Bush leave the *Missouri* at the end of their visit on December 7, 1991. (USS *Missouri* photo by Mark Egan)

hoopla and visitors during that time in Pearl, the mood was quiet during the ensuing trip to Seal Beach, not far from the ship's home port. At the naval weapons station, the ship emptied all her ammunition except for the missiles, which were removed once she returned to Long Beach. Captain Kaiss had insisted that the *Missouri* not go to Hawaii without a load of ammunition in her magazines. Even though her days were obviously numbered, he still wanted her to be a fully capable warship during that last cruise. But now the cruise was over.[29]

The *Missouri* sat at anchor for three days and three nights while the crew manhandled tons of powder and projectiles up from below and over the side into barges. On the evening of December 20, the ship weighed anchor and made the voyage back to her home port. It was the last time a battleship of any nation steamed on her own power. She went in on the evening tide.

The executive officer of the Long Beach Naval Station had arranged a tribute. He sent a message out to the waterfront that all ships were to sound their whistles when the *Missouri* came back in. As she passed through the break-

water and approached the piers, her crew was standing at quarters on deck. It was about six in the evening and dark by then, almost the shortest day of the year. As the battleship passed by the first pier, the first whistle sounded out, and then another, and then another. As the *Missouri* went on into the harbor, more ships joined in the chorus. Most sailors have a special feeling of pride about their own ship but aren't particularly sentimental about others. This tribute was extraordinary.[30]

Finally, tugs pushed the ship in against the pier to be moored. By then it seemed that every ship in the harbor was blasting her whistle in tribute. Now came an announcement over the loudspeaker system: "The last officer of the deck of the last battleship is shifting his watch to the quarterdeck." There was very much a sense of history—that this was the last of a long line.[31]

Chief Machinist's Mate Bill Holland, who had reported to the *Missouri*'s precommissioning crew in 1985, remained in the crew until early 1991. When the ship arrived at the Long Beach Naval Shipyard later that year, he was assigned as one of the ship superintendents for her inactivation. The shipyard planners concluded, rightly so, that he knew the engineering plant well. But he found the process much less enjoyable than the activation period of six years earlier. People were laying up equipment and dismantling things, draining from the ship the vitality that Holland had been part of for so many months while on board. The superintendents went through and signed off compartments one at a time as they were officially declared inactivated.[32]

Part of the job involved in preparing the ship for decommissioning was getting rid of the mountain of spare parts, supplies, and reusable equipment such as deck buffers, consumables, et cetera, that had been involved in operating the battleship. That included sending the ship's silver service back to the state of Missouri and various historical artifacts to the curator of the Navy. All told, the ship's supply officer, Commander Kevin Carman, estimated that the ship had to off-load—and document—close to a quarter of a million items as part of the inactivation process.[33]

Included in the equipment removed were expensive electronic devices and other communication gear. Some would have to be replaced, anyway, if the time ever came to reactivate the ship; it made sense to get some other use out of them. The Tomahawk armored box launchers were left in place; the missiles were removed. The Vulcan/Phalanx system remained, although the external guns were taken off.[34]

Among the many items that were redistributed were computers. By the time the *Missouri* ended her active service, she was loaded with them. The MONET system, including its electronic-mail capability, had grown to forty-two Apple Macintosh terminals, with another eight IBM compatibles piggybacked on. There was a second computer system—called SNAP—in the maintenance, finance, and supply setup; it had one mainframe computer that served fifty-six separate terminals. Added to that were the computers in the various weapon systems, such as Tomahawk, Harpoon, and Vulcan/Phalanx.[35]

One officer who had relatively little to do during that winding-down period was the navigator. The quiet period also gave him a chance to reflect on his relationship with Captain Kaiss. Finn had worked with the skipper on essentially a daily basis and considered him ideally suited for the role as commanding officer of a battleship. On the one hand, he knew the ship and her gun systems thoroughly. On the

A time exposure highlights the *Missouri* and the *Arizona* Memorial on the fiftieth anniversary of the attack on Pearl Harbor. (Photo by John Lewis)

other, he was skilled in leading the crew and looking after their concerns. One example of that concern came during the inactivation period. Kaiss and the command master chief went to Washington to ensure that each crew member—officer or enlisted—received desirable orders for his next duty station after leaving the *Missouri*.[36]

Captain Kaiss and Commander Jordan, the exec, also polled the crew to find out which ones wanted to stay around for the final day and arranged that in as many cases as they could. The Bureau of Personnel wanted to reduce the crew to below two hundred men—as it had been for the 1955 decommissioning— but those at the top of the *Missouri*'s chain of command resisted. They managed to keep the size of the crew from going below six hundred people because they wanted enough remaining on board to mount a suitable decommissioning ceremony when the time came. Two members of the crew served all the way through the *Missouri*'s second time in commission: Senior Chief Electrician's Mate Robert Webber and Gunner's Mate First Class Michael Short.[37]

Commander Jordan persuaded Kaiss to remain to the end, as he had been the one who put the *Missouri* into commission six years earlier. Kaiss himself had planned to depart soon after the *Missouri* returned to Long Beach from the anniversary observance celebration at Pearl Harbor. Six months before that, Jordan had begun working on him to get him to stay.[38]

In early 1992, the crew of the *Missouri* moved off the ship and took up residence in personnel barges moored nearby. During the inactivation process, systems were shut down and preserved for possible future use—however unlikely. In contrast to past inactivations of ships, when large amounts of Cosmoline were introduced into piping and equipment, a more freely flowing chemical was used this time. It was poured into such items as the reduction gears, gun barrels, and fuel tanks, then allowed to sit for a while before being drained out. In the process, it left a coating on the metal surfaces so they would not rust.[39]

Morale went down a few notches during the inactivation period. Although the *Missouri* still had the aura of a battleship, she was just an-

As the last representative of the type known as dreadnoughts, the *Missouri* lies at her pier-six berth in Long Beach, decked out in bunting and shortly to move to the naval shipyard for the decommissioning ceremony. For a few years in the late eighties, the sign at the head of the pier had read "Battleship Country." When this picture was taken, the *New Jersey* had been decommissioned and the sign amended. (Photo in DoD Still Media Records Center: DN-ST-92-07089)

other ship in terms of the procedures her crew was going through. Captain Kaiss sought to combat some of those feelings by trying to instill a sense of pride of ownership. He told the crew, "The ship will come back someday." That at least gave them a sense of hope and purpose as they proceeded through the otherwise dreary chore of laying her up.[40]

On March 31, at the huge Pier Echo of the Long Beach Naval Shipyard, came the last act—the decommissioning ceremony. The ship was bedecked with red, white, and blue bunting. The crew was in dress blues, as their predecessors had been nearly six years earlier in San Francisco. In the audience were hundreds of friends of the ship, many of whom were former crew members who had donned *Missouri* baseball caps and other items tying them to the battleship.

When the ship went into commission in 1986, the officer of the deck had been a lieutenant from the state of Missouri. To carry out that duty on March 31, the captain selected Lieutenant Wes Carey, who had been officer of the deck throughout the many times the *Missouri* was at general quarters during Desert Storm a year earlier. It was Carey who had calmly passed the word for the crew to brace for shock when the Silkworm missile was approaching the battleship on February 25, 1991. He was an appropriate choice for her retirement.

Among those in the audience that day were

Right: The national ensign flies at the stern one final time on decommissioning day, March 31, 1992. The squares just below the ship's name are the outlets for streaming the NIXIE acoustic homing devices. (Courtesy John J. Hayes)

Below: The crewmen line the topside spaces at the decommissioning, just as their predecessors had nearly six years earlier at San Francisco. These men, however, were ending an adventure, not beginning one. (Courtesy Terry Cosgrove)

Herman and Phyllis Leibig from Lebanon, Pennsylvania. They had come across the country because Herm had been a seventeen-year-old seaman when the ship first went into commission in 1944. They arrived early on that sunny California morning. Leibig soon caught sight of the ship in which he had served nearly half a century earlier. He then realized that tears had formed in his eyes. Phyllis also was

impressed by the sight of the ship and the pomp that went with the final goodbye. She was particularly moved by Captain Kaiss's comments on the contributions made by the wives of *Missouri* men during the ship's final period in commission.[41]

As usual there was a parade of speakers, including Missouri Congressman Ike Skelton, who had also been on the program in 1986. Chaplain Jim Nickols delivered the prayer. The experience was doubly hard for him because a year earlier he had gone through the same thing when he was part of the last crew of the *New Jersey.*[42]

Near the end of the ceremony, Kaiss said to Commander Jordan, "XO, haul down the colors." It was similar to the original commissioning, nearly forty-seven years earlier, when Captain Callaghan ended by saying, "Pipe down, Commander Cooper." This time the national ensign had fifty stars instead of forty-eight, and this time the occasion was much sadder. With the playing of taps, down came the flags of the state of California, the horizontal red-white-and-blue-striped Missouri state flag, and that of the United States. As the proceedings closed, the remaining crew members filed off the double brows abreast of turret two. Captain Kaiss was the last crew member to leave. As if they were sideboys, the last officers lined up in a double row at the foot of the bow so they could shake hands and say goodbye to the captain. It was over.

Afterward, Captain Kaiss was glad that the exec had persuaded him to stay to the end. It gave him a rare—probably unique—distinction as far as U.S. battleships were concerned. He was the commanding officer when the ship was commissioned and when it was decommissioned. And, of course, he was the last captain of the last battleship in the history of the U.S. Navy.[43]

Harold Seavers and his wife went to California for the decommissioning of the *Missouri,* in part because he had served in the ship in the mid-fifties, in part because the American Battleship Association was holding a reunion at the same time. A couple of days after the ceremony, Seavers and his wife ate breakfast on board the *Queen Mary,* the long out-of-service

British passenger service that became a water-front hotel in Long Beach. Afterward, they went out for a walk around the liner's deck, and when Seavers looked out into the harbor, he saw the silhouette of a battleship in the distance. A Navy tugboat had the *Missouri* in tow and was beginning the journey that would take her back to Bremerton and the resumption of a berth in the mothball fleet.[44]

After the ship reached Bremerton on April 11, the crew of the inactive-ship maintenance facility had to do a great deal to put the *Missouri* away in a condition that would facilitate reactivation if the call ever came. Altogether, the facility took about two years to complete the process of laying the *Missouri* away in storage.[45]

The overboard discharges, which seemed to be constantly dumping unwanted liquids over the side when the ship was in service, were sealed off by welding flat steel circles over the openings. Thus closed, the discharge openings could not provide an avenue for water to leak into the ship. The semi-cylindrical scuppers that had once directed the flow of water down the side of the ship were removed and stored on the battleship's mess deck for safekeeping.[46]

The inactivation crew carefully sealed up topside fixtures that provided access to below. The cylindrical vents on deck were sealed with glue and tape, the ends of the gun barrels with canvas and glue. The aim was to provide an airtight seal so that the dehumidified inside air would remain as uncontaminated as possible by air from the outside atmosphere. To determine the effectiveness of the sealing process, men from the maintenance facility conducted a vacuum test when they believed the ship was buttoned up. Here and there they heard the telltale hissing that indicated air was leaking through. Systematically they went around and used caulking wherever the leaks appeared.[47]

In addition to sealing the ship and installing the cathodic protection and dehumidification gear, the inactivation crew defueled her. Tank trucks came alongside, and pumps removed as much fuel as they could. Then the workmen went through the voids and tanks, aided by a piece of gear not available to inactivation crews in the past. This was an industrial-strength vac-

uum cleaner hooked onto four-inch flexible piping. It pulled out large quantities of rust, dirt, and just plain gunk that had collected over the years. Harry Ehlert and Ken Ahl, two of the men who maintain the inactive ships at Bremerton, could hear the progress of the trash removal as the pieces of junk were being sucked through the vacuum cleaner's hose.[48]

One day in December 1994, shortly before the official onset of winter, I went aboard the *Missouri* at Bremerton to see how her condition compared with what I had seen when she was still in active service three years earlier. Held in place by heavy, rusting anchor chains, she sat quietly alongside Mooring F, a narrow finger pier in the area of the Puget Sound Naval Shipyard devoted to the preserved ships. Ahead of her, with their wooden hulls showing the signs of years of wear, were the minesweepers *Esteem* and *Enhance*. Across the pier to port, towering over the battleship, was the carrier *Midway*, commissioned in 1945 and by now worn down from nearly a half century of active service. To starboard, at Mooring E, was an even bigger ship, the *Ranger*. Commissioned in 1957, she entered the mothball fleet in 1993, one of the first of the big-deck carriers to do so.

While moored to the pier, the *Missouri* sat far higher out of the water than when she was loaded with fuel, ammunition, food, people,

Members of the last battleship crew file off for the last time at the conclusion of the decommissioning ceremony on March 31. (Photo in DoD Still Media Records Center: DN-ST-92-07090)

The *Missouri* lies in dry dock in the summer of 1982 at Bremerton so that the inactivation crew can seal and preserve the hull. (Puget Sound Naval Shipyard)

stores, and all the other things needed to operate an active ship. Her normal operating draft was in the range of thirty-seven to thirty-eight feet. Now it was a mere twenty-three feet.

The battleship was no longer cleaned as often as during the many years when she was open for the public to stroll around on her main deck and 01 level. Vivid evidence appeared on the forecastle, which bore the unmistakable results of target practice by passing pigeons. For some reason, the pigeons seemed to have a particular affinity for dumping on the long, heavy anchor chains and turning them from black into a mustard color. A walk around topside revealed sheet-metal huts built in various places on deck. Sometimes they covered winches. On the fantail the radar antennas had been put on the helicopter deck and surrounded by a small metal hut to protect them from the elements. On the 01 deck another sheet-metal cover protected the famous round surrender plaque embedded in the wood. A

rectangular plaque looked down from a nearby bulkhead.

Some of the painting done topside was not for the purpose of physical preservation but instead a way of preserving the deeds performed by the ship and her crew members. On each side of the bridge were the rows of multicolored service ribbons earned in three wars and in peacetime periods as well. The after smokestack was adorned with a red E, emblematic of engineering excellence, and hashmarks indicating subsequent awards. A white E with hashmarks—for overall excellence in combat readiness—was on the wing of the bridge. The 16-inch turrets wore outlines of the map of Kuwait and the number of rounds they fired in support of the liberation of that small nation in 1991. The armored box launchers were decorated with drawings of Indian tomahawks, signifying the number of Tomahawk missiles fired by each launcher in Desert Storm.

A good deal of the interior of the *Missouri*

The *Missouri* is shown in her mothball fleet berth in this photo taken September 10, 1993, at Bremerton. Next to her is the aircraft carrier *Midway.* At left and right are the distinctive mast structures of the *Knox*-class frigates. (Naval Inactive Ship Maintenance Facility, Bremerton)

was left in place essentially as it was during operation. On the forward bulkhead of the wardroom, for instance, a large world map still showed the travels that the *Missouri* made during her long service. Now it was protected by a glass case and included extensions to depict Persian Gulf service. In berthing compartments, the bunks and lockers were still there, though the mattresses and blankets had gone elsewhere, as had the ubiquitous television sets that had been in so many spaces. Plumbing equipment was still in the heads.

On the second deck, the galley spaces remained outfitted for food service. I saw coffee machines, dispensers for soda and milk, and ice machines. On the starboard side, a sign over the serving windows still proclaimed this to be the "Truman Line," the place where the president and his wife drew their chow at times when they made the trip north from Brazil in September 1947. Not far away from the eating spaces were the walk-in ship's store and the "Big Mo snack shop," as the gedunk came to be known in later years. The goodies were long since gone.

There was, however, a decided difference in the large mess compartments themselves. The area in which thousands of *Missouri* men sat over the years to eat meals, play cards, watch movies, or just chat with shipmates was now bereft of mess tables. In their place were dozens of wooden crates, because the mess area had become a storage area for battleship spare parts. While the battleships were in commission, a warehouse in Long Beach held these items, many of which had been manufactured years ago and were definitely showing signs of age. Here were replacements for a portion of an electric switchboard. Another crate held a large steam whistle. Over there were giant wrenches, perhaps eight feet long and with heads two feet in diameter. They were for the nuts that hold the ship's propellers on their shafts.

In the plotting rooms for the main and secondary batteries, the old analog computers still stood at the ready. It is for equipment such as this that the dehumidification system was so important. Plywood covers protected the glass gauge covers on top of the range keeper. Tape covered the brass handles used for sounding the salvo alarm and pulling the trigger to fire the guns of the main and secondary batteries. In the combat information center the radar repeaters, dead-reckoning tracer, circular plot, and status boards were just as they have been for decades. Several decks higher up—in the superstructure—was the modern counterpart of CIC. Known as the combat engagement center, it housed computers and the electronic direction equipment for the missile battery. It was still full of equipment, including consoles, computer screens, and a water fountain that has been dry for years.

In the turrets themselves and the barbettes below, corrosion was nonexistent. A light film of oil covered the projectile decks and the interrupted screw threads that formed a gas-tight seal at the breech ends of the big guns. In the magazines, racks appeared ready to accommodate hundreds of cans of powder charges, as they did so many times in the past.

Throughout the ship were numerous examples of the kinds of artwork that seafaring men leave behind as silent reminders that they once lived and worked here. Two different bulkheads were adorned by representations of the Tasmanian Devil, a whirling dervish Warner Brothers cartoon character. (Some thought this was to depict Captain Joe Lee Frank, the perpetual-motion executive officer from 1989 to 1991.) In another place was a leftover from the ship's service in Desert Storm. A smiling Bart Simpson, America's favorite cartoon brat, held up his first two fingers—reminiscent of the old Churchillian victory sign and the Vietnam peace sign. The caption had him saying of the Iraqis, "We kicked some #*!@."

In the captain's cabin, on the 01 level in the superstructure, the state seal of Missouri adorned the bulkhead. The furniture, including a comfortable couch, was waiting for those who would sit here for a chat. Nearby was the cabinet that held the ship's silver service. In the adjoining bedroom was an empty bedframe. That was also the case three decks above in the captain's sea cabin, just aft of the bridge. Mounted on the forward bulkhead of the

In the spring of 1995, before the ultimate disposition of the *Missouri* was decided, the ship was moved back to the Bremerton pier she had occupied for many years prior to her reactivation in the 1990s. She was put on public display in the months leading up to the surrender anniversary in September. Visitors got a limited degree of access to the interior of the ship. (Courtesy Naval Submarine Base Bangor)

cramped cabin was a gyrocompass repeater. It was a help to the captain, who might be doing paperwork in the cabin during the daytime, or when he was awakened by the officer of the deck with a phone call during a night watch. The skipper could instantly look up and see what course the *Missouri* was steaming. Now the compass was frozen motionless on one heading.

Out on the bridge were other compass repeaters, and certainly no one had done anything to alter the conning tower and its massive 17-inch-thick armor. One important item was missing—the steering wheel, gone to be housed with other artifacts from the Navy's past. The ship herself is an artifact from that past. All too soon, I reluctantly walked down from the bridge to the quarterdeck to go ashore.

A month after my visit, the role of the *Missouri* as a sleeping beauty, waiting for yet another wake-up call, finally came to an end. On January 5, 1995, Vice Admiral William Earner, deputy chief of naval operations (logistics), signed a letter containing a proposal from the CNO's staff. The terse two-paragraph document discussed the four mothballed *Iowa*-class battleships and reported that the president of the Navy's Board of Inspection and Survey "has recommended the battleships be disposed of in accordance with the needs of the service due to the expenditure necessary to ensure continued, reliable service, the cost of which would be disproportionate to the ships' value." Therefore, he recommended the four ships be declared excess to the Navy's requirements and be stricken from the Naval Vessel Register.[49]

Ironically, the officer who signed the letter on behalf of the CNO had considerable personal experience with the *Iowa*-class battleships. He was the vice chief of naval operations, Admiral Stanley R. Arthur. In June 1954, as a midshipman third class, he was on board the *Missouri* when she and her three sisters steamed together for the only time in history. In 1968, when he was a lieutenant commander, he flew an A-4 Skyhawk to provide air cover for the *New Jersey* as she fired shore bombardment missions at Vietnam. As a vice admiral in 1991,

Arthur had been the naval component commander in the Persian Gulf for Operation Desert Storm.

On January 12, Secretary of the Navy John H. Dalton signed his name on the line granting approval of the CNO request from Arthur. With those pen strokes from Dalton, the ship was removed from the Navy's list of mobilization assets. Fifty years and seven months after her first commissioning on a sunny day in Brooklyn, the U.S. Navy said it no longer had any need for a battleship named *Missouri*.

But the *Missouri*, which has been largely quiet and neglected since 1992, suddenly became the object of considerable attention and action as 1995 progressed. One of the actions contemplated in the strike decision was that the half-century-old battleships could now become available as museums and memorials. The *Missouri*, not surprisingly, was considered the top prize in the group because of her history as the surrender ship. Contenders emerged, and backers in each location trumpeted their advantages.

Pearl Harbor would afford the opportunity to use the pier built next to Ford Island as a home port. The site would permit the ship to be adjacent to the *Arizona* Memorial and thus put together in one place powerful symbols of the beginning and the end of the Pacific War. But San Francisco has a proven record of attracting thousands of tourists annually, and it is far easier and less expensive to reach than Hawaii. The relative ease of visiting San Francisco appealed to a number of former crew members. Still another contingent argued for keeping the *Missouri* in the Puget Sound area principally because the ship would not need to be towed, thus saving valuable dollars. Moreover, politicians and businessmen in that area wanted to perpetuate the ship's appeal as a tourist attraction.

Meanwhile, members of Congress took a let's-not-be-hasty approach, contending that the *Iowa*-class battleships had not yet outlived their usefulness. The Navy announced plans for a new type of warship, a floating arsenal that would be equipped with 6-inch guns and hundreds of missiles in vertical-launch tubes. But that ship is still only in the conceptual

stage, years away from entering the fleet. In the meantime, argued members of Congress, the Navy should keep at least two of the four remaining battleships as insurance policies—floating mobilization assets. They had been reactivated in the past; perhaps the need for them might arise in the future.

As this book went to press, a compromise appeared possible. According to this plan, the *Iowa* and *New Jersey* would be made available as museums with no further active duty contemplated. The *Missouri* and *Wisconsin* could be in a special status—on public display as memorials but with some mothball-fleet preservation features still in place so that reactivation could be feasible, if necessary. The final decision on the fate of the four ships is due to be made in early 1996.[50]

The *Missouri* emerged from her cocoon in another way as 1995 passed. In May she was towed out from the closed-off area of the mothball fleet in which she had resided since shortly after her decommissioning in 1992. From then until early September she was once again on public display. Her berth was at the same pier she occupied for many years before she was towed to Long Beach in 1984 to be reactivated. Once again, the public could go aboard and walk the *Missouri*'s decks. Once again, the wardroom was opened up so visitors could step in and see the map mural. Large photo displays appeared in the wardroom so people could see pictorial highlights of the ship's long history.

On Saturday, September 2—the fiftieth anniversary of the surrender signing—ceremonies on board the ship coincided with the annual reunion of the USS *Missouri* Association. A number of the former crew members wore replicas of their active-duty white uniforms—the same as the uniform of the day for the ceremony in 1945. It just so happened that the starboard side—including the surrender deck—was facing the pier and the adjacent *New Jersey*. As a result, the ceremonies were moved to the port side 01 level, facing a nearby dock, so the thousands in the audience could see.

A huge American flag was suspended from and hung down the port side of the bridge. It served as a backdrop for the keynote address by General Richard Hearney, assistant commandant of the Marine Corps. He talked of the importance of passing down to future generations the legacies bequeathed by those who served in World War II. With little imagination, he said, one could hear echoes from the sounds of fifty years earlier: shouts of crewmen, Japanese planes, and the firing of the *Missouri*'s big guns. Then he added, "But no echo—none rings as loudly as the quiet scratch of a fountain pen on paper, or General MacArthur's pronouncement that, 'These proceedings are closed.'"[51]

Indeed, the *Missouri* and her myriad crewmen over the years of her service have created a lasting impression. Tens of thousands of men lived and worked on board for varying periods of time. Each carries the memories of his association with a ship that has become part of the national heritage of the United States. For many the memories are sentimental ones about youth, camaraderie, and work toward a common purpose. One former *Missouri* man, a Desert Storm veteran, spoke for many as he sat in the battleship's mess deck shortly before she left active duty for the final time—so far—in 1992. Gunner's Mate Leon Tucker lamented, "It's hard to say goodbye to yesterday."[52]

Appendix A

Chronology, 1944–1955, 1984–1992

This chronology is based on USS *Missouri* deck logs for 1944–45, stored at the National Archives in Washington, D.C.; deck logs for 1946–55, stored at the Washington National Records Center in Suitland, Maryland; and deck logs for 1986–92 and annual command histories for 1984–92, both stored in the Ships Histories Branch, Naval Historical Center, Washington, D.C. The movements of various flag officers embarked in the *Missouri* are not necessarily complete because of the differing standards used for recording such movements at various times in the ship's career.

1944

June 11–July 12 Moored at the New York Navy Yard, Brooklyn, New York. On June 11, the commandant of the navy yard, Rear Admiral Monroe Kelly, USN, placed the *Missouri* into commission; Captain William M. Callaghan, USN, assumed command.

July 12–13 Anchored near the Statue of Liberty in New York harbor.

July 13–24 Drydocked at New York Navy Yard Annex, Bayonne, New Jersey.

July 24–31 Anchored in Gravesend Bay, New York harbor, while taking on ammunition.

July 31–August 3 Alternately under way off New York for structural test firing of guns and anchored in Gravesend Bay.

August 3–4 En route to Norfolk in company with the destroyers *Broome* and *Simpson*.

August 4–5 Moored in deperming pen, Lamberts Point, Norfolk, Virginia.

August 5–17 Alternately under way for various exercises in the Chesapeake Bay and anchored in the Chesapeake Bay.

August 17–18 Anchored in Hampton Roads.

August 18–21 Moored at the Norfolk Naval Station.

August 21–25 En route to Trinidad as part of Task Unit 23.16.1, which also included the large cruiser *Alaska* and destroyers.

August 25–September 17 Alternately under way as part of Task Unit 23.16.1 for training exercises in the Gulf of Paria and anchored at Port of Spain, Trinidad.

September 17–19 En route to Culebra Island as part of Task Unit 23.16.1.

September 19 Shore bombardment practice at Culebra.

September 19–22 En route to Hampton Roads as part of Task Unit 23.16.1.

September 22–26 Anchored in Hampton Roads, except for an underway period on September 24 for a battle problem to test training effectiveness.

September 26–27 En route to New York with the destroyer *Decatur*.

September 27–28 Anchored near the Statue of Liberty.

September 28–November 5 Moored at Bayonne.

November 5–10 Anchored in Gravesend Bay, except for a period under way on November 6 for post-repair trials.

November 10–17 En route to Panama in Task Group 27.7, which also included the battleships *Texas* and *Arkansas*, the escort carriers *Shamrock Bay* and *Wake Island*, and destroyers.

November 17   Anchored at Cristobal, Panama Canal Zone.

November 17–18   Transited the Panama Canal, including overnight anchorage in Gatun Lake.

November 18–19   Moored at Balboa, Panama Canal Zone.

November 19–28   En route to San Francisco in Task Unit 12.7.1, which included the same ships that accompanied the *Missouri* to Panama.

November 28–December 15   Moored at Hunters Point Naval Dry Docks, San Francisco.

December 15–18   Anchored off Oakland Bridge, San Francisco Bay.

December 18–24   En route to Pearl Harbor in Task Unit 12.7.1, which also included the destroyers *Bailey* and *Terry*.

December 24–27   Moored at berth F-2, Ford Island, Pearl Harbor.

December 27–30   Under way in the Hawaiian operating area for exercises with the destroyers *Bailey* and *Bancroft*.

December 30–31   Moored at berth F-2, Pearl Harbor.

Here, the *Missouri* is anchored in Gravesend Bay, New York, while loading ammunition on July 30, 1944. (U.S. Navy photo in the National Archives: 80-G-237646)

1945

January 1–2   Moored at berth F-2, Pearl Harbor.

January 2–13   En route to Ulithi, Caroline Islands, in Task Unit 12.5.9, which also included the heavy cruiser *Tuscaloosa* and destroyers.

January 13–24   Anchored in the Ulithi atoll.

January 24–26   Under way for exercises in Task Unit 30.1.10, which also included the *Tuscaloosa*, ammunition ship *Mount Baker*, and destroyers.

January 26–February 10   Anchored in the Ulithi atoll.

February 10–March 3   Under way as part of Task Group 58.2, which also included the carriers *Lexington*, *Hancock*, and *San Jacinto*; the battleship *Wisconsin*; the cruisers *Boston* and *San Francisco*; and destroyers. On February 16–17, the task group joined on air strikes against Tokyo; on February 19, supported the invasion of Iwo Jima; on February 25, joined on air strikes against the Tokyo area; and on

March 1, joined on air strikes against Okinawa.

March 3–5   Under way for gunnery and maneuvering exercises as part of Task Force 59, commanded by Vice Admiral Willis A. Lee, Jr. This task force comprised the fleet's other fast battleships, as well as a number of destroyers.

March 5–14   Anchored in the Ulithi atoll.

March 14–16   Under way in Task Group 59.7, which also included the *New Jersey* and *Wisconsin,* for tactical exercises.

March 16–24   Under way in Task Group 58.4, which also included the carriers *Yorktown, Intrepid, Langley, Independence,* and *Enterprise;* the battleship *Wisconsin;* the cruisers *Alaska, Guam, St. Louis, Flint,* and *San Diego;* and destroyers. On March 18–19, the task group joined on air strikes against Kyushu.

March 24   Joined Task Unit 59.7.1, which also included the *New Jersey, Wisconsin,* and destroyers, for shore bombardment of Okinawa.

March 24–25   Under way in Task Group 58.1, formed around the carriers *Hornet, Bennington, Wasp,* and *Belleau Wood.*

March 25–26   Under way in Task Unit 59.1.1, which also included the *New Jersey* and *Wisconsin.*

March 26–May 5   Under way in Task Group 58.4 to provide air support for the Okinawa campaign, including the invasion itself on April 1. As of May 1, the task group carriers were the *Yorktown, Shangri-La, Langley,* and *Independence.*

May 5–6   Under way in Task Group 58.3, formed around the carriers *Essex, Bunker Hill,* and *Cabot.*

May 6–9   En route to Ulithi in Task Unit 50.18.77, which also included the destroyer *Stockton* and the destroyer escort *Howard F. Clark.*

May 9–17   Anchored in the Ulithi atoll. On May 14, Stuart S. Murray, USN, relieved Captain William M. Callaghan, USN, as commanding officer of the *Missouri.*

May 17–18   En route to Guam in Task Group 50.2, which also included the destroyers *McNair* and *Wedderburn.*

May 18–21   Moored in Apra harbor, Guam. On May 18, Admiral William F. Halsey, Jr., USN, commander Third Fleet, embarked with his staff in the *Missouri.*

May 21–26   En route to Okinawa in Task Group 30.1, which also included the destroyers *Wedderburn* and *McNair.* Briefly, on May 24–25, the *Missouri* was part of Task Group 50.8, which included the cruiser *Detroit* and destroyers.

May 26–27   Anchored off Okinawa.

May 27–28   Under way in Task Group 30.1, which also included the destroyers *Wedderburn* and *McNair.* Bombarded Okinawa on May 27.

May 28–June 13   Under way in Task Group 38.4, which also included the carriers *Yorktown, Shangri-La, Ticonderoga,* and *Independence;* the battleships *Iowa* and *Wisconsin;* the cruisers *Alaska, Guam, San Diego,* and *Flint;* and destroyers. During this period the task group supported the Okinawa operation and also joined in air strikes against Kyushu on June 2, 3, and 8.

June 13   En route to the Philippines in Task Unit 38.4.2, which included several battleships and cruisers.

June 13–July 1   Anchored in San Pedro harbor, Leyte, Philippines.

July 1–3   Under way as part of Task Unit 34.8.2, which also included the battleships *Iowa* and *Wisconsin* and destroyers.

July 3–August 23   Under way as part of Task Group 38.4, which also included the aircraft carriers *Yorktown, Shangri-La, Bonhomme Richard, Independence,* and *Cowpens;* the battleships *Iowa* and *Wisconsin;* the cruisers *Quincy, Chicago, Flint,* and *San Diego;* and destroyers. The *Missouri* joined Task Unit 34.8.2 on July 15 for a bombardment of Hokkaido and on July 17–18 for a bombardment of Honshu. On August 20, the *Missouri* transferred a bluejacket landing force to the battleship *Iowa* while at sea.

August 23–27   Under way as part of Task Group 30.1, which also included the battleship *Iowa* and the destroyers *Nicholas*, *O'Bannon*, and *Taylor*.

August 27–29   Anchored in Sagami Wan, Honshu, Japan.

August 29–September 6   Anchored in Tokyo Bay. On September 2, the *Missouri* flew the flags of Fleet Admiral Chester W. Nimitz, USN, and General of the Army Douglas MacArthur, USA, during the ceremony in which Japan officially surrendered. The flag of Admiral William F. Halsey, USN, was temporarily in the *Iowa*. On September 5, Admiral Halsey transferred the Third Fleet flag and staff to the battleship *South Dakota*.

September 6–9   En route to Guam with the destroyer *Kimberly*.

September 9–12   Anchored at Apra harbor, Guam.

September 12–20   En route to Hawaii with the *Kimberly*.

September 20–29   Moored at Ten-Ten Dock, Pearl Harbor Navy Yard.

September 29–October 12   En route to Panama with the *Kimberly*.

October 12–13   Moored at Panama Navy Yard, Panama City.

October 13   Transited the Panama Canal.

October 13–18   En route to Norfolk with the *Kimberly*.

October 18–22   Moored at the Norfolk Naval Station.

October 22–23   En route to New York.

October 23–November 14   Moored at pier ninety, New York City, except for the period October 25–28, when the ship was moored to a buoy in the Hudson River. President Harry S Truman was on board October 27 for Navy Day and conducted a fleet review. Admiral Jonas Ingram, USN, commander in chief, Atlantic Fleet, embarked in the *Missouri* October 24–28. Vice Admiral Frederick C. Sherman, USN, commander, Carrier Task Force One, embarked briefly in late October. On November 6, Captain Roscoe H. Hillenkoetter, USN, relieved Captain Stuart

S. Murray, USN, as commanding officer of the *Missouri*.

November 14–16   Moored at Bayonne.

November 16–19   Anchored in Gravesend Bay.

November 19–December 8   Moored at New York Naval Shipyard.

December 8–31   Drydocked at New York Naval Shipyard. Vice Admiral Frederick C. Sherman, USN, commander, Carrier Task Force One, embarked in the *Missouri* December 8–16.

1946

January 1–7   Drydocked at the New York Naval Shipyard.

January 7–10   Moored at the New York Naval Shipyard.

January 10–15   Moored at the New York Naval Shipyard Annex, Bayonne, New Jersey.

January 15–20   Moored at Gravesend Bay while taking on ammunition.

January 20–21   En route to the Hampton Roads area.

January 21–22   Anchored in Lynnhaven Roads.

January 22–25   Moored at the Norfolk Naval Station.

January 25–28   En route to Cuba.

January 28–31   Anchored at Guantánamo Bay, Cuba.

January 31–February 15   Alternately under way for various exercises and anchored at Guantánamo Bay, Cuba; other ships in company at various times were the cruiser *Fargo* and destroyers.

February 15–25   Anchored at Guantánamo Bay, Cuba.

February 25–March 2   Made round trip to the vicinity of Culebra Island for shore bombardment drills.

March 2–4   Anchored at Guantánamo Bay, Cuba.

March 4–7   En route to Norfolk.

March 7–11   Moored at the Norfolk Naval Station.

March 11–12   En route to Bayonne.

March 12–15 Drydocked at Bayonne.

March 15–22 Moored at Bayonne.

March 22–31 En route to Gibraltar.

March 31–April 1 Anchored in Gibraltar Bay; Admiral H. Kent Hewitt, commander, U.S. Naval Forces Europe/commander, 12th Fleet, embarked in the *Missouri* April 1–24.

April 1–5 En route to Istanbul in company with the cruiser *Providence* and destroyer *Power.*

April 5–9 Anchored at Istanbul, Turkey.

April 9–11 En route to Piraeus in company with the *Power* and Turkish destroyer *Sultan Hisar.*

April 10–14 Anchored at Piraeus, Greece.

April 14–15 En route to Naples in company with the *Power.*

April 15–22 Anchored at Naples, Italy.

April 22–23 En route to Algiers in company with the *Power.*

April 23–26 Moored at Algiers, Algeria.

April 26–27 En route to Tangier in company with the *Power.*

April 27–30 Anchored at Tangier, Spanish Morocco.

April 30 En route to Gibraltar.

April 30–May 1 Anchored at Gibraltar.

May 1–9 En route to Norfolk.

May 9–11 Moored at the Norfolk Naval Station.

May 11–14 En route to Culebra.

May 14–18 Participated in training exercises in the Culebra area as part of Task Group 80.3; other ships in company at various times included the carriers *Franklin D. Roosevelt* and *Princeton;* the cruisers *Macon* and *Dayton;* and various destroyers.

May 18–20 Anchored off Culebra.

May 20–27 Participated in training exercises while en route to New York as part of Task Group 80.2.

May 27–June 7 Moored in Hudson River, New York City. On May 31, Captain Tom B. Hill relieved Captain Roscoe H. Hillenkoetter as commanding officer of the *Missouri.*

June 7–8 En route to Cape May, New Jersey.

June 8–10 Anchored off Cape May.

June 10 En route to Assateague, Island, Virginia.

June 10–12 Alternately under way for various exercises and anchored off Assateague Island; at times the gunnery training ship *Wyoming* was in company.

June 12–14 En route to Portland, Maine.

At anchor in the Hudson River, October 26, 1945. The fog-shrouded Empire State Building looms over the guns of turret three. (Photo by Ted Stone)

June 14–24 Moored off Portland.

June 24–27 Alternately under way for various exercises and anchored off Portland.

June 27–July 8 Anchored off Portland.

July 8–9 Alternately under way for various exercises and anchored off Portland.

July 9–15 Anchored off Portland.

July 15–25 Alternately under way for various exercises and anchored off Portland.

July 25–August 2 Moored off Portland.

August 2 En route to Gloucester, Massachusetts.

August 2–12 Anchored off Gloucester.

August 12–13 Under way for drills in Casco Bay, Maine.

August 13–21 Anchored off Portland, Maine. Vice Admiral William M. Fechteler, commander, Battleships–Cruisers, Atlantic Fleet, was embarked in the *Missouri*, August 14–21.

August 21–22 Under way for drills in Casco Bay, Maine.

August 22–24 Anchored off Portland, Maine.

August 24–25 En route to Bar Harbor, Maine.

August 25–30 Anchored at Bar Harbor.

August 30–31 En route to Boston.

August 31–September 9 Moored at Boston. Rear Admiral Maurice E. Curts, commander, South Atlantic Force, was embarked in the *Missouri* approximately September 1–6.

September 9–11 En route to Hampton Roads.

September 11–16 Anchored in Hampton Roads.

September 16–26 Alternately under way for various exercises and anchored off Winter Quarter Shoal, Chesapeake Lightship, Hampton Roads, and Smith Island Shoal.

Sidecleaners have partly completed the task of repainting the hull as the ship lies moored in the Hudson River on May 29, 1946. (Photo by Ted Stone)

September 26–October 5 Anchored in Hampton Roads.

October 5–14 Moored at the Norfolk Naval Station.

October 14–17 Alternately under way for various exercises and anchored off Chesapeake Lightship; in company with the battleship *Wisconsin* part of the time.

October 17–21 Anchored in Hampton Roads.

October 21–24 Alternately under way for various exercises and anchored off Winter Quarter Shoal, Chesapeake Lightship, and the Virginia Capes.

October 24–25 En route to New York.

October 25–29 Moored to pier ninety, New York City, for Navy Day celebration on October 27.

October 29–30 En route to Virginia Capes.

October 30–November 7 Alternately under way for various exercises and anchored or moored off Winter Quarter Shoal, Hampton Roads, and Virginia Capes. Fleet tug *Kiowa* towed target raft for gunnery practice.

November 7–21 Moored at Norfolk Naval Station.

November 21–27 En route to Davis Strait as part of Task Group 20.2, which also included the cruiser *Little Rock* and the destroyer *Fechteler*.

November 27–December 4 Participated in cold-weather exercises in Davis Strait, between Greenland and East Baffin Island, as part of Task Group 20.2.

December 4–7 En route to Argentia, Newfoundland, as part of Task Group 20.2.

December 7–9 Anchored in Placentia harbor, Argentia.

December 9–13 En route to Norfolk; Task

Group 20.2 dissolved December 10, and the *Missouri* and *Fechteler* steamed together to Norfolk.

December 13–31 Moored at the Norfolk Naval Station.

1947

January 1–11 Moored at the Norfolk Naval Station.

January 11–15 En route to Culebra Island.

January 15–17 Alternately anchored off Culebra and under way in the vicinity of the island for shore bombardment drills. En route to Puerto Rico.

January 17–20 Anchored at Ponce, Puerto Rico.

January 20–24 En route to Norfolk.

January 24–February 3 Moored at the Norfolk Naval Station. On January 27, Vice Admiral William H. P. Blandy, commander, Second Task Fleet, and his staff embarked in the *Missouri*.

February 3–26 Under way for fleet maneuvers in the Atlantic as part of Task Force 28. At various times, as war games pitted different ships against each other, the *Missouri* was in Task Group 28.1, 28.2, 28.3, and 28.4. Other ships participating in the maneuvers included the aircraft carriers *Franklin D. Roosevelt, Leyte,* and *Randolph;* the cruisers *Houston, Dayton, Providence, Huntington,* and *Juneau;* and screening destroyers. On February 4, Admiral Blandy was promoted to admiral as he assumed command of the U.S. Atlantic Fleet.

February 26–28 En route to Trinidad.

February 28–March 7 Anchored at Port of Spain, Trinidad, British West Indies. On March 3, Vice Admiral Arthur W. Radford came aboard and relieved Admiral William H. P. Blandy, CinCLantFlt, of his additional duty as commander, Second Task Fleet. The Second Task Fleet staff remained in the *Missouri*.

March 7–14 Alternately under way for training exercises as part of Task Group 28.4, including the *Franklin D. Roosevelt,* *Randolph, Leyte, Houston,* and destroyers, and anchored off Culebra. Included in the training was shore bombardment at Culebra.

March 14–18 En route to Norfolk as part of Task Group 28.4.

March 18–April 2 Moored at the Norfolk Naval Station.

April 2 En route to Hampton Roads.

April 2–7 Anchored in Hampton Roads. On April 2, Captain Robert L. Dennison relieved Captain Tom B. Hill as commanding officer of the *Missouri*.

April 7–11 Alternately under way for various exercises and anchored off the Virginia Capes and at the entrance to the Chesapeake Bay.

April 11–14 Moored at the Norfolk Naval Station. On April 14, Vice Admiral Arthur Radford, commander, Second Task Fleet, shifted his flag to the aircraft carrier *Midway*.

April 14–16 Alternately under way for various exercises and anchored off the Virginia Capes and in Hampton Roads.

April 16–17 En route to New York.

April 17–22 Moored at pier ninety, Hudson River, New York City.

April 22–23 En route to the Virginia Capes operating area.

April 23–25 Alternately under way for various exercises and anchored off the Virginia Capes and at the entrance to the Chesapeake Bay.

April 25–May 19 Moored at the Norfolk Naval Station.

May 19–22 Alternately under way for various exercises and anchored off the Virginia Capes.

May 22–26 Moored in Hampton Roads.

May 26–27 Alternately under way for various exercises and anchored off the Virginia Capes.

May 27–29 En route to Boston.

May 29–June 3 Moored at the South Annex, Boston Naval Shipyard.

June 3–6 En route to Norfolk.

June 6–July 1 Moored at the Norfolk Naval Station.

July 1 En route to Portsmouth, Virginia.

July 1–19 Moored at the Norfolk Naval Shipyard.

July 19 En route to Norfolk.

July 19–August 6 Moored at the Norfolk Naval Station.

August 6–9 En route to Cuba as part of Task Force 84, which also included the destroyers *Dyess* and *Small*.

August 9–20 Alternately under way for various exercises and anchored in Guantánamo Bay, Cuba.

August 20–22 En route to Trinidad as part of Task Force 84.

August 22–23 Anchored at Port of Spain, Trinidad, British West Indies.

August 23–30 En route to Brazil as part of Task Force 84. The *Missouri* crossed the equator on August 26.

August 30–September 8 Anchored at Rio de Janeiro, Brazil. On September 2, President Harry Truman of the United States, President Eurica Gaspar Dutra of Brazil, and various other dignitaries came aboard for a reception and luncheon. On September 7, President Truman, his family, and his official party embarked for transportation to the United States.

September 8–19 En route to Norfolk as part of Task Force 84. On September 11, the *Missouri* held a crossing-the-equator initiation.

September 19–22 Moored at the Norfolk Naval Station. On September 19, President Truman, his family, and his official party left the ship.

September 22–23 En route to New York.

September 23–25 Moored in Gravesend Bay, New York harbor, while off-loading ammunition.

September 25 En route to Bayonne, New Jersey.

September 25–29 Moored at the New York Naval Shipyard Annex, Bayonne, while off-loading ammunition.

September 29 En route to Brooklyn.

September 29–October 18 Moored at the New York Naval Shipyard.

October 18–December 31 Drydocked at the New York Naval Shipyard.

1948

January 1–7 Drydocked at the New York Naval Shipyard.

January 7–February 28 Moored at New York Naval Shipyard. On January 23, Commander John B. Colwell relieved Captain Robert L. Dennison as commanding officer of the *Missouri*. On February 24, Captain James H. Thach, Jr., relieved Commander Dennison as commanding officer.

February 28–29 Alternately under way in New York harbor and anchored in Gravesend Bay.

February 29–March 5 Moored at the New York Naval Shipyard Annex, Bayonne, New Jersey.

March 5 En route to Gravesend Bay.

March 5–10 Anchored in Gravesend Bay while taking on ammunition.

March 10–11 En route to Norfolk, including a period at anchor off Cape Henry on March 11.

March 11–22 Moored at the Norfolk Naval Station.

March 22–31 Alternately under way for various exercises and anchored in Hampton Roads and off Cape Henry.

March 31–April 5 Moored at the Norfolk Naval Station.

The crew mans the rail as the *Missouri* delivers President Truman to Norfolk at the end of his journey from South America in September 1947. (Norfolk Public Library)

April 5–8   En route to Cuba.

April 8–13   Anchored in Guantánamo Bay, Cuba.

April 13–30   Alternately under way for various fleet training group exercises and anchored in Guantánamo Bay, Cuba.

April 30–May 2   En route to Culebra Island.

May 2–4   Alternately under way for various exercises and anchored off Culebra.

May 4–6   En route to Cuba.

May 6–7   Alternately under way for various exercises, including final battle problem of training period, and anchored in Guantánamo Bay, Cuba.

May 7–10   En route to Norfolk.

May 10–June 1   Moored at the Norfolk Naval Station. On May 15, Rear Admiral Heber H. McLean, commander, Cruiser Division Two/commander, Task Force 84, embarked in the *Missouri* with his staff for the upcoming midshipman training cruise.

June 1–2   En route to Annapolis, Maryland, including a period anchored in Hampton Roads.

June 2–5   Anchored off Annapolis, to embark Naval Academy midshipmen for their summer training cruise.

June 5   En route to Hampton Roads.

June 5–7   Anchored in Hampton Roads.

June 7–21   En route to Portugal as part of Task Force 84, which also included the aircraft carrier *Coral Sea*, the cruiser *Macon*, and destroyers.

June 21–26   Anchored at Lisbon, Portugal. Admiral Richard L. Conolly, commander in chief, U.S. Naval Forces Eastern Atlantic and Mediterranean, embarked in the *Missouri*, June 21–26.

June 26–July 5   En route to France as part of Task Force 84, which now included the cruiser *Columbus*, Admiral Conolly's flagship, in addition to those that had crossed the Atlantic together.

July 5–10   Anchored at Villefranche, France. The *Missouri* flew Admiral Conolly's flag July 6–10.

July 10–26   En route to Cuba as part of Task Force 84, which also included the aircraft carrier *Coral Sea*, the cruiser *Macon*, and destroyers.

July 26–August 14   Alternately under way for various training exercises and anchored in Guantánamo Bay, Cuba.

August 14–16   En route to Culebra; fired shore bombardment at Culebra.

August 16–17   Anchored off Culebra.

August 17–21   En route to Lynnhaven Roads as part of Task Force 84.

August 21–23   Alternately under way and anchored in Lynnhaven Roads and Patuxent River, Maryland.

August 23   En route to Annapolis, Maryland.

August 23–24   Anchored off Annapolis to off-load Naval Academy midshipmen after their summer training cruise. Task Force 84 was dissolved on August 24.

August 24–25   En route to Norfolk, includ-

The *Missouri* and the carrier *Coral Sea* steam in formation during the midshipman cruise in the summer of 1948. (U.S. Navy photo in the National Archives: 80-G-396612)

ing a period at anchor in Hampton Roads.

August 25–30 Moored at the Norfolk Naval Station.

August 30–September 2 Under way east of the Virginia Capes while avoiding a hurricane.

September 2–19 Moored at the Norfolk Naval Station.

September 19–22 En route to Cuba.

September 22–23 Anchored in Guantánamo Bay, Cuba.

September 23–25 En route to Panama.

September 25–27 Moored at Cristobal, Panama Canal Zone.

September 27–October 2 En route to Norfolk.

October 2–11 Moored at the Norfolk Naval Station.

October 11–14 Alternately under way for various exercises and anchored in the Chesapeake Bay and Virginia Capes operating areas.

October 14–25 Moored at the Norfolk Naval Station.

October 25–26 En route to New York.

October 26–28 Moored to pier ninety, New York City, for Navy Day celebration on October 27.

October 28–29 En route to Norfolk.

October 29–November 2 Moored at the Norfolk Naval Station. On October 30, Vice Admiral Donald B. Duncan, commander, Second Task Fleet, embarked with his staff in the *Missouri.*

November 2–8 En route to Newfoundland while participating in war games as part of Task Force 28, which also included the aircraft carriers *Kearsarge, Leyte,* and *Philippine Sea;* the cruisers *Juneau* and *Fargo;* and several destroyers.

November 8–9 Lying to off Argentia, Newfoundland, while simulating shore bombardment.

November 9–11 En route to Davis Strait as part of Task Force 28.

November 11–15 Participated in cold-weather exercises in Davis Strait, between Greenland and East Baffin Island, as part of Task Force 28.

November 15–23 En route to Norfolk, including a period at anchor off the entrance to the Chesapeake Bay.

November 23–December 31 Moored at the Norfolk Naval Station. On December 4, President Harry Truman, Missouri Governor Phil Donnelly, and Secretary of the Navy John Sullivan visited the ship in connection with the presentation of the ship's silver service by the state. On December 21, Admiral Duncan, commander, Second Task Fleet, shifted his flag to the aircraft carrier *Midway.*

1949

January 1–10 Moored at the Norfolk Naval Station.

January 10–15 En route to Cuba as part of Task Group 88.1, which also included the aircraft carrier *Kearsarge,* cruisers *Huntington* and *Juneau,* and destroyers.

January 15–18 Anchored in Guantánamo Bay, Cuba.

January 18–21 En route to Norfolk in company with the cruiser *Juneau* and several destroyer minelayers.

January 21–February 1 Moored at the Norfolk Naval Station.

February 1–4 Alternately under way for various ship-handling exercises and anchored in the Virginia Capes operating area.

February 4–7 Moored at the Norfolk Naval Station. On February 5, Captain Harold P. Smith relieved Captain James H. Thach, Jr., as commanding officer of the *Missouri.*

February 7–9 Alternately under way for various exercises and anchored in the Virginia Capes operating area.

February 9 En route to Norfolk.

February 9–21 Moored at the Norfolk Naval Station. On February 20, Admiral William H. P. Blandy, commander in chief, Atlantic Fleet, embarked with his staff in the *Missouri.*

February 21–27 Under way for war games with Task Group 28.1, including the carriers *Franklin D. Roosevelt, Kearsarge,* and *Leyte;* the cruiser *Juneau;* and destroyers. On February 27, the *Missouri* anchored briefly off Culebra Island to transfer Admiral Blandy and his staff to the amphibious group command ship *Pocono.*

February 27–28   Under way for exercises with Task Group 102.7, comprised of amphibious warfare ships. On February 28, the *Missouri* fired shore bombardment at the island of Vieques.

February 28–March 2   Anchored off Vieques. Rear Admiral Felix Johnson, commander, Destroyer Force Atlantic Fleet, embarked in the *Missouri* during this three-day period.

March 2–5   Alternately lying to off Vieques and under way for shore bombardment exercises, firing at Vieques.

March 5–7   En route to Trinidad as part of Task Group 28.1, comprised as before.

March 7–11   Anchored at Trinidad, British West Indies.

March 11–15   En route to Cuba as part of Task Group 28.1, comprised as before.

March 15–17   Anchored in Guantánamo Bay, Cuba.

March 17–21   En route to Hampton Roads as part of Task Group 28.1, comprised as before.

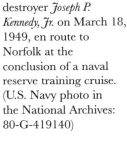

The *Missouri* refuels the destroyer *Joseph P. Kennedy, Jr.* on March 18, 1949, en route to Norfolk at the conclusion of a naval reserve training cruise. (U.S. Navy photo in the National Archives: 80-G-419140)

March 21–23   Alternately under way for various exercises in the Virginia Capes operating area and anchored in Hampton Roads.

March 23–April 4   Moored at the Norfolk Naval Station.

April 4–8   Under way during a naval reserve training cruise, beginning with exercises in the Virginia Capes operating area. The *Missouri* was part of Task Group 88.1, including the carriers *Kearsarge* and *Midway,* the cruiser *Juneau,* and a division of destroyer minesweepers.

April 8–9   En route to New York as part of Task Group 88.1.

April 9–11   Moored to pier ninety, New York City.

April 11–13   Under way for exercises with Task Group 88.1, including time in Narragansett Bay off Rhode Island.

April 13–16   En route to Norfolk, part of the time as a member of Task Group 88.1.

April 16–25   Moored at the Norfolk Naval Station.

April 25–30   En route to Panama for a naval reserve training cruise in company with the cruiser *Rochester.*

April 30–May 2   Moored at Cristobal, Panama Canal Zone.

May 2–7   En route to Hampton Roads in company with the *Rochester.*

May 7–9   Anchored in Hampton Roads. Disembarked naval reservists on May 7.

May 9   En route to Portsmouth, Virginia.

May 9–26   Moored at the Norfolk Naval Shipyard.

May 26   En route to Norfolk.

May 26–31   Moored at the Norfolk Naval Station. On May 27, Rear Admiral Allan E. Smith, commander, Cruiser Force Atlantic Fleet, embarked with his staff in the *Missouri.*

May 31   En route to Annapolis, Maryland.

May 31–June 4   Anchored off Annapolis to embark Naval Academy midshipmen.

June 4   En route to Hampton Roads.

June 4–5   Anchored in Hampton Roads.

June 5 En route to Norfolk.

June 5–6 Moored at the Norfolk Naval Station.

June 6–17 En route to England as part of Task Force 61, which also included the ships of Destroyer Division 81 and Mine Division Two.

June 17–25 Moored at Portsmouth, England, after brief period at anchor off Spithead on June 17.

June 25–July 8 En route to Cuba in Task Force 61, comprised as before.

July 8–11 Anchored in Guantánamo Bay, Cuba.

July 11–15 Under way with Task Force 61 for exercises in the Guantánamo operating area.

July 15–18 Anchored in Guantánamo Bay.

July 18 Under way with Task Force 61 for exercises in the Guantánamo operating area.

July 18–19 Anchored in Guantánamo Bay.

July 19–25 En route to Hampton Roads in Task Force 61. The *Missouri* anchored briefly off Cape Romain on July 23.

July 25 Anchored in Hampton Roads and en route to Norfolk.

July 25–August 3 Moored at the Norfolk Naval Station. On July 26, the *Missouri* disembarked the midshipmen from the first training cruise and on August 2 took aboard those for the second.

August 3–15 En route to France as part of Task Force 61, which also included the ships of Destroyer Division 81 and Mine Division Two.

August 15–22 Anchored at Cherbourg, France.

August 22–September 3 En route to Cuba in Task Force 61.

September 3–6 Anchored in Guantánamo Bay, Cuba.

September 6–15 Alternately under way with Task Force 61 for exercises in the Guantánamo operating area and anchored in Guantánamo Bay.

September 15–20 En route to Norfolk in Task Force 61.

September 20–22 Moored at the Norfolk Naval Station.

September 22 En route to Annapolis, Maryland.

September 22–23 Anchored off Annapolis to disembark Naval Academy midshipmen.

September 23 En route to Norfolk.

September 23–October 4 Moored at the Norfolk Naval Station. Off-loaded ammunition.

October 4 En route to Portsmouth, Virginia.

October 4–November 5 Moored at the Norfolk Naval Shipyard.

November 5–December 2 Drydocked at the Norfolk Naval Shipyard.

December 2–22 Moored at the Norfolk Naval Shipyard. On December 5, Captain William D. Brown relieved Captain Harold P. Smith as commanding officer of the *Missouri*.

December 22–23 Alternately under way for post-repair trials in the Virginia Capes operating area and anchored off Virginia Beach.

December 23–31 Moored at the Norfolk Naval Shipyard.

1950

January 1–10 Moored at the Norfolk Naval Shipyard.

January 10 En route to Norfolk.

January 10–17 Moored at the Norfolk Naval Station. On January 14, the *Missouri* hauled down the flag of Rear Admiral Allan E. Smith, ComCruLant.

January 17 At the beginning of a planned voyage to Guantánamo Bay, Cuba, the *Missouri* ran aground near Old Point Comfort, just outside of Thimble Shoal Channel.

January 17–February 1 Aground off Old Point Comfort. Admiral Smith and his CruLant staff were embarked during this period.

February 1 En route to Portsmouth, Virginia.

February 1–7 Drydocked at the Norfolk Naval Shipyard. On February 4, Captain William D. Brown, USN, was detached; Commander George E. Peckham, USN, assumed duty as acting commanding officer.

February 7–8 Moored at the Norfolk Naval Shipyard. On February 7, Captain Harold P. Smith, USN, reported aboard and assumed command.

February 8 Under way for a post-repair trial run.

February 8–9 Anchored in Hampton Roads.

February 9 En route to Norfolk.

February 9–15 Moored at the Norfolk Naval Station. Took on ammunition.

February 15–18 En route to Cuba.

February 18–20 Anchored in Guantánamo Bay, Cuba.

February 20–25 Alternately under way for exercises in the Guantánamo operating area and anchored in Guantánamo Bay.

February 25–26 En route to Culebra Island.

February 26–March 1 Under way off Culebra while conducting shore bombardment exercises.

March 1–6 Under way with Task Group 104.3, including the carrier *Saipan;* the cruisers *Salem, Des Moines,* and *Worcester;* the amphibious group flagship *Eldorado;* and destroyers, during war games in the Caribbean. The *Missouri* fired shore bombardment at Vieques Island as part of the exercises.

March 6–12 Alternately under way with Task Group 104.3 during war games and anchored off Vieques.

March 12–22 Under way as part of Task Group 21.1, including the carriers *Philippine Sea* and *Wright;* the cruisers *Salem, Des Moines,* and *Worcester;* and destroyers, during war games. On March 12, Vice Admiral Donald B. Duncan, USN, commander, Second Fleet, embarked in the *Missouri.*

March 22–23 En route to Norfolk after being detached from Task Group 21.1.

March 23–April 17 Moored at the Norfolk Naval Station. On April 1, Vice Admiral Robert B. Carney, USN, relieved Vice Admiral Donald B. Duncan, USN, as commander, Second Fleet. On April 10, the Second Fleet flag and staff transferred to the carrier *Franklin D. Roosevelt.*

April 17–19 Alternately under way and anchored in the Virginia Capes during familiarization for the prospective commanding officer.

April 19–24 Moored at the Norfolk Naval Station. On April 19, Captain Irving T. Duke, USN, relieved Captain Harold P. Smith, USN, as commanding officer of the *Missouri.* On April 23, the ship took aboard naval reservists for a two-week training cruise.

April 24–28 Under way for training exercises in the Virginia Capes operating area as part of Task Group 22.1, which also included the destroyers *Gearing, Greene,* and *Bailey.*

April 28–29 En route to New York as part of Task Group 22.1.

April 29–May 1 Moored to pier ninety, New York City.

May 1–2 En route to Virginia Capes.

May 2–6 Alternately under way for training exercises in the Virginia Capes operating area as part of Task Group 22.1 and anchored in Virginia Capes.

May 6–9 Moored at the Norfolk Naval Station. On May 9, Rear Admiral Fred D. Kirtland, USN, commander, Training Command Atlantic Fleet, embarked with his staff in the *Missouri.*

May 9–11 Alternately under way for an operational readiness inspection in the Virginia Capes operating area and anchored in Hampton Roads.

May 11–16 Moored at the Norfolk Naval Station.

May 16–18 Under way for training exercises in the Virginia Capes operating area.

May 18–19 En route to Gravesend Bay, New York harbor.

May 19–22 Moored at Gravesend Bay in connection with Armed Forces day.

May 22–23 En route to Virginia Capes.

May 23–24 Anchored at Virginia Capes.

May 24 En route to Norfolk.

May 24–31 Moored at the Norfolk Naval Station.

May 31 En route to Annapolis, Maryland.

May 31–June 4 Anchored off Annapolis to embark Naval Academy and NROTC midshipmen. On May 31, Admiral Kirtland was designated commander, Task Force 86, for the upcoming midshipman training cruise.

June 4 En route to Hampton Roads.

June 4–5 Anchored in Hampton Roads.

June 5–10 En route to Boston in Task Force 86, including six destroyers.

June 10–12 Moored at the South Annex, Boston Naval Shipyard. On June 11, Admiral Carney, commander, Second Fleet, embarked in the *Missouri*. Admiral Kirtland remained on board as commander, Task Force 86.

June 12–17 En route to New York.

June 17–22 Moored to pier eighty-eight, New York City. On June 17, Admiral Carney transferred his flag off the *Missouri* with Admiral Kirtland remaining on board.

June 22–28 En route to Panama as part of Task Force 86.

June 28–July 1 Moored Cristobal, Panama Canal Zone.

July 1–3 En route to Cuba as part of Task Force 86.

July 3–5 Anchored in Guantánamo Bay, Cuba.

July 5–10 Alternately under way for exercises in the Guantánamo operating area and anchored in Guantánamo Bay.

July 10–14 En route to Norfolk as part of Task Force 86.

July 14–24 Moored at the Norfolk Naval Station. Disembarked midshipmen on July 14. On July 19, Rear Admiral John H. Carson, USN, relieved Rear Admiral Fred D. Kirtland, USN, as commander, Task Force 86. Naval Academy midshipmen and Military Academy cadets embarked on July 22; NROTC midshipmen embarked on July 23.

July 24–29 En route to Canada as part of Task Force 86, including Destroyer Division 101 and Destroyer Division 181.

July 29–August 2 Moored at Halifax, Nova Scotia.

August 2–9 En route to New York, via Narragansett Bay operating area, as part of Task Force 86.

August 9–14 Moored to pier eighty-eight, New York City.

August 14–15 En route to Norfolk independently.

August 15–19 Moored at the Norfolk Naval Station. The midshipmen disembarked August 16. On August 19, Admiral Carson and his staff disembarked. The *Missouri* took on ammunition during this in-port period.

August 19–23 En route to Panama.

August 23 Transited the Panama Canal.

August 23–24 Moored at Balboa, Panama Canal Zone.

August 24–31 En route to Hawaii.

August 31–September 4 Moored at Pearl Harbor.

September 4–14 En route to Japan, including shore bombardment exercises at Kahoolawe, Hawaii, on September 4.

September 14 Lay to off Sasebo, Japan, while Rear Admiral Allan E. Smith, USN, commander, Task Force 95, embarked with his staff. En route to Korea.

September 14–17 Under way off the east coast of Korea, including blockade and shore bombardment of Pohang. Operated with Task Force 95, including the cruiser *Helena* and destroyers.

September 17–18 En route to Japan in company with the destroyer *Maddox*.

September 18 Moored at Sasebo, Japan.

September 18–19 En route to Korea.

September 19–October 4 Anchored at Inchon, Korea; fired shore bombardment missions. On September 21, General of the Army Douglas MacArthur, USA, made an official visit to the ship. On October 1, Rear Admiral John M. Higgins, USN, commander, Task Group 90.6, and commander, Cruiser Division Five, embarked in the *Missouri* with his staff.

October 4–5 En route to Japan in company with the destroyer *Rowan*.

October 5–11 Moored at Sasebo, Japan. On October 7, Admiral Higgins and his staff shifted to the cruiser *Rochester* moored alongside. The same day Vice Admiral Arthur D. Struble, USN, commander, Seventh Fleet, and his staff shifted from the *Rochester* to the *Missouri*.

October 11 En route to Korea.

October 11–17 Under way in the operating area off the east coast of Korea, including shore bombardment of Wonsan and Chongjin and operations with Task Force 77 and Task Force 95. Task Force 77 included the carrier *Valley Forge;* Task Force 95 included the cruisers *Helena* and *Worcester*.

October 17–November 1 Anchored off Wonsan, Korea.

November 1–2 En route to Japan.

November 2–5 Moored at Sasebo, Japan.

November 5–6 En route to Korea.

November 6–20 Under way in the operating area off the east coast of Korea with Task Force 77, including the carriers *Valley Forge* and *Philippine Sea* and the cruiser *Juneau*.

November 20–22 Alternately anchored off Wonsan, Korea, and under way to the eastward.

November 22–25 Anchored off Wonsan, Korea.

November 26–December 23 Under way in the operating area off the east coast of Korea with Task Force 77, including the carriers *Valley Forge, Philippine Sea, Leyte,* and *Princeton* and the cruiser *Juneau*.

December 23–24 Anchored off Hungnam, Korea, while providing shore bombardment.

December 24–25 Under way in the operating area off the east coast of Korea with Task Force 77.

December 25–26 En route to Japan with Task Group 70.9, including the *Philippine Sea* and *Juneau*.

December 26–31 Moored at Sasebo, Japan.

Turret two fires at Chongjin, North Korea, on October 12, 1950. (U.S. Navy photo in the National Archives: 80-G-421279)

1951

January 1–7 Moored at Sasebo, Japan.

January 7–8 En route to Korea.

January 8–22 Under way in the operating area off the east and south coasts of Korea during operations with Task Force 77, including the carriers *Valley Forge, Philippine Sea,* and *Leyte;* the cruisers *Manchester, Juneau,* and *St. Paul;* and destroyers.

January 22–23 En route to Pusan.

January 23 Anchored at Pusan, Korea. On January 23, Admiral Arthur W. Radford, USN, commander in chief, Pacific Fleet, embarked in the *Missouri.*

January 23–25 Round trip to the operating area off the east coast of Korea.

January 25–27 Moored at Sasebo, Japan. Admiral Radford disembarked on January 25.

January 27–28 En route to Korea.

January 28–February 1 Under way in the operating area off the east coast of Korea, including shore bombardment off Kosong and operations with Task Force 77.

February 1–2 En route to Pusan.

February 2–3 Anchored at Pusan, Korea. On February 3, the crew of the *Missouri* manned the rail in honor of President Syngman Rhee of the Republic of Korea and other dignitaries.

February 3–4 En route to Japan in company with destroyers.

February 4 Moored at Sasebo, Japan.

February 4–5 En route to Korea.

February 5–7 Alternately anchored off Kangnung, Korea, and under way for bombardment of Kangnung.

February 7–9 En route to Inchon with destroyers.

February 9–14 Anchored at Inchon, Korea.

February 14–15 En route to east coast operating area with destroyers.

February 15–25 Under way in the operating area off the east coast of Korea, including shore bombardment off Tanchon and Songjin and operations with Task Force 77.

Midshipmen wave goodbye from the bow as they prepare to get under way June 3, 1951, on a summer training cruise. (Courtesy Jack Blumenfield)

February 25–26 Anchored at Pusan, Korea.

February 26–March 1 En route to Japan.

March 1–11 Moored at Yokosuka, Japan. On March 2, Captain George C. Wright, USN, relieved Captain Irving T. Duke, USN, as commanding officer of the *Missouri.*

March 11–13 En route to Korea.

March 13–21 Under way in the operating area off the east coast of Korea, including shore bombardment of Wonsan, Chaho, and Chongjin and operations with Task Force 77.

March 21–24 En route to Japan in company with destroyers, including a brief period on March 22 lying to off Pusan for helicopter operations.

March 24–29 Moored at Yokosuka, Japan. On March 28, Vice Admiral Harold M. Martin, USN, relieved Vice Admiral Arthur D. Struble, USN, as commander, Seventh Fleet. Admiral Struble relieved Admiral Martin as commander, First Fleet. Admiral Struble remained on board the *Missouri* for the upcoming voyage to the West Coast.

March 29–April 5 En route to Hawaii.

April 5–7 Moored at Pearl Harbor.

April 7–12 En route to Long Beach.

April 12–14 Moored at the Long Beach

Naval Shipyard. On April 14, Admiral Struble disembarked from the *Missouri*.

April 14–21　En route to Panama.

April 21–23　Moored at Balboa, Panama Canal Zone.

April 23　Transited the Panama Canal.

April 23–27　En route to Norfolk.

April 27–30　Moored at the Norfolk Naval Station.

April 30　En route to Portsmouth, Virginia.

April 30–May 15　Moored at the Norfolk Naval Shipyard.

May 15　En route to Hampton Roads.

May 15–18　Anchored in Hampton Roads.

May 18　En route to Norfolk.

May 18–31　Moored at the Norfolk Naval Station. On May 19, Rear Admiral James L. Holloway, Jr., USN, commander, Cruiser Force Atlantic Fleet, shifted his flag from the *Albany* to the *Missouri*.

May 31　En route to Annapolis, Maryland.

May 31–June 3　Anchored at Annapolis to embark Naval Academy and NROTC midshipmen.

June 3　En route to Norfolk.

June 3–4　Moored at the Norfolk Naval Station.

June 4–19　En route to Norway as part of Task Group 86.1, including the battleship *Wisconsin*, the cruiser *Albany*, and destroyers.

June 19–23　Anchored at Oslo, Norway. On June 20, the crew manned the rail when Crown Prince Olav of Norway came aboard for an official visit.

June 23–25　En route to France.

June 25–30　Anchored at Cherbourg, France.

June 30–July 16　En route to Cuba as part of Task Group 86.1, comprised as before.

July 16–17　Anchored in Guantánamo Bay, Cuba.

July 17–20　Under way for exercises in the Guantánamo operating area.

July 20–24　Anchored in Guantánamo Bay, Cuba.

July 24–27　En route to Hampton Roads as part of Task Group 86.1, comprised as before.

July 27　Anchored in Hampton Roads to disembark midshipmen.

July 27　En route to Norfolk.

July 27–August 3　Moored at the Norfolk Naval Station to embark NROTC midshipmen.

August 3–8　Under way for exercises in the Virginia Capes operating areas.

August 8–9　En route to New York.

August 9–13　Moored to pier ninety, New York City.

August 13–18　En route to Panama in Task Force 86, including Destroyer Division 42.

August 18–21　Moored at Cristobal, Panama Canal Zone.

August 21–22　En route to Cuba.

August 21–24　Alternately under way for various exercises and anchored at Guantánamo Bay, Cuba.

August 24–27　Anchored in Guantánamo Bay, Cuba.

August 27–September 3　En route to Virginia Capes and then exercises there upon arrival.

September 3–4　Anchored in Hampton Roads to disembark midshipmen.

September 4　En route to Norfolk.

September 4–October 1　Moored at the Norfolk Naval Station.

October 1　En route to Hampton Roads.

October 1–8　Anchored in Hampton Roads.

October 8　En route to Portsmouth, Virginia.

October 8–27　Moored at the Norfolk Naval Shipyard. On October 18, Captain John Sylvester relieved Captain George C. Wright, USN, as commanding officer of the *Missouri*. Captain Wright became chief of staff to Admiral Holloway, embarked in the ship.

October 27–December 8　Drydocked at the Norfolk Naval Shipyard.

December 8–31　Moored at the Norfolk Naval Shipyard.

1952

January 1–11　Moored at the Norfolk Naval Shipyard. On January 2, Rear Admiral James L. Holloway, Jr., who had been embarked in the *Missouri*, returned from leave and broke his flag in the cruiser *Albany*.

January 11–12   Under way for exercises in the Virginia Capes operating area.

January 12–23   Moored at the Norfolk Naval Shipyard.

January 23–24   Under way for exercises in the Virginia Capes operating area.

January 24–29   Anchored in Hampton Roads.

January 29   En route to Norfolk.

January 29–31   Moored at the Norfolk Naval Station.

January 31–February 3   En route to Cuba.

February 3–5   Anchored at Guantánamo Bay, Cuba.

February 5–7   Alternately under way for various exercises and anchored at Guantánamo Bay.

February 7–11   Anchored at Guantánamo Bay.

February 11–14   Alternately under way for various exercises and anchored at Guantánamo Bay.

February 14–19   Anchored at Guantánamo Bay.

February 19–21   Alternately under way for various exercises and anchored at Guantánamo Bay.

February 21–25   Anchored at Guantánamo Bay.

February 25–March 1   Alternately under way for various exercises and anchored at Guantánamo Bay.

March 1–3   Anchored at Guantánamo Bay.

March 3–7   Alternately under way for various exercises and anchored at Guantánamo Bay. On March 4, Rear Admiral H. R. Thurber, commander, Battleship Division Two, and his staff transferred to the *Missouri*.

March 7–8   En route to Haiti.

March 8–9   Anchored at Port au Prince, Haiti.

March 9–10   En route to Cuba.

March 10–12   Alternately under way for various exercises and anchored at Guantánamo Bay, Cuba.

March 12–14   Made trip to the vicinity of Culebra Island for shore bombardment drills.

March 14–18   En route to Norfolk, including a period on March 17–18 anchored in Hampton Roads.

March 18–20   Moored at the Norfolk Naval Station.

March 20   En route to Hampton Roads.

March 20–27   Anchored in Hampton Roads.

March 27   En route to Norfolk.

March 27–April 7   Moored at the Norfolk Naval Station. Embarked naval reservists on April 6 for a two-week training cruise.

April 7–10   Under way for exercises in the Virginia Capes operating area.

April 10–14   Anchored in Hampton Roads.

April 14–17   Under way for exercises in the Virginia Capes operating area, plus a trip

Awnings cover the ship's main and 01 decks as she lies at anchor in Annapolis Roads on June 5, 1952. (Courtesy Jack Blumenfield)

to the vicinity of Cape May, New Jersey, to join in the search for a downed aircraft.

April 17–22   Anchored in Hampton Roads.

April 22   En route to Norfolk.

April 22–28   Moored at the Norfolk Naval Station.

April 28–May 1   Under way for exercises in the Virginia Capes operating area.

May 1–5   Anchored in Hampton Roads.

May 5–8   Under way for exercises in the Virginia Capes operating area. On May 6, Admiral Thurber's flag was hauled down, and Captain John Sylvester, commanding officer of the *Missouri*, became acting commander, Battleship Division Two.

May 8–15   Anchored in Hampton Roads.

May 15–16   En route to New York.

May 16–19   Moored to pier ninety, New York City, for Armed Forces Day on May 17.

May 19–20   En route to Norfolk.

May 20–23   Moored at the Norfolk Naval Station. On May 22, the *Missouri* hauled down the broad pennant of Captain Sylvester and embarked Rear Admiral James L. Holloway, Jr., commander, Cruiser Force Atlantic Fleet, and his staff.

May 23   En route to Hampton Roads.

May 23–26   Anchored in Hampton Roads.

May 26   En route to Norfolk.

May 26–June 3   Moored at the Norfolk Naval Station.

June 3   En route to Annapolis, Maryland.

June 3–7   Anchored off Annapolis. Embarked Naval Academy midshipmen on June 7.

June 7   En route to Norfolk.

June 7–9   Moored at the Norfolk Naval Station. Embarked NROTC midshipmen on June 8.

June 9–23   En route to Norway as part of Task Group 86.1, including the battleship *Wisconsin*, the cruisers *Macon* and *Des Moines*, the carrier *Saipan*, and destroyers.

June 23–28   Anchored at Bergen, Norway.

June 28–July 9   En route to England with elements of Task Group 86.1, including the *Wisconsin, Macon, Des Moines*, and destroyers.

July 9–16   Moored at Portland, England.

July 16–29   En route to Cuba with elements of Task Group 86.1, including the *Wisconsin, Macon, Des Moines, Saipan*, and destroyers.

July 29–August 1   Alternately under way with the *Wisconsin* for various exercises and anchored at Guantánamo Bay, Cuba.

August 1–4   En route to Norfolk with elements of Task Group 86.1, including the *Wisconsin, Macon, Des Moines, Saipan*, and destroyers.

August 4–12   Moored at the Norfolk Naval Station. Disembarked both Naval Academy and NROTC midshipmen August 5.

August 1   En route to Portsmouth, Virginia.

August 12–25   Moored at the Norfolk Naval Shipyard.

August 25–29   Drydocked at the Norfolk Naval Shipyard.

August 29–September 5   Moored at the Norfolk Naval Shipyard. On September 4, Captain Warner R. Edsall, USN, relieved Captain John Sylvester as commanding officer of the *Missouri*.

September 5   En route to Hampton Roads.

September 5–8   Anchored in Hampton Roads.

September 8   En route to Norfolk.

September 8–11   Moored at the Norfolk Naval Station. On September 9, Admiral Holloway shifted his flag and staff to the cruiser *Albany*, moored alongside the *Missouri*.

September 11–16   En route to Panama.

September 16   Transited the Panama Canal.

September 16–17   Moored at Balboa, Panama Canal Zone.

September 17–24   En route to Long Beach. During part of the voyage, the carrier *Shangri-La* was in company with the *Missouri*.

September 24–26   Moored at the Long Beach Naval Shipyard.

September 26–October 1   En route to Hawaii.

October 1–2   Moored at Pearl Harbor.

October 2–4   Under way for exercises in

the Hawaiian operating era, including shore bombardment practice.

October 4–6 Moored at Pearl Harbor.

October 6–17 En route to Japan in company with the destroyer *Hickox*.

October 17–21 Moored at Yokosuka, Japan. On October 18–19, the battleship *Iowa* was moored alongside to facilitate the transfer of the Seventh Fleet staff. On October 19, Vice Admiral Joseph J. Clark, commander, Seventh Fleet, transferred his flag to the *Missouri*.

October 21–25 En route to Korea in company with the *Hickox*.

October 25–November 8 Under way in the operating area off the east coast of Korea, including shore bombardment off Wonsan and Tanchon and operations with Task Force 77.

November 8–9 En route to Japan in company with the destroyer *Rogers*.

November 9–11 Moored at Sasebo, Japan.

November 11–12 En route to Korea in company with the destroyer *Rogers*.

November 12–19 Under way in the operating area off the east coast of Korea, including shore bombardment off Wonsan and Chongjin and operations with Task Force 77.

November 19–20 En route to Pusan.

November 20–23 Anchored at Pusan, Korea. On November 20, the crew of the *Missouri* manned the rail in honor of President Syngman Rhee of the Republic of Korea.

November 23–24 En route to Japan.

November 24–December 6 Moored at Sasebo, Japan.

December 6–7 En route to Korea in company with the destroyer *Eversole*.

December 7–11 Under way in the operating area off the east coast of Korea, including shore bombardment off Wonsan and Songjin.

December 11–12 En route to Japan in company with the *Eversole*.

December 12–15 Moored at Sasebo, Japan.

December 15–16 En route to Korea in company with the *Eversole*.

December 16–22 Under way in the operating area off the east coast of Korea, including shore bombardment off Hungnam and operations with Task Force 77.

December 22–23 En route to Japan.

December 23–27 Moored at Sasebo, Japan.

December 27–28 En route to Korea in company with the destroyer *Tingey*.

December 28–31 Under way in the operating area off the east coast of Korea, including shore bombardment and operations with Task Force 77.

1953

January 1–3 Under way in the operating area off the east coast of Korea, including shore bombardment and operations with Task Force 77.

January 3–5 En route to Inchon in company with the destroyer *Tingey*.

January 5 Anchored at Inchon, Korea.

January 5–6 Under way for shore bombardment of the Chodo-Sokto area.

January 6–8 En route to Japan in company with the *Tingey*.

January 8–11 Moored at Sasebo, Japan.

January 11–13 En route to Yokosuka.

January 13–20 Moored at Yokosuka.

January 20–22 En route to Sasebo.

January 22–24 Moored at Sasebo.

January 24–25 En route to Korea in company with the destroyer *Uhlmann*.

January 25–February 2 Under way in the operating area off the east coast of Korea, including shore bombardment off Wonsan and Tanchon and operations with Task Force 77.

February 2 En route to Japan in company with the *Uhlmann*.

February 2–4 Moored at Sasebo.

February 4 En route to Korea in company with the destroyer *Hopewell*.

February 4–8 Under way in the operating area off the east coast of Korea, including shore bombardment off Wonsan and north of Suwon Dam.

Men on the forecastle spray the newly housed anchor to wash off the Chesapeake Bay mud that covers it. The ship is just leaving Annapolis to begin a midshipman training cruise in June 1953. Notice the "cat whiskers" radio antennas that have sprouted from the 011 level. (Audry Bodine photo courtesy of the Mariners Museum, Newport News, Virginia)

February 8 En route to Japan in company with the *Hopewell*.

February 8–10 Moored at Sasebo.

February 10–12 En route to Yokosuka.

February 12–19 Moored at Yokosuka.

February 19–21 En route to Sasebo.

February 21 Moored at Sasebo.

February 21–22 En route to Korea with the destroyer *Cowell*.

February 22–26 Under way in the operating area off the east coast of Korea, in-

cluding shore bombardment off Wonsan, Tanchon, Yongdae Gap, and Mayangdo; operations with Task Force 77, including the carriers *Kearsarge* and *Philippine Sea;* the cruiser *Los Angeles;* and destroyers.

February 26–27 En route to Japan.

February 27–March 1 Moored at Sasebo.

March 1–2 En route to Korea in company with the destroyer *Prichett*.

March 2–11 Under way in the operating area off the east coast of Korea, including shore bombardment off Wonsan and Tanchon and operations with Task Force 77. Task Force 77 included the carriers *Philippine Sea, Valley Forge,* and *Oriskany;* the cruiser *Rochester;* and destroyers.

March 11–12 En route to Japan.

March 12–14 Moored at Sasebo.

March 14 En route to Korea in company with the destroyer *Samuel N. Moore.*

March 14–25 Under way in the operating area off the east coast of Korea, including shore bombardment off Wonsan, Hungnam, and Kojo; operations with Task Force 77.

March 25–26 En route to Japan. On February 26, Captain Warner R. Edsall, USN, died while on the bridge of the *Missouri;* the ship's executive officer, Commander James R. North, USN, succeeded to command.

March 26 Moored at Sasebo.

March 27–28 En route to Yokosuka.

March 28–April 7 Moored at Yokosuka, Japan. On April 4, Captain Robert Brodie, Jr., USN, relieved Commander James R. North, USN, as commanding officer of the *Missouri.* On April 5–7, the battleship *New Jersey* was moored alongside to facilitate the transfer of the Seventh Fleet staff. On April 6, Vice Admiral Joseph J. Clark, commander, Seventh Fleet, transferred his flag to the *New Jersey.*

April 7–13 En route to Pearl Harbor.

April 13–15 Moored at Pearl Harbor Naval Base.

April 15–20 En route to Long Beach.

April 20–22 Moored at the Long Beach Naval Base.

April 22–28 En route to Panama.

April 28–30 Moored at Balboa, Panama Canal Zone.

April 30 Transited the Panama Canal.

April 30–May 4 En route to Norfolk.

May 4–15 Moored at the Norfolk Naval Station. On May 14, Rear Admiral E. Tyler Wooldridge, USN, commander, Battleship Cruiser Force Atlantic Fleet, embarked in the *Missouri* to command

the upcoming midshipman training cruise.

May 15 En route to Portsmouth, including a brief period anchored in Hampton Roads.

May 15–20 Drydocked at the Norfolk Naval Shipyard.

May 20 En route to Hampton Roads.

May 20–22 Anchored in Hampton Roads.

May 22 En route to Norfolk.

May 22–June 2 Moored at the Norfolk Naval Station.

June 2 En route to Annapolis, Maryland.

June 2–6 Anchored at Annapolis to embark Naval Academy midshipmen.

June 6 En route to Norfolk.

June 6–8 Moored at the Norfolk Naval Station to embark NROTC midshipmen.

June 8–27 En route to Brazil as part of Task Group 40.1, including the battleship *Wisconsin;* the cruisers *Macon* and *Albany;* the carrier *Saipan;* the oilers *Aucilla, Niobrara,* and *Chipola;* and destroyers. Crossed the equator June 19.

June 27–July 5 Anchored at Rio de Janeiro, Brazil.

July 5–23 En route to Panama as part of Task Group 40.1, including the *Wisconsin, Macon, Albany, Saipan, Aucilla, Aldebaran,* and destroyers.

July 23–25 Moored at Colón, Panama Canal Zone.

July 25–28 En route to Cuba as part of Task Unit 40.18.3, including the *Albany, Sabine, Aucilla,* and destroyers.

July 28–29 Anchored at Guantánamo Bay, Cuba.

July 29–August 1 Alternately under way for various exercises and anchored at Guantánamo Bay.

August 1–4 En route to Norfolk with ships of Task Group 40.1.

August 4–13 Moored at the Norfolk Naval Station; disembarked midshipmen.

August 13–15 Under way for exercises in the Virginia Capes operating area.

August 15–17 Anchored in Hampton Roads.

August 17 En route to Norfolk.

August 17–28 Moored at the Norfolk

Naval Station. On August 28, Rear Admiral E. Tyler Wooldridge, USN, shifted his flag to the cruiser *Albany.*

August 28 En route to Hampton Roads.

August 28–September 2 Anchored in Hampton Roads.

September 2 En route to Portsmouth, Virginia.

September 2–14 Moored at the Norfolk Naval Shipyard. On September 10, Rear Admiral Clark L. Green, USN, commander, Battleship Division Two, shifted his flag to the *Missouri.*

September 14–17 Under way for exercises in the Virginia Capes operating area.

September 17–October 10 Moored at the Norfolk Naval Station.

October 10–13 En route to Cuba.

October 13–14 Anchored at Guantánamo Bay, Cuba.

October 14–24 Alternately under way for various exercises and anchored at Guantánamo Bay.

October 24–27 En route to Norfolk.

October 27–30 Moored at the Norfolk Naval Station.

October 30 En route to Hampton Roads.

October 30–November 2 Anchored in Hampton Roads.

November 2–10 Under way for exercises in the Virginia Capes operating area as part of Task Group 44.2, including the carrier *Tarawa* and destroyers.

November 10–12 Anchored in Hampton Roads.

November 12 En route to Norfolk.

November 12–16 Moored at the Norfolk Naval Station. On November 16, Rear Admiral Clark L. Green, USN, shifted his flag to the *New Jersey.*

November 16 En route to Hampton Roads.

November 16–20 Anchored in Hampton Roads.

November 20 En route to Portsmouth, Virginia.

November 20–December 17 Moored at the Norfolk Naval Shipyard.

December 17–31 Drydocked at the Norfolk Naval Shipyard.

1954

January 1–28 Drydocked at the Norfolk Naval Shipyard.

January 28–March 16 Moored at the Norfolk Naval Shipyard.

March 16–17 Under way for exercises, including full-power run, in the Virginia Capes operating area.

March 17–24 Moored at the Norfolk Naval Shipyard.

March 24 En route to Hampton Roads.

March 24–29 Anchored in Hampton Roads to load ammunition.

March 29 En route to Norfolk.

March 29–April 2 Moored at the Norfolk Naval Station. On April 1, Captain Robert T. S. Keith, USN, relieved Captain Robert Brodie, Jr., USN, as commanding officer of the *Missouri.*

April 2–5 En route to Cuba, including brief period anchored in Hampton Roads.

April 5–6 Anchored at Guantánamo Bay, Cuba.

A helicopter flies by in the foreground as the *Missouri* steams under the Golden Gate Bridge on her arrival at San Francisco on September 10, 1954. (U.S. Navy photo in the National Archives: 80-G-649796)

April 6–7   Under way for various exercises in Guantánamo operating area.

April 7–13   Anchored at Guantánamo Bay.

April 13–23   Alternately under way for various exercises and anchored at Guantánamo Bay.

April 23–24   En route to Haiti.

April 24–25   Anchored at Port au Prince, Haiti.

April 25–26   En route to Cuba in company with the carrier *Coral Sea.*

April 26–27   Anchored at Guantánamo Bay, Cuba.

April 27–May 1   Alternately under way for various exercises and anchored at Guantánamo Bay.

May 1–3   Anchored at Guantánamo Bay. During this three-day period, Rear Admiral George R. Cooper, USN, commander, Battleship Division Two, was embarked in the *Missouri.*

May 3–5   Alternately under way for various exercises and anchored at Guantánamo Bay.

May 5–7   En route to Culebra Island.

May 7   Shore bombardment exercise off Culebra.

May 7–9   En route to Cuba.

May 9–14   Alternately under way for various exercises and anchored at Guantánamo Bay.

May 14–17   En route to Norfolk.

May 17–June 1   Moored at the Norfolk Naval Station. On May 17, Rear Admiral Ruthven E. Libby, USN, commander, Battleship Cruiser Force Atlantic Fleet, shifted his flag from the *Albany* to the *Missouri* to command the upcoming midshipman training cruise.

June 1   En route to Annapolis, Maryland.

June 1–5   Anchored at Annapolis to embark midshipmen.

June 5   En route to Norfolk.

June 5–7   Moored at the Norfolk Naval Station.

June 7–19   En route to Portugal as part of Task Group 40.1, including the battleship *New Jersey;* the cruisers *Macon* and *Des Moines;* the carrier *Siboney;* the oilers

Allagash and *Nantahala;* and destroyers. On June 7, in the Virginia Capes operating area, all four ships of Battleship Division Two—*Iowa, New Jersey, Missouri,* and *Wisconsin*—conducted tactical exercises together.

June 19–24   Anchored at Lisbon, Portugal.

June 24–July 3   En route to France as part of Task Group 40.1, including the *New Jersey, Macon,* and *Siboney;* the oiler *Caloosahatchee;* and destroyers.

July 3–10   Moored at Cherbourg, France.

July 10–27   En route to Cuba as part of Task Group 40.1, including the *New Jersey, Macon, Des Moines, Siboney, Nantahala, Caloosahatchee, Denebola,* and destroyers.

July 27–31   Alternately under way for various exercises and anchored at Guantánamo Bay.

July 31–August 3   En route to Norfolk as part of Task Group 40.1, including the *New Jersey, Macon, Des Moines, Siboney,* and destroyers.

August 3–23   Moored at the Norfolk Naval Station.

August 23–28   En route to Panama.

August 28   Transited the Panama Canal.

August 28–30   Moored at Balboa, Panama Canal Zone.

August 30–September 7   En route to Long Beach.

September 7–9   Moored at the Long Beach municipal pier.

September 9–10   En route to San Francisco.

September 10–13   Moored at the San Francisco Naval Shipyard.

September 13–15   En route to Seattle.

September 15–16   Moored at pier ninety-one, Seattle.

September 16   En route to Bangor, Washington.

September 16–17   Moored at Bangor to off-load ammunition.

September 17   En route to Bremerton, Washington.

September 17–18   Anchored at Bremerton.

September 18–22   Moored at the Puget

Sound Naval Shipyard. On September 18, Captain James R. North, USN, relieved Captain Robert T. S. Keith, USN, as commanding officer of the *Missouri*.

September 22–December 31 Drydocked at the Puget Sound Naval Shipyard.

1955

January 1–10 Drydocked at the Puget Sound Naval Shipyard.

January 10–February 26 Moored at the Puget Sound Naval Shipyard. On February 26, the *Missouri* was decommissioned and entered the Pacific Reserve Fleet.

1984

May 14–25 En route to Long Beach under tow.

May 25–August 11 Moored at the Long Beach Naval Shipyard.

August 11–December 31 Drydocked at the Long Beach Naval Shipyard.

1985

January 1–March 22 Drydocked at the Long Beach Naval Shipyard.

March 22–December 31 Moored at the Long Beach Naval Shipyard. On September 12, the *Missouri* was placed "in service active," and the crew moved aboard to occupy messing and berthing spaces.

Navy tugboats herald the arrival of the *Missouri* at San Francisco on May 6, 1986. (Photo by Steve Grzezdzinski in DoD Still Media Records Center: DN-SC-86-06957)

1986

January 1–28   Moored at the Long Beach Naval Shipyard.

January 28–30   Under way off southern California for machinery sea trials.

January 30–March 3   Moored at the Long Beach Naval Shipyard.

March 3–10   Under way off southern California for builder's trials and gun shoot.

March 10–May 5   Moored at the Long Beach Naval Shipyard. On April 30, the *Missouri*'s status was changed to "in service special."

May 5–6   En route to San Francisco.

May 6–12   Moored at San Francisco. On May 10, Secretary of Defense Caspar Weinberger placed the *Missouri* into commission. Captain Albert Lee Kaiss, USN, assumed command.

May 12–13   En route to Long Beach.

May 13–June 27   Moored at the Long Beach Naval Shipyard. On June 20, Captain James A. Carney, USN, relieved Captain Albert Lee Kaiss, USN, as commanding officer of the *Missouri*.

June 27–28   En route to San Francisco.

June 28–July 5   Moored at San Francisco.

July 5–7   En route to Seal Beach, California.

July 7–11   Anchored off of the Naval Weapons Station, Seal Beach, while taking on ammunition.

July 11–14   Moored at the Long Beach Naval Station.

July 14–25   Under way off southern California for performance evaluation.

July 25–28   Moored at the Long Beach Naval Station.

July 28–31   Under way off San Clemente Island for naval gunfire support qualification.

July 31–August 4   Moored at the Long Beach Naval Station.

August 4–15   Alternately under way off southern California for refresher training and anchored off San Diego and Coronado.

August 15–September 10   Moored at the Long Beach Naval Station.

September 10–16   En route to Pearl Harbor.

September 16–19   Moored at the Pearl Harbor Naval Station.

September 19–October 1   En route to Australia.

October 1–6   Moored at Sydney.

October 6–8   En route to Hobart, Tasmania, Australia.

October 8–11   Moored at Hobart.

October 11–15   En route to Albany, Australia.

October 15   Anchored at Albany.

October 15–16   En route to Fremantle (Perth), Australia.

October 16–19   Anchored at Fremantle.

October 19–27   En route to Diego Garcia Island.

October 27–28   Moored at Diego Garcia.

October 28–November 6   En route to Suez, Egypt.

November 6–7   Anchored in Suez Bay, northern Red Sea.

November 7   Transited the Suez Canal into the Mediterranean Sea.

November 7–11   En route to Turkey.

November 11–14   Anchored at Istanbul.

November 14–17   En route to Italy.

November 17–19   Moored at Naples.

November 19–21   En route to Spain.

November 21–23   Moored at Palma, Mallorca.

November 23–25   En route to Portugal.

November 25–28   Anchored at Lisbon.

November 28–December 8   En route to Panama.

December 8–9   Moored at Cristobal.

December 9   Transited the Panama Canal.

December 9–11   Moored at Balboa, Panama.

December 11–19   En route to Long Beach.

December 19–31   Moored at the Long Beach Naval Station.

1987

January 1–5   Moored at the Long Beach Naval Station.

January 5–8   Anchored off of the Naval

Weapons Station, Seal Beach, California, while off-loading ammunition.

January 8–9 Moored at the Long Beach Naval Station.

January 9–May 23 Moored at the Long Beach Naval Shipyard during post-shakedown availability.

May 23–25 Under way in the southern California operating area for post-shipyard sea trials.

May 25–29 Anchored off of the Naval Weapons Station, Seal Beach, California, while taking on ammunition.

May 29–June 1 Moored at the Long Beach Naval Station.

June 1–5 Under way off San Clemente Island for naval gunfire support qualification.

June 5–22 Moored at the Long Beach Naval Station.

June 22–23 Under way for exercises in the southern California operating area.

June 23–July 1 Moored at the Long Beach Naval Shipyard.

July 1–2 En route to San Francisco.

July 2–7 Moored at San Francisco.

July 7 En route to Monterey, California.

July 7–10 Anchored in Monterey Bay.

July 10–17 Under way, along with the cruisers *Long Beach* and *Bunker Hill* and destroyers, in the southern California operating area while participating in READIEX 87-5.

July 17 Anchored off of the Naval Weapons Station, Seal Beach, California, while taking on ammunition.

July 17–25 Moored at the Long Beach Naval Station.

July 25–August 16 En route to the Philippine Islands as part of Task Group 30.7, which also included the cruisers *Long Beach* and *Bunker Hill*, the replenishment oiler *Kansas City*, and destroyers. During the transit, the *Missouri* participated in training exercises in the vicinity of Hawaii and Guam.

August 16–21 Moored at the Subic Bay Naval Station.

August 21–September 2 En route to the North Arabian Sea as part of Task Group 70.10, which also included the cruisers *Long Beach* and *Bunker Hill*, the replenishment oiler *Kansas City*, and destroyers. The *Missouri* joined exercises in the vicin-

Beyond the local sailing fleet, the *Missouri* is anchored at Monterey, California, in early July 1987. (Photo by Rich Pedroncelli)

The *Missouri* prepares to ease in between the carriers *Ranger* and *Constellation* while mooring at the North Island Naval Air Station at Coronado, California, on August 24, 1988. (Photo in DoD Still Media Records Center: DN-SC-94-00545)

ity of Singapore and then transited the Strait of Malacca on August 25–26.

September 2–October 5 Under way with the aircraft carrier *Ranger*'s battle group (Task Group 70.5, later Task Group 800.1) in the North Arabian Sea/Gulf of Oman. The battle group was supporting Operation Earnest Will, the allied convoy escort of tankers. Secretary of the Navy James H. Webb visited the *Missouri* on September 11–12.

October 5–6 Anchored off of Masirah, Oman.

October 6–November 24 Under way in the North Arabian Sea in support of Operation Earnest Will with the *Ranger* battle group (Task Group 800.1) until the *Ranger*'s departure on November 14. The *Missouri* was the major combatant until the arrival of the *Midway* battle group on November 24. Other ships in company included the cruisers *Long Beach* and *Bunker Hill*, the replenishment oiler *Kansas City*, destroyers, and frigates. Admiral David E. Jeremiah, USN, commander in chief, Pacific Fleet, visited the *Missouri* on October 15–16. Admiral Carlisle A. H. Trost,

USN, chief of naval operations, visited November 9.

November 24–30 En route to Diego Garcia Island. The *Missouri* crossed the equator on November 28.

November 30–December 2 Moored at Diego Garcia.

December 2–9 En route to Australia in company with the destroyer *Leftwich*.

December 9–16 Anchored at Fremantle.

December 16–22 En route to Sydney.

December 22–29 Moored at Sydney.

December 29–31 En route to Pearl Harbor in company with the *Bunker Hill*, *Kansas City*, and *Leftwich*.

1988

January 1–10 En route to Pearl Harbor in company with the *Bunker Hill*, *Kansas City*, and *Leftwich*.

January 10–12 Moored at Pearl Harbor.

January 12–19 En route to Long Beach in company with the *Long Beach*, *Bunker Hill*, *Kansas City*, and destroyers.

January 19–March 9 Moored at the Long Beach Naval Station.

Pleasure boats provide an escort as the battleship steams up Puget Sound on September 20, 1988, en route to the shipyard at Bremerton. (Photo by Rick Ellis, Puget Sound Naval Shipyard)

March 9–10 Anchored off of the Naval Weapons Station, Seal Beach, California, while taking on ammunition.

March 10–14 En route to Canada.

March 14–18 Anchored at Vancouver, British Columbia.

March 18–22 En route to Long Beach, California.

March 22–April 19 Moored at the Long Beach Naval Station.

April 19–21 Under way for exercises in the southern California operating area.

April 21–May 16 Moored at the Long Beach Naval Station.

May 16–19 Under way for type training in the southern California operating area.

May 19–23 Moored at the Long Beach Naval Station.

May 23–27 Under way for exercises in the southern California operating area. On May 24, the *Missouri* fired a Tomahawk missile for the first time.

May 27–June 14 Moored at the Long Beach Naval Station.

June 14–20 En route to Pearl Harbor as part of Task Group 334.1, which also included the cruiser *Long Beach* and destroyers.

June 20–24 Moored at Pearl Harbor.

June 24–July 1 Under way for Exercise

RimPac '88 in the Hawaiian operating area. The *Missouri* was part of a surface action group that also included U.S., Canadian, and Australian destroyer-type ships and a U.S. Coast Guard cutter.

July 1–8 Moored at Pearl Harbor. On July 6, Captain John J. Chernesky, USN, relieved Captain James A. Carney, USN, as commanding officer of the *Missouri*.

July 8–16 Under way for continuation of Exercise RimPac '88 in the Hawaiian operating area. The *Missouri* was part of a surface action group that also included the cruiser *Long Beach* and U.S. and Australian destroyers.

July 16–26 Moored at Pearl Harbor.

July 26–August 2 En route to Long Beach, accompanied by the cruisers *Long Beach* and *California* and destroyers, while participating in the continuation of Exercise RimPac '88.

August 2–24 Moored at the Long Beach Naval Station.

August 24 En route to Coronado on dependents' cruise.

August 24–30 Moored at the North Island Naval Air Station. On August 27, on board the *Missouri*, Vice Admiral Robert K. U. Kihune, USN, relieved Vice Admiral George W. Davis, USN, as commander, Naval Surface Force Pacific Fleet.

August 30–September 1   En route to Long Beach, conducting exercises in the southern California operating area.

September 1–10   Moored at the Long Beach Naval Station.

September 10–14   En route to Canada.

September 14–16   Alternately anchored at Nanoose, British Columbia, and under way for exercises.

September 16–17   Anchored at Esquimalt, British Columbia.

September 17   En route to Seattle, Washington.

September 17–20   Moored at pier sixty-six, Seattle.

September 20   En route to Bremerton, Washington.

September 20–23   Moored at the Puget Sound Naval Shipyard.

September 23–26   En route to Long Beach, California.

September 26–October 19   Moored at the Long Beach Naval Station.

October 19–21   Under way in the southern California operating area for cruise missile training and evaluation.

October 21–31   Moored at the Long Beach Naval Station.

October 31–November 4   Under way for exercises in the southern California operating area.

November 4–14   Moored at the Long Beach Naval Station.

November 14–17   Under way for exercises in the southern California operating area.

November 17–December 31   Moored at the Long Beach Naval Station.

1989

January 1–18   Moored at the Long Beach Naval Station.

January 18–19   Under way for exercises in the southern California operating area.

January 19–30   Moored at the Long Beach Naval Station.

January 30–February 2   Anchored off of the Naval Weapons Station, Seal Beach,

California, while off-loading ammunition.

February 2–April 25   Drydocked at the Long Beach Naval Shipyard.

April 25–May 1   Moored at the Long Beach Naval Shipyard.

May 1–24   Moored at the Long Beach Naval Station.

May 24–25   Under way off southern California for sea trials.

May 25–June 5   Moored at the Long Beach Naval Station.

June 5–9   Anchored off of the Naval Weapons Station, Seal Beach, while taking on ammunition.

June 9–12   Moored at the Long Beach Naval Station.

June 12   En route to Coronado, California.

June 12–15   Moored at the North Island Naval Air Station.

June 15   En route to Long Beach, California.

June 15–19   Moored at the Long Beach Naval Shipyard.

June 19   Under way off southern California for dependents' cruise.

June 19–20   Moored at the Long Beach Naval Shipyard.

June 20–23   Under way for battle problem in the southern California operating area.

June 23–24   Anchored in the Long Beach commercial anchorage.

The Missouri is moored at pier six, Long Beach Naval Station, on August 26, 1989. The superstructure of the *New Jersey* can be seen above the number 63 on the *Missouri*'s bow. (Photo by Terry Cosgrove in DoD Still Media Records Center: DN-SN-93-04071)

June 24–29   Under way for exercises in the southern California operating area.

June 29–July 10   Moored at the Long Beach Naval Shipyard.

July 10–14   Under way for exercises off southern California.

July 14–25   Moored at the Long Beach Naval Station.

July 25–August 11   Under way off southern California while participating in READIEX 89. The *Missouri* operated with the carrier *Enterprise,* the cruiser *Long Beach,* the replenishment ships *Wichita* and *Mount Hood,* and Japanese destroyers.

August 11–September 18   Moored at the Long Beach Naval Station.

September 18–October 21   Under way off of the U.S. West Coast, Aleutian Islands, and Okinawa, en route to Pusan, Korea, during PacEx '89. At various times during the cruise, the *Missouri* operated with the battleship *New Jersey;* the aircraft carriers *Enterprise* and *Carl Vinson;* the cruisers *Long Beach* and *California;* the replenishment ships *Wichita, Kansas City, Wabash,* and *Mount Hood;* the amphibious warfare ships *Tarawa,* *Peleliu, Cleveland, Fort Fisher, Schenectady, Coronado, Anchorage,* and *Bristol County;* destroyers; and frigates.

October 21–25   Moored at Pusan, South Korea.

October 25–November 9   En route to Long Beach in company with the *Carl Vinson* and *Wabash.*

November 9–December 4   Moored at the Long Beach Naval Station.

December 4–8   En route to Mexico.

December 8–12   Anchored at Mazatlán, Mexico.

December 12–14   En route to Long Beach, California.

December 14–31   Moored at the Long Beach Naval Station.

1990

January 1–February 5   Moored at the Long Beach Naval Station.

February 5–9   Under way for exercises off southern California.

February 9–12   Moored at the North Island Naval Air Station, Coronado.

A commercial tug eases the ship in toward a berth at the North Island Naval Air Station on February 9, 1990. (Photo by Christopher T. Bolden in DoD Still Media Records Center: DN-SC-90-05719)

February 12–16 Under way for exercises off southern California.

February 16 Anchored off San Diego; en route to Long Beach.

February 16–March 6 Moored at the Long Beach Naval Station.

March 6 Under way for exercises off southern California.

March 6–13 Moored at the Long Beach Naval Station.

March 13 Under way for exercises off southern California.

March 13–22 Moored at the Long Beach Naval Station.

March 22–23 Anchored off of the Naval Weapons Station, Seal Beach, while taking on ammunition.

March 23–30 Moored at the Long Beach Naval Station.

March 30–April 6 En route to Pearl Harbor, participating in Exercise RimPac '90 in company with the cruisers *Texas* and *Princeton* and smaller surface combatants.

April 6–16 Moored at Pearl Harbor.

April 16–24 Under way in company with U.S., Canadian, Australian, and Korean warships for Exercise RimPac '90 in the Hawaiian operating area.

April 24–28 Moored at Pearl Harbor.

April 28–May 12 Under way in company with the Australian *Darwin* for the continuation of Exercise RimPac '90 in the Hawaiian operating area. On May 9, Admiral Charles R. Larson, USN, commander in chief, Pacific, visited the *Missouri.*

May 12–17 Moored at Pearl Harbor.

May 17–23 En route to Long Beach in a continuation of Exercise RimPac '90.

May 23–June 18 Moored at the Long Beach Naval Station. On June 13, Captain Albert Lee Kaiss, USN, relieved Captain John J. Chernesky, USN, as commanding officer of the *Missouri.*

June 18–25 Under way in company with the cruisers *Texas* and *Princeton,* the replenishment ship *Sacramento,* the destroyer *Fletcher,* and the frigate *Downes* for READIEX 90-2A, off southern California.

June 25–28 Moored at the North Island Naval Air Station, Coronado.

June 28 En route to Long Beach.

June 28–July 10 Moored at the Long Beach Naval Station.

July 10–12 En route to San Francisco.

July 12–17 Moored at San Francisco.

July 17–19 En route to Long Beach.

July 19–24 Moored at the Long Beach Naval Station.

July 24–25 Anchored off of the Naval Weapons Station, Seal Beach, California, while taking on ammunition.

July 25–August 27 Moored at the Long Beach Naval Station.

August 27–30 Anchored off of the Naval Weapons Station, Seal Beach, while taking on ammunition.

August 30–September 19 Moored at the Long Beach Naval Station.

September 19–24 Under way for exercises off southern California.

September 24–28 Moored at the Long Beach Naval Station.

September 28 En route to Coronado.

September 28–October 5 Moored at the North Island Naval Air Station.

October 5–6 En route to Long Beach, conducting firing exercises while under way.

October 6–29 Moored at the Long Beach Naval Station.

October 29–November 2 Anchored off of the Naval Weapons Station, Seal Beach, while taking on ammunition.

November 2–4 Under way for exercises off southern California.

November 4–13 Moored at the Long Beach Naval Station.

November 13–21 En route to Pearl Harbor.

November 21–25 Moored at Pearl Harbor.

November 25–December 8 En route to the Philippine Islands.

December 8–12 Moored at the Subic Bay Naval Station.

December 12–17 En route to Thailand.

December 17–22 Anchored at Pattaya Beach.

December 22–31 En route to the Persian Gulf.

1991

January 1–3 En route to the Persian Gulf.

January 3 Transited the Strait of Hormuz.

January 3–5 Under way in the Persian Gulf.

January 5–8 Anchored at Manama, Bahrain.

January 8–15 Under way for operations in the Persian Gulf.

January 15–16 Anchored at Manama, Bahrain.

January 16–March 3 Under way for operations in the Persian Gulf during the Desert Storm air war and ground war. During this period the *Missouri* fired twenty-eight Tomahawk missiles and 759 16-inch projectiles.

March 3–12 Anchored at Manama, Bahrain.

March 12–15 Under way for operations in the Persian Gulf.

March 15–20 Anchored at Manama, Bahrain.

March 20–21 En route to the Strait of Hormuz.

March 21 Transited the Strait of Hormuz.

March 21–April 4 En route to Australia. The *Missouri* crossed the equator March 27.

April 4–8 Moored at Fremantle (Perth), Australia.

April 8–14 En route to Hobart, Tasmania, Australia.

April 14–19 Moored at Hobart.

April 19–May 3 En route to Pearl Harbor.

May 3–6 Moored at the Pearl Harbor Naval Station.

May 6–13 En route to Long Beach in company with the frigate *Ford*.

May 13–July 24 Moored at the Long Beach Naval Station. On July 23, Rear Admiral Phillp Coady, USN, commander, Cruiser-Destroyer Group Five, embarked for the Seattle-Vancouver visit.

July 24–30 En route to Indian Island, Washington, in company with the cruiser *Antietam*, the replenishment ship *Sacramento*, destroyers, and frigates.

July 30–31 Moored at the Indian Island ammunition pier.

July 31 En route to Seattle, Washington.

July 31–August 6 Moored at Seattle.

August 6 En route to Canada.

August 6–10 Anchored at Vancouver, British Columbia.

August 10–14 En route to Long Beach.

August 14–October 9 Moored at the Long Beach Naval Station. From October 8 to 16, Rear Admiral Phillp Coady, USN, commander, Cruiser-Destroyer Group Five, was embarked for Fleet Week in San Francisco.

October 9–11 En route to San Francisco in company with the cruisers *Chancellorsville* and *Jouett*, the tender *Cape Cod*, the amphibious warfare ship *Fort Fisher*, the destroyers *Berkeley* and *O'Brien*, and the frigate *Barbey*.

October 11–12 Anchored in the vicinity of Alcatraz for review of parade of ships. Admiral Robert J. Kelly, USN, commander in chief, Pacific Fleet, visited the *Missouri*.

October 12–17 Moored at San Francisco.

October 17–18 En route to Long Beach.

October 18–November 29 Moored at the Long Beach Naval Station.

November 29–December 5 En route to Pearl Harbor.

December 5–9 Moored at Pearl Harbor. President George Bush visited the *Missouri* on December 7, the fiftieth anniversary of the Japanese attack on Pearl Harbor.

December 9–16 En route to Seal Beach, California.

December 16–20 Anchored off of the Naval Weapons Station, Seal Beach, while off-loading ammunition.

December 20–31 Moored at the Long Beach Naval Station.

1992

January 1–March 24 Moored at the Long Beach Naval Station.

Aerial view of the ship at San Francisco in October 1991. (Photo by Dr. Giorgio Arra via Norman Polmar)

March 24–31   Moored at the Pier Echo, Long Beach Naval Shipyard. On March 31, the *Missouri* was decommissioned for the second time and reentered the reserve fleet. She was subsequently towed to her mothball fleet berth in Bremerton, Washington.

Appendix B

Commanding Officers

CAPTAIN WILLIAM M. CALLAGHAN,
U.S. NAVY
June 11, 1944–May 14, 1945

CAPTAIN STUART S. MURRAY, U.S. NAVY
May 14, 1945–November 6, 1945

CAPTAIN ROSCOE H. HILLENKOETTER,
U.S. NAVY
November 6, 1945–May 31, 1946

CAPTAIN TOM B. HILL, U.S. NAVY
May 31, 1946–April 2, 1947

CAPTAIN ROBERT L. DENNISON, U.S. NAVY
April 2, 1947–January 23, 1948

COMMANDER JOHN B. COLWELL, U.S. NAVY
January 23, 1948–February 24, 1948

CAPTAIN JAMES H. THACH, JR., U.S. NAVY
February 24, 1948–February 5, 1949

CAPTAIN HAROLD P. SMITH, U.S. NAVY
February 5, 1949–December 10, 1949

CAPTAIN WILLIAM D. BROWN , U.S. NAVY
December 10, 1949–February 3, 1950

COMMANDER GEORGE E. PECKHAM,
U.S. NAVY
February 3, 1950–February 7, 1950

CAPTAIN HAROLD P. SMITH, U.S. NAVY
February 7, 1950–April 19, 1950

CAPTAIN IRVING T. DUKE, U.S. NAVY
April 19, 1950–March 2, 1951

CAPTAIN GEORGE C. WRIGHT, U.S. NAVY
March 2, 1951–October 18, 1951

CAPTAIN JOHN SYLVESTER, U.S. NAVY
October 18, 1951–September 4, 1952

CAPTAIN WARNER R. EDSALL, U.S. NAVY
September 4, 1952–March 26, 1953

COMMANDER JAMES R. NORTH, U.S. NAVY
March 26, 1953–April 4, 1953

CAPTAIN ROBERT BRODIE, JR., U.S. NAVY
April 4, 1953–April 1, 1954

CAPTAIN ROBERT T. S. KEITH, U.S. NAVY
April 1, 1954–September 18, 1954

CAPTAIN JAMES R. NORTH, U.S. NAVY
September 18, 1954–February 26, 1955

CAPTAIN ALBERT LEE KAISS, U.S. NAVY
May 10, 1986–June 20, 1986

CAPTAIN JAMES A. CARNEY, U.S. NAVY
June 20, 1986–July 6, 1988

CAPTAIN JOHN J. CHERNESKY, U.S. NAVY
July 6, 1988–June 13, 1990

CAPTAIN ALBERT LEE KAISS, U.S. NAVY
June 13, 1990–March 31, 1992

Appendix C

Ship's Data

Key dates

—keel laid—January 6, 1941, New York
Navy Yard
—launched—January 29, 1944, New York
Navy Yard
—commissioned—June 11, 1944, New York
Navy Yard
—decommissioned—February 26, 1955, Puget Sound Naval Shipyard
—recommissioned—May 10, 1986, San Francisco commercial piers
—decommissioned—March 31, 1992, Long
Beach Naval Shipyard

Displacement

—standard—45,000 tons
—at designer's waterline—54,889 tons
—full-load (in 1945)—57,540 tons
—full-load (in 1988)—57,500 tons

Dimensions

—length overall—887 feet, 3 inches
—length at waterline—860 feet, 0 inches
—maximum beam—108 feet, 2 inches
—frame spacing—4 feet, total of 216 frames
—mean draft at designer's waterline—34 feet,
9.25 inches
—design draft—34 feet, 9.25 inches at
54,889 tons
—maximum draft at full load (in 1945)—37
feet, 9 inches at 57,540 tons
—maximum draft at full load (in 1988)—37
feet, 8.75 inches at 57,500 tons

SOURCES: Robert F. Sumrall, Iowa-*Class Battleships*
(Annapolis: Naval Institute Press, 1988) and USS *New
Jersey* (BB-62) Ship's Data Book.

Machinery

Boilers
eight Babcock and Wilcox

Turbines
four General Electric: high pressure—24,400
horsepower at 4,905 rpms; low pressure—
28,600 horsepower at 3,913 rpms; astern—
11,000 horsepower at 2,375 rpms

Reduction Gears
General Electric: high-pressure ratio—
24.284:1; low-pressure ratio—19,369:1

Shafts
four

Shaft Horsepower
212,000 maximum ahead; 44,000 astern

Maximum Speed
33 knots at 202 shaft rpms

Propellers
four: inboard—two five-bladed, 17 feet, 0
inches diameter; outboard—two four-bladed,
18 feet, 3 inches diameter

Rudders
two, each 340 square feet in area

Generators
eight turbo, 1,250 kilowatt; two diesel, 250
kilowatt

Fuel Oil Capacity
8,624 tons (in 1945)

Diesel Oil Capacity
187 tons (in 1945)

Aviation Gasoline Capacity
8,588 gallons (in 1945)

Armament

—nine 16-inch/50-caliber guns in three triple turrets.

—twenty 5-inch/38-caliber dual-purpose guns in ten twin mounts; the number was reduced to twelve guns in six twin mounts during the 1984–86 modernization.

—eighty 40-mm guns in twenty quad mounts, later reduced in number following World War II and then restored to the original number in 1950 for the Korean War. All the quad mounts were removed during the 1984–86 modernization.

—forty-nine 20-mm guns in single mounts upon completion in 1944. The number was gradually reduced to twenty-two in 1947, when the guns were eliminated. Dual-mount 20-mm guns began appearing in 1945, increasing from eight at that time to thirty-two during the Korean War. The 20-mm guns were eventually eliminated prior to the 1955 decommissioning.

—four Vulcan/Phalanx 20-mm Gatling guns were added during the 1984–86 modernization.

—four quadruple Harpoon antiship missile canister launchers, for a total of sixteen missiles, were added during the 1984–86 modernization.

—eight quadruple Tomahawk armored box launchers, for a total of thirty-two missiles, were added during the 1984–86 modernization.

Armor

Belts

upper side, between second and third decks, frames 50–166: 12.1-inch class A armor

lower side, between third deck and hold: frames 166–89, tapered from 13.5 inches to 5.625 inches at frame 166; tapered from 13.5 inches to 7.25 inches at frame 189, class B armor

lower side, between third deck and hold, frames 50–166: tapered from 12.1 inches to 1.625 inches, class B armor

Turrets

front, 17 inches over 2.5-inch special treatment steel; sides, 9.5 inches; rear, 12 inches; top, 7.25 inches

Barbettes (down to second deck)

11.6 inches forward and aft; 17.3 inches on sides

Deck Plating

second deck, frames 50–166: 4.75-inch class B armor; third deck, frames 166–89: 5.6-inch class B armor; third deck, frames 189–203: 6.2-inch class B armor

Bulkheads

frame 203, between second and third decks: 11.3-inch class A armor

frame 166, between second and third decks: 11.3-inch class A armor

frame 50, between second deck and hold: tapered from 11.3 inches to 8.5 inches, class A armor

Citadel from 03 to 05 level: top, 7.25 inches; bottom, 4 inches; sides, 17.3 inches
Tube from second deck to 03 level, 16 inches all the way around.

Search Radar Antennas

—SK-2 air-search on foremast from 1944 to 1947

—SR-3 air-search on foremast from 1948 to 1955

—SPS-49 air-search on foremast from 1986 to 1992

—SP height-finder on mainmast from 1948 to 1953

—SPS-8 height-finder on mainmast from 1953 to 1955

—SG surface-search on foremast and mainmast from 1944 to 1948

—SG-6 surface-search on foremast from 1948 to 1955

—SPS-67 surface-search on foremast from 1986 to 1992

The *Missouri* as outfitted in June 1944

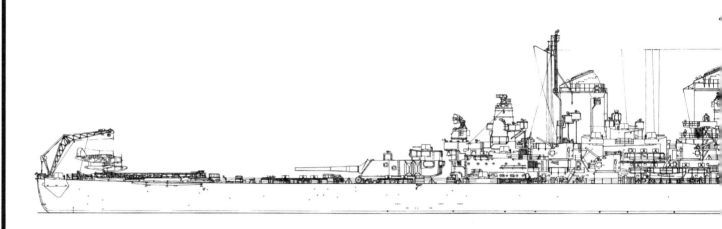

Drawings by Alan B. Chesley

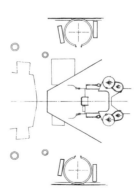

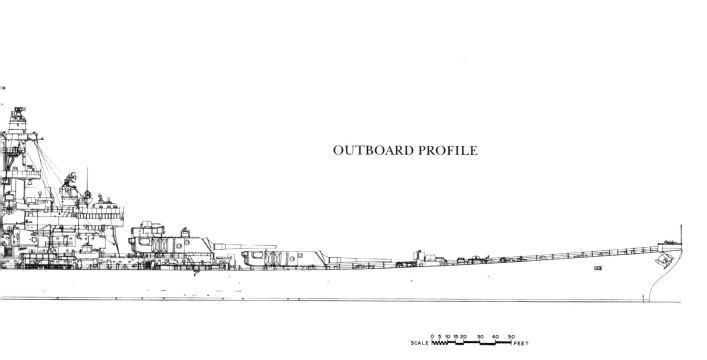

OUTBOARD PROFILE

SCALE 0 5 10 15 20 30 40 50 FEET

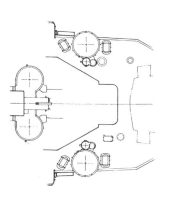

PARTIAL OVERHEAD SHOWING DETAILS AS COMPLETED

The *Missouri* as outfitted circa April 1945

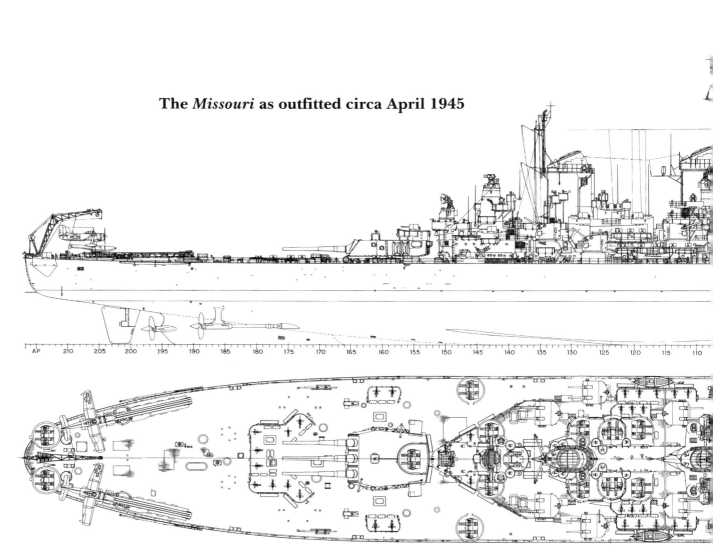

Drawings by Alan B. Chesley

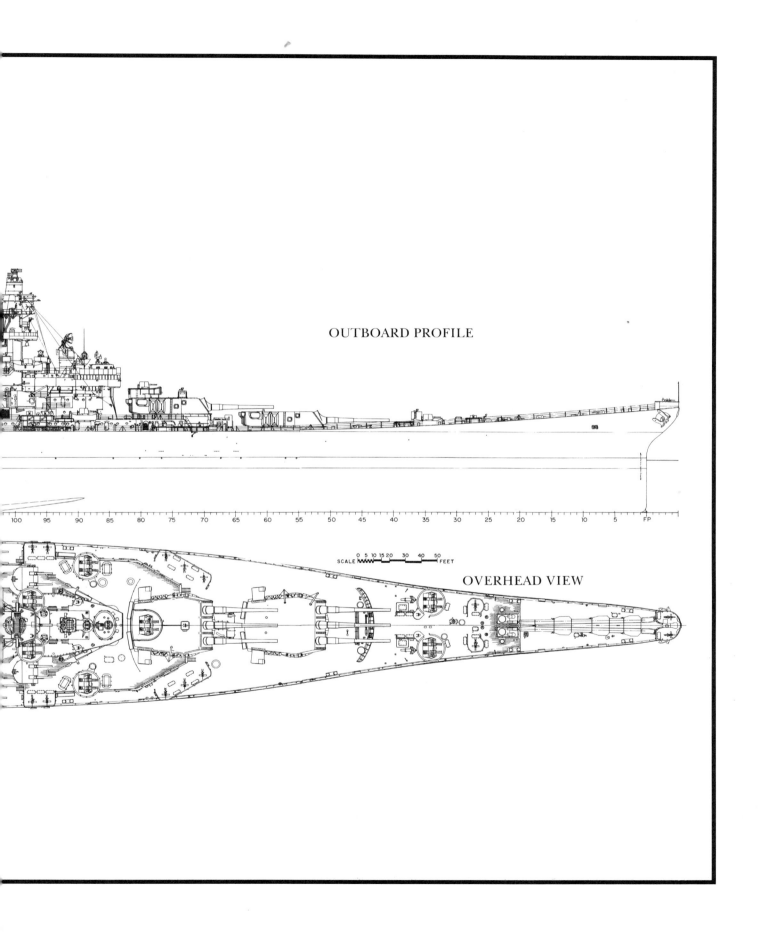

OUTBOARD PROFILE

OVERHEAD VIEW

SCALE 0 5 10 15 20 30 40 50 FEET

100 95 90 85 80 75 70 65 60 55 50 45 40 35 30 25 20 15 10 5 FP

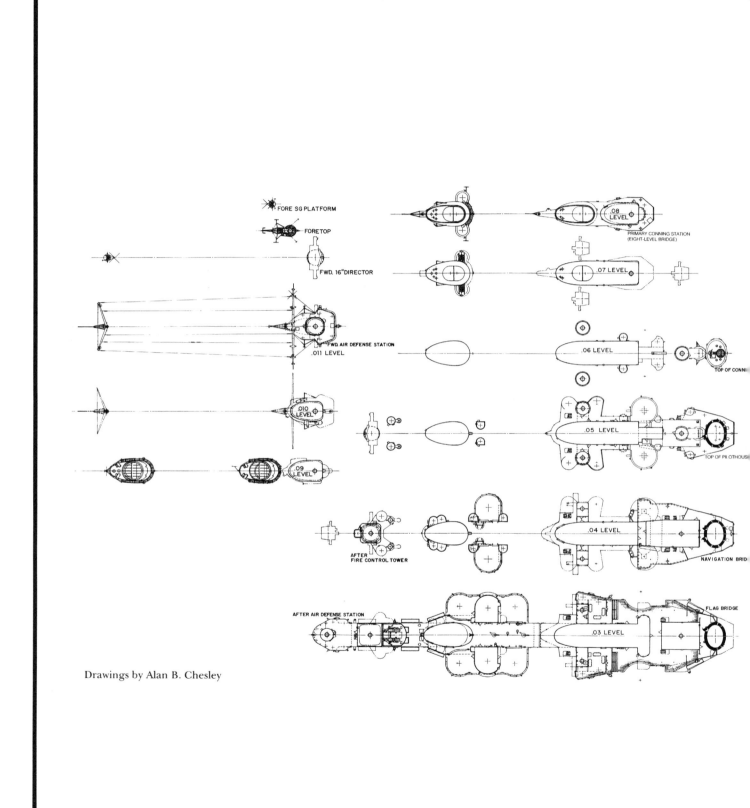

FORE SG PLATFORM

FORETOP

FWD. 16" DIRECTOR

FWD AIR DEFENSE STATION
.011 LEVEL

.010 LEVEL

.09 LEVEL

AFTER
FIRE CONTROL TOWER

AFTER AIR DEFENSE STATION

.08 LEVEL
PRIMARY CONNING STATION
(EIGHT-LEVEL BRIDGE)

.07 LEVEL

.06 LEVEL
TOP OF CONNI

.05 LEVEL
TOP OF PILOTHOUS

.04 LEVEL
NAVIGATION BRID

.03 LEVEL
FLAG BRIDGE

Drawings by Alan B. Chesley

Superstructure Decks and Platforms (1945)

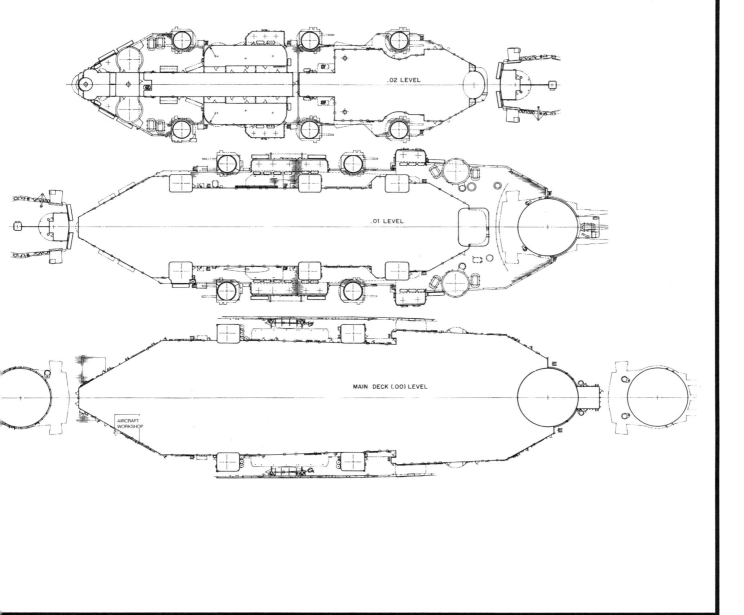

.02 LEVEL

.01 LEVEL

MAIN DECK (.00) LEVEL

AIRCRAFT
WORKSHOP

The *Missouri* as outfitted in 1951

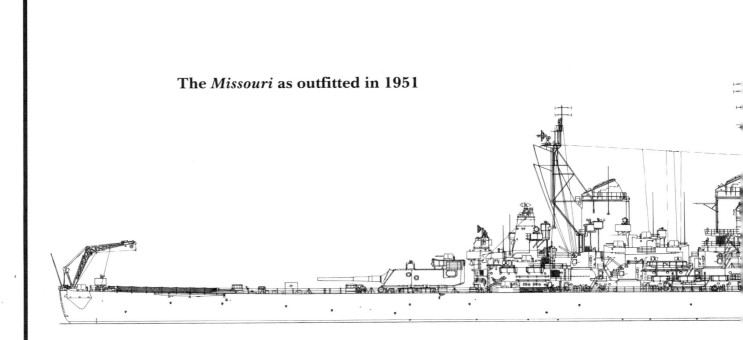

Drawing by Alan B. Chesley

OUTBOARD PROFILE

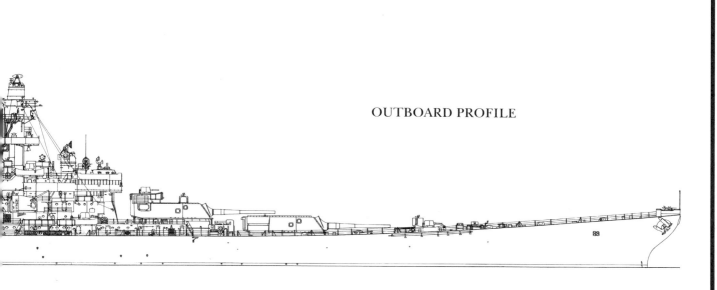

SCALE |—| 0 5 10 15 20 30 40 50 FEET

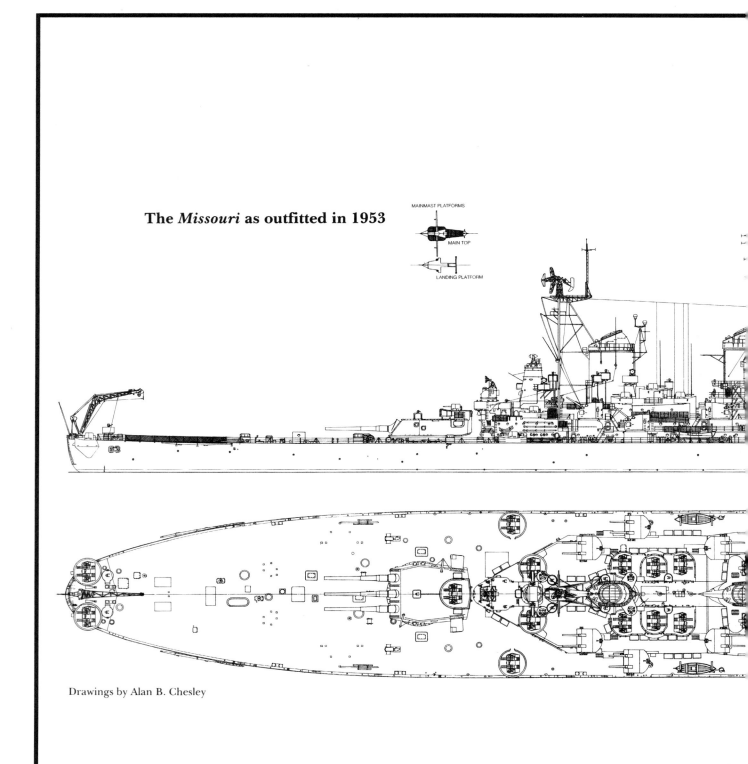

The *Missouri* as outfitted in 1953

MAINMAST PLATFORMS

MAIN TOP

LANDING PLATFORM

Drawings by Alan B. Chesley

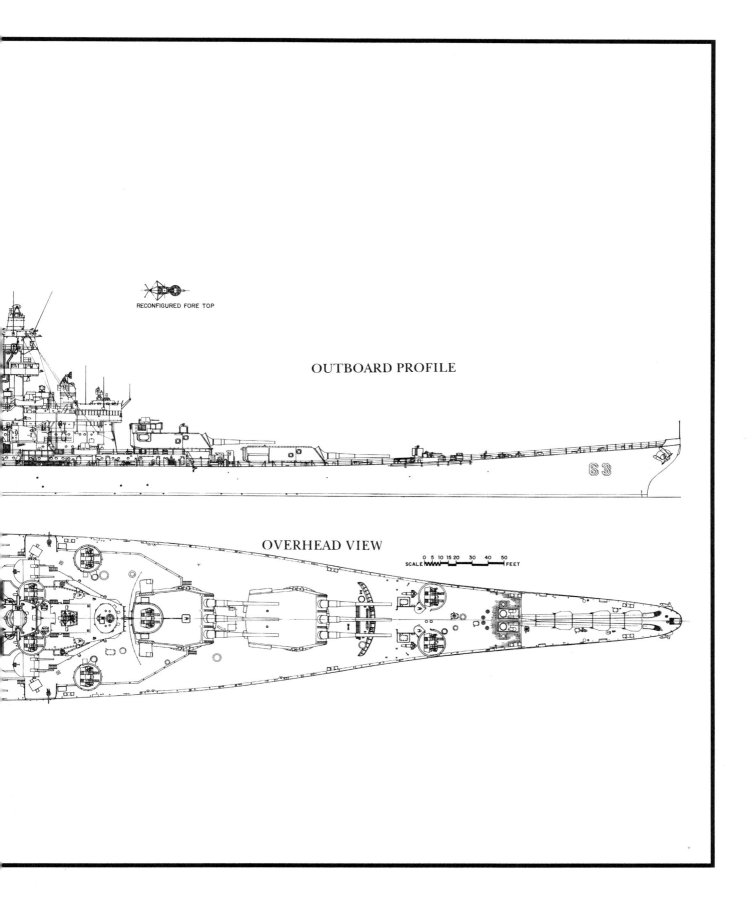

RECONFIGURED FORE TOP

OUTBOARD PROFILE

OVERHEAD VIEW

SCALE 0 5 10 15 20 30 40 50 FEET

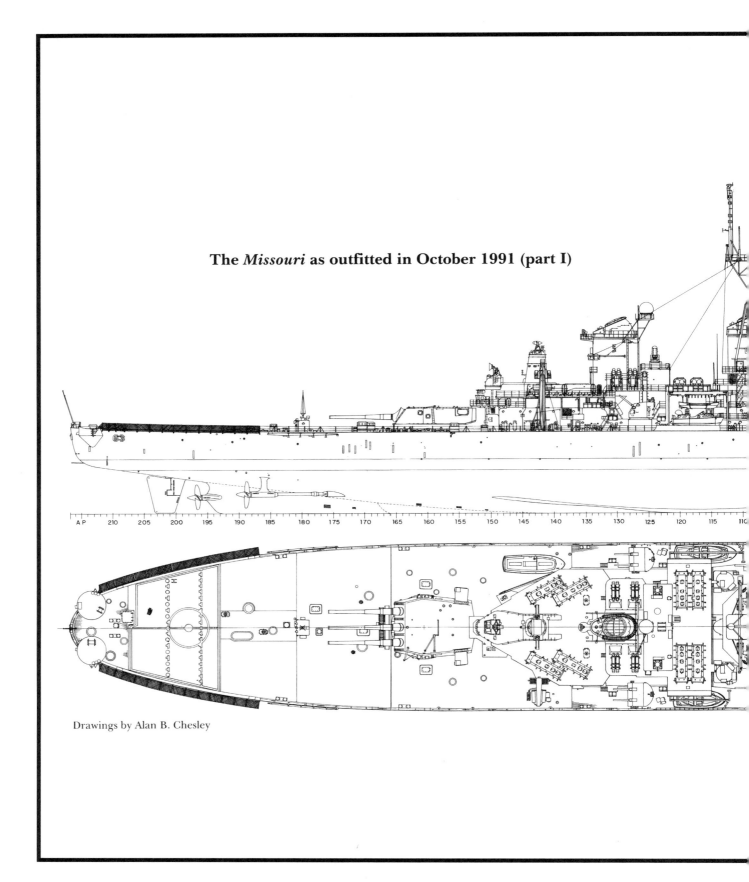

The *Missouri* as outfitted in October 1991 (part I)

Drawings by Alan B. Chesley

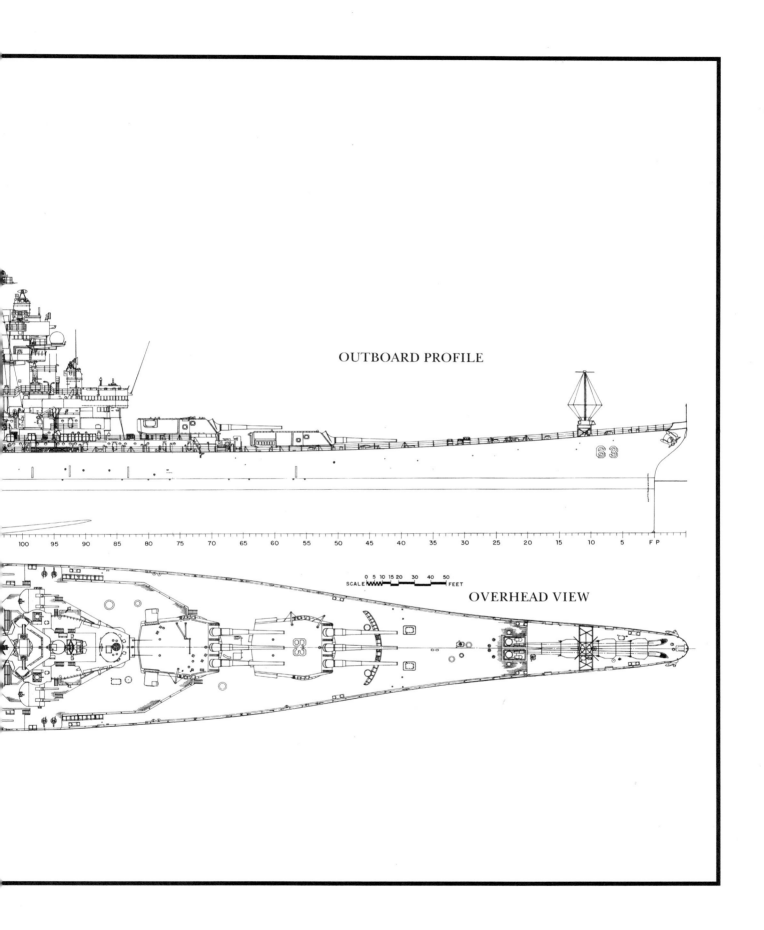

OUTBOARD PROFILE

OVERHEAD VIEW

SCALE |0 5 10 15 20 30 40 50 FEET

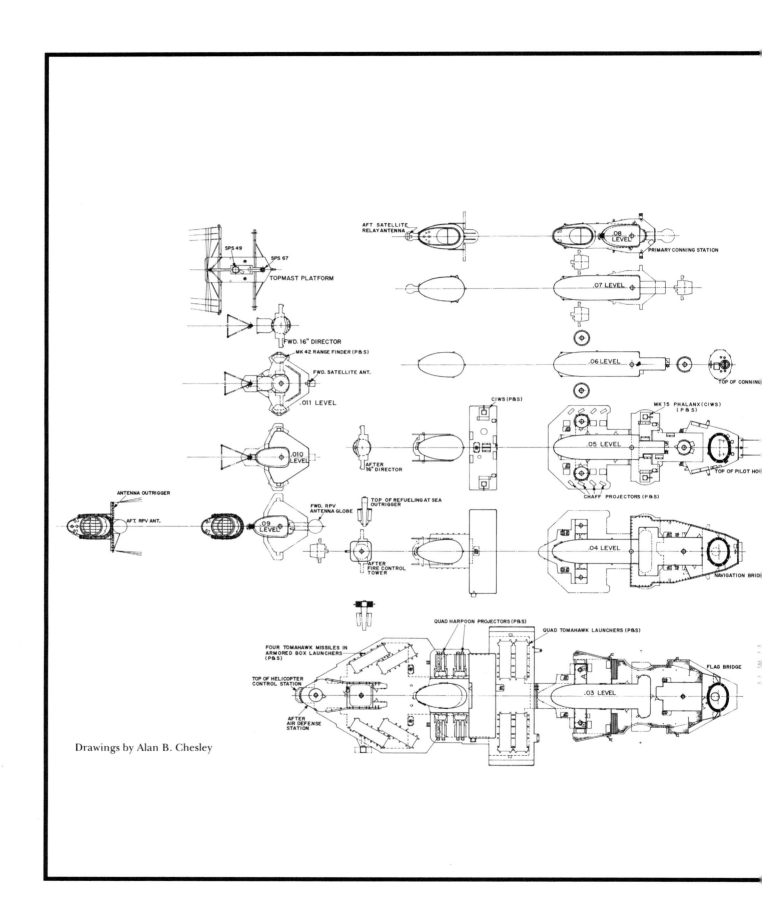

Drawings by Alan B. Chesley

Superstructure Decks and Platforms (1991)

① SPAN WIRE WINCH
② SADDLE WINCHES
③ BOAT HANDLING WINCHES

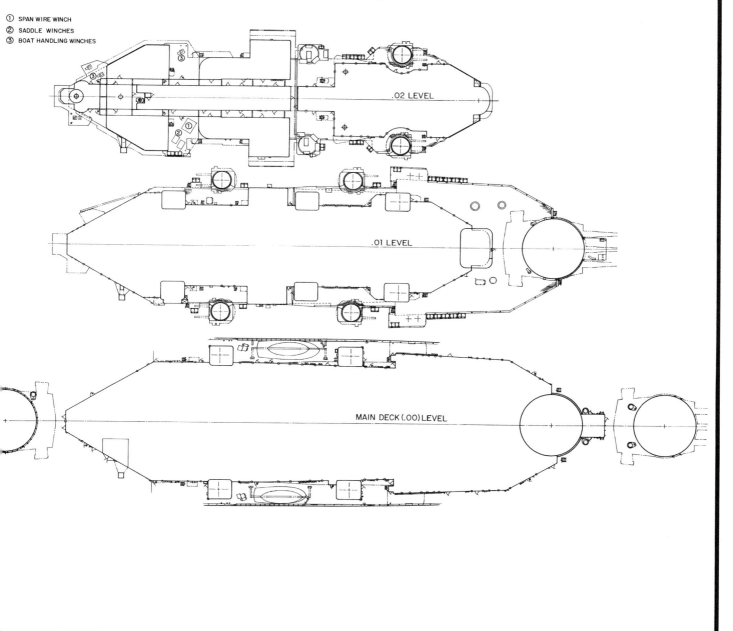

.02 LEVEL

.01 LEVEL

MAIN DECK (.00) LEVEL

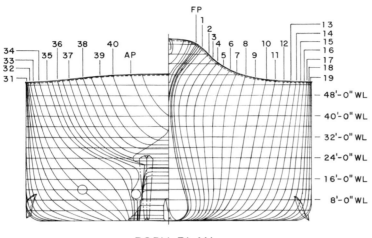

BODY PLAN

TABLE OF DIMENSIONS

A	45.0" (3'-9")
B	220.0" (18'-4")
C	125.0" (10'-5")
D	27.0" (2'-3")
E	62.0" (5'-2")
F	185.0" (15'-5")
G	16.0" (1'-4")
H	18.3" (1'-6 5/16")
I-J	23.5" (1'-11 1/2")
K	30.0" (2'-6")
L	40.0" (3'-4")
M	45.0" (3'-9")
N	49.0" (4'-1")

1 BELL
2 CHASE
3 HOOP
4 LOCKING RING
5 SLIDE CYLINDER

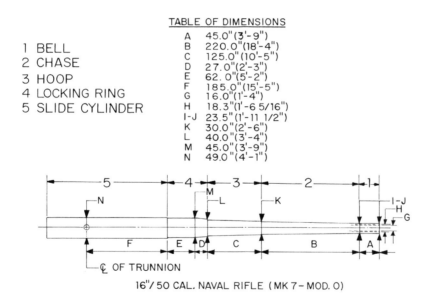

16"/ 50 CAL. NAVAL RIFLE (MK 7 – MOD. 0)

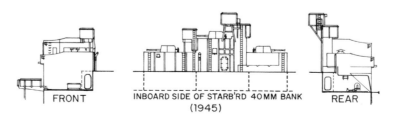

FRONT

INBOARD SIDE OF STARB'RD 40 MM BANK
(1945)

REAR

Drawings by Alan B. Chesley

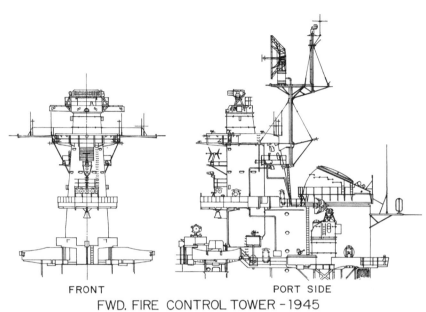

FRONT   PORT SIDE

FWD. FIRE CONTROL TOWER – 1945

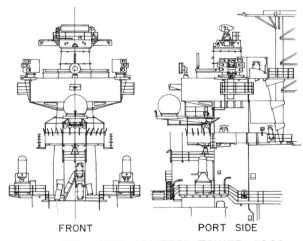

FRONT   PORT SIDE

FWD. FIRE CONTROL TOWER – 1991

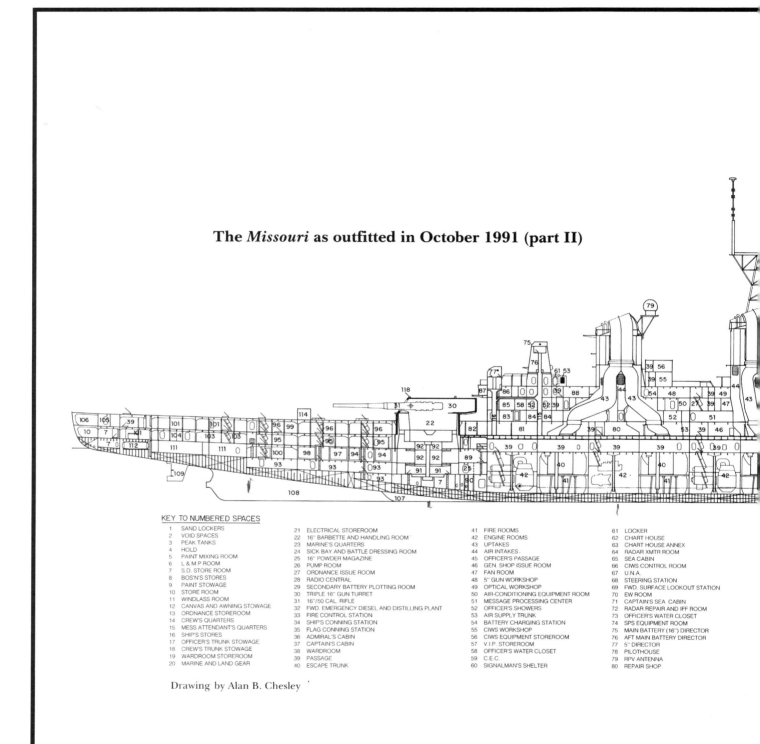

The *Missouri* as outfitted in October 1991 (part II)

KEY TO NUMBERED SPACES

1	SAND LOCKERS	21	ELECTRICAL STOREROOM	41	FIRE ROOMS	61	LOCKER
2	VOID SPACES	22	16" BARBETTE AND HANDLING ROOM	42	ENGINE ROOMS	62	CHART HOUSE
3	PEAK TANKS	23	MARINE'S QUARTERS	43	UPTAKES	63	CHART HOUSE ANNEX
4	HOLD	24	SICK BAY AND BATTLE DRESSING ROOM	44	AIR INTAKES	64	RADAR XMTR ROOM
5	PAINT MIXING ROOM	25	16" POWDER MAGAZINE	45	OFFICER'S PASSAGE	65	SEA CABIN
6	L & M P ROOM	26	PUMP ROOM	46	GEN. SHOP ISSUE ROOM	66	CIWS CONTROL ROOM
7	S.D. STORE ROOM	27	ORDNANCE ISSUE ROOM	47	FAN ROOM	67	U.N.A.
8	BOS'N'S STORES	28	RADIO CENTRAL	48	5" GUN WORKSHOP	68	STEERING STATION
9	PAINT STOWAGE	29	SECONDARY BATTERY PLOTTING ROOM	49	OPTICAL WORKSHOP	69	FWD. SURFACE LOOKOUT STATION
10	STORE ROOM	30	TRIPLE 16" GUN TURRET	50	AIR-CONDITIONING EQUIPMENT ROOM	70	EW ROOM
11	WINDLASS ROOM	31	16"/50 CAL. RIFLE	51	MESSAGE PROCESSING CENTER	71	CAPTAIN'S SEA CABIN
12	CANVAS AND AWNING STOWAGE	32	FWD. EMERGENCY DIESEL AND DISTILLING PLANT	52	OFFICER'S SHOWERS	72	RADAR REPAIR AND IFF ROOM
13	ORDNANCE STOREROOM	33	FIRE CONTROL STATION	53	AIR SUPPLY TRUNK	73	OFFICER'S WATER CLOSET
14	CREW'S QUARTERS	34	SHIP'S CONNING STATION	54	BATTERY CHARGING STATION	74	SPS EQUIPMENT ROOM
15	MESS ATTENDANT'S QUARTERS	35	FLAG CONNING STATION	55	CIWS WORKSHOP	75	MAIN BATTERY (16") DIRECTOR
16	SHIP'S STORES	36	ADMIRAL'S CABIN	56	CIWS EQUIPMENT STOREROOM	76	AFT MAIN BATTERY DIRECTOR
17	OFFICER'S TRUNK STOWAGE	37	CAPTAIN'S CABIN	57	V.I.P. STOREROOM	77	5" DIRECTOR
18	CREW'S TRUNK STOWAGE	38	WARDROOM	58	OFFICER'S WATER CLOSET	78	PILOTHOUSE
19	WARDROOM STOREROOM	39	PASSAGE	59	C.E.C.	79	RPV ANTENNA
20	MARINE AND LAND GEAR	40	ESCAPE TRUNK	60	SIGNALMAN'S SHELTER	80	REPAIR SHOP

Drawing by Alan B. Chesley

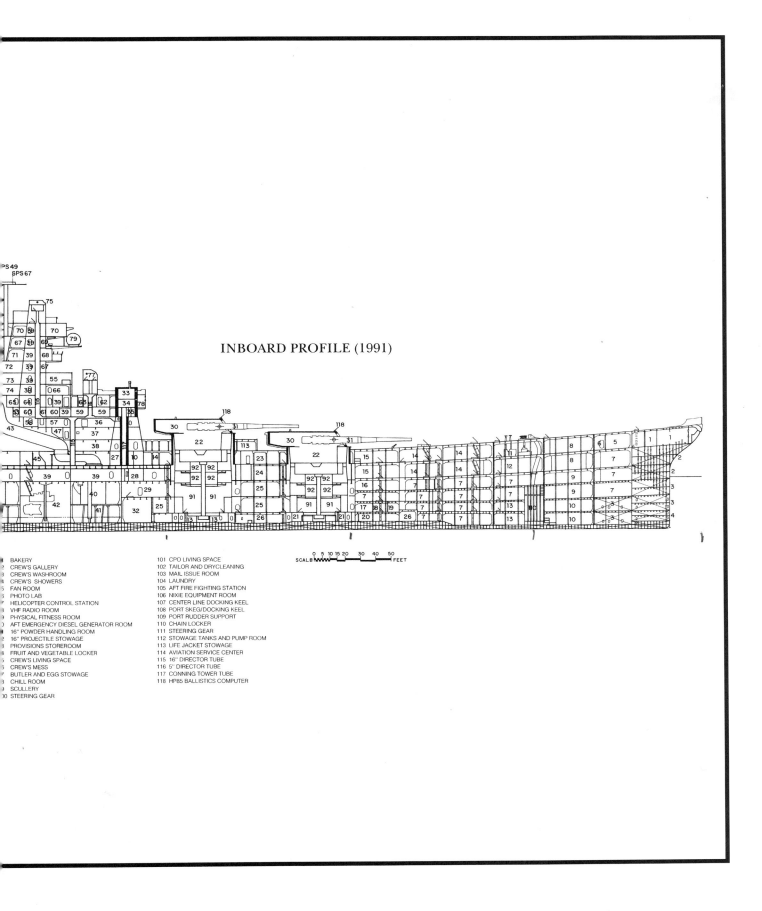

INBOARD PROFILE (1991)

1 BAKERY
2 CREW'S GALLERY
3 CREW'S WASHROOM
4 CREW'S SHOWERS
5 FAN ROOM
6 PHOTO LAB
7 HELICOPTER CONTROL STATION
8 VHF RADIO ROOM
9 PHYSICAL FITNESS ROOM
10 AFT EMERGENCY DIESEL GENERATOR ROOM
11 16" POWDER HANDLING ROOM
12 16" PROJECTILE STOWAGE
13 PROVISIONS STOREROOM
14 FRUIT AND VEGETABLE LOCKER
15 CREW'S LIVING SPACE
16 CREW'S MESS
17 BUTLER AND EGG STOWAGE
18 CHILL ROOM
19 SCULLERY
100 STEERING GEAR

101 CPO LIVING SPACE
102 TAILOR AND DRYCLEANING
103 MAIL ISSUE ROOM
104 LAUNDRY
105 AFT FIRE FIGHTING STATION
106 NIXIE EQUIPMENT ROOM
107 CENTER LINE DOCKING KEEL
108 PORT SKEG/DOCKING KEEL
109 PORT RUDDER SUPPORT
110 CHAIN LOCKER
111 STEERING GEAR
112 STOWAGE TANKS AND PUMP ROOM
113 LIFE JACKET STOWAGE
114 AVIATION SERVICE CENTER
115 16" DIRECTOR TUBE
116 5" DIRECTOR TUBE
117 CONNING TOWER TUBE
118 HP85 BALLISTICS COMPUTER

SCALE 0 5 10 15 20 30 40 50 FEET

Appendix D

The Surrender Signers

The signers of the surrender documents on the morning of September 2, 1945, were as follows:

9:04 Foreign Minister Mamoru Shigemitsu signed for Japan.

9:06 General Yoshijiro Umezo, chief of the army General Staff, signed for the Japanese armed forces.

9:08 General of the Army Douglas MacArthur signed for the Allied Powers.

9:12 Fleet Admiral Chester W. Nimitz signed for the United States.

9:13 General Hsu Yung-Chang signed for China.

9:14 Admiral Sir Bruce Fraser signed for the United Kingdom.

9:16 Lieutenant General Kuzma Nikolaevich Derevyanko signed for the Union of Soviet Socialist Republics.

9:17 General Sir Thomas Blamey signed for Australia.

9:18 Colonel Lawrence Moore Cosgrave signed for Canada.

9:20 General Jacques LeClerc signed for France.

9:21 Admiral C. E. L. Helfrich signed for the Kingdom of the Netherlands.

9:22 Air Vice Marshal Leonard M. Isitt signed for New Zealand.

Notes

Chapter 1—The Birth of a Battleship

1. *The New York Times,* January 7, 1941.
2. Ibid.
3. Ibid.
4. Ibid.
5. *The New York Times,* January 30, 1944.
6. Miller, notes on *Iowa* and *Missouri,* January 19, 1993.
7. Miller, interview with author, January 24, 1993.
8. Ibid.
9. Ibid.
10. Johnson (Herbert), interview with author, January 14, 1995.
11. Ibid.
12. Ibid.
13. *The New York Times,* January 30, 1944.
14. Johnson (Herbert), interview with author, January 14, 1995.
15. Ibid.
16. Ibid.
17. Ibid.
18. Miller, interview with author, January 24, 1993.
19. Stokes, *St. Louis Post-Dispatch,* January 27, 1944.
20. Ibid.
21. Ibid.
22. Margaret Truman, *Truman,* 159.
23. *The New York Times,* January 30, 1944.
24. Margaret Truman, *Truman,* 159.
25. *The New York Times,* January 30, 1944.
26. Daniel, interview with author, November 1, 1994.
27. Ibid; Truman, *Truman,* 159.
28. Kelly, letter to Governor Donnell, January 31, 1944.
29. Margaret Truman, *Truman,* 160.
30. Chinn, interview with author, October 27, 1994.
31. Smith and Newell, *Mighty Mo,* 14.
32. Yucka, interview with author, September 2, 1994.
33. Ibid.
34. Clancy interview, USS *Missouri* oral history project.
35. Vella, interview with author, September 2, 1994.
36. Leibig, interview with author, September 2, 1993.
37. Vella, interview with author, September 2, 1994.
38. Ibid.
39. USS *Missouri* deck log (hereafter, Deck log).
40. Smith and Newell, *Mighty Mo,* 14.
41. Vella, interview with author, September 2, 1994; Yucka, interview with author, September 2, 1994.
42. Plate, interview with author, December 17, 1994.
43. Vella, interview with author, September 2, 1994.
44. Alessandro, interview with author, January 5, 1995.
45. Circelli, interview with author, September 4, 1994.
46. Ibid.
47. Ibid.
48. Leibig, interview with author, September 2, 1993.
49. Schwenk, interview with author, September 3, 1994.
50. Ibid.
51. Plate, interview with author, December 17, 1994.
52. Ibid.
53. Deck log.
54. Smith and Newell, *Mighty Mo,* 14.
55. Ibid., 17; Couture, interview with author, September 1, 1994.
56. Smith, *Mighty Mo,* 17.
57. Leibig, interview with author, September 2, 1993.
58. Ibid.
59. Barron (John), interview with author, October 22, 1994.
60. Albert, interview with author, September 2, 1994.
61. Ibid.
62. Smith and Newell, *Mighty Mo,* 19.
63. Leibig, interview with author, September 2, 1993.

64. Barron (John), interview with author, October 22, 1994.
65. Plate, interview with author, December 17, 1994.
66. Vella, interview with author, September 2, 1994.
67. Barron (John), interview with author, October 22, 1994.
68. Ibid.
69. Barron (Eleanor), interview with author, October 22, 1994.
70. Starnes, interview with author, January 6, 1995.
71. Ibid.
72. *The Missourian,* February 3, 1945.
73. Jong Hwan Jim, news release, August 18, 1945.
74. Deck log; Smith and Newell, *Mighty Mo,* 14.
75. Deck log; Smith and Newell, *Mighty Mo,* 15–16.
76. Deck log.
77. Plate, interview with author, December 17, 1994.
78. Rodrigues interview, USS *Missouri* oral history project.
79. Plate, interview with author, December 17, 1994; Sumrall, interview with author, January 20, 1995; Sumrall, *Proceedings,* February 1973, 67–81.
80. Plate, interview with author, December 18, 1994.
81. USS *Missouri* aviation unit history, Naval Historical Center (hereafter Aviation unit history).
82. Leibig, interview with author, September 2, 1993.
83. Circelli, interview with author, September 4, 1994.
84. Zimmerman interview, USS *Missouri* oral history project.
85. Deck log.
86. Plate, unpublished recollections.
87. Ibid.
88. Ibid.

Chapter 2—Victory in Combat

1. Action report, March 2, 1945; Plate, unpublished recollections; Aviation unit history.
2. Deck log.
3. Action report, March 2, 1945; Plate, interview with author, December 17, 1994.
4. USS *Missouri* war diary (hereafter War diary).
5. Action report, March 2, 1945.
6. Ibid.
7. Plate, unpublished recollections.
8. Deck log.
9. Faulk, interview with Dr. John T. Mason, Jr., November 11, 1974.
10. Yucka, interview with author, September 2, 1994; Plate, interview with author, December 17, 1994.
11. Vella, interview with author, September 2, 1994.
12. Dubensky, interview with author, September 1, 1994.
13. Murray, interview with Etta-Belle Kitchen, October 10, 1970.
14. Action report, May 9, 1945.
15. Leibig, interview with author, September 2, 1993.
16. Smith and Newell, *Mighty Mo,* 28.
17. Starnes, interview with author, January 6, 1995.
18. Action report, March 26, 1945.
19. Action report, May 9, 1945; Plate, interview with author, December 17, 1994.
20. Alessandro, interviews with author, December 1, 1991, and January 5, 1995.
21. Ibid.
22. Action report, March 26, 1945.
23. Starnes, interview with author, January 6, 1995.
24. *The History of USS* Missouri (World War II cruisebook [hereafter, Cruisebook]).
25. Ganas interview, USS *Missouri* oral history project.
26. Circelli, interview with author, September 4, 1994.
27. Conner, interview with author, September 1, 1994; Schwenk, interview with author, September 3, 1994.
28. Alessandro, interview with author, January 5, 1995.
29. Faulk, interview with Dr. John T. Mason, Jr., November 11, 1974.
30. Conner, interview with author, September 1, 1994.
31. Action report, May 9, 1945; *The Missourian,* April 28, 1945.
32. Faulk, interview with Dr. John T. Mason, Jr., November 11, 1974.
33. Starnes, interview with author, January 6, 1995.
34. Action report, May 9, 1945.
35. Ibid.
36. Schmidt, interview with author, September 5, 1993.
37. Albert, interview with author, September 2, 1994.
38. Plate, interview with author, December 17, 1994.
39. Albert, interview with author, September 2, 1994.
40. Faulk, interviews with Dr. John T. Mason, Jr., November 11 and 12, 1974.
41. Deck log.
42. J. C. Truman, letter to Harry Truman, April 22, 1945.
43. Starnes, interview with author, January 6, 1995.
44. Action report, May 9, 1945; Cruisebook.
45. Action report, May 9, 1945.
46. Ibid.
47. Smith and Newell, *Mighty Mo,* 36.

48. Murray, interview with Etta-Belle Kitchen, October 10, 1970.
49. Plate, interview with author, December 17, 1994.
50. Starnes, interview with author, January 6, 1995.
51. Ibid.
52. Murray, interview with Etta-Belle Kitchen, October 10, 1970.
53. Halsey, *Halsey's Story*, 197, 250.
54. Balfour, interview with author, September 4, 1993.
55. Barron (John), interview with author, October 22, 1994; Balfour, interview with author, September 4, 1993.
56. Conner, interview with author, September 1, 1994.
57. Ibid.
58. Murray, interview with Etta-Belle Kitchen, October 10, 1970.
59. Ibid.
60. War diary; Halsey, *Halsey's Story*, 251; Murray, interview with Etta-Belle Kitchen, October 10, 1970.
61. Action report, June 30, 1945; Morison, *Victory*, 298–306; War diary; Murray, interview with Etta-Belle Kitchen, October 10, 1970.
62. Rouse interview, USS *Missouri* oral history project.
63. Barron (John), interview with author, October 22, 1994; Action report, June 30, 1945.
64. Murray, interview with Etta-Belle Kitchen, October 10, 1970.
65. Barron (John), interview with author, October 22, 1994.
66. Ibid.
67. Conner, interview with author, September 1, 1994.
68. Plate, interview with author, December 17, 1994.
69. Ibid.
70. Ibid.
71. Balfour, interview with author, September 4, 1993.
72. Gayler, interview with author, January 30, 1984.
73. Couture, interview with author, September 1, 1994.
74. Action report, July 19, 1945.
75. Plate, interview with author, December 17, 1994.
76. Barron (John and Eleanor), interview with author, October 22, 1994.
77. Action report, July 20, 1945.
78. Ibid.
79. Starnes, interview with author, January 6, 1995.
80. Action report, August 25, 1945.
81. Faulk, interview with Dr. John T. Mason, Jr., November 11, 1974.
82. Action report, August 25, 1945.
83. Ibid.
84. Murray, interview with Etta-Belle Kitchen, February 20, 1971.
85. Action report, August 25, 1945.
86. Morison, *Victory*, 333.
87. Barron (John), interview with author, October 22, 1994.
88. Halsey, *Halsey's Story*, 268–69.
89. Conner, interview with author, September 1, 1994.
90. Halsey, *Halsey's Story*, 272.

Chapter 3—The Surrender

1. Plate, interview with author, December 17, 1994.
2. Action report, August 25, 1945.
3. Conner, interview with author, September 1, 1994.
4. Plate, unpublished recollections.
5. Vella, interview with author, September 2, 1994.
6. Plate, interview with author, December 18, 1994.
7. Harry Truman, *Year of Decisions*, 451.
8. J. C. Truman, letter to Harry Truman, August 18, 1945.
9. Murray, interview with Etta-Belle Kitchen, February 20, 1971.
10. Ibid.
11. Morison, *Victory*, 353–54, 357–58.
12. Barron (John), interview with author, October 22, 1994.
13. *Dictionary*, 416.
14. Barron (John), interview with author, October 22, 1994.
15. Ibid.
16. Ibid.
17. Ibid.
18. Ibid.
19. Kase, *Journey*, 264.
20. Deck log; Balfour, interview with author, September 4, 1993.
21. Halsey, *Halsey's Story*, 275.
22. Faulk, interview with Dr. John T. Mason, Jr., November 11, 1974.
23. Dubensky, interview with author, September 1, 1994.
24. Plate, interview with author, December 18, 1994.
25. Halsey, *Halsey's Story*, 276.
26. Carney, *Proceedings*, December 1983, 41–50.
27. Murray, interview with Etta-Belle Kitchen, February 20, 1971.
28. Bremyer, interview with the Navy Office of Public Information, September 18, 1945.
29. Ibid.
30. Starnes, interview with author, January 6, 1995.

31. Murray, interview with Etta-Belle Kitchen, February 20, 1971.
32. USS *Missouri* plan of the day, September 2, 1945.
33. Cruisebook; *The Missourian*, September 10, 1945; Murray, interview with Etta-Belle Kitchen, February 20, 1971.
34. Mackey, letter to John Mason, January 21, 1987.
35. Circelli, interview with author, September 4, 1994; Mackey, letter to John Mason, January 21, 1987.
36. Starnes, interview with author, January 6, 1995.
37. Plate, interview with author, December 18, 1994.
38. Faulk, interview with Dr. John T. Mason, Jr., November 12, 1974.
39. Murray, interview with Etta-Belle Kitchen, February 20, 1971.
40. Lee, interview with Etta-Belle Kitchen, July 11, 1970.
41. Murray, interview with Etta-Belle Kitchen, February 20, 1971.
42. Kase, *Journey*, 4–5.
43. Ibid., 6.
44. Smith-Hutton, interview with Paul Ryan, October 17, 1974.
45. Schwenk, interview with author, September 3, 1994.
46. Manchester, *American Caesar*, 451.
47. Murray, interview with Etta-Belle Kitchen, February 20, 1971.
48. *Life*, September 17, 1945.
49. Kase, *Journey*, 7.
50. Ibid.; *Life*, September 17, 1945.
51. Kase, *Journey*, 7–9.
52. *Newsweek*, September 10, 1945; Manchester, *American Caesar*, 453.
53. Kase, *Journey*, 1.
54. *Life*, September 17, 1945.
55. Dennison, interview with Dr. John T. Mason, Jr., January 17, 1973.
56. *Life*, September 17, 1945.
57. Mydans, *Life*, April 17, 1964.
58. Murray, interview with Etta-Belle Kitchen, February 20, 1971.
59. Kalisch, *Proceedings*, August 1955, 868–69; Kalisch, interview with author, August 10, 1975.
60. *Newsweek*, September 10, 1945.
61. Conner, interview with author, September 1, 1994; Kase, *Journey*, 10.
62. Halsey, *Halsey's Story*, 283.
63. Starnes, interview with author, January 6, 1995; Balfour, interview with author, September 4, 1993.
64. Yucka, interview with author, September 2, 1994.

Chapter 4—Homecoming

1. Murray, interview with Etta-Belle Kitchen, February 20, 1971.
2. Ibid.
3. Bremyer, interview with the Navy Office of Public Information, September 18, 1945.
4. Conner, interview with author, September 1, 1994.
5. Balfour, interview with author, September 4, 1993.
6. Ibid.
7. War diary; Murray, interview with Etta-Belle Kitchen, March 27, 1971.
8. Faulk, interview with Dr. John T. Mason, Jr., November 12, 1974.
9. Conner, interview with author, September 1, 1994.
10. Ibid.
11. Schwenk, interview with author, September 3, 1994; Murray, interview with Etta-Belle Kitchen, March, 27 1971.
12. Plate, interview with author, December 18, 1994.
13. Schwenk, interview with author, September 3, 1994.
14. Plate, interview with author, December 18, 1994.
15. Schwenk, interview with author, September 3, 1994.
16. Ibid.
17. Ibid.
18. Ibid.
19. Conner, interview with author, September 1, 1994.
20. J. C. Truman, letter to Harry Truman, October 9, 1945.
21. Murray, interview with Etta-Belle Kitchen, March 27, 1971.
22. Plate, interview with author, December 18, 1994.
23. Murray, interview with Etta-Belle Kitchen, March 27, 1971.
24. Hartson, interview with author, January 17, 1995.
25. Ibid.
26. Plate, interview with author, December 18, 1994.
27. Ibid.
28. *New York Times*, October 17, 1945; *Time*, November 5, 1945.
29. Murray, interview with Etta-Belle Kitchen, March 27, 1971.
30. George Elsey file, Presidential Papers, Harry S. Truman Library.
31. *Time*, November 5, 1945; George Elsey, letter to author, November 14, 1994.
32. *New York Times*, October 28, 1945.
33. Hird, interview with author, October 30, 1994.

34. Ibid.
35. Ibid.
36. Daniel, interview with author, November 1, 1994.
37. Hird, interview with author, October 30, 1994.
38. Ibid.
39. Faulk, interview with Dr. John T. Mason, Jr., November 12, 1974.
40. Leibig, interview with author, September 2, 1993; *Time,* November 12, 1945.
41. Murray, interview with Etta-Belle Kitchen, March 27, 1971.
42. Schmidt, interview with author, September 5, 1993.
43. Hartson, interview with author, January 17, 1995.
44. Schmidt, interview with author, September 5, 1993.
45. Hillenkoetter, interview with author, February 26, 1977.
46. Ibid.
47. Johnson (Clarence), interview with author, February 4, 1995.
48. Hillenkoetter, interview with author, February 26, 1977.
49. Faulk, interview with Dr. John T. Mason, Jr., November 12, 1974; *St. Louis Globe-Democrat,* December 18, 1945, and January 7, 1946; Newspaper clippings from Missouri Historical Society.
50. Ibid.
51. Hartson, interview with author, January 17, 1995.
52. Ibid.
53. *The New York Times,* January 29, 1946.
54. Faulk, interview with Dr. John T. Mason, Jr., November 12, 1974.
55. Ibid.
56. Ibid.
57. Ibid.
58. Hartson, interview with author, January 17, 1995.
59. Deck log.
60. Vella, interview with author, September 2, 1994.

Chapter 5—Postwar Diplomat

1. Fisher, *Decision,* 72.
2. McCrea, letter to State Dept., February 7, 1946.
3. Messages in *Missouri* files at Naval Historical Center.
4. Fisher, *Decision,* 69–70, 73.
5. Ibid., 70, 74–76.
6. Ibid., 82, 91, 94.
7. *The New York Times,* March 22, 1946.
8. Hillenkoetter, interview with author, February 26, 1977.
9. Ibid.
10. *St. Louis Post-Dispatch,* April 6, 1946.
11. Ibid.
12. Hartson, interview with author, January 17, 1995; Hillenkoetter, interview with author, February 26, 1977.
13. Faulk, interview with Dr. John T. Mason, Jr., November 12, 1974.
14. Hartson, interview with author, January 17, 1995.
15. Schmidt, interview with author, September 5, 1993.
16. Alessandro, interview with author, January 5, 1995.
17. Ibid.
18. Ibid.
19. Conner, interview with author, September 1, 1994.
20. Hillenkoetter, interview with author, February 26, 1977.
21. Conner, interview with author, September 1, 1994.
22. Faulk, interview with Dr. John T. Mason, November 12, 1974; Albert, interview with author, September 2, 1994.
23. Schmidt, interview with author, September 5, 1993.
24. Ibid.
25. Faulk, interview with Dr. John T. Mason, Jr., November 12, 1974.
26. Wiernik, interview with author, June 25, 1994
27. Merritt, interview with author, February 8, 1995.
28. Klug, interview with author, September 5, 1993.
29. Hill official biography, Naval Historical Center.
30. Merritt, interview with author, February 8, 1995.
31. Schwenk, interview with author, September 3, 1994.
32. Deck log.
33. Merritt, interview with author, February 8, 1995.
34. Deck log.
35. Ibid.; Fletcher, interview with author, September 5, 1993.
36. Travis interview, USS *Missouri* oral history project.
37. Deck log.
38. Dennison, interview with Dr. John T. Mason, Jr., January 17, 1973.
39. Dennison, interview with Dr. John T. Mason, Jr., January 17, 1973.
40. Dennison, interview with Dr. John T. Mason, Jr., January 30, 1973.
41. Ibid.
42. Fletcher, interview with author, September 5, 1993.
43. Merritt, interview with author, February 8, 1995.

44. Colwell, interview with Dr. John T. Mason, Jr., June 14, 1973.
45. Albert, interview with author, September 2, 1994; Klug, interview with author, September 5, 1993.
46. Fletcher, interview with author, September 5, 1993.
47. Margaret Truman, *Truman*, 375.
48. Merritt, interview with author, February 8, 1995.
49. Dennison, interview with Dr. John T. Mason, Jr., January 30, 1973.
50. Daniel, interview with author, November 1, 1994; *Time*, September 22, 1947.
51. Merritt, interview with author, February 8, 1995.
52. Margaret Truman, *Truman*, 380; Rigdon, *Sailor*, 231.
53. Daniel, interview with author, November 1, 1994.
54. Ibid.
55. Colwell, interview with Dr. John T. Mason, Jr., June 14, 1973.
56. Dennison, interview with Dr. John T. Mason, Jr., January 30, 1973; *Time*, September 22, 1947.
57. *Time*, September 22, 1947; Deck log.
58. Margaret Truman, *Truman*, 378.
59. Ibid.
60. Rigdon, *Sailor*, 236–37.
61. Margaret Truman, *Truman*, 379–80; *Time*, September 22, 1947.
62. Margaret Truman, *Truman*, 380.
63. Fletcher, interview with author, September 5, 1993.
64. Klug, interview with author, September 5, 1993.
65. Ibid.; *Time*, September 22, 1947.
66. Travis interview, USS *Missouri* oral history project.

Chapter 6—Training Ship

1. Dennison, interview with John T. Mason, Jr., January 30, 1973.
2. Colwell, interview with Dr. John T. Mason, June 14, 1973.
3. Thach, biography.
4. Colwell, interview with Dr. John T. Mason, June 14, 1973.
5. Thach, letter to author, November 7, 1994.
6. Lee (Alan), interview with author, December 27, 1994.
7. Ibid.
8. Ibid.
9. Ibid.
10. Ibid.
11. Barker, interview with author, September 5, 1993.
12. Williams (John), interview with author, September 5, 1993.
13. Seagren, interview with author, October 29, 1994.
14. Ibid.
15. Ibid.
16. Ibid.
17. Dunn, interview with author, March 15, 1990.
18. Seagren, interview with author, October 29, 1994.
19. Williams (John), interview with author, September 5, 1993.
20. Ibid.
21. Eichenlaub, interview with author, October 6, 1993.
22. Smoot, interview with Etta-Belle Kitchen, February 21, 1971.
23. Ibid.
24. Klug, interview with author, September 5, 1993.
25. Deck log.
26. Graham, interview with author, March 8, 1994.
27. *St. Louis Globe-Democrat*, December 5, 1948.
28. Ibid.; *Time*, December 13, 1948.
29. Thach, letter to author, November 7, 1994.
30. Smith (Harold), interview with author, July 12, 1988.
31. Ibid.
32. Smith (Harold), interview with author, July 12, 1988.
33. Ibid.; Deck log.
34. Hughes, interview with author, September 12, 1994.
35. Ibid.
36. Smith (Harold), interview with author, July 12, 1988.
37. Smith and Newell, *Mighty Mo*, 61.
38. Fisher, interview with author, August 5, 1994.
39. Ibid.
40. Fisher, interview with author, August 5, 1994.
41. Ibid.
42. *St. Louis Post-Dispatch*, June 18, 1949.
43. Royal, interview with author, November 12, 1994.
44. Smith and Newell, *Mighty Mo*, 62.
45. Ibid., 62–63.
46. Hughes, interview with author, September 12, 1994.
47. Ibid.
48. Williams (John), interview with author, September 5, 1993.
49. Smith (Harold), interview with author, July 12, 1988.
50. Fisher, interview with author, August 5, 1994.
51. Koch, interview with author, November 20, 1994.
52. Dolan interview, USS *Missouri* oral history project.

Chapter 7—Aground

1. Brown, official biography, Naval Historical Center.
2. Ibid.
3. Muir, *Naval History* (Fall 1991), 31.
4. Fisher, interview with author, August 5, 1994.
5. Smith and Newell, *Mighty Mo,* 69–70.
6. Ibid., 70.
7. Ibid.
8. Ibid., 70–71.
9. Ibid. 71–72.
10. Deck log.
11. Smith, *Mighty Mo,* 73.
12. Ibid., 73–74; Muir, *Naval History* (Fall 1991), 32.
13. Smith and Newell, *Mighty Mo,* 73–74; Muir, *Naval History* (Fall 1991), 32.
14. Smith and Newell, *Mighty Mo,* 78; Muir, *Naval History* (Fall 1991), 31–32.
15. *The Washington Post,* February 14, 1950; Smith and Newell, *Mighty Mo,* 78; Muir, *Naval History* (Fall 1991), 32.
16. Travis interview, USS *Missouri* oral history project.
17. Koch, interview with author, November 20, 1994.
18. Ibid.
19. Eichenlaub, interview with author, October 6, 1993.
20. Drachnik, letter to author, September 3, 1991; Smith and Newell, *Mighty Mo,* 79.
21. Smoot, interview with Etta-Belle Kitchen, March 21, 1971; BuShips, "Refloating," 3.
22. Smoot, interview with Etta-Belle Kitchen, March 21, 1971.
23. Ibid.
24. Little, telegram to White House, January 18, 1950.
25. Smith and Newell, *Mighty Mo,* 81–82.
26. Weschler, interview with author, February 23, 1983.
27. Ibid.
28. Goffredo, interview with author, September 3, 1993.
29. Lee (Warren), interview with author, September 5, 1993.
30. Ibid.
31. Ibid.
32. Smoot, interview with Etta-Belle Kitchen, March 21, 1971.
33. Williams (John), interview with author, September 5, 1993.
34. Foley, unpublished manuscript.
35. Ibid.
36. Smoot, interview with Etta-Belle Kitchen, March 21, 1971.
37. BuShips, "Refloating," 13–14, 33–34.
38. Smoot, interview with Etta-Belle Kitchen, March 21, 1971.
39. Weschler, interview with author, February 23, 1983.
40. Goffredo, interview with author, September 3, 1993; BuShips, "Refloating," 14
41. Smoot, interview with Etta-Belle Kitchen, March 21, 1971.
42. Weschler, interview with author, February 23, 1983.
43. *The Washington Post,* February 14, 1950.
44. *Washington Times-Herald,* February 19, 1950.
45. *Washington Times-Herald,* February 21, 1950.
46. (Washington) *Evening Star,* February 28, 1950.
47. Ibid.
48. Muir, *Naval History* (Fall 1991), 34–35; Smith (Harold), interview with author, July 12, 1988.
49. Smoot, interview with Etta-Belle Kitchen, March 21, 1971.
50. Smith (Harold), interview with author, July 12, 1988.
51. Koch, interview with author, November 20, 1994.
52. Muir, *Naval History* (Fall 1991), 34.
53. Fisher, interview with author, August 5, 1994.
54. Ibid.
55. Fisher, interview with author, August 5, 1994.
56. Smith (Harold), interview with author, July 12, 1988.
57. Ibid.
58. Ibid.
59. *St. Louis Post-Dispatch,* February 15, 1950.
60. *New York Herald Tribune,* February 2, 1950.
61. Smith (Harold), interview with author, July 12, 1988.
62. Giles, interview with author, November 2, 1994.

Chapter 8—The Korean War Begins

1. Hammond, interview with author, November 3, 1994.
2. Lawrence, interview with author, September 19, 1990.
3. Deck log; Royal, interview with author, November 12, 1994.
4. Royal, interview with author, November 12, 1994.
5. Ibid.
6. Giles, interview with author, November 2, 1994; War diary.
7. O'Malley, interview with author, September 3, 1994.
8. Royal, interview with author, November 12, 1994; *Missouri* storm damage report, August 23, 1950 (hereafter Storm damage report).
9. Giles, interview with author, November 2, 1994.
10. Storm damage report.
11. Ibid.
12. Royal, interview with author, November 19,

1994; Travis, interview with author, February 16, 1995.

13. Ibid.

14. War diary.

15. Royal, interview with author, November 12, 1994.

16. Ibid.

17. War diary.

18. Royal, interview with author, November 12, 1994.

19. Ibid.

20. Debenedetto interview, USS *Missouri* oral history project.

21. Field, *Korea*, 212; Karig, Cagle, and Manson, *Battle Report*, 244–45; Action report, October 1, 1950.

22. Karig, Cagle, and Manson, *Battle Report*, 254–55.

23. Giles, interview with author, February 16, 1995.

24. Cagle and Manson, *Sea War*, 108.

25. Giles, interview with author, November 2, 1994.

26. Royal, interview with author, November 12, 1994.

27. Ibid.

28. Ibid.

29. Karig, Cagle, and Manson, *Battle Report* 336.

30. Ibid., 338.

31. War diary.

32. Karig, Cagle, and Manson, *Battle Report* 332.

33. Manson, interview with author, December 10, 1987.

34. Lee (Warren), interview with author, September 5, 1993.

35. Ibid.

36. Giles, interview with author, November 2, 1994.

37. Royal, interview with author, November 12, 1994.

38. Giles, interview with author, November 2, 1994.

39. Eichenlaub, interview with author, October 6, 1993.

40. Royal, interview with author, November 19, 1994.

41. Ibid.

42. Koch, interview with author, November 20, 1994.

43. Ibid.

44. Giles, interview with author, November 2, 1994.

45. Royal, interview with author, November 12, 1994.

46. Eichenlaub, interview with author, October 6, 1993.

47. Giles, interview with author, November 2, 1994.

48. Royal, interview with author, November 19, 1994.

49. Lee (Warren), interview with author, September 5, 1993.

50. Giles, interview with author, November 2, 1994.

51. Ibid.

52. Royal, interview with author, February 16, 1995.

53. Ibid.

54. Ibid.

55. Houghton interview, USS *Missouri* oral history project.

56. Royal, interview with author, February 16, 1995.

57. Ibid.

58. Ibid.

59. Ibid.

60. Wright, official biography, Naval Historical Center; Giles, interview with author, February 16, 1995.

61. Houghton interview, USS *Missouri* oral history project.

62. Royal, interview with author, November 12, 1994.

63. Giles, interview with author, February 16, 1995

64. Royal, interview with author, November 19, 1994.

65. Ibid.

66. Giles, interview with author, February 16, 1995

Chapter 9—Midshipmen and More Korea

1. Thumudo, interview with author, September 1, 1994.

2. Ibid.

3. Hessman, interview with author, October 4, 1994.

4. Ibid.

5. Ibid.

6. Houghton interview, USS *Missouri* oral history project.

7. Travis, interview with author, February 16, 1995; Hessman, interview with author, October 4, 1994.

8. Hessman, interview with author, October 4, 1994.

9. Ibid.

10. Ibid.

11. Ibid.

12. Ibid.

13. Ibid.

14. Treadwell, interview with author, February 25, 1995.

15. Ibid.

16. Ibid.

17. Ibid.

18. Deck log; Eichenlaub, interview with author, October 6, 1993.

19. Eichenlaub, interview with author, October 6, 1993.

20. Deck log.

21. Treadwell, interview with author, February 25, 1995.
22. Reisig, interview with author, January 17, 1995.
23. Thumudo, interview with author, September 1, 1994.
24. Clem, interview with author, September 1, 1994; Thumudo, interview with author, September 1, 1994.
25. Houghton interview, USS *Missouri* oral history project.
26. Treadwell, interview with author, February 25, 1995.
27. Deck log.
28. Treadwell, interview with author, February 25, 1995; Sylvester, official biography, Naval Historical Center.
29. Holcomb, interview with author, February 16, 1995.
30. Ibid.
31. Treadwell, interview with author, February 25, 1995; Giles, interview with author, November 2, 1994.
32. Holcomb, interview with author, February 16, 1995.
33. Nau interview, USS *Missouri* oral history project.
34. Travis interview, USS *Missouri* oral history project.
35. Thumudo, interview with author, September 1, 1994.
36. Holcomb, interview with author, February 16, 1995.
37. Ibid.
38. Ibid.
39. Ibid.
40. Reisig, interview with author, January 17, 1995.
41. Ibid.
42. Edsall, official biography, Naval Historical Center.
43. Deck log.
44. Treadwell, interview with author, February 25, 1995.
45. Smith (Harry), interview with author, February 20, 1995.
46. Ibid.; Smith (Harry), interview with author, February 23, 1995.
47. McCarron, interview with author, February 18, 1995.
48. Ibid.
49. Ibid.
50. Smith (Harry), interview with author, February 20, 1995.
51. Ibid.
52. Ibid.
53. McHugh interview, USS *Missouri* oral history project.
54. Allen interview, USS *Missouri* oral history project.
55. Ibid.
56. McHugh interview, USS *Missouri* oral history project.
57. Smith (Harry), interview with author, February 20, 1995.
58. Thumudo, interview with author, September 1, 1994.
59. Ibid.
60. Ibid.
61. Treadwell, interview with author, February 25, 1995.
62. Smith (Harry), interview with author, February 20, 1995.
63. War diary; Action report, January 25, 1953.
64. Smith (Harry), interview with author, February 23, 1995; Travis interview, USS *Missouri* oral history project.
65. Smith (Harry), interview with author, February 20, 1995.
66. Zeldes, interview with author, February 22, 1995.
67. McCarron interview, USS *Missouri* oral history project.
68. McCarron, interview with author, February 18, 1995.
69. Treadwell, interview with author, February 25, 1995.
70. Ibid.
71. Ward, interview with author, February 23, 1995.
72. Smith (Harry), interview with author, February 20, 1995; War diary; Action report, April 28, 1953.
73. Ward, interview with author, February 23, 1995.
74. Ibid.; Action report, May 8, 1953; War diary.
75. Zeldes, interview with author, February 22, 1995.
76. Ibid.
77. Ibid.
78. The totals for the 1952–53 deployment were derived by adding together the daily ammunition expenditures recorded in individual action reports.
79. Ward, interview with author, February 23, 1995; Mrs. Sybil-Carmen North, letter to author, January 31, 1995; Treadwell, interview with author, February 25, 1995.
80. Travis interview, USS *Missouri* oral history project.
81. Ward, interview with author, February 23, 1995.
82. Ibid.; Brodie, official biography, Naval Historical Center.
83. Houghton interview, USS *Missouri* oral history project.

Chapter 10—The Long Farewell

1. Rogers, unpublished manuscript.
2. Ibid.
3. Ibid.
4. Ibid.
5. Ibid.
6. Ibid.
7. Smith (Harry), interview with author, February 20, 1995.
8. O'Malley, interview with author, September 3, 1994.
9. Ibid.
10. Smith (Harry), interview with author, February 20, 1995.
11. Rogers, unpublished manuscript; Deck log.
12. Ibid.
13. Zeldes, interview with author, February 22, 1995.
14. Williams (Daniel), interview with author, February 26, 1995.
15. Williams (Daniel), interview with author, February 28, 1995.
16. *The New York Times,* March 29, 1954.
17. Ibid.
18. Clark, interview with author, February 26, 1995.
19. Keith, interview with author, January 13, 1987.
20. Ibid.
21. Roth, interview with author, September 5, 1993.
22. Fahr, interview with author, September 3, 1993.
23. Clark, interview with author, February 26, 1995.
24. Koenninger, interview with author, February 27, 1995.
25. Clark, interview with author, February 26, 1995.
26. Koenninger, interview with author, February 27, 1995.
27. Ibid.
28. Ibid.
29. Ibid.
30. Fahr, interview with author, September 3, 1993.
31. Keith, interview with author, January 13, 1987.
32. Ibid.
33. Fahr, interview with author, September 3, 1993.
34. Williams (Daniel), interview with author, February 26 1995.
35. Ibid.
36. Ibid; Williams (Daniel), interview with author, February 28, 1995.
37. Renner, interview with author, February 25, 1995.
38. Ibid.
39. *The Jerseyman,* July 23, 1954.
40. Keith, interview with author, January 13, 1987.
41. Ibid.
42. Fahr, interview with author, September 3, 1993.
43. Ibid.
44. Keith, interview with author, January 13, 1987.
45. O'Malley, interview with author, September 3, 1994.
46. Renner, interview with author, February 25, 1995.
47. Ibid.
48. *Norfolk Virginian-Pilot,* August 24, 1954.
49. Williams (Daniel), interview with author, February 26, 1995.
50. Ibid.
51. Ibid.
52. Fahr, interview with author, September 3, 1993.
53. Ibid.; Keith, interview with author, January 13, 1987.
54. Keith, interview with author, January 13, 1987.
55. Ibid.
56. Williams (Daniel), interview with author, February 26, 1995.
57. *Seattle Post-Intelligencer,* September 16, 1954.
58. Williams (Daniel), interview with author, February 26, 1995.
59. Clark, interview with author, February 26, 1995.
60. Ibid.
61. Fahr, interview with author, September 3, 1993.
62. Ibid.
63. Williams (Daniel), interview with author, February 26, 1995.
64. Ibid.
65. Smith and Newell, *Mighty Mo,* 138; Deck log.
66. Deck log.
67. *Seattle Post-Intelligencer,* February 27, 1955.
68. Clark, interview with author, February 26, 1995.
69. Williams (Daniel), interview with author, February 26, 1995.

Chapter 11—Mothballs

1. Kohrt, interview with author, December 4, 1994.
2. Smith and Newell, *Mighty Mo,* 144.
3. Ibid.
4. Spencer, *St. Louis Globe-Democrat,* August 28, 1955.
5. *The Salute,* September 14, 1956.
6. Harry Truman, letter to John Connally, August 29, 1961.
7. Dunsire, *Seattle Post-Intelligencer,* January 8, 1963.
8. *Kansas City Star,* April 4, 1963.
9. Weller, *Seattle Times,* September 3, 1963.
10. Landgraff, interview with author, March 7, 1995; *Salute,* August 27, 1976.
11. "Changing the Guard," *Winds of War.*
12. Stillwell, unpublished manuscript.
13. Ibid.
14. Ibid.

15. Kohrt, interview with author, December 4, 1994.
16. Ibid.
17. Ibid.
18. Ibid.
19. Ibid.
20. Ibid.
21. Ibid.
22. Ibid.
23. Ehlert, interview with author, December 5, 1994.
24. Ibid.
25. Ibid.
26. Ibid.
27. Ibid.
28. Ibid.
29. *The Trentonian*, September 2, 1984.

Chapter 12—Around the World

1. *Los Angeles Times*, May 26, 1984.
2. O'Malley, interview with author, September 3, 1994.
3. Ibid.
4. Stillwell, "Battleships" in George, *The U.S. Navy*, 103–5.
5. Ibid., 114–16.
6. Kaiss, interview with author, December 3, 1991.
7. Kaiss, official biography; Kaiss, interview with author, December 3, 1991.
8. Kaiss, interview with author, December 3, 1991.
9. Holland, interview with author, January 21, 1995.
10. Webber, interview with author, December 4, 1991.
11. Lewis, interview with author, December 3, 1991.
12. Ibid.
13. Ibid.; Holland, interview with author, January 21, 1995.
14. Holland, interview with author, January 21, 1995.
15. Landgraff, letter to author, November 3, 1994.
16. Ibid.
17. Ibid.
18. Landgraff, letter to author, November 3, 1994.
19. Landgraff, letter to author, January 3, 1995.
20. Ibid.
21. Landgraff, letter to author, November 3, 1994.
22. Ibid.
23. Kaiss, interview with author, December 3, 1991.
24. McDermott, interview with author, February 18, 1995.
25. Ibid.

26. Holland, interview with author, January 21, 1995.
27. Ibid.
28. Lewis, interview with author, December 3, 1991; Kaiss, interview with author, December 3, 1991.
29. Ibid.
30. Kaiss, interview with author, December 3, 1991.
31. Ibid.; Holland, interview with author, January 21, 1995.
32. Stockton, interview with author, December 1, 1991.
33. McDermott, interview with author, February 18, 1995; Kaiss, interview with author, December 3, 1991.
34. Lewis, interview with author, December 3, 1991.
35. *Time*, June 2, 1986.
36. Kaiss, interview with author, December 3, 1991.
37. Lewis, interview with author, December 3, 1991.
38. Kaiss, interview with author, December 3, 1991; Carney, interview with author, March 22, 1995.
39. Egan, interview with author, January 28, 1995.
40. Ibid.
41. McDermott, interview with author, February 18, 1995.
42. Holland, interview with author, January 21, 1995.
43. Lewis, interview with author, December 3, 1991; McDermott, interview with author, February 18, 1995.
44. Fahr, interview with author, September 3, 1993.
45. Kaiss, interview with author, December 3, 1991.
46. Carney, interview with author, February 4, 1993.
47. Carney, official biography.
48. Lewis, interview with author, December 3, 1991.
49. McDermott, interview with author, February 18, 1995; Holland, interview with author, January 21, 1995.
50. McDermott, interview with author, February 18, 1995.
51. Carney, interview with author, February 4, 1993.
52. Ibid.
53. McDermott, interview with author, February 18, 1995; *Honolulu Star-Bulletin*, September 20, 1986; USS *Missouri* official history, 1986.
54. Carney, interview with author, February 4, 1993.
55. Lewis, interview with author, December 3, 1991.

56. Anderson, interview with author, December 3, 1994.

57. Ibid.

58. Anderson, interview with author, December 3, 1994.

59. Carney, interview with author, February 4, 1993.

60. Ibid.

61. Egan, interview with author, January 28, 1995; Webber, interview with author, December 4, 1991; Carney, interview with author, February 4, 1993.

62. Lewis, interview with author, December 3, 1991.

63. Egan, interview with author, January 28, 1995.

64. McDermott, interview with author, February 18, 1995.

65. Ibid.

66. Ibid.

67. *Who's Who in America, 1993–94.*

68. McDermott, interview with author, February 18, 1995.

69. Carney, interview with author, February 4, 1993.

70. Ibid.

71. Lewis, interview with author, December 3, 1991.

72. McDermott, interview with author, February 18, 1995.

73. Carney, interview with author, February 4, 1993; McDermott, interview with author, February 18, 1995.

74. McDermott, interview with author, February 18, 1995.

75. Carney, interview with author, February 4, 1993.

76. McDermott, interview with author, February 18, 1995.

Chapter 13—With the Fleet Again

1. USS *Missouri* command history (hereafter Command history), 1987.

2. *Long Beach Navy Dispatch,* April 30, 1987.

3. Lewis, interview with author, December 3, 1991.

4. McDermott, interview with author, February 18, 1995.

5. *Proceedings,* May 1988, 30–34.

6. McDermott, interview with author, February 18, 1995.

7. Carney, interview with author, February 4, 1993.

8. Ibid.; Command history, 1987.

9. Carney, interview with author, March 22, 1995.

10. Walker, interview with author, October 19, 1992.

11. Ibid.

12. Carney, interview with author, February 4, 1993; Command history, 1987.

13. Price, interview with author, December 3, 1991.

14. Walker, interview with author, October 19, 1992.

15. Carney, interview with author, February 4, 1993.

16. Holland, interview with author, January 21, 1995.

17. Walker, interview with author, October 19, 1992.

18. Carney, interview with author, February 4, 1993.

19. Ibid.

20. Ibid.

21. Ibid.

22. Ibid.

23. Webber, interview with author, December 4, 1991.

24. Command history, 1987.

25. Walker, interview with author, October 19, 1992.

26. Egan, interview with author, January 28, 1995.

27. Ibid.

28. Ibid.

29. Ibid.

30. Walker, interview with author, October 19, 1992.

31. Ibid.; Egan, interview with author, January 28, 1995.

32. Walker, interview with author, October 19, 1992.

33. Webber, interview with author, December 4, 1991.

34. Holland, interview with author, January 21, 1995.

35. Command history, 1988.

36. Walker, interview with author, October 19, 1992.

37. Command history, 1988.

38. Chernesky, official biography, Naval Historical Center.

39. Chernesky, interview with author, October 12, 1994.

40. Ibid.

41. Walker, interview with author, October 19, 1992.

42. Price, interview with author, December 3, 1991; Walker, interview with author, October 19, 1992.

43. Walker, interview with author, October 19, 1992.

44. Ibid.

45. Price, interview with author, December 3, 1991.

46. *Navy Times,* January 11, 1988; *Long Beach Press-Telegram,* March 29, 1989.

47. Command history, 1988.
48. *Broadside,* September 1989.
49. Frank, interview with author, December 17, 1994; *Broadside,* May, June–July 1989.
50. Chernesky, interview with author, April 11, 1995.
51. Hofman, interview with author, December 3, 1991.
52. Ibid.
53. Holland, interview with author, January 21, 1995; Raskin, interview with author, December 1, 1991.
54. Frank, interview with author, December 17, 1994.
55. Mobilia, interview with author, August 28, 1994.
56. Ibid.
57. Walker, interview with author, October 19, 1992.
58. Ibid.
59. Ibid.; Anderson and Van Atta, *The Washington Post,* January 5, 1990.
60. Chernesky, interview with author, October 12, 1994.
61. O'Malley, interview with author, September 3, 1994; Chernesky, letter to Robert Kaplan, August 25, 1989.
62. Walker, interview with author, October 19, 1992.
63. Chernesky, interview with author, October 12, 1994.
64. Farmer, interview with author, December 2, 1991.
65. Taylor, interview with author, December 2, 1991.
66. Ibid.
67. Command history, 1989.
68. Mobilia, interview with author, August 28, 1994; Hofman, interview with author, December 3, 1991.
69. Chernesky, interview with author, October 12, 1994.
70. Ibid.
71. Frank, interview with author, December 17, 1994.
72. Ibid.
73. Command history, 1989.
74. Woodard, interview with author, December 4, 1991.
75. *Broadside,* April 1990.
76. Mobilia, interview with author, August 28, 1994.
77. Ibid.
78. Stockton, interview with author, December 1, 1991.
79. Frank, interview with author, December 17, 1994.
80. Chesser, interview with author, August 18, 1994; Allen, letter to author, February 3, 1995.
81. Holland, interview with author, January 21, 1995.

Chapter 14—Desert Storm

1. Kaiss, official biography; Carney, interview with author, February 4, 1993; Kaiss, interview with author, December 3, 1991.
2. Kaiss, interview with author, December 3, 1991.
3. Command history, 1990; *Navy Times,* September 17, 1990; Kaiss, interview with author, December 3, 1991.
4. Kaiss, interview with author, December 3, 1991.
5. Kaiss, interview with author, March 18, 1995.
6. Ibid.
7. Hofman, interview with author, December 3, 1991; Price, interview with author, December 3, 1991.
8. Kaiss, interview with author, March 18, 1995.
9. Bergren, interview with author, December 4, 1991.
10. Ibid.
11. Ibid.
12. Wilson, interview with author, December 4, 1991.
13. Chesser, interview with author, August 18, 1994.
14. Stockton, interview with author, December 1, 1991.
15. Price, interview with author, December 3, 1991.
16. Hofman, interview with author, December 3, 1991; "Meeting the Challenge," videotape.
17. Command history, 1991.
18. Wilson, interview with author, December 4, 1991.
19. Wilson and Crozier, interview with author, December 4, 1991.
20. Wilson, interview with author, December 4, 1991.
21. Tucker, interview with author, December 4, 1991.
22. Frank, interview with author, December 17, 1994.
23. Hofman, interview with author, December 3, 1991.
24. "Meeting the Challenge," videotape.
25. Finn, interview with author, December 1, 1991.
26. Carey, interview with author, December 2, 1991; Raskin, interview with author, December 1, 1991.
27. Finn, interview with author, December 1, 1991.
28. Mobilia, interview with author, August 28, 1994; Hofman, interview with author, December 3, 1991.
29. *Broadside,* February–March 1991.

30. Caffey, interview with author, December 4, 1991.
31. Marchese, interview with author, December 4, 1991; Mobilia, interview with author, August 28, 1994; Hays, interview with author, December 4, 1991.
32. Mobilia, interview with author, August 28, 1994.
33. Carey, interview with author, December 2, 1991; Finn, interview with author, December 1, 1991.
34. Mobilia, interview with author, March 15, 1995.
35. Tucker, interview with author, December 4, 1991.
36. Dreier, interview with author, December 3, 1991.
37. Taylor, interview with author, December 2, 1991.
38. Finn, interview with author, December 1, 1991.
39. Jordan, interview with author, March 12, 1995.
40. Ibid.; Mobilia, interview with author, August 28, 1994.
41. Roswell, interview with author, January 14, 1995; Jordan, interview with author, March 12, 1995; Price, interview with author, December 3, 1991.
42. Marchese, interview with author, December 4, 1991.
43. Tucker, interview with author, December 4, 1991.
44. Farmer, interview with author, December 2, 1991.
45. Price, interview with author, December 3, 1991.
46. Nickols, interview with author, February 3, 1995.
47. Green, interview with author, December 1, 1991.
48. Nickols, interview with author, February 3, 1995.
49. Bulkeley, interview with author, January 29, 1995.
50. Ibid.
51. Carey, interview with author, December 2, 1991; Bulkeley, interview with author, January 29, 1995.
52. Bulkeley, interview with author, January 29, 1995; Nickols, interview with author, February 3, 1995.
53. Bulkeley, interview with author, January 29, 1995.
54. Finn, interview with author, December 1, 1991.
55. Ibid.
56. Carey, interview with author, December 2, 1991.
57. Raskin, interview with author, December 1, 1991.
58. Kaiss, interview with author, March 18, 1995.
59. Ibid.
60. Finn, interview with author, December 1, 1991.
61. Carey, interview with author, December 2, 1991.
62. Kaiss, interview with author, March 18, 1995.
63. Green, interview with author, December 1, 1991.
64. Stockton, interview with author, December 1, 1991.
65. Bulkeley, interview with author, January 29, 1995.
66. Kaiss, interview with author, March 18, 1995.
67. Ibid.; Raskin, interview with author, December 1, 1991.
68. Raskin, interview with author, December 1, 1991.
69. Ibid.
70. Rhoden, interview with author, December 3, 1991.
71. Mobilia, interview with author, March 15, 1995; Bulkeley, interview with author, January 29, 1995.
72. Stockton, interview with author, December 1, 1991.
73. Bulkeley, interview with author, January 29, 1995.
74. Ibid.
75. Ibid.
76. Marchese, interview with author, December 4, 1991.
77. Tucker, interview with author, December 4, 1991.
78. Ibid.
79. Price, interview with author, December 3, 1991.
80. Taylor, interview with author, December 2, 1991.
81. Stockton, interview with author, December 1, 1991; Marchese, interview with author, December 4, 1991.
82. Bulkeley, interview with author, January 29, 1995.
83. Finn, interview with author, December 1, 1991.
84. Ibid.
85. Ibid.
86. Carey, interview with author, December 2, 1991.
87. Mobilia, interview with author, August 28, 1994.
88. Kaiss, interview with author, December 3, 1991.
89. Mobilia, interview with author, August 28, 1994.
90. Ibid.
91. Ibid.
92. Nickols, interview with author, February 3, 1995.
93. Mobilia, interview with author, August 28, 1994.
94. Hofman, interview with author, December 3, 1991.

95. Roswell, interview with author, January 14, 1995.
96. Price, interview with author, December 3, 1991.
97. Finn, interview with author, December 1, 1991.
98. Green, interview with author, December 1, 1991.
99. Ibid.
100. Chesser, interview with author, August 18, 1994.
101. Kaiss, interview with author, March 18, 1995.
102. Price, interview with author, December 3, 1991.

Chapter 15—The Last Battleship

1. Mobilia, interview with author, August 28, 1994; Finn, interview with author, December 1, 1991.
2. Mobilia, interview with author, August 28, 1994.
3. Caffey, interview with author, December 4, 1991.
4. Kaiss, interview with author, December 3, 1991.
5. Hofman, interview with author, December 3, 1991.
6. Ibid.
7. Ibid.
8. Kaiss, interview with author, March 18, 1995.
9. Carman, interview with author, December 4, 1991.
10. Ibid.
11. Mobilia, interview with author, August 28, 1994.
12. Ibid.
13. Ibid.
14. Alpert, interview with author, December 4, 1991.
15. Ibid.
16. Ibid.
17. Jordan, interview with author, March 12, 1995.
18. Stockton, interview with author, December 1, 1991.
19. Ibid.
20. *St. Louis Post-Dispatch Magazine,* February 16, 1992, 6.
21. Carey, interview with author, December 2, 1991.
22. Lewis, interview with author, December 3, 1991.
23. Command history, 1991; *St. Louis Post-Dispatch Magazine,* February 16, 1992, 7–8.

24. *St. Louis Post-Dispatch Magazine,* February 16, 1992, 11.
25. Mobilia, interview with author, August 28, 1994.
26. Kaiss, interview with author, March 18, 1995; Nickols, interview with author, February 3, 1995.
27. Jordan, interview with author, March 12, 1995.
28. Kaiss, interview with author, March 18, 1995; Nickols, interview with author, February 3, 1995.
29. Mobilia, interview with author, August 28, 1994.
30. Chesser, interview with author, August 18, 1994.
31. Ibid.
32. Holland, interview with author, January 21, 1995.
33. Carman, interview with author, December 4, 1991.
34. Mobilia, interview with author, August 28, 1994.
35. Hays, interview with author, December 4, 1991.
36. Finn, interview with author, December 1, 1991.
37. Webber, interview with author, December 4, 1991.
38. Jordan, interview with author, March 12, 1995.
39. Mobilia, interview with author, August 28, 1994.
40. Ibid.; Jordan, interview with author, March 12, 1995.
41. Leibig, interview with author, September 2, 1993.
42. Nickols, interview with author, February 3, 1995.
43. Kaiss, interview with author, March 18, 1995.
44. Seavers, interview with author, September 5, 1993.
45. Ahl and Ehlert, interview with author, December 5, 1994.
46. Ibid.
47. Ibid.
48. Ibid.
49. Battleship *New Jersey* Historical Museum Society *Newsletter,* January 1995, contains a copy of the official strike document.
50. "Three Cities Wage One Last Battle for the Mighty Mo," *The Olympian,* September 3, 1995.
51. "Symbols of the End," *The Sun* (West Puget Sound), September 3, 1995.
52. Tucker, interview with author, December 4, 1991.

Sources

Interviews with Author

Albert, Machinist's Mate Arthur C., Sr., USN (Ret.), at San Antonio, Texas, September 2, 1994.

Alessandro, Tony, on board the USS *Missouri* at sea, December 1, 1991, and by telephone, January 5, 1995.

Alpert, Fire Controlman Third Class Larry, USN, on board the USS *Missouri* at sea, December 4, 1991.

Anderson, Commander Robert, USN, at Seattle, Washington, December 3, 1994.

Balfour, Robert, at Kissimmee, Florida, September 4, 1993.

Barker, Lander F., Jr., at Kissimmee, Florida, September 5, 1993.

Barron, Eleanor McDonald, at Annapolis, Maryland, October 22, 1994.

Barron, John C., at Annapolis, Maryland, October 22, 1994.

Bergren, Lieutenant Commander Richard J., USN, on board the USS *Missouri* at sea, December 4, 1991.

Bulkeley, Captain Peter W., USN, by telephone, January 29, 1995.

Caffey, Master Chief Journalist John L., USN, on board the USS *Missouri* at sea, December 4, 1991.

Carey, Lieutenant Ralph W., USN, on board the USS *Missouri* at sea, December 2, 1991.

Carman, Commander Kevin R., SC, USN, on board the USS *Missouri* at sea, December 4, 1991.

Carney, Captain James A., USN (Ret.), at Alexandria, Virginia, February 4, 1993, and by telephone, March 22, 1995.

Chernesky, Captain John J., USN, by telephone, October 12, 1994, and April 11, 1995.

Chesser, Lieutenant Commander Steven B., USN (Ret.), by telephone, August 18, 1994.

Chinn, Mrs. Carol, by telephone, October 27, 1994.

Circelli, Albert, at Kissimmee, Florida, September 4, 1993.

Clark, Commander Willard H., Jr., USN (Ret.), by telephone, February 26, 1995.

Clem, Norman, at San Antonio, Texas, September 1, 1994.

Conner, Richard, at San Antonio, Texas, September 1, 1994.

Couture, Roland O., at San Antonio, Texas, September 1, 1994.

Daniel, Margaret Truman, at New York City, November 1, 1994.

Dreier, Lieutenant Armin F., USN, on board the USS *Missouri* at sea, December 3, 1991.

Dubensky, John A., at San Antonio, Texas, September 1, 1994.

Dunn, Vice Admiral Robert F., USN (Ret.), at Annapolis, Maryland, March 15, 1990, U.S. Naval Institute oral history program.

Egan, Journalist First Class William, USNR (Ret.), by telephone, January 28, 1995.

Ehlert, Harry, at Bremerton, Washington, December 5, 1994.

Eichenlaub, Robert, at Annapolis, Maryland, October 6, 1993.

Fahr, Herbert, Jr., at Kissimmee, Florida, September 3, 1993.

Farmer, Chief Gunner's Mate Carl, USN, on board the USS *Missouri* at sea, December 2, 1991.

Finn, Lieutenant Commander Michael, USN, on board the USS *Missouri* at sea, December 1, 1991.

Fisher, Captain Allan J., SC, USN (Ret.), at Coronado, California, August 5, 1994.

Fletcher, Eddie, at Kissimmee, Florida, September 4, 1993.

Frank, Captain Joe Lee, USN, by telephone, December 17, 1994.

Gayler, Admiral Noel A. M., USN (Ret.), at Washington, D.C., January 30, 1984, U.S. Naval Institute oral history program.

Giles, Donald T., Jr., at Annapolis, Maryland, November 2, 1994, and by telephone, February 16, 1995.

Goffredo, Angelo, at Kissimmee, Florida, September 3, 1993.

Graham, Staff Sergeant Robert D., Army National Guard (Ret.), at St. Charles, Missouri, March 8, 1994.

Green, Ship's Serviceman First Class Gregory, USN, on board the USS *Missouri* (BB-63) at sea, December 1, 1991.

Hartson, Almon C., by telephone, January 17, 1995.

Hays, Lieutenant Verlyn R., SC, USN, on board the USS *Missouri* at sea, December 4, 1991.

Hessman, James, by telephone, October 4, 1994.

Hillenkoetter, Vice Admiral Roscoe H., USN (Ret.), at Weehawken, New Jersey, February 26, 1977.

Hird, John II, by telephone, October 30, 1994.

Hofman, Master Chief Personnelman Timothy C., USN, on board the USS *Missouri* at sea, December 3, 1991.

Holcomb, Vice Admiral M. Staser, USN (Ret.), by telephone, February 16, 1995.

Holland, Chief Machinist's Mate William, USN, by telephone, January 21, 1995.

Hughes, Captain Wayne P., USN (Ret.), by telephone, September 12, 1994.

Johnson, Captain Herbert L., SC, USN (Ret.), by telephone, January 14, 1995.

Johnson, Chief Quartermaster Clarence E., USN (Ret.), by telephone, February 4, 1995.

Jordan, Captain Kenneth S., USN, by telephone, March 12, 1995.

Kaiss, Captain Albert Lee, USN/USN (Ret.), on board the USS *Missouri* at sea, December 3, 1991, and by telephone, March 18, 1995.

Kalisch, Colonel Bertram, USA (Ret.), at Brandywine, Maryland, August 10, 1975.

Keith, Vice Admiral Robert T. S., USN (Ret.), at Coronado, California, January 13, 1987, U.S. Naval Institute oral history program.

Klug, Richard C., at Kissimmee, Florida, September 5, 1993.

Koch, F. Ludwig, Jr., by telephone, November 20, 1994.

Koenninger, Tom, by telephone, February 27, 1995.

Kohrt, Senior Chief Hull Technician Larry, USN (Ret.), at Bremerton, Washington, December 4, 1994.

Landgraff, Richard A., by telephone, March 7, 1995.

Lawrence, Vice Admiral William P., USN (Ret.), at Annapolis, Maryland, September 19, 1990, U.S. Naval Institute oral history program.

Lee, Commander Alan S., USN (Ret.), by telephone, December 27, 1994.

Lee, Warren, at Kissimmee, Florida, September 5, 1993.

Leibig, Herman B., at Kissimmee, Florida, September 2, 1993.

Lewis, Yeoman Second Class John, USN, on board the USS *Missouri* at sea, December 3, 1991.

McCarron, Chief Gunner John, USN (Ret.), by telephone, February 18, 1995.

McDermott, Lieutenant Commander Michael R., USN, by telephone, February 18, 1995.

Manson, Captain Frank A., USN (Ret.), at Annapolis, Maryland, December 10, 1987, U.S. Naval Institute oral history program.

Marchese, Lieutenant Commander Henry, USN, on board the USS *Missouri* at sea, December 4, 1991.

Merritt, Captain Robert G., USN (Ret.), by telephone, February 8, 1995.

Miller, Captain Richards T., USN (Ret.), at Annapolis, Maryland, January 24, 1993.

Mobilia, Lieutenant Commander Ross F. at Arnold, Maryland, August 28, 1994, and by telephone, March 15, 1995.

Nickols, Captain James, CHC, USN, by telephone, February 3, 1995.

O'Malley, Martin T., at San Antonio, Texas, September 3, 1994.

Plate, Vice Admiral Douglas C., USN (Ret.), by telephone, December 17 and 18, 1994.

Price, Journalist Second Class Gary, USN, on board the USS *Missouri* at sea, December 3, 1991.

Raskin, Lieutenant (junior grade) Joseph, USNR, on board the USS *Missouri* at sea, December 1, 1991.

Reisig, Richard, by telephone, January 17, 1995.

Renner, Gerald, by telephone, February 25, 1995.

Rhoden, Lieutenant Horace O., USN, on board the USS *Missouri* at sea, December 3, 1991.

Roswell, Master Chief Machinist's Mate James D., USN (Ret.), by telephone, January 14, 1995.

Roth, David, at Kissimmee, Florida, September 5, 1993.

Royal, Lee R., by telephone, November 12 and 19, 1994, and February 16, 1995.

Schwenk, Robert L., Jr., at San Antonio, Texas, September 3, 1994.

Seagren, Major Leonard W. USAF (Ret.), by telephone, October 29, 1994.

Seavers, Harold A., at Kissimmee, Florida, September 5, 1993.

Smith, Admiral Harold P., USN (Ret.), at Virginia Beach, Virginia, July 12, 1988, U.S. Naval Institute oral history program.

Smith, Harry J., by telephone, February 20 and 23, 1995.

Starnes, James L., Jr., by telephone, January 6, 1995.

Stockton, Ensign Edward J., USN, on board the USS *Missouri* (BB-63) at sea, December 1, 1991.

Sumrall, Robert, at Annapolis, Maryland, January 20, 1995.

Taylor, Lieutenant Commander John E., USN, on board the USS *Missouri* at sea, December 2, 1991.

Thumudo, Mario, at San Antonio, Texas, September 1, 1994.

Travis, Lieutenant Bevan E., USN (Ret.), by telephone, February 16, 1995.

Treadwell, Captain Lawrence P., Jr., USN (Ret.), by telephone, February 25, 1995.

Tucker, Gunner's Mate First Class Leon, USN, on board the USS *Missouri* at sea, December 4, 1991.

Vella, Joseph, at San Antonio, Texas, September 2, 1994.

Walker, Lieutenant Mark, USN, at the Pentagon, October 19, 1992.

Ward, Commander Arthur T., USN (Ret.), by telephone, February 23, 1995.

Webber, Senior Chief Electrician's Mate Robert, USN, on board the USS *Missouri* (BB-63) at sea, December 4, 1991.

Weschler, Vice Admiral Thomas R., USN (Ret.), at Annapolis, Maryland, February 23, 1983, U.S. Naval Institute oral history program.

Wiernik, Edwin, by telephone, June 25, 1994.

Williams, Commander Daniel N., MSC, USN (Ret.), by telephone, February 26, 1995.

Williams, John L., at Kissimmee, Florida, September 5, 1993.

Wilson, Lieutenant Steve, USN, on board the USS *Missouri* (BB-63) at sea, December 4, 1991.

Yucka, Walter, at San Antonio, Texas, September 2, 1994.

Zeldes, Jacob D., by telephone, February 22, 1995.

Other Interviews

Allen, Thomas, USS *Missouri* oral history project, interview date unknown.

Clancy, John, USS *Missouri* oral history project, interview date unknown.

Colwell, Vice Admiral John B., USN (Ret.), interview with Dr. John T. Mason, Jr., June 14, 1973, U.S. Naval Institute oral history program.

Debenedetto, Joseph J., USS *Missouri* oral history project, interview date unknown.

Dennison, Admiral Robert L., USN (Ret.), interviews with Dr. John T. Mason, Jr., January 17 and 30, 1973, U.S. Naval Institute oral history program.

Faulk, Captain Roland W., CHC, USN (Ret.), interview with Dr. John T. Mason, Jr., November 11, 1974, U.S. Naval Institute oral history program.

Ganas, Julian J., USS *Missouri* oral history project, interview date unknown.

Houghton, Amory M. III, USS *Missouri* oral history project, interview date unknown.

Lee, Vice Admiral Fitzhugh, USN (Ret.), interview with Etta-Belle Kitchen, July 11, 1970, U.S. Naval Institute oral history program.

McCarron, Chief Gunner John, USN (Ret.), USS *Missouri* oral history project, interview date unknown.

McHugh, John J., Jr., USS *Missouri* oral history project, interview date unknown.

Nau, Arthur, USS *Missouri* oral history project, interview date unknown.

Rouse, Donald B., USS *Missouri* oral history project, interview date unknown.

Smith-Hutton, Captain Henri, USN (Ret.), interview with Paul B. Ryan, October 17, 1974, U.S. Naval Institute oral history program.

Smoot, Vice Admiral Roland N., USN (Ret.), interviews with Etta-Belle Kitchen, February 21, 1971, and March 21, 1971, U.S. Naval Institute oral history program.

Travis, Lieutenant Bevan E., USN (Ret.), USS *Missouri* oral history project, interview date unknown.

Zimmerman, Ernest, USS *Missouri* oral history project, interview date unknown.

Books

Battleship Missouri: RimPac '88. Booklet published by the USS *Missouri*, 1988.

Battleship Missouri: RimPac '90. Booklet published by the USS *Missouri*, 1990.

Cagle, Malcolm, and Frank A. Manson. *The Sea War in Korea.* Annapolis: U.S. Naval Institute, 1957.

Garzke, William H., Jr., and Robert O. Dulin, Jr. *Battleships: United States Battleships, 1935–1992* (revised and updated edition). Annapolis: Naval Institute Press, 1995.

Halsey, Fleet Admiral William F., USN, and J. Bryan III. *Admiral Halsey's Story.* New York: McGraw-Hill, 1947.

The History of USS MISSOURI. Pamphlet published by the USS *Missouri*, 1945. Copy on file in the Harry S. Truman Library.

The History of USS MISSOURI. World War II cruisebook written and edited by the USS *Missouri*. Atlanta: Albert Love Enterprises, 1946.

Karig, Walter, Malcolm W. Cagle, and Frank A. Manson. *Battle Report: The War in Korea.* New York: Rinehart and Company, 1952.

Kase, Toshikazu. *Journey to the Missouri.* Edited by David Nelson Rowe. New Haven: Yale University Press, 1950.

Manchester, William. *American Caesar: Douglas MacArthur, 1880–1964.* Boston: Little, Brown, 1978.

Navy Department, Office of the CNO, Naval History Division. *Dictionary of American Naval Fighting Ships.* Vol. 4: Washington, D.C.: Government Printing Office, 1969.

Rigdon, William M. *White House Sailor.* Garden City, New York: Doubleday, 1962.

Smith, Allan E., and Gordon Newell. *The Mighty Mo: The U.S.S. Missouri: A Biography of the Last Battleship.* Seattle: Superior, 1969.

Stillwell, Paul. "Battleships for the 1980s: Symbol and Substance." In James L. George, *The U.S. Navy: The View from the Mid-1980s.* Boulder, Colorado: Westview Press, 1985.

Sumrall, Robert F. *Iowa-Class Battleships: Their Design, Weapons, and Equipment.* Annapolis: Naval Institute Press, 1989.

————USS Missouri (BB 63): Part I, 1941–1984. Missoula, Montana: Pictorial Histories Publishing Company, 1986.

Truman, Harry S. Year of Decisions. Vol. 1. New York: Doubleday, 1955.

Truman, Margaret. Harry S. Truman. New York: William Morrow, 1973.

USS Missouri (BB 63): Charting a New Course, 1987–1988. Cruisebook published by the USS Missouri, 1988.

USS Missouri: 1952–1953 Far Eastern Cruise. Cruisebook published by the USS Missouri, 1953.

USS Missouri (BB 63): Meeting the Challenge, a Call to Crisis, 1990–1991. Cruisebook published by the USS Missouri, 1991.

USS Missouri (BB 63): Strength for Freedom, 1985–1986. Cruisebook published by the USS Missouri, 1987.

Who's Who in America: 1993–94.

Magazine Articles

"Battle of the Hudson." Time (November 12, 1945).

Carney, Admiral Robert B. "Under the Cold Gaze of the Victorious." U.S. Naval Institute Proceedings (December 1983).

Kalisch, Colonel Bertram, USA. U.S. Naval Institute Proceedings (August 1955).

Muir, Dr. Malcolm, Jr. "Hard Aground on Thimble Shoal." Naval History (Fall 1991).

"No. 1 Pollywog." Time (September 22, 1947).

O'Rourke, Ronald. "The Tanker War." U.S. Naval Institute Proceedings (May 1988).

"Peace Be Now Restored." Time (September 10, 1945).

"The Presidency." Time (November 5, 1945).

Price, Gary. "'Mo' Joins Recycling Effort." Broadside (September 1989).

————"Automatic Teller Machines Streamline Pay on board USS Missouri." Broadside (April 1990).

"Show in the Oval Room." Time (December 13, 1948).

Sumrall, Robert F. "Ship Camouflage (WWII): Deceptive Art." U.S. Naval Institute Proceedings (February 1973).

"The Sun Shines Bright." Newsweek (September 10, 1945).

Witteman, Paul A. "In California: A Battleship Comes Alive." Time (June 2, 1986).

Newspaper Articles

Associated Press. "Big Mo Skipper Tells Distrust of Ship's Navigator." Washington Times-Herald (February 19, 1950).

Associated Press. "4th Officer of Big Mo Is Defendant." The Washington Post (February 14, 1950).

Associated Press. "Missouri Captain Takes All Blame for Grounding." (Washington) Evening Star (February 28, 1950).

Associated Press. "Truman's Slight Opens a 'Closet.'" Kansas City Star (April 5, 1963).

Baldwin, Hanson W. "World's Greatest Warship Is Launched in Brooklyn." The New York Times (January 30, 1944).

"Battleship Missouri Out of Mothballs." The Trentonian (September 2, 1984). Reprinted in Ship's Newsletter (Battleship New Jersey Historical Museum Society, October 1984).

"Body of Ertegun Put on Missouri." The New York Times (March 22, 1946).

Egan, Bill. "Sailors, Marines Answer the Call of Bright Lights." Long Beach Navy Dispatch (April 30, 1987).

Einstein, David. "Battleship Missouri Home for a Face-Lift." Los Angeles Times (May 26, 1984).

Jim, Jong Hwan. "Reporting for Duty." Navy Department news release (August 18, 1945).

"Keel Is Laid Here for Great Warship: 45,000-Ton Missouri Started Ahead of Plan." The New York Times (January 7, 1941).

Lawrence, David. "Today in Washington." New York Herald Tribune (February 2, 1950).

Levins, Harry. "Aboard the Missouri: A Legendary Battleship Makes Its Final Voyage." St. Louis Post-Dispatch Magazine (February 16, 1992).

"'Man Overboard' Is OK Again." The Missourian (April 28, 1945).

Matthews, William. "Mayor Says No to Missouri." Navy Times (January 11, 1988).

"'Mighty Mo' Pays a Call on Little Kalaupapa." Honolulu Star-Bulletin (September 20, 1986).

"Missouri to Join Mothball Fleet." The New York Times (March 29, 1954).

Mitchell, Brian. "Navy Lifts Moratorium on Firing Wisconsin's Guns." Navy Times (September 17, 1990).

"Operations Dep't—Innovation on Mo." The Missourian (February 3, 1945).

Parker, Lloyd. "Missouri Sails from Norfolk on 'Curtain' Cruise: Departure, to Pretty Lass at Pier, 'Is Sad, Really.'" Norfolk Virginian-Pilot (August 24, 1954).

Schulze, William. "Seattle Gives Mighty Mo Wet Welcome." Seattle Post-Intelligencer (September 16, 1954).

Shoults, Darrell. "'Mighty Mo' Makes a Comeback." St. Louis Globe-Democrat (May 17–18, 1986).

Stokes, Richard L. "Donnell Passed Up for Truman on Warship Sponsor." St. Louis Post-Dispatch (January 27, 1944).

"Truman Squelches Idea of Junking USS Missouri." St. Louis Globe-Democrat (December 5, 1948).

Weller, Oree C. "Security Wraps on Navy's Most-Photographed Ship." Seattle Times (September 3, 1963).

Official Records

Bureau of Ships, "Refloating of the U.S.S. *Missouri* (BB-63)." June 1, 1950.

USS *Missouri* (BB-63) plan of the day, September 2, 1945. Courtesy of Vice Admiral Douglas Plate.

USS *Missouri* (BB-63) deck logs, 1944–45. National Archives, Washington, D.C.

USS *Missouri* (BB-63) deck logs, 1946–55. Washington National Records Center, Suitland, Maryland.

USS *Missouri* (BB-63) deck logs, 1986–92. Ships Histories Branch, Naval Historical Center, Washington, D.C.

USS *Missouri* action report BB63/A16-3, serial 047, March 2, 1945. Operational Archives Branch, Naval Historical Center.

USS *Missouri* action report BB63/A16-3, serial 060, March 26, 1945. Operational Archives Branch, Naval Historical Center.

USS *Missouri* action report BB63/A16-3, serial 087, May 9, 1945. Operational Archives Branch, Naval Historical Center.

USS *Missouri* action report BB63/A16-3, serial 0121, June 30, 1945. Operational Archives Branch, Naval Historical Center.

USS *Missouri* action report BB63/A16-3, serial 0127, July 19, 1945. Operational Archives Branch, Naval Historical Center.

USS *Missouri* action report BB63/A16-3, serial 0130, July 20, 1945. Operational Archives Branch, Naval Historical Center.

USS *Missouri* action report BB63/A16-3, serial 0162A, September 8, 1945. Operational Archives Branch, Naval Historical Center.

USS *Missouri* action report BB63/A16-3, serial 0153, August 25, 1945. Operational Archives Branch, Naval Historical Center.

USS *Missouri* war diaries, 1945–46. Operational Archives Branch, Naval Historical Center.

USS *Missouri* trip report BB63/A4-3, serial 1770, December 8, 1947. Operational Archives Branch, Naval Historical Center.

USS *Missouri* storm damage report BB63/A9-8, serial 1188, August 23, 1950. Operational Archives Branch, Naval Historical Center.

USS *Missouri* action report BB63:15/A12-1, serial 086, October 1, 1950. Operational Archives Branch, Naval Historical Center.

USS *Missouri* action report BB63:15/A12-1, serial 0106, November 23, 1950. Operational Archives Branch, Naval Historical Center.

USS *Missouri* action report BB63:15/A16, serial 034, January 25, 1953. Operational Archives Branch, Naval Historical Center.

USS *Missouri* action report BB63:20/A16, serial 0112, April 28, 1953. Operational Archives Branch, Naval Historical Center.

USS *Missouri* action report BB63:20/A16, serial 0120, May 8, 1953. Operational Archives Branch, Naval Historical Center.

USS *Missouri* war diaries, 1950–53. Operational Archives Branch, Naval Historical Center.

USS *Missouri* command history (OpNav report symbol 5750-1), calendar year 1985, serial 13/0282, April 25, 1986. Ships Histories Branch, Naval Historical Center.

USS *Missouri* command history (OpNav report symbol 5750-1), calendar year 1986, serial 13/278, April 21, 1987. Ships Histories Branch, Naval Historical Center.

USS *Missouri* command history (OpNav report symbol 5750-1), calendar year 1987, serial 13/1102, October 23, 1988. Ships Histories Branch, Naval Historical Center.

USS *Missouri* command history (OpNav report symbol 5750-1), calendar year 1988, serial 11/430, May 26, 1989. Ships Histories Branch, Naval Historical Center.

USS *Missouri* command history (OpNav report symbol 5750-1), calendar year 1989, serial 11/125, April 14, 1991. Ships Histories Branch, Naval Historical Center.

USS *Missouri* command history (OpNav report symbol 5750-1), calendar year 1990, serial 11/199, July 10, 1991. Ships Histories Branch, Naval Historical Center.

USS *Missouri* command history (OpNav report symbol 5750-1), calendar year 1991, serial 11/016, January 15, 1991. Ships Histories Branch, Naval Historical Center.

Letters

Allen, Lieutenant Commander Max, USN (Ret.). To author, February 3, 1995.

Arthur, Admiral S. R., USN. To Battleship *New Jersey* Historical Museum Society, April 26, 1993. Reprinted in May 1993 issue of the society's newsletter.

Chief of naval operations to the secretary of the Navy, 4730, serial N431L/5U589703, January 5, 1995. Printed in *Ship's Newsletter*, Battleship *New Jersey* Historical Museum Society, January 1995.

Drachnik, Captain Joseph B., USN (Ret.). To author, September 3, 1991.

Giles, Donald T., Jr. To author, November 12, 1994.

Hartman, Captain C. C., USN. To Harry S Truman, February 25, 1944. Senatorial File, Box 174, Harry S. Truman Library.

Kelly, Rear Admiral Monroe, USN. To Governor Forrest C. Donnell, January 31, 1944. F. C. Donnell Gubernatorial Papers, 1941–45, Subject File M., University of Missouri Western Historical Manuscript Collection-Columbia.

Landgraff, Richard A. To author, November 3, 1994, and January 3, 1995.

Little, Thomas F. Telegram to the White House, January 18, 1950. Folder 736, Presidential Papers, Harry S. Truman Library.

McCrea, Rear Admiral John (OpNav). To State Department, serial 068P21, 2-7-46. CNO files, also in *Missouri* files at Naval Historical Center.

Thach, James H., III. To author, November 7, 1994.

Truman, Harry S. To Secretary of the Navy John B. Connally, August 29, 1961. Box 60, Post-Presidential Papers, Harry S. Truman Library.

Truman, John C. To Harry S Truman, April 22, 1945. Family Correspondence (PSF), Box 332, Harry S. Truman Library.

————. To Harry S Truman, October 9, 1945. Family Correspondence (PSF), Box 332, Harry S. Truman Library.

Unpublished Manuscripts

Fisher, Robert E., Jr. *Decision in the Northern Tier: Administration and Navy Policies Converge, 1945–1947.* San Diego State University master of arts thesis, 1993.

Foley, Rear Admiral Francis D., USN (Ret.). "Helicopter Anecdote."

Miller, Captain Richards T., USN (Ret.). "Notes on *Iowa* and *Missouri*" (January 19, 1993).

Rogers, Robert W. "Le USS Miserie," chapter VIII of a book-length memoir titled *I'll Find Out, Sir!*

Stillwell, Paul. "The Last of a Mighty Breed" (1969).

Videotapes

"Changing the Guard" (episode six), *Winds of War* (Paramount, televised 1983).

"Meeting the Challenge: A Call to Crisis." Documentary history of the *Missouri*'s 1990–91 Middle East deployment, produced by the ship's public affairs office.

Index

About the Author

Paul Stillwell joined the staff of the U.S. Naval Institute in 1974 and is now director of the history division, including the oral history program, photo archive, reference library, and photo sales program.

Stillwell has a bachelor's degree in history from Drury College, Springfield, Missouri, and a master's degree in journalism from the University of Missouri-Columbia. From 1962 to 1988 he participated in the Naval Reserve, officially retiring in 1992 with the rank of commander. He served in the tank landing ship *Washoe County* (LST-1165) and the battleship *New Jersey* (BB-62) during the Vietnam War. In early 1988 he was recalled to active duty for a month and sent to the Persian Gulf as a historian to document the U.S. Navy's role during the Iran-Iraq War.

Stillwell is editor or author of several Naval Institute Press books, including *Air Raid: Pearl Harbor!* (1981), *Battleship New Jersey: An Illustrated History* (1986), *Battleship Arizona: An Illustrated History* (1991), *The Golden Thirteen: Recollections of the First Black Naval Officers* (1993), *Sharks of Steel* (coauthored with Vice Admiral Robert Y. Kaufman, 1993), and *Assault on Normandy: First-Person Accounts from the Sea Services* (1994).